GUATEMALA
AND BELIZE
THE ROUGH GUIDE

KU-5?-995

ROUGH GUIDE CREDITS

Series Editor: Mark Ellingham
Editorial: Martin Dunford, John Fisher, Jack Holland, Jonathan Buckley
Production: Susanne Hillen, Kate Berens, Greg Ward, Andy Hilliard
Typesetting: Gail Jammy
Series Design: Andrew Oliver

This book is dedicated to Kate, with love and affection.

Thanks to all our friends in Guatemala and Belize who made this book possible. Special thanks to the people of Hopkins and the Belize City Hospital, to the British High Commission in Belmopan, the Belize High Commission in London, British Forces Belize, the Belize Tourist Board, especially Michelle Garbut, John and Dorothy Jackson, Bill and Julie from California, Beth LaCroix, Winnel Branche, Careerwise of Dunstable, Bob Jones at Eva's in San Ignacio for generous helpings of food and advice, to Julio Godoy and Julian at the Montana in Sayaxché, Mike Shawcross for his help in Guatemala and proofreading, Nick Hanna, to Des for a much improved but unpublishable back cover, to Matt, Anita and Penelope for putting up with the early draft, and to Ladislaus for carrying it, to Adrian for his unflagging enthusiasm, to Vernon Nunn for the generous and extended loan of his tent, to the staff at Inguat in Guatemala City, to Survival International, Amnesty international, the Guatemalan Commission for Human Rights, and to everyone at Rough Guides, especially John Fisher, for his stamina and patience, without whom this book would never have happened.

Published by Harrap Columbus, Chelsea House, 26 Market Square, Bromley, Kent BR1 1NA

Typeset in Linotron Univers and Century Old Style
Printed by Cox & Wyman, Reading, Berks

Small incidental illustrations in Part One and Part Four by Ed Briant
Other illustrations by Henry Iles (Contexts) and Mark Whatmore

432pp
includes index

British Library Cataloguing in Publication Data
   Whatmore, Mark
   Guatemala and Belize: the rough guide.
   1. Guatemala – visitors guides 2. Belize – Visitors guides
   I. Title II. Eltringham, Pete
   ISBN 0–7471–0085–3

GUATEMALA
AND BELIZE
THE ROUGH GUIDE

written and researched by

MARK WHATMORE
and PETER ELTRINGHAM

with additional research and accounts from

Kate Ivens and Ronnie Graham

Edited by
John Fisher
with Jonathan Buckley

HARRAP-COLUMBUS ■ LONDON

CONTENTS

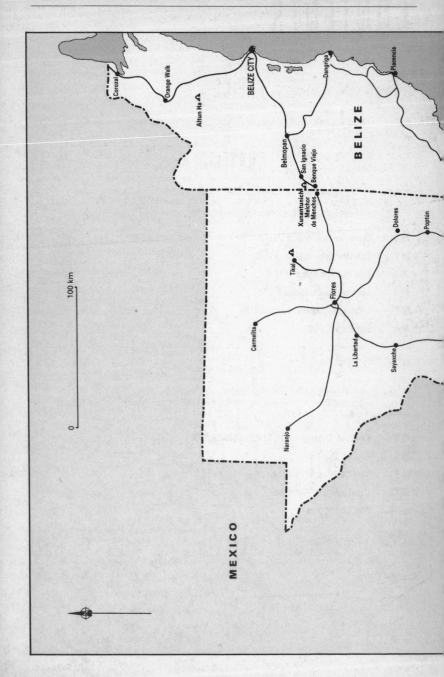

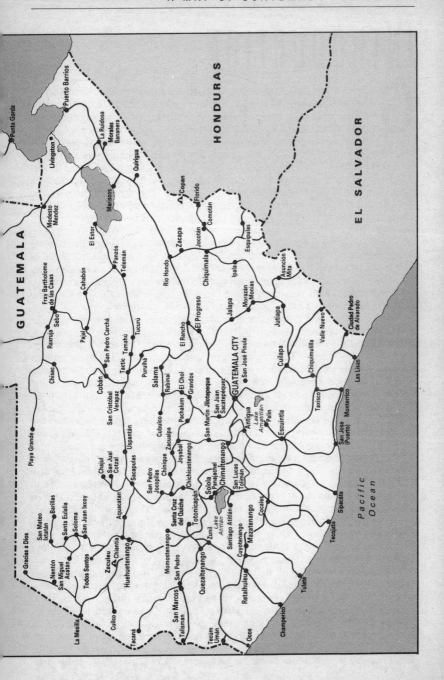

INTRODUCTION

Guatemala and Belize, spanning the narrowing Central American isthmus, don't take up very much space, but they make the most of what they have with a range of scenery, wildlife, cultural traditions and archaeological remains that would do justice to an entire continent. They also have a way of defying your expectations at every turn. The two countries are very different from each other – not just in language, but in mood and pace as well – and from anywhere else you might have been. If you're coming from the north, the surprise is perhaps greatest: you're an awfully long way from the United States here, but also a surprising distance from Mexico. The serene beauty of the Guatemalan highlands undermines the image created by newspaper reports, but beneath the surface, and clearly felt at times, a very real tension exists between the two sharply contradictory cultures which coexist throughout the nation, between western values and indigenous ones, *Ladino* and Indian. Belize feels more easy-going, and while there are less obvious places of interest there is plenty of awesomely wild scenery and a breathtaking coastline. It's a country that, especially compared to the densely populated Guatemalan highlands, sometimes feels half empty: until you reach Belize City – no longer the capital but still the centre of all activity – a rough, bustling and decidedly streetwise town.

Both Guatemala and Belize offer an astonishing range of **landscape**; from the volcanic cones and sweeping valleys of the Guatemalan highlands to the lush tropical forests of the Petén lowlands and the interior of Belize. One of the world's longest and loveliest **barrier reefs** runs off the Caribbean coast of Belize, dotted with islands – known locally as cayes – which provide divers, snorkellers and fishermen with access to an amazingly rich marine environment. Both at sea and inland Guatemala and Belize support a tremendous array of **wildlife**. The rainforests are among the best preserved in Latin America, affording protection to a huge number of species including jaguars, tapir, toucans, howler monkeys, jabiru storks, and the elusive quetzal, national symbol of Guatemala. The forest itself is spellbinding, and for both the uninitiated and the expert a visit is an unforgettable experience.

The region also offers an astonishing wealth of archaeological remains. The **Maya** civilisation, which dominated the area from at least 2000 BC until the arrival of the Spanish – but above all during the so-called Classic Period from 300 to 900 AD – has left its traces everywhere. Both Guatemala and Belize are scattered with ruins, rising mysteriously out of the rainforest and marking out the more fertile of the highland valleys. These ancient cities – some of them, like **Tikal**, reasonably well known, others just as exciting yet hardly ever visited – are a fascinating testament to a civilisation of great complexity and with a tremendous enthusiasm for architectural grandeur.

Culturally, Guatemala and Belize are quite distinct. **Indigenous groups** still make up half of the Guatemalan population. Their language, costumes and crafts, which dominate the highland regions, remain astonishingly distinct: setting them entirely apart from the country's *Ladino* rulers. In the cities and lowlands it's *Ladino* culture, a distinctively aggressive blend of Spanish colonial customs, native American traditions and North American enterprise that sets the less relaxing pace. Belize, on the other hand, seems to sit uneasily in Central America. Its tiny population includes Lebanese, Chinese, Afro-Caribbeans, indigenous

Indians, *mestizos* and even a collection of Mennonites from Canada and Germany. But it's the rhythm and pace of the Caribbean that characterise the country; relaxed and easy-going on a steady diet of rum, reggae and superb seafood.

As for **where to go**, each country has its established attractions. In Guatemala it's the Indian-dominated highlands that most people head for, and rightly. The colour, the markets, the culture shock, and above all the people make it an experience wholly unique. And it seems almost an unfair bonus that all this is set in countryside of often mesmerising beauty: for photographers, it's heaven. **Guatemala City** is not somewhere you'll want to hang around: most people head instead for one of two centres – **Antigua**, the former capital, now thriving again but still with a ruined colonial building on every corner; or **Panajachel** on Lake Atitlán, a growing (but still small) resort in a setting of exceptional beauty. Either makes a good base from which to visit markets and villages around – or to learn Spanish – but there are plenty of more adventurous options covered in detail in the guide. Certainly you should try to get to the rainforest: **Tikal**, certainly the most accessible of the great Maya cities, lies right in its midst, and handily on the way to Belize.

In Belize it's the water which is the main draw, and many people arrive and head straight out to the **cayes**, without even spending one night on the mainland. Certainly the cayes are the chief attraction, with crystal-clear waters, diving and snorkelling as good as any in the world, and an atmosphere where time simply stops. But the country deserves more than this. There's a great deal that is less well known but equally worthwhile, and it's again covered fully in the text.

Climate – when to go and where

Guatemala and Belize lie in subtropical latitudes, so the weather is always warm by European standards and can often be hot and humid, though rarely to the point of being uncomfortable.

The immediate climate is largely determined by **altitude**. In the highlands of Guatemala the air is almost always fresh and the nights cool, and despite the heat of the midday sun humidity is never a problem. In the lowlands, particularly in the rainforests of the Petén area, the **humidity** can be exhausting. Both coasts can also be sweltering, but here at least you can usually rely on a sea breeze to dry the sweat. Humidity is most marked in the **rainy season**, which officially lasts from May to November, when clear mornings are soon obscured by gathering cloud and afternoons are often drenched by downpours. The worst of the rain falls in September and October, when these cloudbursts are often impressively dramatic, though still usually confined to the late afternoon. Fortunately the rainy season is never serious enough to disrupt your travels too badly. In the more out of the way places, such as the Cuchumatanes in Guatemala or the remote south of Belize, rain may slow you down by flooding dirt roads or converting them to a sea of mud, but it rarely puts a stop to anything. In the middle of the rainy season, usually in August, there's a mini dry season, when a couple of weeks of clear, fine weather interrupt the rains.

The very best **time of year** to go is from November to Christmas, when the hills are still lush with vegetation but the skies are clear. The tourist season, which is perhaps more marked in Belize, runs from December to April, though there are also plenty of people taking their summer holidays here, from July to September.

Perhaps the most serious weather threat is from **hurricanes**, which occasionally sweep through the Caribbean in the late summer and autumn. If you're on the cayes or in the coastal area of Belize, which are really the only areas which are at all endangered, you'll hear about it long before the storm hits. Wind speeds can exceed 119km/h but the country has an efficient system of warning and a network of shelters. Elsewhere, particularly in the highlands of Guatemala, there's some danger from **earthquakes**, which shake the country on a regular basis. Minor tremors are a regular event and you'll probably only recognise them after they've passed. You're highly unlikely to experience anything more serious, and there's really nothing you can do to guard against the threat.

AVERAGE TEMPERATURE (°C), HUMIDITY AND RAINFALL

Guatemala City

	Jan	Feb	Mar	Apr	May	Jun	Jul	Aug	Sep	Oct	Nov	Dec
Maximum temperature	23	25	27	28	29	27	26	26	26	24	23	22
Minimum temperature	12	12	14	14	16	16	16	16	16	16	14	13
Humidity (%) at 2pm*	69	62	51	51	55	70	67	72	71	72	71	70
Rainfall (mm)	8	3	13	31	152	274	203	198	231	173	23	8
Number of rainy days	4	2	3	5	15	23	21	21	22	18	7	4

Belize City

	Jan	Feb	Mar	Apr	May	Jun	Jul	Aug	Sep	Oct	Nov	Dec
Maximum temperature	27	28	29	30	31	31	31	31	31	30	28	27
Minimum temperature	19	21	22	23	24	24	24	24	23	22	20	20
Humidity (%) at 7pm*	89	87	87	87	87	87	86	87	87	88	91	90
Rainfall (mm)	137	61	38	56	109	196	163	170	244	305	226	185
Number of rainy days	12	6	4	5	7	13	15	14	15	16	12	14

*Humidity is always greater in the early morning, when the wind is usually calm, decreasing to the lowest level at mid afternoon, then rising in the early evening.

PART ONE

THE

BASICS

GETTING THERE

FROM BRITAIN AND EUROPE

There are no direct flights from London to Guatemala or Belize, so it's not all that cheap to fly there, although with a little creative routing it's possible to bring the price down. For example, fares to Guatemala and Belize are always a little higher than those to Mexico City, so you might want to consider travelling down overland from there, or even from the States if you want to see some of Mexico along the way.

For a scheduled flight from London to Guatemala City or Belize City you should expect to pay between £450 and £550 return, if you book through a travel agent or "bucket shop". Official fares, quoted direct by the airlines, are generally much higher. In the low season, from around September or October (excluding the Christmas period), the price can come down to around £400, occasionally less. And there's always some deal available for young people or students, though don't expect massive reductions (*STA* and *Campus Travel* are specialists in this field). Tickets are usually valid for between three and six months, and you'll pay more for one that allows you to stay for up to a year.

Scheduled flights **to Guatemala City** are operated from Europe by *Iberia* via Madrid, and *KLM* via Amsterdam, with other airlines, such as *British Airways*, offering deals that connect in the States with American airlines. As yet there are no scheduled flights from Europe **to Belize City**, and all available flights go via Miami or Houston:

they usually cost around £50 more than flights to Guatemala City. For the cheapest deals, on these or any others, you'll need to go through an agent, and the more specialised they are the better – see the list of operators for details. It's also worth looking through the classified ads in magazines and newspapers, where the cheapest of flights sometimes crop up. In London the most comprehensive lists are in *Time Out* and the *Evening Standard*, and nationally in the *Guardian*, the *Independent*, and the *Observer*. *LAW* and *TNT*, two magazines distributed free in London, also have useful lists of flights and travel agents.

An alternative is to fly **to Mexico City** and continue overland. It's not that much cheaper, but you do get to see the splendours of southern Mexico (see below). Several airlines fly from Europe to Mexico City, although none go direct from London. *Aeroflot*, via Moscow, is usually the cheapest, but more comfortable and direct routings include *Continental* from Gatwick via Houston, *KLM* via Amsterdam, *Air France* via Paris and *Iberia* via Madrid. For this you should expect to pay between £50 and £100 less than you would for a flight to Guatemala or Belize, through much the same agents. Bear in mind, however, that Guatemala and Belize are at least two days by bus from Mexico City: as an alternative you could fly to **Mérida** or **Cancún** (via Miami or Houston), each of which is less than a day from the border with Belize.

If you want to travel through several countries in Central America, or continue into South America, then it's worth considering an **"open jaw"** ticket, which lets you fly into one city and out of another. Engineering one of these can be a little complex, but on some routes you can end up paying little more than you would for a normal return. *Journey Latin America* is the best first call to sort out the possibilities.

Yet another option is **flying to the States**, which might well work out cheaper, particularly if you decide to head south overland. From London, **New York** is the cheapest destination, but hardly the most convenient, unless you're planning a tour of the entire continent. **Los Angeles** or **Houston** make more sense if you plan to continue overland, and **Miami** if you want to fly south, either to Mexico or directly to Belize or Guatemala. Also worth checking out are US **air passes**, which are

TRAVEL OPERATORS TO GUATEMALA AND BELIZE

Flight Specialists

Campus Travel 52 Grosvenor Gardens, London SW1 (☎071/730 3402). Offices throughout the UK and Ireland.

Journey Latin America 14–16 Devonshire Road, London W4 (☎081/747 3108).

Latin American Travel 28 Conduit Street, London W1 (☎071/629 1130).

Nouvelles Frontières 1–2 Hanover Street, London W1 (☎071/629 7772). Offices throughout Europe.

STA 74 Old Brompton Road, London SW7 (☎071/937 9962). Offices throughout England.

Steamond Travel 23 Eccleston Street, London SW1 (☎071/730 8646).

Packages and Tours

Journey Latin America 14–16 Devonshire Road, London W4 (☎081/747 8315).

Explore Worldwide 7 High Street, Aldershot, Hampshire (☎0252/319448).

Twickers World 23 Church Street, Twickenham, Middlesex (☎081/892 8164).

Virgin Holidays 3rd Floor, Sussex House, High Street, Crawley, West Sussex (☎0293/775511).

World Challenge Exhibitions Walham House, Walham Grove, London SW6 (☎071/386 9828).

Eco Safaris, 146 Gloucester Road, London SW7 45Z (☎ 071 370 5032)

sometimes cheaper if they're bought in Europe, and can cover Mexico. *Continental*, *Delta* and *Eastern* are the most likely candidates.

PACKAGES

Very few companies offer **package tours** to either Belize and Guatemala, and few of those that do are likely to offer what you're really after in visiting these countries. Nonetheless there is increasing interest – especially in Belize – and if your time is short some of the offers can be exceptionally good value.

Among the more interesting operators are *Virgin Holidays* and *Twickers World* – who offer a fair degree of comfort to go with tours that take in wildlife and archaeology – *Eco Safaris*, a long-established operator offering comfortable reef and rainforest trips in Belize, and the more basic offerings of the likes of *Journey Latin America* and *Explore Worldwide*, whose overland tours are relaxed and friendly, making use of local transport and taking in most of the main sites. *Nouvelles Frontières* also offer several tours of Guatemala in varying degrees of luxury, with departures from points all over Europe.

These tours do offer company and a degree of security, but it's worth remembering that there are plenty of local travel agents who operate day or overnight trips to the main places of interest; especially the ones that are hard to get to on your own.

World Challenge Expeditions organise expeditions to Belize for young people to encourage environmental awareness and to carry out research in areas off the beaten track.

FROM AUSTRALIA AND NEW ZEALAND

There are no direct flights from Australasia to anywhere in Central America or Mexico, and consequently you've little choice but to fly via the States. Los Angeles is usually the easiest connection for Guatemala City: you may have to continue to Houston or Miami to get to Belize. Most airlines flying the Pacific should be able to offer connections south, but only on *Continental* (who fly daily Sydney–Auckland–Honolulu–LA) are you likely to be able to continue with the same airline. For overland travel and more detail on flights from the States, see below.

A good place to look for cheap fares is *STA*, with offices at 1a Lee Street, Railway Square, Sydney 2000 (☎02/212 1255); 10 O'Connell Street, Auckland (☎09/399 191); and in Adelaide, Brisbane, Canberra, Christchurch, Hobart, Melbourne, Perth, Townsville and Wellington.

FROM THE USA

If you travel via the States you've still got a long way to go, and you face the choice of doing it overland – seeing something of the USA and Mexico along the way – or flying straight down.

BY AIR

Direct flights **to Guatemala City** are available from **Miami** with *Aviateca, Eastern, Taca* and *Pan Am*, from **Houston** with *Continental* and *Aviateca*, from **New Orleans** with *Aviateca*, and from **Los Angeles** with *Pan Am*. Flights from these southern cities shouldn't come to much more than $450 round trip – sometimes considerably less for a special deal – but if you're coming from New York then expect to pay around $700 return. There are direct flights **to Belize City** from **Miami, Houston** and **New Orleans**, and you should expect to pay around $400 for a return. As in the UK it's a good idea to shop around between travel agents, as there's a bewildering array of fare options. The cheapest deals often include accommodation – which of course you don't have to use if you don't want it.

Once again it's cheaper and easier to fly to **Mexico City**, which is served by daily flights from most major US cities. The cost of a flight from, say, New Orleans works out around $350 return.

OVERLAND

It's a long haul to Guatemala and Belize **from the States** and not something to be recommended if you're in a hurry. However, if you want to see something of Mexico on the way, it might be worth doing. There are numerous possible routes through Mexico, almost all of which pass through Mexico City along the way. From every border crossing there are constant **buses** to the capital (generally at least 24 hours away) and it's also possible to take the **train** – more comfortable but less convenient.

Beyond Mexico City the train is not recommended, but there are good bus connections to all the main border crossings: Tapachula on the Pacific coast; the Pan-American highway via San Cristóbal de las Casas into central Guatemala; and Chetumal on the Caribbean coast for the border with Belize.

As you can imagine there are infinite routes you could take through Mexico, combining bus and train travel, or even taking an internal flight if the distances get the better of you. If you decide to opt for the **buses** then you should realistically expect a journey of three days from New York to the border, a couple of days from there to Mexico City, and two more to reach Belize or Guatemala. But if you've got a few weeks to spare then it's well worth doing.

Travelling south by **car** may give you a lot more freedom, but it does entail a great deal of bureaucracy. You need separate insurance for Mexico (sold at the border) and again for Belize or Guatemala; and everywhere there are strict controls to make sure you're not importing the vehicle – if you attempt to leave without it (even if it's been destroyed in a crash) you'll face a massive duty bill. The shortest route from the States to Guatemala and Belize sets out from Brownsville in Texas, heading south along the Gulf of Mexico.

Finally you could try and **hitch** your way through Mexico, although this is certainly not an easy option.

FROM MEXICO

The simplest way to get from Mexico City to Belize and Guatemala is to **fly**, and there are two or three daily flights for which you should expect to pay around $130 one way.

If, on the other hand, you'd like to get a closer look at southern Mexico then take a **bus**. Probably the best route into Guatemala takes you along the Pan-American highway through Oaxaca to San Cristóbal de las Casas, and then on to Huehuetenango in Guatemala. The other main road crossings are on the Pacific coast, through Tapachula, and on the Caribbean coast, from Chetumal into Belize. A more exotic option is to visit the Mayan site of Palenque, and from there travel via the Rio San Pedro to a remote border crossing that brings you into the department of El Petén in Guatemala (see p.231).

Entering Guatemala or Belize **by car**, you and the car require separate entry permits, which are often valid for different lengths of time – you may be allowed to stay for just a month while the car gets three months. Cars are usually granted between thirty and ninety days, and you'll need to show the registration and your licence. If necessary the permit can then be extended at a customs office.

BETWEEN BELIZE AND GUATEMALA

There are two border crossings that join Belize and Guatemala. The first is between **Benque Viejo** (in Belize) and **Melchor de Menchos** (in Guatemala), which takes you fairly directly between Belize City and the Petén: this border is well connected to Belize City, and to Flores in

Guatemala, by a regular bus service. The second option is the twice-weekly ferry between the town of **Punta Gorda** (in southern Belize) and **Livingston** and **Puerto Barrios** in Guatemala.

It's also possible to fly between Belize and Guatemala, either directly between the capitals or from **Flores** to or from Belize City, a service which is fairly new and has four or five flights a week.

RED TAPE AND ENTRY REQUIREMENTS

GUATEMALA

Even the Guatemalans seem unsure of their country's exact entry requirements, and each embassy or consulate is likely to give you a different answer about what you need. Basically, British, Australian, New Zealand, US and Canadian citizens need either a tourist card or visa to enter. The tourist card is easier, and is routinely issued at the airport on arrival (though you can also get one in advance from a consulate). Most other EC

nationals need no documentation, although Irish citizens must obtain a visa before travelling.

In short, it's always worth a phone call to an embassy or consulate to check before leaving, but there's rarely any need to go there. If you travel down through Mexico, there are Guatemalan consulates in Mexico City, and in Comitán and Tapachula close to the major crossings.

Tourist cards are also routinely issued at the border: officially they're free but border guards usually charge a small fee. The card is valid for between one and three months, and can always be extended up to three months if you weren't granted that much initially – apply to the immigration office in Guatemala City (8 Avenida 12 Calle, Zona 1). Visas are normally valid for one month, and can be extended for a second month. Staying any longer is a complex process for which you need a guarantor, the signature of a lawyer, and proof of adequate funds. All this is extremely long-winded – it's usually much easier to leave the country for a day or two and get a new tourist card at the border when you re-enter.

Arriving in Guatemala you must go through immigration (*migración*) and customs (*aduana*), where your tourist card will be issued and your passport stamped. After this you should keep

GUATEMALAN CONSULATES ABROAD

United Kingdom 13 Fawcett Street, London SW10 (☎071/351 3042).

United States 9700 Richmond Avenue, Suite 218, Houston, TX 77042 (☎713/953 9531).
584 South Spring Street, Office 1030, Los Angeles, CA 90013 (☎213/489 1891.
300 Sevilla Avenue, Oficina 210, Coral Gables, Miami, FLA 33134 (☎305/443 4828).
57 Park Avenue, New York, NY 10016 (☎212/686 3837).
10405 San Diego Mission Road, Suite 205, San Diego, CA 92108 (☎415/282 8127).
2220 R Street Northwest, Washington DC 20008 (☎202/745 4952).

Australia 39 Ocean Street, Woollahra, Sydney NSW 2025 (☎02/322965).

Canada 1140 Maisonneuve Ouest, Suite 1040, Montreal, P.Q. Canada 113A IM 8 (☎514/228 7327).

Mexico Avenida Esplanada 1025, Lomas de Chapultepec 11000, Mexico D.F. 4 (☎05/520 2794).
Alvarado Obregon No.342, Apartado Postal 226, Chetumal Q.R. (☎0052/98321365).
2 Avenida Poniente Norte No. 28, Comitán, Chis.
2a Calle Oriente No. 33, Tapachula, Chis (☎61252).

your passport or tourist card with you at all times, as you may be asked to show them. If you lose your tourist card you can get a new one from the immigration office in Guatemala City.

BELIZE

Getting into Belize the situation is similar. Visas are not needed by citizens of the US, Britain or most EC and commonwealth countries. Officially visitors are required to prove that they can afford to stay in Belize – estimated at a cost of £50 a day – and you may be asked to show your travellers' cheques at the border. If you have more than a couple of hundred pounds or dollars then it should be no problem; if not you might only be allowed a few days in the country. The penniless sometimes get as little as 24 hours – to pass through.

Entering Belize you pass through customs and immigration, a far more straightforward process than at the average Central American border crossing, though still sometimes slow.

BELIZEAN REPRESENTATIVES ABROAD

United Kingdom Belize High Commission, 200 Sutherland Avenue, London W9 (☎071/226 3485).

Washington Embassy of Belize, 3400 International Drive NW, Suite 2-J, Washington DC 20008 (☎202/363 3982).

New York Suite 401-02, 801 Second Avenue, New York, NY 10017 (☎212/599 0233).

Mexico Avenida Theirs No 152-B, Col Anzures 2P 11590, Mexico D.F. (☎05/531 8115).

COSTS AND MONEY

By European standards the cost of living in Belize and Guatemala is low, and by Latin American standards their currencies, the Belizean dollar and the Guatemalan *quetzal*, are surprisingly stable. However fluctuations can and do take place, particularly in Guatemala, so prices quoted in the Guatemala section of this book are in US dollars (for Guatemala) and Belizean dollars (worth exactly US$0.50) in Belize. The American dollar is the most widely accepted foreign currency in both countries, and by far the easiest to take. Travellers' cheques are the safest way to carry your money, but it's also a good idea to have some dollars cash, in case you run short of local currency a long way from the nearest bank, when you're more likely to persuade a taxi driver to take cash than travellers' cheques.

PRICES

Under any circumstances, life in Guatemala and Belize is cheaper than in North America and Europe. And prices in Guatemala are on the whole about half those in Belize (or Mexico). To an extent, what you spend will obviously depend on where, when and how you choose to travel. Peak tourist seasons, such as Christmas and Holy Week, tend to push up hotel prices, and certain towns, most notably Belmopan, San Pedro, Guatemala City and the tourist centres of Antigua and Panajachel, are noticeably more expensive.

In Guatemala it's possible to get by on around $50 a week, and in Belize on around $80: if you run a really tight budget you could make do for less. On the other hand, for $10 a day in Guatemala – say $20 in Belize – you can expect to live well. The following prices should give you a rough idea of what you might end up paying in Guatemala – in Belize you'll find things are between one and a half and two times as expensive. Travelling alone tends to make things a little more expensive: single hotel rooms are often unavailable, and you'll save money by sharing food, excursions and the like too.

Basic **rooms** cost anything from $1 to $4 for a single, $1.50 to $6 double. **Food** prices vary tremendously, but in a simple *comedor* you can always eat for a couple of dollars. Processed food, often imported, is expensive, but fresh produce from the market is very good value – although local prices fluctuate in accordance with the growing seasons. A bottle of Guatemalan **beer** costs a little under $1, but local fire-water, such as the ubiquitous *Quezalteca*, is a lot cheaper. **Travel** is probably the greatest bargain in Central America, providing you stick to the buses and the train. Buses charge around 30¢ an hour, or 3 cents per kilometre, although again prices vary throughout the country. Pullman buses charge almost double, and in general the more remote the area the cheaper it is to get around. Travelling by car is expensive, and the cost of renting a car is higher in Belize and Guatemala than it is in the USA, as is the cost of petrol – although this is still cheaper than in Europe.

In general locally produced goods are cheap while those that are imported are overpriced. This applies to most tinned food, American clothing – although plenty of imitations are produced inside Guatemala – and high-tech goods such as cameras, film and radios. Almost everything is available at a price, from French wine to canned baby food, but unless it's made in Central America you'll have to pay over the odds. **Cigarettes** cost 50¢ a pack for local brands, and $1 for North American imports.

A **Student Card** is worth carrying if you have one, as it sometimes opens the way for a reduction, but it won't save you a great deal.

CURRENCY

The **Guatemalan** *quetzal*, named after the endangered and sacred bird, is one of the most stable currencies in Latin America, strangely defying the nation's inherent instability. The monetary symbol is "Q", and the *quetzal* is divided into 100 *centavos*. The notes come in denominations of Q0.50, Q1, Q5, Q10, Q20, Q50, and Q100. One *quetzal* is often called simply a *billete* or bill. Coins include the 5 centavo, the 10 and the 25, which is sometimes referred to as a *choco* or *choca*.

For a long time the *quetzal* was fixed at one US dollar, but a worsening economic situation led to its collapse in the mid-1980s, and in 1985 the government officially legalised exchange-houses. A further deterioration of the economic situation in 1988 and 1989 meant a further decline in the value of the *quetzal*, which at the time of writing stands at Q3.50 to $1. Cash and travellers' cheques can be changed easily at banks in the main towns and with street traders in Guatemala City, who can be found around the main post office, sometimes offering a better rate than the bank – but they're reluctant to exchange travellers' cheques. Outside the main towns, it can be hard to change money at all.

The US dollar is the best currency to take, but in Guatemala City you should be able to **change** other currencies at the main branch of the *Banco de Guatemala* – the state bank. All the other banks are privately run and most of them will exchange dollars, although in small towns it's always simplest to make for the local branch of the *Banco de Guatemala*. Opening hours for this and most other banks are Monday to Thursday 8.30am to 2pm, with an extra half-hour on Friday: in Guatemala City and Quezaltenango some banks, detailed in the relevant sections, stay open later. *Lloyds Bank* has branches in Guatemala, which may make you feel at home but are in practice little different from any other Guatemalan bank.

Even more than the *quetzal*, the **Belizean dollar** has remained remarkably stable: firmly fixed at two to one with the US dollar (BZ$2=US$1). US dollars are again much the best foreign currency to carry – most banks will also change pounds sterling, but at a worse rate. Cash and travellers' cheques are easily exchanged at banks in all of the main towns, and you'll even find branches of *Barclays Bank* in Belize City and Belmopan. If you bank with *Barclays* you can use your regular cheque book or cash card at these to withdraw Belizean dollars, and a limited amount of US dollars. Most banks in Belize are open Monday to Friday from 9am to 1pm, with an additional session on Friday afternoons. Again there's a small black market for cash, operated by street dealers in Belize City, but as always you run the risk of being ripped off.

CHEQUES, PLASTIC AND PROBLEMS

Travellers' cheques are certainly the best way to bring money, as they offer the added security of a refund if they're stolen. To facilitate this you want to make sure that you have cheques issued by one of the big names, which are also more readily accepted. *Thomas Cook*, with offices at the *Banco Nacional de la Vivienda* (6 Avenida 1-22, Guatemala City) or *American Express* (Reforma 9-00, Zona 10, Guatemala City and *Belize Global Travel*, 41 Albert Street, Belize City) are probably the most widely recognised.

Personal cheques are useless in Guatemala, but *Barclays Bank* customers can use theirs in branches in Belize. **Credit cards** are widely accepted and always good in an emergency. *Access/Mastercard* is the most useful, enabling you to get cash advances from several banks and from *Credomatic* (7 Avenida 6-23, Zona 9, Guatemala City), but both *American Express* and *Visa/Barclaycard* are also accepted fairly widely. You'll only be able to use them in upmarket places, as plastic carries no weight in the ordinary hotels and restaurants of Belize and Guatemala.

If you manage to run out of money altogether, then it's not too hard to get someone back home to **send money**, and in a real emergency you just might persuade your embassy to lend you some. Most British banks will be able to telex funds to a bank in Belize or Guatemala, but it's a great deal more straightforward if you use *Lloyds* to send money to a branch of *Lloyds* in Guatemala, or *Barclays* in Belize. *American Express* is also a very efficient place to have money sent.

TAX

There's a seven percent **value added tax** on all goods and services sold in Guatemala – you'll see it on bills as I.V.A. Market goods are exempt from tax. In Belize, hotel rooms and restaurant bills are subject to a five percent tax. When leaving either country by air you have to pay a Q20 **exit tax** (in dollars or *quetzales*), and a tax of a few cents at land borders.

HEALTH AND INSURANCE

There are no obligatory inoculations for either Guatemala or Belize, but there are several that you should have anyway.

Cholera/typhoid is always a sensible precaution, and you should also check that you're up-to-date with polio, tetanus and smallpox. *Gamma-globulin*, which protects against hepatitis A, is also recommended, although the protection wears off fairly fast – in about two months. For this reason it's best to leave it until just before you set off, and if you're staying longer to arrange for a booster locally. If you're arriving from a country where yellow fever is endemic, you'll also have to have a vaccination certificate for this (only specialist centres can do this – see the list below, or check with your local health authority).

All these inoculations, and *gamma-globulin* boosters, are available from the *Centro de Salud* in Guatemala City (No.1 9 Calle 2-64, Zona 1) or from any doctor in Belize City or Belmopan.

If you're planning to visit the Pacific Coast, the rainforests of the Petén, or practically anywhere in Belize, then **Malaria pills** are a good idea. You have to take these for a month before you arrive and stick with it for another month after you leave the country; but it's worth it. Get advice from a knowledgeable doctor about which pills most effectively combat the local strains.

Your own doctor will be able to provide most of these shots (for the price of a prescription), or you can get any of the above, and good up-to-date advice, from a **British Airways Travel Clinic**: they charge from £5 for the basic injections to £20 and up for the more exotic ones.

London 156 Regent Street, London W1 (☎071/439 9584).

101 Cheapside, London EC2 (☎071/606 2977). Hospital for Tropical Diseases, 4 St Pancras Way, London NW1 (☎071/388 9600).

Manchester 19–21 St Mary's Gate, Market Street, Manchester M1 1PU (☎061/832 3019).

Milton Keynes The Health Centre, Marsh End Lane, Newport Pagnell, Bucks MK16 8EA (☎0908/211005).

Glasgow 5–6 Park Terrace, Glasgow G3 6BY (☎041/332 8010).

Edinburgh 4 Drumsheugh Gardens, Edinburgh EH3 7QJ (☎031/68249).

Once **in Guatemala and Belize** you're far more likely to experience a dose of **diarrhoea**, which is endemic and all too easy to contract. Its main cause is simply the change of diet: the food in Belize and Guatemala contains a whole new set of bacteria, as well as perhaps rather more of them than you're used to. Everyone has their own ideas about which particular ingredient should take the blame, whether it's the water or the salads, but in truth you can pick it up almost anywhere. Standard remedies may have some effect, but the best cure is the simplest one: take it easy for a day or two, drink lots of bottled water, and eat only the blandest of foods — papaya is good for soothing the stomach and also crammed with vitamins. Only if the symptoms last more than four or five days do you really need to worry.

More serious is **amoebic dysentery**, which is also endemic in many parts of the country. The symptoms are more or less the same as a bad dose of diarrhoea but include bleeding. On the whole, a course of antibiotics will cure it, and if you plan to visit the far-flung corners of either country then it's worth carrying these, just in case. If possible get some, and some advice on their usage, from a doctor before you go: local pharmacists can sell things which in Europe would be available only on prescription, but you may not get correct instructions on dosage and the like.

To avoid the worst stomach problems it's advisable to exercise a degree of caution, particularly during the first week or so, when your system is still adjusting. You should also be careful with **tap-water**, which is not always drinkable. In the main cities it should be all right, and you can often taste the chlorine, but even here it's safer to stick to purified water and bottled

drinks. **Altitude and sun** can also be a cause of illness, and if you're struck down by either of these two then there's little you can do other than take it easy and wait until you start to acclimatise.

For simple medical problems head for the *farmacía* (chemist), where you'll find some common brand names and reasonably knowledgeable advice. If you need the services of a doctor, you'll find that many Guatemalan doctors were trained in the States and speak good English, as were almost all Belizean doctors. Your embassy will always have a list of recommended doctors, and some are included in the listings sections for Guatemala City and Quezaltenango. Both of these cities have good hospitals, as do Belize City and Belmopan. Elsewhere even the smallest of villages has a *Centro de Salud* (health centre) where health care is free, although you can't rely on finding an English-speaking doctor or nurse.

INSURANCE

Medical insurance is a must as there are no reciprocal health arrangements between European countries and Guatemala or Belize. Public health care in both countries is very basic, and the private hospitals are expensive. Any travel agent or insurance broker will sell you a comprehensive policy to cover you for medical expenses, loss and theft — most also include the cost of repatriation should you pick up anything serious. *ISIS* travel insurance, available from branches of *STA Travel* (see *Getting There*) or *Endsleigh Insurance* (☎071/436 4451), is one of the best cheap policies available in Britain, at around £30 a month. But it's usually easiest to buy a policy when you get your ticket.

MAPS AND INFORMATION

Information about Guatemala and Belize is not easily obtained, either inside or outside the countries.

For **Guatemala** the only place to turn to in London is the Guatemalan Embassy (13 Fawcett Street, London SW10; ☎071/351 3042), where you have to struggle to get any real assistance. You could also try writing to *Inguat*, the Guatemalan Tourist Board, at 7 Avenida 1–17, Centro Civico, Guatemala City, although communication will inevitably take a week or two: for the limited help you get you might as well wait until you arrive.

In Guatemala *Inguat* have offices in Guatemala City, Antigua, Quezaltenango, Panajachel and Flores. The quality of the information they dispense is highly variable, though in general the main office and the Antigua branch are the most reliable.

For **maps** of Guatemala *Inguat* is again the main source. Their "tourist map" (1:1,000,000), which includes a map of the whole country (including Belize), a detailed map of the central area and plans of the main cities, is the best you're likely to find. It's sold for $1 from *Inguat* offices and some shops in Guatemala, but sadly it's often out of print – there's no real alternative. **In London** *Stanford's* (12 Long Acre, London WC2; ☎071/836 1321) may have copies of this map, or of a simple four-sheet version, at a scale of 1:5,000,000, which is produced for use in Guatemalan schools and includes the national anthem in one corner. The only **large-scale maps** of Guatemala (1:50,000) are produced by the *Instituto Geografico Militar* (Avenida de las Americas 5-76, Zona 13, Guatemala City). These cover the country in 250 sections and are accurately contoured, although some aspects are now out of date. You can consult these maps at the offices of the Instituto, but without special permission from the Ministry of Defence they're not generally on sale to the public. You can, however, buy photocopies of most of them from the *Casa Andinista* in Antigua (4 Calle Oriente 5A, Apartado Postal 343, 03901 Antigua).

Information on **Belize** isn't particularly forthcoming either. The Belizean High Commission in London (15 Thayer Street, London W1; ☎071/486 8381) is extremely friendly but not really geared up as a tourist office; and you can buy good maps of Belize from *Stanford's*. In Belize itself there's a well-organised Tourist Board in Belize City, where they have a fair amount of information, and good general maps are widely available. Larger scale sheets are sold from an office above the main post office in Belize City.

PART TWO

GUATEMALA

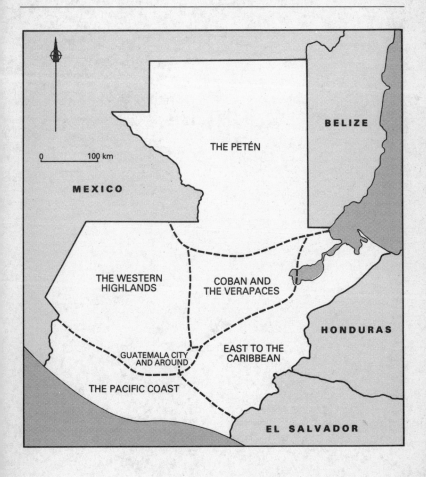

THE PETÉN

BELIZE

MEXICO

0   100 km

THE WESTERN
HIGHLANDS

COBAN AND
THE VERAPACES

HONDURAS

GUATEMALA CITY
AND AROUND

EAST TO THE
CARIBBEAN

THE PACIFIC COAST

EL SALVADOR

Introduction

Guatemala is a physical and cultural micro-cosm of Latin America, incorporating an astonishing array of contradictions in a country roughly the size of Ireland. Uniquely, it still has a population which is at least half Indian, and the strength of indigenous American culture is greater here than perhaps anywhere else in the world. More than anywhere, Guatemala is the product of the merger of sophisticated pre-Columbian cultures with Spanish colonialism and the consumerist influences of modern America.

Today, **Indian society** is a strange hybrid of pre-conquest pagan traditions and more recent cultural and religious influences, which combine – above all in the highlands – to form perhaps the most distinctive culture in all of Latin America. At the other end of the scale, *Ladino* Guatemala supports a culture of equal strength, a blend of Latin machismo that is economically aggressive and decidedly urban. At the edges, there is a certain blurring between the two cultures, but the contrast between the urban hustle of Guatemala City and the murmur of village markets could hardly be more extreme.

All of this exists against the nagging back-ground presence of Guatemala's turbulent and bloody **history**. Over the years, between indige-nous and "western" culture, has produced bitter conflict, and even today this is a violent country where political killings are commonplace. However, as a visitor you're as safe in Guatemala as in almost any other Latin American country. The victims of violence are clearly defined politi-cal targets, and to outsiders the country seems relaxed and peaceful. Highland culture remains essentially introspective but this is still a varied, easy, enjoyable and friendly place to travel.

Physically, Guatemala is also defined by extremes, and by regular earthquakes and volcanic eruptions (though you're extremely unlikely to encounter either of these). In the south, the narrow, steamingly hot Pacific coastal plain rises inland towards a string of magnificent volcanic peaks. These mark out the southern limit of the central highlands, and beyond them lies a series of rolling hills and larger granite peaks that form the country's heartland – and home to the vast majority of the Indian population. The scen-ery here is astonishingly beautiful with lakes, forests and lush green hills that at times seem almost too picturesque. Further to the north the peaks of the last great mountain range, the Cuchumatanes, drop off into the lowlands of the Petén – a huge, sparsely populated area of virgin rainforest, which was once the centre of Maya civilisation.

■ Where to go

The **attractions** of each area are discussed at greater length in the relevant chapter introductions but the following, briefly, are the highlights.

The **Pacific Coast** (usually taken to mean the entire coastal plain) is hot and dull. The coastline is a single strip of black volcanic sand, and behind this a smattering of mangrove swamps rise into the country's finest farmland. The area is devoted to commercial agriculture and dotted with bustling urban centres such as **Escuintla**, **Mazatenango** and **Retalhuleu**. Points of inter-est are thin on the ground: confined mainly to the pre-Columbian ruins around the town of **Santa Lucía Cotzumalguapa** (which can't compare with the ruins in the Petén), the **beaches** (scrubby and desolate for the most part, and not how you imagine a Pacific beach ought to be), and the wild-life reserve at **Monterrico**, where you can explore the maze of mangrove swamps.

It is in the **central highlands** that things really get interesting, particularly to the west of Guatemala City, where Indian culture dominates. Not only is the scenery wildly beautiful, but the Indian villages, with an endless array of fiestas

and markets, are fascinating. Among the highlights are **Lake Atitlán**, the jewel of the highlands; **Antigua**, the old colonial capital, devastated by earthquakes but still scattered with superb architecture and the remains of huge churches; and the vast market in **Chichicastenango**, though there are literally hundreds of other markets that are worth visiting. The ideal way to explore the highland area is to base yourself in one of the larger towns – **Antigua, Quezaltenango, Huehuetenango**, or even the lakeside village of **Panajachel** – and set out on day trips to the smaller places. If you want to explore the more remote regions, such as the **Ixil triangle** or the **Cuchumatanes** to the north of Huehuetenango, you'll need to stay in the small villages along the way. In the highlands you'll also find an interesting collection of pre-Columbian ruins, the capital cities of the various tribal groups. Among the best of these are **Iximché, Utatlán and Zaculeu**.

None of these, however, can compete with the archaeological wonders of the **Petén**. This unique lowland area, which makes up about a third of the country, is covered with dense rainforest only now threatened by development – which is alive with wildlife and dotted with superb Maya ruins. The only town of any size is **Flores**, from where you can easily reach **Tikal**, the most impressive of all Maya sites and a ruin that rivals any in Latin America. There are hundreds of other smaller sites, though many are hard to reach. From **Sayaxché**, for example, you can take river trips to the ruins of **Ceibal** or **Yaxchilán** (just across the border in Mexico); from Tikal you can hike through the jungle to **Nakum** or **Uaxactún**, both of them largely buried in the forest.

Finally, the **east** includes a seldom visited highland area, which has little to offer the visitor, though in the **Motagua** valley you'll find the superb Maya site of Quiriguá, and you can cross the border into Honduras to visit the ruins of Copán. You can also travel up into the rain-soaked highlands of the **Verapaces**, similar in many ways to the central highlands, though fresher and greener. Here also Lake Izabal drains, via the Río Dulce, through a dramatic gorge to the **Caribbean**. At its mouth is the town of **Livingston**, an outpost of Caribbean culture which is home to Guatemala's only black community. Yet again, however, the Caribbean beaches are a disappointment – if it's white sand and blue seas you want, head north from here into Belize.

Getting around

Travel within Guatemala is as diverse as the country itself. There are buses plying the Pan-American highway every half-hour or so – some of them quite fast and luxurious – but once you leave the central routes, and head off on the byways, things are sure to slow down. The only really long journey is to the Petén, and for this one you might want to consider flying. Otherwise you can rely on the bus system almost exclusively: despite occasional frustrations it's a pleasure to use and offers a real insight into the country and its energy. Details of travel schedules and bus company offices are given in the relevant sections of the guide.

■ Buses

Buses are by far the best way to get around: cheap, convenient, and wildly entertaining. In Guatemala private cars are owned only by the privileged few, and for the rest of the population, along with their possessions and livestock, buses are the only mode of transport. For the most part the service is extremely cheap and amazingly good, reaching even the smallest of villages.

There are two classes of bus. The so-called **pullman** is usually an old *Greyhound*, and rated as first-class: each passenger gets a seat to him or herself, and in some cases tickets can be bought in advance. They're more expensive but considerably faster than regular buses, not only because the buses themselves are better, but also because they make fewer stops along the way. Pullmans usually leave from the company's own offices – addresses are listed in the text – and on the whole they serve only the main routes, connecting the capital with the Mexican border, Huehuetenango, Quezaltenango, Puerto Barrios, Esquipulas and San Salvador. This means that most long journeys can be done at least part of the way by pullman.

Second-class buses, known as *camionetas*, are open to all and stop for every possible passenger, cramming the seats, aisles and occasionally even the roofs. These buses are often old school buses from the States, their seats designed for the under-fives, so you're liable to have bruised knees after a day or two's travel – especially if you're tall. Nevertheless, travel by second-class bus offers you a real taste of Guatemalan life, and if many trips are uncomfortable and frustratingly slow, they are never dull. There are hundreds of small bus companies, each determined to outdo the next in the garishness of the paint jobs with which they decorate their vehicles. Almost all of them operate out of **bus terminals**: usually on the edge of town, and often adjacent to the market. Tickets are bought on the bus, and are always a bargain: between towns you can hail buses and they'll almost always stop for you. Be warned, though, that bus traffic is almost non-existent after dark.

■ Trains

Until relatively recent times, **trains** provided an essential link between the capital and the two coasts, but these days the service is in rapid decline and before too long the state railway company, steadily accumulating hefty debts, may close down altogether.

For the moment they run a twice-weekly service to **Tecún Umán** on the Mexican border and to **Puerto Barrios** on the Caribbean coast. The trains themselves are in a dreadful state and the trip, scheduled to take a full day, can sometimes continue well into the evening. It is, however, astoundingly cheap.

■ Planes

The only **internal flight** you're at all likely to take in Guatemala – indeed the only flight available – is from the capital to **Flores**. The flight costs about $50 and takes only 45 minutes (as opposed to some 18 hours on the bus), with four rival companies offering services. Their addresses and other details can be found in the chapter on the Petén: tickets can be bought from any travel agent in Guatemala City, and several outlets in Flores.

You might also want to fly **between Belize and Guatemala**, on planes connecting Belize City with Flores or Guatemala City several times a day. Again, fuller details are given in the text.

■ Cars

If you've succeeded in getting your car to Guatemala (see "Getting There"), any further problems you face are likely to seem fairly minor. On the whole, **driving** inside the country is straightforward and it certainly offers unrivalled freedom – traffic is rarely heavy outside the capital, although local driving practices can be alarming at times.

Most of the main routes are paved, but beyond this the roads are often extremely rough.

Petrol stations (*gasolineras*), too, are scarce once you venture away from the main roads: the fuel itself is extremely cheap by European standards, though marginally more expensive than in the States. Should you break down there'll usually be an enthusiastic local mechanic, but **spare parts** can be a problem, especially for anything beyond the most basic of models – *Toyotas*, *Dodges*, *Fords* and *VWs* are all fairly common in this part of the world so you might be able to find someone who has some spares – for other makes you'd be sensible to bring a basic spares kit. Tyres in particular suffer badly on the burning hot roads and rough dirt tracks. If you plan to head up into the mountains or along any of the smaller roads in the Petén then you'll need high clearance and four-wheel drive.

Parking and security constitute a further problem, particularly in the cities where theft and vandalism are fairly common. If possible you should get your car shut away in a guarded car park – of which there are plenty in the centre of Guatemala City. Some hotels also have protected parking space.

Local **warning signs** are also worth getting to know. The most common is placing a branch in the road, which indicates the presence of a broken-down car. Most other important road signs should be fairly recognisable: you'll see many *Alto* (meaning stop) signs still in place to mark military checkpoints from more troubled times. Locals usually know which to ignore, but if in doubt it's safest to stop anyway. *Derrumbes* means landslides, *frene con motor* brake with motor (meaning a steep descent) and *tumulos* bumps in the road, a favourite technique for slowing down traffic.

Hiring a car takes some of the worries out of driving but is expensive in Guatemala: generally at least $50 a day by the time you've added in the extras. Nonetheless it can be worth doing if you can get a few people together – even better value if you get a larger group and hire a minibus. If you do hire, make sure to check the details of the insurance, which often does not cover damage to your vehicle at all. Local rental companies are listed for the main towns.

Motorbike is arguably an even better way of getting around – they can handle the terrain better, and since many locals ride them you may well be able to locate parts and expertise. Motorbikes too can be hired in Guatemala City and Antigua.

■ Taxis

Taxis are available in all the main towns and their rates are fairly low. Meters are a rarity so you should try and fix a price before you set off, particularly in Guatemala City, where the drivers are most likely to try to rip you off. Local taxi drivers will almost always be prepared to negotiate a price for a half-day or day excursion to nearby villages or sites, and if time is short this can be a good way of seeing places where bus services are awkwardly timed (if you have enough time and patience, it's possible to get just about anywhere by bus). Again, if you can organise a group this need not be an expensive option – possibly even cheaper than hiring a car for the day.

■ Bikes

Bikes are very common indeed in Guatemala, and cycling has to be one of the most popular sports. You'll be well received almost anywhere if you travel by bike, and if you've got the energy to make your way through the highlands it's a great way to see the country. Since cycling is so popular most towns will have a repair shop where you can get hold of spare parts, although you still need to carry the basics for emergencies on the road. Mountain bikes make the going easier, as even the main roads include plenty of formidable potholes, and it's a rare ride that doesn't involve at least one steep climb. Second-class buses will carry bikes on the roof, so if you can't face the hills then there's always an easy option. If you didn't bring your own bike they can be hired in both Antigua and Panajachel. If you want to hire long-term then head for Antigua, where mountain bikes are on offer by the day, week or month.

■ Hitching

It's perfectly possible to **hitch** around Guatemala and on the main routes it's a good way to get around, although you might end up on a bus as they are almost as frequent as private cars. Off the main routes private cars are rare, and many of those that do take passengers provide a bus service, charging all of their passengers. So under most circumstances you should anticipate paying for the trip, and it's always polite to offer. If you face a long wait for the next bus then it's almost always worth a try – lots of locals hitch rides (again they usually expect to pay) and the occasional discomfort of riding in the back of a pick-up or truck is worth it for the time saving and the contact with local fellow passengers.

■ Boats and ferries

Ferries operate on several different routes inside Guatemala. The two major routes take you across Lake Izabal, from Mariscos to El Estor, and between Puerto Barrios and Livingston. Both of these are daily passenger-only services and very reasonably priced. From Puerto Barrios there's also a twice-weekly service to Punta Gorda in Belize. Once again the precise details of schedules are given in the text.

Smaller boats also run a regular service along the Río San Pedro, from Naranjo in the Petén to the Mexican border and beyond, and you can hitch a ride, or hire a boat, on the Río Salinas from Sayaxché to Benemerito on the Mexican bank of the Usumacinta. You'll also find plenty of boats offering to take passengers along the Río Dulce to and from Livingston. On almost any of the other navigable waterways you should be able to hire a boat somewhere.

On the Pacific coast the Chiquimulilla canal separates much of the shoreline from the mainland. If you're heading for the beach you'll find that a regular shuttle of small boats takes people across the canal. If the village is also on the other side then arriving buses are met by boats.

Sleeping

Guatemalan hotels come in all shapes and sizes, and it doesn't take long to find yourself in tune with what's on offer and able to recognise the style that suits your needs. Accommodation comes under a range of names: *hotels, pensiones, posadas, hospedajes* **and** *huespedes*. **The names don't always mean a great deal: in theory a** *hospedaje* **is less formal than a** *hotel*, **but in practice the reverse is almost as common.**

Prices for rooms vary as much as anything else. On the whole you can expect the cheapest places to charge $1 per person, and to get a reasonable but basic room for $2–4. But price and quality are not always as closely linked as you might expect, and despite the fact that prices are officially regulated you'll find both bargains and rip-offs at almost every level. It's often worth trying to haggle a little, or asking if there are any cheaper rooms. If you think you're being ripped off then ask to see the official prices, which should be set by *Inguat*, the national tourist board, and are meant to be displayed in the room. If you have been overcharged you can register a complaint with *Inguat*, although it's unlikely that much will happen. If you're travelling in a group you can often save money by **sharing** a larger room, which almost all of the cheaper hotels can offer.

Prices tend to be at their highest in Guatemala City, where it's sometimes difficult to find a room at all, and are also higher than average in Antigua and Flores. At fiesta and holiday times, particularly Holy Week and Christmas, prices tend to be inflated and it can be hard to find a room. The summer tourist season also tends to be crowded. At these times, particularly if you're going to arrive in Guatemala City at night, it's worth booking a room by phone, but in other parts of the country it's hardly worth it.

When you arrive at a hotel you should always insist on seeing the room before any money changes hands, otherwise they'll dump you in the noisiest part of the building and save the good rooms for more discerning customers. In general the hotels recommended in this book are not the very cheapest – which are often genuinely squalid – but one step up, at about $2 per person. The rooms in these places will be simple, with a shared toilet and bathroom usually at the end of the corridor. In the main tourist centres some more upmarket options are also included, while in some other places there's no alternative to squalor. On the whole, though, it's not hard to find somewhere reasonable, and you soon learn to recognise the promising places.

A major problem in all but the most expensive, air-conditioned hotels is the insects, usually fleas in the highlands and mosquitoes in the lowlands. You can often spot the worst places by the remains splattered on the wall. There's not a lot you can do about this, although anti-mosquito devices (either pyrethrin coils which burn all night, or the more modern electronic equivalents) sold widely and cheaply throughout Guatemala are reasonably effective. Ceiling fans can also help to keep flying insects at bay. Mosquito nets are never provided by hotels, but only really essential if you're going to be sleeping out in the Petén.

■ Camping, hostels and towns without hotels

Youth hostels are non-existent in Guatemala, and in a country so heavily populated you rarely need to **camp**. The main cities certainly don't have campsites, and the only places with any decent formal provision for camping are Panajachel and Tikal.

If you decide to set off into the wilds, then a **tent** is certainly a good idea, although even here it's by no means essential. Hiking **in the highlands** is usually from village to village, and everywhere you go it's possible to find somewhere to sling a hammock or bed down for the night. In villages that don't have hotels you should track down the mayor (*Alcalde*) and ask if you can stay in the town hall (*municipalidad*) or local school. If that isn't possible then he'll almost certainly find you somewhere else. If you do have a tent the Guatemalan countryside offers plenty of superb spots to camp, although you should take care in politically sensitive areas and also try and ask the owner of the land. In some places, such as Semuc Champey and the ruins of Mixco Viejo, there are thatched shelters where you can sling a hammock or bed down out of the rain.

When it comes to **hiking in the jungle** you'll need to hire a guide. They usually sleep out in the open, protected only by a mosquito net, so you can either follow suit or use a tent. At most of the smaller Maya sites there are guards who will usually let you sleep in their shelters and cook on their fires. If you plan to use their facilities then bring along some food to share with them.

The other occasion for which a tent is useful is climbing **volcanoes**, which often entails a night under the stars. On the lower cone of Acatenango there's a small hut that provides shelter for sleeping out, but it sometimes fills up at weekends. Tents, sleeping bags, stoves and backpacks can be hired from the *Casa Andinista* in Antigua.

Communications – post, phones and media

Keeping in touch with home shouldn't be a problem in Guatemala, although outside the capital the post and phone services are a bit thin on the ground. International phone calls, however, are expensive and it's usually cheaper to reverse the charges.

■ Mail

Guatemalan postal services are fairly efficient by Latin American standards, and you can **send mail** easily from even the smallest of towns – though it's probably safer to send anything of importance from the capital. Letters generally take a couple of weeks to Europe, around one week to the States. To ensure that it won't take

any longer make sure that you send your letters *express*, which costs twice the normal fee but is still cheap, and mark them *correo aereo* (air mail). The main post office (*Correo Central*) in Guatemala City is open weekdays from 8am to 6pm, but most local branches close at 4.30pm.

Receiving mail is also straightforward. You can have it sent to any post office in the country, although once again Guatemala City is the best bet. Letters to be picked up from the post office should be addressed to you at the *Lista de Correos, Guatemala City, Central America*, and it's important to use only one initial before your surname. Otherwise you should check under all your initials as letters are all too easily mislaid. A small fee is charged by the post office and you'll need some proof of identity in order to pick up your mail. You should also bear in mind that letters are only kept at the post office for one month, after which they're returned to the sender.

Alternatively you could have your mail sent to the *American Express* office, which is a much more efficient and reliable service, and where letters are kept for several months. The address of the office is *American Express, Avenida Reforma 9–00, Zona 9, Central America*. The one snag is that you need to show either an *American Express* card or travellers' cheques: the latter are a good idea anyway, and in the end it's unlikely that they'll actually refuse to hand over any letters.

Sending parcels is less easy, as there are complex regulations about the way in which they should be wrapped. Normally this entails cardboard boxes, brown paper and string, although you can also pack things in a flour sack (both boxes and sacks can be bought in shops and markets). The parcel has to be taken to the post office for inspection by the customs department, and is then sealed. The rates for shipment are

reasonable, but parcels sent by air are fairly expensive. In the end the whole process is so time-consuming and frustrating that you're almost invariably better off using one of the agencies in Antigua or Panajachel. The better of them is *Get Guated Out* in Panajachel; slightly more expensive than Antigua's longer-established *Pink Box*, but considerably more reliable.

Telegrams are a much used and very cheap mode of communication within the country, and once you get into the swing of it they are a good way to get in touch with misplaced travelling partners – by addressing them to assorted hotels – and to book hotel rooms. Telegrams within the country are handled by the post office and cost next to nothing: **international telegrams** have to be sent from *Guatel* (the phone company) and cost far more.

■ Phones

Local phone calls in Guatemala are cheap, but outside Guatemala City there are hardly any pay-phones so all calls have to be made from the offices of *Guatel*, the national phone company. Where you do find a pay-phone you'll need 10 or 15 centavo coins. Some shops, bars and restaurants also allow customers to use their phones, and international calls can be made from upmarket hotels (though usually at a considerable premium). At *Guatel* offices you tell the operator who it is that you want to phone, wait until your name is announced and go to the booth they point out. Afterwards they present you with the bill. *Guatel* offices are open from 7am to 10pm, with some staying open until midnight.

For **long-distance and international calls** the procedure is pretty much the same, and you have the option to reverse the charges.

■ Media

For finding out what's happening both inside and outside the country, Guatemala is equipped with several daily papers, a handful of TV channels, and more than enough radio stations.

Of the **daily papers** the most popular are *La Prensa Libre* and *El Grafico*, which are both available in the early morning throughout the country and published in tabloid format. Their stance on national issues is well to the right of centre, and to find a more balanced view you need to read the "marginal" papers. *La Hora* is the oldest of these, available only in Guatemala City, and *7 Dias* is an impressive new weekly that regularly takes the authorities to task. Finally the *Diario de CentroAmerica* is published weekly by the government, and is unashamed in its propaganda, filling many pages with official announcements. The left remains unrepresented in the Guatemalan media and the most recent attempt, *La Epoca*, survived for a mere month before its offices were bombed and the editor driven into exile.

There are also several **periodicals** that have substantial sales: none more so than *Extra*, which catalogues the horrors of the previous week and includes graphic pictures of mutilated corpses. More respectable journalism is peddled by *La Cronica*, a monthly magazine that deals with regional issues from a politically central standpoint, and *This Week*, the main locally produced **English-language** paper. It's actually more of a news-sheet, but manages to take a stridently progressive stance and cover most of the main issues. It is published every Monday and can be bought from the paper's offices at 12 Calle 4–53, Zona 1, Guatemala City. Copies are also available by post from Apartado 1156, Guatemala City. Also in English are *Central America Report*, a long-established but rather stodgy publication, available from their offices at 9 Calle A 3–56, Zona 1, Guatemala City; and *Viva Guatemala*, a six-monthly magazine published by *Fundesa*, a local business organisation, to encourage foreign investment. It does this by consistently singing the praises of the country and the stability of its economy. Copies are available for free from their office at Ruta 6, 9–21, Zona 4, Guatemala City.

As for **foreign publications**, *Newsweek*, *Time* and *The Economist* are all sold in the streets of Guatemala City, particularly around the main plaza. Some American newspapers are also available, in particular *USA Today*, the *Miami Herald*, the *New York Times* and the *Wall Street Journal* – all sold at the *Pan-American Hotel*, the *Camino Real*, and the *Sheraton* in Guatemala City. Some are also available in Antigua, or you can read them at the *Instituto Guatemalteco Americano* library at Ruta 4, 4–05, Zona 4, Guatemala City. No British papers are sold in Guatemala although the British Embassy has recent copies.

Guatemala has an abundance of **radio stations**. There are 43 of them in Guatemala City alone, with another 105 in the rest of the country. Some of them are religious stations, but most transmit a steady stream of Latin rock, and whether you have a radio or not you're certain to hear plenty of it. Two of the best are *Radio Conga*

(99.7FM) and *Radio Fiesta* (98.1FM). If you yearn for the voice of the BBC, the World Service transmits on 9915 Khz and 9640 Khz.

Television stations are also in plentiful supply, and in Guatemala City viewers can choose between six local channels and ten satellite channels, all of them dominated by American programmes. In other parts of the country the local channels are rivalled by regional cable networks. Guatemala's most notorious TV station is *Aqui El Mundo*, a staunchly right-wing channel which was shut down by the Cerezo government and now beams into Guatemala from Miami. Many upmarket hotels and some bars in tourist areas (Antigua for example) also have direct satellite or cable reception of US stations – handy, for example, for catching up on the news on *CNN*.

Eating and drinking

Food doesn't come high in the list of reasons for visiting Guatemala, and although Guatemalan cuisine does have its high points they're not easy to come by. But at least you're unlikely to go hungry: there's plenty of international food on the menu and, given enough time, you may even end up liking the beans.

■ Where to eat

The most important distinction in Guatemala is between the **restaurant** and the **comedor**. The latter translates as an "eatery", and in general these are simple local cafés serving the food of the poor at rock-bottom prices. In a *comedor* there is normally no menu, and you simply ask to see what's on offer, or look into the bubbling pots. Restaurants, in general, are slightly more formal and expensive. As usual, however, there are plenty of exceptions to this rule: many a restaurant has a very *comedor*-like menu, and vice-versa. On the whole you'll find restaurants in the towns, while in small villages there are usually just one or two *comedores*, clustered around the market area. *Comedores* generally look scruffier, but the food is almost always fresh and the turnover is fast.

In the cities you'll also find **fast food** joints, modelled on the American originals and often owned by the same companies. When you're travelling you'll also come across a local version of fast food; when buses pause they're besieged by vendors offering a huge selection of drinks,

A LIST OF FOODS AND DISHES

Basics

Azucar	Sugar	Mantequilla	Butter	Queso	Cheese
Carne	Meat	Pan	Bread	Sal	Salt
Ensalada	Salad	Pescado	Fish	Salsa	Sauce
Huevos	Eggs	Pimienta	Pepper	Verduras/Legumbres	Vegetables

Soups (*Sopas*) and starters

Sopa	Soup	Entremeses	Hors d'oeuvres
de Fideos	with noodles	Caldo	Broth (with bits in)
de Lentejas	Lentil	Consome	Consomme
de Verduras	Vegetable	Ceviche	Raw fish salad, marinated
de Arroz	Plain Rice		in lime juice

Meat (*Carne*) and Poultry (*Aves*)

Alambre	Kebab	Codorniz	Quail	Pato	Duck
Bistec	Steak	Conejo	Rabbit	Pavo/Guajalote	Turkey
Cabrito	Kid	Cordero	Lamb	Pechuga	Breast
Carne (de res)	Beef	Costilla	Rib	Pierna	Leg
Carnitas	Stewed	Guisado	Stew	Pollo	Chicken
	chunks	Higado	Liver	Salchicha	Hot dog or
Cerdo	Pork	Lengua	Tongue		salami
Chorizo	Sausage	Milanesa	Breaded	Ternera	Veal
Chuleta	Chop		escalope	Venado	Venison

Specialities

Chile Relleno	Stuffed Pepper	Pan de Coco	Coconut bread
Chuchitos	stuffed maize	Pan de Banana	Banana bread
	dumplings	Quesadilla	Cheese-flavoured sponge
Enchilada	flat, crisp tortilla piled	Taco	Rolled and stuffed tortilla
	with salad or meat	Tamale	Boiled and stuffed maize
Mosh	Porridge		pudding

Vegetables (*Legumbres, verduras*)

Ago	Garlic	Hongos	Mushrooms
Aguacate	Avocado	Lechuga	Lettuce
Casava/Yuca	Potato-like root vegetable	Pacaya	Bitter-tasting local vegetable
Cebolla	Onion	Papas	Potatoes
Col	Cabbage	Pepino	Cucumber
Elote	Corn on the cob	Tomate	Tomato
Frijoles	Beans	Zanahoria	Carrot

Fruit (*Fruta*)

Ciruelas	Greengages	Limon	Lime	Piña	Pineapple
Coco	Coconut	Mamey	Pink, sweet,	Pitahaya	Sweet, purple
Frambuesas	Raspberries		full of pips		fruit
Fresas	Strawberries	Mango	Mango	Platano	Banana
Guanabana	Pear-like	Melocoton	Peach	Sandia	Watermelon
	cactus fruit	Melon	Melon	Toronja	Grapefruit
Guayaba	Guava	Naranja	Orange	Tuna	Cactus fruit
Higos	Figs	Papaya	Papaya	Uvas	Grapes

Eggs (*Huevos*)

Fritos	fried	a la Mexicana	scrambled with mild tomato, onion and chilli sauce
con Jamon	with ham		
Revueltos	scrambled	Rancheros	fried and smothered in hot chilli sauce
con Tocino	with bacon		
Tibios	lightly boiled	Motuleños	fried, served on a tortilla with ham, cheese and sauce

Common terms

Asado/a	Roast	Empanado/a	Breaded
Al Horno	Baked	Picante	Hot and spicy
Al Mojo de Ajo	fried in garlic and butter	Recado	A sauce for meat made from garlic, tomato and spices
A la Parilla	Grilled		

Sweets

Crepas	Pancakes	Helado	Ice cream
Ensalada de Frutas	Fruit salad	Platanos al Horno	Baked plantains
Flan	Creme caramel	Platanos en Mole	Plantains in chocolate sauce

sweets, local specialities and complete meals. Many of these are delicious, but you do need to treat this kind of food with a degree of caution, and bear in mind the general lack of hygiene.

Traditionally Guatemalans eat a **breakfast** of tortillas and eggs, accompanied by the inevitable beans – and sometimes including a sauce of sour cream. **Lunch** is the main meal of the day, and this is the best time to fill your belly as restaurants often offer *comidas corridas*, a set two- or three-course meal that sometimes costs as little as a dollar. It's always filling and occasionally delicious. Sometimes the same deal is on offer in the evenings, but in general only at midday; so **evening meals** are likely to be more expensive.

Vegetarians are hardly catered for specifically, except in the tourist restaurants of Antigua and Panajachel and at a couple of places in Guatemala City. It is, however, fairly easy to get by eating plenty of beans and eggs, which are always on the menu (although you should know that these things, beans especially, are often fried in lard). The markets also offer plenty of superb fruit, and tortillas, which are the basic ingredient of most Guatemalan diets.

■ What to eat

There are three distinct **types of cooking** in Guatemala, and although they overlap to an extent it's still clear enough which one it is that you're eating.

MAYA CUISINE

The first and oldest style is **Maya cooking**, in which the basic staples of beans and maize dominate. **Beans** (*frijoles*) are the black kidney-shaped variety and are served in two ways: either *refritos*, which are boiled up, mashed, and then refried in a great dollop, or *enteros*, which are boiled up whole, with a few slices of onion, and served in their own black juice. For breakfast, beans are usually served with eggs and cream, and at other times of the day they're offered up on a separate plate to the main dish. Almost all truly Guatemalan meals include a portion of beans, and for many highland Indians beans are the only regular source of protein.

Maize is the other essential; a food which for the Maya (and many other American Indians) is almost as nourishing spiritually as it is physically. In Indian legends, mankind was originally made from maize. It appears most commonly as the **tortilla**, a thin pancake of maize, which is mixed with small quantities of lime and eaten with chillies. The maize is traditionally ground by hand and shaped by clapping it between two hands, although these days machines are equally common. It's cooked on a **comale**, which is a sheet of metal placed over the fire, and the very best tortillas are eaten while warm, usually brought to the table wrapped in cloth. While beans may be part of many a Guatemalan meal, it's tortillas that are the country's staple, and for

Indians it's the tortilla that forms the hub of a meal, with beans or the odd piece of meat as accompaniments to spice it up. Some people never get to like them, but the burnt, smoky taste of tortillas will become very much a part of your trip; and the smell of them is enough to revive memories years later. Where there's an option local people often serve gringos with bread, assuming they wouldn't want tortillas.

Maize is also used to make a number of traditional **snacks**, which are sold on buses, at markets and during fiestas. The most common of these is the *tamale*, a pudding-like cornmeal package sometimes stuffed with chicken. It's wrapped in a banana leaf and then boiled. Slightly more exciting is the *chuchito*, which is similar but tends to include a bit of tomato and a pinch of hot chilli. Other popular snacks are *chiles rellenos*, stuffed peppers, and *pacaya*, which is a rather stodgy local vegetable.

Chillies are the final essential ingredient of the Indian diet, usually placed (raw or pickled) in the middle of the table in a jar, but also served as a sauce – *salsa picante*. The strength of these can vary tremendously, so treat them with caution until you know what you're dealing with.

Other traditional Maya dishes include a superb range of **stews** – known as *caldos* – made with duck, beef, chicken or turkey; and *fiambre*, which is the world's largest salad, traditionally served on the Day of the Dead (November 1). The best chance to sample traditional food is at a market or fiesta, when makeshift *comedores* serve freshly cooked food. A highland breakfast often includes a plate of *mosh*, which is made with milk and oats and tastes rather like porridge. It's the ideal antidote to an early morning chill.

COLONIAL CUISINE

Guatemala's second culinary style is **Ladino food**, which is indebted to the great range of cultures that go to make up the *Ladino* population. Most of the food has a mild Latin American bias, incorporating a lot of Mexican ideas, but the influence of the United States and Europe is also strongly felt. At its most obvious Ladino food includes *bistek* (steak), *hamburguesa* and *chao mein*, all of which are readily available in most Guatemalan towns. But you'll also find **German** influence in the widespread availability of frankfurter-type sausages and plenty of **Italian** restaurants offering pasta and pizza. In the main tourist towns, Antigua and Panajachel, you'll also find some fairly unusual additions including Tex-Mex, Japanese, vegetarian, and even a European-style deli.

CREOLE CUISINE

The final element is the **Creole cooking** found on Guatemala's Caribbean coast. Here it's **bananas**, **coconuts** and **seafood** that dominate the scene, all of them, if you're lucky, cooked superbly. You have to hunt around to find true Creole cooking, which incorporates the influences of the Caribbean with those of Africa, but it's well worth the effort. Some of the more obvious elements have also penetrated the mainstream: you'll get fried plantains everywhere (*platanos fritos*) as well as *ceviche*, a delicious dish of raw fish marinated in lemon juice and onions.

■ Drink

To start off the day most Guatemalans drink a cup of hot **coffee**, **chocolate** or **tea** (all of which are usually served with plenty of sugar), but in the highlands you'll also be offered *atol*, a warm, sweet drink made with either rice or maize and sugar. Some travellers swear by it. At other times of day **soft drinks** and beer are usually drunk with meals. *Coca-cola*, *Pepsi*, *Sprite* and *Fanta* are all common, and mineral water (*agua mineral*) is almost always available in bottles (in many of the larger towns the tap water is safe to drink, but as a general rule it's a good idea to stick with the bottled version). There are two main varieties of bottled **beer** on sale in Guatemala: *Cabro* (Goat) and *Gallo* (Cockerel). If you venture into the more upmarket bars you may also come across some premium brands, including *Moza*, the country's only dark beer.

As for **spirits**, rum (*ron*) and *aguardiente*, a clear and lethal spirit, are very popular, and correspondingly cheap. Hard drinkers will soon get to know *Quezalteca*, an *aguardiente* sold and drunk everywhere, whose power is at the heart of many a fiesta. If you're after a real bargain then try locally brewed alcohol (*chicha*), which is practically given away. Its main ingredient can be anything: apple, cherry, sugar cane, peach, apricot or quince are just some of the more common.

Wine is also made in Guatemala, from local fruits or imported concentrates. It's interesting to try, but if you hope to find anything drinkable it's best to stick to the more expensive imports.

Opening hours and holidays

Guatemalan opening hours are subject to considerable local variations but in general many places, including shops and museums, open around 9 or 10am, close for a siesta of an hour or so in the early afternoon, and stay open until around 7pm. Others, including most offices, work a standard 9am to 5pm eight-hour day. In general opening times are stricter in the capital, where you need to check up on museums and banks before you set out.

Museums and **galleries** are usually open from 9am to noon and from 2 to 6pm. They stay open at weekends but tend to close on either Monday or Wednesday. **Banks** are mostly open from 9am, closing any time between 3pm and 8pm, and government offices close at around 3.30pm. Outside the main towns, branches of the *Banco de Guatemala* are open 8.30am to 2pm from Monday to Thursday, with an extra half-hour on Friday afternoon. The main **post office** in Guatemala City is open from 8am to 6pm, while branches in other parts of the country are open from 8am to 4.30pm. **Archaeological sites** are open every day, usually from 8am to 5pm.

The principal public holidays, when almost all businesses close down, are given below, but each village or town will also have its own fiestas or saints' days when everything will be shut. These can last anything from one day to two weeks.

PUBLIC HOLIDAYS

Jânuary 1 New Year's Day

January 6 Epiphany

Semana Santa The four days of Holy Week leading up to Easter

May 1 Labour Day

June 30 Army Day, anniversary of 1871 revolution

August 15 Guatemala City fiesta, Guatemala City only

September 15 Independence Day

October 12 Discovery of America

October 20 Revolution Day

November 1 All Saints' Day

December 24 From noon

December 25 Christmas

December 31 From noon

Fiestas and entertainment

Traditional fiestas are one of the great excitements of a trip to Guatemala, and every town and village, however small, devotes at least one day a year to celebration. The date is normally prescribed by the local saint's day, but the party often extends to a week or two around that date, although the main day is always marked by a climactic event. On almost every day of the year there's a fiesta in some forgotten corner of the country, and with a bit of planning or a stroke of luck you should be able to witness at least one. Most of them are well worth going out of your way for.

The **format** of fiestas varies between two basic models. In towns with a largely *Ladino* population, fairs are usually set up and the days are filled with processions, beauty contests and perhaps the odd marching band, while the nights are dominated by dance halls and salsa rhythms. In the highlands, where the bulk of the population is Indian, you'll see traditional dances, costumes and musicians, and a blend of religious and secular celebration that incorporates elements which predate the arrival of the Spanish. What they all share is an astonishing energy and an unbounded enthusiasm for drink, dance and fireworks: all three of which are virtually impossible to escape during the days of fiesta.

One thing you shouldn't expect is anything too dainty or organised: fiestas are above all chaotic, and the measured rhythms of traditional dance and music are usually obscured by the crush of the crowd and the huge volumes of alcohol consumed by participants. If you can join the mood there's no doubt that fiestas are wonderfully entertaining and what's more that they offer a real insight into Guatemalan culture, *Ladino* or Indian.

Many of the best fiestas include some specifically local element, such as the giant kites at Santiago Sacatepéquez, the religious processions in Antigua and the horse race in Todos Santos. The dates of most fiestas, along with their main features, are listed at the end of each chapter. At certain times virtually the whole country erupts simultaneously: Easter Week is perhaps the most important, particularly in Antigua, but both All Saints' Day (November 1) and Christmas are also marked by partying across the land.

■ Dance

Dance is the subject of yet another cultural divide. In the nightclubs of Guatemala City it's Latin-rock and salsa that gets people onto the dance floor, and once they're there they dance a mixture of disco and Latin styles. Outside the city, dance is usually confined to fiestas, and in the highland villages this means traditional dances, heavily imbued with history and symbolism.

The drunken dancers may look out of control, but the process is taken very seriously and involves great expense on the part of the dancers – who have to hire their ornate costumes. The most common dance is the *Baile de la Conquista*, which re-enacts the victory of the Spanish over the Indians. At the same time the dance manages to ridicule the *conquistadores* and, according to some studies, it is based in pre-Columbian traditions. Other popular dances are the *Baile de los Gracejos*, the dance of the jesters, the *Baile del Venado*, the dance of the deer, and the *Baile de la Culebra*, the dance of the snake; all of them again rooted in pre-Columbian traditions.

In some places local dances have been developed, and one of the most impressive is the *Palo Volador*, in which men swing by ropes from a thirty-metre pole. Today this is only performed in Chichicastenango, Joyabaj and Cubulco.

■ Music

Guatemalan **music** combines many different influences, but yet again it can be broadly divided between Ladino and Indian. For fiestas bands are always shipped in, complete with a crackling PA system and a strutting lead singer.

Traditional music is dominated by the **marimba**, a type of wooden xylophone that may well have originated in Africa (although many argue that it developed independently in Central America). The oldest versions use gourds beneath the sounding board and can be played by a single musician, while modern models, using hollow tubes to generate the sound, can need as many as seven players. The marimba is at the heart of traditional music, and marimba orchestras play at every occasion, for both *Ladino* and Indian communities. In the remotest of villages you sometimes hear them practising well into the night, particularly around market day. Other important instruments, especially in Indian bands, are the *tun*, a drum made from a hollow log; the *tambor*, another drum traditionally covered with the skin of a deer; *los chichines*, a type of maracas made from hollow gourds; the *tzijolaj*, an Indian piccolo; and the *chirimia*, a flute.

Modern, or Ladino, music is a blend of north American and Latin sounds, much of it originating in Miami and Puerto Rico, although there are plenty of local bands producing their own version of the sound. It's fast-moving, easy-going and very rhythmic, and on any bus you'll hear many of the most popular tracks. It draws on *merengue*, a rhythm that originally came from the Dominican Republic, and includes elements of Mexican *mariachi* and the *cumbia* and *salsa* of Colombia and Cuba.

Finally, on the Caribbean coast, you'll hear the sound of reggae, which reaches Livingston from island radio stations. Reggae has also made it to Guatemala City where there are a couple of nightclubs run by people from the Caribbean coast.

■ Sport

Guatemalans have a furious appetite for spectator sport and the daily papers always devote four or five pages to the subject. **Football** tops the bill and if you get the chance to see a major game it's a thrilling experience, if only to watch the crowd. Otherwise North American sport predominates – **baseball**, **American football**, and **basketball** are all popular.

On a more local level **bullfights**, which are staged in Guatemala City in October and December, draw large crowds. The *matadores* are usually from Spain or Mexico, and entrance fees are high. The main bull ring is beside the Parque Aurora in Guatemala City.

As a participatory sport, **fishing** is popular. Good sea fishing is available on either coast, while in the Petén the rivers and lakes are packed with sport fish, including snook, tarpon and

peacock bass. Lake Petexbatún and Lake Yaxja both offer superb fishing, as do the Usumacinta and Dulce rivers. On the Pacific coast there are yellow and black tuna, snappers, bonito and dorado, while further offshore there are marlin and sailfish. For more information on the waters of the Caribbean coast see the section on Belize. If you have plenty of money you can find superb sea fishing in the Caribbean off Belize.

Crafts, markets and shops

Guatemalan craft traditions, locally known as *artesania*, are very much a part of modern Indian culture, stemming from practices that in most cases predate the arrival of the Spanish. Many of these traditions are highly localised, with different regions and even different villages specialising in particular crafts.

■ Artesania

The best place to buy Guatemalan **crafts** is in their place of origin, where the quality is usually highest, the prices reasonable, and above all else the craftsmen and women get a greater share of the profit. But if you haven't the time or the energy to travel to remote highland villages then there are plenty of places where you can find a superb selection from all around the country. The markets in Chichicastenango (on Thursday and Sunday) are always good, but you'll also find good quality *artesania* in Guatemala City, Antigua, Panajachel and Huehuetenango. In all of these places it's well worth shopping around – and bargaining – as prices can vary wildly.

The greatest craft in Guatemala has to be **weaving**, with styles and techniques developed consistently since Maya times, and now prac- tised at an astonishingly high standard through- out the western highlands. Each village has its own traditional designs, woven in fantastic patterns and with superbly vivid colours. One thing to bear in mind is that for the Indians cloth- ing has a spiritual significance and the pattern is specific to the weaver and the wearer, casting

them in a particular social role. If you go into a village and buy local clothing you may well cheapen the value that's placed on it, and it is deeply insulting to offer to buy the clothes that someone is wearing. Having said this there are plenty of Indian weavers who are very keen to expand their market by selling to tourists, and for them you offer a ideal supplement to a meagre income. All the finest weaving is done on the backstrap loom, and the quality and variety are so impressive that you'll be spoilt for choice.

Alongside Guatemalan weaving most **other crafts** suffer by comparison. However if you hunt around you'll also find good ceramics, baskets, mats, silver and jade. The last two are easiest to come by in Antigua, although most of the silver is mined in Alta Verapaz. The others are produced by Indian craftsmen and women in the villages of the highlands, and sold in local markets through- out the country.

■ Markets

For shopping – and simply sightseeing – the **markets** of Guatemala are some of the finest anywhere. Most towns and villages, particularly in the highlands, have weekly markets – some of the larger ones are held twice a week, although one day is always the more important. Traditional markets are the focus of economic and social activity in rural Guatemala, and people come from miles around to sell, buy and have a good time. You really should make the effort to see a few: the mood varies tremendously, from the frenetic tourist markets in Chichicastenango to the calm of San Juan Atitán, but all markets have an air of fiesta about them and incorporate a great deal of chaotic celebration as well as hard-nosed busi- ness deals. Above all else markets offer a real glimpse of Indian culture, as they are at the heart of the Indian economy and social structure.

Prices are almost always lower in markets than in shops or on the streets in tourist areas (although in Chichicastenango real bargains are becoming increasingly scarce), but you'll still need to **bargain** if you want to avoid being severely ripped off. Everyone claims to have perfected a bargaining technique, but few stand a chance against the masters of the market: obvious tips are to have some idea of the shop price of similar items before you start to haggle, and always offer way below what's asked and expect to meet somewhere in the middle. However badly you do it's always good entertainment, and if approaching gringos are a major cause of inflation – why not?

■ Everyday goods

For ordinary **shopping** and your everyday needs you can buy just about everything in Guatemala that you could buy in Europe or the United States – at a price. For **food** you need to look no further than the market, where things are fresh and the prices are low. For other things you should stick to the shops. Basic items are always cheaper but imported goods command a higher price and luxuries, like electrical goods and cameras, are often very expensive. **Film** is available – though not black-and-white and nothing beyond 64–400 ASA. Video film can be bought in Guatemala City but Video 8 is very hard to come by as is cine film. Books in English – a rather limited selection – are sold in Guatemala City and Antigua, but prices are high. For anything out of the ordinary it's a good idea to do your shopping in the capital, where there's a much greater range on offer.

Trouble, and sexual harassment

The problem of personal safety in Guatemala is part of a strange contradiction. While the country has a horrific record on human rights, visitors are very safe indeed. Violence still claims a life each day but the victims are clearly defined and violent crime is not particularly common. Certainly the chances of becoming involved are extremely slim. In fact for the tourist Guatemala is one of the safest countries in Latin America, particularly compared to the horrors of Peru and Colombia. Nevertheless you should be aware that there are areas of danger and ways of avoiding potentially dangerous situations.

■ Crime

Despite the alarmingly high murder rate, you – as a visitor – are very unlikely to run into any trouble in Guatemala. Theft is not a serious problem but you should still take all the normal precautions, particularly around bus stations and in Guatemala

City. **Petty theft** and **pickpockets** are your biggest worry. Again the risk is highest in the capital, though markets and fiestas are also favourite haunts of pickpockets – large gangs sometimes descend on villages for such events. It's never a good idea to flash your money around, and you should avoid leaving cameras and cash in hotel rooms: most hotels will have somewhere to lock up valuables, although even this may not be too secure. You are also particularly vulnerable when travelling so try and keep your bag, or at least your most valuable stuff, with you in the bus, and keep an eye on anything that goes up top.

Muggings and **violent crime** are said to be on the increase in Guatemala City. There's little to worry about during the day, providing you don't visit the slum areas, but you should think twice before wandering outside the central area after dark. Stick to the main streets and use the buses and taxis to get around.

If you are robbed then you'll have to report it to the police, which can be a very long process. In the end it's worth it, though, as many insurance companies will only pay out if you can produce a police statement.

Drivers are perhaps more likely to run into trouble and cars left unattended are often relieved of a wing mirror or two. To avoid this it's a good idea to search out hotels that can accommodate your car as well as you.

Drug offences are dealt with severely. Even the possession of marijuana could land you in jail, a sobering experience in Guatemala.

■ Police and soldiers

For Europeans and North Americans expecting to enter a police state, Guatemala may come as something of a surprise. Though there are a lot of police and soldiers on the streets there's rarely anything intimidating about their presence, and if you do have any dealings with them you'll probably find them surprisingly helpful.

Travelling in Guatemala you'll inevitably pass through many **road blocks** and **checkpoints**, though these are by no means an intimidating experience and in almost all cases it's a routine process. At some you may be asked to get out of the bus and line up, with men and women separated. If this happens you'll be frisked and have to show your passport, but again it's a routine procedure that Guatemalans have learned to live with. It's also possible that your bus will be stopped by the guerrillas, and though this is a little unnerving it's again nothing to worry about. Under normal circumstances you'll hear a short lecture on their aims and be allowed to go on your way.

It's important to **carry your passport** at all times, as you never know when someone might demand to see it. If for any reason you do find yourself **in trouble with the law**, be as polite as possible and do as you're told. At the first possible opportunity get in touch with your embassy and negotiate through them: they will understand the situation better than you. The addresses of embassies and consulates in Guatemala City are listed in the section on the city.

■ Sexual harassment

So many oppressive limitations are imposed on women travellers that any advice or warning would seem only to reinforce the situation. However, it has to be said that **machismo** is very much a part of Guatemalan culture. The hassle is usually confined to comments on the street and perhaps the occasional pinch or grab, and unless your Spanish and nerve are up to a duel it's a good idea to ignore such things.

The worst areas are those dominated by *Ladino* culture: the Pacific coast, Guatemala City and the eastern highlands. Indian society is conditioned into being more deferential so you're unlikely to experience any hassle in the western highlands.

There's little in the way of a **feminist movement** in Guatemala, and no formulated groups.

Directory

ADDRESSES in Guatemala are almost all based on the grid system that's used in most towns, with *Avenidas* running in one direction and *Calles* in the other. The address specifies the street first, then locates the block, and ends with the zone. For example, the address *Avenida Reforma 3–55 Zona 1*, means that house is on Avenida Reforma, between 3 and 4 Calles, at No. 55, in Zona 1. Almost all towns have numbered streets, but in some places the old names are also used. In Antigua the Calles and Avenidas are also divided according to their direction from the central plaza – north, south, east or west (*norte, sur, oriente* and *poniente*).

AIRPORT TAX has to be paid before departure on all international flights. It's currently set at Q20, payable in *quetzales* or US dollars.

BAGS If you're planning to travel around by bus – and certainly if you're going to do some walking with your gear as well – then a backpack is the best option. But you might also bear in mind that there is some prejudice against "hippies", and backpacks are often seen as their trademark. Whatever you decide to pack your stuff in, make sure it's tough enough to handle being thrown on and off the top of buses. Or better still carry something small enough to fit inside a bus, on the luggage rack, which is both easier and safer.

BEGGARS are fairly common in Guatemala, particularly on the streets of the main towns and around church entrances, though they rarely hassle anyone. Local people tend to be generous, and it's worth having some change handy.

CONTRACEPTION Condoms are available from chemists (*farmacías*) in all the main towns, although it's safest to get them in Guatemala City, where shortages are less common. Some makes of the pill are also available, mostly those manufactured in the States, but it's obviously sensible to take enough to last for your entire stay. Bear in mind that diarrhoea can reduce the reliability of the pill (or any other drug) as it may not be in your system long enough to be fully absorbed.

DRUGS are increasingly available in Guatemala as the country is becoming a centre for both shipment and production. Marijuana, which mostly comes in from South America and Mexico, is readily available and cheap – especially as in recent years the Petén has become a marijuana producing area and there is a plentiful supply across the border in Belize. Cocaine, which is shipped to the States through Guatemala, is also available within the country, although heroin, which is said to be produced here, is as yet barely known on the streets. Bear in mind that the drugs problem is now viewed increasingly seriously by the government and users will be dealt with harshly. If you're caught, expect to go to jail.

ELECTRICITY in Guatemala is theoretically 110 volts AC, although the nature of the supply varies from place to place. In some smaller towns the current is at 220 volts, so ask before you plug in any vital equipment. Anything from Britain will need a transformer and a plug adaptor as well. Cuts in the supply and wild fluctuations in the current are fairly common, while in some isolated villages, where they have their own generator, the supply only operates for part of the day (usually the early evening and morning).

EMBASSIES AND CONSULATES are listed under Guatemala City, where almost every country, except Belize, is represented. In addition there are Mexican consulates in Quezaltenango and Retalhuleu, and a Honduran consul in Esquipulas.

GAY LIFE There is a small gay community in Guatemala City but they have no clubs or public meeting places and homosexuality is publicly strongly frowned upon – although not theoretically illegal. Macho attitudes incorporate an overwhelming prejudice against gays and the newspapers occasionally include accounts which might read "the arrest of prostitutes and gays". Extreme discretion is the only answer.

LAUNDRY Hotels occasionally offer a laundry service, and most cheap places will have somewhere where you can wash and dry your own clothes. In Guatemala City and Quezaltenango there are self-service launderettes, and several places that will do your washing for you – on the whole these are much easier and cost about the same. There are also laundry services in Panajachel, Huehuetenango and Antigua.

ODD ESSENTIALS Insect repellent is a must – you can buy it in markets, particularly in the Petén, which is where you'll really need it. You can also buy coils that burn through the night to keep the beasts at bay, although if you plan to sleep out then there's no substitute for a mosquito net – which you can also buy in the markets in the Petén. A torch and alarm clock are worth having for catching those pre-dawn buses, and it's always a good idea to carry toilet paper with you. It's easy enough to buy in Guatemala but it's never there when you need it.

STUDENT CARDS can get you discounts from time to time, particularly in the expensive private museums in Guatemala City. But it's hardly worth struggling to obtain one as there are few discounts available outside the capital.

TAMPONS are sold at most *farmacías* (chemists), although outside Guatemala City the supply is unpredictable. Several brand names are available including *Tampax*.

TIME ZONES Guatemala is on the equivalent of US Central Standard Time, which puts it six hours earlier than London. There are no seasonal changes and it gets light around 6.30am, with sunset at 7pm.

TIPS In upmarket restaurants a ten-percent tip is appropriate, but in most places, especially the cheaper ones, tipping is the exception rather than the rule. Taxi drivers are not normally tipped.

TOILETS vary greatly throughout the country, but in general the further you are from the city the lower the standard. Public toilets are few and far between, and the majority of them are filthy. Toilet paper is usually sold by the attendant, who also charges a small entrance fee. The most common name is *baños*, and the signs are *damas* (women) and *caballeros* (men).

TOURIST OFFICES are to be found in Guatemala City, Panajachel, Antigua, Flores and Quezaltenango. They are all very friendly but can't always be relied on to come up with the solution to your problem.

WATER Tap water in the main towns is purified and you can usually taste the chlorine. However, this doesn't mean that it won't give you stomach trouble, and it's always safest to stick to bottled water, at least until your body has begun to adapt.

WORK is generally badly paid, and unless you have something very special to offer your best bet is to teach English. All the English schools in Guatemala City, which are listed in the phone book, are constantly on the lookout for new teachers, and there are also schools in Antigua. If you'd like to work as a volunteer for one of the relief agencies in Guatemala then contact Mike Shawcross at the *Casa Andinista* in Antigua.

METRIC WEIGHTS AND MEASURES

1 ounce = 28.3 grams	1 pint = 0.47 litres	1 inch = 2.54 centimetres (cm)	1.09 yards = 1m
1 pound = 454 grams	1 quart = 0.94 litres	1 foot = 0.3 metres (m)	1 mile = 1.61 kilometres (km)
2.2 pounds = 1 kilogram	1 gallon = 3.78 litres	1 yard = 0.91 metres	0.62 miles = 1 km

Guatemalan Indians also use the *lengua*, a distance of about four miles, which is roughly the distance a person can walk in an hour. Indigenous fabrics are often sold by the *vara*, an old Spanish measure of about 33 inches, while land is sometimes measured by the *cuerda*, a square with sides of 32 *varas*. A larger unit, the *manzana*, is equivalent to three-quarters of a hectare or 1.73 acres.

CHAPTER ONE

GUATEMALA CITY AND AROUND

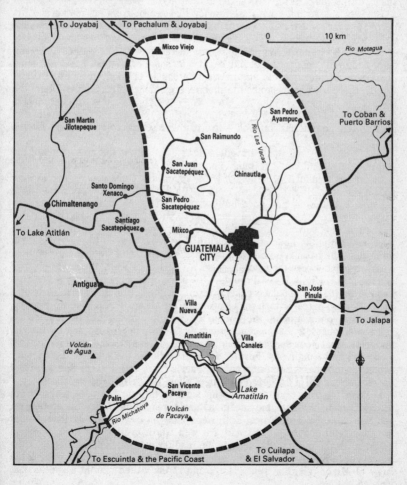

Guatemala's capital is splayed out across a sweeping highland basin, surrounded on three sides by low hills and volcanic cones. Cosmopolitan and congested, the city has an atmosphere that seems somehow ill-suited to the country as a whole. Today it's home to around two million people, a quarter of Guatemala's population, and is the established centre of politics, power and wealth.

The modern city was founded in 1776, after the devastation of Antigua, but its site – on a natural trade route between the Pacific and the Caribbean – had been of importance long before the arrival of the Spanish. In its early years the capital grew slowly, and it wasn't until the beginning of this century that it really began to dominate the country. These days its shapeless and swelling mass, ringed by shanty towns, ranks as the largest city in Central America.

The city has an intensity and vibrancy that are both its fascination and its horror, and for some travellers a trip to the capital is an exercise in damage limitation, struggling through a swirling mass of bus fumes and beggars. The city centre is now run-down and polluted – and the affluent middle classes have long since fled to the suburbs – but it does have its share of "sights", including some impressive architecture, old and new, and a couple of good museums. Beyond this the real attraction has to be the sheer energy of life on the streets, where the calm of the highlands is long forgotten. The city's population is truly cosmopolitan, with its aspirations firmly rooted in the United States, and incorporating an aggressively commercial outlook – two of the essential components of *Ladino* culture.

Like it or not – and many travellers don't – the city is the crossroads of the entire country, and you'll certainly end up here at some time, if only to hurry between bus terminals or negotiate a visa extension. Once you get used to the pace it can offer a welcome break from life on the road, with decent restaurants, cinemas, hot showers and good hotels. And if you really can't take the city it's easy enough to escape, with buses leaving every few minutes, day and night.

The hills that surround the city have somehow managed to remain unaffected by it, and within an hour or two you'll find yourself back in the highlands. On three sides the basin is hemmed in by a horseshoe of hills, while to the south, in a narrow gap between the volcanic peaks of Agua and Pacaya, the Rio Michatoya and the Pacific Highway cut through to the ocean. Heading out this way you pass **Lake Amatitlán**, a popular weekend resort for those who don't have their own *fincas*. Beyond here a branch road leads up to the village of **San Vicente Pacaya**, from where you can climb the **Volcán Pacaya**, the most active of Guatemala's volcanoes. Its size and appearance aren't particularly impressive, but for the last few years it has been spewing a fountain of sulphurous gas and molten rock that glows red in the night sky. Further down the valley is the village of **Palín**, after which you emerge at **Escuintla** and the Pacific coast, with **Puerto San José** and the chance of a dip in the ocean just three or four hours from the capital.

Leaving the city from the opposite side, to the northwest, you travel out through rolling hills and pine forests to the villages of **San Pedro Sacatepéquez** and **San Juan Sacatepéquez**. Both were badly hit by the 1976 earthquake but are now returning to normal and are well worth visiting for their weekend markets. To the north of the villages the road divides, one half heading over the mountains to **Rabinal**, and the other heading on towards **Pachalum**, passing the ruins of **Mixco Viejo**, a well restored but rarely visited site, in a spectacular, isolated setting.

GUATEMALA CITY

Guatemala City, an extremely horizontal place, is like a city on its back. Its ugliness, which is a threatened look (the low morose houses have earthquake cracks in their facades; the buildings wince at you with fright lines), is ugliest on those streets where, just past the toppling houses, a blue volcano's cone bulges. I could see the volcanoes from the window of my hotel room. I was on the third floor, which was also the top floor. They were tall volcanoes and looked capable of spewing lava. Their beauty was undeniable; but it was the beauty of witches. The rumbles from their fires had heaved this city down.

Paul Theroux, The Old Patagonian Express.

While much has changed since Theroux was here, Guatemala City, though by no means as black as he implies, is certainly not somewhere you visit for its beauty or architecture. The city is built in a massive highland basin, on a site that was a centre of population and political power long before the arrival of the Spanish. The pre-conquest city of **Kaminaljuyú**, its ruins still scattered amongst the western suburbs, was well established here two thousand years ago. In early Classic times (250–550 AD), through an alliance with the great northern power of Teotihuacán (near to present-day Mexico City), the city came to dominate the highlands, and eventually provided the political and commercial backing that fostered the rise of Tikal. Kaminaljuyú was situated at the crossroads of the north–south and east–west trade routes, and also controlled the obsidian mine at El Chayal, giving it a virtual monopoly of this essential commodity. To further ensure its wealth, the city also had access to a supply of quetzal feathers, another highly valued item.

At the height of its prosperity Kaminaljuyú had a population of some 50,000, but following the decline of Teotihuacán around 600 AD it was surpassed by the great lowland centres that it had helped to establish. Soon after their rise it was abandoned, some time between 600 and 900 AD.

Seven centuries later, when Alvarado entered the country, the fractured tribes of the west controlled the highlands and preoccupied the *conquistadores*. The nearest centre of any importance was the Pokoman capital of **Mixco Viejo**, about 60km to the northwest. Mainly because of the need to keep a close watch on the western tribes, the Spanish ignored the possibility of settling here, founding their capital instead at Iximché, and later at two sites in the Panchoy valley.

In the early years of Spanish occupation the only new building in this area was a church in the village of La Ermita, founded in 1620. For over a hundred years the village remained no more than a tiny cluster of Indian homes, but in 1773, following months of devastating earthquakes, Captain Mayorga and some 4200 followers, fleeing the disease-ridden ruins of Antigua, established a temporary headquarters in the village. From here they despatched envoys and scouts in all directions, seeking a site for the new capital, and eventually decided to settle in the neighbouring Valley of the Virgin.

By royal decree the new city was named **Nueva Guatemala de la Asunción**, in honour of the Virgin of the Ascension, whose image stood in the church at La Ermita. On January 1, 1776, the city was officially inaugurated, and the following day its "fathers" held their first council to administer construction. The plan was typical of the Spanish colonial model, and identical to that used in the two previous, ill-fated cities. A main plaza was boxed in by the Cathedral, the Palace of the Captains General and the town hall, and around this, on a strict grid pattern, was a

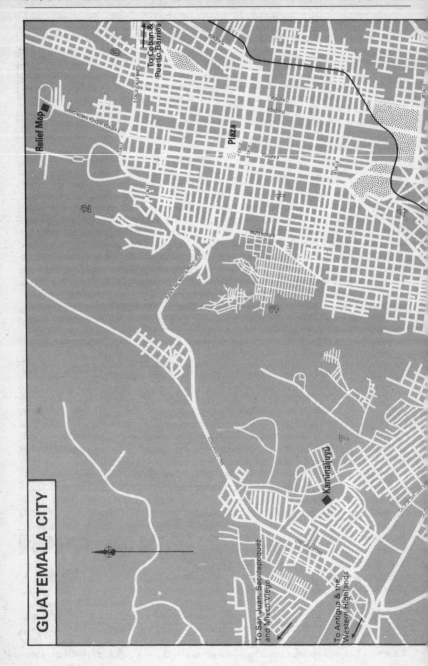

GUATEMALA CITY

Relief Map

To Cobán &
Puerto Barrios

Plaza

Kaminaljuyú

To San Juan, Sacatepéquez
and Mixco-Viejo

To Antigua & the
Western Highlands

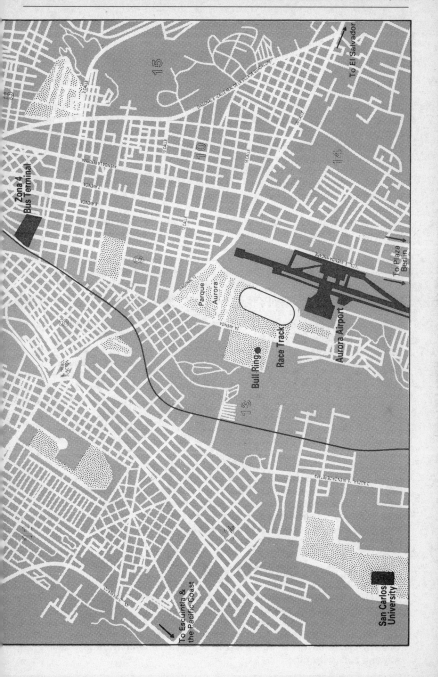

city fifteen streets long and fifteen wide. Early development was slow: the people of Antigua were reluctant to leave, despite being bullied by endless decrees and deadlines, although waves of smallpox and cholera eventually persuaded some. By 1800, however, the population of the new capital was still only 25,000.

The splendour of the former capital was hard to re-establish and the new city's growth was steady but by no means dramatic. An 1863 census listed the main structures as 1206 residences, 7 warehouses, 130 shops, 28 churches, 1 slaughter-house, 2 forts, 12 schools, and 25 fountains and public laundries. The author, Enrique Palacios, concluded that it was "a delightful city and a pleasant place to live". Boddam-Wetham, on the other hand, living here in 1877, claimed that it was "gloomy and dull; owing to the uniformity of the houses . . . the regularity of the streets . . . and the absence of traffic", adding that "the few signs of life are depressing". When Eadweard Muybridge took some of the earliest photographs in 1875 the city was still little more than a large village, with a theatre, a government palace and a fort.

One of the factors retarding the city's growth was the existence of a major rival, Quezaltenango. Stimulated by the coffee boom and large numbers of German immigrants, Quezaltenango competed with the capital in both size and importance. However in 1902, this too was razed to the ground by a massive earthquake, prompting many wealthy families to move to the capital, and finally establishing it as the country's primary city. Its population had by then been boosted by two major **earthquakes** – in Antigua and Quezaltenango – and inevitably its turn had to come. On Christmas Eve 1917 the capital itself was shaken by the first in a series of devastating tremors, and not until early February, after six long weeks of destruction, did the ground stabilise and the dust settle. This time however there was nowhere to run; and spurred on by the need to celebrate 100 years of independence, and the impetus of the eccentric President Ubico, reconstruction began.

Since then Guatemala City has grown at an incredible rate, tearing ahead of the rest of the country at a pace that still shows little sign of letting up. The flow from the fields, characteristic of all Third World countries, was aided and abetted here by the chronic shortage of land or employment in the countryside, and has in the past been swollen by rural violence (though in practice it's far more dangerous to live in the city than anywhere in the highlands). The deep ravines that surround the city, thought by the original Spanish planners to offer protection from the force of earthquakes, are now filling rapidly with rubbish and shanty towns. The streets, choked with jet-black bus fumes, tunnel beneath neon signs; while the wealthy, as ever, have abandoned the scramble of the city centre to take refuge in relaxed suburbs. Glass skyscrapers rise alongside colonial churches, and while the rich bask in the joys of an all-American lifestyle, the poor struggle to earn a living on its fringes. The contrasts of poverty and extravagance are extreme.

Arrival and orientation

Arriving in Guatemala City for the first time it's easy to feel overwhelmed by its scale, with suburbs sprawled across some nineteen **zones**. In fact, once you've got your bearings, the layout is straightforward and you'll find that the central area, which is all that you need to worry about, is really quite small. Like almost all Guatemalan towns it's laid out on a strict grid pattern, with **avenidas** running one way and **calles** the other.

ADDRESSES IN THE CAPITAL

The system of street numbers in the capital may seem a little confusing at first as the same numbers are given to different streets in different zones. However once you get the hang of things there is a degree of method to the apparent madness.

When it comes to finding an address always check the zone first and then check out the street. For example "4 Avenida 9–14, Zona 1" is in Zona 1, on 4 Avenida between 9 and 10 Calle, house number 14.

You may see street numbers written as 1a, 7a etc, rather than simply 1, 7. This is technically more correct, since the names of the streets are not One Avenue and Seven Street, but First (*primera*), Seventh (*séptima*) and so on. A capital "A" used as a suffix indicates a smaller street between two large ones: 1 Calle A is a short street between 1 and 2 Calles.

Broadly speaking the city divides into two distinct halves. The northern section, centred on **Zona 1**, is the old part of town, containing the central plaza – the **Parque Central** – most of the budget hotels, shops, restaurants, cinemas, the post office, immigration, and many of the bus companies. This part of the city is cramped and congested, but bustling with activity. The two main streets are 5 and 6 avenidas, both thick with street traders and neon.

To the south, acting as a buffer between the two halves of town, and on the border of Zona 1 and Zona 4, is the **Centro Municipal**, where you'll find all the main administrative buildings, the **tourist office**, the central market and the National Theatre. The avenidas of Zona 1 are brought together at several junctions in this section and then fan out into the southern city.

The southern section, starting in **Zona 4**, is the modern city, where the streets are broad and tree-lined. To complicate matters slightly, this southern half of the city is itself divided into two halves, split down the middle by 7 Avenida. On the eastern side is the main **Avenida La Reforma**, which leads on into the Avenida las Americas. Here it's the wealthy who dominate the scene, with expensive offices, private museums, banks, travel agents, smart hotels and embassies. The other half of the modern city, to the west, is dominated by trade and transport, including the **airport** and the Zona 4 **bus terminal**. The **railway** line to the coast runs out through this area, as does Avenida Bolívar, one of the main traffic arteries bringing buses from the western highlands into the heart of the city.

Maps of the city are available from the **tourist office**, 7 Avenida 1–17, Zona 4.

Transport termini

Arriving in Guatemala City is always a bit disconcerting, but the hotels and bus companies are, for the most part, close together in Zona 1, so you'll find that settling in isn't as daunting as it might at first appear. If you're laden with luggage then it's probably not a good idea to take on the bus system, and a taxi is well worth the extra cost.

Bus

If you arrive in the city by second-class bus prepare yourself for the jungle of the **Zona 4 bus terminal**, which as to rate as Guatemala City's most chaotic corner. On the whole it's only second-class buses from the western and eastern highlands that arrive here, so if you're coming from the Pacific coast or the Petén you'll be spared, arriving instead at the terminal at 18 Calle and 9 Avenida, in Zona 1. However if you do end up in Zona 4, and decide not to take a taxi – there are always plenty around at the entrance to the terminal – then you have to walk a couple of blocks to the corner of 2 Calle and 4 Avenida, from where local buses go to the centre of town (the #17 is one, but always ask the driver if he's going to *Zona Uno*). To get to the Zona 4 bus terminal from the centre of town take any bus marked *terminal*: you'll find these heading south along 4 Avenida in Zona 1.

Most of the buses that don't use the Zona 4 terminal will end up somewhere in Zona 1, close enough to walk to a hotel, or at least a cheap taxi ride away. The Zona 1 bus terminal is at 18 Calle and 9 Avenida, but many companies, especially first-class ones, have their own offices.

Plane

The **Aurora Airport**, which handles all domestic and international flights, is on the edge of the city in Zona 13, some way from the centre. Much the easiest way to get to and from the airport is by taxi: if you're **leaving** for the Petén you'll certainly want to do this as departures are mostly in the early morning, when the bus service is poor; **arriving**, you'll find plenty of taxis lying in wait as you emerge from the terminal.

During the day the #5 **bus** goes past the airport terminal – you can catch it in Zona 1, on 4 Avenida, but make sure that the word *aeropuerto* is displayed in the window of the bus as there are numerous variations on route #5. Coming from the airport to the centre of town you can catch the bus outside the terminal, across the open patch of grass, and it'll drop you in Zona 1, either on 5 Avenida or 9 Avenida.

Inside the airport terminal the check-in desks are upstairs and the customs and departure gates are in the basement. There's also a bank here, open seven days a week, and lots of duty-free and souvenir shops. If you're leaving the country there's a Q20 **departure tax** on all international flights, payable in either *quetzals* or dollars.

Train

Trains to and from Guatemala City were once an important component in the national transport network, but these days only two lines are still in service, to **Puerto Barrios** and to the Mexican border at **Tecún Umán**. These journeys are really only for genuine train enthusiasts, as the scheduled time of eight hours often extends to 18 or 20 (compared to a six-hour bus trip), and sooner or later the heavily indebted railway company will probably call a halt to its passenger service altogether. However, if you've more patience than money, and would like to spend the day rattling through the countryside, it can be an enjoyable trip, and you can always opt out somewhere along the way.

For the moment trains leave from the **railway station** at 9 Avenida and 18 Calle, Zona 1, to Puerto Barrios on Tuesday, Thursday and Saturday at 7.30am, and to Tecún Umán Tuesday and Saturday at 7am. Check the time and schedule in advance, however, as they tend to be unreliable. Heading to Guatemala City by train the schedules are more or less the same from the other end of the track, and you'll arrive in the early evening, all being well.

Local transport – buses and taxis

One of Guatemala City's greatest nightmares is the **bus system**, and even local people, who've lived in the city all their lives, are baffled by it.

One major complication is that the city authorities regularly re-route the buses in order to control traffic congestion, and another is that each route, or bus number, includes many possible variations. The easiest way to handle it is to accept that getting on the wrong bus isn't the end of the world, and that you can always cross the road and go back to where you started. Above all else the buses are cheap, so you'll need some small change to hand. In Zona 1 all the main avenidas are one-way; buses going south towards the newer parts of the city run down 4 Avenida and 10 Avenida; those coming up into Zona 1 run along 5 Avenida and 9 Avenida.

Buses **run** from around 6 or 7am until about 10pm, and after this there are **minibuses**, effectively operating as taxis along vaguely defined routes until around 1am. The minibuses also operate during the day, alongside the buses, serving similar routes.

USEFUL BUS ROUTES

#5 Runs along 4 Avenida in Zona 1, takes you out past the Parque Aurora and then to the airport – but make sure it says *aeropuerto* in the window, as other #5s go out into Zona 12.

#2 Runs along 10 Avenida and 12 Avenida in Zona 1, goes past the train station at 18 Calle and 9 Avenida, through Zona 4 along 6 Avenida, and then all the way down Avenida La Reforma to the Parque Independencia. This route is particularly handy as it takes you past many of the embassies, the office of *American Express*, the Popol Vuh and Ixchel museums, and to within walking distance of any address on Avenida las Americas.

#17 Marked *Kaminaljuyú* – runs along 4 Avenida in Zona 1, and will take you out west into Zona 7, and to the ruins of Kaminaljuyú.

Terminal Any bus marked *terminal*, and there are plenty of these on 4 Avenida in Zona 1, will take you to the main bus terminal in Zona 4.

Bolívar or Trébol Any bus with either of these written on will take you along the western side of the city, down Avenida Bolívar and to the Trébol junction.

Taxis

If you can't face the complexities of the bus system then **taxis** are always an easier option and aren't necessarily that expensive, providing you arrange a deal beforehand (meters are non-existent). There are plenty to be found around any of the bus terminals and in the Parque Central and the Parque Concordia, 6 Avenida 14 Calle, Zona 1.

Hotels

Hotels in Guatemala City come in all shapes and sizes, but the majority of the budget choices are conveniently grouped on the eastern side of Zona 1. There are also a few in the area of the two main bus terminals, but these are really for emergency use only (or for very early starts) as the neighbourhoods are neither convenient nor safe.

A personal favourite has always been the *Chalet Suizo*, at 14 Calle 6–82 (☎86371), a friendly and comfortable sort of place that's certainly very safe. Rooms start at about $4 – more for a private bathroom – but the hotel is often booked up in advance, so it's worth phoning to reserve a room. A couple of blocks to the south the *Hotel Fenix*, at 7 Avenida 15–81, is a bit more run-down, in an old wooden building, but still perfectly reasonable at $3. In the streets between the *Fenix* and the *Suizo* you'll find a whole bunch of budget hotels which are worth a try if the other two are full, but are somewhat downmarket. On 7 Avenida there's the *El Virrey* and the *Santa Ana*, while around the corner on 16 Calle are some rather more sleazy options, the *Copan*, the *Washington* and the *Mundial* – very much a last resort. If on the other hand you're looking for something slightly more upmarket then try the *Colonial*, 7 Avenida 14–19, where most rooms have private showers and the price is correspondingly high.

Heading further north, on 8 Avenida the *Hotel Spring* ($4), 8 Avenida 12–65, is another relaxed hotel, popular with budget travellers. Even further over, off 10 Avenida, the *Pension Meza* is a legendary hang-out that has to be the cheapest of the budget hotels. The ambience is distinctly Sixties, and it's rumoured that Fidel Castro and Che Guevara stayed here even earlier than that, in the days before the Cuban revolution. None of the rooms have private showers and many of them are shared. To add to the atmosphere there's music all day and a cheap restaurant next door.

Back in the heart of Zona 1 there are several cheapish places just off 6 Avenida, all of which are fairly good and charge around $8 for a double. The *Hotel Ritz*, at 6 Avenida 9–28, could hardly be more central. Further north are the *Hotel Posada Real*, 12 Calle 6–21, and the *Hotel Berlin*, 11 Calle 6–33, both of which are clean and good, charging three or four dollars.

The City – a guide to the sites

It's unlikely that you'll have come to Guatemala City for the sites, but while you're here there are some places that are well worth visiting. The Ixchel and Popul Vuh **museums** are particularly good and much of the city's **architecture** is impressive and unusual, with the older buildings huddled together in Zona 1 and some outlandish modern structures dotted across the southern half of the city. What follows is a guide to the city as a whole, from which you can pick and choose.

Zones 1 and 2: the Old City

The hub of the old city is **Zona 1**, which is also the busiest and most claustrophobic part of town. Here the two main streets, 5 and 6 avenidas, are still the city's principal shopping area, despite the fact that the really exclusive places have moved out into Zona 10. Nevertheless the old city is still the most exciting part of the capital, throbbing with activity as it falls steadily into disrepair.

The zone's northern boundary runs behind the Palacio Nacional, taking in the central square, the **Parque Central**, the country's political and religious centre, dominated by the Palace and the Cathedral. This plaza, which now covers an underground car park, was originally the scene of a huge central market: this still operates from a covered concrete site behind the Cathedral. Most of the imposing structures that face the plaza today, however, were put up after the 1917 earthquake.

One of the few exceptions to this is the **Cathedral** itself; started on St James' Day 1782, and not completed until 1868. For years its grand facade, merging the Baroque and the Neoclassical, dominated the plaza, dwarfing all the other structures. The solid, squat design was intended to resist the force of earthquakes, and for the most part it has succeeded. In 1917 the bell towers were brought down and the cupola fell, destroying the altar, but the central structure, though cracked and patched over the years, remains intact. Inside there are three main aisles, all lined with arching pillars, austere colonial paintings and intricate altars supporting an array of saints. Some of this collection was brought from the original cathedral in Antigua when the capital was moved in 1776.

These days however the most striking building in the plaza is the **Palacio Nacional**, its solid stone-faced structure looking south towards the neon maze of Zona 1. The Palace was started in 1939 under the auspices of President Ubico – a characteristically grand gesture from the man who believed that he was a reincarnation of Napoleon – and completed a year before he was ousted in 1944. Today it houses the executive branch of the government, and from time to time its steps are fought over by assorted coupsters. The interior of the Palace is open to the public, and once you've offered the security guard a glimpse of your passport you can simply wander in and stroll around the two courtyards, on any of three floors. Inside, things are astonishingly relaxed, with the various ministries housed in the chambers around these courtyards, their doorways guarded by waiting journalists. Most impressive are the **Salas de Recepción** (the state reception rooms), and unless they're being prepared for use you can see inside. The rooms occupy the front of the second floor and the stained glass of their windows tells the story of Guatemalan history. Along one wall is a row of flags and the country's coat of arms, topped with a stuffed quetzal. (If the reception rooms are closed up ask the guards to let you take a look.) Back in the main body of the building the stairwells are decorated with murals, again depicting aspects of Guatemalan history mixed in with images of totally unrelated events. One wall shows a group of idealised pre-conquest Indians, and another includes a portrait of Don Quixote.

Opposite the Cathedral is the **Parque del Centenario**, currently undergoing restoration behind walls of corrugated iron. The Palace of the Captains General once stood here, a long single-storey building that was finished at the end of the nineteenth century and intended to serve the function of the National Palace. It was, however, promptly destroyed in the 1917 earthquake. For the 1921 centenary celebration a temporary wooden structure replaced it, but once this had served its purpose it went up in flames. After that it was decided to create a park instead, with a bandstand, gardens and a fountain, and it's these that are being revamped at the moment. On the other side of the Parque del Centenario is the **Biblioteca Nacional** (the National Library), a fairly unattractive modern building which houses the archives of Central America.

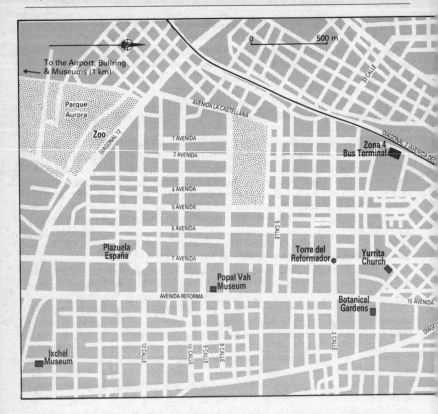

Around the back of the Cathedral the **Mercado Central**, a new building that replaced an earlier version destroyed in the 1976 earthquake, is housed in a couple of layers of sunken concrete. The architect – taking no chances – apparently modelled the structure on a nuclear bunker, sacrificing any aesthetic concerns to the need for strength. The top level is given over to a car park, and beneath that are the **handicraft** sellers. Unexpectedly, this is a good spot to buy traditional weaving and there's an astonishing range of cloth from all over the country. The market is hardly ever visited by tourists so prices are reasonable and the traders very willing to bargain. On the bottom layer, beneath the handicrafts, is the market proper, a great spread of food stalls and *comedores*. This was once the city's main food market but these days it's just one of many, and by no means the largest.

Towards the new city
Heading south from the Parque Central are **6 and 7 avenidas**, thick with clothes shops, restaurants, cinemas, neon signs and bus fumes. What you can't buy in the shops is sold on the pavements, with *McDonalds*, *Wimpy* and *Pizza Hut* all very much part of the scene. It's here that most people head on a Saturday night, when the traffic squeezes between hordes of pedestrians. By 11pm,

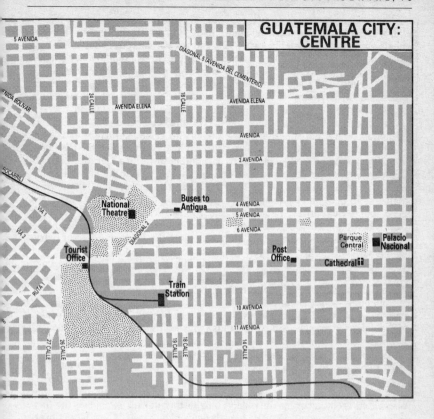

though, the streets are largely deserted, left to the cigarette sellers and prostitutes.

6 Avenida is the more overwhelming of the two: halfway along, strangely out of place at the corner of 13 Calle, is the **Iglesia de San Francisco**. The church is famous for its carving of the Sacred Heart, which, like several of its paintings and statues, was brought here from Antigua. Building began in 1780, but was repeatedly interrupted by seismic activity – it's said that cane syrup, egg whites and cow's milk were mixed with the mortar to enhance its strength. For the most part it fared well, but in 1917 a tremor brought down one of the arches, revealing that the clergy had used the roof to store banned books.

Another block to the south is the **Police Headquarters**, an outlandish looking castle built in imitation of medieval battlements. The next block is taken up by the **Parque Concordia**, a leafy square, one side of which is lined with cheap *comedores*. Plenty of people spend their time hanging out here, and there's always a surplus of shoeshine boys, taxi drivers and lottery tickets – the prizes, usually cars, are sometimes on display in a corner of the park. Concordia is also a favourite spot for street performers and travelling preachers, and at weekends you can see the snake charmers, clowns and rabid evangelicals, all competing furiously for an audience.

Beyond the park, as you head south, things go into steady decline. The pavements are swamped by temporary stalls, and the commercial chaos starts to get out of control. At this end of 6 Avenida electrical shops predominate, gradually giving way to clothes stalls, and finally emerging in the madness of 18 Calle. On the other side of 18 Calle is the **Tipografía Nacional**, the government's printing press and media centre: a marvellous, crumbling building, where bureaucrats beaver away at their task of disseminating information and propaganda.

Heading to the left, beneath the trees, **18 Calle** becomes distinctly sleazy. The cheap food stalls and shoeshine boys mix in with grimy nightclubs and "streaptease" joints. By night the streets are patrolled by prostitutes and the local hotels are protected by prison-like grilles. In daylight, however, it's a grubby but harmless part of town (though you may still encounter the odd highly skilled pickpocket) with a collection of the very cheapest restaurants and hotels. At the corner of 18 Calle and 9 Avenida is the **eastern bus terminal**, from where buses head to Puerto Barrios, Esquipulas and the Mexican border (via the Pacific coast). In the surrounding streets are the offices of several bus companies; *Monja Blanca* for Coban, and *Fuente del Norte* who go to the Petén and Puerto Barrios. On the east side of the open square is the **train station**, an inconspicuous whitewashed wooden building, from where trains leave to Tecún Umán and Puerto Barrios three times a week. Further to the east, behind the railway station, lies **Zona 5**, a run-down residential suburb.

Continuing south along 6 Avenida, crossing the deadly flow of 18 Calle, you pass the **main food market** in a vast, pale-green hangar. Those traders who can afford it pay for a space inside, while those who can't spread themselves along the pavements, soggy with rotten fruit. At the end of this extended block the character of the city is radically transformed. The ageing and claustrophobic streets of Zona 1 give way to the broad tree-lined Avenues of Zona 4 and the new city.

Elsewhere in Zona 1 there are just a couple of other buildings of note. The **post office**, at 7 Avenida and 12 Calle, is a spectacular Moorish building with a marvellous arch that spans the road. A little further down 7 Avenida is the *Guatel* office, from where you can make long-distance phone calls. A few blocks further to the east are the churches of **La Merced**, at 11 Avenida and 5 Calle, and **Santo Domingo**, 12 Avenida and 10 Calle, both of which are very impressive. And also out this way are the museums of National History and Popular Art, for more on which see p.50.

The Centro Municipal – Zona 4

At the southern end of the old city, separating it from the newer parts of town, the **Centro Municipal**, also known as the **Centro Cívico**, marks the boundary between Zones 1 and 4. At this point the avenidas from the north are brought together at a couple of roundabouts, from where they fan out into the more spacious southern city. Bunched around these junctions are a collection of multistorey office blocks that house the city's main administrative buildings. The long building in the centre is the **Municipalidad**, the City Hall, the others are the main **Banco de Guatemala**, the **Institute of Social Security**, the **National Mortgage Bank** and the **Ministry of Finance**. It's unlikely that you'll want to visit any of these, but you'll also find the main office of *Inguat*, the **Guatemalan Tourist Board**, on the ground floor at 7 Avenida 1–17. Here you can buy maps of the city and the country (though they're often out of stock), and there's usually someone on hand who speaks English to answer any queries.

Overlooking all this, a block or so to the west, is the **National Theatre**, the city's most prominent and unusual building. Built on top of the **San José Fortress**, and still surrounded by the original battlements, it's designed along the lines of a huge ship, painted in blue and white, with portholes as windows. Finding an entrance that isn't locked is not always easy, but it's well worth it, as the views across the city are superb. The structure is also home to the **Military Museum**, a strange homage to the Guatemalan army which rarely sees any tourists.

South of the Centro Municipal is the **Olympic City**, a complex of swimming pools, tennis courts and gymnasiums, none of which, sadly, are open to the general public.

North to Zona 2 and the Parque Minerva

To the north of the old city centre is Zona 2, bounded by a deep-cut ravine that prevents the sprawl spreading any further in this direction. Right out on the edge is the **Parque Minerva**, a scruffy little park and sports complex where fairs are held on public holidays and fiestas. The main point of interest is the **relief map of the country**, which covers 2500 square metres and has a couple of special viewing towers so that you can get a good look. The map was finished in 1905, designed to have running water flowing in the rivers. Its vertical scale is out of proportion to the horizontal, making the mountains all look incredibly steep. It does however give you a good idea of the general layout of the country, from the complexity of the highlands to the sheer enormity of the Petén.

To get to the Parque Minerva take bus #1 from anywhere along 5 Avenida in Zona 1.

The New City

The southern half of the city is far more spacious, but though you may have more room to breathe, the air is no less noxious. Roughly speaking, it divides into two halves, split down the middle by 7 Avenida. The eastern half, centred on Avenida La Reforma, is the smartest part of town, with the banks, hotels, restaurants, boutiques and walled residential compounds that belong strictly to Guatemala's wealthy elite. The western half of the new town is rougher, incorporating the bus terminal, zoo and airport.

The eastern side, along 7 Avenida and Avenida La Reforma

Heading to the south of the Centro Civico and into Zona 4 proper, 6 Avenida runs into the modern city, with Ruta 6 branching off to the east, towards Avenida La Reforma. As it does so Ruta 6 crosses 7 Avenida beside the **Edificio El Triangulo**, a local landmark. From here 7 Avenida heads south beneath the **Torre del Reformador**, Guatemala's answer to the Eiffel Tower. The steel structure, built in honour of President Barrios along the same lines as its Parisian model, stands at the junction of 7 Avenida and 2 Calle. A bell in the top of the tower is rung every year on June 30 to commemorate the Liberal victory in the 1871 revolution.

Heading on towards Avenida La Reforma, Ruta 6 passes the **Iglesia Yurrita**, an outlandish building designed in an exotic neo-Gothic style that belongs more to horror movies than to the streets of Guatemala City. It was built as a private chapel by a rich philanthropist: his house, in the same style, stands alongside. The church is also known as **Nuestra Señora de las Angustias**, and is usually open to the public. It's well worth a look, as the inside is just as wild.

The junction where Ruta 6 meets Avenida La Reforma is marked by a roundabout and the *Cine Reforma*, now an Evangelical church plastered with the words *Jesus es Rey*. On the opposite side of Avenida La Reforma are the **Botanical Gardens** (Mon–Fri 8am–noon & 2–6pm) of the San Carlos University. The entrance is on 0 Calle. Inside you'll find a beautiful, small garden with quite a selection of species, all neatly labelled in Spanish and Latin. There's also a small but not terribly exciting **Natural History Museum**, which has a selection of stuffed birds, including a quetzal and an ostrich, some geological samples, wood types, live snakes and a small library which includes some books in English.

Heading south along Avenida La Reforma you pass the *Politecnica*, a school for the training of young military officers built in the style of a toy fort. Beyond this is the smart part of town, with boutiques, travel agents, the American Embassy, banks, office blocks, smart hotels and the offices of *American Express* (at Avenida La Reforma 9–00). While there's a steady flow of traffic along Avenida La Reforma, the surrounding streets are quiet and the lawns mown. This part of town has clearly escaped from the Third World. A little to the east, around 10 Calle and 3 Avenida, is the so-called **Zona Viva**, a tight bunch of upmarket hotels, restaurants and nightclubs.

It's also in this part of town, at the southern end of Avenida La Reforma, that you'll find two of the city's finest museums, the **Popul Vuh Archaeological Museum**, at Avenida La Reforma 8–16, Zona 9, and the **Ixchel Museum of Indian Weaving**, at 4 Avenida 16–27, Zona 10, both of which are privately owned. (For more information on the museums see p.49). Out to the west side of Avenida La Reforma the **Plaza España** occupies the the junction of 7 Avenida and 12 Calle. Now marked by a fountain, this crossroads used to be the site of a statue of King Carlos III of Spain, torn down when independence was declared. At the four corners of the plaza you can still see some superb tiled benches, dating originally from colonial times but now in a state of some disrepair.

To get to Avenida La Reforma from Zona 1 take bus #2, which runs along 8 and 10 Avenidas in Zona 1, past the Yurrita Church, and all the way along Avenida La Reforma. Avenida La Reforma is two-way, so you can return by the same means.

Zona 14

Heading further south, into Zona 14, the end of Avenida La Reforma is marked by the **Parque Independencia**, at the junction with 20 Calle. Below this it runs on as the **Avenida las Americas**. Here things are even more exclusive, and many of the large walled compounds belong to embassies. At the southern end of the Avenida, behind a statue of Pope John Paul II, is the **Plaza Berlin**, a small park with spectacular views across the valley to the south, taking in the corner of Lake Amatitlán and the peak of the Volcán Pacaya. 14 Calle, running parallel to the Avenida las Americas, is better known as **Avenida Hincapié**. To the west of this is Aurora Airport. The passenger terminal is on the far side of the airport, reached through Zona 9, but down here is the main airforce base, the entrance to which is marked by the shell of a plane and a helicopter, impaled on steel spikes.

To the east, the main highway to the border with El Salvador runs out through Zona 10. As this road leaves the city it climbs a steep hillside and passes through some of the most exclusive and expensive housing in the country, all of which has a superb view of the city below, and most of which is ringed by ferocious fortifications. Out beyond this, at the top of the hill, is the country's main (if not only) motor-racing track.

The western side of the new city; traffic and trade

Out to the west of 6 Avenida it's quite another story, and while there are still small enclaves of upmarket housing, and several expensive shopping areas, things are really dominated by transport and commerce. The **railway** to the coast, its tracks lined with bedraggled slums, runs out this way. The airport, the bullring, the zoo and the infamous Zona 4 bus terminal all rub shoulders. Perhaps the most important of these is the **Zona 4 Bus Terminal**, at 1 Calle and 4 Avenida in Zona 4. This is certainly the country's most impenetrable and intimidating jungle, a swirl of petty thieves, bus fumes and sleeping vagrants. From here there are second-class buses to all parts of the country, with departures every minute of the day. (For detailed schedules, check the "Travel Details" at the end of each chapter.) If you're setting out to find a bus remember that only some of them leave from the terminal itself, while others park in the streets around. There's no real pattern to all this but people are always keen to help, and if you look lost someone will eventually point you in the right direction.

Around the terminal the largest **market** in the city spreads out across several blocks. If you can summon the energy it's a real adventure to wander through this maze of alleys, but don't carry too much money as this is a relatively risky part of town. To get to the bus terminal take any of the buses marked *terminal* from 4 Avenida or 9 Avenida in Zona 1, all of which will pass within a block or two of it.

Behind the bus terminal are railway tracks heading towards the coast, and behind these is **Avenida Bolívar**, an important traffic artery that runs out to the **Trébol junction**, where it meets the main highways from the western highlands and the Pacific coast. Up above the bus terminal here is the **Santuario Expiatorio**, a superb modern church designed (by a then unqualified Salvadorean architect) in the shape of a fish. It's part of a church-run complex that includes clinics and schools, and is well worth taking a look inside, above all for the fantastic mural running down the side of the interior.

Further to the south, in Zona 13, the **Parque Aurora** houses the city **zoo** (free), with a collection including lions, crocodiles, monkeys and wild boar: as you might expect it's a cramped and vaguely depressing gathering of beasts. The zoo's main gate is marked by a huge statue of Tecún Umán, the great Quiché warrior.

On the other side of the Parque Aurora, reached along 7 Avenida, is a collection of state-run museums: the **Museum of Natural History**, the **Museum of Archaeology and Ethnology** and the **Museum of Modern Art**, all of which are open daily from 9am to 4.30pm, but closed on Monday. (For more on the museums see p.49.) Beside the park there's also a **bullring**, where there are bullfights towards the end of the year (October to December), and a running track, while to the south is the **Aurora Airport**. To get to Parque Aurora take bus #5 from 4 Avenida in Zona 1.

The final point of interest in the southern half of the city is the **Ciudad Universitária**, the campus of the San Carlos University. A huge, purpose-built complex situated in Zona 12, it's heavily decorated with vivid political graffiti. The students here have been victims of repression and political killing on several occasions and many right-wing politicians still regard the campus as a centre of subversion. Buses marked *Universitária* travel through Zona 1 along 4 Avenida, heading for the campus.

Zona 7, the Ruins of Kaminaljuyú

Way out on the western edge of the city, beyond the stench of the rubbish dump, is the long thin arm of Zona 7, a well established but run-down part of town that wraps around the ruins of **Kaminaljuyú**. Archaeological digs on this side of the city have revealed the astonishing proportions of a Maya city that once housed around 50,000 people and includes over three hundred mounds and thirteen ball courts. Unlike the massive temples of the lowlands these structures were built of adobe, and most of them have been lost to centuries of erosion and a few decades of urban sprawl. Today the archaeological site, incorporating only a tiny fraction of the original city, is little more than a series of earth-covered mounds, a favourite spot for football and romance. A couple of sections have been cut into by archaeologists, and peering through the fence you can get some idea of what lies beneath the grassy exterior, but it's virtually impossible to get any impression of Kaminaljuyú's former scale and splendour.

Despite their nondescript appearance, the ruins are those of a particularly important site, once the largest Maya city in the Guatemalan highlands. The history of Kaminaljuyú falls neatly into two sections; a first phase of indigenous growth, and a later period during which migrants from the north populated the site. In the Late Preclassic era, 400 BC to 100 AD, the city had already grown to huge proportions with some 200 flat-topped pyramids, the largest reaching to a height of about 18 metres. Beneath each of these a member of the nobility lay entombed, and a few have been unearthed to reveal the wealth and sophistication of the culture. The corpses were wrapped in finery, covered in cinnabar pigment and surrounded by an array of human sacrifices, pottery, jade, masks, stingray spines, obsidian and quartz crystals. A number of carvings have also been found, proving that the elite of Kaminaljuyú were fully literate at a time when other Maya had perhaps no notion of writing. Many of the gods, ceramic styles and hieroglyphic forms from these early days at Kaminaljuyú are thought to prefigure those found in the flowering of Maya art at later centres such as Tikal and Copán. But the power of the city, pre-eminent during the Late Preclassic era, faded throughout the second and third centuries and the site may even have been abandoned.

Kaminaljuyú's renaissance took place shortly after 400 AD, when the Guatemalan highlands suffered a massive influx of migrants from the north and fell under the domination of Teotihuacán (in central Mexico). The migrants seized the city of Kaminaljuyú and established it as their regional capital, giving them control of the obsidian mines and access to the coastal trade routes and the lowlands of the Petén. With the weighty political and economic backing of Teotihuacán the city once again flourished, as the new rulers constructed their own temples, tombs and ball courts. Numerous artefacts have been found from this period, including some pottery that's thought to have been made in Teotihuacán itself and endless imitations of the style. Kaminaljuyú's new-found power also played a crucial role in shaping the lowlands of the Petén: it was only with the backing of the great Teotihuacán-Kaminaljuyú alliance that Tikal was able to grow so large and so fast. This role was considered of such importance that some archaeologists suggest that Curl Nose, one of the early rulers at Tikal (who ascended to power in 387 AD), may actually have come from Kaminaljuyú. The fortunes of Kaminaljuyú itself, however, were so bound up with those of its northern partner that the fall of Teotihuacán around 600 AD weakened and eventually destroyed the city.

To get to the ruins take bus #17, from 4 Avenida in Zona 1. The #17 has several different destinations so be sure to get on one marked *Kaminaljuyú*, with a small sign in the windscreen. Officially the site is open daily from 8am to 6pm, but in practice the park is ringed by such a patchy fence that you can get in easily at any time – and no-one seems to mind.

Museums

Guatemala city's **museums** fall into two distinct groups; the very best are the Popol Vuh and Ixchel museums, both of which are privately owned, superbly presented, and fairly expensive. In the second category are the state museums, some of which also have very impressive collections but all of which are a touch run-down: and the bottom end are really very poor. The bulk of the state-run museums are in the Parque Aurora, so as a group they are worth visiting at least briefly.

Museo Ixchel

4 Avenida 16–27, Zona 10; Mon–Fri 8.30am–5.30pm, Sat 9am–1pm; $1, less for students with a card; bus #2 from 10 Avenida in Zona 1 to the end of Avenida La Reforma, and walk south for several blocks.

Probably the capital's best museum, the Museo Ixchel is dedicated to Indian culture, with particular emphasis on traditional weaving. On display is a collection of hand-woven fabrics, including some very impressive ceremonial costumes, with explanations in English. There's also information about the techniques used, and the way in which the costumes have changed over the years. Despite the fact that it's by no means comprehensive, and that the costumes lose a lot of their impact and meaning when taken out of the villages in which they're made, this is a fascinating exhibition.

A private institution dedicated to the study and preservation of Indian culture, the museum also has a large library and collections of cloth and pictures. The organisation also provides funds for research programmes.

Museo Popol Vuh

Avenida La Reforma 8–16, 6th floor – in the black office block; Mon–Sat 9am–5.30pm; $1, less for card carrying students; bus #2 from 10 Avenida in Zona 1.

The city's other private museum works in association with the Francisco Marroquin University, and the standards are just as high as at the Ixchel museum. This time the subject is archaeology, with an outstanding collection of artefacts from sites all over the country. Among the best pieces are some incredible ceramics and several ball-court markers. The museum also goes beyond the Maya into the colonial era, with a few musty colonial costumes and Indian exhibits.

Museo Nacional de Antropologia y Etnologia

Parque Aurora; Tues–Fri 9am–4.30pm, Sat & Sun 9am–noon & 2–4.30pm; bus #5 from 4 Avenida in Zona 1; 30¢.

The state's answer to the Popol Vuh may not be quite as slick, but it does have a good selection of Maya artefacts, including some fantastic *stelae*, as well as a display on Indian culture showing traditional masks and costumes. Compared to the Popol Vuh it looks a bit dowdy, but the exhibits are just as impressive and make it well worth a visit for Maya enthusiasts. Several vast pieces of Maya stonework are included in the collection, some of them from the more remote sites such as Piedras Negras.

Museo de Arte Moderno

Parque Aurora, opposite the Museum of Anthropology and Ethnology; Tues–Fri 9am–4.30pm, Sat & Sun 9am–noon & 2–4.30pm; entrance free; bus #5 from 4 Avenida in Zona 1.

The modern art museum is a little disappointing and seems sadly neglected. It's not worth a special trip, but if you're in the area you might as well drop in to see some impressively massive murals as well as an abundance of twee images of Indian life. The works cover the last couple of centuries of Guatemalan art, including most of the modern movements.

Museo de Historia Natural

Parque Aurora; Tues–Fri 9am–4.30pm, Sat & Sun 9am–noon & 2–4pm; entrance free; bus #5 from 4 Avenida in Zona 1.

Third of the state-run museums in the park, the Natural History collection shares the general air of neglect. It includes a range of mouldy looking stuffed animals from Guatemala and elsewhere, and a few mineral samples.

A second natural history museum is attached to the **Jardín Botánico**, in 0 Calle just off the northern end of Avenida Reforma. This is a slightly more tempting proposition, with the added attraction of the Gardens themselves, and a display that includes a couple of stuffed quetzals, more mineral samples, wood types and some horrific pickled rodents (see p.46 for more).

Museo Nacional de Artes e Industrias Populares

10 Avenida 10–72, Zona 1; Tues–Sun 9am–noon & 2–4pm.

A collection of painting, weaving, ceramics, musical instruments and Indian masks, which ought to be interesting but somehow manages not to be. Again the museum is sadly neglected and very small, and it's not really worth going out of your way for.

Museo Nacional de Historia

9 Calle 9–70; Tues–Sun 9am–noon & 2–4pm.

A selection of painting and artefacts relating to Guatemalan history, including documents, clothes and paintings. Amongst the exhibits are some photographs by Eadweard Muybridge, who, in 1875, was one of the first people to undertake a study of the country. These are probably the most interesting exhibits, but from time to time they put on other exhibitions here, some of which are excellent.

The Military Museum

Part of the National Theatre, Zona 4, reached through the main gate of the theatre; Mon–Fri 8am–6pm; entrance free.

Last, and probably least, this museum houses a small collection of weapons and uniforms used by the Guatemalan army over the years. Considering the importance of the army the museum is very low-key, and really only for military buffs.

The Facts

Above all Guatemala City is the place to get things done. Whether you've run out of film, your visa has expired, or you're simply hungry for news of home, this is the place to sort it out. Listed below is the information that should make such things possible, along with a selection of restaurants, nightclubs and cinemas.

Eating and drinking

Restaurants are everywhere in Guatemala City, and they invariably reflect the type of neighbourhood that they're in. Cheap and filling food can be easily found around any of the bus stations and on many of the streets in the centre, and in Zona 1 you'll find a concentration of cheap *comedores* around 18 Calle and 9 Avenida. In the smarter parts of town, particularly Zonas 9 and 10, the emphasis is on upmarket cafés and overpriced hamburgers, and cheap places are hard to find. When it comes to eating well and cheaply, stick to Zona 1, where the restaurants tend to reflect the cosmopolitan side of the capital's population.

Many of the best are **Chinese**, and of these there's a major cluster on 6 Calle, between 4 and 3 avenidas, which must rank as the city's Chinatown. In this area both the *China Hilton* and the *Long Wax* are good, but there are plenty of others to choose from. In the very centre of Zona 1, on 6 Avenida at the corner of 12 Calle, the *Fu Lu Sho* also does good Chinese, as do the *Mundial*, 6 Avenida and 15 Calle, and the *Ruby*, 11 Calle 5–56, although the latter is a bit short on atmosphere.

For **Mexican** food try *El Gran Pavo*, 13 Calle 4–41, which serves massive portions of genuinely Mexican cuisine in a decidedly Mexican atmosphere. For a more subdued meal you can eat **Spanish** food at the *Altuna*, 5 Avenida 12–31, where the atmosphere is wonderfully civilised and the prices, although by no means cheap, are still reasonable.

Italian restaurants have also established themselves in the city, and the *Piccadilly*, 6 Avenida and 11 Calle, Zona 1, is one of the most popular with both tourists and Guatemalans. It serves a delicious range of pastas and pizzas, along with huge jugs of beer. Slightly more upmarket is *A Guy From Italy*, 12 Calle 6–23, part of a chain of restaurants throughout the city.

Vegetarian restaurants are scarce in a city so obsessed with the macho aspects of meat eating, but there are a couple. In Zona 1 there's a place at the corner of 11 Calle and 6 Avenida, or try *El Arbol de la Vida*, a much better alternative at 7 Avenida 13–56 in Zona 9.

Fast food is perhaps at the heart of life in Zona 1, and there's plenty to choose from, the vast majority of it imported directly from the States. *McDonald's* is at 10 Calle 5–56, *Burger Shop* at 6 Avenida 13–40, and there's a branch of *Pizza Hut* on 6 Avenida between 12 and 13 Calles. *Pollo Campero*, the Guatemalan version of *Kentucky Fried Chicken*, has branches throughout the city: in Zona 1 you'll find them at 9 Calle and 15 Avenida, and 6 Avenida and 15 Calle.

Finally, for a more Guatemalan meal, there's *Delicadezas Humburgo*, at 15 Calle 5–34, which serves a hybrid of Guatemalan and German food, including set meals that are particularly good value. They also do a good deal on a set breakfast, offering a number of menus from cornflakes to beans and eggs. The *Cafe Penalba*, 6 Avenida 11–71, and the *Selecta*, 14 Calle 6–24, also serve cheap set meals: the latter is the better.

Bars and nightlife

Despite appearances, Guatemala City quietens down very quickly in the evenings, and **nightlife** is certainly not one of its strengths. The best plan is to **drink** in one of the restaurants on 6 Avenida, and perhaps move on later to zone 9 or 10 in search of a **club**. What little nightlife there is divides into two distinct parts: in the southern half of the city, particularly in the so-called *Zona Viva* (Zona 10), there are a handful of western-style nightclubs and bars, while in Zona 1 "Streap Tease" clubs and sleazy bars are all that's on offer.

La Quinta, in the centre of Zona 1 on 5 Avenida between 13 and 14 Calles, is a club that typifies this part of town: weary and middle-aged. But at least there's usually live music, and you can buy overpriced food and drink. Slightly rougher, but still very much in the same mould, is *El Zócalo* at the corner of 18 Calle and 4 Avenida, where they blast out Marimba music. And that much more tacky is *Las Vegas*, on the corner of 18 Calle and 5 Avenida.

If you still crave the low life then stroll on down 18 Calle, to the junction with 9 Avenida, and you're in the heart of the Zona 1 **red light district**, where there are plenty of truly sleazy bars and clubs.

Heading into the newer part of town, the nightclubs have a more western flavour. In the *Zona Viva*, which is just off Avenida La Reforma in Zones 9 and 10, there are bars and discos in the *Sheraton* (Zona 9) and *Camino Real* (Zona 10) hotels. A popular spot with young and wealthy Guatemalans is the *Dash Disco*, in the basement at 12 Calle and 1 Avenida, and on the other side of Avenida La Reforma the *Establo*, Reforma 14–34, is a good rock-and-roll bar where you can get delicious food at any time of day. You could also try the *Kahlua*, a notorious bar at 1 Avenida 13–29, Zona 10, or the *Le Pont Disco* at 13 Calle 0–48, Zona 10, a good dance spot.

Lastly, if you're looking for somewhere a bit more relaxed, but not as worn out as the clubs of Zona 1, there's a great **reggae club** on Via 4, between 6 Avenida and Ruta 6 in Zona 4. It's a favourite haunt of Guatemalans from Livingston and the Caribbean coast, and radiates rhythm.

Listings

Airport Aurora airport is in Zona 13, and both domestic and international flights leave from the sole terminal on the west side. Bus #5, marked *Aeropuerto*, runs irregularly to the airport from 4 Avenida in Zona 1. If you've a plane to catch you'd be better off taking a taxi, which costs around $10. There's a Q20 departure tax on all international flights.

Airlines Airlines are scattered throughout the city, with a vague concentration along Avenida Reforma. It is however fairly straightforward to phone them and there will almost always be someone in the office who speaks English. The addresses are as follows:

Aerolineas Argentinas, 10 Calle 3–17, Zona 10; ☎311276.
Aeronica, 10 Calle 6–20, Zona 9; ☎325541.
Air France, Avenida Reforma 9–00, Zona 9 (8th floor); ☎367667.
Aerovias, Avenida Hincapié at 18 Calle, Zona 13; ☎347936.
Aviateca, 10 Calle y 6 Avenida, Zona 1 (3rd floor); ☎81372.
British Airways, Avenida Reforma 8–60, Zona 9 (11th floor); ☎312555.
Continental, at the airport; ☎312051/3.
Copa, 7 Avenida, 6–53, Zona 4; ☎366256.
Iberia, Avenida La Reforma 8–60, Zona 9; ☎373911 (airport ☎325517/8).
Japan Airlines, 7 Avenida 15–45, Zona 9; ☎318597.

Eastern, at the airport; ☎317455/8.

LanChile, Avenida La Reforma 9–00, Zona 9, Edificio Plaza Panamericana; ☎312070.

Lufthansa, 20 Calle 6–20, Zona 10, Edificio Plaza Maritima; ☎370113/6.

Mexicana, 12 Calle 4–55, Zona 1; ☎518824.

KLM, 6 Avenida 20–25, Zona 10, Edificio Plaza Maritima; ☎370222 (airport ☎319247).

Lacsa, 7 Avenida 14–44, Zona 9, Edificio La Galeria; ☎373905/7.

Pan Am, 6 Avenida 11–43, Zona 1; ☎ 82181/4.

Sabena, 7 Avenida 6–26, Zona 9 (7th floor); ☎347081.

SAM, Avenida La Reforma 12–01, Zona 10, Edificio Reforma Montufar; ☎323242.

Sahsa, 12 Calle 1–25, Zona 10; ☎352671/3.

Scandinavian Airlines, 7 Avenida 6–26, Edificio Plaza El Roble; ☎347067.

Taca, 7 Avenida 14–35, Zona 9; ☎322360 (airport ☎364613).

Tapsa, Avenida Hincapié, Zona 13; ☎314860.

Virgin Atlantic, Avenida La Reforma 9–00, Zona 9, Edificio Plaza Panamericana (8th floor); ☎312070.

Varig, Avenida La Reforma 9–00, Zona 9, Edificio Plaza Panamericana (8th floor); ☎311912.

American Express have their main office in the *Banco del Café*, Avenida Reforma 9–00, Zona 9 (not, as some would have you believe, at *Clarke Tours*). The office, which includes the mail service, is in the basement, and the bank on the first floor. To get there take bus #2 from 10 Avenida in Zona 1.

Baggage If you want to leave a bag then you'll have to trust it to your hotel as there's no central left luggage facility.

Banks throughout the city open and close at varying hours, some shutting as early as 3pm, and others staying open until after dark. For cashing travellers' cheques the *Banco Industrial*, 7 Avenida 11–20, Zona 1, is fairly straightforward but closes around 4pm. The *Banco del Quetzal* and the *Banco Promotor* are opposite each other in 9 Calle, between 6 and 7 Avenidas, Zona 1 – both are open weekdays until around 7pm. Other major banks are the *Banco de Guatemala* in the Civic Centre on 7 Avenida, Zona 1, and *Lloyds Bank*, 8 Avenida 10–67, Zona 1. If you need to change money on a Sunday or public holiday then try the bank at the airport, which is open every day. Back in Zona 1, on 7 Avenida between 12 and 13 Calles, there's also a legal black market which at times offers a better rate than the banks – although only for cash. Here you can also exchange other Central American currencies.

Books and Newspapers. The best bookshop for fiction in English and German is *Arnel*, in the basement of the Edificio El Centro on 9 Calle, at the corner of 8 Avenida, in Zona 1. Otherwise the bookshops in Antigua are probably better than those in the capital. Second-hand English books can be bought from *El Establo*, Avenida La Reforma 14–34, Zona 10, a café with an impressive selection lining its walls. Guatemalan newspapers are sold everywhere on the streets, but European ones are hard to come by. Copies of *Time*, *Newsweek* and *The Economist* are usually on sale in the main plaza, and the British Embassy usually has copies of the *Times*, *Independent* and *Guardian*. American papers are fairly readily available both in Guatemala City and Antigua. The *Hotel Panamerican*, 9 Calle 5–63, Zona 1, and *El Dorado* in Zona 4, both sell US papers, as do some of the street sellers in the centre.

Guatemala's two English-language publications can be bought from their offices; *This Week*, a weekly summary of the regional news, is available from 12 Calle 4–53 Zona 1, while *Central American Report* is available from 9 Calle "A" 3–56, Zona 1.

Bullfights are staged from October to December, and are advertised well in advance. The main arena is beside the Parque Aurora – #5 bus from 4 Avenida in Zona 1. Tickets start from around $10.

Buses There are two principal bus terminals, one outside the train station at 18 Calle and 9 Avenida, Zona 1 – which on the whole serves the coastal and eastern routes – the other the chaotic Zona 4 terminal at 1 Calle and 3 Avenida, which serves the highlands. The main bus companies and their services are listed on p.60; for information on local bus services see p.39.

Camera repairs Try *Foto Sittler*, 12 Calle 6–20, Zona 1, who offer a three-month guarantee on their work.

Car Hire Hiring a car in Guatemala is an expensive business, and you should keep a sharp eye on the terms, particularly when it comes to insurance. *Budget* have an office at Avenida Reforma 15–00, Zona 9, and a branch at the airport. They rent Jeeps for a little under $100 a day, and also have cars and minibuses. *Hertz*, who are a touch more expensive, have one branch opposite the *Hotel Dorado* on 7 Avenida in Zona 9 and another at the airport. *Avis*, at 12 Calle 2–73, Zona 9, rent minibuses and cars. *National* is at 14 Calle 1–24, Zona 10, and *Tally*, who offer the best value and also rent motorbikes, are at 7 Avenida 14–60, Zona 1.

Cinemas Films are very popular in the capital. Most are in English with Spanish subtitles, including some that you can see here before they're released in Europe. There are four cinemas on 6 Avenida between the main plaza and the Parque Concordia, and plenty of others scattered throughout the city: *Cine Las Americas* (2 screens), 8–9 Calle and Avenida las Americas, Zona 13; *Cine Bolívar*, Avenida Bolívar y 28 Calle, Zona 8; *Cine Plaza*, 7 Avenida 6–7 Calle, Zona 9; *Cine Tropical*, Avenida Bolívar 31–71, Zona 8; *Cines Taurus, Leo* and *Aires*, are all at 9 Calle and 4 Avenida, Zona 1; *Cine Lido*, 11 Calle 7–34, Zona 1; *Cine Lux* (3 screens), 11 Calle and 6 Avenida, Zona 1; *Cine Capri*, 8 Calle 3 Avenida, Zona 1; *Cine Capitol* (6 screens), 6 Avenida 12 Calle, Zona 1; *Cine Palace*, opposite this last. The programmes are listed in the two main newspapers, *El Grafico* and *Prensa Libre*.

Doctors Your embassy should have a list of bilingual doctors, but if you need emergency medical assistance then the *Centro Medico*, a private hospital with 24-hour cover is at 6 Avenida 3–47, Zona 10; ☎ 323555. They can also provide booster vaccinations.

Embassies Most of the embassies are located in the southeastern quarter of the city, along Avenida La Reforma and Avenida las Americas, and they tend to open weekday mornings only. If the opening time isn't listed below then it might be worth phoning before you set off in search of the address. All embassies and consulates are listed in the blue pages of the phone book.

Belgium, Avenida Reforma 13–70, Zona 9; ☎316597.

Brazil, 18 Calle 2–22, Zona 14; ☎370949.

Canada, 7 Avenida 11–59 (6th floor), Zona 9; ☎321411.

Colombia, 12 Calle 1–25, Zona 10; ☎353602 (Mon–Fri 9am–1pm).

Costa Rica, Avenida La Reforma 8–60 (3rd floor), Zona 9; ☎319604 (Mon–Fri 9am –3pm).

Denmark, 7 Avenida 20–36, Zona 1; ☎81091.

Ecuador, 6 Avenida 4–29, Zona 10; ☎316119.

El Salvador, 12 Calle 5–43 (7th floor), Zona 9; ☎325848.

Spain, 4 Calle 7–73, Zona 9; ☎318784.

Finland, Ruta 2 (24 Calle) 0–70, Zona 4; ☎313116.

France, 16 Calle 4–53 (11th floor), Zona 10; ☎373639.

Honduras, 16 Calle 8–27, Zona 10; ☎373919 (Mon–Fri 8.30am–1.30pm).

Italy, 5 Avenida 8–59, Zona 14 (Mon, Wed & Fri 8am–2.30pm; Tues & Thurs 8am–1.30pm & 3–6pm).

Mexico, 13 Calle 7–30, Zona 9; ☎363573.

Netherlands, 12 Calle 7–56 (4th floor), Zona 9; ☎374092.

Nicaragua, 10 Avenida 14–72, Zona 10; ☎680785.

Norway, 6 Avenida 7–02, Zona 9; ☎310064.

Panama, Edificio Maya (7th floor), Via 5 4–50, Zona 4; ☎325001.

Peru, 2 Avenida 9–42, Zona 9; ☎318409.

Sweden, 8 Avenida 15–07, Zona 10; ☎370555.

Switzerland, 4 Calle 7–73, Zona 9; ☎365726.

United Kingdom, 7 Avenida 5–10 (7th floor), Zona 4; ☎321601.

United States, Avenida Reforma, 7–01, Zona 10; ☎311541/4.

Venezuela, 8 Calle 0–56, Zona 9; ☎316505.

Emergencies Police ☎120, Fire ☎123, *Centro Medico* 24-hour service ☎323555.

Film Colour slide and print film is easy to buy in Guatemala City (though expensive) and there are several camera shops on 6 Avenida in Zona 1. None of them stock anything beyond the basics, though, and black-and-white or very fast film is almost impossible to find.

Immigration The main immigration office (*Migracion*) is at 8 Avenida and 12 Calle, Zona 1. Here you can extend your tourist card up to a total maximum of ninety days, or extend a visa for a month.

Language courses There are at least five different schools in Guatemala City if you want to learn Spanish, probably the best of which is the IGA (the Guatemalan American Institute) which is on Ruta 1 and Via 4, Zona 4. If you've come to learn Spanish, though, you're far better off in Antigua.

Laundry Laundries are hard to come by in the capital. The *Lavanderia Internacional*, 18 Calle 11–12, Zona 1, is one of the best, although when business is good they'll insist that you pay for a complete service including ironing. The *Lavanderia Pichola*, 18 Calle 11–60, Zona 1, is cheaper and more basic, or there's a do-it-yourself place at 4 Avenida 13–89, Zona 1, which costs much the same and takes a lot longer.

Libraries The best library for English books is in the IGA, the Guatemalan American Institute, at Ruta 1 and Via 4, Zona 4. There's also the national library in the Parque Central, another big library alongside the main branch of the *Banco de Guatemala*, and specialist colections at the Ixchel and Popul Vuh museums.

Maps of the city and the country are available from the tourist board – *Inguat* – at 7 Avenida 1–17, Zona 4. For a really detailed map of the country try the *Instituto Geografico Militar*, Avenida las Americas 5–76, Zona 13. Most of their sheets are restricted and sold only with express permission. You can, however, look at them at the institute. Photocopies of them are sold at the *Casa Andinista* bookshop in Antigua.

Opening hours Most shops and businesses are open Monday to Friday from 9am to 6pm, with a siesta from noon to 1pm, 2pm or 3pm.

Police The main police station is in a bizarre castle on the corner of 6 Avenida and 14 Calle, Zona 1. To telephone the police in an emergency dial ☎120.

Post The main post office is on the corner of 7 Avenida and 12 Calle, Zona 1. The *lista de correos*, where you go to pick up a letter, is at the back on the ground floor. *American Express*, Avenida La Reforma 9–00, Zona 9, run a more efficient service where you can receive mail.

Taxis can be found in the Parque Central or Parque Concordia, or you could try phoning on ☎29290, ☎26213, ☎23226: other numbers are in the phone book. Taxis don't have meters so arrange a price before you get in.

Telegrams within the country are sent from the main post office at 7 Avenida and 12 Calle, Zona 1, and international telegrams from *Guatel*, next door at 8 Avenida and 12 Calle, Zona 1.

Telephones Local calls can be made from booths around the city, which take 5, 10 and 25 *centavo* coins. For long-distance calls you need the *Guatel* office, at 8 Avenida and 12 Calle, Zona 1.

Tourist Information *Inguat* have a single office at 7 Avenida 1–17, Zona 4. The information desk is on the ground floor and here you can buy maps of the country and the city, or put your questions to the staff – there will usually be someone who speaks English. The office is open Mon–Fri 8am–4.30pm, Sat 8am–1pm.

Trains leave to Puerto Barrios and Tecún Umán from the station at 18 Calle and 10 Avenida, Zona 1.

Travel Agents There are plenty of these both in the centre and along Avenida La Reforma in zones 9 and 10. Flights to the Petén can be booked through all of them. They include *Clarke Tours*, who run tours of the city and many parts of the country (*Edificio El Triangulo* on 7 Avenida, Zona 4, and 10 Calle 6–34, Zona 1), *Ceibal Tours* (Avenida Reforma 8–95, Zona 10), *Ronel Tours* (7 Avenida 1–52, Zona 9), *Setsa Travel* (8 Avenida 14–11, Zona 1) and *Proviasa* (11 Calle 5–16, Zona 1).

Work is hard to come by in the city: the best bet is to try and teach at one of the English schools, most of which are grouped on 10 and 18 Calles in Zona 1.

AROUND THE CITY

Heading out of the capital in any direction you escape its atmosphere almost immediately. There are just two trips that are suited to excursions from the city, while the rest of the surrounding hills are easily visited from other towns.

To the south the main road runs to Escuintla and the Pacific coast, passing through a narrow valley that separates the cones of the Pacaya and Agua volcanoes. Out this way is **Lake Amatitlán**, a popular weekend resort just half an hour from the capital. A few kilometres to the south of the lake is the village of **San Vicente Pacaya**, from where you can climb Pacaya itself, one of Guatemala's three active cones and currently the most impressive, spouting a plume of lava.

To the northwest of the capital are the villages of **San Juan Sacatepéquez** and **San Pedro Sacatepéquez**, both of which have impressive markets. Further to the west are the ruins of **Mixco Viejo**, the ancient capital of the Pokoman Maya.

South to Lake Amatitlán

Heading out through the southern suburbs, the **Pacific highway** runs past the clover-leaf junction at El Trébol and leaves the city through its industrial outskirts. The land to the south of the capital is earmarked for new housing projects, but as yet this skeletal ground plan has drawn only one or two takers, and elaborate advertising posters on empty lots sing the merits of suburban life. Further to the south lies the small town of **Villa Nueva**, which is a lot older than its name might suggest, and beyond this the valley starts to narrow, overshadowed by the volcanic cones of Agua and Pacaya.

A few kilometres to the east of the highway, **Lake Amatitlán** nestles at the base of the Pacaya volcano, encircled by forested hills. It's a superb setting, but one that has been sadly undermined by the abuses that the lake has suffered at the hands of holidaymakers. In the not-too-distant past its delights were enjoyed by a handful of the elite, whose retreats dotted the shoreline, but since then the bungalows have proliferated at an astonishing rate, and the waters of the lake are now grossly polluted. The wealthy have now moved on, seeking their seclusion at Lake Atitlán instead, while here at Amatitlán the weekends bring buses from the capital every ten minutes or so, spewing out families who spend the day eating, drinking, barbecueing, boating and swimming. If you want to enjoy the view then come during the week, but if you want to watch Guatemalans at play drop by on a Sunday.

Where the road arrives on the lakeshore the beach is lined with grimy *comedores* and *tiendas*. Boat trips across the lake are a popular pastime, as are the thermal baths said to cure rheumatism and arthritis. Considerably less healthy are the black waters of the lake, and although the brave (or foolhardy) still swim in them, I'd recommend the swimming pools, where you can pay to take a dip in cleaner waters.

High above the lake, to the north, is the **Parque de las Naciones Unidas** (the United Nations Park, formerly the Parque El Filón), connected to the lakeside by an Austrian-made bubble-lift that looks strangely out of place so far from the ski slopes. The trip itself, and the park above, offer incredible views of the lake and the volcanic cones. The lift is open on Saturday and Sunday only, from 10am to 12.45pm.

A kilometre or so from the lake is the village of **AMATITLÁN**, where you'll find restaurants and hotels, as well as a seventeenth-century church housing El Niño de Atocha, a saintly figure with miraculous powers.

Buses run to Lake Amatitlán every ten minutes or so, from 20 Calle 3 Avenida in Zona 1, returning from the plaza in Amatitlán and the lakeshore. The trip takes around 45 minutes.

The Pacaya Volcano

Heading further down the valley, towards the Pacific coast, a branch road leaves the main highway to the left, heading for the village of **SAN VICENTE PACAYA**. From here you can climb the Pacaya volcano, one of the smallest and most impressive of Guatemala's peaks. The track to the village winds its way up from the highway through lush coffee plantations and clouds of dust. San Vicente itself is a fairly miserable place, but if you're planning to climb the cone and make it back down the same day then you might be able to find somewhere to stay. There's no hotel in the village and people don't seem particularly friendly, but it's worth asking around for a room anyway – if you don't succeed you can always try one of the villages higher up.

To climb the volcano you need to rejoin the road (which actually bypasses San Vicente) and then turn left at the fork after a hundred metres or so. You'll come to a second bedraggled village, **CONCEPCIÓN EL CEDRO**, where you want to head straight on, walking up the track to the right of the church. This track moves around to the left as it leaves the village, and then climbs in a narrow rocky gully, coming out at the village of **SAN FRANCISCO**, the last settlement and the highest point accessible by motor vehicles. Here you'll pass the last *tienda* and your last chance of finding a bed for the night – ask in the *tienda* and they'll point you towards someone with a room to rent.

From San Francisco the path is a little harder to follow, but it's only another couple of hours to the top. After you pass the *tienda* the path goes up to the right, beside an evangelical church, above which you want to head diagonally across the open grassland – bearing to the left. From this left-hand corner a clear-cut path heads on towards the cone, and where it first forks you want to go left, along a path that climbs diagonally. After a while this meets a barbed-wire fence, where you turn sharply to the right and continue up, through a thickish forest. This time you head straight on for a kilometre or so (moving diagonally across the hill) until the path goes over a hump, and then down the other side. On the second hump you turn to the left, onto a smaller path, which you follow up through the woods, scrambling up the slippery cinder, until you reach the top.

All of a sudden you emerge on the lip of an exposed ridge. In front of you is a massive bowl of cooled lava, its fossilised currents flowing away to the right, and opposite is the cone itself, a jet black triangle that occasionally spouts molten rock and sulphurous fumes. From here you can head on around to the left, across lava fields and between the charred stumps of trees. The path runs around the lip of the bowl to a concrete post, and then up the side of the dormant cone, which is a terrifying but thrilling ascent, eventually bringing you face to face with the eruptions – although you should watch the eruptions for a while beforehand to ensure that you wont be hit.

The best time to watch the eruptions is at night, when the sludge that the volcano spouts is seen in its full glory as a plume of brilliant orange. But to see this you need either to camp out – there are several good sites near the top – or to find somewhere to stay in one of the villages, which is possible but not that easy: you just have to ask around. If you do find somewhere to stay then I'd recommend spending the first hours of darkness at the top and coming down by torchlight. (Tents can be rented from the *Casa Andinista* bookshop in Antigua.)

A **bus** leaves Guatemala City for Concepción daily at 8.45am, and returns from there at noon; a later service runs to San Francisco at 3.30pm, coming back at 5am the following day.

On towards the coast and the village of Palín

Continuing towards the coast the main highway passes through the village of **PALÍN**, where the road is lined with restaurants and *tiendas*. Palín was once famous for its weaving, but these days the only *huipiles* that you'll see are the purples of Santa María de Jesus, to which it's connected by a rough back road. The original Palín *huipiles* were particularly short, exposing the women's breasts when they raised their arms, and it's said that President Ubico, witnessing this when a woman tried to sell pineapples to his train, ordered that they be lengthened.

The best time to visit Palín is for the Wednesday market, which takes place under a magnificent Ceiba tree in the plaza. Buses pass through every ten minutes or so, heading between the capital and the coast, so it's worth dropping in even if you just happen to be passing on a Wednesday morning. The name Palín derives from the word *palinha*, meaning water that holds itself erect, a reference to a nearby waterfall.

Northwest of the city

To the northwest of the capital is a hilly area that, despite its proximity, is little tainted by the influence of the city. Here the hills are still covered by lush pine forests, and heading out this way you'll find a couple of interesting villages, both badly scarred by the 1976 earthquake but with markets well worth visiting. Further afield are the Mixco Viejo ruins, impeccably restored but seldom visited.

San Pedro Sacatepéquez and San Juan Sacatepéquez

Leaving the city to the northwest you travel out through the suburb of Florida, which bears little relation to its North American namesake. Once you escape the confines of the city the road starts to climb into the hills, through an area that's oddly uninhabited. To the south the high ground has been colonised by the rich, but here there are only one or two mansions, lost in the forest.

The first of the two villages is **SAN PEDRO SACATAPÉQUEZ**, where the impact of the earthquake is still painfully felt. The market here – which takes place on a Friday – is by some way the smaller of the two. Another six kilometres takes you over a ridge and into the village of **SAN JUAN SACATEPÉQUEZ**. As you approach, the road passes a number of makeshift greenhouses where flowers are grown: an industry that has become the local speciality. The first carnation was brought to Guatemala by Andrés Stombo, some sixty years ago. He employed the three Churup brothers, all from San Juan, and seeing how easy it was they all set up on their own. Since then the business has flourished, and there are flowers everywhere in San Juan.

By far the best time to visit is for the Friday market, when the whole place springs into action and the village is packed. Keep an eye out for the *huipiles* worn in San Juan, which are unusual and impressive, with bold geometric designs of yellow, purple and green. **Buses** to both villages run every half-hour or so from the Zona 4 terminal in Guatemala City.

Mixco Viejo

Beyond San Juan the road divides, one branch heading north to EL CHOL and RABINAL – one bus a day takes this route, leaving the Zona 4 terminal in Guatemala City at 5am – and the other branch going west towards **Mixco Viejo** and **Pachalum**. Heading out along this western route the scenery changes dramatically, leaving behind the pine forests and entering a huge dry valley. Small farms are scattered here and there and the *Politecnica*, Guatemala's military academy, is also out this way. Several hours beyond San Juan, in the bottom of a massive valley, are the ruins of Mixco Viejo.

MIXCO VIEJO was the capital of the Pokoman Maya, one of the main preconquest tribes. The original Pokoman language has all but died out – it's now spoken only in the villages of Mixco and Chinautla – and the bulk of their original territory is swamped by Cakchiquel speakers. The site itself is thought to date from the thirteenth century, and its construction, built to withstand siege, bears all the hallmarks of the troubled times before the arrival of the Spanish. Protected on all sides by deep ravines, it can be entered only along a single-file causeway. At the time the Spanish arrived, in 1525, this was one of the largest highland centres, with nine temples, two ball courts and a population of around 9000.

The Spanish historian Fuentes y Guzman actually witnessed the conquest of the city, so for once we have a detailed account. At first Alvarado sent only a small force, but when they were unable to make any impact he launched an attack himself, using his Mexican allies, 200 Indians from Tlaxcala. With a characteristic lack of subtlety he opted for a frontal assault, but his armies were attacked from behind by a force of Pokoman warriors who arrived from Chinautla. The battle was fought on an open plain in front of the city, and by sunset the Spanish cavalry had won the day, killing some 200 Pokoman warriors, although the city remained impenetrable. According to Fuentes y Guzman the Pokoman survivors then pointed out a secret entrance to the city, allowing the Spanish to enter the city virtually unopposed, and to unleash a massacre of its inhabitants. The survivors were resettled at a site on the edge of the capital, in the village of Mixco Viejo, were Pokoman is still spoken.

Today the site has been delicately restored, with its plazas and temples laid out across several flat-topped ridges. Like all the highland sites the structures are fairly low – the largest temple reaches only about ten metres in height – and devoid of decoration. It is, however, an interesting site in a spectacular setting, and during the week you'll probably have the ruins to yourself, which gives the place all the more atmosphere.

Getting there

Mixco Viejo is by no means an easy place to reach, and if you can muster enough people it's worth hiring a car or trying to arrange for a travel agent to ferry you to and from the ruins. If you're determined to travel by bus there's one a day, leaving the Zona 4 terminal in Guatemala City at around 10am, and passing the site on its way to Pachalum. (Make sure that it will pass *las ruinas*, as there are buses that go to Pachalum without doing so.) If you opt to travel by bus then you'll have to stay overnight at the ruins, or try to hitch out again in the afternoon – and there's desperately little traffic. The bus itself returns at about 2am, passing the ruins at about 3am, and arriving in the capital for dawn.

fiestas

Despite its modern appearance Guatemala City has firmly established traditions, and in accordance with this there are one or two fiestas. Also listed are some of those in the surrounding villages, which aren't necessarily covered in the text but may well be worth visiting for their fiestas.

January
The fiesta year around Guatemala City starts from the 1st to 4th in the villages of **Fraijanes**, and there's also a moveable fiesta in **San Pedro Ayampuc**, at some stage during the month.

March
Villa Canales has its fiesta from the 6th to 14th, and **San Pedro Pinula** has its fiesta from the 16th to 20th, with the main day on the 19th. **San José del Golfo** has a fiesta from the 18th to 20th, with the main day on the 19th.

April
The only April fiesta is in **Palencia**, from the 26th to 30th.

May
May 1st, Labour Day, is marked in the capital by marches and protests, while the fiesta in

Amatitlán is from the 1st to 7th, with the main day on the 3rd.

June
Once again there's only one fiesta in this month, this time in **San Juan Sacatepéquez**, from the 22nd to 27th, with the main day on the 24th.

July
Palín has its fiesta from the 24th to 30th, a fairly traditional one which climaxes on the final day.

August
Mixco, an interesting Pokoman village on the western side of town, has its fiesta on the 4th, while the main **Guatemala City** fiesta, involving all sorts of parades and marches, is on the 15th.

November
The end of the year has very few fiestas in this part of the country but there is one in **San Catarina Pinula**, from the 20th to 28th, with the main day on the 25th.

December
The year ends with a fiesta in **Chinautla**, from the 4th to 9th, with the main day on the 6th, and **Villa Nueva**, where they have a fiesta from the 6th to 11th, with the last day as the main day.

travel details

Guatemala City is at the transport heart of the country and even the smallest of villages is connected to the capital. Hence there are literally thousands of buses into and out of the city. Most of these are covered in the "Travel Details" of other chapters; the following are the main services.

Buses
The main **bus companies**, their addresses and departure times, are as follows.

The western highlands
San Marcos. *Transportes Marquensita*, 21 Calle 12–41, Zona 1, run direct pullmans every hour or so from 4.30am to 3pm.
Antigua. Every half-hour or so from 15 Calle between 3 and 4 avenidas in Zona 1, from 6am until around 8pm. Arriving here you are close enough to walk to any of the hotels in Zona 1.
Chichicastenango and **Santa Cruz del Quiché**. Second-class buses leave every hour or so from the Zona 4 terminal.

Lake Atitlán and **Panajachel**. *Transportes Rebuli* have direct buses every hour from 20 Calle 3–42, Zona 1, from 5.30am to 4pm; or you can go to the Zona 4 terminal and board any bus going to the western highlands, and then change buses at the Los Encuentros junction.

Santiago Atitlán. *Rebuli*, 20 Calle 3–42, Zona 1, at 5am, 11.30am and 3pm. These go via Escuintla and Cocales, a roundabout route to say the least.

Quezaltenango. Several pullman companies run buses: *Galgos*, 7 Avenida 19–44, Zona 1, have departures at 5.30am, 8am, 11.30am, 2.30pm, 5pm, 7pm and 9pm; *Lineas Americas*, 2 Avenida 18–74, Zona 1, at 5am, 8am, 5pm and 7.30pm; *Rutas Lima*, 8 Calle 3–63, Zona 1, at 8am, 3pm, 4.30pm and 8pm.

Huehuetenango. Only a few regular pullman services, the best of which is *Los Halcones*, 7 Avenida 15–27, Zona 1, who have buses at 7am and 2pm. *Rapidos Zaculeu*, 9 Calle 11–42, Zona 1, have buses at 6am and 3pm and *Transportes El Condor*, 2 Avenida 19 Calle, Zona 1, run second-class buses to Huehuetenango at 4am, 8am, 1pm and 5pm.

The Pacific Coast and the Mexican border

The bus service to this part of the country is one of the best, and the bulk of the bus companies are also conveniently sited on the edge of Zona 1, outside the train station, at the junction of 19 Calle and 9 Avenida. There are buses to both **Tecún Umán** and **Talisman** hourly from 5am to 5pm. These pass through all the main towns in the coastal region between Escuintla and the border, where you can change buses for smaller places off the main highway.

The Motagua Valley, the Caribbean and the Petén

Buses for the **Petén** are run by *Fuente del Norte*, 7 Calle 8–46, Zona 1, close to the main area of budget hotels. There are three or four buses a day and you need to get a ticket in advance in either direction.

Puerto Barrios, **Zacapa**, **Chiquimula** and **Esquipulas**. Hourly buses, most of them pullmans, leave from the train station terminal at 19 Calle 9 Avenida in Zona 1.

The eastern highlands and San Salvador

For all the towns between the capital and the border with El Salvador there are second-class buses that leave from the terminal in Zona 4. If you're heading across the border then several bus companies run a direct service to **San Salvador**; *Melva*, *Taca Internacional*, *Mermex*, *El Condor* and *Transcomer* are the main ones, all around the junction of 1 Calle and 4 Avenida, a block or so from the main terminal in Zona 4. Between them they offer an hourly service from 5.30am to 3.30pm. It's an eight-hour trip and the buses take you directly to the *Terminal Occidente* in San Salvador.

Planes

There are frequent international flights from Guatemala City's Aurora airport, to Mexico, Central America and North America, and four daily flights to **Flores** in the Petén. Three of these leave at around 7am, and one at about 4pm. Tickets can be bought from virtually any travel agent in the capital. It's a fifty-minute flight, and tickets cost around $50.

Train

There are trains three times a week to Puerto Barrios and Tecún Umán. Departures from the station at 9 Avenida and 18 Calle, Zona 1, are at 7.30am (Tues, Thurs & Sat) for Puerto Barrios and 7am (Tues & Sat) for Tecún Umán: both trips can take anything between 8 and 20 hours.

CHAPTER TWO

THE WESTERN HIGHLANDS

Guatemala's western highlands, stretching from Guatemala City to the Mexican border, are perhaps the most fascinating and beautiful part of the entire country. The area is defined by two main features; the string of volcanoes that run along the southern side, and the mountain ranges that mark out the northern boundary. The greatest of these are the **Cuchumatanes**, whose granite peaks rise to some 3600 metres. Strung between the two is a series of twisting ridges, lakes, sweeping bowls, forests, gushing streams and deep valleys.

It's an astounding, brooding landscape, blessed with tremendous fertility but cursed by instability. The hills are regularly shaken by earthquakes and occasionally showered by volcanic eruptions. Of the thirteen cones that run through the western highlands, three are still active: **Pacaya**, **Fuego** and **Santiaguito**, all oozing plumes of sulphurous smoke and occasionally throwing up clouds of molten rock. Two major **fault lines** also cut through the area, making earthquakes a regular occurrence. The most recent major quake was centred around **Chimaltenango**, in 1976 – it left 25,000 dead and around a million homeless. But despite its sporadic ferocity the landscape is outstandingly beautiful and the atmosphere is calm and welcoming, with irrigated valleys and terraced hillsides carefully crafted to yield the maximum potential farmland.

The highland landscape is controlled by many factors, all of which affect its appearance. Perhaps the most important is **altitude**. At lower levels the vegetation is almost tropical, supporting dense forests, **coffee**, **cotton**, **bananas** and **cacao**, while higher up the hills are often wrapped in cloud and the ground is sometimes hard with frost. Here trees are stunted by the cold, and maize and potatoes are grown alongside grazing herds of sheep and goats. The seasons also play their part. In the rainy season, from May to October, the land is superbly green, with young crops and lush forests of **pine**, **cedar** and **oak**, while during the dry winter months the hillsides gradually turn to a dusty yellow.

The Indian highlands

The western highlands are home to a substantial percentage of Guatemala's population, of whom the vast majority are Indians. Their life and culture are strongly separated from the world of *Ladinos*, and their history is bound up with the land on which they live. In the days of Classic Maya civilisation (300–900 AD) the western highlands were a peripheral area, with the great developments taking place in the lowlands to the north. Apart from the city of **Kaminaljuyú**, on the site of modern Guatemala City, little is known about the highlands at this time, and there are no archaeological remains that date from the Classic Period.

Towards the end of the eleventh century the **Toltec Maya** moved south, from what is now central Mexico, and conquered the Maya of the western highlands, installing themselves as an elite ruling class. Under Toltec rule a number of rival empires emerged, each speaking a separate language and based around a ceremonial centre. The most powerful of these groups were the **Quiché**, whose capital city **Utatlán** was situated to the west of the modern town of **Santa Cruz del Quiché**. Between 1400 and 1475 the Quichés embarked on an aggressive campaign of expansion and managed to bring most of the other tribes under their control, with perhaps one million subjects bowing to the Quiché king. But 1475 saw the death of Quicab, the most successful of the Quiché rulers, and as a result of this the smaller tribes, including the **Cakchiquel**, **Mam**, **Rabinal** and **Tzutujil**, were able to assert their independence. From then on they lived in a world of constant conflict, consistently competing for control of the dwindling supply of farmland. By the time the Spanish arrived the highlands were in a state of crisis, with population growth starting to outstrip the food supply. The highland tribes had been forced to expand onto the Pacific coast, and their rivalries had never been more serious. All the archaeological remains from this period reflect the bitter conflict, with cities built on inaccessible hilltops and surrounded by protective ditches.

Even today the highlands are divided up along traditional tribal lines. The **Quiché language** is still spoken by the largest number, centred on the town of Santa Cruz del Quiché and reaching into the Quezaltenango valley. The highlands around Huehuetenango are **Mam-speaking**, the Tzutujiles occupy the southern shores of Lake Atitlán, with the **Cakchiqueles** to the east. **Smaller tribal groups**, such as the Ixiles and the Aguatecas, also occupy clearly defined areas in the Cuchumatan mountains, where the language and costume are distinct.

The Spanish highlands

Though pre-conquest life was certainly hard, the **arrival of the Spanish** was a total disaster for the Indian population. In the early stages Alvarado and his army met with a force of Quiché warriors in the Quezaltenango basin, and defeated them in open warfare. The defeated Quichés took the Spanish to their capital, Utatlán, hoping to negotiate some kind of deal. Alvarado, however, was not to be seduced by such subtlety and promptly burnt the city along with many of its inhabitants. The next move was made by the Cakchiqueles, who formed an alliance with the Spanish, hoping to exploit the newcomers' military might to overcome former rivals. As a result of this the Spanish made their first permanent base at the site of the Cakchiquel capital Iximché. But in 1527 the Cakchiqueles, provoked by demands for tribute, rose up against the Spanish and fled to the mountains, from where they waged a campaign of guerrilla war against their former allies. The Spanish then moved their capital into the Almolonga valley, to a site near the modern town of Antigua, from where they gradually brought the rest of the highlands under a degree of control.

Meanwhile the damage done by Spanish swords was nothing when compared to that of the **diseases** they introduced. Waves of smallpox, typhus, plague and measles swept through the indigenous population, reducing their numbers by as much as ninety percent in the worst hit areas. The population was so badly devastated that it only started to recover at the end of the seventeenth century, and didn't get back to pre-conquest levels until the middle of the twentieth century.

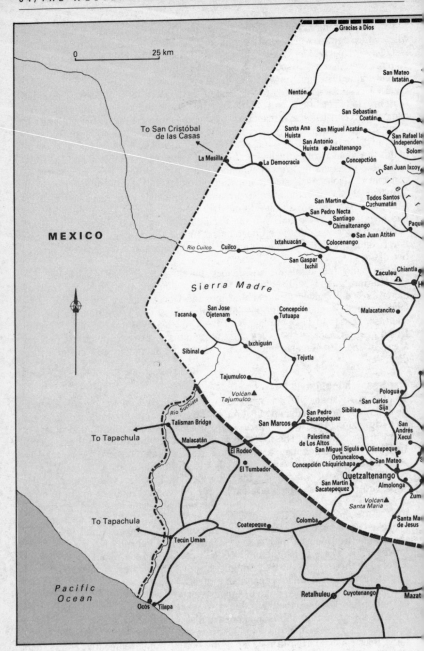

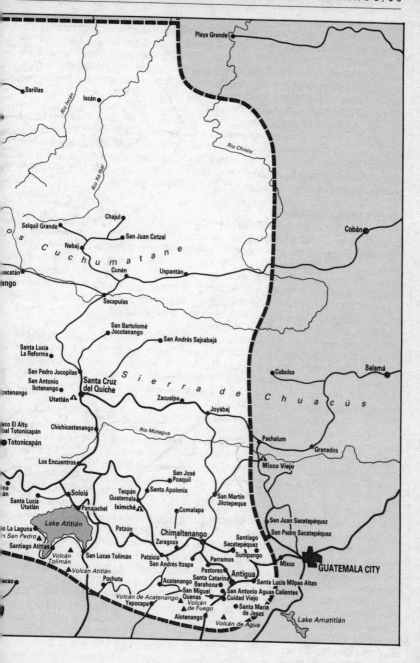

In the long term the **Spanish administration** of the western highlands was no gentler than the conquest, as Indian labour became the backbone of the Spanish empire. Guatemala offered none of the gold and silver that was available in Peru or Mexico, but there was still money to be made from **cacao** and **indigo**. Indian labourers were forced to travel to the Pacific coast to work the plantations, while priests moved them from their scattered homes into new villages and attempted to transform them into devout Catholics. At the heart of all this was the colonial capital of **Antigua**, then known as Santiago de los Caballeros, from where the whole of Central America and Chiapas (now in Mexico) was administered. In its day Antigua must have been a truly impressive city, with a massive cathedral and hundreds of other chapels and churches, the ruins of which are still scattered across the modern town. But in 1773 the city was destroyed by a massive earthquake, and the capital moved to its modern site.

Independent highlands

By the time the Spanish left Guatemala, in 1821, three centuries of colonial rule had left a permanent imprint on the western highlands. The entire social structure had been radically transformed. The Spanish had attempted to remove the power of large regional centres, replacing it with that of the church, but a lack of clergy, particularly in the seventeenth and eighteenth centuries, had enabled the villages to establish their own authority and allowed traditional religion to continue. As a result of this the Indian population had developed strong village-based allegiances: these, along with the often bizarre hybrid of Catholicism and paganism, are still at the heart of highland life.

At the village level **independence** brought little change. *Ladino* authority replaced that of the Spanish, but Indians were still required to work the coastal plantations and when labour supplies dropped off they were simply press-ganged (or more subtly lured into debt) and forced to work, often in horrific conditions. It's a state of affairs that has changed little even today, and remains a major burden on the Indian population.

In the last few decades fresh pressures have emerged as the Indians have been caught up in the waves of political violence. In the late 1970s **guerrilla movements** began to develop in opposition to military rule, seeking support from the Indian population and establishing themselves in the western highlands, particularly the departments of Quiché, Huehuetenango, Sololá and Totonicapán. The Indians became the unwilling victims of the process, caught between the guerrillas and the army. A total of 440 villages were destroyed; thousands died and thousands more fled the country, seeking refuge in Mexico. Indian communities have also been besieged by American **evangelical churches**, whose influence undermines local hierarchies and threatens to destroy indigenous culture.

Today the level of violence has dropped off significantly although some areas are still hotly fought over. Despite intense pressure and bitter racism, Indian society remains largely intact; traditional structures are still in place, local languages still spoken, and traditional costume still worn. It is this, above all else, that is Guatemala's most fascinating feature. **Indian society** is inward-looking and conservative, operating, in the face of adversity, on its own terms. Rejecting *Ladino* commercialism, the Indians see trade as a social function as much as an economic one. They live in a world that is centred on the village, with its own civil and religious hierarchy. Subsistence farming of maize and beans is at its heart, and the land its life-blood. Today Guatemala's Indians face immense cultural and economic pressures, which may even threaten their survival; however it is their culture, moulded by centuries of struggle, which shapes the western highlands and gives them a totally unique atmosphere.

Visiting Indian **villages** during the week you'll find them almost deserted – their permanent populations are generally small, though they may support five or ten times as many scattered rural homesteads. This wider populace is regularly brought together by markets and fiestas, and at such times the villages fill to bursting. This is when you can most clearly sense the values of the Indian world – in the subdued bustle of the market or the intense joy of celebration.

Where to go

Travelling in the western highlands you're spoilt for choice, with beautiful scenery and interesting villages at every turn. It's the villages that are the main attrac-

---

MARKET DAYS

Throughout the western highlands weekly markets are the main focus of economic and social activity, drawing huge crowds from the area around the town or village where they're held. Second only to fiestas it's market days that you should make for when visiting a village.

Monday
Antigua. Chimaltenango. San Juan Atitán. Zunil. Santa Barbara.

Tuesday
Acatenango. Comalapa. El Tejar. Olintepeque. Patzún. Salcajá. San Andrés Semetabaj. San Antonio Llotenango. San Pedro Jocopolis. San Lucas Toliman. San Marcos. Yepocapa. Totonicapán. Chajul.

Wednesday
Chimaltenango. Colotenango. Patzicia. Momostenango. Palestina. Sacapulas. Cotzal. Palestina de los Altos. San Sebastián Huehuetenango. Almolonga.

Thursday
Aguacatán. Antigua. Chichicastenango. Chimaltenango. El Tejar. Jacaltenango. La Libertad. Nebaj. Panajachel. Patulul. Patzún. Sacapulas. San Juan Atitán. San Luis Jilotepeque. San Mateo Ixtatán. Uspantán. Santa Cruz del Quiché. San Pedro Necta. San Pedro Pinula. San Pedro Sacatepéquez. Santa Barbara. Tajamulco. Tecpán. Totonicapán. Soloma. Patzite. San Miguel Ixtahuacán. Zacualpa. San Rafael La Independencia.

Friday
Chimaltenango. Chajul. San Andrés Itzapa. Jocotenango. San Francisco el Alto. San Lucas Toliman. Sololá. Tacaná. Santiago Atitlán.

Saturday
Colotenango. Ixchiguan. Malacatán. Nentón. Olintepeque. Patzicia. Palestina de los Altos. Cotzal. Yepacapa. Santa Cruz del Quiché. Santa Clara La Laguna. Sumpango. Todos Santos. Totonicapán. Almolonga.

Sunday
Acatenango. Cantel. Cuilco. Sumpango. Chichicastenango. Chimaltenango. El Jacaltenango. Joyabaj. Aguacatán. San Bartolo. La Libertad. Malacancito. San Pedro Necta. Tecpán. Tejar. San Pedro Sacatepequez. Momostenango. Nebaj. Nahualá. Patzite. Nentón. Panajachel. San Carlos Sija. Patzún. Parramos. San Cristóbal Totonicapán. Comalapa. San Martin Jilotepeque. Ostuncalco. San Luis Jilotepeque. San Miguel Acatán. San Miguel Ixtahuacán. Soloma. San Mateo Ixtahuacán. Tucuru. Uspantán. Santa Eulalia. Tacaná. Huehuetenango. Santa Barbara. Santa Cruz del Quiché. Zacualpa. Sibilia. Yepocapa. Sacapulas.

tion, but there are also historical sites: the pre-conquest cities of **Iximché**, **Utatlán** and **Zaculeu**, as well as the colonial ruins in **Antigua**. The ancient cities don't bear comparison to Tikal and the lowland sites, but they're nevertheless fascinating in their own way.

The **Pan-American highway** runs through the middle of the western highlands so it's easy enough to get around. There's a constant flow of buses along this main artery, with others branching off along minor roads to more remote areas. Travel in some of these can be a gruelling experience, particularly in northern Huehuetenango and Quiché, but the scenery makes it well worth the discomfort. The best plan of action is to base yourself in one of the larger places and then make day trips to markets and fiestas, although even the smallest of villages usually have some kind of accommodation of their own.

Travelling west from Guatemala City the first place of interest is **Antigua**, where it's easy to settle into the relaxed pace of things, visiting the surrounding villages, climbing the volcanoes, or taking in the colonial ruins. Further to the west is the department of **El Quiché**, with the famous market at **Chichicastenango** and the ruins of **Utatlán**, near the departmental capital of **Santa Cruz del Quiché**. To the south of Quiché, **Lake Atitlán** is the jewel of the western highlands, ringed by volcanoes and villages, and reached through **Sololá** and **Panajachel** – the latter a growing but still low-key resort. To the north are the wildly beautiful peaks of the **Cuchumatanes**, between which are the towns of the **Ixil triangle**, in a superb world of their own. Heading on to the west you pass the strongly traditional town of **Nahualá** and go up over the mountains to **Quezaltenango**, Guatemala's second city, an ideal base for visiting local villages or climbing the **Santa María Volcano**. Beyond this the border with Mexico is marked by the departments of **San Marcos** and **Huehuetenango**, both of which offer some superb mountain scenery, dotted with isolated villages, through which you can travel on into Mexico.

ANTIGUA AND AROUND

At the base of a broad U-shaped valley, suspended between the Agua, Acatenango and Fuego volcanoes, lies Guatemala's colonial capital, **ANTIGUA**. In its day this was one of the great cities of the Spanish empire, ranking alongside Lima and Mexico City, and serving as the administrative centre for the entire *Audiencia de Guatemala*, which included all of Central America and Chiapas.

Antigua was actually the third capital of Guatemala. The Spanish first settled at the site of **Iximché** in July 1524, so that they could keep a close eye on their Cakchiquel allies. In November 1527, when the Cakchiqueles rose up in defiance of their new rulers, the capital was moved into the Almolonga valley, to the site of **Ciudad Vieja**, a few kilometres from Antigua. In 1541, shortly after the death of Alvarado, this entire town was lost beneath a massive mud slide. Only then did the capital come to rest in Antigua, known in those days as *La Muy Noble y Muy Leal Ciudad de Santiago de los Caballeros de Goathemala*. Here, despite the continued threat from the instability of the bedrock – the first earthquake came after just twenty years – it settled, and began to achieve astounding prosperity.

As the heart of colonial power in Central America, Antigua grew slowly but steadily. One by one the religious orders established themselves, competing in the construction of schools, churches, monasteries and hospitals. Bishops built themselves grand palaces which were soon rivalled by the homes of local merchants and corrupt government officials. The city reached its peak in the middle of the eighteenth century, after the 1717 earthquake prompted an unprecedented building boom, and the population rose to around 50,000. By this stage it was a genuinely impressive place, with a university, a printing press, a newspaper, and streets that were seething with commercial and political rivalries.

But as is so often the case in Guatemala **earthquakes** brought all of this to an abrupt end. For the best part of a year the city was shaken by tremors, with the final blows delivered by two severe shocks on September 7 and December 13, 1773. The damage was so bad that the decision was made to abandon the city in favour of the modern capital: fortunately, despite endless official decrees, there were many who refused to leave and the city was never completely deserted.

Since then the city has been gradually repopulated, particularly in the last hundred years or so. As Guatemala City has become increasingly congested, many of the conservative middle classes have moved to Antigua, where they've been joined by a large number of foreigners, attracted by its relaxed and sophisticated atmosphere. In recent years concern has mounted for the fate of the city's ancient architecture and many of the old buildings have been meticulously restored, or their ruins carefully landscaped. Antigua was the first planned city in the Americas, originally built on a rigid grid pattern, with neatly cobbled streets and superb architecture. Of this some now lies in shattered ruins, some is steadily decaying, and yet more is impeccably restored. Here alone you can sense the splendour and affluence of the colonial years, in a city that's totally unique. Local laws protect the streets from the intrusion of overhanging signs, and every effort is made to recreate the architectural splendour of the past.

Once regarded as the cultural and religious centre of the country, these days Antigua has stepped aside from the forefront and become a haven of tranquillity. It offers a welcome break from the unrelenting energy of the capital. Popular with tourists, retired Americans, and above all language students, the town has managed to become one of the most picturesque in Central America. By Guatemalan standards it is highly organised, clean and peaceful, too. The downside of this settled, comfortable affluence is perhaps a loss of vitality – it's a great place to wind down and eat well for a few days if you've been travelling hard, or to learn Spanish at some of the best language schools in Latin America – but after a while it can come to seem too secure, too smug. Still, it's certainly somewhere you should visit, and the surrounding **countryside** is superbly beautiful.

Semana Santa in Antigua

Antigua's **Semana Santa (Holy Week) celebrations** are perhaps the most extravagant and impressive in all of Latin America. The celebrations start with a procession on Palm Sunday, representing Christ's entry into Jerusalem, and continue through to the really big processions and pageants on Good Friday. On Thursday night the streets are carpeted with carefully drawn patterns of coloured sawdust, and on Friday morning a procession re-enacts the progress of Christ to the cross. Images of Christ and the cross are carried on massive platforms, borne on the shoulders of solemn penitents, and watched by thousands. The pageant leaves the church of La Merced at 8am, the penitents dressed in purple. After 3pm, the hour of the crucifixion, they change into black.

The tourist office has more exact details of the events. During Holy Week hotels in Antigua are often full, but even if you have to make the trip from Guatemala City or Panajachel, it's well worth being in Antigua for Good Friday.

Antigua

Antigua is laid out on the traditional grid system, with *avenidas* running north–south, and *calles* east–west. Each street is numbered and has two halves, either a north and south (*norte/sur*) or an east and west (*oriente/poniente*), with the plaza, the **Parque Central**, regarded as the centre. To complicate matters the old names for some streets have been revived, and are occasionally used instead of the numbering system. In reality the town is small and it's all a lot simpler than it sounds, but just in case you get confused the Agua volcano, the one that hangs most immediately over the town, is to the south. The only problem with finding your way around is that overhanging signs are outlawed, in a bid to preserve the colonial ambience, so specific places can be a little hard to locate.

Arriving by bus, whether from Guatemala City or Chimaltenango, you'll end up in the main **bus terminal**, a large open space behind the market, which is three long blocks to the west of the plaza. To get to the centre of town, cross the broad tree-lined street outside the terminal and walk straight up the street opposite, which will bring you into the plaza.

BUSES

The bus terminal is beside the market at the western end of 4 Calle Poniente. The main bus schedule is as follows.
To Guatemala City (45min) buses leave every half-hour or so from 3am to 7pm, except on Sunday, when the first one leaves at 6am.
To Chimaltenango (50min) hourly buses from 5.30am to 5.30pm.
To Escuintla (via El Rodeo) at least one bus a day, at 12.30pm – returning at 7am.
To Yepocapa and **Acatenango** buses leave in the late afternoon, around 3 or 4pm.
Local buses, to the villages within the valley, also leave from the terminal. The times are listed in the relevant sections below.

Finding a place to stay

Hotels in Antigua are in plentiful supply, although like everything else they can be a bit hard to find due to the lack of overhanging signs, and be warned that rooms get scarce around Holy Week.

Many of the cheaper places are around the bus terminal. To your right as you emerge from the terminal, on Alameda Santa Lucía, is *La Casa de Santa Lucía* ($3), a gorgeous but small place, built with dark wood around a leafy courtyard. It's not only spotlessly clean but also has hot showers – some rooms even have private bathrooms. Next door is the cheaper *Hospedaje El Pasaje*, a little less polished, a little cheaper, but still very friendly and also with hot water. Along the street that runs from the bus terminal to the Parque Central, 4 Calle Poniente, are a selection of other places. The first on the right is the *Hotel Doña Angelina* ($3), a newish and pleasant sort of place, and further up on the other side of the street is *El Refugio* ($1), vast and laid back, with a variety of rooms, although the ones out the back are to be avoided – "decency" is included in the price of a room. If you turn left at the corner of the plaza, and follow 5 Avenida Norte for two and a half blocks, under the arch, you come to the *Pension El Arco* ($2), which is clean and good value. Also on this side of town is the *Hotel Placido* on Avenida del

Deseungano, an immaculate family business with rooms set around a beautiful courtyard. The one drawback is that it's on the main road out of town: the noise doesn't penetrate so much to the back rooms, but the whole building still shakes as buses thunder past. (Not a good place to stay if you're worried about earthquakes.) If you're on a tight budget then head for 2 Calle Poniente and the *Posada La Antigueñita*, which is undoubtedly the cheapest place in town and equally certainly not the most luxurious: if you're looking for a bargain look no further.

There are dozens of **others** – most of them perfectly good – as you're likely to discover when you step off the bus into a horde of would-be guides offering to take you to a room (or a language school). At busy times it can be worth taking up one of these offers – you can always move later.

The City – ruins, restorations and museums

In accordance with its position of importance, Antigua was once a centre of secular and religious power, trade, and above all wealth. Here the great institutions competed with the government to build the county's most impressive buildings. Churches, monasteries, schools, hospitals and grand family homes were once spread throughout the city, all built with tremendously thick walls to resist earthquakes. Today Antigua is scattered with an incredible number of ruined and restored colonial buildings, and although these constitute only a fraction of the city's original architectural splendour they do give you an idea of its former extravagance. Listed below are only some of the remaining examples; armed with a map from the tourist office you could spend days exploring the ruins (there's a small entrance fee to most of them).

The Parque Central

As always the focus of the colonial city was its **central plaza**. Old prints show it as an open expanse of earth, which became a sea of mud in the rainy season. For centuries this was the hub of the city, bustling with constant activity. A huge market spilled out across it, cleared only for bullfights, floggings and public hangings. The calm of today's tree-lined **Parque Central** is a relatively recent creation, and the fountain, originally set to one side so as not to interfere with the action, was moved to the centre in 1936.

The most imposing of the surrounding structures is the **Cathedral of San José**, on the western side. The first cathedral was begun in 1545, making use of some of Alvarado's vast fortune after his death. However the workmanship was so poor that the structure was in a constant state of disrepair, and an earthquake in 1583 brought down much of the roof. In 1670 it was decided to start on a new cathedral, worthy of the town's importance. For eleven years the town watched and the Indians laboured, as the most spectacular building in Central America took shape. The sheer scale of the new building was astounding; a huge dome, five naves, eighteen chapels, and a central chamber 90 by 20 metres. Its altar was inlaid with mother-of-pearl, ivory and silver, while carvings of the saints and paintings by the most revered of European and colonial artists covered the walls.

The new cathedral was strong enough to withstand the earthquakes of 1689 and 1717, but the walls were weakened and the 1773 earthquake brought them crashing to the ground. Today two of the chapels have been restored as the **Church of San José**, inside which is a figure of Christ by Quirio Cataño, who carved the famous black Christ of Esquipulas. This opens off the Parque Central;

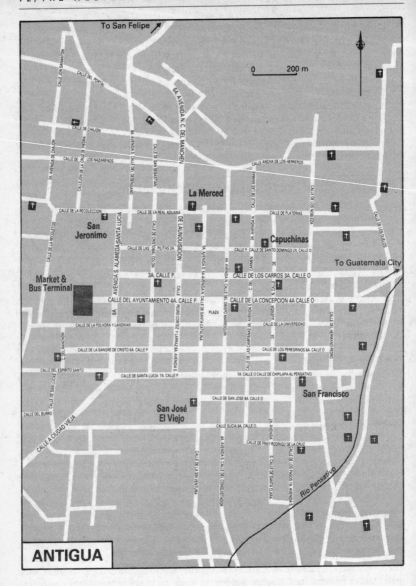

ANTIGUA

behind (entered from 5 Calle Oriente) are the remains of the rest of the structure, a mass of fallen masonry, rotting beams, broken arches and hefty pillars, cracked and moss-covered. Buried beneath the floor are some of the great names of the conquest, including Alvarado, his wife Beatriz de la Cueva, Bishop Marroquín and Bernal Díaz del Castillo, famous historian of the conquest.

Along the entire south side of the Parque Central runs the **Palace of the Captains General**, a squat two-storey facade with 27 arches on each floor. It was originally built in 1558, but as usual the first version was destroyed by earthquakes. It was rebuilt in 1761, only to be damaged again in 1773, and then restored along the lines of the present structure. The Palace was home to colonial rulers, and also housed the barracks of the dragoons, law courts, tax offices, great ballrooms, a large bureaucracy, and a lot more besides. Today it contains the local government offices, the headquarters of the Sacatepéquez police department, and the tourist office.

Directly opposite, on the north side of the plaza, is the **Ayuntamiento**, the city hall, also known as the *Casa del Cabildo* or town house. Dating from 1740, its metre-thick walls balance the solid style of the Palace of the Captains General. Unlike most others this building was damaged quite recently, in the 1976 earthquake, but has been repaired since. Above the arches you can see Saint James (Santiago), the emblem of the colonial city, spurring his horse over three volcanoes, with the middle one in eruption. The city hall was abandoned in 1779 when the capital was moved to its modern site, but it later held the police headquarters, and now that they've moved across the plaza the building is again used by the city's administration.

The Ayuntamiento also houses a couple of museums. The first of these is the **Museo de Santiago** (daily 9am–noon & 2–6pm), which has a collection of colonial artefacts, including bits of pottery, a sword said to have been used by Alvarado, portraits of stern-faced colonial figures, and some paintings of warfare between the Spanish and the Indians. At the back of the museum is the old city jail, beside which there was a small chapel where condemned prisoners passed their last moments before being hauled off to the gallows in the plaza. Also under the arches of the city hall is the **Museo del Libro Antiguo**, in the rooms that held the first printing press in Central America. This arrived here in 1660, from Puebla de los Angeles in Mexico, and churned out the first book three years later. A replica of the original is on display alongside some copies of other early works.

South and east of the plaza

Across the street from the ruined Cathedral, in 5 Calle Oriente, is the **Seminario Tridentino**, one of the great colonial schools. It was founded at the start of the seventeenth century for some fifteen students, and later expanded to include the School of the Indians, so that local people could share in the joys of theology. The structure is still in almost perfect condition, but it's currently divided up into several separate homes, so the elaborate stucco doorway is all you'll get to see.

A little further up the same street is the **University of San Carlos Borromeo**, which now houses the **Museo de Arte Colonial**. The founding of a university was first proposed by Bishop Marroquín in 1559, but met with little enthusiasm as the Jesuits, Dominicans and Franciscans couldn't bear the thought of rivals to their own colleges. It wasn't until 1676 that the plan was authorised, using money left by the Bishop, and classes started in 1681 with seventy students applying themselves to everything from law to the Cakchiquel language. For a while only pure-blooded Castilians were admitted, but later entry requirements were changed to include a broader spectrum of the population. After the 1751 earthquake the university's original building was beyond repair, and the rector of the Seminary donated the house next door to his own. Since then the university has moved to Guatemala City, and in 1832 this building became a grammar school, and then a museum in 1936. The deep-set windows and beautifully ornate arched corridor surrounding the patio make it one of the finest survivors in Antigua. The museum contains a collection of dark and brooding religious art, sculpture, murals of life on the colonial campus, and a seventeenth-century map of Antigua by the historian Antonio de Fuentes y Guzmán.

The next turning to the right takes you onto 3 Avenida Sur, and another block brings you to the **San Pedro Church** and hospital. Originally built in 1680, and periodically crammed full of earthquake victims, it was finally evacuated when one of the aftershocks in 1976 threatened to bring down the roof – reconstruction is still in progress. In front of the hospital a tree-lined plaza leads to **Santa Clara**, a convent and church founded in 1699 by nuns from Puebla in Mexico. In colonial times this became a popular place for well-to-do young ladies to take the veil, as the hardships were none too hard and the nuns earned a reputation for their cooking, selling their bread to the aristocracy. The original huge convent was totally destroyed in 1717, as was the second in 1773, but the current building was spared in 1976, and the ornate exterior remains intact.

Walking around the front of the church and to the left, along 7 Calle Oriente, you arrive at **San Francisco**, one of the few churches that has recently come back into service. The most recent phase of reconstruction began in 1960, and is still the subject of much controversy. The nave has been restored in its entirety, but the ornate mouldings and sculpture have been left off, so although you get a rough idea of its former splendour, in actuality it would have been considerably more decorative. The remains of Pedro de Betancourt (a Franciscan from the Canary Islands who founded the Hospital of Belén in Antigua) are buried here, and pilgrims from all over Central America come to ask for the benefit of his powers of miraculous intervention. The earliest building on the site was begun in 1579 by the Franciscans, who were the first religious order to arrive in the city. It grew into a vast religious and cultural centre including a school, a hospital, music rooms, a printing press and a monastery, covering four blocks in all. All of this, though, was lost in the 1773 earthquake.

Heading out of town, in the direction of the Agua volcano, you can follow the **stations of the cross**, signifying Christ's route to crucifixion at Calvary. Along the way are twelve little chapels representing the stations, in assorted states of disrepair, and at the far end is **El Calvario**, a small functioning church with magnificently thick walls. Outside the church, sunk in the middle of the road and looking oddly out of place, is a beautifully carved stone fountain.

Heading back towards the centre of town you can drop in at the **Casa Popenoe** (Mon–Sat 3–5pm), a superbly restored colonial mansion on the corner of 1 Avenida Sur and 5 Calle Oriente. Not only does this offer a welcome break from church ruins, but it's also an interesting insight into domestic life in colonial times. The house, set around a gorgeous courtyard, was restored in 1932, and decorated with Señor Popenoe's incredible collection of colonial furniture and art. Among the collection are portraits of Bishop Marroquín and the fierce-looking Alvarado himself. Every last detail has been authentically restored, down to the original leather lampshades that are painted with religious musical scores, and the great wooden beds, decorated with a mass of accomplished carving. The kitchen and servants' quarters have also been carefully renovated, and you can see the bread ovens, the herb garden and the pigeon loft, which would have provided the original occupants with their mail service. Señor Popenoe died in 1972, but two of his daughters still live in the house.

Around the corner, on 5 Calle Oriente heading back towards the Parque Central, between 1 and 2 Avenidas, is the house that once belonged to **Bernal Díaz del Castillo**, one of the soldiers who served under Alvarado in Mexico and Guatemala and in his later years wrote an account of the conquest.

North from the plaza
Setting out northwards from the Parque Central, along 4 Avenida Norte, you'll find the hermitage of **El Carmen**, down to the right after the first block. This was originally one of the city's great churches, first built in 1638, and rebuilt many times since: the facade finally collapsed in 1976, and today only the ruined nave stands.

Back on 4 Avenida the convent of **Santa Teresa** lies another block to the north. Founded with funds from a Peruvian philanthropist, it was originally filled with Carmelite nuns from Lima: these days its occupants are a quite different bunch, as the building is now used as the city jail.

A block to the east, at the junction of 2 Calle Oriente and 2 Avenida Norte, is **Las Capuchinas**, the largest and most impressive of the city's convents. The Capuchin nuns, who came from Madrid, were rather late on the scene, founding the fourth convent in the city in 1726. They were only granted permission because the women would not need dowries to pay their way into religious life. The ruins themselves are some of the best preserved and least understood in Antigua. The two-storey circular tower is the most unusual point. On the top floor eighteen tiny cells are set into the walls, each with an independent sewage system, while the lower floor is dominated by a massive pillar that supports the structure above and incorporates seventeen small recesses, some with stone rings set in the walls. Theories about the use of this part are plentiful: a warehouse, a laundry room, a communal bath, a pantry, or even a torture chamber.

Further out along 1 Avenida Norte, for the real devotee, are the badly damaged ruins of the churches of **Santa Rosa, Candelaria** and **Nuestra Señora de los Dolores del Cerro**.

Back into the centre, leaving the plaza along 5 Avenida Norte, you pass under the arch of **Santa Catalina**, which is all that remains of the original convent, founded here in 1609. By 1697 it had reached maximum capacity with 110 nuns and six novices. The arch was built so that they could walk between the two halves of the establishment without exposing themselves to the pollution of the outside world. Somehow it managed to defy the constant onslaught of earthquakes, and was restored in the middle of the nineteenth century.

Walking under the arch and to the end of the street, you reach the church of **La Merced**, with one of the most intricate and impressive facades in the entire city, crammed with plaster moulding of interlaced patterns. The church is still used and has been restored, but the cloisters and gardens are ruined and lie exposed to the sky. In the centre of one of the courtyards is a fountain surrounded by four pools, known as the *Fuente de Pescados*; the pools were used by the Mercedarian brothers for breeding fish. There's a colonial fountain in front of the church, which is worth a look as the stone carving that decorates it is superbly preserved.

West of the plaza
Back in the Parque Central again, the last of the ruins are to the west, towards the bus station. At the junction of 4 Calle Poniente and 6 Avenida Norte is **La Compañia de Jesús**, an educational establishment and church that was operated by the Jesuits until the King of Spain, feeling threatened by their tremen-

dous power, expelled them from the colonies in 1767. In this century the market, moved out of the plaza, was housed in the cloisters until the 1976 earthquake: nowadays most of the ruins are closed off, though one or two rather touristy *artesania* stalls have recently moved back in.

Turning to the right in front of the bus station, and to the end of the tree-lined street, you reach the spectacular remains of **San Jeronimo**, a school built in 1739. Well-kept gardens are woven between the huge blocks of fallen masonry and crumbling walls. Down behind San Jeronimo a dirt track leads to the even more chaotic ruin **La Recolección**, where the middle of the church is piled high with the remains of the roof and walls. Recolect friars first arrived here, asking permission to be allowed to build, in 1685, but it wasn't until 1701 that they started the church, finishing it in 1715. Months later it was brought to the ground by a huge earthquake. This second version was destroyed in 1773, and has been steadily decaying ever since.

On the other side of the bus station (to its south) is an imposing monument to Rafael Landivar (1731–93), a Jesuit composer who is generally considered the finest poet of the colonial era. Along with all the other Jesuits he was banished from the Americas in 1767.

Finally, walking back to the plaza along 5 Calle Poniente, you'll pass the **Iglesia de San Agustin**, the remains of a vast convent complex that once occupied about half the block but has stood derelict since the earthquake of 1773, after which the Augustinians followed the government in the exodus to Guatemala City.

Eating and entertainment

In Antigua the food is even more cosmopolitan than the population, and the only thing that's hard to come by is an authentic Guatemalan *comedor*. Here you can eat your way around the world in a series of sedate, sophisticated and fairly expensive **restaurants**. For a healthy start to the day the best breakfast, of fruit salad and granola, is at the *Peroleto*, Alameda Santa Lucía 36, which also does fantastic fruit juices and sandwiches. Right in the centre, at 4 Calle Oriente 12, *Doña Luisa's* is probably the most popular place in town, frequented by foreigners, whether residents or tourists, and local people alike. The menu is simple, the setting relaxed, and the food tasty; chilli con carne, baked potatoes, salads, hamburgers, and superb bread and pastries. For **Chinese** food there's *La Estrella*, 5 Calle Poniente 6, or the *Gran Muralla*, at 4 Calle Poniente 3, just off the plaza. The latter is a strongly Guatemalan hard-drinking bar that also serves good steaks and pasta, generous portions at low prices. Also along Oriental lines is *Zen*, 3 Avenida del Norte 3, a delicious and fairly authentic **Japanese** restaurant.

If you hunger for something more European, then **Italian** food is always at hand. The *Angeletti*, on 5 Calle Poniente, does a good range of pizza and pasta, and if you want to dine in style and disregard the cost then *El Capuchino*, on 6 Avenida del Norte, is one of the most spectacular places in town, serving delicious Italian food. Moving into northern Europe you can eat **French** food at the *Mistral*, 4 Calle Oriente 7, or **German** at *Welten*, 4 Calle Oriente 21. Both are good, but neither is particularly cheap.

Among the best **bars** in town are *Mio Cid*, at 5 Calle Oriente and 3 Avenida Sur, a popular, yuppie-style hang-out that sometimes has live music; *Moscas y Miel*, 5 Calle Poniente 5; *La Chimenea*, 4 Calle Poniente and 7 Avenida; *Picasso's*

Café, 7 Avenida Norte; and *Bianco*, 6 Avenida Norte. For drinking in more Guatemalan surroundings try again the *Gran Muralla*, at 4 Calle Poniente 3. On Sundays there are sometimes Marimba concerts in the *Hotel Antigua* and there's a **disco** in the *Hotel Ramada*.

The only functioning **cinema** is the *Colonial*, to the south of the plaza on 5 Avenida Sur, but **videos** and **satellite TV** are shown in the early evening at the *Welten* and *Mistral*. For whiling away the daylight hours there's a public open-air **swimming pool** at the *Club Viejo*, down the end of 5 Calle Oriente.

Other practicalities

The **tourist office**, open daily from 8am to noon and 2pm to 6pm, is on the south side of the plaza.

The **language school** business is currently booming in Antigua, with a total of 26 in operation, and it's an inescapable subject around town where the intricacies of Spanish grammar are one of the main topics of conversation. Most schools offer a weekly deal that includes up to seven hours tuition a day and full board with a local family, with prices ranging from $50 to $100 a week. It's very hard to recommend anywhere in particular as the success of the whole exercise is totally dependent on hitting it off with your teacher. (Some programmes offer a change of teacher at the end of each week.) You can get hold of a complete list from the tourist office, but some of the most respected schools are: the *Tecún Umán Linguistic School*, 6 Calle Poniente 34, the *Projecto Linguístico Francisco Marroquín*, 4 Avenida Sur 4, the *Centro Linguístico Maya*, 5 Calle Poniente 20, and the *Professional Spanish Language School*, 7 Avenida Norte 82.

The best English-language **bookshop** is undeniably the *Casa Andinista*, at 4 Calle Oriente 5A, which also sells **maps** of Guatemala, including photocopies of detailed government maps (many of which are officially unavailable). *Un Poco de Todo*, in the plaza, also stocks some titles, as does the *Librería Pensativo*, on 5 Avenida Norte just beyond the arch. The best guidebook to the city, called simply *Antigua Guatemala* and written by Trevor Long and Elizabeth Bell, is available in all the bookshops, and human guides are also fairly ubiquitous. (If you're looking for a guide it's best to hire one through the tourist office to avoid cheap imitations of the real thing.) There's an exceptionally good **library** at *CIRMA* (*Centro de Investigaciones Regionales de Mesoamerica*), a research centre with facilities for students of Central America, that also publishes their work. The library and reading room are to one side of a gorgeously peaceful courtyard at 5 Calle Oriente 5.

In the Parque Central are branches of *Lloyds* **bank**, the *Banco de Guatemala*, the *Banco del Agro* and the *Banco Industrial*, all of which will change travellers' cheques and are open from 9am to 3pm, Monday to Friday. The *Banco del Agro* also has a branch beside the post office, which is open until 6pm and on Saturday mornings. The **post office** is on Alameda de Santa Lucía opposite the bus terminal. (If you're sending a parcel home be warned that the *Pink Box* agency has an unfortunate reputation for losing things, so either send them yourself or use *Get Guated Out* in Panajachel.) For long-distance **phone calls** *Guatel* is at the corner of 5 Avenida Sur and 5 Calle Poniente. To get your **laundry** done try the *Summer Laundry* at 5 Avenida Sur 24, or the *Lavarapido* at 5 Calle Poniente 7a. If you need to see a **doctor**, Miguel Angel Soto speaks some English and has his surgery at 4 Avenida del Sur 6: there's an English-speaking **dentist**, Julio Paredes, at 4 Calle Oriente 9.

Several alternatives to bus travel are on offer in Antigua; *Avis* **car hire** have an office half a block from the plaza on 5 Avenida Sur, with vehicles from around $80 a day. If this puts it out of your price range then **motorbikes** and **bicycles** can be hired from 2 Calle Oriente, or *Chinto's* mountain bike hire at 5 Avenida Sur 7, who rent out their bikes by the day, week or month. For long-distance travel there's a **travel agent** upstairs in *Un Poco de Todo*, in the plaza. If you're setting out on foot and feel the need of a **guide** they can be arranged through the tourist office or from *Club Chicag* at 6 Avenida del Norte 34. **Camping equipment** can be hired here or at the *Casa Andinista*, 4 Calle Oriente 5A.

There are **noticeboards** advertising everything from private language tuition to apartments, but especially flights home or shared rides for onward journeys, in various popular tourist venues. Probably the most read are at *Doña Luisa's* and the *Casa Andinista*.

Around Antigua: villages and volcanoes

The countryside surrounding Antigua is superbly fertile and breathtakingly beautiful, and the valley is dotted with small villages, ranging from the *Ladino* coffee centre of Alotenango to the traditional Indian village of Santa María de Jesús. None are more than an hour or two away and they all make interesting day trips. For the more adventurous, the volcanic peaks of Agua, Acatenango and Fuego offer strenuous but superb hiking.

The first of the villages, **SAN FELIPE DE JESÚS**, is so close that you can walk there, just a kilometre or so north of Antigua following 6 Avenida Norte (or catch one of the minibuses from the bus terminal). San Felipe has a small Gothic-style church housing a famous image of Christ: severely damaged in the 1976 earthquake, the church has been well restored since, and there's a fiesta here on August 30 to celebrate the anniversary of the arrival of the image in 1670. The village's other attraction is the **silver workshop**, where silver, mined in the highlands of Alta Verapaz, is worked and sold. To find the workshop follow the sign to the *Platería Típica La Antigueña*.

Ciudad Vieja and Alotenango

To the south of Antigua the Panchoy valley is a broad sweep of farmland, over-shadowed by three volcanic cones and covered with olive-green coffee bushes. A single road runs out this way, eventually reaching Escuintla and the Pacific coast, and passing a string of villages along the way.

The first of these, 5km from Antigua, is **CIUDAD VIEJA**, a scruffy and unhurried village with a distinguished past. It was near here that the Spanish established their second capital, Santiago de los Caballeros, in 1527. Today there's no trace of the original city, and all that remains is a solitary tree, in a corner of the plaza, which bears a plaque commemorating the site of the first mass ever held in Guatemala. The plaza also boasts a colonial church, built in the eighteenth century, which has recently been restored.

The history of the site, however, is so extraordinary that it deserves to be told in full. The Spanish first settled near the Cakchiquel capital of Iximché. Within a year, however, the Cakchiqueles had turned against them, and the Spanish decided to base themselves elsewhere, moving their capital to the valley of

Almolonga, 35km to the east between the Acatenango and Agua volcanoes. Here, on Saint Celia's Day 1527, in a landscape considered perfect for pasture, and with plentiful supplies of building materials, the first official capital, **Santiago de los Caballeros**, was founded.

The new city was built in a mood of tremendous confidence, with building plots distributed according to rank, and Alvarado's Mexican allies given the suburban sites. Within twenty years things had really started to take shape, with a school, a cathedral, monasteries, and farms stocked with imported cattle. But while the bulk of the Spaniards were still settling in, their leader, the rapacious **Alvarado**, was off in search of action. His lust for wealth and conquest sent him to Peru, Spain and Mexico, and in 1541 he set out for the Spice Islands, travelling via Jalisco, where he met his end, crushed to death beneath a rolling horse. When news of his death reached his wife, Doña Beatriz, at home in Santiago, she plunged the capital into an extended period of mourning, staining the entire palace with black clay, inside and out. She went on to command the officials to appoint her as her husband's replacement, and on the morning of September 9, 1541, she became the first governess in the Americas. On the official declaration she signed herself as *La sin ventura Doña Beatriz*, and then deleted her name to leave only *"La sin ventura"* (the unlucky one) – a fateful premonition.

From the announcement of Alvarado's death the city had been swept by storms, and before the night of his wife's inauguration was out an earthquake added to the force of the downpour. A tremor shook the surrounding volcanoes and from the crater of the Volcán de Agua a great wave of mud and water slid down, accelerating as it surged towards the valley floor, and sweeping away the capital. Today the exact site of the original city is still open to debate, but the general consensus puts it about 2km to the east of Ciudad Vieja, although one of the Indian suburbs would probably have reached out as far as the modern village.

Further down the valley, the ragged-looking village of **ALOTENANGO** is dwarfed by the steaming, scarred cone of the Volcán de Fuego, which has been in a state of constant eruption since the arrival of the Spanish. A path leads from the village up the volcano, but it's extremely hard to find and follow, so unless you're with a guide it's a lot easier to climb from La Soledad on the side of Acatenango (see p.80).

Beyond Alotenango a rough dirt road continues down the valley to **Escuintla**, passing through the village of **El Rodeo**. One, and sometimes two, buses a day connect Antigua and Escuintla, leaving Antigua at around 12.30pm and leaving Escuintla at 7am. To get to Ciudad Vieja or Alotenango there's a steady stream of **buses** leaving from outside the terminal in Antigua (opposite the post office): the last returns from Alotenango at around 7pm.

San Antonio Aguas Calientes

Out to the west of Antigua is the village of **SAN ANTONIO AGUAS CALIENTES**, set to one side of a steep-sided bowl beneath the peak of Acatenango. San Antonio is famous for its weaving, and stalls in the plaza sell a complete range of the output. This is also a good place to learn traditional back-strap weaving, and the best way to find out about possible tuition is by simply asking the women in the plaza.

Adjoining San Antonio is the village of **SANTA CATARINA**, which has a superb ruined colonial church. Out on the edge of the village there's also a small swimming pool which is open to the public – daily except Monday, 9am to 6pm – a superb place for a chilly dip. To get to the pool, walk along the main street in San Antonio until you come to the plaza in Santa Catarina and continue up the street that goes up the far side of the church. Turn left at the end and you'll reach the pool (on the right) in five minutes or so.

Minibuses from the terminal in Antigua run a regular service to San Antonio and Santa Catarina.

San Miguel Dueñas and La Soledad: climbing the volcanoes

To the south of Antigua, branching off the road to Ciudad Vieja, a dusty dirt track runs to **SAN MIGUEL DUEÑAS**, a dried-out, scrappy-looking sort of place where the roads are lined with bamboo fences and surrounded by coffee *fincas*. There's little to delay you in San Miguel itself, but you may well pass through here on your way to La Soledad, from where you can climb the Acatenango and Fuego volcanoes. **Buses** head out to San Miguel every half-hour or so from the terminal in Antigua, but beyond the village traffic is scarce at the best of times. If you're making for the volcanoes then you'll have to either take a taxi from Antigua to La Soledad, or walk for a couple of hours up the road from San Miguel Dueñas.

Acatenango
The trail for **Acatenango** actually starts in **LA SOLEDAD**, an impoverished village which is perched on an exposed ridge high above the valley. Walking up the road from San Miguel Dueñas you come upon a cluster of bamboo huts, with a football field to the right. Here you'll find a small *tienda* and the last tap – so fill up on water. A short way beyond the *tienda* a track leads up to the left, heading above the village and towards the wooded lower slopes of Acatenango. It crosses another largish trail and then starts to wind up into the pine trees. Just after you enter the trees you have to turn onto a smaller path that goes away to the right, and a hundred metres or so further on take another small path that climbs to the left. This brings you onto a low ridge, where you meet a thin trail that leads to the left, away up the volcano – this path eventually finds its way to the top, somewhere between six and nine hours away. At times it's a little vague, but most of the way it's fairly easy to follow.

There are only two other important spots on the ascent, the **campsites**, which are also the easiest places to lose the trail. The first, a beautiful grassy clearing, is about one and a half hours up – the path cuts straight across so don't be tempted by the larger track that heads off to the right. Another hour and a half above this is the second campsite, a little patch of level ground in amongst the pine trees, which is about halfway to the top.

The trail itself is an exhausting climb, a thin line of slippery volcanic ash that rises with unrelenting steepness through the thick forest. Only for the last fifty metres or so does it emerge above the tree line, before reaching the top of the lower cone. Here there's a radio mast and a small yellow shelter, put up by the *Guatemalan Mountaineering Club*, where you can shelter for the freezing nights – though at weekends there's the possibility that it will be full. To the south, another hour of gruelling and gasping ascent, is the main cone, a great grey bowl that rises to a height of 3975 metres. From here there's a magnificent view stretching out across the valley below. On the opposite side is the Volcán de Agua, and to the right the fire-scarred cone of Fuego. Looking west you can see the three cones that surround Lake Atitlán, and beyond that the Volcán de Santa María, high above Quezaltenango.

When it comes to getting down again, the direct route towards Alotenango may look invitingly simple but is in fact very hard to follow. It's easiest to go back the same way that you came up.

Fuego

In the unlikely event that you have any remaining energy you can continue south and climb the neighbouring cone of **Fuego** (3763m). From the top of Acatenango it looks comfortingly close, but the dip between the two peaks takes a good few hours to cross, and you should be wary of getting too close to Fuego's cone as it oozes overpowering sulphur fumes, and occasionally spits out molten rock. Descending from Fuego is fairly problematic as the trail that leads down to Alotenango is very hard to find. The bottom of the gully, which looks tempting, is impassable – the actual trail is on the Fuego side of this dip. The only way to be really sure of a trouble-free descent is to go back over Acatenango, and down the way you came up.

Fuego can also be climbed by a direct ascent from the village of Alotenango, but the climb is very hard going and the trail difficult to follow. Hire a guide if you plan to take this route.

East: San Juan del Obispo, Santa María de Jesús and the Volcán de Agua

East of Antigua the dirt road to Santa María de Jesús runs out along a narrow valley, sharing the shade with acres of coffee bushes. Before it starts to climb the road passes the village of **SAN JUAN DEL OBISPO**, invisible from the road, but marked by what must rank as the country's finest bus shelter, beautifully carved in local stone. The village is unremarkable, although it does offer a good view of the valley below. What makes it worth a visit is the **Palacio de Francisco Marroquín**, who was the first Bishop of Guatemala. The place is currently home to about 25 nuns, and if you knock on the great wooden double doors one of them will come and show you around.

Marroquín arrived in Guatemala with Alvarado and is credited with having introduced Christianity to the Indians, as well as reminding the Spaniards about it from time to time. On the death of Alvarado's wife he assumed temporary responsibility for the government, and was instrumental in the construction of Antigua. He spent his last days in the vast palace that he'd built for himself here in San Juan, and died in 1563. The palace, like everything else, has been badly damaged over the years, and serious reconstruction only began in 1962. The interior, arranged around two small courtyards, is spectacularly beautiful, and several rooms still contain their original furniture. Attached to the palace is a fantastic church and chapel with ornate wood carvings, plaster mouldings, and austere religious paintings.

To get to San Juan take any of the buses going to Santa María de Jesús from the terminal in Antigua, and ask them to drop you.

Santa María de Jesús

Up above San Juan the road arrives in **SANTA MARÍA DE JESÚS**, starting point of the ascent of the Volcán de Agua. Perched high on the shoulder of the volcano, the village is some 500 metres above Antigua, with magnificent views over the Panchoy valley and east towards the smoking cone of Pacaya. It was founded at the end of the sixteenth century for Indians transported from Quezaltenango: they were given the task of providing firewood for Antigua, and the village earned the name of *Aserradero*, lumber yard. Since then it has developed into a farming community where the women wear beautiful purple *huipiles*, although the men have recently abandoned traditional costume. The only place to stay is the *Hospedaje Oasis* (just off the plaza on the road into town), a clean and friendly institution that also serves meals, of beans, eggs and tortillas, that are as simple as its rooms.

Buses run from Antigua to Santa María every hour or so from 6am to 5pm, and the trip takes forty minutes. Beyond Santa María, the road continues down the east side of the volcano to the village of Palín, on the Guatemala City–Escuintla highway. There are no buses that cover this route, but there's a chance that you might be able to hitch a lift on a truck.

The Volcán de Agua

The **Volcán de Agua** is the easiest and by far the most popular of Guatemala's big cones to climb: on Saturday nights there are sometimes hundreds spending the night at the top. Even so it's an exciting ascent with a fantastic view to reward you at the top. The trail starts in the village of **Santa María de Jesús**, and to reach it you head straight across the plaza, between the two ageing pillars, and up the street opposite the church doors. Take a right turn just before the end, and then continue past the cemetery and out of the village. From here on it's a fairly simple climb on a clear path, cutting across the road that goes some of the way up. The climb can take anything from four to six hours, and the peak, at 3766 metres, is always cold at night: there is a shelter (though not always room) and the views certainly make it all worth the struggle.

Antigua to Chimaltenango

To the northwest, a second road connects Antigua with the Pan-American highway, this time intersecting it at **Chimaltenango**. On its way out of town the road passes through the suburb of **JOCOTENANGO**, where many of the locally produced coffee beans are processed. There's a magnificent, crumbling church on the plaza. In colonial times Jocotenango was the gateway to the city, where official visitors would be met to be escorted into Antigua.

Another 4km brings you to **SAN LORENZO EL TEJAR**, which has some superb hot springs. To reach the springs turn right in the village of SAN LUIS CARRETAS, and then right again when the road forks: they're at the end of a narrow valley, a couple of kilometres from the main road. If you want to bathe in the steamy and sulphurous waters you can either use the cheaper communal pool or hire one of your own – a little private room with a huge tiled tub set in the floor. The baths are open daily from 6am to 5pm, but closed for cleaning on Tuesday and Friday afternoons.

From San Luis the main road climbs out of the Antigua valley through PASTORES and PARRAMOS, a couple of dusty farming villages, after which a dirt track branches to **SAN ANDRÉS IZTAPA**, one of the many villages badly hit by the 1976 earthquake. San Andrés shares with Zunil and Santiago Atitlán the honour of revering San Simón or Maximón, the wicked saint, who is usually housed here in a chapel of his own (ask around for the *casa de San Simón*). The weaving of the women's *huipiles* is particularly intricate and the patterns are both delicate and bold, similar in many ways to those around Chimaltenango. The local Tuesday market is also worth a visit.

Tragically San Andrés hit the headlines at the end of 1988, when it was the scene of the largest massacre since the present government came into office. On a hillside above the nearby hamlet of El Aguacate, 22 corpses were found in a shallow grave. Blame was passed back and forth between the army and the guerrillas, but nothing has been proved by either party.

After the turning for San Andrés the main road drops through pine trees into the bottom of a dip and to the **LAGUNA DE LOS CISNES**, a small boating lake surrounded by cheap *comedores* and swimming pools. The lake is very popular with the people of Antigua and Chimaltenango, who flood out here for weekends and public holidays – something of a local version of Lake Amatitlán. Above the lake is the local army base, and beyond that is the Pan-American highway and **Chimaltenango**, 19km and 45 minutes from Antigua. **Buses** run hourly between Antigua and Chimaltenango from around 5.30am, with the last one leaving Antigua at 5.30pm, and Chimaltenango at 6.30pm. Buses for San Andrés Iztapa also leave hourly, between 6am and 4pm, from the market in Chimaltenango.

The Pan-American Highway

Leaving Guatemala City to the west, the **Pan-American Highway** cuts right through the central highlands as far as the border with Mexico. In its entirety this road stretches from Alaska to Chile (with a short break in southern Panama), and here in Guatemala it forms the backbone of transport in the highlands. As you travel around, the highway and its junctions will inevitably become all too familiar, since wherever you're going it's invariably easiest to catch a local bus to the Pan-American and then flag down one of the buses heading along the highway.

There are four major junctions which you'll soon get to know well. **Chimaltenango** is the first major town on the highway and it's here that you make connections to or from Antigua. Heading west, **Los Encuentros** is the next main junction, where one road heads off to the north for Chichicastenango and Santa Cruz del Quiché, while another branches south to Panajachel and Lake Atitlán. Beyond this the highway climbs high over a mountainous ridge before dropping to **Cuatro Caminos** (p.126), from where side roads lead to Quezaltenango and Totonicapán. The Pan-American itself continues to Huehuetenango before it reaches the Mexican border.

Between Guatemala City and Chimaltenango

Heading west from Guatemala City along the Pan-American highway to Chimaltenango, you travel through one of the central highland valleys, where a number of large villages devote themselves to market gardening. The villages themselves are particularly scruffy, but their fields are meticulously neat, churning out vegetables for both the domestic and export markets.

Leaving Guatemala City the first "village" that you pass is **MIXCO**, now absorbed into the capital's suburban sprawl. Founded in 1525 to house Pokoman refugees from Mixco Viejo, Mixco still has a large Indian population today. Next along the way is **SAN LUCAS SACATEPÉQUEZ**, just before the turning for Antigua. This village dates back to before the conquest but these days it bears the scars of the 1976 earthquake, with cheap *comedores* and family restaurants lining the highway. Beyond this is **SANTIAGO SACATEPÉQUEZ**, whose centre lies a kilometre or so to the north of the highway. The road to Santiago actually branches off the highway at San Lucas Sacatepéquez, but it's easier to walk to the village from a point overlooking it, a couple of kilometres further on. The best time to visit is on November 1, when massive paper kites are flown in the cemetery as part of a local fiesta to honour the Day of the Dead. Finally the Pan-American highway goes on past SUMPANGO, and through EL TEJAR, which is famous for its bricks, before reaching Chimaltenango.

Chimaltenango

CHIMALTENANGO was founded by Pedro de Portocarrero in 1526, on the site of the Cakchiquel centre of Bokoh, and was later considered as a possible site for the new capital. It has the misfortune, however, of being positioned on a continental divide: in 1976 it suffered terribly at the hands of the earthquake that shook and flattened much of the surrounding area. Today's town, its centre just to the north of the main road, is dominated by that fact, and like so much of the area its appearance testifies to rapid and unfinished reconstruction, with dirt streets, breeze block walls and an air of weary desperation. But it remains busy, a regional centre of transport and trade whose prosperity is boosted by the proximity of the capital.

The town's plaza is an odd mix of architectural styles, with a police station that looks like a medieval castle, a church that combines the Gothic and the Neoclassical, and a superb colonial fountain – the waters of which drain half to the Pacific and half to the Caribbean. The **post office**, *Banco de Guatemala* and *Guatel* are all on the plaza, and if you want to stay here the *Hotel La Predilecta*, one block to the south, is good value at $2.

Chimaltenango's second focal point is the Pan-American highway, which cuts through the southern side of the town, dominating it with an endless flow of trucks and buses. The town extracts what little business it can from this stream of traffic, and the roadside is crowded with cheap *comedores*, mechanics' workshops, and sleazy bars that become brothels by night.

Buses passing through Chimaltenango run to all points along the Pan-American highway: for Antigua they leave hourly from 5.30am to 6.30pm from the market in town – though you can also wait at the turn-off on the highway. To get to Chimaltenango from Guatemala City take any bus heading to the western highlands from the Zona 4 bus terminal.

San Martín Jilotepeque

To the north of Chimaltenango a rough dirt road runs through nineteen kilometres of plunging ravines and pine forests to the village of **SAN MARTÍN JILOTEPEQUE**. The village itself is still badly scarred by the events of 1976, but the sprawling Sunday market is well worth a visit and the weaving here, the women's *huipiles* especially, is some of the finest you'll see – with intricate and ornate patterning, predominantly in reds and purples.

Buses to San Martín leave the market in Chimaltenango every hour or so from 4am to 2pm, with the last one returning at about 3pm. The trip takes around an hour. To the north of San Martín the road continues **Joyabaj** (p.95). One bus a day covers this route, leaving the capital in the morning and passing through San Martín around 12.30pm: the return leaves Joyabaj early the following morning.

San Juan Comalapa, Patzicía and Patzún

Heading west from Chimaltenango, the Pan-American highway runs past a series of turns to interesting but seldom-visited villages. The first of these, 16km to the north of the main road, on the far side of a deep-cut ravine, is **SAN JUAN COMALAPA**. The village was founded by the Spanish, who brought together the population of several Cakchiquel centres here: a collection of eroded pre-Columbian sculptures are displayed in the plaza. There's also a small monument to Rafael Alvarez Ovalle, a local man, who composed the Guatemalan national anthem. Like so many of the villages in this area, Comalapa's appearance is still dominated by the impact of the 1976 earthquake, and the plaza is overshadowed by the crumbling facade of the ruined church.

In the last few decades the villagers of Comalapa have developed something of a reputation as "primitive" artists, and there are several galleries in the streets around the plaza where their work is exhibited and sold. The whole thing started in 1930, when Andrés Curuchich was the first of the Comalapans to take to painting, depicting village scenes with a simplicity that soon attracted the attention of outsiders. Throughout the Fifties he became increasingly popular, exhibiting in Guatemala City, and later as far afield as Los Angeles and New York. Today, inspired by his example and the chance of boosting their income, there are forty to fifty painters working here, including two or three women – although it's considerably harder for the women as painting is generally perceived as a man's task.

The Maya Goddess Ixchel (goddess of weaving)

Comalapan weaving is also of the highest standards, using styles and colours that are characteristic of the Chimaltenango area. Traditionally the weavers work in silk and a natural brown cotton called *cuyuxcate*, although these days they increasingly use ordinary cotton and synthetic fabrics.

As ever the best time to visit is for the **market**, on Tuesday, which brings the people out in force. **Buses** to Comalapa run hourly from Chimaltenango (1hr) and the service is always better on a market day. There's nowhere to stay in the village and the last bus back leaves at 3 or 4pm.

Patzicía and Patzún: a route to the lake

Further to the west another branch road runs down towards Lake Atitlán, connecting the Pan-American highway with several small villages. At the junction with the main road is **PATZICÍA**, a ramshackle sprawl still reeling from the impact of the 1976 earthquake. Despite its bedraggled appearance the village has a history of independent defiance, and in 1944 it was the scene of an Indian uprising that left some 300 dead. Villagers were led to believe that Indians throughout Guatemala had risen up against their *Ladino* rulers, and charged through the village putting to death any they could set hands on. Armed *Ladinos*, arriving from the capital, managed to put down the uprising, killing the majority of the rebels. Ironically enough, over a hundred years earlier, in 1871, the Declaration of Patzicía was signed here, setting out the objectives of the liberal revolution.

PATZÚN, 11km from the main highway heading towards Lake Atitlán, also suffered terrible losses in 1976. A monument in the plaza remembers the 172 who died, and a new church stands beside the shell of the old one, which somehow seems an even more poignant memorial. Traditional costume is still worn here and the colourful Sunday market is well worth a visit. Outside the twin churches the plaza fills with traders, with the majority of the women dressed in the brilliant reds of local costume.

Beyond Patzún it's possible to continue all the way to the small village of **Godínez**, high above the northern shore of Lake Atitlán, and from there by road to Panajachel and San Lucas Tolimán. A couple of buses a day do this trip but the road is fairly rough and often closed by landslides. **Buses** to Patzún leave the Zona 4 terminal in Guatemala City every hour or so, and you can pick them up in Chimaltenango or at the turning for Patzicía.

Back at Patzicía there's a second branch road that leaves the Pan-American highway to head south, past huge coffee plantations, to the villages of **ACATENANGO** and **YEPOCAPA**. It's a fairly obscure part of the country and there's no very good reason to travel this way, although there are several daily buses that go as far as Acatenango, and one that goes all the way through to the Pacific coast, heading back to the capital via Escuintla. Buses or trucks going to Yepocapa also pass through La Soledad, on the lower slopes of the Acatenango volcano, which is the starting point for a climb to the cone (see p.80). The bus that covers the round trip, Guatemala City–Chimaltenango–Acatenango–Yepocapa– Escuintla, leaves the capital daily at 5am, passing through Chimaltenango at 6am and Patzicía at around 7.30am.

Tecpán and the ruins of Iximché

An hour and a half or so from the capital, the town of **TECPÁN** lies a few hundred metres to the south of the Pan-American highway. This may well have been the site chosen by Alvarado in 1524 as the first Spanish capital to which the Spanish forces retreated in August 1524, after they'd been driven out of Iximché. Today it's a place of no great interest, and you're unlikely to do more than pass through on your way to the ruins. Tecpán again suffered severely in the 1976 earthquake and in the centre a new church stands alongside the cracked remains of the old one.

The ruins of **IXIMCHÉ**, the pre-conquest capital of the Cakchiqueles, are about five kilometres to the south. The site is positioned on an exposed hillside, protected on three sides by steep slopes, and surrounded by pine forests. From the early days of the conquest the Cakchiqueles allied themselves with the *conquistadores*, so the structures here suffered less than most at the hands of the Spanish. Since then, however, time and weather have taken their toll and the majority of the buildings, originally built of adobe, have disappeared, leaving only a few stone-built pyramids and the clearly defined plazas. Nevertheless the site is strongly atmospheric, and its grassy plazas, ringed with pine trees, are marvellously peaceful. At weekends this is a favourite local picnic spot.

The Cakchiqueles were originally based further west, around the modern town of Chichicastenango, and the language of Cakchiquel is still spoken throughout the central highlands and along the eastern side of Lake Atitlán. But when their villages came under the control of the Quichés, the Cakchiqueles were the first to break away, moving their capital to Iximché in order to establish their independence. They founded the new city in about 1470 and from then on they were almost continuously at war with other tribes. Despite this, they managed to devote a lot of their energy to building and rebuilding their new capital, and trenches dug into some of the structures have revealed as many as three superimposed layers. In fact war may have helped in this, as most of the work was done by slave labourers captured in battle. When the Spanish arrived, the Cakchiqueles were quick to join forces with Alvarado in order to defeat their old enemies the Quiché. Grateful for their assistance, the Spanish established their first headquarters near here on May 7, 1524. The Cakchiqueles referred to Alvarado as *Tonatiuh*, the son of the sun, and as a mark of respect he was given the daughter of a Cakchiquel king as a gift.

On July 25 the Spanish renamed the settlement **Villa de Santiago**, declaring it their new capital. But before long the Cakchiqueles rose in rebellion, outraged by demands for tribute. They abandoned their capital and fled into the mountains, from where they waged a guerrilla war against the Spanish until 1530, when the Spanish moved their capital to the greater safety of Ciudad Vieja, a short distance from Antigua.

The ruins of Iximché are made up of four main plazas, a couple of ball courts, and several pyramids. In most cases only the foundations and lower parts of the original structures were built of stone, while the upper walls were of adobe, with thatched roofs supported by wooden beams. You can make out the ground plan of many of the buildings, but it's only the most important all-stone structures that still stand. The most significant buildings were those clustered around courts A and C, which were probably the scene of the most revered rituals. On the sides of **Temple 2** you can make out some badly eroded murals, the style of which is very similar to that used in the codices.

It's thought that the site itself, like most of the highland centres, was a ceremonial city used for religious rituals and inhabited only by the elite. The rest of the population would have lived in the surrounding hills, and come to Iximché only to attend festivals and defend the fortified site in times of attack. Archaeological digs here have unearthed a number of interesting finds, including the decapitated heads of sacrifice victims, grinding stones, burial sites, obsidian knives, a flute made from a child's femur, and large numbers of incense burners. There was surprisingly little sculpture, but most of it was similar to that found in the ruins of Zaculeu and Mixco Viejo, both of which were occupied at around the same time.

The ruins are open daily from 9am to 4pm, and **to get there** you can take any bus travelling along the Pan-American highway between Chimaltenango and Los Encuentros: ask to be dropped at Tecpán, from where you can walk. From Guatemala City any of the buses going to Sololá or Quiché will do: they leave the Zona 4 terminal hourly, passing through Chimaltenango. If you're coming from Los Encuentros take any bus heading for Guatemala City.

To get to the ruins simply walk through Tecpán and out the other side of the plaza, passing the *Centro de Salud*, and follow the road through the fields for about five kilometres, an hour or so on foot. With any luck you'll be able to hitch some of the way, particularly at weekends when the road can be fairly busy.

There's nowhere to stay at the site and nothing to eat, so take a picnic; and be back at the Pan-American highway before 6pm to be sure of a bus out.

EL QUICHÉ

At the heart of the western highlands, sandwiched between the Verapaces and Huehuetenango, is the **Department of El Quiché**. Like its neighbours El Quiché includes the full range of Guatemalan scenery. In the south, only a short distance from Lake Atitlán, is a section of the sweeping central valley, a fertile and heavily populated area that forms the upper reaches of the Motagua valley. To the north the landscape becomes increasingly dramatic, rising first to the **Sierra de Chuacús**, and then to the massive peaks of the **Cuchumatanes**, beyond which the land drops away into the inaccessible rainforests of the **Ixcán**.

The department takes its name from the greatest of the pre-conquest tribal groups, the **Quichés**, for whom it was the hub of an empire. From their capital **Utatlán**, which stood to the west of the modern town of Santa Cruz del Quiché, they overran much of the highlands and were able to demand tribute from most of the other tribes. By the time the Spanish arrived their empire was in decline, but they were still the dominant force in the region and challenged the *conquistadores* as soon as they entered the highlands, at a site near Quezaltenango. They were, however, easily defeated, and the Spanish were able to negotiate alliances with their former subjects, playing one tribe off against another, and eventually overcoming them all. Today these highlands remain a stronghold of Indian culture and the department of Quiché, scattered with small villages, is the scene of some superb fiestas and markets.

For the Spanish, though, it remained an unimportant backwater, with little to offer in the way of plunder: only in later years, when large-scale commercial farming began on the Pacific coast, did it grow in importance as a source of cheap labour. This role has had a profound impact here for the last two hundred years, and forced the population to suffer horrific abuses. Perhaps not surprisingly it became a centre of guerrilla activity in the late 1970s, and subsequently the scene of unrivalled repression.

For the traveller El Quiché has a lot to offer, both in the accessible south and the wilder north. **Chichicastenango**, one of the country's most popular destinations, is the scene of a vast twice-weekly market and remains a relatively undisrupted centre of Indian religion. Beyond this, at the heart of the central valley, is the departmental capital of **Santa Cruz del Quiché**, stopping-off point for trips to a string of smaller towns and to the ruins of **Utatlán**. Continuing to the north the paved road ends and the mountains begin, and although travelling here can be hard work the extraordinary scale of the scenery makes it all well worthwhile. Here the isolated villages, set in superb mountain scenery and sustaining a wealth of Indian culture, seem to occupy a world of their own. Passing over the **Sierra de Chuacús**, and down to the **Río Chixoy**, you reach **Sacapulas** at the base of the **Cuchumatanes**. From here you can travel across the foothills to **Cobán** or **Huehuetenango**, or up into the mountains to the three towns of the **Ixil triangle** – **Nebaj**, **Chajul** and **Cotzal**.

The road for Chichicastenango and the department of El Quiché leaves the Pan-American highway at the **Los Encuentros** junction. From here it drops off the southern volcanic ridge and runs into the broad central valley, a great stretch of land suspended between the volcanoes and the mountains. From a distance this open expanse looks like a bed of pine trees, but as you head north the truth is revealed as the bus plunges into deep ravines and struggles out around endless switchbacks.

Chichicastenango

Seventeen kilometres from Los Encuentros is **CHICHICASTENANGO**, Guatemala's *"Mecca del Turismo"*. It's a compact and traditional town of cobbled streets, adobe houses and red-tiled roofs, where the calm of day-to-day life is shattered on a twice-weekly basis by the **Sunday and Thursday market**. The town is conveniently placed, a short hop from the Pan-American highway, and the market attracts tourists and commercial traders on day trips out of Antigua, Panajachel and Guatemala City, as well as Indian weavers from throughout the central highlands. The streets are packed with buyers and lined with stalls, and the choice is overwhelming, ranging from superb quality Nebaj *huipiles* to wooden dance masks, and including pottery, gourds, machetes, belts and a gaudy selection of recently invented "traditional" fabrics. You can still pick up some authentic and beautiful weaving, but you need to be prepared to wade through a lot of trash and to bargain hard – easier said than done, but your chances are better before 10am when the tourist buses arrive from the capital, or in the late afternoon once things have started to quieten down. Even at the best of times prices here are by no means the lowest in the country, and for a real bargain you need to head further into the highlands: while for western-style clothes the markets in Panajachel and Guatemala City are also worth a look.

The market has existed here for hundreds, if not thousands, of years, and local people continue to trade their wares, despite the weekly invasions. Their market is held in the centre of the plaza. This is not only much more interesting than the bulk of the market (at least if you haven't come to buy) but also a great place for lunch in one of the makeshift *comedores*, where you'll find cauldrons of stew, rice and beans.

Indian traditions

The market is by no means all that sets Chichicastenango apart, and for the local Indian population it's an important centre of culture and religion. Long before the arrival of the Spanish this area was inhabited by the Cakchiqueles, whose settlements of Patzak and Chavier were threatened by the all-powerful Quichés. In a bid to assert their independence the Cakchiqueles abandoned these villages and moved south to Iximché in 1470 and from there mounted repeated campaigns against their former masters. Chichicastenango itself was founded by the Spanish in order to house the Quiché refugees from Utatlán, which they conquered and destroyed in 1524. The town's name is a Nahuatl word meaning "the place of the nettles", given to the place by Alvarado's Mexican allies.

Over the years Indian culture and folk Catholicism have been treated with a rare degree of respect in Chichicastenango, although inevitably this blessing has been mixed with waves of arbitrary persecution and exploitation. Today the town has an incredible collection of Maya artefacts, parallel Indian and *Ladino* governments, and a church that makes no effort to disguise its acceptance of unconventional

Indian worship. Traditional weaving is also adhered to in Chichicastenango and the women wear superb heavily embroidered *huipiles*. The men wear short trousers and jackets made of black wool embroidered with silk. Their costume looks highly distinguished although sadly it's very expensive to make, and these days most men opt for western dress. However for fiestas and market days a handful of *cofradías* (elders of the religious hierarchy) still dress traditionally.

The main **Santo Tomás Church**, in the southeast corner of the plaza, was built in 1540 on the site of a Maya altar, and rebuilt in the eighteenth century. Here the Indians have been left to adopt their own style of worship. It's said that local Indians became interested in the church after Francisco Ximenez (a priest here from 1701 to 1703) started reading the Popul Vuh, their own holy book. Seeing that he had considerable respect for their religion they moved their altars from the hills and set them up inside the church.

Before entering the building it's customary to make offerings in a fire at the base of the steps or burn incense in perforated cans, a practice that leaves a cloud of thin, sweet smoke hanging over the entrance. Inside is an astonishing scene of avid worship. A soft hum of constant murmuring fills the air, as Indians kneel to offer candles to their ancestors and the saints. For these people the entire building is alive with the souls of the dead, each located in a specific part of the

CHICHICASTENANGO

To Santa Cruz del Quiché (19 km)

Cemetery

El Calvario

PLAZA

Santo Tomas

Pascual Abaj

0   200 m

To Los Encuentros & Guatemala City

church. The place of the "first people", the ancient ancestors, is beneath the altar railing; former officials are around the middle of the aisle; common people to the west in the nave; and deceased native priests beside the door. Alongside these, and equally important, are the Catholic saints, which receive the same respect and are continuously appealed to with offerings of candles and alcohol. Last, but by no means least, specific areas within the church, and particular patterns of candles, rose petals and *chicha*, are used to invoke certain types of blessings such as those for children, travel, marriage, harvest or illness. It's polite to enter the church by the side door and it's deeply offensive to take photographs inside the building – don't even contemplate it.

Beside the church is a former monastery, now used by the parish administration. Here the Spanish priest Francisco Ximenez became the first outsider to be shown the **Popol Vuh**, the holy book of the Quichés. His copy of the manuscript is now housed in the Newberry library in Chicago: the original was lost some time later in the eighteenth century. The text itself was written in Santa Cruz del Quiché shortly after the arrival of the Spanish, and is a brilliant poem of over nine thousand lines that details the cosmology, mythology and traditional history of the Quichés. Broadly speaking it's split into two parts; the first is an account of the creation of man and the world, and the second describes the wanderings of the ancestors of the Quichés, as they migrate south and settle in the highlands of Guatemala. The opening lines give an impression of the book's importance, and the extent to which it sets out to preserve a threatened cultural heritage:

> *This is the beginning of the Ancient World, here in this place called Quiché. Here we shall ascribe, we shall implant the ancient word, the potential and source of everything done in the citadel of Quiché.*
> *And here we shall take up the demonstration, revelation, and account of how things were put in shadow and brought to light . . . We shall write about this amid the preaching of God, in Christendom now. We shall bring it out because there is no longer a place to see it, a Council book.*

(As translated by Dennis Tedlock)

On the south side of the plaza is the **museum** (8am–noon and 2–5pm, closed Tuesday), housing a broad-ranging collection of pre-Columbian artefacts, mostly small pieces of ceramics that local people had kept in their homes, some as much as two thousand years old. The collection is based on that of Ildefonso Rossbach, an accountant turned priest, who served in Chichicastenango from 1894 until his death in 1944. Most of the pieces here were donated to him by local people.

Opposite Santo Tomás is **El Calvario**, a smaller chapel exclusively for the Indians. Inside there's a large image of Christ, in a glass case, that's paraded through the street during Holy Week. The steps are the scene of incense-burning rituals and the chapel is considered good for general confessions and pardons.

Chichicastenango's appetite for religious fervour is most in evidence during the **fiesta** of Santo Tomás, from 14 to 21 December, a particularly good time to visit. While it's not the most spontaneous of fiestas it's certainly one of the most spectacular, with attractions including the *Palo Volador* (in which men dangle by ropes from a sixty-foot pole), a live band or two, clouds of incense, gallons of *chicha*, a massive procession, traditional dances, and endless deafening fireworks. On the final day, all babies born in the previous year are brought to the church for christening. Easter is also celebrated here with tremendous energy and seriousness.

Beyond the plaza: the cemetery and the shrine of Pascual Abaj

The town **cemetery**, which is down the hill behind El Calvario, offers further evidence of the strange mix of religions which characterises Chichicastenango. The graves are marked by anything from a grand tomb to a small earth mound, and in the centre is an Indian shrine where the usual offerings of incense and alcohol are made. At the back, in a large yellow building, the body of Father Rossbach is entombed.

The churches and cemetery are certainly not the only scenes of Indian religious activity, and the hills that surround the town, like so many throughout the country, are topped with shrines. The closest of these, less than a kilometre from the plaza, is known as **Pascual Abaj**. The site is fairly regularly visited by tourists, but you should still keep your distance from any ceremonies and ask permission to take photographs. It's laid out in a typical pattern with several small altars facing a stern pre-Columbian sculpture. Offerings are usually overseen by a *brujo*, a type of traditional shaman, and range from flowers to sacrificed chickens, always incorporating plenty of incense, alcohol and incantations. In 1957, during a bout of religious rivalry, the shrine was raided and smashed by reforming Catholics, but the traditionalists gathered the scattered remains and patched them together with cement and a steel reinforcing rod.

To get to Pascual Abaj, walk down the hill beside the Santo Tomás church, take the first right, 9 Calle, and follow this as it winds its way out of town. You soon reach a football field where two pine-clad hills face you, and the shrine is on top of the left-hand one. If there's a ceremony in progress a thin plume of smoke will pick it out. A path goes up the right-hand side of the hill.

Practical details

Hotels are in fairly short supply in Chichicastenango, and if you can't find a room you might find it easier to stay in Santa Cruz del Quiché, just half an hour away. In Chichicastenango itself the cheapest is the *El Salvador*, down the street beside the church, a vast and business-like place with rooms from $1 to $4, depending on the degree of luxury. The *Pension Giron*, 6 Calle 4–52, is friendlier and smaller, and charges around $2, as does the *Posada Santa Marta*, on 5 Avenida – on the left down the hill under the arch. They're all fairly basic, but the real problem is that they fill up fast.

The eating situation is no better, and the only place that I'd recommend is the **restaurant** *Tapena*, 5 Avenida 5–21, although there are also plenty of basic *comedores* in and around the market. If you're bitten by market fever and need to change some more money there's a *Banco del Ejercito* on 6 Calle, a block from the plaza, and the **post office** and *Guatel* – for phone calls – are on 6 Avenida, up behind the church.

Buses heading between Santa Cruz del Quiché and Guatemala City pass through Chichicastenango every hour or so, and you can pick them up anywhere along the way. In Guatemala City they leave from the terminal in Zona 4, hourly from 4am to about 5pm. Coming from Antigua you can pick them up in Chimaltenango, and from Panajachel you can go up to Los Encuentros. There are also several direct buses from Panajachel. When it comes to leaving

Chichicastenango catch any bus as far as Los Encuentros and make a connection there: there are plenty of direct buses to Guatemala City – the last leaves from Chichicastenango at around 7pm. If you're heading north take a bus to Santa Cruz del Quiché, from where buses go up towards the mountains.

Santa Cruz del Quiché and around

The capital of the department, **SANTA CRUZ DEL QUICHÉ**, lies half an hour to the north of Chichicastenango. A good paved road connects the two towns, running through pine forests and ravines, and past the **Laguna Lemoa**: a lake which, according to local legend, was originally filled with tears wept by the wives of Quiché kings after their husbands were slaughtered by the Spanish.

Santa Cruz del Quiché itself is a pleasant sort of place where not a lot goes on. It is, however, the hub of transport for the department and really the only practical place to base yourself while exploring it. There's a busy market here on the same days as in Chichicastenango – Thursday and Sunday – and palm weaving is a local speciality: Indians can often be seen threading a band or two as they walk through town. Many of the palm hats that are sold throughout the country were originally put together here, but if you want to buy you'll have to look hard and long to find one that fits a gringo head.

On the plaza there's a large colonial church, built by the Dominicans with stone from the ruins of Utatlán. Inside is a permanent tribute to the priests who lost their lives in the department during the violence of the late Seventies and early Eighties. Priests were singled out during those years, as they were often connected with the cooperative movement. The situation was so serious that in 1981 the Church decided to withdraw its priests from the whole department, although they've now returned to their posts.

Sleeping, eating, and getting around

There's a good range of **hotels** in Quiché, and right beside the bus terminal you'll find the cheapest ones; the *hospedajes Tropical* and *Hermano Pedro* are better than the *Centro America*, but all three are very simple and charge around $1. Further into town are a couple of more luxurious places, both very good value at $2: the *San Pascual*, 7 Calle 0–43, and the *Posada Calle Real*, 2 Avenida 7–36, which is the only one with hot showers.

Restaurants are less easy to find: the *Cafeteria Maya Quiché*, on the plaza, is fairly good though with a somewhat limited menu, or you can try the *Restaurant Lago Azul*, 2 Avenida 2–12, and the *Video Bar*, 4 Calle 2–35, a garish sort of place that does pizza and occasionally shows a film or two. The only other source of evening entertainment is the cinema at 3 Avenida and 6 Calle. If you need to change **money** there's a branch of the *Banco de Guatemala* in the corner of the plaza.

Second-class **buses** to all over the highlands run from the terminal on the edge of town: departures to Guatemala City hourly from 5am to 5pm; to Joyabaj hourly from 9am to 5pm; to Nebaj at 9am and 10am; to Uspantán at 9am, 11am and 3pm; to Quezaltenango at 8.30am, 1pm and 2pm; and to San Marcos at 5am. If you're heading for anywhere outside the department then it's generally easiest to take any bus to Los Encuentros and catch another from there.

The Ruins of Utatlán

Early in the fifteenth century, riding on a wave of successful conquest, the Quiché king Gucumatz (feathered serpent) founded a new capital, Gumarcaaj. A hundred years later the Spanish arrived, renamed the city **Utatlán**, and then destroyed it. Today the ruins still stand about 4km to the west of Santa Cruz del Quiché.

According to the Popol Vuh, Gucumatz was a lord of great genius assisted by powerful spirits.

> *"The nature of this king was truly marvellous, and all the other lords were filled with terror before him . . . And this was the beginning of the grandeur of the Quiché, when Gucumatz gave these signs of his power. His sons and his grandsons never forgot him."*

There's no doubt that this was once a great city, with several separate citadels spread across neighbouring hilltops. It housed the nine dynasties of the tribal elite, in which there were four main Quiché lords, and included a total of 23 palaces. The splendour of the city embodied the strength of the Quiché empire, which at its height encompassed a population of around a million.

By the time of the conquest, however, the Quichés had been severely weakened and their empire fractured. They first made contact with the Spanish on the Pacific coast, suffering a heavy defeat at the hands of Alvarado's forces near Quezaltenango, with the loss of their hero Tecún Umán. The Quichés then invited the Spanish to their capital, a move that made Alvarado distinctly suspicious. Seeing the fortified city he feared a trap and captured their leaders, Oxib-Queh and Beleheb-Tzy. Next he adopted a characteristically straightforward approach.

> *"As I knew them to have such a bad disposition to service of his Majesty, and to ensure the good and peace of this land, I burnt them, and sent to burn the town and destroy it."*

Since then little has been done to restore the ruins, and only a few of the main structures are still recognisable, while most lie buried beneath grassy mounds and shaded by pine trees. The site is surrounded by deep ravines, with stunning views across the valley. The central plaza, which includes all the remaining buildings, is parcelled off by three **temples**, the Great Monuments of Tohil, Auilix and Hacauaitz, all of which were simple pyramids topped by thatched shelters. In the middle of the plaza there used to be a circular **tower**, the Temple of the Sovereign Plumed Serpent, but these days you can only make out the foundations of the original structure. The only other feature that is still vaguely recognisable is the **ball court**, which lies beneath grassy banks to the south of the plaza.

Perhaps the most interesting thing about the site is that *brujos*, traditional Indian priests, still come here to perform religious rituals – practices that predate the arrival of the Spanish by thousands of years. The entire area is covered in small burnt circles – the ashes of incense – and chickens are regularly sacrificed in and around the plaza.

Beneath the plaza is a long man-made tunnel that runs underground for about 100 metres. Why it was made remains a mystery but these days it's become a favourite spot for sacrifice, the floor carpeted with chicken feathers, and candles burning in the alcoves at the end. To get to the tunnel follow the signs to *La Cueva*; it's probably best to go with one of the guards to make sure you don't disturb any secret acts.

Coming from Santa Cruz del Quiché, you can reach Utatlán by taxi or on foot. To walk, head south from the plaza along 2 Avenida, and then turn right down 10 Calle which will take you all the way out to the site – with luck you might hitch a lift some of the way. At the site there's a small museum with a scale model of the original city, and you're welcome to **camp** amongst the ruins.

East to Joyabaj

An astonishingly good paved road runs east from Santa Cruz del Quiché, beneath the impressive peaks of the Sierra de Chuacús, through a series of interesting villages set in beautiful rolling farmland. The first of the villages is **CHICHÉ**, a sister village of Chichicastenango, with which it shares costumes and traditions, although the market here is on Wednesday. Next is **CHINIQUE**, just outside which are the natural **hot springs** of the *Baños del Chorro Blanco* – a sign on the road points the way. Another 20km brings you to the larger village of **ZACUALPA**, which has markets on Thursday and Sunday in a beautiful broad plaza. The name of the village means "where they make fine walls", and in the hills to the north are the remains of a pre-conquest settlement. There's a *pension* down the street beside the church should you want to stay here.

The last place out this way is the small town of **JOYABAJ**, again with a small archaeological site to the north.

During the colonial period Joyabaj was an important staging post on the royal route to Mexico, but all that remained of its former splendour was lost in 1976 when the earthquake almost totally flattened the town, and hundreds of people lost their lives: the crumbling facade of the colonial church that still stands in front of the new prefabricated version is one of the few physical remains. In recent years the town has staged a miraculous recovery and is once again a prosperous and traditional centre: the Sunday **market**, which starts up on Saturday afternoon, is a huge affair well worth visiting, as is the fiesta in the second week of August – five days of unrelenting celebration that includes some fantastic traditional dancing and the spectacular *Palo Volador*, in which men spin to the ground from a huge wooden pole, a pre-conquest ritual that's now performed only in three places in the entire country.

There's a good unmarked *pension* ($2) on the plaza, beside the *"King Express"* sign, and plenty of *comedores* scattered around: one of the best is just off the main street beside the petrol station.

Buses run between Guatemala City and Joyabaj, passing through Santa Cruz del Quiché, every hour or so (9am to 6pm from the capital and 5am to 4pm from Joyabaj). For Panajachel and connections to the Pacific coast, buses leave Joyabaj at 8.30am and 12.30pm, heading for Cocales. It's also possible to head back to the capital along two rough and seldom travelled routes. The first of these is **via San Martín Jilotepeque**, with a daily bus that leaves Joyabaj at 3am, while the second option takes you **to Pachalum**, with buses at 2pm on Tuesday, Thursday and Sunday. There's nowhere to stay in Pachalum but onward buses leave to the capital at 2am, passing the ruins of Mixco Viejo (the driver may let you sleep in the bus while you wait).

Finally you can **walk** from Joyabaj, over the Sierra de Chuacús, to Cubulco in Baja Verapaz. It's a superb but exhausting hike, of at least a day, though it's perhaps better done the other way around (which is described on p.200).

To the Cuchumatanes: Sacapulas and Uspantán

The land to the north of Santa Cruz del Quiché is sparsely inhabited and dauntingly hilly, with a single rough road running to Sacapulas. About 10km out of town this road passes through SAN PEDRO JOCOPILAS, and then struggles on, skirting the western end of the Sierra de Chuacús and dropping to the riverside town of **SACAPULAS**, two hours from Quiché in the dusty foothills of the Cuchumatanes. Sacapulas has a small colonial church, and a good market is held beneath a huge ceiba tree in the plaza, every Thursday and Sunday. The women wear impressive *huipiles* and tie their hair with elaborate pom-poms, similar to those of Aguacatán.

Since long before the arrival of the Spanish, **salt** has been produced here in beds beside the Río Negro, and as salt has always been a valuable commodity in the highlands it earned the town a degree of importance. Legend has it that the people originally migrated from the far north, fleeing other savage tribes. The town's original name was Tajul, meaning hot springs, but the Spanish changed it to Sacapulas, "the grassy place", as they valued the locally made straw baskets. Along the river bank, downstream from the bridge, there are several little pools in which warm water bubbles to the surface and local people wash themselves and their clothes. On the opposite bank there are some ramshackle *comedores* and fruit stalls, where trucks and buses break for lunch. If you want to **stay** in Sacapulas the *Comedor Gloria* has some grimy but cheap rooms. The village is also at the junction of two crucial backroads, with **buses** leaving for Huehuetenango in the early morning (4am and 5am), and others passing through en route between Quiché, Nebaj and Uspantán. To get to Sacapulas you can catch any bus heading for Uspantán or Nebaj, which leave Santa Cruz del Quiché throughout the morning. Getting out of Sacapulas can take a while, particularly if you arrive in the morning.

East to Uspantán, and on to Cobán

East of Sacapulas a dirt road rises steeply, clinging to the mountainside and quickly leaving the Río Negro far below. As it climbs the views are superb, with the tiny riverside town of Sacapulas dwarfed by the sheer enormity of the landscape. Eventually the road reaches a high valley and arrives in **USPANTÁN**, a small town lodged in a chilly gap in the mountains, and often soaked in steady drizzle. The only reason you'll end up here is in order to get somewhere else, and with the bus for Cobán and San Pedro Carcha leaving at 2.30am the best thing to do is go to bed. (The return bus, from San Pedro Carcha to Uspantán, leaves at 12.30pm.) There are two friendly and good *pensiones*: the *Casa del Viajero* and the *Golinda*, both of which charge around $1. **Buses** for Uspantán, via Sacapulas, leave Quiché at 9am, 11am and 3pm, returning at 7pm, 11.30pm and 3am – a five-hour trip.

The Ixil triangle: Nebaj, Chajul and Cotzal

High up on the spine of the Cuchumatanes, in a landscape of steep hills, bowl-shaped valleys and gushing rivers, is the **Ixil triangle**. Here the three small towns of Nebaj, Chajul and Cotzal, remote and conservative, share a language spoken nowhere else in the country. These lush and rain-drenched hills are hard to reach and notoriously difficult to control, and the relaxed atmosphere of provincial charm conceals a bitter history of protracted conflict. It's an area that embodies some of the very best and worst characteristics of the Guatemalan highlands.

On the positive side is the beauty of the landscape and the strength of indigenous culture, both of which are overwhelming. When Church leaders moved into the area in the 1970s they found very strong community structures in which the people were reluctant to accept new authority, and women were included in the process of decision-making. To counterbalance these strengths are the horrors of the human rights abuses that took place here over the last decade, which must rate as some of the worst anywhere in Central America.

Figures from pottery vases excavated at Nebaj

Before the **conquest** the town of Nebaj was a sizeable centre of population, producing large quantities of jade, and possibly allied to Zaculeu in some way. The Spanish conquest, however, was particularly brutal in these parts, and not only was the town burnt to the ground, but the survivors were condemned to slavery as a punishment for their resistance. In the years that followed their land was repeatedly invaded by the Lacandones and swept by disease. Things didn't improve with the coming of independence, when the Ixiles were regarded as a source of cheap labour, and forced to work on the coastal plantations. It is estimated that between 1894 and 1930 six thousand labourers migrated annually to work on the harvest, suffering not only the hardship of the actual work, but also exposed to a number of new diseases. Many never returned, and even today large numbers are forced to migrate in search of work, and conditions on many of the plantations remain appalling. More recently, since about 1978, the Ixil triangle has been the main theatre of operation for the **EGP** (the Guerrilla Army of the Poor). Caught up in the horrors of the conflict, the people have suffered enormous losses, with the majority of the smaller villages destroyed by the army and their inhabitants herded into "protected" settlements. In the last few years the EGP have been

driven back into the wilderness to the north and a degree of normality has returned to the area. New villages are springing up in the old sites and a precarious cease-fire is sporadically maintained.

Despite all this, the fresh green hills are some of the most beautiful in the country and the three towns are friendly and accommodating, with a relaxed and distinctive atmosphere in a misty world of their own.

NEBAJ is the centre of Ixil country and by far the largest of the three, a beautiful old town of white adobe walls and cobbled streets. The weaving done here is unusual and intricate, its greatest feature being the women's *huipiles* which are a mass of complex geometrical designs in superb purples, reds, yellows, greens and oranges, while their *cortes* (skirts) are a brilliant red. The men's jackets, which are fast going out of use, are formal-looking and ornately decorated, modelled on those worn by Spanish officers. (The red cloth used in both the jackets and the women's sashes originates in Germany and keeps its colour incredibly well. If you look closely at the cloth it's easy to recognise the use of "Alemania"). The people of Nebaj are keen to establish a market for their weaving, but most of them can't afford to travel as far as Chichicastenango, and as soon as you arrive in town an army of young girls, desperate to sell their cloth, will hassle you with unrelenting and disarming charm.

There's not really much to do in Nebaj itself. The market is interesting, one block from the plaza under a covered building, although it's fairly quiet most days. On Thursday and Sunday the numbers swell and the action moves out into the open air. The church is also worth a look, although it's fairly bare inside. If you can arrange to be here for the second week in August then you'll witness the **Nebaj fiesta** which includes processions, dances, drinking and fireworks.

Sleeping, eating, and getting there
Undoubtedly the best **hotel** in Nebaj is the *Pension Las Tres Hermanas*, a delight-ful place with damp rooms set around a large muddy courtyard, in the centre of which is a vast *pila*. Rooms go for about $1 and the sisters also serve delicious warming food, with early morning porridge to shake off the dawn chill. If this is full then try the *Las Gemelitas* which is further out towards the edge of town, the *Little Corner Hostel*, nearby, or the *Hotel Ixil* on the road into town.

The town has no **restaurants** as such, but there are a couple of *comedores* off the plaza, and you can always get something to eat in the market.

Buses to Nebaj leave Santa Cruz del Quiché between 9am and 10am, taking around five hours, and one of them usually goes on to Cotzal. From Nebaj to Quiché buses leave between 12.30am and 3am.

Some nearby walks
In the hills that surround the town there are several beautiful **walks**, the most interesting of which takes you to the village of Acul, two hours away. Starting from the church in Nebaj, you cross the plaza and turn to the left, taking the road that goes downhill between a shop and a *comedor*. At the bottom of the dip it divides, and here you take the right-hand fork and head out of town along a dirt track.

Just after you pass the last houses there are some pre-Columbian burial mounds to your right. They're still used for religious ceremonies and if you take a close look you'll find burnt patches marking the site of offerings. Since the mounds are usually planted with maize they can be a bit hard to spot, but once you get up above the town they're easier to make out.

Beyond this the track carries on, switchbacking up a steep hillside, and heads over a narrow pass into the next valley, where it drops down into the village. ACUL was one of the original so-called "model villages" into which the people were herded after their homes had been destroyed by the army, and despite the spectacular setting, and the efforts of the United Nations, amongst others, to improve the standard of living, it's a sad, weary, disease-ridden place. If you walk on through the village and out the other side you arrive at the *Finca San Antonio*, a bizarre Swiss-style chalet set in a neat little meadow. For the last fifty years this has been home to an Italian who makes some of the country's best cheese: visitors are welcome to have a look around – especially if they buy some of the produce.

A second, shorter walk takes you to a beautiful little **waterfall** about an hour from Nebaj. Take the road to Chajul and turn left just before it crosses the bridge. Shortly before the main set of falls is a smaller version, so don't be fooled into thinking you've seen it prematurely.

West to Salquil Grande

A third possible excursion takes you out to the village of **SALQUIL GRANDE**, 23km to the west. A newish road runs out this way, through the village of TZALBAL, and across two huge and breathtaking valleys. But the view is over-shadowed by evidence of the scale of the recent violence, which dominates the landscape. The hills beside the road are dotted with brand new villages, their tin roofs still clean and rust free. All of these were built to replace those burnt to the ground, and are inhabited by people who have spent the last few years starving in the mountains or shut away in the refugee camps of Nebaj. Trucks run out to Salquil Grande, leaving from the market or plaza in Nebaj, on most days, and certainly for the Tuesday market. There's nowhere to stay in the village but the trucks usually return a couple of hours later.

Cotzal and Chajul

Of the other two towns in the Ixil triangle, **COTZAL** is the easier to reach. The bus that leaves Quiché at 10am passes through Nebaj at about 3pm, and in theory continues to Cotzal. However, the 20km from Nebaj to Cotzal can take as long as two hours by bus, as the road, curving its way around the jutting green hills, is sometimes a sea of mud, and in practice this bus often doesn't show, or decides to go no further than Nebaj. Cotzal itself is a huddle of steep streets, built along the shoulder of a sharp ridge and often wrapped in a damp blanket of mist. The women wear intricate green *huipiles*, and weave bags and rope from the fibres of the maguey plant. If you head out this way you'll almost certainly have to stay the night, and the *Farmacía* in the corner of the plaza rents out rooms for about $1. The owners also run a *comedor*, so let them know if you'd like a meal.

Last but by no means least of the Ixil villages is **CHAJUL**. This is the hardest to reach as there's no regular bus service, but you can either hitch a ride on a truck from the market in Nebaj, or walk the two hours from Cotzal. Chajul, made up almost entirely of old adobe houses, with wooden beams and red-tiled roofs blackened by the smoke of cooking fires, is the friendlier of these two villages. The streets are usually bustling with activity; you'll be met by an army of small children, and local women gather to wash clothes in the stream which cuts through the middle of the village. Here boys still use blowpipes to hunt small birds, a skill that dates from the earliest of times, but is now little used elsewhere. The women of Chajul dress entirely in red, filling the streets with colour, and wear old coins as earrings, strung up on lengths of wool. The traditional red jackets of the men, however, are a rare sight these days.

The colonial church, a massive old structure, is home to the **Christ of Golgotha**, and is the scene of a large pilgrimage on the second Friday of Lent, which is a particularly good time to be here. The two angels that flank the image were originally dressed as policemen, after a tailor who'd been cured through prayer donated the uniforms so that his benefactor would be well protected. Later they were changed into army uniforms, and recently they've been toned down to look more like boy scouts.

Once again you'll almost certainly have to stay, as transport into and out of Chajul is sporadic. You can rent a **room** from one of the men who works in the post office. Other than a steady flow of unscheduled trucks, the only transport between Chajul and Nebaj is on Sundays when a bus leaves Chajul for Nebaj at 5am, returning at noon. There are markets in Chajul on Tuesday and Friday.

To the north of the Ixil triangle is a thinly populated area known as the **Ixcán**, dropping away towards the Mexican border to merge with the Lacandon rainforests. The last vestiges of the EGP are still fighting to maintain control this region, gradually driven deeper into the wilderness and threatened by the prospect of a new road cutting through from Playa Grande to Barillas.

LAKE ATITLÁN

"Lake Como, it seems to me, touches the limit of the permissibly picturesque; but Atitlán is Como with the additional embellishments of several immense volcanoes. It is really too much of a good thing. After a few days of this impossible landscape one finds oneself thinking nostalgically of the English Home Counties."

Aldous Huxley, *Beyond the Mexique Bay*, 1934.

Whether or not you share Huxley's refined sensibilities there's no doubt that Lake Atitlán is astonishingly beautiful, and most people find themselves captivated by its scenic excesses. Indeed the effect is so overwhelming that a handful of devotees have been rooted to its shores since the Sixties. The lake, just three hours from Guatemala City and a few kilometres to the south of the Pan-American highway, rates as the country's number one tourist attraction. It's a source of much national pride, and some Guatemalans claim that it ranks with the Seven Wonders of the World.

The water itself is an irregular shape, with three main inlets. It measures 18km by 12km at its widest point, and shifts through an astonishing range of blues, greys and greens as the sun moves across the sky. Hemmed in on all sides by steep hills and massive volcanoes, it's at least 320 metres deep and has no visible outlet, draining as it does through an underground passage to the Pacific coast. In the morning the surface of the lake is normally calm and clear, but by early afternoon the *Xocomil*, "the wind that carries away sin", blows from the coast, churning the surface and making travel by boat a hair-raising experience. A north wind, say the Indians, indicates that the spirit of the lake is discarding a drowned body, having claimed its soul.

On the shores of the lake are a total of thirteen villages, with many more in the hills behind. They range from the cosmopolitan resort-style of **Panajachel**, to the tiny, traditional and isolated **Tzununá**. Around the southwestern shores, from **Santiago** to **San Pedro**, the Indians are **Tzutujil** speakers, the remnants of one of the smaller pre-conquest tribes, whose capital was on the slopes of the San Pedro volcano. On the other side of the water, from **San Marcos** to **Cerro de Oro**, **Cakchiquel** is spoken, marking the eastern barrier of this tribe. With the exception of Panajachel the villages are traditional farming communities: it's easy to travel around the lake staying in a different one each night.

This area has been heavily populated since the earliest of times, but it's only recently that it has attracted large numbers of tourists. For the moment things

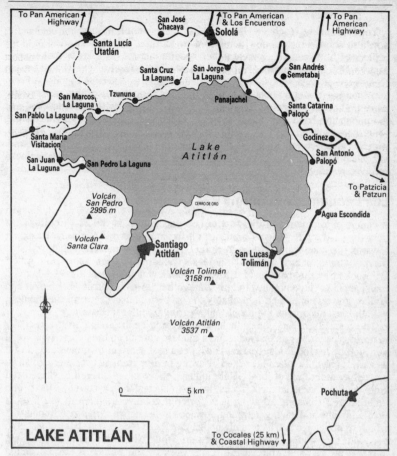

To Pan American
Highway

San José
Chacaya

To Pan American
& Los Encuentros

Sololá

To Pan
American
Highway

Santa Lucía
Utatlán

Santa Cruz
La Laguna

San Jorge
La Laguna

San Andrés
Semetabaj

San Marcos
La Laguna

Tzununa

Panajachel

San Pablo La Laguna

Santa Catarina
Palopó

Santa María
Visitación

*Lake
Atitlán*

Godínez

San Antonio
Palopó

San Juan
La Laguna

San Pedro La Laguna

To Patzicia
& Patzun

*Volcán
San Pedro
2995 m*

CERRO DE ORO

Agua Escondida

*Volcán
Santa Clara*

Santiago
Atitlán

San Lucas
Tolimán

*Volcán Tolimán
3158 m*

*Volcán Atitlán
3537 m*

0   5 km

Pochuta

LAKE ATITLÁN

To Cocales (25 km)
& Coastal Highway

are still relatively undisturbed and the beauty remains overwhelming, but some of the new pressures are decidedly threatening. The fishing industry, once thriving on the abundance of small fish and crabs, was crippled by the introduction of black bass, which not only eat the smaller fish and water birds, but are also much harder to catch. The fish stick to the deeper water and have to be speared by divers. (The intention of introducing them was to create a sport fishing industry.) The increase in population has also had a damaging impact on the shores of the lake, as the desperate need to cultivate more land leads to deforestation and accompanying soil erosion.

In the last year or so the shores have suffered at the hands of yet another invasion. The fashionable and wealthy have abandoned the blackened waters of Lake Amatitlán and moved across to Atitlán. Weekend retreats are springing up around the shores and Saturday afternoons see the waters dotted with speedboats and skiers. In 1955 the Atitlán basin was declared a national park in a bid to preserve its wealth of cultural and natural characteristics, but this seems to have had little effect on development.

You'll probably reach the lake through **Panajachel**, a small village on the northern shore which is now dominated by tourism. It makes an ideal base for exploring the surrounding area, either heading across the lake or making day trips to **Chichicastenango**, **Nahualá**, **Sololá** and **Iximché**. The village has an abundance of cheap hotels and restaurants and is well served by buses. From here you can travel by boat or road to the southern shores of the lake and the more traditional villages of **Santiago** and **San Pedro**, where the landscape and the population have maintained a degree of harmony. The western shoreline is even more isolated but it's possible to walk from **San Pedro** to **San Marcos**, which is a superb way to absorb the splendours of Atitlán. Each of the surrounding villages has a distinctive character and from every angle the lake looks completely different.

Los Encuentros to Sololá

A couple of kilometres to the west of Los Encuentros, at the **El Cuchillo** junction, the road for Panajachel branches off the Pan-American highway. Dropping towards the lake it arrives first at **SOLOLÁ**, the departmental capital, which is perched on a natural balcony some six hundred metres above the water. Overlooked by the majority of travellers, Sololá is nonetheless a fascinating and unusual place. In common with only a few other towns it has parallel Indian and *Ladino* governments, and is probably the largest "Indian" town in the country, with the vast majority of the people still wearing traditional costume.

The town itself isn't much to look at; a wide central plaza with a recently restored clock tower on one side, and a modern church on the other. However, if you stop by for the Friday market you'll get a real sense of its importance. From as early as 5am the plaza is packed, drawing traders from all over the highlands, as well as thousands of local Sololá Indians; the women covered in striped red cloth and the men in their distinctive jackets, outlandish cowboy shirts, and embroidered trousers. Weaving is a powerful creative tradition in the lives of Sololá Indians and each generation develops a distinctive style, based upon that which went before. You'll certainly notice that there are several styles of jacket in use, with the younger men preferring pure white cloth with heavy embroidery, and that the red and white striped cloth worn by the women is also becoming more elaborate. Aldous Huxley described the market here as "a walking museum of fancy dress".

Tradition still dominates daily life in Sololá which is said to be divided into sections, each administered by an Indian clan, just as it was before the conquest.

Little, though, is known about the details of this system and its secrets are well kept. The design on the back of the men's jacket is an abstraction of a bat, the symbol of the royal house of *Xahil*, the rulers of the Cakchiqueles at the time of the conquest, and to the north of town is the pre-conquest site of **Tecpán-Atitlán**, which was abandoned in 1547, when Sololá was founded by the Spanish.

Bat design found on traditional men's jackets

Another interesting time to visit Sololá is on Sunday, when the *Cofradías*, the elders of the Indian religious hierarchy, parade through the streets in ceremonial costume to attend the 10am mass. They're easily recognisable, carrying silver-tipped canes and wearing broad-brimmed hats with particularly elaborate jackets. Inside the church the sexes are segregated, and the women wear shawls to cover their heads.

If you'd rather not immerse yourself in Panajachel there are a couple of **hospedajes** in Sololá itself, the *Santa Ana* and the *Paty*, both of which have *comedores*, charge a little over a dollar, and are a couple of blocks up from the plaza. There's also a **post office** and a *Banco de Guatemala*. For bus times look at the Panajachel schedules, as all **buses** going between Panajachel and Los Encuentros pass through Sololá. There are also minibuses that run regularly between Sololá and Los Encuentros. The last bus to Panajachel passes through Sololá at around 6pm.

Nearby villages

Several other villages can be reached from Sololá, most of them within walking distance. About 8km to the east is **CONCEPCIÓN**, an exceptionally quiet farming village with a spectacularly restored colonial church. The restoration was finished in 1988 and the facade is still a shiny white. The walk out there, along a dirt track skirting the hills above Panajachel, offers superb views across the lake.

To the west of Sololá, along another dirt road and across a deep-cut river valley, SAN JOSÉ CHACAYÁ (4km from Sololá) has a tiny colonial church with thick crumbling walls, but little else. Further along the track, another 8km, is SANTA LUCÍA UTATLÁN (which can also be reached along a second dirt track that branches off the Pan-American highway). From Santa Lucía the road continues around the lake, set back from the ridge of hills overlooking the water, to SANTA MARÍA VISITACIÓN and SANTA CLARA LA LAGUNA. The latter is connected by a steep trail to San Pablo on the lakeshore below: if you're planning to walk to San Pablo via Santa Clara set out early as it's a full day's hike.

On the hillside below Sololá is the village of **SAN JORGE**, a tiny hamlet perched above the lake. The inhabitants of San Jorge have been chased around the country by natural disasters. The village was founded by refugees from the 1773 earthquake in Antigua, and the previous lakeside version was swept into the water by a landslide, persuading the people to move up the hill.

Panajachel

Ten kilometres beyond Sololá, separated by a precipitous descent, is **PANAJACHEL**, gateway to the lake. Over the years what was once a small Indian village has become something of a resort, with a sizeable population of long-term foreign residents, whose numbers are swollen in the winter by an influx of seasonal migrants. The same pleasures that attract the Americans have earned the town a bad reputation amongst some sections of Guatemalan society, and it's often regarded as a haven of drug-taking drop-outs. In the past the army has raided hotels in Panajachel, and banished some of the occupants, but these days they're a touch more tolerant. Other locals are keen to associate themselves with the scene, and at weekends you'll see the blacked-out cars cruising the streets, and riotous drinking sessions in lakeside *comedores*.

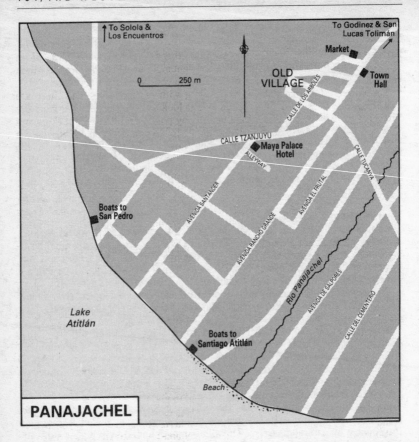

To Solola &
Los Encuentros

To Godinez & San
Lucas Tolimán

Market

OLD
VILLAGE

Town
Hall

0   250 m

CALLE DE LOS ARBOLES

CALLE TZANJUYU

Maya Palace
Hotel

ALLEYWAY

CALLE IUCANTA

AVENIDA SANTANDER

AVENIDA EL FRUTAL

Boats to
San Pedro

AVENIDA RANCHO GRANDE

Rio Panajachel

AVENIDA DE SAPORES

Lake
Atitlán

CALLE DEL CEMENTERIO

Boats to
Santiago Atitlán

Beach

PANAJACHEL

Not so long ago (although it seems an entirely different age) Panajachel was a
quiet little village of Cakchiquel Indians, whose ancestors were settled here after
the Spanish crushed a force of Tzutujil warriors on the site. In the early days of the
conquest the Franciscans established a church and monastery here, using the
village as the base for their regional conversion campaign. Today the old village is
enveloped by the new building boom but it still has a traditional feel, and most of
the Indians farm in the river delta behind the town. The Sunday market, bustling
with people from all around the lake, continues oblivious to the tourist invasion.

For travellers Panajachel is one of those inevitable destinations, and although
no-one ever owns up to actually liking it, everyone seems to stay for a while. The
old village is still attractive and although most of the new building is fairly nondescript its lakeside setting is superb. There's an abundance of cheap hotels, restaurants and bars, even a few cinemas, and the streets are lined with walls of weaving.
It's a comfortable place to be based for exploring the lake and the central highlands. The markets in **Nahualá** – Sunday – and **Chichicastenango** – Thursday
and Saturday – are both within an hour or two, and the ruins at **Santa Cruz del
Quiché** – Utatlán – and **Tecpán** – Iximché – can also be visited as day trips.

Arrival, rooms and the rest

Arriving in Panajachel the bus drops you on the main street, outside the *Maya Palace Hotel*. To the right are the avenidas Santander and Rancho Grande which run parallel towards the lake, and in front and to your left is the old village.

The streets of Panajachel are overflowing with cheap **hotels**, and there are huge numbers of **"rooms"**. The latter tend to look as if they're left over from the Sixties, their wooden walls adorned with trippy poetry and bizarre drawings, but they still offer the best deal in town, almost invariably charging a little over a dollar, with a few cents more for a hot shower. The nicest of them is the *Hospedaje Mi Chosita*, down a side street off the middle of Avenida Santander, and further along the same street is the *Hospedaje Garcia*, a bit more expensive but still well worth it. Around the corner from these two, on Santander itself, is *Mario's Rooms*, and towards the centre of town is *Rooms Santander*, while further down Avenida Santander, towards the beach, are the *hospedajes Londres, Santa Clara* and *San Francisco*, all a touch scruffier, but still good value. If Sixties nostalgia doesn't thrill you, then the *Hotel Casa Linda* (down an alley behind the *Maya Palace*) is a slightly more upmarket sort of place. Even better, for around $3, is *Las Casitas*, at the back of the old village, near the market. If you're in a group, and planning to stay for a while, then check the noticeboards for houses to rent or try *Los Geranios*, which charges $20 a week for a bungalow that sleeps six and has its own kitchen.

If you have a tent then you can either take your chances on the public beach in Panajachel or pay $4 to **camp** at the *Vision Azul*, which is in the next bay in the shadow of the two concrete towers. The fee also entitles you to use the pool and private beach.

TRANSPORT AROUND PANAJACHEL

Buses arriving in Panajachel drop their passengers outside the *Maya Palace Hotel*, and those on their way out of town leave from here. Throughout the day there are also **minibuses** shuttling between Panajachel and Los Encuentros, and much of the time it's easier to catch one of these and flag down another bus on the Pan-American highway.

To and from Guatemala City. *Rebuli* run hourly buses from 5am to 2pm. There are also *Higueros* buses that go to Guatemala City at 6am and 6pm. The offices of *Rebuli* in Guatemala City are at 20 Calle and Avenida Bolívar in Zona 1.

To Chichicastenango there are buses at 7am, 8am, 9am, 4pm and 5pm. If these don't materialise or you want to travel at some other time then take any bus to Los Encuentros, where buses to Chichicastenango pass every hour.

To San Lucas Tolimán and Cocales there are buses at 5.45am, 8am, 4.30pm and 5.45pm.

To Quezaltenango there are buses at 5am, 6am and 5.45pm.

Boats to Santiago Atitlán leave the public beach daily at 9am, returning at around midday. Boats to San Pedro leave from the beach beside the *Hotel Tzanjuyu* at 3am and 3pm, returning at around 5am and 6pm: there are often others that shuttle back and forth throughout the day, some calling in at the smaller villages on the western shore, or you can easily take the morning boat to Santiago and travel on from there.

Eating and entertainment

Panajachel has plenty of restaurants, all catering to the cosmopolitan tastes of its floating population. Several of the most popular are on Avenida Santander, where you'll find the *Restaurante los Amigos*, which does simple pasta dishes, fish, guacamole and salads. Just off Santander, beyond the *Guatel* office, is *The Last Resort*, probably the most popular place in Panajachel. The menu and the portions are vast and the coffee is free, but don't expect to see many Guatemalans. Further down Santander is *Mario's*, which does a limited range of cheap food, including huge salads and pancakes. Back at the top of Calle Santander (opposite the *Maya Palace Hotel*), *Zen* is a Japanese restaurant whose menu includes all sorts of traditional Japanese food including teriyaki, fish and beef dishes.

Heading up into the old village there are plenty more good places to eat. The first of these is *La Unica Deli*, on the main street opposite the health centre, which has an unusual but fairly expensive menu. They serve a delicious range of salads, sandwiches and pastries, as well as bagels, wines and excellent coffee. A couple of blocks to the left is the *Blue Bird*, a favourite budget restaurant that does good, cheap plates of fish, chicken and beef. Further into the old village, also on the main street, the *Cafe Xocomil* has a video cinema and a restaurant that serves delicious food, including some **vegetarian** dishes.

For really cheap and authentically Guatemalan food there are plenty of *comedores* in the market, and several on the beach, although the latter are more expensive, catering for local day-trippers and drinking parties.

The main daytime activity in Panajachel is hanging out at the **public beach**, where you can swim and sunbathe, although really it's far nicer on the other side of the lake in San Pedro. You can also pay a few dollars to use the swimming pool and private beach at *Vision Azul*, in the bay before Panajachel.

For **evening entertainment** there are two **video bars**, one on Calle Santander, and the other in the *Cafe Xocomil* in the old part of town, each showing three English films a night. There's also a local cinema that specialises in Mexican horror films. But the best place to head for in the evening is the *Circus Bar*, where they have **live music**. (A larger nightclub, *La Posada del Pintor*, with cabaret as well as music, has just opened opposite, and should be good as it's run by the same people.) The only **disco** in town is *Past Ten*, down by the beach at the end of the Avenida Rancho Grande, but the *Circus Bar* has cabaret and live music until well into the small hours.

Finally there's a **pool hall** in the old village, near the post office and next to *The Pink Box*.

Other practicalities

The *Inguat* office, which offers a fairly limited **tourist information** service, is at the top of Avenida Santander: *Toro Pinto*, a shop on the entrance road near the *Kodak* sign, is also handy for information, particularly bus schedules, and to **change money**. An official **bank**, the *Banco Agricola Mercantil*, is open in the centre of town from 9am to 3pm, Monday to Friday. The **post office** is in the old village, down a side street beside the church, but for **sending parcels** the safest way is through *The Pink Box* or *Get Guated Out*, two companies who take care of the hassle. The latter is reputedly safer, although a little more expensive. For long-distance phone calls *Guatel* on Avenida Santander is open from 7am to midnight. If you find yourself in need of **medical attention**, Doctor Hernandez has his surgery from 2 to 3pm on the road into town, just before the petrol station, and there's also a homeopathic health centre in the old village which has its own doctors, and offers Shiatsu reflexology and Swedish acupuncture.

The streets of Panajachel are a **shoppers'** paradise. There's **weaving** from all over Guatemala as well as western-style clothes made with Guatemalan cloth. Much of the weaving is of the very highest standards with the weavers themselves, from places like Todos Santos, Nebaj and Chajul, travelling down to sell their wares. Prices, however, can be high, so bargain hard. If you're in the market for **books**, second-hand or new, try the *Galería Bookstore* or *El Mundo Real*, both of which are in the old village. The main market day in Panajachel is Sunday, when the old village is alive with activity, although things are also busy on Saturday.

When it comes to washing, most hotels will either let you do your own or provide a **laundry** service, but if not try the *Hospedaje Londres*, which is down an alley off Avenida Santander, near the beach.

If you'd rather travel around under your own steam then **bikes** can be hired from *Moto Servicio Quiché*, on the main street opposite the bank, and from *Bicicletas Gaby*, just off Avenida Santander. **Boats**, **canoes** and **windsurfers** can be hired on the main beach. **Taxis** usually wait outside the post office, or you can call one on ☎621571.

If you'd like to learn Spanish in Panajachel there's only one **language school**, *The Spanish Academy*, which is just off the entrance road on Calle Principal.

In the event of an **emergency** the police station is on the plaza in the old village and you can phone it on ☎621120.

Around the Lake

The villages that surround the lake are all easily accessible. For a short afternoon outing a trip to **San Antonio** and **Santa Catarina Palopó** takes you out along the shore to the southeast of Panajachel. Or if you want to spend a day or two exploring the area then it's well worth crossing the lake to **Santiago**, and going on to **San Pedro**. The more adventurous can walk back along the western shore – a spectacular and exhausting hike that takes a full day. These southern and western shores are by far the most beautiful and it would be a shame to visit the lake without seeing them.

The Eastern shore

Two roads run from Panajachel around the lake's eastern shore: one clings to the shoreline while the other, parallel to the first, heads up along the ridge of hills. Beside the lake, backed up against the precipitous slopes, are a couple of villages, the first of which is **SANTA CATARINA PALOPÓ**, just four kilometres from Panajachel. The people of Santa Catarina used to live almost entirely by fishing and trapping crabs, but these days the black bass has put an end to all that and they've turned to farming and migratory work, while many of the women travel to Panajachel to peddle their weaving. The traditional purple costume, designed in bold zig-zags, is worn by both the men and the women. Much of the shoreline out this way has been developed by the wealthy, and great villas, ringed by impenetrable walls, have come to dominate the village.

Another five kilometres brings you to **SAN ANTONIO PALOPÓ**, a larger and more traditional village, squeezed in beneath the steep slope behind. The hillside above the village is neatly terraced and irrigated, and a range of vegetables are farmed here. Again the men and women dress traditionally in beautiful costumes; the men in red woven shirts and short woollen skirts, similar to those in Nahualá.

The best way to visit these two villages is on foot – catch a bus from Panajachel heading towards Godínez, and get off at the *mirador* (about a kilometre before Godínez). From here you can enjoy some of the best lake views of all, and a path drops through the terraces, for about an hour, to San Antonio. From there it's another hour's walk, through Santa Catarina, back to Panajachel.

Alternatively you can stick to the lower road that runs through the villages themselves. **Buses** run out along it around mid-morning, heading back as soon as they arrive. If you decide to stay in San Antonio the *Hotel Terrazas del Lago*, down by the water, is fairly upmarket, charging around $10, and also has a restaurant.

The higher road – to Godínez and beyond to San Lucas Tolimán

The higher of the two roads heads back into the delta behind Panajachel, before climbing up above the lake to **SAN ANDRÉS SEMETABAJ**, which has a fantastic ruined colonial church. A path opposite the church's main entrance leads back to Panajachel, winding down through fields and coffee bushes, a nice walk of an hour or so. Beyond here the road curves around the edge of the ridge, with an incredible sweeping view of the lake below, and the irregular cone of the Tolimán volcano opposite, arriving eventually in Godínez. A short distance before this is the *mirador* mentioned before, from where the path leads down to the lakeside village of **San Antonio Palopó**.

At **GODÍNEZ**, a ramshackle and wind-blown village, the road splits, one side running out to the Pan-American highway (through Patzicía and Patzún), and the other on around the lake to the village of **SAN LUCAS TOLIMÁN** in the southeast corner. Set apart from the other villages in many ways, this is probably the least attractive of the lot. The land roundabout is almost all planted with coffee, which dominates the flavour of the place. The Indians take a poor second place to the sizeable *Ladino* population, and the easy-going atmosphere of the lake is tempered by the influence of the Pacific coast. The setting, however, is as spectacular as always. The village is at the back of a small inlet of reed beds, with the Tolimán volcano rising above. There's a weekly market here on Friday, which is certainly the best time to drop by, although sadly it clashes with the market in Santiago. If you want to stop off here the best place to stay is the *Cafeteria Santa Ana*, and you can either eat there or in the *Cafe Tolimán*, down by the lake shore. San Lucas is also the junction of the coast road and the road to Santiago Atitlán, and **buses** to both thunder through the village on a regular basis. On the whole, buses head out towards Cocales and the coast in the early morning, making their way back to Santiago in the afternoon. There are also buses that run between here and Panajachel, mostly in the morning.

Santiago Atitlán

Over on the other side of the lake, **SANTIAGO ATITLÁN** is set to one side of a sheltered horseshoe inlet, overshadowed by the towering cones of the San Pedro, Atitlán and Tolimán volcanoes. It's the largest and most important of the lakeside villages, and also one of the most traditional, being the main centre of Tzutujil-speaking Indians. At the time of the conquest the Tzutujiles had their fortified capital, **Chuitinamit-Atitlán**, on the slopes of the San Pedro volcano, but the bulk of the population lived spread out around the site of today's village. Alvarado and his crew, needless to say, destroyed the capital and massacred the Indians, assisted this time by a force of Cakchiqueles, who arrived at the scene in some 300 canoes.

Today Santiago is an industrious but relaxed sort of place, in a superb setting, and if you're planning a trip around the lake it's probably the best place to spend the first night, heading on to San Pedro in the morning. During the day it becomes fairly commercial and the **main street**, which runs from the dock to the plaza, is lined with weaving shops. There's nothing like the Panajachel overkill, but the persistence of underage gangs can still be a bit much. By mid-afternoon, once the ferries have left, things revert to normal and the whole village becomes a lot more friendly. There's not a lot to do in Santiago other than strolling around and soaking up the atmosphere, but if you're here for a Friday morning then the market is well worth a look, and the old colonial church is interesting. If you're here for the day then you can walk out of town along the track to San Lucas Tolimán, or hire a canoe and paddle out into the lake – just ask around at the dock.

Religion, both Catholic and pagan, plays an important role in the life of Santiago and the town is famous as one of the few places where the Indians still pay homage to Maximón, the drinking and smoking saint. **Easter** celebrations in Santiago are particularly special, and as Holy Week draws on the town is alive with expectation and excitement. Maximón has an important role in the proceedings. On the Monday of Holy Week his image is taken to the lakeshore to be washed, on the Tuesday he's dressed, and on the Wednesday he's housed in a small chapel in the plaza. Here he waits until Good Friday, when Santiago is the scene of a huge and austere religious procession. The town's plaza is packed, with everyone dressed in their finest traditional costume. Christ's image is paraded solemnly through the streets, arriving at the church around noon, where he's tied to a cross and raised above the altar. At around 3pm he's cut down from the cross and placed in a coffin, which is then paraded through the streets, accompanied by the Virgin Mary and Maximón.

The presence of **Maximón**, decked out in a felt hat and western clothes, with a cigar in his mouth, is scorned by reforming Catholics and revered by the traditionalists. The precise origin of Maximón is unknown, but he's also referred to as San Simon, Judas Iscariot and Pedro de Alvarado, and always seen as an enemy of the church. Some say that he represents a Franciscan friar who chased after young Indian girls, and that his legs are removed to prevent any further indulgence. "Max" in the Mam dialect means tobacco and Maximón is always associated with *Ladino* vices such as smoking and drinking; more locally he's known as *Rij Laj*, the powerful man with a white beard. Throughout the year he's looked after by a *cofradía* (a type of local religious society), and if you'd like to drop in and pay your respects ask for "*La Casa de San Simón*", and someone will show you the way. Take along a packet of cigarettes and a bottle of *Quezalteca* for the ever-thirsty saint and his minders.

The traditional costume of Santiago, still worn a fair amount, is both striking and unusual; the men wear long shorts which, like the women's *huipiles*, are white and purple striped, superbly embroidered with birds and flowers. The women also wear a *tocayal*, a band of red cloth approximately ten metres in length, wrapped around their heads, which has the honour of being depicted on the 25 Centavo coin. Sadly this headcloth is going out of use and on the whole you'll probably only see it at fiestas and on market days, worn by the older women.

Around Santiago: the volcanoes and the nature reserve

The land around Santiago is mostly volcanic, with only the odd patch of fertile soil mixed in with the acidic ash. Farming, fishing and the traditional industry, the manufacture of *cayucos* (canoes), are no longer enough to provide for the population, and a lot of people travel to the coast, or work on the coffee plantations that surround the volcano. The Tolimán and Atitlán **volcanoes** can both be climbed from here, but you'll need a couple of days to make it to the top of the latter. It's always best to take a guide to smooth the way, as *ORPA* guerrillas are often camped out on the slopes*. If you're looking for a guide ask in the hotel *Chi-Nim-Ya*, or at either of the restaurants.

To the north of Santiago is a **nature reserve** designated for the protection of the *Poc*, or **Atitlán grebe**, a flightless water bird found nowhere else in the world. The *Poc* used to thrive in the waters of the lake but two factors have threatened its chances of survival; the overcutting of the reeds where it nests, and the introduction of the fierce black bass which eat the young birds. The reserve is surrounded by an underwater fence to keep out the marauding fish.

Practical details

The best **place to stay** in Santiago is the *Hospedaje Chi-Nim-Ya* (on the left as you enter the village from the lake), an old wooden building on two floors, where rooms go for a little over $1. If this is full there's also the *Pension Rosita* beside the church. There are two **restaurants** at the entrance to the village, just up from the dock, both of which are reasonable.

Boats go daily to Santiago from the beach in Panajachel, leaving at 9am and returning some time after noon – the trip takes about an hour. For San Pedro boats leave Santiago mid-morning, and sometimes in the early afternoon.

The village is also astonishingly well connected by **bus**, with almost anywhere except Panajachel. Buses mostly leave from the central plaza and head via San Lucas Tolimán and Cocales towards Guatemala City or Quezaltenango. There are no direct buses between Santiago and Panajachel, and all those that leave the village, whether for Guatemala City or Quezaltenango, go via Cocales and the coastal highway. From Guatemala City to Santiago (4hr), *Rebuli* buses leave the capital (from 20 Calle 3–24, Zona 1) at 5am, 11.30am and 3pm, and for Guatemala City they leave Santiago at 3am, 6am and noon. They also run to Quezaltenango at 3.30am and 4.30am, leaving from Quezaltenango for Santiago at 11am and 12.30pm.

---

*The village itself has seen a fair amount of fighting and was briefly occupied by the army in 1981, after it was claimed that the guerrillas held a meeting here. Many people from Santiago have lost their lives as a result of political killings and the work of "death squads". Today the village remains a centre of resistance and is still regularly visited by the army.

San Pedro La Laguna

Around the other side of the San Pedro volcano is the village of **SAN PEDRO LA LAGUNA**. Far fewer tourists make it here and those who do have little impact, making it the most relaxed of the lakeside villages. Tradition isn't as powerful here either, and only a few old people, mostly men, still wear the old costume. Nevertheless there's a sense of permanence in the narrow cobbled streets and old stone houses. The people of San Pedro have a reputation for driving a hard bargain when trading their coffee and avocados, and have managed to buy up a lot of land from neighbouring San Juan, with which there's endless rivalry. They're also famed for the *cayucos* (canoes) made from the great cedar trees that grow on the slopes of the San Pedro volcano.

The setting is again spectacular, with the volcano rising to the east and a ridge of steep hills running behind the village. To the left of the main beach, as you look towards the lake, a line of huge white boulders juts out into the water; an ideal spot for an afternoon of swimming and sunbathing.

There are three **hotels** in San Pedro. Two are on the main beach, facing the dock – the *Hospedaje Chuasinahu* is the newer at a little over $1, the *Ti-Kaaj*, right next door, is a little cheaper and scruffier. Here you can also camp or sling a hammock. On the other side of the village, beside the alternative dock, is the *Pension Johanna*, also a touch cheaper, with an excellent restaurant that serves wholemeal bread, spaghetti and yoghurt amongst other things. Other possible places to eat are the restaurant in the *Chuasinahu* and the *Comedor Michel*, a little further around from the twin hotels.

The western shoreline: San Pedro to Sololá

The western side of the lake is the only part that remains largely inaccessible by car. From San Pedro a rough dirt road runs as far as San Marcos, and from here a spectacular path, a bit vague in parts, continues all the way to Sololá. Some of the boats between San Pedro and Panajachel call in to the larger villages but the best way to see the string of isolated villages along this route is on foot, and it makes a fantastic day's walk. Most of the way a narrow strip of level land is wedged between the water and the steep hills behind, but where this disappears the path is cut into the slope with dizzying views of the lake below. At several of the villages along the way, *tiendas* sell Coke and biscuits, so there's no need to carry water. The only hotel on this side of the lake is in Santa Cruz.

From San Pedro you follow the road to **SAN JUAN**, just a kilometre or so away at the back of a sweeping bay surrounded by shallow beaches – the area is known as *Aguas Cristalinas*. The village of San Juan specialises in the weaving of *petates*, mats made from lake reeds, and there's a market here on Tuesday and Saturday. Leaving the lakeside here a trail leads high up above the village to SANTA CLARA LA LAGUNA, which is connected to Sololá by a seldom used road. The lakeside road, however, runs on through coffee plantations to **SAN PABLO LA LAGUNA**, where the speciality is the manufacture of rope from the fibres of the *maguey* plant, and you can sometimes see great lengths being stretched and twisted in the streets. Beyond this point the villages shrink significantly, starting with **SAN MARCOS**, about two hours' walk from San Pedro, which is no more than a loose group of houses clustered around a small, ancient church. This far the road is still passable for vehicles and with a bit of luck you might get a lift in a truck: beyond

San Marcos, though, it starts to deteriorate and the villages along the way have a still greater feeling of isolation. If you continue you'll find the people along the way astonished to see outsiders and all eager for a glimpse of passing gringos. Nowhere is this more true than in **TZUNUNÁ**, the next place along the way, where the women run from oncoming strangers, taking shelter behind the nearest tree in giggling groups. They all wear beautiful red *huipiles* striped with blue and yellow on the back. The village was originally built at the lakeside, but after it was badly damaged by a flood in 1950 the people rebuilt their homes on the higher ground. Here the road indisputably ends, giving way to a narrow path, cut out of the steep hillside. At some points this can be a little hard to follow as it descends to cross small streams and then climbs again around the rocky outcrops.

The next village is JAIBALITO, a ragged-looking place lost amongst the coffee bushes, and beyond here, set well back from the lake on a shelf a hundred metres or so above the water, is **SANTA CRUZ LA LAGUNA**, the largest of this line of villages. On the shore, opposite a thatched jetty, is the *Hotel Arco de Noe*, a lovely little place owned by an Austrian couple. The food, the hospitality and the setting are all wonderful, with beautiful twin-bedded bungalows for $9. Whether you drop in for a snack or stay a week, you'll be glad you did, and there's certainly no better place to soak up the scenery. The walk from San Pedro to Santa Cruz takes about five hours in all, so by the time you get here you'll probably be ready to take a swim and relax for the rest of the day.

Beyond Santa Cruz there are two ways to reach Panajachel, either by boat or on foot. Boats travelling between Panajachel and San Pedro call in, or you can hire a boat to Panajachel for $4. The path that runs directly to Panajachel is hard to follow and distraught walkers have been known to spend as long as seven hours scrambling through the undergrowth. A much better bet is to walk up through the village to Sololá, a spectacular and easy-to-follow path that takes around three hours, and catch a bus back to Panajachel from there.

If you want to do this walk in the other direction – **from Sololá to San Pedro** – then you should head west out of Sololá along the dirt road towards San José Chacayá, and as you come up out of the river valley, about 1km out of Sololá, follow the track branching off to the left. This eventually brings you to Santa Cruz, from where you simply follow the shoreline.

The Highway: Los Encuentros to Cuatro Caminos

Heading west from the Los Encuentros junction to Cuatro Caminos and the Quezaltenango valley, the Pan-American highway runs through some fantastic high mountain scenery. The views alone are superb, and if you have a Sunday morning to spare then it's well worth dropping into Nahualá for the market. **LOS ENCUENTROS** itself is an all-important staging point on the Pan-American highway, and typical of the junctions along the way, with wooden *comedores*, an army base, and a team of enthusiastic sales people who besiege waiting buses. Here a branch road heads north to Chichicastenango, while the main highway continues west towards Quezaltenango, Huehuetenango and the Mexican border. Only a kilometre or so beyond this turning, at the **EL CUCHILLO** junction, a second road runs south to Sololá, Panajachel and the shores of Lake Atitlán.

These junctions are likely to feature heavily in your travels as it's here that you transfer from one bus to another heading between Panajachel, Chichicastenango and the rest of the country. There are direct buses to and from all of these places, but if their schedule doesn't coincide with yours then it's easier to take any bus to the junction and intercept one going your way – all buses stop here and their destinations are yelled by the driver's assistant, touting for business. The last buses to Chichicastenango, Panajachel and Guatemala City pass through Los Encuentros at around 7pm, and if you miss those you'll have to negotiate with a taxi.

Nahualá and Alaska

West of Los Encuentros and El Cuchillo the Pan-American highway runs through some spectacular and sparsely inhabited countryside. The only place of any size is **NAHUALÁ**, a small and intensely traditional town a kilometre or so to the north of the highway. It sits at the base of a huge, steep-sided and intensely farmed bowl.

The town itself isn't much to look at, a sprawl of cobbled streets and adobe houses, but the Indians of Nahualá have a reputation for fiercely preserving their independence, and have held out against *Ladino* incursions with exceptional tenacity. Under President Barrios, the government confiscated much of their land at the end of the nineteenth century (as they did throughout the country) and sold it to coffee planters. In protest, the entire male population of Nahualá walked the 150 kilometres to Guatemala City and demanded to see the President in person, refusing his offers to admit a spokesman and insisting that they all stood as one. Eventually they were allowed into the huge reception room and knelt with their foreheads pressed to the floor, refusing to leave until they were either given assurances of their land rights or allowed to buy the land back, as they'd done twice before. The action saved their land that time, but since then much of it has gradually been consumed by coffee bushes all the same.

On another occasion, this time during the 1930s under President Ubico, *Ladinos* were sent to the town as nurses, telegraph operators and soldiers. Once again the Nahualáns appealed directly to the President, and insisted that their own people should be trained to do these jobs, and once again their request was granted. Ubico also wanted to set up a government-run drink store, but the Indians chose instead to ban alcohol, and Nahualáns who got drunk elsewhere were expected to confess their guilt and face twenty lashes in the town's plaza.

These days the ban has been lifted, and if you're here for the fiesta on November 25 you'll see that the people are keen to make up for all those dry years. Nevertheless only a handful of *Ladino*s live in the town, and the Indians still have a reputation for hostility, with rumours circulating about the black deeds done by the local shamen. You don't have much to worry about if you drop in for the Sunday market, however, as this is one time that the town is full to bursting and the people seem genuinely pleased to welcome visitors. The unique atmosphere of isolation from and indifference to the outside world make it well worth taking a look. It's a combination that makes Nahualá one of the most impressive and unusual Quiché towns.

The town's **weaving** is outstanding: the *huipiles*, designed in intricate geometrical patterns of orange on white, particularly impressed the Spanish because they featured a double-headed eagle, the emblem of the Hapsburgs, who ruled Spain at the time of the conquest. The men wear bright shirts with beautifully embroidered collars, and short woollen skirts.

To **get to Nahualá** take any bus along the Pan-American highway between Los Encuentros and Cuatro Caminos, and get off at the *Puente Nahualá*, from where it's a kilometre or so up the path behind the old bus shelter. There's a very basic *pensión* in the centre of town, but it's easier to visit as a day trip from Chichicastenango, Panajachel or Quezaltenango.

Santa Catarina and the Alaskan heights

Beyond Nahualá the road continues to the west, climbing a mountainous ridge and passing the entrance to **SANTA CATARINA IXTAHUACAN**, a sister town and bitter rival of Nahualá, 8km to the other side of the highway. The costumes and traditions of the two places, which are together known as the *Pueblos Chancatales*, are fairly similar, and they're both famous as producers of *metates*, the stones used for grinding corn. These days much corn-grinding is done by machine and they've turned to making smaller toy versions and wooden furniture – both of which you'll see peddled by the roadside.

As it continues west, the road climbs above Santa Catarina and into the most impressive section of the Pan-American highway, coming out on a flat plateau high up in the hills. Known as **Alaska**, this exposed tract of land, where the men of Nahualá farm wheat and graze sheep, shines white with frost in the early mornings. Raised up to a height of 3671 metres and almost level with the great cones, the view is of course fantastic. Away to the east a string of volcanoes runs into the distance, and to the west the Totonicapán valley is stretched out below you.

Further on, as the road drops over the other side of the ridge, the Quezaltenango valley opens out to the left, a broad plain reaching across to the foot of the Santa María volcano. At the base of the ridge the Pan-American highway arrives at the Cuatro Caminos crossroads, the crucial junction of the extreme western highlands. Right here leads to Totonicapán, left to Quezaltenango, and straight on for Huehuetenango and the Mexican border.

QUEZALTENANGO AND AROUND

To the west of Lake Atitlán the highlands rise to form a steep-sided ridge topped by a string of forested peaks. On the far side of this is the **Quezaltenango basin**, a sweeping expanse of level ground that forms the natural hub of the western highlands. The Quezaltenango basin is perhaps the most hospitable area in the western highlands, encompassing a huge area of fertile farmland that has been densely populated since the earliest of times. Originally it was part of the Mam kingdom, administered from their capital **Zaculeu** (at a site adjacent to the modern city of Huehuetenango); but sometime between 1400 and 1475 the area was overrun by the Quichés, and was still under their control when the Spanish arrived. Today the western side of the valley is Mam-speaking and the east Quiché. It was here that Pedro de Alvarado first struggled up into the highlands, having already confronted one Quiché army on the coast and another in the pass at the entrance to the valley. Alvarado and his troops came upon the abandoned city of Xelaju (near Quezaltenango) and were able to enter it without encountering any resistance. Six days later they fought the Quichés in a decisive battle on the nearby plain, massacring the Indian warriors and killing their hero Tecún Umán. The old city was then abandoned and the new town of Quezaltenango soon established in its place. The name means "the place of the quetzals" in

Nahuatl, the language spoken by Alvarado's Mexican allies. Quetzals may well have existed here then but the name is more likely to have been chosen because of the brilliant green quetzal feathers worn by Quiché nobles and warriors, including, no doubt, Tecún Umán himself.

Nowadays the valley is heavily populated, with three major towns; the departmental capital of **Quezaltenango**, and the textile centres of **Salcajá** and **San Francisco Totonicapán**. In the surrounding hills are numerous smaller towns and villages, mostly Indian agricultural communities and weaving centres. To the south, straddling the coast road, are **Almolonga**, **Zunil** and **Cantel**, all overshadowed by volcanic peaks, where you'll find superb natural hot springs. To the north are **Totonicapán**, capital of the department of the same name, and **San Francisco el Alto**, a small market town perched on an outcrop overlooking the valley. Beyond that, in the midst of a pine forest, is **Momostenango**, the country's principal wool-producing centre. Throughout this network of towns and villages Indian culture remains strong, based on a simple rural economy that operates in a series of weekly markets, bringing each town to life for one day a week. To the west, up against the Mexican border, the **department of San Marcos** is a rather neglected region that's far less visited – it's a potential route to Mexico by the coastal crossing, and the home of the country's highest volcano.

Set in some of the finest highland scenery, the area also offers excellent hiking. The most obvious climb is the **Santa María volcano**, towering above Quezaltenango itself. It's just possible to make this climb as a day trip, but to really enjoy it, and increase your chances of a good view from the top, you should plan to take two days over it, camping on the way. If you haven't the time, energy or equipment for this then try instead the hike to **Laguna Chicabal**, a small lake set in the cone of a extinct volcano. The lake is spectacularly beautiful, and can easily be reached as a day trip from Quezaltenango, setting out from the village of **San Martín Sacatepéquez**.

Quezaltenango is the obvious place to base yourself, as from here buses run to all parts of the western highlands. It's easy enough to spend a week or two exploring this part of the country; making day trips to the markets and fiestas, basking in the Almolonga hot springs, or hiking in the mountains. If you yearn for a dip in the Pacific it's also possible to reach **Tulate** as a day trip, or stay overnight if you can handle the heat. Leaving Quezaltenango you can head west to the department of **San Marcos**, or follow the Pan-American highway to **Huehuetenango**, and on into **Mexico**.

Quezaltenango – Guatemala's second city

Totally unlike Guatemala City, and only a fraction of its size, **QUEZALTENANGO** has the subdued provincial atmosphere that you might expect in the capital of the highlands. The city is ringed by high mountains and in the early mornings the air is bitterly cold. It wakes slowly, getting going once the warmth of the sun has made its mark. The city's plaza, heavily indebted to Neoclassicism, is a monument to stability, with great slabs of grey stone that look reassuringly permanent defying a history of instability and struggle. The heart of town has the calm of a regional administrative centre, while its outskirts are ruffled by the bustle of an Indian market and bus terminal. Locally, the city is usually referred to as *Xela* (pronounced "shey-la"), a shortening of the Quiché name of a nearby pre-conquest city, Xelaju. The Quiché word means "under the ten", and is probably a reference to the surrounding peaks.

Under colonial rule Quezaltenango flourished as a commercial centre, benefiting from the fertility of the surrounding farmland and its good connections to the port at Champerico. When the prospect of independence eventually arose the city was set on deciding its own destiny. At first it declared its allegiance to Mexico and then joined the Central American Federation as the capital of the independent state of **Los Altos**, which incorporated the modern departments of Huehuetenango, Sololá, San Marcos and Totonicapán. But the separatist movement was soon brought to heel by President Carrera in 1840, and a later attempt at secession, in 1848, was put down by force. Despite having to accept provincial status, the town remained an important centre of commerce and culture, consistently rivalling Guatemala City. The coffee boom at the end of the last century was particularly important, as the town controlled some of the richest coffee land in the country. Its wealth and population grew rapidly, incorporating a large influx of German immigrants, and by the end of the nineteenth century Quezaltenango was firmly established as an equal to Guatemala City.

All of this, however, came to an abrupt end in 1902 when the city was almost totally destroyed by a massive earthquake. It was rebuilt in a mood of high hopes, and all the grand and ancient-looking architecture dates from this period, with a heavy indulgence in the Neoclassical. A new railway was built to connect the city with the coast, but this was washed out in 1932–33 and the town never regained its former glory, gradually falling further and further behind the capital.

Today it has all the trappings of wealth and self-importance; the grand imperial architecture, the great banks, and a list of famous sons. But it is completely devoid of the rampant energy that binds Guatemala City to the all-American twentieth century. Instead the city finds itself suspended in the late nineteenth century, with a calm and dignified air that borders on the pompous. *Quezaltecos* have a reputation for formality and politeness, and pride themselves on the restrained sophistication of their cultured semi-provincial existence. If the chaos of Guatemala City gets you down then Quezaltenango, relaxed and easy-going, is an ideal antidote. The flip side of this is that while it may be an ideal base from which to explore the western highlands, the city itself has nothing to detain you for more than a day, and certainly none of the pace and energy that characterises the capital. It's nevertheless a pleasant enough place to stay if you don't mind going to bed early, with plenty of hotels and restaurants, few tourists, and good bus connections to every corner of the western highlands.

Arrival and orientation

There are two bus terminals in Quezaltenango, one for local second-class buses and the other for longer distance ones, and in addition to this there are several first-class bus companies, which operate from offices scattered throughout the city. The main point of arrival is the **Minerva bus terminal** in Zona 3, which is on the western side of town. It's quite some way from the centre so you'll need to catch a local bus to and from the plaza. The actual terminal is on the northern side of the Parque Minerva, just off 6 Calle, and the local buses heading into town stop on the other side, on 4 Calle. Separating the two is a large covered market: walk down the passage that runs through the middle of this, and on the south

Minerva Bus
Terminal

To San Pedro &
San Marcos

CALZADA REVOLUCION   4A CALLE

CALLE CUESTA BLANCA

To Los Encuentros &
Guatemala City

Roundabout &
Marimba Monument

CALLE RODOLFO ROBLES   CALLE RODOLFO ROBLES

CALZADA SINFOROSO AGUILAR   4A CALLE

CALLE CIRILO FLORES

0   200 m

PLAZA
Cathedral

QUEZALTENANGO

To Almolonga

side cross a large patch of open ground to reach the road. Any of the small buses going to the left will take you to the plaza (local buses charge 10 centavos and you need to have some change to hand). The second bus terminal is only a block from the plaza, beside the Cathedral at 10 Avenida and 6 Calle in Zona 1. This is used only by local second-class buses running to Zunil, Cuatro Caminos, Totonicapán and San Francisco el Alto: unless you're coming from one of these places you won't arrive here, but it's convenient for short trips out of town.

If you arrive by **first-class** or pullman bus you'll find yourself at the office of the particular company. *Lineas Americas* and *Rutas Lima* are both just off Calzada Independencia (7 Avenida), on the eastern side of town, and from here any local bus going west will bring you to the plaza. *Galgos* are at Calle Rudolfo Robles 17–43, Zona 1 (☎0612248), which is close to the plaza. From here it's easier to walk into town than waste time searching for a bus.

The city itself is laid out on a standard grid pattern, somewhat complicated by a number of steep hills. Basically, avenidas run north–south, and calles east–west. The oldest part of the city, focussed around the plaza, is made up of narrow twisting streets, while in the newer part, reaching out towards the Minerva terminal and sports stadium, the blocks are larger. The city is also divided up into zones, although for the most part you'll only be interested in 1 and 3, which contain the plaza and the bus terminal.

When it comes to getting around the city, most places are within easy walking distance. To get to the Minerva terminal you can take any bus that runs along 13 Avenida between 8 Calle and 4 Calle in Zona 1. To head for the eastern half of town, along 7 Avenida, catch one of the buses that stops in front of the Casa de la Cultura, at the bottom end of the plaza. You pay the driver, and it's a good idea to have some small change handy.

TRANSPORT

As the focus of the western highlands, Quezaltenango is served by literally hundreds of buses. **Getting to Quezaltenango** is fairly straightforward: there are direct pullmans from Guatemala City – listed below – and at any point along the Pan-American highway you can flag down a bus to take you to Cuatro Caminos, from where you'll find buses to Quezaltenango every half-hour (the last at around 7pm). Coming from the coast you can catch a bus from the El Zarco junction, Mazatenango or Retalhuleu. **Leaving the city**, there are plenty of direct buses (listed below) but it's often easier to head for Cuatro Caminos and go on from there.

Pullman buses
Rutas Lima have buses from Quezaltenango to Guatemala City at 5.30am, 6.30am, 8am, 2.30pm and 8.30pm; to Huehuetenango and La Mesilla at 5am and 6.30pm; and to Talisman at 5am. In Guatemala City their office is at 8 Calle 3–63, Zona 1.
Galgos have buses from Quezaltenango to Guatemala City at 5am, 8.30am, 10.15am, 12.15am, 3pm, 4.30pm and 7pm. In Guatemala City their office is at 7 Avenida, 19–44, Zona 1.
Lineas Americas have buses to Guatemala City at 5.15am, 9.45am, 1.15pm and 3.45pm.Their office in Guatemala City is at 2 Avenida 18–74, Zona 1.

Second-class buses
Buses for **Zunil** (25min), **San Francisco el Alto** (45min) and **Totonicapán** (1hr) leave every half-hour between 8am and 6pm from the small terminal at 10 Avenida and 6 Calle in Zona 1.
From the main Minerva terminal in Zona 3 there are hourly buses to **Huehuetenango** (2hr 30min), **San Marcos** (2hr), **Mazatenango** (2hr), **Retalhuleu** (2hr), **Coatepeque** (2hr) and **Guatemala City** (5hr). There are also buses to **Santiago Atitlán** at 11am and 12.30pm, and to **Panajachel** at 6.15am, noon and 1pm (you can also take a *Higueros* bus to Guatemala City via Panajachel, although their buses were built in the 1950s apparently with midgets in mind – they leave from the office at 12 Avenida and 7 Calle at 4am and 3.30pm). To **Momostenango** (2hr) there are hourly buses from 9am to 5pm.
Heading for **Santa Cruz del Quiché**, **Chichicastenango** or **Antigua** you can catch any bus going to Guatemala City and change buses at the relevant junction. (Los Encuentros for Chichicastenango and Quiché, Chimaltenango for Antigua.)
To the Mexican border at Talisman. It's possible to travel via San Marcos to the border in a day, but the quickest route is to take a bus to the coast, and intercept a pullman on the Coastal Highway (*Rutas Lima* have one daily bus to the Talisman border at 5am).
To the Mexican border at La Mesilla. The easiest way is to take a direct bus to Huehuetenango and catch another from there to the border. However *Rutas Lima* have direct buses to La Mesilla at 5am and 6.30pm.

Sleeping and eating

Once you've made it to the plaza you can set about looking for somewhere to stay. Quezaltenango's **hotels** are basically divided into two groups, one to each side of the plaza. A block or two to the southeast of the plaza you'll find the *Pension Altense*, at the corner of 9 Calle and 9 Avenida, a clean and friendly place that's good value at $2. Another block to the east is the *Casa del Viajero*, similarly priced and just as good, at 10 Calle 8 Avenida. This one also has a *comedor*, although it can be a bit hard to get inside – ring the bell beside the black garage doors. Next is the *Pension Quijote*, further up the same road, which is cheaper but smells a bit. If you're on a really tight budget there are plenty of other horrible places for around $1, and two that are worth recommending; the *Pension Regia*, 9 Avenida 8–26, is certainly the best of the really cheap places, and the *Pension Fenix*, 9 Avenida 6–29, an old building with huge cold rooms, is also cheap and reasonably good. The other group of hotels is on the opposite side of the plaza – off the top left-hand side – the northwest. Here you'll find the *Casa Kaehler* at 13 Avenida 3–33, a lovely place with rooms for $3, spotlessly clean with hot showers – knock on the door to get in. Further up the same street is *Radar 99*, not as good but a little bit cheaper. A few blocks further over are the *Hotel Modelo*, 14 Avenida A 2–31, and *Pension Casa Suiza*, in the same street, both of which are popular with Guatemalan businessmen and have rooms from around $3, more with a private bathroom.

As for eating, there are more than enough **restaurants**, with four pizza places on 14 Avenida alone, all of which are fairly good. Also on 14 Avenida is *Deli Crepe*, which does good fruit juices, sweet and savoury pancakes, and delicious sandwiches. For Chinese the best is the *Shanghai*, at 4 Calle 12–22, half a block from the plaza; *Chao Mein*, further along the same street, is cheaper, but somewhat bland. For something with a more Guatemalan flavour there's the *Comedor Capri*, 8 Calle 1–39, which has a rigidly set meal, and opens early for breakfast, as does the *Coffee Centre*, 4 Calle 13–50, which serves small meals until around 11pm. There's also the *Cafe Ut'z Hua*, up the hill above the plaza at 12 Avenida 3–02, which is simple, good and cheap, if a little scruffy. If you want to sample some of the city's upmarket pomposity, tea at the *Pension Bonifaz* (in the corner of the plaza) is always a sedate and civilised affair.

There's not much to do in the evenings, and the streets are quiet by about 9pm. A couple of **bars**, though, are worth visiting; at the *Don Rodrigo*, 1 Calle and 14 Avenida, you can eat sandwiches and drink draught lager with the sophisticated and wealthy; while at the *Tecún*, on the west side of the plaza, you can down *Quezalteca* with the boys, in the company of the odd rat or two. The city is the home of this all-pervasive spirit and of *Cabro* beer, both of which have been brewed here for well over a century.

There are also three **cinemas**; the *Cadore* at 7 Calle 13 Avenida just off the plaza, which specialises in violence, horror and soft porn; the *Roma*, a beautiful old theatre at 14 Avenida A 34; and the *Alpino*, at 4 Calle and 24 Avenida, part of a new complex in Zona 3 out near the bus terminal.

Other practicalities

Banks surround the plaza: the *Banco de Guatemala*, *Banco del Café*, *Banco Inmobiliario* and *Banco del Occidente* all change travellers' cheques. The **post office** is at 15 Avenida and 4 Calle in Zona 1, and for long- or short-distance phone calls *Guatel* is on the main plaza. You can get your **laundry** done at the *Lavandería Minimax*, 13 Avenida 0–47. Simple **camera repairs** can be handled by *Fotocolor*, 15 Avenida 3–25, and there are several shops on 14 Avenida that sell a good range of film. If you need medical attention, **doctors** Cohen and Molina at the *Policlinica*, A Calle 13–15, speak some English, and for real emergencies the *Hospital Privado* is at Calle Rudolfo Robles 23–51 Zona 1 (☎4381). The only **travel agent** is *SAB Tours*, 1 Calle 12–35, Zona 1. The **Mexican Consulate** is in the *Pension Bonifaz* at the top of the main plaza: they charge $1 for a Mexican tourist card and are open 8am to noon, Monday to Friday. There are several **language schools** operating in Quezaltenango, the most established being *SAB*, 1 Calle 12–35, Zona 1, and *Casa Xelaju*, 6 Calle 7–32, Zona 1. Both run courses for about $150 a week, including food and accommodation. The *English Club* (3 Calle and 15 Avenida, Zona 1) is a little cheaper and also offers lessons in Quiché and Mam.

The City

There aren't many specific things to do or see in Quezaltenango, but if you have an hour or two to spare then it's well worth wandering through the streets, soaking up the atmosphere or taking in the museum. The hub of the place is, obviously enough, the **central plaza**, officially known as the **Parque Centro América**. It's a mass of Greek columns, banks and shoeshine boys, with a wonderfully dignified calm. It's here that you can best sense the mood of self-importance in which the city was rebuilt after the 1902 earthquake. The buildings have a look of defiant authority, although there's none of the buzz of business that you'd expect. The Greek columns were probably intended to symbolise the city's cultural importance, and its role as the heart of the liberal revolution, although today many of them do nothing more than support street lights. The northern end of the plaza is dominated by the grand *Banco del Occidente*, complete with sculptured flaming torches. On the west side are the *Banco de Guatemala* and the *Pasaje Enriquez*. The latter, planned as a sparkling arcade of upmarket shops, is these days abandoned and decaying, housing a single, rat-infested bar.

At the bottom end of the plaza is the **Casa de la Cultura del Occidente**, the city's most blatant impersonation of a Greek temple, with a bold grey frontage that radiates stability and strength. The **tourist office** (8am–noon & 2–5pm weekdays – half day Saturdays) is here, to the right of the main entrance, where you can get a map of the town and some information on trips to the surrounding villages. The main part of the building is given over to an odd mixture of local **museums**. On the ground floor, to the left-hand side, you'll find a display of assorted documents from the liberal revolution and the State of Los Altos, some sports trophies, and a museum of Marimba. Upstairs there are some interesting Maya artefacts, a display about local industries, and a fascinating collection of old photographs.

Along the other side of the plaza is the **Cathedral**, with the new cement version set behind the spectacular crumbling front of the original. A little further up is the **Municipalidad** or town hall, another unashamed piece of Greek grandeur. Take a look inside at the courtyard, which has a neat little garden set out around a single palm tree. Back in the centre of the plaza are rows and circles of redundant columns, a few flowerbeds, and a monument to President Barrios, who ruled Guatemala from 1873 to 1885.

In the bottom left-hand corner of the plaza, between the cathedral and the Casa de la Cultura, the **Mercadito** is an old market that still functions, although nowadays it's eclipsed by a larger version in Zona 3. Beside it, the shape of things to come is represented by the **Centro Comercial Municipal**, a new three-storey shopping centre.

Away from the plaza the city spreads out, a mixture of the old and new. 14 Avenida is the commercial heart, complete with pizza restaurants and neon signs in pale imitation of the capital. At the top of this strip the **Teatro Municipal** stands at the junction with 1 Calle, yet another spectacular example of the Neoclassical. The plaza in front of the theatre is dotted with busts of local artists, in another bid to assert Quezaltenango's cultural superiority.

Further afield, the city's role as a regional centre of trade is more in evidence. Out in Zona 3 is the **La Democracía Market**, a vast covered complex with stalls spilling out onto the streets. And a couple of blocks beyond the market is the modern **Church of San Nicolás**, at 4 Calle and 15 Avenida, a bizarre and ill-proportioned neo-Gothic building, sprouting sharp Norman arches.

Right out on the edge of town, also in Zona 3, the **Minerva Temple** is yet another Greek-style structure. This one makes no pretence at serving any practical purpose, but was built to honour President Barrios' enthusiasm for education. Beside the temple is the **Zoo** (free), a little place that doubles as a childrens' playground. Crammed into the tiny cages are a collection of foxes, sheep, birds, wild boar and big cats, including a pair of miserable-looking lions. Below the temple is the sprawling **market** and **bus terminal**, and it's here that you can sense the city's role as the centre of the western highlands, with Indian traders from all over the area doing business, and buses heading to or from every imaginable village and town. To get out to this side of the city take any of the local buses that run along 13 Avenida between 8 Calle and 4 Calle in Zona 1.

Olintepeque and the old road to Huehuetenango

To the north of Quezaltenango, on the edge of the flat plain, is the small textile-weaving town of **OLINTEPEQUE**. According to some accounts this was the site of the huge and decisive battle between the Spanish and Quiché warriors and legend has it that the Río Xequijel, the "river of blood", ran red during the massacre of the Quichés. These days, however, it's a peaceful little village with a small colonial church and a market on Tuesdays. **Buses** for Olintepeque leave from the Minerva terminal in Quezaltenango every half-hour.

Olintepeque was a staging post on the old road to Huehuetenango, and although only local traffic heads this way nowadays you can still follow the route. Leaving Olintepeque it heads up the steep hillside onto a plateau above, where it reaches the village of **SAN CARLOS SIJA**, 22km from Quezaltenango and the hub of a fertile and isolated area. There's nowhere to stay in San Carlos, but five buses a day connect it with Quezaltenango – leaving from the Minerva terminal in Zona 3 – the last returning at about 4pm. The only real reason to head out this way would be for the wonderful views or to visit the small Sunday market. Heading on, you can hitch a ride to the Pan-American highway, just 10km away, where there's plenty of traffic to Quezaltenango via Cuatro Caminos or on to Huehuetenango. The old road itself continues more or less due north, rejoining the Pan-American highway about 40km before Huehuetenango – but there's very little traffic.

Climbing the Santa María Volcano

Due south of Quezaltenango, the perfect cone of the Santa María volcano rises to a height of 3772m. From the town only the peak is visible, but seen from the rest of the valley the whole cone seems to tower over everything around. The view from the top is, as you might expect, spectacular, and if you're prepared to sweat out the climb you certainly won't regret it. It's possible to climb the volcano as a day trip, but to really see it at its best you need to be on top at dawn, either sleeping on the freezing peak, or camping at the site below and climbing the final section in the dark by torchlight. Either way you need to bring enough food, water and stamina for the entire trip; and you should be acclimatised to the altitude before attempting it.

To get to the start of the climb you should take a local bus to **Llanos del Pinal**, a twenty-minute ride: they leave every hour or so between 7am and 5.30pm from the market side of the Minerva terminal. The village of Llanos del Pinal is set on a high plateau beneath the cone, and the bus driver will drop you at a crossroads from where you head straight down the road towards the right-hand side of the volcano's base. The track passes a small plaque dedicated to the Guatemalan Mountaineering Club and then bears up to the left, becoming a rocky trail. At the end of a confined rocky stretch (a few hundred metres in length) the path goes across an open grassy area and then curves further around to the left. All along this first section painted arrows mark the way – those painted with a fierce "NO" mean what they say and you should backtrack until you find an alternative.

As you push on, the path continues to climb around to the left, up a rocky slope and under some trees, arriving at a flat and enclosed grassy area about the size of small football pitch. There's a grass bank to the right, a wooded area to the left, and a big boulder at the other end. This point is about one and a half to two hours from the start, and an ideal place to **camp** if you want to make the final ascent in the hours before dawn. From here the path cuts off to the right, leaving from the start of this level patch of grass. (Another path goes across the grassy patch, but this isn't the one for you.) From here on the route is a little harder to follow, but it heads more or less straight up the side of the cone, a muddy and backbreaking climb of two or three hours: avoid the tempting alternative that skirts around to the right.

At the top the cone is a mixture of grass and volcanic cinder, usually frozen solid in the early morning. The highest point is marked by an altar where Indians burn copal and sacrifice animals, and on a clear day the **view** will take your breath away – as will the cold if you get here to watch the sun rise. In the early mornings the Quezaltenango valley is blanketed in a layer of cloud, and while it's still dark the lights of the city create a patch of orange glow. As the sun rises, its first rays eat into the cloud, revealing the land beneath. To the west, across a chaos of twisting hills, are the cones of Tajumulco and Tacaná, marking the Mexican border. But most impressive of all is the view to the east. Wrapped in the early morning haze are four more volcanic cones; two above Lake Atitlán, and two more above Antigua. The right-hand cone in this last pair is Fuego, which emits a stream of smoke, rolling down the side of the cone in the early morning. If you look south, you can gaze down over the smaller cone of **Santiaguito**, which has been in constant eruption since 1902. Every now and then it spouts a great grey cloud of rock and dust hundreds of metres into the air.

Towards the coast: hot baths

The most direct route from Quezaltenango to the coast takes you through a narrow gash in the mountains to the village of **ALMOLONGA**, sprawled around the sides of a steep-sided, flat-bottomed valley just 5km from Quezaltenango. Almolonga is Quiché for "the place where water springs", and streams gush from the hillside, channelled to the waiting crops. It's the market garden of the western highlands, where the flat land is far too valuable to live on, and is parcelled up instead into neat, irrigated sections.

In markets throughout the western highlands the women of Almolonga corner the vegetable trade. It's easy to recognise them, dressed in their bold, orange zig-zag *huipiles*, and wearing beautifully woven headbands. The village itself has markets on Wednesday and Saturday – the latter being the larger – when the plaza is ringed by trucks and crammed with people, while piles of food and flowers are swiftly traded between the two. The Almolonga market may not be Guatemala's largest, but it has to be one of the most frenetic, and is well worth a visit.

A couple of kilometres beyond the village lie **Los Baños**, where about ten different operations offer a soak in waters heated naturally by the volcano. Two good ones are *Fuentes Saludable* and *El Recreo*. For a dollar you get a private room, a sunken concrete tub, and enough hot water to drown an elephant. In a country of lukewarm showers it's paradise, and the baths echo to the sound of Indian families who queue barefoot for the pleasure of a good scrub. Below the baths is a communal pool, usually packed with local men, and a *pila* where the women wash their clothes in warm water. Between the baths and the village there's also a warm swimming pool below the road – follow the sign to *Agua Tibia* – which you can use for a small fee.

If on the other hand you'd prefer to immerse yourself in steam, then this too emerges naturally from the hillside. To get to the "*vapores*", as they're known, get off the bus halfway between Quezaltenango and Almolonga at the sign for LOS VAHOS, and head off up the track. Take the right turn after about a kilometre, follow this track for another twenty minutes, and you'll come to the steam baths. Here you can sweat it out for a while in one of the cubicles and then step out into the cool mountain air, or have a bracing shower to get the full sauna effect.

Buses to Almolonga run every twenty minutes from Quezaltenango, leaving from the Minerva terminal in Zona 3 and stopping to pick up passengers at the junction of 10 Avenida and 10 Calle in Zona 1. They pause in Almolonga itself before going on to the baths, which are open from 5am to 10pm, although the last bus back is at around 6pm. Beyond Los Baños the road heads through another narrow gully to join the main coast road in Zunil.

Cantel, Zunil and the Fuentes Georginas

Most buses to the coast avoid Almolonga, leaving Quezaltenango via the **Las Rosas junction** and passing through **CANTEL FABRICÁ**, an industrial village built up around an enormous textile factory. The factory's looms produce a range of cloths, using Indian labourers, German dyes, English machinery and a mixture of American and Guatemalan cotton. The village was originally known as Chuijullub, a Quiché word meaning "on the hill", and this original settlement (now called Cantel – Cantel Fabrica simply means "Cantel Factory") can still be seen on a height overlooking the works.

Further down the valley is **ZUNIL**, another centre for the production of vegetables. As at Almolonga, the village is split in two by the need to preserve the best land. The plaza is dominated by a beautiful colonial church with an intricate silver altar protected behind bars. The women of Zunil wear vivid purple *huipiles* and carry incredibly bright shawls, and for the Monday market the plaza is awash with colour. The village is reputed to be one of the few remaining places where Maximón, the evil saint, is still worshipped. The practice is frowned upon by the Catholic church, which makes the Indians reluctant to display their Judas, who's also known as Alvarado. However his image is usually paraded through the streets during Holy Week, dressed in western clothes and smoking a cigar.

In the hills above Zunil are the **FUENTES GEORGINAS**, another set of luxurious hot springs, state-owned and named after the dictator Jorge Ubico (1931–44). A turning to the left off the main road, just beyond the entrance to the village, leads up into the hills to the baths, 8km away. You can walk it in a couple of hours, or hire a truck from the plaza in Zunil for about $4.

The baths are surrounded by fresh green ferns, thick moss and lush forest, and to top it all there's a restaurant and bar beside the main pool. You can swim in the pool for 30¢ or rent a bungalow for the night for $9, complete with bathtub, double bed, fireplace and barbecue. In the rainy season it can be cold and damp, but with a touch of sunshine it's a beautiful place to spend the night.

Buses to Cantel and Zunil leave Quezaltenango from the small bus terminal in Zona 1, just behind the cathedral. They run every hour or so, the last bus back from Zunil leaving at around 5pm. All buses that run to and from the coast also pass through this way. Just below Zunil the road from Almolonga joins the main coastal highway, so you can easily walk between the two villages, a trek of little more than half an hour.

West to Ostuncalco, and to Coatepeque and the coast via San Martín Sacatepéquez

Heading west from Quezaltenango, a good paved road runs 15km along the valley floor, through SAN MATEO, to the prosperous village of **SAN JUAN OSTUNCALCO**, the commercial centre for this end of the valley. There's a large Sunday market that draws people from all the surrounding villages and where you can see locally made furniture, of wood and rope painted in garish primary colours. The village's other famous feature is the Virgen de Rosario, housed in the church, which is reputed to have miraculous powers for the granting of prayers. Barely 2km away, on the far side of the coast road, is the quiet and traditional village of **CONCEPCIÓN CHIQUIRICHAPA**, which has a very local market on Thursday, attended only by a few outsiders and conducted in hushed tones.

Buses and minibuses run every half-hour between Quezaltenango and Ostuncalco. Beyond the village the road splits, one branch running to Coatepeque on the coast, and the other over a high pass to San Marcos and San Pedro Sacatepéquez. The road to the coast climbs into the hills and through a gusty pass before winding down to **SAN MARTÍN SACATEPÉQUEZ**, also known as San Martín Chile Verde, an isolated Mam-speaking village set in the base of a natural bowl and hemmed in by steep, wooded hills. The village was abandoned in 1902 when the eruption of the Santa María volcano buried the land beneath a metre-thick layer of sterile pumice stone, killing thousands. These days both the people and the fertility have returned to the land, and the village is once again devoted to farming. The men of San Martín wear a particularly unusual costume; a long white tunic with thin red stripes, ornately embroidered around the cuffs, and tied around the middle with a red sash; the women wear beautiful red *huipiles* and blue *cortes*.

About an hour's walk from San Martín is **LAGUNA CHICABAL**, a spectacular lake set in the cone of the Chicabal volcano which is the site of Indian religious rituals. To get there head down the side of the church and turn right onto the track at the end, which takes you out of the village. When the track crosses a small bridge take the path that branches off to the right on the other side, and follow this as it goes up and over a range of hills, then drops down and bears around to the left – several kilometres from the village. Once over the lip the path carries on under a ridge and then crosses a flat pass before disappearing into the trees. Just as it enters the trees, take the smaller path that branches off to the right: this goes up through the forest and curves around to the right before finally cutting up to the left and crossing over into the cone itself. All of a sudden you pass into an different world, eerily still, disturbed only by the soft buzz of a hummingbird's wings or the screech of parakeets. From the rim the path drops precipitously, through thick, moist forest, to the water's edge, where charred crosses and bunches of fresh-cut flowers mark the site of ritual sacrifice. On May 3 every year *brujos* from several different tribes gather here for ceremonies to mark the fiesta of the Holy Cross: on this date especially, but to a lesser extent at any time, you should take care not to disturb any ceremonies that might be taking place – the site is considered holy by local Indians.

San Martín can be visited either as a day trip from Quezaltenango or on your way to the coast – if you want to stay, the woman who runs the *Farmacia Municipal* has a room that she rents out. **Buses** run along the road between Coatepeque and Quezaltenango every couple of hours, passing San Martín, with the last in either direction at about 5pm. From Quezaltenango buses for Coatepeque leave from the Minerva terminal in Zona 3.

Quezaltenango to Cuatro Caminos

Between the Cuatro Caminos junction and Quezaltenango, **SALCAJÁ**, a small *Ladino* town lined along the road, is one of Guatemala's main commercial weaving centres, producing much of the cloth used in the dresses worn by Indian women. The lengths of cloth are often stretched out by the roadside, either being prepared for dyeing or laid out to dry, and on market day they're an exceptionally popular commodity.

Salcajá's other claim to fame is that (according to some historians at least) it was the site of the first Spanish settlement in the country, and the church is therefore regarded as the first Catholic foundation in Guatemala. If you're staying in Quezaltenango and travelling out to the surrounding villages then the sight of Salcajá will become familiar as you pass through heading to and from Cuatro Caminos. But the ideal time to stop off is for the market on Tuesday.

A few kilometres beyond Salcajá the main road turns sharply to the right, beside a petrol station. At this point a dirt track branches off to the left, running to the edge of the valley and the village of **SAN ANDRÉS XECUL**. Bypassed by almost everything, and hemmed in on three sides by steep dry hills, it is to all appearances an unremarkable farming village. But two features set it apart. The first is little more than rumour and hearsay, set in motion by the artist Carmen Petterson when she was painting here in the 1970s. She claimed to have discovered that a "university" for Indian *brujos* was operating in the village, with young students of shamanism arriving from Quiché villages throughout the country. There's little sign of this when you're here, though, beyond perhaps an atmosphere which is even more hushed and secretive than usual. The second feature is the village church, a beautiful old building with incredibly thick walls. Its facade is painted an outrageous mustard yellow, with vines dripping plump, purple fruit, and podgy little angels scrambling across the surface. If you decide that you have to see it for yourself there are a few daily **buses** that leave the Minerva terminal in Quezaltenango for San Andrés, although the easiest way to get there is to take any bus as far as the petrol station beyond Salcajá and hitch a ride from there.

Cuatro Caminos and San Francisco Totonicapán

At **CUATRO CAMINOS** the Pan-American highway is met by the main roads from Quezaltenango and Totonicapán. This is the most important junction in the western highlands and you'll find all the usual characteristics of Guatemalan road junctions, including the cheap meals, the hustlers and the shanty-like *comedores*. More importantly, up until about 7pm there's a stream of buses heading for Quezaltenango, Huehuetenango, Guatemala City and smaller villages along the way. Wherever you are, this is the place to make for in search of a connection.

One kilometre to the west, the *Ladino* town of **SAN FRANCISCO TOTONICAPÁN** is built at the junction of the Río Sija and the Río Salama. Similar in many ways to Salcajá, San Francisco is a quiet place that holds a position of importance in the world of Indian tradition as a source of costumes for fiestas, which are rented out from various *Morerias*. If you'd like to see one of these you can drop in at 5 Calle 3–20, from where costumes are rented out for around $50 a fortnight, depending on their age and quality. The colonial church, which is on the other side of the river, has some fantastic ancient altars, including ornate silverwork and images of the saints. The market here is on Sunday, and **buses** going to San Francisco el Alto pass the village – these leave Quezaltenango from the small terminal in Zona 1, beside the cathedral.

San Francisco el Alto and Momostenango

From a magnificent hillside setting, the small market town of **SAN FRANCISCO EL ALTO** overlooks the Quezaltenango valley. It's worth a visit for the view alone, with the great plateau stretching out below, and the cone of the Santa María volcano marking the opposite side of the valley. At times a blanket of early-morning cloud fills the valley, and the volcanic cone, rising out of it, is the only visible feature.

The best time to visit San Francisco is for the **Friday market**, the largest weekly market in the country. Traders from every corner of Guatemala make the trip, many arriving the night before, and some starting to sell as early as 4am, by candlelight. Throughout the morning a steady stream of buses and trucks fills the town to bursting, and by midday the market is at its height, buzzing with activity.

The town is set into the hillside, with steep cobbled streets connecting the different levels, and two areas in particular are monopolised by specific trades. At the very top is an open field used as an animal market, where everything from pigs to parrots changes hands. The teeth and tongues of animals are inspected by the buyers, and at times the scene degenerates into a chaotic wrestling match, with pigs and men rolling in the dirt. Below this is the town's plaza, dominated by textiles. These days most of the stalls deal in imported denim, but under the arches and in the covered area opposite the church you'll find a superb selection of traditional cloth. Below this the streets are filled with vegetables, fruit, pottery, furniture, cheap *comedores*, and plenty more. By early afternoon the numbers start to thin out, and by sunset it's all over – until the following Friday.

There are plenty of **buses** from Quezaltenango to San Francisco, leaving every twenty minutes or so from the small bus terminal in Zona 1 beside the cathedral – the first is at 6am, and last bus back leaves at about 5pm. If you'd rather stay in the town itself then there are two **hotels**. The cheaper is the *Hospedaje San Francisco* on the main street, a roughish sort of place that charges $1; the *Hotel Vista Hermosa*, a block or so below the plaza, is a much smarter option, charging $2. As its name suggests, some of the rooms (especially at the front) really do have magnificent views.

Momostenango

Up above San Francisco a dirt road continues over the ridge, dropping down on the other side through lush pine forests. The road is deeply rutted, and the journey painfully slow, but within an hour you arrive in **MOMOSTENANGO**. This small and isolated town is the centre of wool production in the highlands, and *Momostecos* travel throughout the country peddling their blankets, scarves and rugs. Years of experience have made them experts in the hard sell, and given them a sharp eye for tourists. The wool is also used in a range of traditional costume, including the short skirts worn by the men of Nahualá and the jackets of Sololá. The ideal place to buy Momostenango blankets is in the Sunday market, which fills the town's two plazas.

A visit at this time will also give you a glimpse of Momostenango's other feature, its rigid adherence to tradition. Opposite the entrance to the church, on a small fire, people make offering of incense and alcohol, muttering their appeals to the gods. The town is famous for this unconventional folk-Catholicism, and it has been claimed that there are as many as 300 Indian shamen working here. Momostenango's religious **calendar** is, like only one or two other villages, still based on the 260-day *Tzolkin* year (which is made up of thirteen 20-day months and has been in use since Mayan times). The most celebrated ceremony is *Guaxaquib Batz*, "Eight Monkey", which marks the beginning of a new year. Originally this was a purely pagan ceremony, starting at dawn on the first day of the year, but the Church have muscled in on the action and it now starts with a Catholic service the night before. The next morning the people make for Chuitmesabal, "little broom", a small hill about 2km to the west of the town. Here offerings of broken pottery are made before age-old altars (Momostenango's name means "the place of the altars"). The entire process is overseen by *brujos*, shamen who are responsible for communicating with the gods. At dusk the ceremony moves to Nim Mesabal, "big broom", where the *brujos* pray and burn incense throughout the night.

As a visitor, however, even if you could plan to be in town at the right time, you'd be unlikely to see any of this, and it's best to visit Momostenango for the market, or for the fiesta on August 1. If you decide to stay for a day or two then you can take a walk to the *riscos*, a set of bizarre sandstone pillars, or beyond to the **hot springs** of PALA CHIQUITO. The springs are about 3km away to the north, and throughout the day weavers work there washing and shrinking their blankets – it's always best to go early, before most people arrive and the water is discoloured by soap.

There are two **hotels** in Momostenango, the *Hospedaje Roxana* on the main plaza and the *Hospedaje Paclom*, up the hill above the smaller plaza, and there's really not much to choose between them. Both are simple, cheap and clean. There are plenty of small *comedores* on the main plaza, and the *Hospedaje Paclom* also has a restaurant.

Buses to Momostenango run from Quezaltenango, passing through San Francisco el Alto on the way. They leave from the Minerva terminal in Quezaltenango every hour or so from 10am to 4pm, and from Momostenango from 6am to 3pm. On Sunday a special early morning bus leaves Quezaltenango at 6am: you can catch this at the *rotunda*, a roundabout at the eastern the edge of town (although you'll need to take a taxi as far as the *rotunda*).

Totonicapán

TOTONICAPÁN, capital of one of the smaller departments, is reached down a direct road leading north from Cuatro Caminos. Surrounded by rolling hills and pine forests, the town stands at the heart of a heavily populated and intensely farmed little region. There is only one point of access and the valley has always held out against outside influence, shut off in a world of its own. In 1820 it became the scene of one of the most famous **Indian rebellions**. The early part of the nineteenth century had been marked by a series of revolts throughout the area, and particularly in Momostenango and Totonicapán; in 1820 the largest of these erupted, sparked by demands for tax. The Indians expelled all of the town's *Ladino*s, crowning their leader Atanasio Tzul the "king and fiscal king", and making his assistant, Lucas Aquilar, president. His reign lasted only 29 days before it was violently suppressed.

Today, Totonicapán is a quiet place whose faded glory is ruffled only by the Tuesday market, which fills the two plazas to bursting. Until fairly recently a highly ornate traditional costume was worn here. The women's *huipiles* were some of the most elaborate and colourful in the country, and the men wore trousers embroidered with flowers, edged in lace, and decorated with silver buttons. Today, however, all this has disappeared and the town has instead become one of the chief centres of commercial weaving. Along with Salcajá it produces much of the *Jasped* cloth worn as skirts by the majority of Indian women: the machine-made *huipiles* of modern Totonicapán are used throughout the highlands as part of the universal Indian costume. On one side of the old plaza is a workshop where young men are taught to weave on treadle looms, and visitors are always welcome to stroll in and take a look around. The building is labelled *Centro de Capacitacion Artesanal, Cooperativa Kato Kirl*. This same plaza is home to the crumbling municipal theatre, a grand Neoclassical structure echoing that in Quezaltenango. On the second square is the modern *Banco de Guatemala*.

There are good conections between Totonicapán and Quezaltenango, with buses shuttling back and forth every half-hour or so. If you want to stay you have a choice of two hotels. The *Hospedaje San Miguel*, 8 Avenida 7–49, is the grander, charging around $3, the *Pension Blanquita* is cheaper – a friendly and basic place opposite the petrol station at 3 Avenida and 4 Calle. **Buses** for Totonicapán leave Quezaltenango from the small terminal in Zona 1, down the side of the cathedral. Entering the village you pass one of the country's finest *pilas* (communal washing places), ringed with Gothic columns.

The Department of San Marcos

Leaving Quezaltenango to the west the main road heads out of the valley through **San Mateo** and **Ostuncalco** and climbs a massive range of hills, dropping down on the other side to the village of PALESTINA DE LOS ALTOS. Beyond this it weaves through a U-shaped valley to the twin towns of San Marcos and San Pedro Sacatepéquez. These towns form the core of the country's westernmost department, a neglected region that once served as a major trade route, and includes Guatemala's highest volcano and a substantial stretch of its border with Mexico.

San Pedro Sacatepéquez and San Marcos

SAN PEDRO SACATEPÉQUEZ is the larger and busier of the two towns, a bustling and unattractive commercial centre with a huge plaza that's the scene of a market on Thursday and Sunday. In days gone by this was a traditional Indian settlement, and famed for its brilliant yellow weaving, in which silk was used. Over the years the town has been singled out for some highly questionable praise; in 1543 the King of Spain, Carlos V, granted the headmen special privileges as thanks for their assistance during the conquest, and in 1876 the town was honoured by President Rufino Barrios, who with a stroke of his pen raised the status of the people from Indians to *Ladinos*.

A dual carriageway road connects San Pedro with its sister town of San Marcos, 2km to the west. Along the way, a long-running dispute about the precise boundary between the two towns has been solved by the construction of the departmental headquarters at **La Union**, halfway between the two. The building, known as the **Maya Palace**, is an outlandish and bizarre piece of architecture that goes some way to compensate for the otherwise unrelenting blandness of the two towns. The structure itself is relatively sober, but its facade is covered in imitation Maya carvings. Elaborate decorative friezes run around the sides, two great roaring jaguars guard the entrance, and above the main doors is a fantastic clock with Maya numerals and snake hands. Minibuses run a continuous shuttle service between the two towns, and they'll drop you at the Maya Palace if you want to take a look.

SAN MARCOS, officially the capital of the department, once stood proud and important on the main route to Mexico, but these days articulated lorries roar along the coastal highway and the focus of trade has shifted to San Pedro, leaving San Marcos to sink into provincial stagnation. There's little to detain you in either of these towns, other than a trip into the mountainous countryside to the north. But if you're passing through, the market in San Pedro and the Maya Palace are worth a look, and a few kilometres away there's a spring-fed swimming pool where you can while away an hour or two: to get there walk from the plaza in San Pedro down 5 Calle in the direction of San Marcos, and turn left in front of the Templo de Candelero along 2 Avenida. Follow this road through one valley and down into a second, where you take the left turn to the bottom. The pool – marked simply as *Agua Tibia* – is open from 6am to 6pm, and there's a small entrance fee.

Most of the activity and almost all the transport are based in San Pedro so it's best to stay in one of the **hotels** here. The cheapest, at $1, is the *Pension Mendez*, a very basic place at 4 Calle and 6 Avenida. The *Hotel Samaritano*, 6 Avenida 6–44, is a clean but characterless modern building, though definitely better than the *Hotel Bagod*, 5 Calle and 4 Avenida – both charge around $2. In San Marcos the *Hotel Palacio*, on 7 Avenida opposite the police station, is an amazing old place, friendly, decaying and cheap ($1), with big, musty rooms and peeling wallpaper. There's also a relatively luxurious hotel, the *Perez*, at 9 Calle 2–25 – it charges around $4.

For **eating** there are plenty of cheap *comedores* in San Pedro, fewer in San Marcos. The latter, though, makes up for it with the restaurant *Mah Kik*, an elegant, subdued and fairly expensive place behind the *Chevron* station. Both towns have **cinemas**: the *Cine T-manek* on the plaza in San Pedro, and the *Cine Carua*, beside the *Hotel Perez* in San Marcos. There are **banks** on both plazas.

Second-class **buses** run hourly from San Pedro to Malacatán, Quezaltenango (both 1hr 30min) and Guatemala City, between 5am and 5pm, from a small chaotic terminal one block behind the church. *Marquensita* pullmans go direct from San Marcos to Guatemala City, passing through the plaza in San Pedro, at 2am, 2.30am, 3am, 6.30am, 9am, 11am, noon, 1.30pm and 3pm: in the capital, they leave from 21 Calle 12–41, Zona 1 at 4.30am, 6.30am, 8.30am, 10am, 11am, noon, 1.30pm, 3.30pm and 5pm.

To Tacaná and the high country

To the northwest of San Pedro is some magnificent high country, strung up between the Tajumulco and Tacaná volcanoes, and forming an extension of the Mexican Sierra Madre. A rough dirt road runs through these mountains, connecting a series of isolated villages that lie exposed in the frosty heights.

Leaving San Pedro the road climbs steeply, winding up through thick pine forests, and emerging onto a high grassy plateau. Here it crosses a great boggy expanse to skirt around the edge of the **Tajumulco volcano** whose 4210-metre peak is the highest in Guatemala. It's best climbed from the roadside hamlet of TUCHAN, from where its about four hours to the summit, not a particularly hard climb as long as you're acclimatised to the altitude.

Up here the land is sparsely inhabited, dotted with adobe houses and flocks of sheep and goats. The rocky ridges are barren and the trees twisted by the cold. At this altitude the air is thin and what little breath you have left is regularly taken away by the astonishing views which – except when they're consumed in the frequent mist and cloud – open up at every turn. The village of **IXCHIGUÁN**, on an exposed hillside at 3050m, is the first place of any size, surrounded by bleak rounded hills and in the shadow of the two towering volcanic cones. Buses generally stop here for lunch, giving you a chance to stretch your legs and thaw out with a steaming bowl of *caldo*.

Moving on, the road climbs to the **CUMBRE DE COTZIL**, a spectacular pass that marks the highest point on any road in Central America. From here on it's downhill all the way to the scruffy village of **TACANÁ**, a flourishing trading centre that marks the end of the road – 73km from San Marcos and less than 10km from the Mexican border. Cross-border ties are strong and at the end of 1988 the inhabitants threatened to incorporate themselves into Mexico if the road to San Pedro wasn't paved, claiming that this had been promised to them by the Christian Democrats in the run-up to the 1985 election. Up above the village, spanning the border, is the **Tacaná volcano** (4064m), which can be climbed from the village of SIBINAL. It last erupted in 1855, so it should be safe enough. Unless you're setting out to climb one of the volcanoes there's not much to do out this way, but the bus ride alone, bruising though it is, offers some great scenery. Three **buses** a day leave the terminal in San Pedro for Tacaná, at 10am, 11am and noon, returning at 3am, 4am and 5am. The trip takes about five hours, and there is also a bus service to Sibinal and Concepción Tutiapa – at similar times. In Tacaná there's a simple unmarked *pension* in the green house next to *Foto Estudio Galvez*.

Towards the Mexican border

The main road through San Pedro continues west, through San Marcos and out of the valley. Here it starts the descent towards the Pacific plain, dropping steeply around endless hairpin bends and past acre after acre of coffee bushes. Along the way the views towards the ocean are superb. Eventually you reach the sweltering lowlands, passing through SAN RAFAEL and EL RODEO with their squalid shacks for plantation workers. About an hour and a half out of San Pedro you arrive in **MALACATÁN**, a relatively sedate place by coastal standards. If you get stuck here on your way to or from the border, try the *Pension Lucía* or the *Hotel America*, both on the plaza and both charging around $2. Contrary to popular belief, there is no Mexican Consul in Malacatán.

Buses between Malacatán and San Marcos run every hour from 5am to 5pm. From Malacatán to the border at Talisman (see p.156) trucks and minibuses run every half-hour, and plenty of pullmans pass through on their way between the border and the capital. *Galgos*, for example, go to Guatemala City at 5am, 8.30am, 10am, noon, 3.30pm and 5.30pm.

HUEHUETENANGO AND THE CUCHUMATANES

The **department of Huehuetenango**, slotted into the northwest corner of the highlands, is a wildly beautiful part of the country that's bypassed by the majority of visitors. The area is dominated by the mountains of the **Cuchumatanes**, but the department also includes a limestone plateau in the west and a strip of dense jungle to the north. The vast majority of this is inaccessible to all but the most dedicated of hikers, but there's plenty that's easy to see too.

The Pan-American highway, cutting through from **Cuatro Caminos** to the **Mexican border**, is the only paved road in the department, and if you're heading through this way you'll get a glimpse of the mountains, and perhaps a vague sense of the isolating influence of this massive landscape.

With more time and energy to spare, a trip into the mountains to **Todos Santos**, or even all the way out to **San Mateo Ixtatán**, reveals an exceptional wealth of Indian culture. It's a world of jagged peaks and deep-cut valleys, where Spanish is definitely the second language and traditional costume is still rigidly adhered to. Heavily populated before the conquest, the area now has pre-Columbian ruins scattered throughout the hills, with the largest at **Zaculeu**, immediately outside **Huehuetenango**. Despite the initial devastation, the arrival of the Spanish had surprisingly little impact here, and traditional ways are still well preserved. A visit to these mountain villages, either for a market or fiesta (and there are plenty of both) offers one of the best opportunities to see Indian life at close quarters.

Heading on from Huehuetenango you can be at the **Mexican border** in a couple of hours, reach **Guatemala City** in five or six, or use the back roads to travel across the highlands through **Aguacatán** towards **Santa Cruz del Quiché**, **Nebaj** or **Cobán**.

From Cuatro Caminos to Huehuetenango

Heading west from Cuatro Caminos, the Pan-American highway climbs steadily, passing the entrance to **San Francisco el Alto** and stepping up out of the Xela valley onto a broad plateau thick with fields of wheat and dotted with houses. The only village along the way is **POLOGUA**, where they have a small weekly market, a *pension* – the *Pologuita* – and a fiesta from the 21st to the 27th of August.

About a kilometre before the village, an unmarked dirt track leads north to **SAN BARTOLO**, a small agricultural centre down amongst the pine trees, some 12km from the road. The place is virtually deserted during the week, but on Sundays the farmers who live scattered in the surrounding forest gather in the village for the market. There's a small unmarked *pension* and some thermal springs a couple of kilometres away. Another track, branching from the first a couple of kilometres before San Bartolo, connects the village with Momostenango, which is about two hours' walk, and there is a bus service between San Bartolo and Quezaltenango. (From Quezaltenango to San Bartolo there are buses at noon, 3pm, 4pm and 5pm, all going back again between 6am and 6.30am.)

Beyond Pologua the road turns towards the north and leaves the corn-covered plateau, crossing the crest of the hills and skirting around the rim of a huge sweeping valley. To the east a superb view opens out across a sea of pine forests, the last stretch of levellish land before the mountains to the north. Way out there in the middle is **Santa Cruz del Quiché** and closer to hand, buried in the trees, is **Momostenango**. Once over the ridge the road winds its way down towards Huehuetenango. The first place inside the department is the *Ladino* village of **Malacatancito**, where Mam warriors first challenged the advancing Spanish army in 1525.

Huehuetenango: the Town

In the corner of a small agricultural plain, five kilometres from the main road at the foot of the mighty Cuchumatanes, **HUEHUETENANGO**, capital of the department of the same name, is the focus of trade and transport for a vast area. Nonetheless its atmosphere is provincial and relaxed. The name is a Nahuatl word meaning "the place of the old people", and before the arrival of the Spanish it was the site of one of the residential suburbs that surrounded the Mam capital of Zaculeu. Under colonial rule it was a small regional centre with little to offer other than a steady trickle of silver, and a stretch or two of grazing land. The supply of silver dried up long ago, but other minerals are still mined, and coffee and sugar have been added to the area's produce.

Today's town has two quite distinct functions – and two contrasting halves – each of which serves a separate section of the population. The large majority of the people are *Ladino*s, and for them Huehuetenango is an unimportant regional centre far from the hub of things; a mood which is summed up in the unhurried atmosphere of **the plaza**, where shaded walkways are surrounded by administrative offices. This is the heart of the *Ladino* half of town. Overlooking it, perched above the pavements, are a shell-shaped bandstand, a clock tower and a grandiose Neoclassical church, a solid whitewashed structure with a facade that's crammed with Doric pillars and Grecian urns. In the middle of the plaza there's a **relief map** of the department with flags marking the villages – the details are vague and the scale a bit warped, but it gives you an idea of the mass of rock that dominates the region, and the deep river valleys that slice into it.

A few blocks to the east, the town's atmosphere could hardly be more different. Here the neat little rows of arches are replaced by the pale green walls of the **market**, hub of the Indian part of town, and the streets are crowded with traders, drunks and travellers, shuffling between buses as they make their way to and from the mountains, or set off for the coast in search of work. This part of Huehuetenango, centred on 1 Avenida, is always alive with activity, its streets packed with people from every corner of the department and littered with rotten vegetables.

Arrival, departure and orientation

Like all Guatemalan towns, Huehuetenango is laid out on a strict grid pattern, with avenidas running one way and calles the other. It's fairly small so you shouldn't have any real problems finding your way around, particularly once you've located the plaza.

Arriving, you'll probably find yourself on 1 Avenida, which is four blocks to the east of the plaza, and where you'll find the main concentration of **second-class bus** companies. When it comes to **leaving**, it's again on 1 Avenida that you'll find a bus to the Mexican border (2hr), Quezaltenango (3hr) or Guatemala City (6hr), with departures every hour or so from 5am to around 4pm – although there tends to be more traffic in the mornings. If you want to go to Antigua, Lake Atitlán or Chichicastenango, take a bus heading for Guatemala City and change buses at the appropriate junction (Los Encuentros for Chichicastenango and Lake Atitlán, Chimaltenango for Antigua). The times for other second-class buses, to the nearby villages, are listed under the relevant sections. *El Condor*, at 5 Avenida 1–

15, is one of the few second-class bus companies that isn't on 1 Avenida. They run buses to Guatemala City at 4am, 8am, 9.30am, 11am and 1pm, and to La Mesilla at 6am, 10am, 2pm and 4pm.

For a faster and more luxurious service, **pullman buses** leave from offices in other parts of the city. *Los Halcones*, 7 Avenida 3–62, run pullmans to Guatemala City at 7am and 2pm, and *Rapidos Zaculeu*, 3 Avenida 5–25, have departures to the capital at 6am and 3pm.

There is a vague plan to move all the bus companies to a new purpose-built **bus terminal** halfway between the Pan-American highway and town, which might have happened by the time you read this, in which case local buses will ferry people to and from the centre of town.

Getting to Huehuetenango you'll probably be coming from elsewhere in the highlands, in which case you might be able to pick up a direct bus somewhere along the Pan-American highway – or you can catch any bus to Cuatro Caminos, from where you'll be able to find a bus for Huehuetenango. There's also a regular service, with hourly departures, from the terminal in Quezaltenango.

Coming direct **from Guatemala City** the best way to travel is by pullman. *Los Halcones*, 7 Avenida 15–27, Zona 1, in Guatemala City, run buses at 7am and 2pm; *Rapidos Zaculeu*, 9 Calle 11–42, Zona 1, at 6am and 3pm; and *El Condor*, 19 Calle 2–01, Zona 1, have second-class buses five times a day. There are also fairly regular departures, every two hours or so, from the main bus terminal in Zona 4. Coming from the **Mexican border** at La Mesilla there's a bus every hour from 4am to 4pm.

Sleeping and eating

For those on a really tight budget, Huehuetenango has an abundance of incredibly cheap **hotels**. Most of these are clustered around 1 Avenida and crowded with Indian traders, but they're scruffy, chaotic places with little to recommend them. Better rooms are in shorter supply, and are mostly in the streets immediately around the plaza. The *Hotel Central*, at 5 Avenida 1–33, is good, with large rooms in a creaking old wooden building and a fantastic *comedor* downstairs, although with a bus company on one side and a disco on the other it can at times be hard to get a good night's sleep. Double rooms go for $3 – there are no singles but there are larger, multi-bedded rooms. The *Pension Familiar*, 4 Calle 6–83, is similarly priced, but also has some more expensive rooms with private showers. If you're looking for something more upmarket, the *Hotel Maya*, 3 Avenida 3–53, is a modern hotel charging around $5; or there's the *Hotel Zaculeu*, 5 Avenida 1–14 opposite the *Central*, which has comfortable rooms off a beautiful leafy courtyard and charges around $10.

Similarly most of the better **restaurants** are in the central area around the plaza. *Las Brasas*, 4 Avenida 5–11, serves Chinese food, reasonably good but not all that cheap. There are also three places along 2 Calle, just off the plaza, which are all fairly reasonable; the *Ebony* and *Los Alpes* both do sandwiches and hamburgers, and the *Maxi Pizza* does just what you'd expect it to. Perhaps the best places to eat, though, are the *Pizza Hogareña*, 6 Avenida 4–45, and the *Restaurante Rincon*, 6 Avenida A 7–21. Both are under the same management and offer the same delicious sandwiches, churrascos, fruit juices and pizzas. For cheap Guatemalan-style food the market area has plenty of *comedores* or there's the *Hotel Central* which does very tasty, cheap set meals, including a particularly good breakfast served from 7.30am.

Other practicalities

The **post office** is at 2 Calle 3–54 (regular mail service round the back), and the
Guatel office, for long-distance phone calls, is right next door. For **changing
money** there's *Banco de Guatemala* on the plaza at 6 Avenida and 3 Calle, and a
collection of other banks, including the *Banco del Cafe*, *Bandesa* and the *Banco del
Ejercito*, at the junction of 5 Avenida and 4 Calle. The **Mexican Consulate** is in the
Farmacía El Cid, which is on the plaza at 5 Avenida and 4 Calle: here they'll charge
you $1 for a tourist card that's usually free at the border. Huehuetenango's only
language school is the *Fundacion 23*, 7 Calle 6–23, and if you want to avoid the
student overkill of Antigua this is certainly a good place to learn. The best place to
do your **laundry** is *Lavandería San Vicente*, 8 Avenida 2–39 (8am–noon & 2–5pm;
half day Sat). Finally **shopping**: superb weaving is produced throughout the
department, and it can be bought here in the market, or at a shop on 5 Avenida
opposite the *Hotel Central*, where both the prices and the quality are high. If you
have time, though, you'd be better advised to travel to the villages and buy direct
from the producers.

Zaculeu

A few kilometres to the west of Huehuetenango are the ruins of **ZACULEU**, capital of the Mam, who were one of the principal pre-conquest highland tribes. The
site (daily 8am–6pm; free) includes several large temples, plazas and a ball court,
but unfortunately it has been restored with an astounding lack of subtlety (or
accuracy). The walls and surfaces have been levelled off with a layer of thick

white plaster, leaving them stark and undecorated. The entire site looks more like an ageing film set than an ancient ruin. There are no roof-combs, carvings or stucco mouldings, and only in a few places does the original stonework show through. Even so, the site does have a peculiar atmosphere of its own and is well worth seeing: surrounded by trees and neatly mown grass, with fantastic views of the mountains, it's an excellent spot for a picnic.

Not all that much is known about the early history of Zaculeu as no Mam records survived the conquest. The site is thought to have been a religious and administrative centre housing the elite, while the bulk of the population lived in small surrounding settlements or scattered in the hills. Zaculeu was the hub of a large area of Mam speakers, its boundaries reaching into the mountains as far as Todos Santos and along the Selegua and Cuilco valleys, an area throughout which Mam is still the dominant language today.

When it comes to putting together a history of the site you have to rely on the records of the Quichés, a more powerful neighbouring tribe. According to Quiché mythology, the Quichés conquered most of the other highland tribes, including the Mam, some time between 1400 and 1475. The Popol Vuh tells that, "our grandfathers and fathers cast them out when they inserted themselves among the Mam of Zakiulew". In 1475 the Quiché leader Quicab died. Under his rule the Quichés had maintained their authority, but once he died the subjugated tribes began to break away from the fold. As a part of this trend the Mam

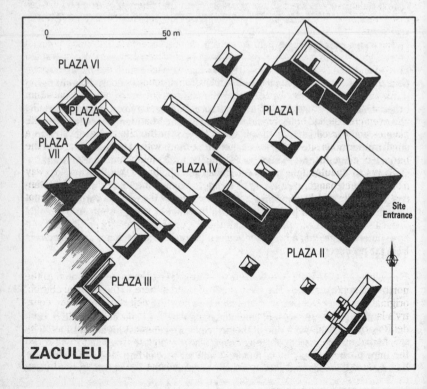

0   50 m

PLAZA VI

PLAZA V

PLAZA VII

PLAZA I

PLAZA IV

Site Entrance

PLAZA II

PLAZA III

N

ZACULEU

managed to reassert their independence, but no sooner had they escaped the clutches of one expansionist empire than the Spanish arrived with a yet more brutal alternative.

For the first few months the Spaniards devoted themselves to conquering the Quiché, who were still the dominant force in the highlands. But once they'd achieved this they turned their attention to the Mam, especially after they were told by Sequechul, leader of the Quichés, that a plan to burn the Spanish army in Utatlán had been suggested to his father by Caibal Balam, king of the Mames. As his answer, Pedro de Alvarado despatched an army under the command of his brother Gonzalo to mete out punishment. They were met by about 5000 Mam warriors near the village of Malacatancito, and promptly set about a massacre. Seeing that his troops were no match for the Spanish, Caibal Balam withdrew them to the safety of Zaculeu, where they were protected on three sides by deep ravines, and on the other by a series of walls and ditches. The Spanish army settled in outside the city, preparing themselves for a lengthy siege, while Gonzalo offered the Indians a simple choice – they either became Christians "peacefully" or faced "death and destruction".

Attracted by neither option they struggled to hold out against the invading force. At one stage a relief army of 8000 arrived from the mountains, but again they were unable to ruffle Gonzalo's well disciplined ranks. Finally, in mid-October, after about a month and a half under siege, his army starving to death, Caibal Balam surrendered to the Spanish. With the bitterest of ironies a bastardised version of his name has been adopted by one of Guatemala's crack army regiments – the "Kaibils".

The ruins of Zaculeu owe their current appearance to a latter-day colonial power, the *United Fruit Company*, under whose auspices they were reconstructed in 1946 and 1947. The company is, of course, notorious for its heavy-handed practices throughout Central America, and this reconstruction is no exception.

Excavations at the site have unearthed hundreds of burials carried out in an unusual variety of ways; bodies were crammed into great urns, interred in vaults and even cremated. These burials, and artefacts found at the site including pyrite plaques and carved jade, have suggested links with the site at Nebaj. There's a small **museum** on site (daily 8am–noon and 1–6pm) with examples of some of the burial techniques used and some interesting ceramics found during excavation.

To get to Zaculeu take one of the trucks and minibuses that head out this way from Huehuetenango, picking up passengers outside the *Rico Mac Pollo* restaurant at 4 Calle and 3 Avenida. Usually these go all the way to the ruins, if not make sure they at least point you in the right direction when they drop you.

Chiantla

The village of **CHIANTLA** is backed right up against the mountains 5km to the north of Huehuetenango. The main point of interest here is the colonial church, originally built by Dominican friars, which is now the object of one of the country's largest pilgrimages, made annually on February 2 to its image of the Virgen del Rosario. Legend has it that the image of the Virgin was given to the church by a Spaniard named Almengor, who owned a silver mine in the hills. Not only did the mine proceed to yield a fortune, but on his last visit to it, just after Almengor had surfaced, the entire thing caved in – thus proving the power of the Virgin.

She is also thought to be capable of healing the sick, and at any time of the year you'll see people who've travelled from all over Guatemala asking her assistance. A mural inside the church depicts a rather ill-proportioned Spaniard watching over the Indians toiling in his mines, while on the wall opposite the Indians are shown discovering God. The precise connection between the two is left somewhat vague, but presumably the gap is bridged by the Virgin. **Buses** from Huehuetenango to Chiantla leave from 1 Avenida and 1 Calle, running every twenty minutes between 6am and 6.30pm.

The Cuchumatanes

The **Cuchumatanes**, rising to a frosty 3600m just to the north of Huehuetenango, are the largest non-volcanic peaks in Central America. The mountain chain rises from a limestone plateau close to the Mexican border, reaches its full height above Huehuetenango, and falls away gradually to the east, continuing through northern Quiché to form part of the highlands of Alta Verapaz. Appropriately enough the name translates as "that which was brought together by great force", from the Mam words *cucuj*, to unite, and *matan*, superior force.

The mountain scenery is magnificent, ranging from exposed craggy outcrops to lush river valleys. The upper slopes are barren, scattered with boulders and shrivelled cypress trees, while the lower levels are richly fertile, cultivated with corn, coffee and sugar. Between the peaks, in the deep-cut valleys, are hundreds of tiny villages, isolated by the enormity of the landscape. This area had little to entice the Spanish, and even at the best of times they only managed to exercise vague control, occasionally disrupting things with bouts of religious persecution or disease, but rarely maintaining a sustained presence. Following the initial impact of the conquest, the people were, for the most part, left to revert to their old ways, and their traditions are still very powerful today, showing through in the fiestas, costumes and folk-Catholicism.

More recently the mountains have been the scene of bitter fighting between the army and the guerrillas. In the late 1970s and early 1980s the area was struck by a wave of violence and terror that sent thousands fleeing across the border to Mexico. These days things have calmed down, and some families have returned from exile, but many remain in refugee camps on the other side of the border. It is, however, once again safe to travel into the mountains, discovering some of the country's most spectacular scenery and fascinating villages. A single rough road runs through the range, climbing the steep south face, crossing the exposed central plateau, and dropping into the isolated valleys to the north. Travel here is not easy – the distances are large, hotels and restaurants basic at best, buses are packed and frequent cloudbursts often make the roads impassable – but if you can summon the energy it's an immensely rewarding area, offering a rare glimpse of Indian life and including some of the country's finest fiestas and markets. The mountains are also ideal for hiking, particularly if you've had enough of struggling up volcanoes.

The most accessible of the villages, and the only one to receive a steady trickle of tourists, is **Todos Santos**, which is also one of the most interesting. At any time of year the Saturday market here is well worth a visit, and the fiesta on November 1 has to be one of the most outrageous in Guatemala. Once established, you can walk over the hills to **San Juan Atitán** and **Santiago Chimaltenango**, or head on down the valley to **San Martín** and **Jacaltenango**. Further into the mountains are the villages of **Soloma** and **San Mateo Ixtatán**, both of which have markets on Thursday and Sunday. Another good hike takes you from **San Miguel Acatán** along the edge of the hills to **Jacaltenango**. Beyond San Mateo Ixtatán the road comes to an end at **Barillas**, a *Ladino* town from where the jungle lowlands beyond are being colonised.

Huehuetenango to Barillas

Heading north out of Huehuetenango the road for the mountains passes through Chiantla before starting to climb the arid hillside, and as the bus sways around the switchbacks the view across the valley is superb. In the distance you can sometimes make out the perfect cone of the Santa María volcano, towering above Quezaltenango some 60 kilometres to the south.

At the top of the slope the road slips through a pass into the *región andina*, a desolate grassy plateau suspended between the peaks, strewn with boulders and segregated with neat earth walls. At this height the air is cool, thin and fresh, the ground often hard with frost and occasionally dusted with snow. In the middle of the plain is the *Comedor de los Cuchumatanes*, where buses stop for a chilly lunch before pressing on through PAQUIX, junction for the road to Todos Santos.

Beyond Paquix the road runs through a couple of magical valleys, where great grey boulders are scattered between ancient-looking oak and cypress trees, their trunks gnarled by the bitter winds. A few families manage to survive the rigours of the altitude up here, collecting firewood and tending flocks of sheep. Sheep have been grazed here since they were introduced by the Spanish, who prized this wilderness as the best pasture in Central America.

Continuing to the north the road gradually winds down off the plateau, emerging on the other side at the top of an incredibly steep valley. Here the track clings to the hillside, cut out of the sheer rock face that drops hundreds of metres to the valley floor. This northern side of the of the Cuchumatanes contains some of the most dramatic scenery in the entire country, and the road is certainly the most spine-chilling. A little further down, as if to confirm your worst fears, the rusting wreck of a bus lies a hundred metres or so beneath the road.

The first village that the road reaches is **SAN JUAN IXCOY**, an apple-growing centre drawn out along the valley floor. There's no particular reason for breaking the journey here, but there is a small *pension*, where you can get a bed and a meal. In season, around the end of August, passing buses are besieged by an army of fruit-sellers. The history of this innocent-looking village is marked by violence. On the night of July 17, 1898, following a dispute about pay, the Indians of San Juan murdered the local labour contractor, and in a desperate bid to keep the crime secret they slaughtered all but one of the village's *Ladino* population. The authorities responded mercilessly, killing about ten Indians for the life of every *Ladino*. In local mythology the revolt is known as *la degollación*, the beheading.

Over another range of hills and down in the next valley is **SOLOMA**, largest, busiest and richest of the villages in the northern Cuchumatanes, with a population of around 3000. Its flat valley floor was once the bed of a lake, and the steep hillsides still come sliding down at every earthquake or cloudburst. Soloma translates (in Kanjobal, the dominant language on this side of the mountains) as "without security", and its history is blackened by disaster; it was destroyed by earthquakes in 1773 and 1902, half burnt down in 1884, and decimated by smallpox in 1885. The long white *huipiles* worn by the women of Soloma are similar to those of San Mateo Ixtatán and the Lacandones, and are probably as close as any in the country to the style worn before the conquest. These days they are on the whole worn only for the market days, on Thursday and Sunday: yet again this is far the best time to visit.

About four hours from Huehuetenango, Soloma makes a good place to break the trip. The *Río Lindo* is a good, friendly hotel ($3) that also does food, or there's the cheaper *Hotel Central* ($1), or as a last resort the *Hospedaje San Juan*. A microbus for Soloma leaves Huehuetenango at 11.30am, from the *Hospedaje San Jorge* at the bottom of 1 Avenida. It returns in the middle of the night. Buses going on to San Rafael La Independencia and Barillas also pass through.

Leaving Soloma the road climbs again, on a steadily deteriorating surface, over another range of hills, to the hillside village of SANTA EULALIA. Beyond this it pushes on, past the junction to SAN RAFAEL LA INDEPENDENCIA, and through another misty, rock-strewn forest. On the other side it emerges at **SAN MATEO IXTATÁN**, the most traditional, and for me the most interesting, of this string of villages. Little more than a thin sprawl of wooden-tiled houses on an exposed hill-side, it's strung out beneath a belt of ancient forest and craggy mountains. The people here speak Chuj, and form part of a tribe of Indians who occupy the extreme northwest corner of the highlands and some of the jungle beyond. Their territory borders on that of the Lacandones, a jungle tribe never subjugated by the Spanish, who constantly harassed these villages in colonial times. The only industry is the manufacture of salt from some communally owned springs in the hills, and life at these heights is hard at the best of times. The only time to visit, other than for the fiesta on September 21, is on a market day, Thursday or Sunday. The rest of the week the village is virtually deserted. The women here wear unusual and striking *huipiles*, long white gowns embroidered in brilliant reds, yellows and blues, radiating out from a star-like centre. The men wear short woollen tunics called *capixays*, often embroidered with flowers around the collar and quetzals on the back. Below the village is a beautiful Maya ruin, the unrestored remains of a small pyramid and ball court, shaded by a couple of cypress trees. If you stay, there's an extremely basic *pension* – don't expect sheets – and a *comedor*.

Beyond San Mateo the road drops steadily to **BARILLAS**, a *Ladino* frontier town in the relative warmth of the lowlands. Further still, the land slopes into the Usumacinta basin through thick, uninhabited jungle. Rough tracks penetrate a short distance into this wilderness (and a local bus runs out as far as San Ramón), opening it up for farming, and eventually a road will run west across the **Ixcán** (the wilderness area that stretches between here and the jungles of the Petén) to PLAYA GRANDE. For the moment, however, this land is still hotly fought over, with some of the surviving guerrillas hiding out in the forest. The cheapest place to stay in Barillas is the *Tienda las Tres Rosas*, which charges around $1, and the best is the *Hotel Monte Cristo* at double the price.

Buses to Barillas, passing through all the villages en route, leave Huehuetenango at midnight, 1.45am and 3.30am, taking around four hours to reach Soloma and at least eight hours to Barillas. All buses leave from 1 Avenida in Huehuetenango, and it's well worth buying your ticket in advance as they operate a vague system of seat allocation. It's a rough and tortuous trip, the buses usually filled to bursting, and the road invariably appalling. Buses leaving Barillas for Huehuetenango depart at the same times as those going the other way, and the bus companies also have offices in Barillas, where you can get a ticket in advance.

San Rafael La Independencia, San Miguel Acatán and on foot to Jacaltenango

Between Santa Eulalia and San Mateo Ixtatán a branch road cuts off to the left, heading over the spine of the Cuchumatanes and curving around the other side to **SAN RAFAEL LA INDEPENDENCIA**, a small village perched on a cold outcrop. In San Rafael you'll find a couple of *comedores* and a Thursday market but nowhere to stay: however, if you ask in the office of the bus company they'll usually be able to find you a concrete floor on which you can rest your weary bones. The next morning you can walk on down the valley, following the road or taking the path towards the larger village of **SAN MIGUEL ACATÁN**. Here there's a Sunday market and a small *pension* in the house behind the Municipalidad. It may be possible to get a bus this far – *Rutas San Rafael* have services leaving Huehuetenango at 2am and 11am, returning at 11.30pm and 2am, and taking around eight hours – but when the road is bad they often go no further than San Rafael.

From San Miguel Acatán a spectacular walk takes you along the edge of the mountains to JACALTENANGO (p.144). Setting out from San Miguel, cross the river and follow the trail that bears to the right as it climbs the hill opposite. At the fork, halfway up, take the higher path that crosses the ridge beside a small shelter. On the other side it drops down into the head of the next valley. Here you want to follow the path down the valley on the near side of the river, and through the narrow gorge to an ancient wooden bridge. Cross the river and climb up the other side of the valley, heading down towards the end of it as you go. The path that heads straight out of the valley runs to NENTÓN, and the other path, up and over the ridge to the left, heads for Jacaltenango. Along the way there are scintillating views of the rugged peaks of the southern Cuchumatanes and the great flat expanse that stretches into Mexico – on a clear day you can see the Lagunas de Montebello, a good 50 kilometres away on the other side of the border. On the far side of the ridge the path eventually drops down to Jacaltenango through the neighbouring village of San Marcos Huista: some eight or nine tough but worthwhile hours in all from San Miguel.

Todos Santos and a hike over the mountains to San Juan Atitán and Santiago Chimaltenango

If you turn off at the **Paquix** junction, about 20km from Huehuetenango, you can follow a road heading west to **TODOS SANTOS**. This western road slopes down through **La Ventosa**, a narrow gully lined with pine and cedar trees, where almost immediately you'll begin to see the traditional red costume of Todos Santos: the men in their red-and-white striped trousers, black woollen breeches and brilliantly embroidered shirt collars; the women in dark blue *cortes* and superbly intricate red *huipiles*. Further down, at the bottom of the steep-sided, deep-cut river valley, is the village itself – a single main street with a few *tiendas*, a plaza, a church and a loose collection of houses and corn fields. Above the village flocks of sheep are grazed and below it the crops are farmed. It's a pretty typical highland village, but better known than most because of the writer Maud Oakes (whose *The Two Crosses of Todos Santos* was published in 1951) and the photographer Hans Namuth, who has been recording the faces of the villagers for over forty years – some of his pictures have recently been published in a book, *Los Todos Santeros* (Nishan, 1989).

As usual, most of the people the village serves don't actually live here. The immediate population is probably around 1200, but there are perhaps ten times that many in the surrounding hills who are dependent on Todos Santos for trade, supplies and social life. This population is more than the land can support, and many travel to the coast in search of work. All over the country you'll see them, always dressed in *traje* – traditional costume. However there's one event that brings them all home, the famous November 1 **fiesta** for All Saints (Todos Santos). For three days the village is taken over by unrestrained drinking, dance and Marimba music. The whole event opens with an all-day horse race, which starts out as a massive stampede. The riders tear up the course, thrashing their horses with live chickens, pink capes flowing out behind them. At either end of the run they take a drink before burning back again. As the day wears on some riders retire, collapse, or tie themselves on, leaving only the toughest to ride it out. On the second day, "The Day of the Dead", the action moves to the cemetery, with Marimba bands and drink stalls setting up amongst the graves for a day of intense ritual that mixes grief and celebration. On the final day of the fiesta the streets are littered with bodies and the jail packed with brawlers.

If you can't make it for the fiesta then the Saturday market, although nothing like as riotous, also fills the village, and the night before you might catch some Marimba. During the week the village is fairly quiet, although it's a pleasant and peaceful place to spend some time and the surrounding scenery is superb. Above the village – follow the track that goes up behind the *Comedor Katy* – is the small Maya site of **Tojcunanchén**, where you'll find a couple of mounds sprouting pine trees. The site is occasionally used by *brujos* for the burning of incense and the ritual sacrifice of animals. Todos Santos is one of the few places where people are still said to use the 260-day *Tzolkin* Calendar, which dates back to Maya times.

There are two **hotels** in the village, which charge well under $1 and are usually full during the fiesta – so arrive early. The *Hospedaje La Paz* has one solid double bed and some smaller cots, and *Los Olguitas* has plenty of tiny rooms suspended in a wooden maze above the kitchen – you can either eat here or at the *Comedor Katy* in the corner of the plaza, both of which are simple but good. **Buses** leave Huehuetenango for Todos Santos at 11.30am and 12.30pm from the *Pension San Jorge*, near the junction between 1 Avenida and 4 Calle – get there early to mark your seat. They carry on through the village, heading further down the valley, and pass through Todos Santos on their way back to Huehuetenango at 5am and 6am.

Three hikes from Todos Santos

The scenery around Todos Santos is some of the most spectacular in all Guatemala and there's no better place to leave the roads and set off on foot. In a day you can walk across to **San Juan Atitán**, and from there continue to the Pan-American highway or head on to **Santiago Chimaltenango**. If you go to the highway you'll be able to catch a bus back to Huehuetenango for the night, and if you make it to Santiago you shouldn't have any problem finding somewhere to stay. This is the more interesting walk, particularly if you set out early on a Thursday morning and arrive in San Juan before the market there has finished.

Alternatively you can walk down the valley from Todos Santos to **San Martín** and on to **Jacaltenango**, a route which offers superb views. In Jacaltenango there's a hotel, so you can stay the night and then catch a bus back to Huehuetenango in the morning.

Walking to San Juan Atitán

The village of **SAN JUAN ATITÁN** is about four hours away, across a beautiful isolated valley. The walk follows the path that bears up behind the *Comedor Katy*, passes the ruins and climbs steeply above the village through endless muddy switchbacks, bearing gradually across to the right. You reach the top of the ridge after about an hour. From here you drop down, past some huts, to cut straight across the head of the next valley. The route takes you up and down endless exhausting ridges, through lush green forests, and over a total of five gushing streams – only the first and third of which are bridged. Beside the first of these, about an hour and a half out of Todos Santos, is an ideal campsite, a flat patch of grass right by the water. The valley is thinly inhabited, and mostly used by the people of San Juan to graze their sheep. Having crossed the valley the path swings up to the left and on to the top of another pass, about three hours from Todos Santos. From here you can see the village of San Juan, strung out along the steep hillside in a long thin line. To head down into the village follow one of the left-hand trails that goes out along the hillside, and then drops down amongst the houses. There are several alternative paths – all cross a series of deep ravines before emerging onto the main track that runs through the village.

San Juan, built on treacherously unstable land, is regularly hit by landslides that sweep whole houses into the valley below. The government has proposed that the entire village be moved, but the people have so far resisted this idea. It's an intensely traditional place: all the men wear long woollen coats (similar in style to the habits worn by Spanish friars), red shirts and plain white trousers. The high-backed sandals worn by both the men and the women, and also by a lot of people in Todos Santos, are a style depicted in ancient Maya carving – they are also worn in some of the villages around San Cristóbal de las Casas in Mexico. Like most of these mountain villages, San Juan is active only on market days, Monday and Thursday.

Maya sandal taken from classic stone carving

There's nowhere to stay in the village so, unless you walk on to Santiago Chimaltenango, make your way back to Huehuetenango before night. The road that leads on down the valley finds its way to the Pan-American highway, about three hours' walk from the village, following the side of the valley and then dropping sharply down to the main road. If you want to walk the other way – from San Juan to Todos Santos – or just walk from San Juan to Santiago Chimaltenango, two pick-ups leave Huehuetenango for San Juan – a two-hour trip – some time after 11am, from the *Cafeteria Tacaná* at 2 Calle 2–15 (from San Juan for Huehuetenango they leave at around 5am).

On to Santiago Chimaltenango

SANTIAGO CHIMALTENANGO makes a good alternative destination, with the added bonus of somewhere to stay at the end. The newly built visitors' accommodation should be finished by now: if not, speak to the mayor (*alcalde*) who will let you stay in the Municipalidad. If you want to go straight here from Todos Santos, turn right when you reach the top of the pass overlooking San Juan, head along the side of the hill and over another pass into a huge bowl-like valley. The village lies on the far side. If you're coming from San Juan, follow the track straight through the village and you'll come to the same pass in just over an hour.

From the top of the pass, follow the main track down into the valley as it bears around to the right, toward the village, around one and a half hours from the top. Although not as traditional as the other villages of the region, Santiago is nevertheless a beautiful old place, a compact mass of narrow cobbled streets and adobe houses.

Two **buses** a day run between Huehuetenango and Santiago, leaving Huehuetenango at noon from the *Hospedaje San Jose* – at the bottom of the dip on 1 Avenida – and returning from Santiago at 5am. If you don't want to catch the early morning bus out of Santiago you can walk on down the valley through coffee plantations to the village of SAN PEDRO NECTA, and beyond to the Pan-American highway, which should take two or three hours.

Hiking from Todos Santos to San Martín and Jacaltenango

Heading down the valley from Todos Santos the road comes to the one-street village of **SAN MARTÍN**, three hours away. The village is inhabited entirely by *Ladinos*, but it has a Friday market that attracts Indians from the land all around, including many from Todos Santos. A little beyond the village the road down the valley divides, with a right fork that leads 11km around the steep western edge of the Cuchumatanes. On a clear day there are spectacular views reaching well into Mexico. At the road's end, on a rocky outcrop, is the poor and ragged village of **CONCEPCIÓN**: the final destination of one of the Todos Santos buses, which arrives here at around 7pm, and leaves for the return to Huehuetenango at about 3am. Passing through Concepción the track doubles back beneath itself, heading around the side of the valley as it drops a thousand metres or so to the small town of Jacaltenango.

Perched on a plateau overlooking the limestone plain that stretches out across the Mexican border, **JACALTENANGO** is the heart of an area that was once very traditional, inhabited by a small tribe of Jacaltec speakers. However in recent years the surrounding land has been planted with coffee and waves of *Ladinos* have swelled the population of the town. Today the place has a calm and prosperous feel to it. There are two *pensiones* – one in the large *tienda* on the corner of the plaza and the other up the hill opposite it – and plenty of cheap *comedores* along the side of the market, which is at its busiest on Sunday.

The town can also be reached by road, along a branch route that leaves the Pan-American highway close to the Mexican border. **Buses** leave Huehuetenango for Jacaltenango at 5am and noon (from 2 Calle 2–35) and return from Jacaltenango to Huehuetenango at 3am and 10am.

East to Aguacatán and Sacapulas

To the east of Huehuetenango, a dirt road turns off at Chiantla to weave along the base of the Cuchumatanes, through dusty foothills, to **AGUACATÁN**. This small agricultural town is strung out along two main streets, shaped entirely by the dip in which it's built. The village was created by Dominican friars, who in the early years of the conquest merged several smaller settlements inhabited by two distinct peoples. The remains of one of the pre-conquest settlements can still be seen a couple of kilometres to the north, and minute differences of dress and dialect still linger – indeed the village remains loosely divided along pre-Columbian lines, with the Chalchitecs to the east of the market and the Aguatecs to the west. The language of Aguateca (used by both) is spoken only in this village and its immediate surrounds, by a population of around 15,000. During the colonial period gold and silver were mined in the nearby hills, and the Indians are said to have made bricks of solid gold for the king of Spain, to persuade him to let them keep their lands. These days the town is still steeped in tradition and the people survive by growing vegetables, including huge quantities of garlic, much of it for export.

Aguacatán's huge Sunday **market** gets under way on Saturday afternoon, when traders arrive early to claim the best sites. On Sunday morning a steady stream of people pours down the main street, cramming into the market and plaza, and soon spilling out into the surrounding area. Around midday the tide turns as the crowds start to drift back to their villages, with donkeys leading their drunken drivers. Despite the scale of the market its atmosphere is subdued and the pace unhurried: for many it's as much a social event as a commercial one.

The traditional costume worn by the women of Aguacatán is for the most part unusually simple: their skirts are made of dark blue cotton and the *huipiles*, which hang loose, are decorated with bands of coloured ribbon on a plain white background. This plainness, though, is set off by the local speciality – the *cinta*, or headdress, in which they wrap their hair; an intricately embroidered piece of cloth combining blues, reds, yellows and greens.

Aguacatán's other attraction is the source of the **Río San Juan**, which emerges from beneath a nearby hill, fresh and cool. The source itself, bubbling up beneath a small bush and then channelled between concrete walls, looks a bit disappointing to the layman (though as far as a caver or geologist is concerned it's a big one) but if you have an hour or two to kill it's a good place for a chilly swim – for which you have to pay a tiny fee. To get there walk east along the main street out of the village for about a kilometre, until you see a sign directing you down a track to the left. Follow this round a sharp bend to the left and then take the right turn, towards the base of the hills. From the village it takes about twenty minutes.

Both minibuses and regular **buses** run from Huehuetenango to Aguacatán. The minibuses leave (every twenty minutes or so on market day, but only in the mornings otherwise) from the Calvario in Huehuetenango, at the junction of 1 Avenida and 1 Calle; the first bus leaves 1 Avenida at 10am, and the last at about 4pm. The 25-kilometre journey takes around an hour. In Aguacatán the best place to stay is the *Hospedaje Aguateco*, a simple little place with small rooms off a courtyard, which charges around a dollar. If that's full then try the *Hospedaje La Paz*. **Beyond Aguacatán** the road runs out along a ridge, with fantastic views stretching out below. Eventually it drops down into the Río Chixoy valley, to the riverside town of **SACAPULAS** (p.96).

West to the Mexican border

From Huehuetenango the Pan-American highway runs for 79km through the narrow Selegua valley to the Mexican border at La Mesilla. Travelling direct this takes about two and a half hours, and buses thunder out of Huehuetenango every hour or so between 5am and 4pm. Along the way, just off the main road, are some interesting traditional villages largely oblivious to the international highway that carves through their land. Most are best reached as day trips out of Huehuetenango.

The first of these is SAN SEBASTIAN HUEHUETENANGO, a quiet little place barely 200 metres north of the highway. The village was the site of a pre-conquest centre, and of a settlement known as Toj-Jol, which was swept away by the Río Selegua in 1891. Further on the road runs through a particularly narrow part of the valley known as **El Tapón**, the cork, and past a turning for San Juan Atitán (12km) and another for SAN RAFAEL PETZAL, 2km from the main road. Beyond this it passes roads that lead to Colotenango, Nentón and Jacaltenango, all of which are covered below.

There's just one last roadside village, LA DEMOCRACIA, before **LA MESILLA** and the border. The two sets of customs and immigration are just a short walk apart here, and on the Mexican side you can pick up buses which run through the border settlement of **Ciudad Cuauhtemoc** to **Comitán** or even direct to **San Cristóbal de las Casas**. Heading into Guatemala the last bus leaves La Mesilla for Huehuetenango at around 4pm, but if you manage to get stuck there's a small hotel on the Guatemalan side. Wherever you're heading in Guatemala it's best to take the first bus to Huehuetenango and catch another from there.

Colotenango, San Ildefonso Ixtahuacán, and Cuilco

The most important of the villages reached from the highway is **COLOTENANGO**, perched on a hillside a kilometre or so from the main road. The municipality of Colotenango used to include San Rafael and San Ildefonso, until 1890 when they became villages in their own right. The ties are still strong, however, and the red *cortes* worn by the women of all three villages are almost identical. Colotenango also remains the focal point for all of the smaller settlements, and its Saturday market is the largest in the Selegua valley. From early Saturday morning the plaza is packed, and the paths that lead into the village are filled with a steady stream of traders, Indian families, cattle, chickens, reluctant pigs and the inevitable drunks. Here you'll see people from all of the surrounding villages, and most of them will be wearing traditional costume. The village is also worth visiting during Holy Week, when elaborate and violent re-enactments of Christ's Passion take place (the bravest of villagers takes the role of Judas, and is shown no mercy by the rest), and for its fiesta from the 12th to the 15th of August.

To get to Colotenango from Huehuetenango take any bus that's heading towards the Mexican border, and ask them to drop you at the village. They'll usually leave you on the main road just below, from where you have to cross the bridge and walk up the hill. The journey from Huehuetenango takes around 45 minutes.

On to San Ildefonso and Cuilco

Behind Colotenango a dirt road goes up over the hills and through a pass into the valley of the Río Cuilco. Here it runs high above the river along the top of a ridge, with beautiful views up the valley: below you can make out the tiny village of SAN GASPAR IXCHIL, which consists of little more than a church and a graveyard.

Another few kilometres brings you to the larger village and mining centre of **SAN ILDEFONSO IXTAHUACÁN**. Similar in many ways to Colotenango, it has a large and traditional Indian population; but in 1977 the place achieved a certain notoriety after the miners were locked out of the mine because they'd tried to form a union. In response to this they decided to walk the 260km to Guatemala City, and put their case to the authorities. At the time this was a bold gesture of defiance and it captured the imagination of the entire nation. When they eventually arrived in the capital one hundred thousand people turned out to welcome them.

Beyond San Ildefonso the road slopes down towards the bottom of the valley and crosses the river before arriving at **CUILCO**, 36km from the Pan-American highway, a sizeable *Ladino* town marking the end of the road. The Mexican border is only 15km away, and the town maintains cross-border trade links both inside and outside the law. Beyond today's village are the ruins of an earlier settlement known as Cuilco Viejo. Three **buses** a day run between Huehuetenango and Cuilco, and if you come out this way you'll probably end up having to stay: the *Hospedaje Osorio*, which charges around a dollar, is on the main street.

Cuilco has also earned itself something of a reputation, although this time it's for producing heroin. As a result of the successful anti-drug campaigns in Mexico, poppy growers have moved across the border, and the American *Drug Enforcement Agency* has estimated that the area may provide enough opium to supply three times the number of heroin addicts in the US. Crop spraying programmes, which were suspended in 1988 after the planes were shot at, were restarted in the middle of 1989 using specially protected aircraft.

North to Nentón and Jacaltenango

A short distance before the border, from the roadside village of **CAMOJA GRANDE**, a dirt road leads off to the north, heading parallel to the border. It runs across a dusty white limestone plateau to the village of **NENTÓN**, and right up into the extreme northwest corner of the country to the **GRACIAS A DIOS**. There are buses (three a day to Jacaltenango, one or two to Gracias a Dios), but the only possible reason to venture out this way would be to walk back into the Cuchumatanes. Halfway between the Pan-American highway and Nentón, at a dreary junction called **Cuatro Caminos**, a branch road heads west towards the mountains, through lush foothills, passing the entrance to SANTA ANA HUISTA, continuing through rich coffee country to SAN ANTONIO HUISTA (with the *Pension Victoria* should you want to stay), and ending up in **Jacaltenango**, from where you can walk to Todos Santos (see p.40). The trip out to Jacaltenango takes you into some beautiful country, but as it's something of a dead end there's little point in heading out here unless you plan a hike into the mountains.

fiestas

The western highlands are the home of the traditional Guatemalan fiesta. Every village and town, however small, has its own saint's day, and based on this it has a fiesta that can last anything from a single day to two weeks. All of these involve traditional dances that mix pre-Columbian moves with more modern Spanish styles, and each fiesta has its own speciality, whether it's a horse race or a firework spectacular. Travelling in the western highlands at any time of year you'll find a fiesta or two coincides with your trip, and it's well worth

going out of your way to get to one of these. It's here that you'll get the best idea of the true strength of Indian culture and the vitality that lies at its heart.

January

January is a particularly active month, and the fiesta year kicks off in the western highlands in **Santa María de Jesus**, near Antigua, where they have a fiesta from the 1st to 5th, with the main action on the first two days. The fiesta is as traditional as the village and includes plenty of dancing and a procession in honour of the sweet name of Jesus. In **El Tumbador**, in the department of San Marcos, there's a fiesta from the 3rd to 8th, and in **San Gaspar Ixchil**, a tiny village on the road to Cuilco in the department of Huehuetenango, they have their fiesta from the 3rd to 6th. In **Sibilia**, in the department of Quezaltenango, they have a fiesta from the 9th to 15th, with the main day on the 13th, and **Santa María Chiquimula**, near Totonicapán, has its fiesta from the 10th to 16th, in honour of the Black Christ of Esquipulas. **Nentón**, to the northwest of Huehuetenango, has a fiesta from the 13th to 16th, and **La Libertad**, to the west of Huehuetenango, from the 12th to 16th. In the central highlands **Chinique**, to the east of Santa Cruz del Quiché, has a very traditional fiesta from the 12th to 15th, with the final day as the main day. **Colomba**, in the department of Quezaltenango, has a fiesta from the 12th to 16th. The village of **San Antonio Llotenango**, which is to the west of Santa Cruz del Quiché, has its fiesta from the 15th to 17th, with the last day as the main day. **San Sebastián Coatan**, in the department of Huehuetenango, has a fiesta from the 18th to 20th. **El Tejar**, on the Pan-American highway near Chimaltenango, has a fiesta from the 18th to 20th, with the final day as the main day, and **Santa Lucía La Reforma**, in the department of Totonicapán, has its fiesta from the 19th to 21st. The village of **Ixtahuacán**, which is on the road to Cuilco in the department of Huehuetenango, has a traditional fiesta from the 19th to 24th. **San Pablo La Laguna**, on the shores of Lake Atitlán, has a fiesta from the 22nd to 26th, with the main day on the 25th. **San Pablo**, in the department of San Marcos, has its fiesta from the 23rd to 27th. The village of **Chiantla**, which is just to the north of Huehuetenango, has its fiesta from the 28th January to 2nd February, with the final day as the main day, and finally **Jacaltenango**, to the west of Huehuetenango, also has a fiesta that starts on the 28th and goes on until the 2nd of February.

February

The celebratory season in February starts in **Cunen**, in the department of Quiché, with a fiesta from the 1st to 4th, with the main day on the 2nd. **Ostuncalco**, in the department of Quezaltenango, has a fiesta on the 8th. **Santa Eulalia** in Huehuetenango, has its fiesta from the 8th to 13th, with the main day on the 8th, and **Patzite**, in Quiché, has a fiesta from the 6th to 10th, in which the main action is also on the 8th. **Antigua** has a fiesta to celebrate the first Friday in Lent, as does **Palestina de Los Altos**, in the department of San Marcos.

March

In March fiestas are relatively scarce. Things start off in **San Jose El Rodeo**, in the department of San Marcos, where they have a fiesta from the 14th to 20th, with the main day on the 19th. **La Democracía**, between Huehuetenango and the Mexican border, has a movable fiesta sometime during the month. **San Jose Paoquil**, which is near Chimaltenango, has a fiesta on the 19th. The second Friday in Lent is marked by fiestas in **Chajul** and **La Democracía**. Holy Week is celebrated throughout the country but with extreme fervour in **Antigua**.: here the main processions are marched over carpets of painted sawdust and involve huge numbers of people engulfed in clouds of incense. **Santiago Atitlán** is also worth visiting during Holy Week to see Maximón paraded through the streets, usually on the Wednesday.

April

San Marcos has its fiesta from the 22nd to 28th, with the main day on 25th, **San Jorge La Laguna** on the 24th, and **San Marcos La Laguna** on the 25th. **Barillas**, far to the north of Huehuetenango, has a fiesta from 29th April to 4th May, and both **Zacualpa** and **Aguacatán** have moveable fiestas to mark forty days from Holy Week: **Zacualpa** also has a moveable fiesta at some stage during the month. Finally **La Esperanza**, in the department of Quezaltenango, has its fiesta from 30th April to 4th May.

May

Cajola, a small village in the department of Quezaltenango, has its fiesta from the 1st to 3rd, with the final day as the main day. **Uspantán** has a busy and traditional fiesta from the 6th to 10th, with the main day on the 8th. **Santa Cruz La Laguna**, on the shores of Lake Atitlán, has its fiesta from the 8th to 10th, with the main day on the last day, as does **Santa Cruz Balanya**, in the department of Chimaltenango. **Patzún** has a fiesta on the 20th.

June

Things start to hot up again in June, starting in **San Antonio Palopó**, to the east of Panajachel, which has a fiesta from the 12th to 14th, with the main day on the 13th. The same days are celebrated in **San Antonio Huista**, while **San Juan Ixcoy**, in the department of Huehuetenango, has its fiesta from the 21st to 25th, with the main day on the 24th. **Olintepeque**, a few kilometres from Quezaltenango, has its fiesta from the 21st to 25th. Towards the end of the month there are two very interesting fiestas high up the mountains: the first, at **San Juan Cotzal**, a very traditional village to the north of Nebaj, lasts from the 22nd to 25th, with the main day on the 24th; the second, in **San Juan Atitán** near Huehuetenango, runs from the 22nd to 26th, with the main day on the 24th. **Comalapa**, near Chimaltenango, has a fiesta on the 24th; **San Juan la Laguna**, on the shores of Lake Atitlán, from the 23rd to 26th, with the main day on the 24th; **San Pedro Sacatepéquez** from the 24th to 30th; and the isolated village of **Soloma**, to the north of Huehuetenango, from the 26th to 30th, with the main day on the 29th. At the end of the month three villages share the same dates; **Yepocapa** in the department of Chimaltenango, **San Pedro Jocopilas** to the north of Santa Cruz del Quiché, and **San Pedro La Laguna** on Lake Atitlán all have fiestas from the 27th to 30th, with the main day on the 29th. Finally in **Almolonga**, near Quezaltenango, there's a fiesta from the 28th to 30th, with the main day on the 29th, which is always a good one. Corpus Christi celebrations, held throughout Guatemala at some stage in June, are particularly spectacular in **Patzún**.

July

In July things start off in **Santa María Visitación**, near Sololá, where they have a fiesta from the 1st to 4th, with the main day on the 2nd. In **Huehuetenango** there's a fiesta from the 12th to 17th, and in **Momostenango** from the 21st July to 4th August, a particularly traditional celebration that is well worth going out of your way for, especially on the 25th. The village of **Tejutla**, high above San Marcos, has a fiesta from the 22nd to 27th, with the main day on the 25th, as does **San Cristóbal Totonicapán**, in the department of Totonicapán. **Chimaltenango** has a fiesta from the 22nd to 27th, with the main day on 26th; **Malacancito**, a small *Ladino* town

on the border of the department of Huehuetenango, celebrates from the 23rd to 26th, with the last day as the main day; **Santiago Atitlán** has its excellent fiesta from the 23rd to 27th, most enjoyable on the 25th; and **Antigua** has a one-day fiesta on the 25th in honour of Santiago. **Patzicía** has a fiesta from the 22nd to 27th, with the main day on the 27th, and **Santa Ana Huistan**, in the department of Huehuetenango, has its fiesta from the 25th to 27th, with the main day on the 26th. Finally **Ixchiguan**, in the department of San Marcos, has a fiesta from the 29th to 31st, in which the final day is the main day.

August

August is a particularly good month for fiestas and if you're in the central area you can visit three or four of the very best. The action starts in **Sacapulas**, which has a fiesta from the 1st to 4th, with the last day as the main day. **Santa Clara La Laguna** has its fiesta from the 10th to 13th, with the main day on the 12th. **Joyabaj** has its fiesta from the 9th to 15th, with the last day as the main day. This is the first of August's really special fiestas and fills Joyabaj with Indians from throughout the valley: traditional dances here include the *Palo Volador*, in which men swing from a huge pole. The second major fiesta is in **Sololá**, from the 11th to 17th, with the main day on the 15th. This is another massive event and also well worth visiting for a day or two. The next is in **Nebaj**, a spectacular spot at any time of the year, where the fiesta is from the 12th to 15th, with the main day on the last day. In **Colotenango**, near Huehuetenango, they have a fiesta from the 12th to 15th, with the final day as the main day. **Cantel**, near Quezaltenango, has a fiesta from the 12th to 18th, with the main day on the 15th, and **Tacaná** has a fiesta from the 12th to 15th, with the main day on the 15th. In **Santa Cruz del Quiché** there's a fiesta from the 14th to 19th, with the main day on the 18th, and in **Jocotenango** the fiesta is for a single day on the 15th. **San Bartolo** has its fiesta from the 18th to 25th, climaxing on the 24th, while **Salcajá** has a fiesta from the 22nd to 28th, with the principal day on the 25th. **Sipacapa**, in the department of San Marcos, has its fiesta from the 22nd to 25th, and **Sibinal**, also in the department of San Marcos, has its fiesta from the 27th to 30th, with the main day on the 19th.

September

The fiesta in **Quezaltenango** lasts from the 12th to 18th, with the main day on the 15th. **San Mateo**, to the west of Quezaltenango, has a fiesta on the 21st, **San Mateo Ixtatán**, to the north of Huehuetenango, from the 17th to 21st, with the last day as the main day, and the departmental capital of **Totonicapán** from the 24th to 30th, with the main day on the 29th. **San Miguel Acatán**, in the department of Huehuetenango, has a fiesta from the 25th to 30th, with the main day also on the 29th. Finally **Tecpán** has its fiesta from 26th September to 5th October.

October

The action in October starts up in **San Francisco el Alto**, which has its fiesta from the 1st to 6th, with its main day on the 4th. **Panajachel** has a fiesta from the 2nd to 6th, which also has its main day on the 4th. **San Lucas Toliman**, on the shores of Lake Atitlán, has its fiesta from the 15th to 20th, with the main day on the 18th. Finally the fiesta in **Todos Santos**, one of the best in the country, starts on the 21st of October and continues into the first few days of November. The 29th is the main day and includes a wild and alcoholic horse race, while on the 1st the action moves to the village's cemetery.

November

The 1st is the scene of intense action in **Todos Santos** (see above) and in **Santiago Sacatepéquez**, where they fly massive paper kites in the village cemetery. **San Martín Jilotepeque** has its fiesta from the 7th to 12th, with the main day on the 11th. **Malacatancito**, in the department of Huehuetenango, has a fiesta from the 14th to 18th, with the last day as the main day. **Nahualá** has a very good fiesta from the 23rd to 26th, with the main day on the 25th. **Santa Catarina Ixtahuacán**, in the department of Sololá, has its fiesta from the 24th to 26th, with the principal day on the 25th. **Zunil** has a fiesta from the 22nd to 26th, again with the chief action on the 25th, and **Santa Catarina Palopo** has a fiesta on that day. Finally **Cuilco**, **San Andrés Semetabaj**, **San Andrés Itzapa** and **San Andrés Xecul** all have their fiestas from the 27th November to 1st December. The main day in Cuilco is on the 28th, and in all the San Andréses on the 30th.

December

Santa Barbara, in the department of Huehuetenango, has its fiesta from the 1st to 4th, culminating on the final day. **Huehuetenango** has a fiesta from the 5th to 8th, again with the last day as the main one, as does **Concepción Huista**, in the department of Huehuetenango. **Concepción**, in the department of Sololá, has its fiesta from the 7th to 9th, and **Malacatán**, in the department of San Marcos, has a fiesta from the 9th to 14th. **Santa Lucía Utatlán**, in Sololá, has its fiesta from the 11th to 15th, with the main day on the 13th. **Chichicastenango** has its fiesta from the 13th to 21st, with the last day as the main day. This is another very large and impressive fiesta, with an elaborate procession and a mass of fireworks. Chichicastenango's sister village, **Chiche**, has its fiesta from the 25th to 28th, with the last day as the main day. From the 7th December men dressed as devils chase around highland towns, particularly in those around Quezaltenango, and the night of the 7th is celebrated with bonfires throughout the country – The Burning of the Devil.

travel details

Travel in the western highlands is fairly straightforward, and moving along the Pan-American highway there's an almost constant stream of buses heading in both directions: certainly between about 8am and 6pm you should never have to wait more than twenty minutes. The main towns are generally just off the highway, and it's the main connections to these that are covered below: other, more local schedules, have been given in the text. The best way to explore the western highlands is to base yourself in one of these main towns and then do a series of day trips into the surrounding area.

Buses

Antigua and Chimaltenango

Direct buses from **Guatemala City to Antigua** (45min) run every half-hour from 18 Calle and 4 Avenida in Zona 1 (between 3am & 6pm). The service is less regular at weekends, when the first buses leave at around 7am. Buses to Antigua **from Chimaltenango** (the junction through which you must pass to reach the rest of the highlands) leave every hour from 5.30am to 6.30pm. One daily bus to Antigua also leaves **Escuintla**, from the terminal at 7am.

From Antigua buses to Guatemala City every half-hour from 3am to 6pm – 7am to 6pm at weekends. Buses **to Chimaltenango** (1hr) leave hourly from 5.30am and 5.30pm. The times of buses to local villages around Antigua are listed in the text. Heading between Antigua and other places in the western highlands you need to go to Chimaltenango to catch another bus: they run every ten minutes or so to and from the Zona 4 terminal in Guatemala City, and heading west you can hop onto any of the passing buses to Quiché, Panajachel, Quezaltenango or Huehuetenango. Buses to **Tecpán**, **Patzicía** and **Patzún** pass through Chimaltenango every hour or so. .

Santa Cruz del Quiché and Chichicastenango

Buses for Santa Cruz via Chichicastenango leave **Guatemala City** every hour or so from 5am to 5pm. In Santa Cruz they leave from the main bus terminal and in Guatemala City from the terminal in Zona 4. Along the way they can be picked up in Chimaltenango or at **Los Encuentros**, the junction for this part of the country. **From Santa Cruz del Quiché** buses to **Nebaj** leave Santa Cruz at 9am and 10am, returning at 3am. Buses to **Uspantán**, which all pass through **Sacapulas**, leave Santa Cruz at 9am, 11am and 3pm, returning at 7pm, 11.30pm and 3am. **From Uspantán** there's a bus for **San Pedro Carcha** at 2.30am, returning at 12.30am. **From Sacapulas** to **Huehuetenango** there are buses at 4am and 5am. Direct buses from Santa Cruz to **Quezaltenango** leave at 8.30am, 1pm and 2pm, but it's easier to get to Los Encuentros and change there. Buses to **Joyabaj** pass through Santa Cruz hourly from 9am to 5pm. The last bus back from Joyabaj leaves at 4pm.

Lake Atitlán

Buses **to Panajachel** via **Sololá** are run by the *Rebuli* company, whose offices in Guatemala City are at 20 Calle 3–24, Zona 1. Direct buses between Guatemala City and Panajachel leave hourly from 5am to 2pm, and at other times you can travel via Los Encuentros. **From Panajachel** there are departures to **Quezaltenango** at 5am,

6am and 5.45pm, and four buses a day to **Cocales**, passing through **San Lucas Tolimán**. Direct buses to **Chichicastenango** leave Panajachel at 7am, 8am, 9am and 4pm.
Buses **to Santiago Atitlán** are also run by *Rebuli*: from Guatemala City they leave at 5am, 11.30am and 3pm, and from Santiago to Guatemala City at 3am, 6am and noon. There are also buses from Santiago Atitlán to **Quezaltenango** at 3.30am and 4.30am, returning at 11am and 12.30am.
To get to **Nahualá** take any bus heading along the Pan-American highway to the west of Los Encuentros.

Quezaltenango

Pullman buses from **Guatemala City to Quezaltenango** via Chimaltenango, Los Encuentros and Cuatro Caminos are run by a number of companies. *Rutas Limas*, who have offices in Guatemala City at 8 Calle 3–63, Zona 1, and in Quezaltenango off 7 Avenida (Calzada Independencia) have services from Guatemala City at 8am, 3pm, 4.30pm and 8pm, and from Quezaltenango at 5.30am, 6.30am, 8am, 2.30pm and 8.30pm. *Galgos*, with offices in Guatemala City at 7 Avenida 19–44, Zona 1, and in Quezaltenango at Calle Rudolfo Robles 17–43, Zona 1, leave Guatemala City at 5.30am, 8am, 11.30am, 2.30pm, 5pm, 7pm and 9pm, and Quezaltenango at 5am, 8.30am, 10.15am, 12.15am, 3pm, 4.30pm and 7pm. *Lineas Americas* have their offices in Guatemala City at 2 Avenida 18–74, Zona 1, and in Quezaltenango off 7 Avenida: their buses leave Guatemala City at 5.15am, 9am, 5pm and 7.30pm, and Quezaltenango at 5am, 9.45am, 1.15pm and 3.45pm.
From Quezaltenango there are second-class buses, departing from the Minerva terminal in Zona 3, that leave hourly for San Pedro, San Marcos, Retalhuleu, Mazatenango, Huehuetenango and Guatemala City. Other bus times, to the smaller towns, are covered in the text. Travelling from Quezaltenango **to the Mexican border** it's quickest to take a bus for Mazatenango or Coatepeque, and then catch another from there. From Quezaltenango to the border shouldn't take much more than 2 hours.

San Marcos

Transportes Marquensita run pullman buses from **Guatemala City to San Marcos** at 4.30am, 6.30am, 8.30am, 10am, 11am, noon, 1.30pm,

3.30pm and 5pm. From San Marcos to Guatemala they leave at 2am, 2.30am, 3am, 6.30am, 9am, 11am, noon, 1.30pm and 3pm. In Guatemala City their office is at 21 Calle 12–41, Zona 1.

From San Marcos there are hourly buses to **Malacatán** and **Quezaltenango**. To get to the Mexican border you need to travel first to Malacatán, from where there are regular buses to the Talisman bridge.

Huehuetenango

Pullman buses from **Guatemala City to Huehuetenango** are run by two companies. *Los Halcones*, who have offices in Guatemala City at 7 Avenida 15–27, Zona 1, and in Huehuetenango at 7 Avenida 3–62, have two departures daily, leaving from both ends at 7am and 2pm. *Rapidos Zaculeu*, whose offices in Guatemala City are at 9 Calle 11–42, and in Huehuetenango at 3 Avenida 5–25, also run twice daily, at 6am and 3pm. Second-class buses to Huehuetenango run from the Minerva terminal in Quezaltenango and the Zona 4 terminal in Guatemala City every hour or so.

From Huehuetenango there are buses to the border at **La Mesilla** every hour or so, with the last bus from La Mesilla to Huehuetenango at 4pm. There are minibuses to **Aguacatán** from 1 Avenida and 1 Calle, as well as buses from 1 Avenida, frequently between 10am and 4pm. Departures to **Sacapulas** at 11.30am and 12.30pm, returning at 4am and 5am.

CHAPTER THREE

THE PACIFIC COAST

B
eneath the volcanoes that mark the southern side of the highlands is a strip of sweltering, low-lying land some 300 kilometres long and on average 50 kilometres wide. Known by Guatemalans simply as **La Costa Sur**, this featureless yet supremely fertile coastal plain separates the highlands from the Pacific Ocean. The shoreline, a stretch of black volcanic sand pounded by the Pacific surf, is unrelentingly straight, and behind it is the coastal plain itself, an area that was once a wilderness of swamp, forest and savannah.

Prior to the arrival of the Spanish, the Pacific coast was similar in many ways to the jungles of the Petén, and certainly as rich in wildlife and archaeological sites, but history has treated the two areas to completely different fates. While the jungles of the Petén have lain undisturbed, the Pacific coast has been ravaged by development. Today its landscape is dominated by large-scale commercial agriculture – including sugar cane, palm oil, cotton and rubber plantations – that accounts for a significant proportion of the country's exports. Only in some isolated sections, where mangrove swamps have been spared the plough, can you still get a sense of the way it once looked, a maze of tropical vegetation. And in only one area, the **Monterrico Reserve**, is the environment specifically protected.

As for the archaeological sites, they too have largely disappeared, lost in a rapidly changing landscape. The earliest history of the Pacific coast remains something of a mystery, with the only real hints offered by the remnants of two distinct languages: **Zoquean**, still spoken by a tiny population on the Mexico–Guatemala border, and **Xincan**, which is thought to have been used throughout the eastern area. However the extent to which these languages can be seen as evidence of independent tribes, and how they might have developed the coast, remain mere speculation. It's generally held that the cultural sophistication of the peoples to the north – in what is now Mexico – spread along the Pacific coast, giving birth to the **Ocós** and **Iztapa** cultures, which thrived here some time around 1500 BC. These were small, village-based societies that had developed considerable skills in the working of stone and pottery. It's also generally believed that great cultural developments, including writing and the basis of the Maya calendar, reached the southern area via the Pacific coast.

What is certain is that some time between 400 and 900 AD the entire coastal plain was overrun by the **Pipiles**, who migrated south from the Central Highlands and Veracruz area of Mexico, possibly driven out by the chaos that followed the fall of Teotihuacán. (The Pipil language is actually an antiquated form of Nahuatl, the official language of the Aztec Empire.) These migrants brought with them the architectural styles and artistic skills that characterised their northern world, and the remains of their civilisation show that they still used a foreign calendar and worshipped the gods familiar in Mexico. The Pipiles built half a dozen sites, all compact ceremonial centres with rubble-filled pyramids. Their main produce was cacao, from which they extracted the beans to make a chocolate drink and to use as a form of currency. But by the time of the

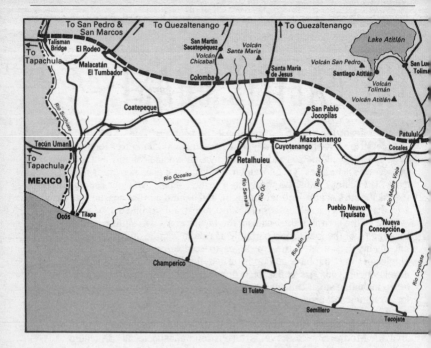

conquest the ever-expanding tribes of the highlands had started to encroach upon the coastal plain with the Mames, Quichés, Tzutujiles and Cakchiqueles all claiming a slice of the action.

A great deal of mystery still surrounds the Pipiles and their world, but a glimpse of their extraordinary art can be had at the sites around the town of Santa Lucía Cotzumalguapa. The **ceremonial centres** have been lost beneath the fields of sugar cane, and all that remains to be seen are some fragments of carving and a number of stern-faced stone heads, but these alone justify the trip.

The first Spaniards to set foot in Guatemala did so on the Pacific coast, arriving overland from the north. Alvarado's first confrontation with Quiché warriors came here in the heat of the lowlands, before he headed up towards Quezaltenango. Once they'd established themselves, the Spanish despatched a handful of Franciscans to convert the populace of the coast, although the Pipiles fought hard and long against colonial control.

In **colonial times** the land was mostly used for the production of indigo and cacao, and for cattle ranching, but the inhospitable climate and accompanying disease soon took their toll, and for much of that era the coast remained a miserable backwater. It was only after **independence** that commercial agriculture really began to dominate this part of the country. In the first phase of development the lower slopes of the mountains, known as the *Boca Costa*, were covered in huge plantations of coffee; later, rubber, banana and sugar-cane plantations spread across the land below. By 1880 the area was important enough to justify the construction of a railway to connect Guatemala City with Puerto San José, subsequently extended all the way to the Mexican border.

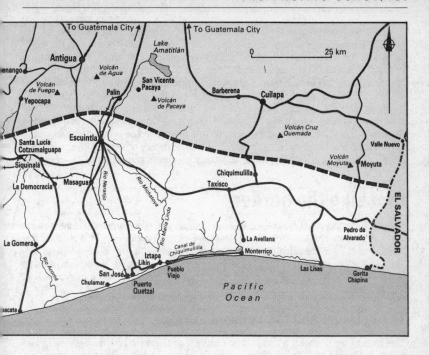

Today the coastal strip is the country's most intensely farmed region, where vast *fincas* have whole villages for their workforce and private airstrips for their owners. Much of the nation's income is generated here, as is most of the misery that inspires Indians to take up arms. The people of the highlands have always been the backbone of this agricultural activity, providing essential seasonal labour. In the past they were forcibly recruited, but today the land shortage drives them to migrate "voluntarily" for several months a year in search of work. A labourer's life, whether cutting cane or picking coffee, is harsh, dangerous and poorly paid.

Getting about: where to go

The main transport link is the **coastal highway** (CA2), which covers the entire length of the coastal strip. It's probably the fastest road in the country, connecting the capital with the Mexican border, and is packed with pullman buses thundering between the two. Along the way are a string of towns, mostly commercial centres that are a mass of energetic activity, noise, and bus fumes. The resident population is almost entirely *Ladino*, and in every way this part of the country has more in common with the chaos of Guatemala City than the calm of the highlands.

The main attraction for travellers is inevitably the **beach**, although frankly it's a disappointment; exposed banks of black volcanic sand, dotted with filthy palm huts and occasionally shaded by palm trees. The hotels are some of the country's worst, to such an extent that it's far better to try to make it to the beach as a day trip. From Guatemala City it's easy enough to visit **San José** or **Iztapa**, take a swim, feast on a plate of fresh shrimp, and head back in the afternoon. A handful of beaches can also be reached from Quezaltenango, the best of them at **El Tulate**.

The second point of interest is **Santa Lucía Cotzumalguapa**, or more specifically the archaeological sites around the town. Totally unlike the sites in the highlands and the Petén, these remains are a hotch-potch of carvings, some of which are still used for religious rituals. Several of them are astonishingly well preserved and the designs are fantastically vivid, although it has to be said that the overall effect is nowhere near as impressive as the great temples of the Petén.

Finally there's a single opportunity to see the wildlife and scenery of the mangrove swamps that once covered much of the area: the **Monterrico Reserve**. The original aim of the reserve was to protect the sea turtle, and with a bit of luck you might even catch sight of one of these; otherwise the wildlife is mostly of the winged variety, including many species of migrants.

Crossing the border

Approaching the coast from the Mexican border, you face some of the very worst that the region has to offer. Breathless and ugly **Coatepeque** is typical of the towns you'll find; **Retalhuleu** somewhat more sedate. If you plan to spend any time on the coast, head east to the area around Escuintla; but if you just want to head for the beach then **Tulate** and **Champerico** are both within easy reach of Quezaltenango.

Tecún Umán and the Talismán Bridge

The coastal border with Mexico is the busiest of Guatemala's frontiers, with two points, Talismán and Tecún Umán, open 24 hours. Tourist cards for either country can be obtained at the immigration posts, but if you require a visa you'll need to get hold of one beforehand – there's a Guatemalan consulate in Tapachula on the Mexican side, and Mexican consulates in Retalhuleu, Quezaltenango, Huehuetenango and Guatemala City.

The northernmost of the two crossings is the **Talismán Bridge**, where the two sets of customs and immigration posts face each other from opposite banks of the Río Suchiate. This tends to be the more relaxed of the two, as there's nothing here but a few huts and a couple of basic *pensiones*. It's also marginally better for first-class buses to Guatemala City, though on the Mexican side there's little difference, as both crossings are half an hour from Tapachula and well connected by a stream of minibuses. On the Guatemalan side there's a regular flow of trucks, minibuses and buses to **Malacatán**, where there are hotels, and buses for San Marcos and the western highlands. If you're heading for Guatemala City there's usually a bus waiting at the border – if not go to Malacatán and catch one from there.

The **Tecún Umán** border crossing, on the edge of the dusty and bustling border town of Ciudad Tecún Umán, is the crossing favoured by most Guatemalans and all commercial traffic. The streets are almost permanently choked with a chaos of articulated lorries and buses, and everything and everyone is on the move: mostly trying to get out as soon as they've arrived. If you do get stuck there are plenty of cheap **hotels** and restaurants – the *Hotel Vanessa 2*, which charges $3 for a room with a fan, is one of the better ones; the *Vanessa 1* is cheaper but has no fans. Once again there's a steady stream of buses connecting the border with Guatemala city.

South to the beach; Ocós and Tilapa

To the south of Tecún Umán a rough dirt road, running parallel to the border, bounces through clouds of thick white dust, and past endless palm-oil plantations, to **OCÓS** on the beach. The village is one of the most forlorn and miserable in the country, with sand streets that run past rows of filthy palm huts. Before the conquest this was the site of a Mam settlement called Ucez, and prior to that it was part of the so-called Ocós culture, one of the earliest civilisations on the Pacific coast. There is no evidence of this nowadays, however, and if you do end up in Ocós it'll probably be by mistake. The quickest way out is to take the boat across the Río Naranjo to the resort of **TILAPA**, a much better bet for spending an hour or two by the sea. If you decide to stay there's a single horrific *pension* in Ocós, and a better one in Tilapa.

You can also travel to and from Tilapa without passing through Ocós, on a good paved road that connects it with the coastal highway. **Buses** run between here and Coatepeque every hour or so from 5am to 6pm, and several times a day between Coatepeque and Ocós.

The Coastal Highway; Coatepeque and Retalhuleu

As you head east from the Mexican border, **COATEPEQUE** is the first place of any importance on the main road, a town that's in many ways typical of the coastal strip. A furiously busy, purely commercial centre, this is where most of the locally produced coffee is processed. The action is centred on the **bus terminal**, an intimidating maelstrom of sweat, mud and energetic chaos: buses run every half-hour from here to the two border crossings, hourly between 4am and 5pm to Quezaltenango (via Santa María and Zunil), and hourly from 2.30am to 6pm to Guatemala City. Local buses also run regularly to **Colomba**, which is in the coffee-producing foothills of the highlands, and four times a day they go on through there to Quezaltenango (via San Martín Sacatepéquez). The best place to stay in Coatepeque is the *Hotel Europa* ($2), on 4 Avenida just off the plaza; slightly cheaper options are the *Pension Sarita* ($1) and the seedy *Hospedaje El Dorado* ($1). For changing money there's a branch of the *Banco del Occidente* on the plaza, and if you're bored in the evening there's a cinema a short distance from the plaza, down the hill on 4 Avenida.

Beyond Coatepeque lies the most densely populated section of the Pacific strip, where a branch road leads to **RETALHULEU**, the largest town in this western section (Retalhuleu is usually referred to as "Reu", pronounced "ray-oo", which is what you should look for on the front of buses). Set away from the highway, and surrounded by the walled homes of the wealthy, Retalhuleu has managed to avoid the worst excesses of the coast. The town was founded by the Spanish, merging the villages of Santa Catarina Sacatepéquez and San Antonio, and the women of these two villages maintained, until recently, the tradition of wearing no blouse – though they were banned from appearing topless in public. This traditionalism marks a real division in the town between a *Ladino* population said to be proud of a lineage untainted by Indian blood, and the Indians who have repeatedly risen up against their control. Today, however, things seem astonishingly peaceful and the town is something of an oasis of civilisation in the chaos of life on the coast. Its plaza epitomises all this, with towering Greek columns on a shiny white Municipalidad, a covered bandstand, and an attractive colonial church.

When it comes to staying in Retalhuleu cheap **accommodation** is in short supply, and there are certainly no bargains on offer. The cheapest place in town is the *Hotel Pacífico* ($1), close to the market on 7 Avenida between 9 and 10 Calles. It's fairly scruffy but if you're on a tight budget there's really no option. Otherwise the price goes up steeply: the *Hotel Astor* ($4), the more upmarket *Don José* ($5), and the *Modelo* ($5) are all just off the plaza. For something to eat try the **restaurants** on the plaza, which is also where you'll find three **banks** and the **post office**, with the *Guatel* office just around the corner. To while away the evenings there's the *Cine Moran* on the plaza, and the *Rex* at 5 Avenida 6–46. The only **Mexican Consulate** on the Pacific coast is in Retalhuleu, on the eastern edge of town at 5 Calle and 3 Avenida, open Monday to Friday 4 to 6pm.

Buses running along the coastal highway almost always pull in at Retalhuleu, running through to the bus terminal on the southern side of the town. To get to the terminal you can either walk, or catch a ride with any bus going south through town on 7 Avenida. There's an hourly service to and from Guatemala City and the Mexican border, and there are also hourly buses to Quezaltenango, Champerico and Tulate – the last to all of these places leave at around 5pm.

The El Zarco junction

Between Retalhuleu and Cuyotenango is the **El Zarco** junction, from where the main road to Quezaltenango heads up into the highlands. If that is your destination then it's generally quickest to take any bus to El Zarco and change – you shouldn't have to wait more than about twenty minutes. You can also catch a direct bus for Quezaltenango from Mazatenango, Coatepeque or Retalhuleu.

Champerico

To the south of Retalhuleu a paved road reaches to the beach at **CHAMPERICO**, which, though it certainly doesn't feel like it, is the country's third port. Founded in 1872, it enjoyed a brief period of prosperity based on the export of coffee. In 1934 Aldous Huxley passed through, but was distinctly unimpressed;

> *Then suddenly, vast and blank, under a glaring white sky, the Pacific. One after another, with a succession of dreary bumps, the rollers broke on a flat beach.*

Huxley was fortunate enough to board a steamer and escape what he called "the unspeakable boredom of life at Champerico". If anything things have got worse, as barely any trade passes through the port these days, and the rusting pier, the only feature to disturb the coastline, will doubtless soon sink beneath the waves. Champerico still supports a handful of fishermen, but spends most of its time waiting for the weekend, when hordes of weary city dwellers descend on the coast. The **beach** is much the same as anywhere else, although its sheer scale is pretty impressive. When you tire of testing your strength against the fury of the surf, there are plenty of places that serve delicious meals of shrimp or fish.

The finest **hotel** in Champerico is the *Martita* ($2), a lovely old building with a fantastic dark wood **bar**; there's no better place to take on your thirst than this. The *Miramar* ($4) is a little more upmarket, or you can try your luck at the *Hospedaje Buenos Aires* ($1), a seedy little boarding house.

Buses from Champerico run directly to Quezaltenango, passing through Retalhuleu, on an hourly basis from 4am to 2.30pm – coming the other way most buses leave Quezaltenango in the mornings, though there's a service from

Retalhuleu throughout the day. If you're heading anywhere else, catch a bus from Champerico to Retalhuleu and then another along the coastal highway.

Cuyotenango, Tulate, Mazatenango and Cocales

Beyond Retalhuleu the highway runs east to **CUYOTENANGO**, one of the older towns along the way. This started life as the site of a pre-conquest Cakchiquel village, and later became an important colonial town. The narrow streets and some of the older buildings still bear witness to this distinguished past, but the thunder of the highway, which cuts right through the town, now overwhelms all else, and its larger neighbours have long since consumed any importance that Cuyotenango once held.

Another branch road to the beach turns off here, heading 45km south to **EL TULATE**. Here the village and the ocean are separated from the mainland by a narrow expanse of mangrove swamp, and this isolation means that El Tulate must rate as the nicest of the beaches that can be reached in a day from Quezaltenango. (Although Champerico, with its direct bus service, is perhaps more convenient.) The beach itself, lined with palm trees and cheap hotels, is again a featureless strip of black sand. **Buses** to El Tulate run every hour or so from Mazatenango and Retalhuleu, with the last bus back to Mazatenango at 4pm, and the last to Retalhuleu at 5pm: small boats run a shuttle service between the end of the road and the village, meeting buses to ferry their passengers.

Back on the highway, the next stop is **MAZATENANGO**, another seething commercial town. There are two sides to "Mazate", as it's generally known. The main street, which runs down the side of the market, past the petrol stations and bus terminal, is characteristic of life along the coastal highway, redolent of diesel fumes and cheap commercialisation. The other half of town, centred around the plaza, is quieter, calmer and more sophisticated, with long shaded streets. There's no particular reason to linger in Mazatenango, but if you do find yourself here for the night the *Hotel Costa Rica* ($2), on the corner opposite the petrol stations, is fairly good, and further down the hill you'll find the *Hotel Moce* ($1), with more possibilities beyond. There are two cinemas in Mazatenango, and plenty of banks.

Buses can be caught at the small terminal above the market on the main street, or outside the petrol stations – where most of the pullmans stop. They run regularly in both directions along the coastal highway, and to Quezaltenango, El Tulate, Chicacao and Pueblo Nuevo Tiquisate. To most of these places buses run every hour or so from 8am to 4 or 5pm.

East to Cocales

Continuing east from Mazatenango the main road passes the junction for CHICACAO, a coffee centre with close links to Santiago Atitlán, and PUEBLO NUEVO TIQUISATE, which was once the local headquarters of the all-powerful *United Fruit Company*, whose banana plantations stretched almost as far as their political influence. The company planted huge numbers of bananas in this area after their plantations on the Caribbean coast were hit by disease, although modern techniques have enabled them to switch many back to their original locations – the company is now under the ownership of *Del Monte*. To the south of Tiquisate, branch roads run to the coast at SEMILLERO and TECOJATE.

About 30 kilometres beyond Mazatenango is **COCALES**, a crossroads from where a road runs north to San Lucas Tolimán and Lake Atitlán, and south to the agricultural centre of **NUEVA CONCEPCIÓN**. Concepción is an inconspicuous little town that has lately been catapulted into the headlines as the home parish of Guatemala's most radical and controversial priest, **Padre Andrés Girón**. Girón is one of the few remaining priests willing to speak out on the political left, and particularly on the touchy issue of land reform. His future remains uncertain, with the Bishop of Escuintla apparently unhappy about his stance, and the death squads dogging his footsteps. Several attempts have been made to kill him, but there are currently rumours that he'll stand for president.

From Cocales buses run to **Santiago Atitlán**, **Panajachel** and **San Lucas Tolimán**. If you're heading this way you can wait for a connection at the junction, but don't expect to make it all the way to Panajachel unless you get here by midday. The best bet is to go to Santiago, which is where most of the buses will be heading, stay the night there, and take a boat across the lake in the morning. The last bus to Santiago Atitlán leaves Cocales at around 4pm.

Santa Lucía Cotzumalguapa and around

Another 23 kilometres brings you to **SANTA LUCÍA COTZUMALGUAPA**, a typically grimy Pacific town a short distance to the north of the highway. The main reason for visiting Santa Lucía is to explore the archaeological sites that are scattered in the surrounding cane fields. **Buses** passing along the highway will drop you at the entrance road to town, while direct buses from the capital go straight into the terminal, a few blocks from the plaza. Buses from the terminal go to Guatemala City hourly from 3am to 5.30pm, or you can pick up a bus on the highway. In the streets around the plaza you'll find several cheap and scruffy hotels, the best of which is the *Pension Reforma* ($1), where for some reason the light switches are outside the rooms. There's a **bank** in the plaza, and the *Comedor Lau* on 3 Avenida does reasonable Chinese meals: the only other way to pass the evening is watching a film at the *Cine Victoria* on 3 Avenida.

As for visiting the **sites**, a tour can be an exhausting and frustrating process, taking you wandering through a sweltering maze of cane fields. Doing it on foot is certainly the cheapest way to see them, but it's also by far the hardest. It's well worth doing the round trip by taxi instead, and if you bargain well it need not be prohibitively expensive. If you opt for a taxi – you'll find plenty in the plaza – then make sure the trip will include all the sites, and fix a firm price beforehand. If you want to see just one of the sites then Bilbao is the closest, only a kilometre or so from the centre of town, and includes some of the best carving. The sites are listed below, with directions, in the best order for visiting them on foot, but it's still fairly easy to get lost. If you do just ask for *las piedras*, as they tend to be known locally.

Bilbao
Bilbao lies just to the north of Santa Lucía Cotzumalguapa. In 1880, more than thirty of the Late Classic stone monuments were removed from this site, and nine of them, probably the very finest of the Pacific coast stelae, were deemed far too good to waste on Guatemala and shipped instead to Germany. One was lost at sea, and the others are currently on display in the Dahlem Museum in Berlin. Four sets of stones are still visible *in situ*, however, and two of them perfectly illustrate the magnificent precision of the carving, beautifully preserved in slabs of black rock.

To get there walk uphill from the plaza, along 4 Avenida, and bear right at the end, where a dirt track takes you past a small red-brick house and along the side of a cane field. About 200 metres further on is a fairly wide path leading left into the cane for about 20 metres. It brings you to two large stones carved in bird-like patterns, with strange circular glyphs arranged in groups of three. The majority of the glyphs are recognisable as the day-names once used by the people of southern Mexico. Numbers are expressed using dots and circles only, without the bar that was used by the Maya to represent five. This is further evidence that the Pipiles, who carved these stones some time between 400 and 900 AD, had more in common with the tribes of the far north than with those of the Guatemalan highlands or the Petén.

This cane field also contains two other sets of stones, reached along similar paths further up this side of the field. The first of these is badly eroded, so that it's only possible to make out the raised border and little or nothing of the actual carving. But the second is the best of the lot, a superbly preserved set of figures and interwoven motifs. The Mexican migrants, who were responsible for all this, shared with the Maya a fascination for the ball game, and on this stone a player is depicted, reaching up to decidedly Mexican divinities – a fairly clear indication that the game was regarded as a form of worship. The player is wearing a heavy protective belt, which would have been made from wood and leather, and you can clearly make out several birds and animals, as well as pods of cacao beans – which were used as currency.

One final stone is hidden in the cane, reached by heading back down the side of the field and turning right at the bottom, along the other side. Here you'll find another entrance, opposite *Casa No. 13*, which brings you to this last carving, another incredibly well defined set of figures. The face of this stone has been cut into, presumably in an attempt to remove it.

Finca El Baul

The second site is also out on this northern side of town, though somewhat further afield, at the **Finca El Baul**. The *finca* is about five kilometres from Santa Lucía and has its own collection of artefacts, as well as a small but fascinating site out in the cane fields. To get there from the last of the Bilbao stones, walk on beyond *Casa No. 13* and onto the tarmacked road (if you're coming out of town this is a continuation of 4 Avenida). At the T-junction straight ahead of you, turn right and follow the road for three or four kilometres until it comes to a bridge. Cross this and take the right-hand fork for another kilometre or so, past all the houses. Out here a dirt track crosses the road, and you want to turn right along this to the base of a small hill. The site is on top of this hill, but you need to walk round to the other side to find the path that takes you up. Once there you'll see the two stones: one flat and carved in low relief, the other a massive half-buried stone head, with wrinkled brow and patterned head-dress. In front of them is a set of small altars on which local people make animal sacrifices, burn incense, and leave offerings of flowers. The faces of the stones are stained with wax dripped from candles.

Drawing from Stela 10 Xultun 889 AD

The next place of interest is the *finca* itself, a few kilometres away. This can be reached either by making your way back to the fork in the road, just after it crosses the bridge, and taking the left-hand branch, or by following the track back and continuing along it straight across the road – after a while this track emerges on the tarmacked road, and you want to turn right for the *finca*. Once you reach the *finca*, walk beyond the rows of shanty-like huts to the huge furnace, behind which the main administration building is protected by an armed guard or two. Ask in here to see the collection, which is housed in a special compound under lock and key: despite the fierce-looking security measures they're always willing to oblige. The carvings include some superb heads, a stone skull, a massive jaguar and many other interesting pieces jumbled together. Alongside all this is the *finca*'s old steam engine, a miniature machine that used to haul the cane along a system of private tracks. A visit is also interesting for the rare glimpse it offers of what a working *finca* looks like. About 900 people are employed here, with their own bus service laid on from town. You may be able to get a ride on this – from Cotzumalguapa buses leave from the *Tienda El Baul*, a few blocks uphill from the plaza, four or five times a day, the first at around 7am and the last either way at about 6pm.

Finca Las Illusiones
The remaining site is on the other side of town, to the east, so if you've been exploring on foot you'll probably want to leave it for another day. This final site is at the **Finca Las Illusiones**, where there's another private collection of artefacts and some stone carvings. To get there walk east along the highway for about a kilometre, out beyond the two *Esso* stations and past a small football field to the north of the road. After this a track leads off to the left (north) to the *finca* itself. Outside the buildings are some copied carvings and several originals, including some fantastic stelae. The building to the left houses a small museum – ask around to unearth the man who looks after the key. Inside is a tiny room crammed with literally thousands of small stone carvings and pottery fragments. More carvings are leant against the walls of a courtyard, reached by crossing the bridge and turning to the left. Some of the figures have the flattened foreheads that are so common in Maya art, while others look like nothing you'd expect to find in the Maya heartland.

La Democracía and the coast at Sipacate

Heading east from Cotzumalguapa the coastal highway arrives next at SIQUINALÁ, a run-down sort of place that straddles the road, and from which another branch road heads to the coast. Along the way, 9km to the south, is **LA DEMOCRACÍA**, which is of particular interest as the home of another collection of archaeological relics. To the east of town is the archaeological site of **Monte Alto**, and many of the best pieces found there are now spread around the plaza under a vast ceiba tree. These so-called "fat boys" are massive stone heads with simple, almost childlike faces. Some are attached to smaller rounded bodies and rolled over on their backs clutching their swollen stomachs. The figures resemble nothing in the Maya world, but are strikingly similar to the far more ancient Olmec sculptures found near Villahermosa in the Gulf of Mexico. In academic circles debate still rages about the precise origins of these traits, but for the moment even less is known about these relics than about the sites around

Cotzumalguapa. However it seems likely that they predate almost all other archaeological finds in Guatemala. The faces of the "fat boys" have a bizarre, almost Buddha-like appearance of contentment, and could well be as much as 4000 years old.

Also on the plaza is the town's **museum** (daily except Mon 9am–noon & 2–5pm), which houses a collection of carvings, including some ceremonial yokes worn by ball-game players, pottery, grinding stones and a few more carved heads.

Further to the south, the road continues to LA GOMERA, a medium-sized agricultural centre where buses usually wait for a while, and beyond there to the coast at **SIPACATE**. The beach at Sipacate is separated from the village by the black waters of the Chiquimulilla Canal, across which boats ferry a constant stream of passengers. The *Hospedaje and Cafetería Mary* ($3), in the village, is the best of a poor bunch of places to stay, but certainly nothing special. On the beach itself the *Rancho Carillo* is just as bad and outrageously overpriced. There are **buses** to Sipacate, passing through La Democracía, from both Guatemala City and Cotzumalguapa, so if you want to head down this way the best thing to do is catch a bus to Siquinalá and wait outside the market there for one heading this way. The trip from the main highway to Sipacate can take as long as two hours, with the last bus back to the highway leaving at 5pm.

East from Escuintla to the border with El Salvador

The southern section of the Pacific coast is dominated by **Escuintla** and **San José**, the largest town and formerly the most important port in the region. If you're heading for the coast from Guatemala City this is probably the route you'll take, and it's a fairly easy day trip. However neither town is particularly attractive so you're unlikely to stay more than a single night, if that. Further to the east is **Monterrico**, an impressive beach where you'll find the coast's one and only wildlife reserve; a protected area of mangrove swamps that's home to some superb birdlife. Beyond that the coastal highway runs to the border with El Salvador, with branch roads running to a couple of small seashore villages.

Escuintla

At the junction of two principal coastal roads, **ESCUINTLA** is the largest and most important of the Pacific towns, and although there's really nothing to do here you do get a good sense of life on the coast. It lies at the heart of the country's most productive region, both industrially and agriculturally, and the department includes cattle, sugar, light industry and even a small *Texaco* oil refinery. The town is also one of the oldest on the Pacific coast, built on the site of a pre-conquest Pipil settlement. Its modern name is a contraction of Isquitepeque, "the hill of the dogs", given to the village because the Pipiles kept dog-like animals for their meat. These days there's no doubt about the commercial bustle of Escuintla's streets, but they look as though the inhabitants, swept up in all this activity, have completely forgotten about the town itself, leaving it to crumble to the ground. One side of the plaza is taken up by the mossy ruins of an old school, and the entire town is in a state of advanced decay, with a worn-out and well-used feel to it.

Below the plaza a huge and frenetic **market** sprawls across several blocks, spilling out into 4 Avenida, the main commercial thoroughfare, which is lined with places where you can **eat** anything from feasts of Guatemalan seafood to the inevitable *Chao Mein* and hamburgers. There are plenty of cheap **hotels** nearby, most of them sharing in the general air of dilapidation. The *Hospedaje El Centro* ($1), painted in imitation of a bus terminal, is one of the better cheap places, on 3 Avenida a block behind the market. Or if you feel the need to escape into a world of overhead fans and private bathrooms try the *Hotel Izcuintla* ($4), 4 Avenida 6–7. A branch of the *Banco de Guatemala* is at 4 Avenida and 7 Calle, and there's a branch of *Lloyds* at 7 Calle 3–07. There are also a couple of cinemas – the *Rialto* at 5 Calle and 3 Avenida, and the *Lux* on 7 Calle opposite the bank.

Buses to Escuintla leave from the Treból junction in Guatemala City every half-hour or so from 4am to 7pm. In Escuintla they leave, at the same times, from the plaza. For other destinations there are two terminals: for places to the Mexican border buses run through the north of town and stop by the *Esso* station (take a local bus up 3 Avenida); buses serving the coast road and the inland route to El Salvador are best caught at the main terminal on the southern side of town, reached by catching a local bus along 4 Avenida. From the latter buses leave every half-hour for Puerto San José and Iztapa, hourly for the eastern border, and daily at 6.30am for Antigua, via El Rodeo.

To the coast: Puerto San José

South from Escuintla the coast road heads through acres of cattle pasture to **PUERTO SAN JOSÉ**, another run-down and redundant port. In its prime San José, which opened as a port in 1853, was Guatemala's main shipping terminal, funnelling goods to and from the capital; but it has now been made virtually redundant by the new container port a few kilometres to the east. Today both town and port are somewhat sleazy, and the main business is tourism: formerly rough sailors' bars pander to the needs of day-trippers from the capital, who fill the beaches at weekends.

The shoreline is again separated from the mainland by the narrow strip of water known as the **Canal de Chiquimulilla**. The canal starts near Sipacate, to the west of San José, and runs as far as the border with El Salvador, cutting off all the beaches in between. For the most part it is nothing more than a narrow strip of water, but in some places it fans out into a maze of mangrove swamps, providing an ideal home for a wide array of wildlife.

Here in San José the main resort area is on the other side of the canal, directly behind the beach. This is where all the bars, restaurants and hotels are, most of them crowded at weekends with large *Ladino* groups feasting on seafood and playing the jukebox until the small hours. The hotels are not so enjoyable, catering, as they do, to a largely drunken clientele. Prices are usually high and standards low: you'll be lucky if you get a sheet, and are normally expected to use a reed mat. Personally I'd recommend sampling the delights of San José as a day trip from the capital, and making it back to civilisation in time for bed. Or if you really want to spend a day or two on the coast then head along to Iztapa, or to Monterrico.

Buses between San José and Guatemala City run every hour or so throughout the day. From Guatemala City they leave from the terminal in Zona 4, and in San José from the plaza. Most of these buses go on to Iztapa, so there's a bus every hour heading that way.

Chulamar and Likin

Leaving San José and following the coast in either direction you come upon the beach resorts of the rich. Guatemala's wealthy elite abandoned Puerto San José to the day-trippers long ago, establishing instead their own enclaves of holiday homes in pale imitation of California.

The first of these is **CHULAMAR**, about five kilometres to the west of Puerto San José, reached only by private car or taxi. Here you'll find another strip of sand separated from the land by the muddy waters of the canal. On the beach there's a single upmarket **hotel** and a string of small *cabañas*, which sleep up to six and are rented for around $50 a day.

To the east of San José, past the container terminal at PUERTO QUETZAL, is the second of these resorts, **BALNEARIO LIKIN**. Here a complete residential complex has been established, based around a neatly planned grid of canals and streets. The ranks of second homes have speedboats and swimming pools, and the entire compound comes complete with an armed guard. There are no buses to Likin itself but any of those going from San José to Iztapa will drop you at the entrance. Like all these places it's deserted during the week, when there are no boats to shuttle you to the beach, but at weekends you can drop by to watch the rich at play. There's a single hotel on the beach, but it's by no means cheap.

Iztapa and along the coast to Monterrico

Further east the road comes to an end at **Iztapa,** another old port that now serves the domestic tourist industry. Of all the country's redundant ports Iztapa is the oldest, as it was here that the Spanish chose to harbour their fleets. In the early days Alvarado used the port to build the boats that took him first to Peru and then on the trip to the Spice Islands from which he never returned. In 1839 the English explorer and diplomat John Lloyd Stephens passed through on his way to Nicaragua, and found the inhabitants far from happy:

> *The captain of the port as he brushed them away (the swarming moschetoes), complained of the desolation and dreariness of the place, its isolation and separation from the world, its unhealthiness, and the misery of a man doomed to live there.*

While for some this might be a fitting description of the entire Pacific coast, there are certainly places that it fits better than Itzapa these days. If not exactly beautiful, the village is at least one of the nicer Pacific beach resorts, smaller and quieter than San José, but with none of the elitist overtones of Likin or Chulamar.

There are also two reasonable **hotels**, another rarity in this part of the country. The *María del Mar* ($4) is a new family hotel with rooms set around a small pool, while the *Hotel Brasilia* ($2) has fewer pretensions to class but is still perfectly good. **Buses** from Guatemala City run to Iztapa every hour or so from 5am to 5pm, leaving from the Zona 4 bus terminal.

Beyond Iztapa the path of the coast road is blocked by the mouth of the **Río Naranjo**. But it is possible to continue along the coast as far as Monterrico, by catching a boat across the river and then a bus on the other side. You have to walk a little way east to the edge of Iztapa, and when you reach the river bank you'll have to look for a boatman to ferry you across – there are usually plenty of canoes and their owners are all too willing to earn a quetzal or two. On the other side is the village of PUEBLO VIEJO, and it's important to make sure that this is where you're being taken, or you might end up on the beach. From Pueblo Viejo buses go three or four times a day to **Monterrico** – usually at 5am, 11am, 2pm and 6pm, although the buses are old and the schedule uncertain at the best of times.

Monterrico, the beach and nature reserve

The setting of **MONTERRICO** is one of the finest on the Pacific coast, perched above a stretch of clear black sand, pounded by the surf. But like all of these seaside villages it's a scruffy sort of place, separated from the mainland by the waters of the Chiquimulilla canal, which in this case weaves through a fantastic network of mangrove swamps. The village itself is friendly and relaxed and it's one of the better places to spend some time by the sea. The main drawback is yet again **accommodation**. The two very basic *pensiones* down by the seafront, both charging around $3 for a miserable room and a filthy mattress, must rate as some of the very worst you could find. As compensation, however, there's the *Hotel Baule Beach*, a few hundred metres along the shore. This is perhaps the best hotel on the entire Pacific shoreline, run by an American woman who used to work for the Peace Corps in Monterrico and was so taken by the place that she decided to stay. Rooms go for about $5 and there are plans for a restaurant and swimming pool.

The beach apart, Monterrico's chief attraction is the **nature reserve**. The swamp behind the town, and a large stretch of the coastline, form a protected area of some 2800 hectares. The mangrove swamp is a bizarre and rich environment that acts as a kind of marine nursery, offering small fish protection from their natural predators. Above the water a dense mat of branches provides an ideal home for hundreds of species of birds, and amongst the mangroves are various species of bulrush and water lily. This maze of roots and branches also supports some mammals; these are extremely difficult to see but their numbers include racoons, iguanas and opossums. At any time of day a trip into the swamp is an astonishing adventure, taking you through a complex network of channels, and beneath a dense canopy of vegetation.

The best way to travel through it is in a small *cayuco*, and there are always plenty of children hanging around the dock in Monterrico who'll be willing to take you on a trip into the wilds, or you can hire a larger boat with an engine – but you won't see as much. You shouldn't expect to see the anteaters and racoons, however you travel, but you probably will see a good range of birdlife including kingfishers, white herons and several species of duck. Failing all else the trip is well worth it just to watch the local fishermen casting their nets.

The reserve is also designed to protect the beach, and in fact it was originally established for the benefit of the **sea turtles** that nest here. These are also rarely seen, as they usually emerge from the ocean at night and lay their eggs as fast as they can before making a dash back to the water. Wandering the shoreline is the only way to increase your chances of seeing a turtle and the woman who runs the *Baule Beach* hotel has plans to hire out horses so that people can go in search of nest sites. The turtle is an endangered species in these parts and along with iguanas they are bred and released in the reserve, in a bid to increase their numbers.

Further along the beach, about 5km to the east, is the isolated village of **HAWAII**, accessible only by boat. This is another relaxed fishing village where the ocean life has attracted a handful of regular tourists, notably some wealthy Argentinians from Guatemala City who have built second homes on the beach. There are no hotels in Hawaii but it's easy enough to visit the village as a day trip from Monterrico, by hiring a boat from the dock.

Getting to and from Monterrico

There are two ways to get to Monterrico, either by ferry and bus from Iztapa or from the coastal highway at **Taxisco**, from where trucks and buses run to **LA AVELLANA**. La Avellana is a couple of kilometres from Monterrico itself on the opposite side of the mangrove swamp, and boats shuttle passengers back and forth. There's a steady of flow of traffic between Taxisco and La Avellana – if you don't want to wait for a bus it's usually easy enough to hitch a ride with a truck.

From Escuintla to El Salvador

Heading east from Escuintla the coastal highway brings you to **TAXISCO**, a quiet farming centre set to the north of the main road. From here a branch road runs to **La Avellana** from where you can catch a boat to Monterrico – see above. If you're heading for Monterrico then take a bus as far as Taxisco and hitch from there or ask around in the plaza. **Buses** to Taxisco leave from the Zona 4 terminal in Guatemala City, calling at Escuintla and usually going on to the border with El Salvador.

Beyond Taxisco is **CHIQUIMULILLA**, from where another branch road heads up into the eastern highlands, through acres of lush coffee plantations, to the town of CUILAPA. Chiquimulilla is another fairly nondescript town that serves as a market centre for the surrounding area, but you might easily end up here in order to change buses – if you get stuck there are a couple of decent hotels. From the small bus terminal a block or so from the plaza there's a steady flow of traffic to both the border and Guatemala City, with departures every hour or so. There are also buses every hour to Cuilapa, departing from the other side of the market.

Heading on towards the border, the highway is raised slightly above the rest of the coastal plain, giving great views towards the sea. A short distance before the border the road divides, with one branch running to the seashore village of **LAS LISAS**, which is another good spot for spending some time by the sea. Like all of these villages Las Lisas is separated from the mainland by the murky waters of the Chiquimulilla canal, again bridged by a shuttle of small boats. On the sandbank itself the village follows a standard pattern, with a collection of scruffy huts and palm trees behind a beautiful black sand beach. As always it's a great place to relax for an afternoon but accommodation is high in price and very low in quality. **Buses** run between Las Lisas and Chiquimulilla hourly from 9am to 4pm, and the journey takes about an hour and a half.

The border with El Salvador

The coastal highway finally reaches the border with El Salvador at **CIUDAD PEDRO DE ALVARADO**, a quiet and easy-going crossing point. Most of the commercial traffic and all the pullman buses use the highland route to El Salvador, and consequently things are fairly relaxed here. Should you get stuck for the night the *Hospedaje Yesina* is right opposite the immigration post. There are second-class buses to and from the Zona 4 terminal in Guatemala City every hour or so from 1am to 4pm, all of them going via Escuintla. If you're not ready to leave the country just yet, there's another branch road from here to the coast, ending up at a couple of small seaside villages, GARITA CHAPINA and BARRA DE LA GABINA.

fiestas

Since, despite the presence of a massive migrant labour force, *Ladino* culture is strongly dominant on the Pacific coast, fiestas here tend to be more along the lines of fairs, with parades, fireworks, sporting events and heavy drinking. You'll see very little in the way of traditional costume or pre-Columbian dances, although marimba bands are popular even here and many of the fiestas are still based on local saints' days. Nevertheless there's no doubt that the people of the coast like to have a good time and know how to enjoy themselves. Allegiances tend to be less local than those of the Indian population, and they celebrate national holidays as much as local ones.

January
The year starts off in **Taxisco** from the 12th to 15th, with a fiesta in honour of the Black Christ of Esquipulas: events include bullfighting and plenty of macho bravado. In **Colomba** (a few kilometres from Coatepeque) they have a fiesta from the 12th to 16th that honours the same Black Christ and also involves bullfighting. In **Cuyotenango** there's a fiesta from the 11th to 18th, with the main day on the 15th – unlike most coastal fiestas this one includes some traditional dancing.

February
A moveable fiesta takes place in **Tecún Umán** some time during the month.

March
Holy Week is celebrated everywhere with a combination of religious ritual and secular partying, while in **Coatepeque** they have a local fiesta from the 11th to 19th, with the main day on the 15th. In **Puerto San José** the fiesta is from the 16th to 22nd, with the principal day on the

19th, and **Ocós** has a moveable fiesta some time during the month.

April
Chiquimulilla has a fiesta at the end of the month from the 30th April to 4th May.

July
Coatepeque has a single day of fiesta on the 25th, in honour of Santiago Apostol.

August
The port of **Champerico** has its fiesta from the 4th to 8th, with the main day on the 6th, in honour of *El Salvador del Mundo*.

October
Iztapa has its fiesta from the 20th to 26th, with the 24th as the main day.

November
November 1st, All Saints' Day, is celebrated throughout the country, and people gather in cemeteries to eat, drink and honour the dead. In **Siquinalá** they have a local fiesta from the 23rd to 26th.

December
Retalhuleu has a fiesta from the 6th to 12th, with the main day on the 8th. **Chicacao** has its fiesta from the 18th to 21st, which includes some traditional dancing as the town has close links with Santiago Atitlán. **Escuintla** has a fiesta from the 6th to 15th, with the main day on the 8th, and in **Santa Lucía Cotzumalguapa** the main fiesta is held on the 25th. Finally it's the turn of **La Democracía** on the 31st.

travel details

Buses are certainly the best way to get around on the Pacific coast, and the main highway, from Guatemala City to the Mexican border, is served by a constant flow of pullmans. Heading in the other direction, to the border with El Salvador, there are no pullmans, but there is a regular stream of second-class buses. On either of these main routes you can hop between buses and

expect one to pass every half-hour or so, but if you plan to leave the highways then it's best to travel to the nearest large town and find a local bus from there. If you're heading up into the highlands take any bus to the relevant junction and wait for a connection there – **El Zarco** for buses to Quezaltenango and **Cocales** for Lake Atitlán – but set out early.

Buses
Tecún Umán and Talismán

There are buses every hour **from Guatemala City** (5hr), calling in at all the main towns along the way – including **Escuintla**, **Santa Lucía Cotzumalguapa**, **Cocales**, **Mazatenango**, **Retalhuleu** and **Coatepeque**. The bulk of these leave from the terminal at 19 Calle and 9 Avenida, in Zona 1. *Fortaleza del Sur* run buses to Talismán every hour from 4.30am to 7pm, and *Rapidos del Sur* have buses to Tecún Umán hourly between 2am and 4pm: both companies have offices at 8 Calle 22, Zona 1, Guatemala City. **To Guatemala City** the service is just as good, with hourly departures throughout the day, from 4am to 5pm. **Journey times** along the main highway are: Coatepeque to Tecún Umán 40min, Coatepeque to Retalhuleu 50min, Retalhuleu to Mazatenango 30min, Mazatenango to Cocales 50 min, Cocales to Escuintla 30min, and Escuintla to Guatemala City 1hr.

Heading from the border **to Quezaltenango** you can either travel to **Malacatán** and then up through **San Marcos**, or come along the coast road and catch a direct bus to Quezaltenango from Retalhuleu, Coatepeque or Mazatenango. If you're coming from the Talismán border it's easy enough to find a truck or bus to Malacatán, and from there there are hourly buses to San Marcos, but if you're coming from Tecún Umán it's more straightforward to travel via Retalhuleu, from where there are buses every hour to Quezaltenango.

To Ocós and Tilapa (2hr from Coatepeque) there are hourly buses to Tilapa from Coatepeque, and three or four a day to Ocós: boats connect the two.

To Champerico (1hr 20min from Retalhuleu) there are buses every hour from Retalhuleu, and throughout the morning from Quezaltenango. Buses returning from Champerico to Quezaltenango leave hourly from 4am to 2.30pm, although later in the afternoon there are still buses from Champerico to Retalhuleu.

To Escuintla (1hr from Guatemala City) buses leave every hour from El Treból or the Zona 4 terminal in Guatemala City. They return from the plaza in Escuintla and run until around 7pm. From Escuintla there's also a direct bus to **Antigua**, which leaves the Escuintla bus terminal at 7am, returning from Antigua at around 1pm. All buses to Puerto San José pass through Escuintla.

To Puerto San José (2hr from Guatemala City) there are hourly buses from the Zona 4 terminal in Guatemala City, and most of these go on **to Iztapa** (30min from San José), and return from there – the last bus from Iztapa to Guatemala City leaves at 5pm.

To Monterrico (2hr from Iztapa) there are buses four times a day from **Puerto Viejo**, across the Río Naranjo from Iztapa. Monterrico can also be reached from Taxisco, by taking a bus or truck to **La Avellana** and a boat from there.

To Taxisco and Chiquimulilla there are buses every hour or so from the Zona 4 terminal in Guatemala City, many of which go on to the border with El Salvador.

To Las Lisas there are buses every hour or so from Chiquimulilla (1hr) between 9am and 4pm. Most of them start out from the Zona 4 terminal in Guatemala City.

To Ciudad Pedro de Alvarado (1hr from Chiquimulilla) there are buses every hour or so from the Zona 4 terminal in Guatemala City, which come via **Escuintla** and **Taxisco**. Buses from the border to Guatemala City leave hourly from 6am to 4pm.

Trains

The other travel option on the coast is the train, although be warned that the service is deadly slow and very unreliable. The only remaining route runs from **Guatemala City to Tecún Umán**, calling at all the main towns along the way. The entire trip takes 12 hours at least – twice as long as the bus. The train service between Guatemala City and Puerto San José is no longer carrying passengers.

Trains officially leave from both Guatemala City and Tecún Umán on Tuesday, Thursday and Saturday at 7pm, but these times are subject to change, and in indeed the entire service may soon close, so check them out before you travel.

CHAPTER FOUR

EAST TO THE CARIBBEAN

Connecting Guatemala City with the Caribbean is the **Motagua Valley**, a broad corridor of low-lying land that separates the Sierra del Espíritu Santo, marking the border with Honduras, from the Sierra de Las Minas. In actual fact the valley starts in the central highlands, around Santa Cruz del Quiché, cutting east through a particularly arid section of the mountains, and meeting the Caribbean highway at the El Rancho junction, where the river is surrounded by desert. From here on the valley starts to take its true form, opening out into a massive floodplain with the parallel ridges rising on either side. The land is fantastically fertile and lush with vegetation at all times of the year, and the air is thick with humidity.

This final section, dampened by tropical heat and repeated cloudbursts, was densely populated in Maya times, forming the southern limit of their civilisation. The valley served as an important trade route, connecting the highlands with the Caribbean coast just as it does today, and it was also one of the main sources of jade. Following the decline of Maya civilisation the area lay disease-infested and virtually abandoned until the end of the nineteenth century. Its revival was part of the masterplan of the *United Fruit Company*, who cleared and colonised the land, planting thousands of acres with bananas and reaping massive profits. At the height of its fortune the company was powerful enough to bring down the government, and effectively monopolised the country's trade and transport. Today bananas are still the main crop, though cattle are becoming increasingly important, and the Caribbean highway, thundering through the valley, is also a vital resource, carrying the bulk of foreign trade from both Guatemala and El Salvador.

For the traveller the Motagua valley is the main route to and from the Petén and most people get no more than a fleeting glimpse of it through a bus window. But two of the greatest Maya sites are in this area: **Quiriguá**, just 5km from the main road, and **Copán**, across the border in Honduras (a side trip of a day or two). Also out towards the frontier is the holy city of **Esquipulas**, home of the famous Black Christ and the scene of Central America's largest annual pilgrimage.

Beyond the Motagua valley is Guatemala's slice of **Caribbean coastline**, where the old banana port of **Puerto Barrios** is now outdated by its squeaky-clean replacement at **Santo Tomás del Castillo**. The main point of interest in Puerto Barrios is the ferry to **Livingston**, the country's only enclave of Caribbean culture, a laid-back seaside town set beneath beautiful lush green hills and reached only by boat.

The final section covered in this chapter is the **Eastern Highlands**, a seldom visited part of the country that shares little with the highlands of the west. Here the bulk of the population are *Ladino*, living in small towns and surviving through small-scale commercial farming. There's little specific to see, but the scenery, dominated by eroded volcanic cones, is superb. If you do see it, however, it'll probably be only in passing, as you head south to El Salvador.

THE MOTAGUA VALLEY

The main road to the Caribbean leaves the capital in conjunction with the road for Cobán, splitting at the **El Rancho junction** beneath the parched hills of the upper Motagua – one half heading up into the rain-soaked highlands of the Verapaces and the other continuing to the Caribbean coast. Heading on down the Motagua valley for another twenty kilometres or so the land is bleak, dry and distinctly inhospitable, with the road keeping well to the left of the river and bypassing the villages that line the railway. The first place of any note is the **Río Hondo junction**, a smaller version of El Rancho, where a waiting army of food sellers swarms around every bus that stops. Here again the road divides, with one arm heading west to Esquipulas and the three-way border with Honduras and El Salvador.

On down the valley the landscape starts to undergo a radical transformation; the floodplain opens out and the occasional cacti are gradually overwhelmed by a profusion of tropical growth, as the warm air becomes thick with humidity. It is this supremely rich floodplain that was chosen by both the Maya and the *United Fruit Company*, to the great benefit of both. Here the broad expanse of the river valley is overshadowed by two parallel mountain ranges; to the northwest is the Sierra de las Minas, and over on the other side, marking out the Honduran border, is the Sierra del Espíritu Santo.

The ruins of Quiriguá

Of one thing there is no doubt; a large city once stood there; its name is lost, its history unknown; and no account of its existence has ever before been published. For centuries it has lain as completely buried as if covered with the lava of Vesuvius. Every traveller from Yzabal to Guatimala has passed within three hours of it; we ourselves had done the same; and yet there it lay, like the rock-built city of Edom, unvisited, unsought, and utterly unknown.

John L. Stephens (1841).

In 1841 John Stephens was so impressed with the ruins at **Quiriguá** that he planned to take them home, using the Motagua river to float the stones to the Caribbean so that "the city might be transported bodily and set up in New York". Fortunately the asking price was beyond his means and the ruins remained buried in the rainforest until 1909, when the land was bought by the *United Fruit Company.*

Today things are somewhat different: the ruins themselves partially restored and reconstructed, and banana plantations stretching to the horizon in all directions. But as far as most travellers are concerned the site is still "unvisited" and "unsought". While Quiriguá certainly can't compete with the enormity of Tikal, it does have some of the finest of all Maya carving, with stelae, altars and so-called zoomorphs that are covered in well preserved and superbly intricate glyphs and portraits. Matched only by Copán, the site offers a look at the complexity of Maya design, an experience which is just as evocative in its way as the scale of Tikal. The vivid portraiture and bizarre glyphs illustrate the sophistication of Maya culture, a permanent riddle, tantalising those who seek to understand it.

Getting to Quiriguá and staying there

The ruins are situated some 70km beyond the junction at Río Hondo, and three or four kilometres from the main road, reached down a dirt track that supplies the banana industry. All buses running between Puerto Barrios and Guatemala City pass by – just ask the driver to drop you at the ruins and you'll end up at the entrance road, about four hours from Guatemala City, from where there's a fairly regular bus service to the site itself (5km), as well as a shuttle of motorbikes that carry passengers to and from the main road. The site is surrounded by a dense stand of rainforest and the weather conditions are decidedly tropical; cloudbursts are the rule and the buzz of mosquitoes is almost uninterrupted – take repellent. The entrance to the ruins is marked by a couple of cheap *comedores* and a car park. The site is open daily and there's a small entrance fee.

There's nowhere to stay at the ruins themselves, but if for some reason you want to stay nearby then there's a **hotel** in the village – also known as QUIRIGUÁ – which is about halfway between the site and the main road. To get there ask to be dropped off at the railway line (which crosses the dirt track about 1km from the main road) and walk south along the tracks for a further kilometre – by car the village is reached from the main road along a separate entrance road.

Nowadays the village is a ramshackle and run-down sort of place, strung out along the railway track, but in the past it was famous for its hospital of tropical diseases, run by the *United Fruit Company*. The imposing building still stands on the hill above the track, now a state-run workers' hospital. Up beside the hospital is the plaza, and here you'll find the *Hotel Royal*, a surprisingly good and spot-lessly clean place, with rooms for about $2.

Trains heading between Guatemala City and Puerto Barrios pass through the village three times a week. The timetable is totally unreliable, though, so if you want to leave the site by train ask someone in the village what time it's expected.

Quiriguá's past – a short history

Quiriguá's history starts a short distance from the existing site, near the hospital, where two stelae and a temple have been unearthed, marking the site of an earlier ceremonial centre. From there it moved to a second location nearby, where another stela has been found, before finally settling at the main site you see today.

The early history of Quiriguá is still fairly vague, and all that is certain is that at some time during the Late Preclassic period (250 BC to 300 AD) migrants from the north, possibly Putun Maya from the Yucatán peninsula, established them-selves as the rulers here. Thereafter, in the Early Classic Period (250–600AD), the centre was dominated by Copán, and doubtless valued for its position on the banks of the Motagua river, an important trade route, and as a source of jade, which is found throughout the valley. At this stage the rulers themselves may well have come from Copán, just 50km away, and there certainly seem to have been close ties between the two sites: the architecture, and in particular the carv-ing which adorns it, makes this very clear.

In the Late Classic Period (600–900 AD) Quiriguá really started to come into its own. The site's own name glyph is first used in 731, just six years after its greatest leader, **Cauac Sky**, ascended to the throne. As a member of the long-standing Sky dynasty he took control of a city that was already embarked upon a campaign of aggressive expansion, and in the process of asserting its indepen-dence from Copán. In 737, matters were brought to a head when he captured 18 Rabbit, Copán's ruler, and made the final break. For the rest of his sixty-year reign the city experienced an unprecedented building boom: the bulk of the great stelae date from this period and are decorated with his portrait. For a century Quiriguá dominated the lower Motagua valley and its highly prized resources. Cauac Sky died in 784 and was succeeded 78 days later by his son, Sky Xul, who ruled for eleven years. He was usurped by Jade Sky, who took the throne in 800. Under Jade Sky Quiriguá reached its peak, with fifty years of extensive building, including a radical reconstruction of the Acropolis. But from the end of Jade Sky's rule, in the middle of the ninth century, the historical record fades out, as does the period of prosperity and power.

The ruins

Entering the site beneath the ever-dripping trees you emerge at the northern end of the **Great Plaza**. To the left-hand side of the path is a badly ruined pyramid and directly in front of this are the **stelae** for which Quiriguá is rightly famous. The nine stelae in the plaza are the tallest in the Maya world, and their carving is arguably the best. The style is similar in many ways to that of Copán, always following a basic pattern, with portraits on the main faces and glyphs covering the sides. As for the figures, they represent the city's rulers, with Cauac Sky depicted on no less than seven (A, C, D, E, F, H and J). Two unusual features are particularly clear, the vast headdresses, which dwarf the faces, and the beards, a fashion that caught on in Quiriguá thirty years after it became popular in Copán. Many of the figures are shown clutching a ceremonial bar, the symbol of office, at one end of which is a long-nosed god, possibly Chaac the rain god, and at the other the head of a snake. The glyphs, crammed into the remaining space, record dates and events during the reign of the relevant ruler.

Largest of the stelae is E, which rises to a height of eight metres and weighs 65 tons – it was originally sunk about three metres into the ground, and set in a foundation of rough stones and red clay, but was reset in 1934 using concrete. The stelae are carved from an ideal fine-grained sandstone, mined in a quarry about 5km from the site. The stones were probably rolled to the site on skids, set up, and then worked by sculptors standing on scaffolding. Fortunately for them the stone was soft once it had been cut, and fortunately for us it hardened with age.

Another feature that has earned Quiriguá its fame are the bizarre **zoomorphs**, six blocks of stone carved with interlacing animal and human figures. Some, like the turtle, frog and jaguar, can be recognised with relative ease, while others are either too faded or too elaborate to be accurately made out. The best of the lot is P, which shows a figure seated in Buddha-like pose, interwoven with a maze of others. The zoomorphs are sometimes referred to as altars and connected with the stela altar complexes at Tikal, but their size and shape make this seem unlikely.

Around the plaza are several other interesting features; along the eastern side are some unrestored structures that may have been something to do with Quiriguá's river **port** – since the city's heyday the river has moved at least a kilometre from its original course. At the southern end of the plaza, near the main zoomorphs, you can just make out the shape of a **ball court** hemmed in on three sides by viewing stands, still buried beneath tons of accumulated soil. The **Acropolis** itself, the only structure of any real size that still stands, is bare of decoration. Trenches dug beneath it have shown that it was built on top of several

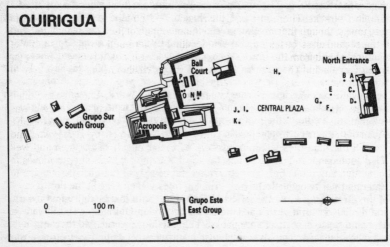

previous versions, the earliest ones built of
rough river stones.

Apart from these central structures there
are a few smaller unrestored complexes scattered in the surrounding forest, but nothing
that's of any particular interest. To get back
to the main road just wait outside the
entrance to the ruins until a bus or motorbike turns up. Buses, often packed with plantation workers, are most likely to stop at the
barrier – some go only as far as the road,
others all the way to Morales/Bananera.

Glyph from Quiriguá

On to the coast: Puerto Barrios

Heading on towards the Caribbean, another 15km brings you to **La Trinchera**,
junction for the branch road to **MARISCOS** on the shores of **Lake Izabal**. The
only reason that you might want to head this way is to take the ferry across the
lake to **El Estor**, from where early morning buses run to Cobán in Alta Verapaz.
In its day Mariscos was an important stopping-off point, where travellers heading
for the capital would disembark and continue overland, but nowadays it's
bypassed by modern transport routes. There are a couple of cheap and scruffy
hotels in the village, and the ferry, which takes passengers only, leaves at 1pm –
returning at 5am. One direct bus a day runs from Guatemala City to Mariscos,
departing at 6am from outside the railway station, 18 Calle and 9 Avenida; and
one from Puerto Barrios at 3pm. Both return after the arrival of the boat from El
Estor at 7am. At other times take any bus along the Caribbean highway, ask to be
dropped at La Trinchera, and hitch from there to Mariscos.

Further down the Motagua valley the road pushes on through a blooming landscape of cattle ranches and fruit trees, splitting again at the junction for the twin
towns of **MORALES** and **BANANERA**, a ramshackle collection of wooden shacks
and railway tracks. There's no particularly good reason for visiting the squalor of
these towns, though they do serve as the transport hub of the lower Motagua, with
all the second-class buses for the Petén calling in here and a regular shuttle of
minibuses to and from Río Dulce. There's also, of course, a steady flow of buses for
Puerto Barrios and Guatemala City, so you might easily end up here, if only to
change buses.

If however you have a passionate interest in Guatemalan history, then
Bananera, innocent though it might appear, is a place of particular potency. It was
here that the **United Fruit Company** made its headquarters and developed a
substantial empire. The company's land is currently owned by *Del Monte*, and
they still maintain the local headquarters here, in a neatly landscaped and well
sealed compound, and still dominate the town. A company store offers supplies to
the faithful, and a one-hole golf course, at the bottom of the airfield, testifies to
the presence of foreign executives.

The *United Fruit Company*, who muscled in on the Motagua valley in the early
part of this century, developed huge tracts of unused land, waging war on
endemic diseases and making millions of dollars in the process. The company's
fingers were in so many pies that it became known as "el pulpo", the octopus, and

its political lobby was so powerful that it secured exemption from almost all tax, controlling not only the banana industry but also the country's railways and the crucial port at Puerto Barrios. So profitable was the company that its assets multiplied fourteen times between 1900 and 1930. Its tentacles held Central America so firmly that when the socialist government of Arbenz proposed confiscating the company's unused lands in 1954, it engineered a coup and replaced the government. *Del Monte*, as inheritors of the empire, have kept their hands relatively clean, limiting themselves to exporting around two billion bananas a year.

A short distance beyond the turning for Morales/Bananera you pass the **Ruidosa** junction, from where the highway to the Petén heads to the northwest, running out over the Río Dulce before being engulfed by the jungles of the Petén. Another fifty kilometres brings you to the Caribbean itself, with the road dividing for the last time, right to the old port of Puerto Barrios and left to Puerto Santo Tomás, the modern town and dock.

Unless you happen to be driving a truck **PUERTO BARRIOS** is the one to make for. Founded in the 1880s by President Rufino Barrios, the port soon fell into the hands of the *United Fruit Company*, who used their control of the railways to ensure that the bulk of trade passed this way. Puerto Barrios was Guatemala's main port for most of this century, and while the Fruit Company was exempt from almost all tax the users of its port were obliged to pay heavy duties. In the 1930s it cost as much to ship coffee from Guatemala to New Orleans as it did from Brazil to New Orleans. These days the boom is definitely over and the town distinctly forlorn, although you'll still find all the services that are associated with ports, including an array of strip clubs and brothels. The streets are still wide, but they're poorly lit and badly pot-holed; one or two fine old Caribbean houses are outnumbered by the abundance of grimy hotels and hard-drinking bars.

Across the bay is **PUERTO SANTO TOMÁS**, the newest port facility in the country. To look at the concrete plaza, the planned housing and the fenced-off docks, you'd never guess that the place had a moment's history, but oddly enough it's been around for a while. It was originally founded by the Spanish in 1604, who inhabited it with some black Caribs, the survivors of an expedition against pirates on Roatan Island. The pirates in turn sacked Santo Tomás, but it was revived in 1843, when a Belgian colony was established here. Today it's connected by a regular shuttle of local buses to Puerto Barrios, though other than the docks themselves there's nothing much to see – certainly no famous Belgians.

Sleeping, eating and entertainment

Cheap hotels are in plentiful supply in Puerto Barrios, designed to accommodate a typically impoverished port population. The best of them is probably the *Hotel Xelaju*, on 9 Calle, a big and basic sort of place where they charge $2. There are plenty of others in the same mould, including the *Pension Xelaju* and the *Hospedaje Central*, both on 9 Calle. Slightly more expensive, but well worth the difference, is the *Hotel Europa* on 8 Avenida, which is clean and comfortable, charging $4 for a room with a private shower. The *Hotel Canada*, on 6 Calle, is similarly priced and also good.

When it comes to **eating** the situation is pretty much the same, with an abundance of cheap and rough places, and a few better but more expensive ones. Puerto Barrios also has more than its fair share of **bars**, pool halls and night clubs, offering the full range of late-night sleaze. None of these are hard to find. There are also a couple of **cinemas**, both on 7 Calle, one of them housed in a superbly misshapen wooden building. If you need to change money there are several banks on 7 Calle, and if you want to make a phone call there's a *Guatel* Office on 8 Avenida. The **post office** is on 6 Calle.

Getting there and getting away – by land and sea

The Caribbean highway is served by the *Litegua* bus company, owners of the country's finest and fastest pullman **buses**, and also by *Fuente del Norte*. In Guatemala City they leave from the plaza in front of the railway station at 9 Avenida and 18 Calle hourly from 5.30am to 5pm. In Puerto Barrios they leave from 6 Avenida, between 9 and 10 calles, hourly from 1am to 4pm. The journey takes around six hours and tickets can be bought in advance, although on the whole it's not necessary. *Litegua* buses don't pass through Morales or Bananera, which is where you want to make for if you want to connect with buses for the Petén, but both places have good second-class connections. Other buses from Puerto Barrios go to Zacapa and Chiquimula: if there's no direct connection take a Guatemala City bus as far as the Río Hondo junction, from where an endless stream of pullmans heads out to Esquipulas and all points in between, for connections to Copán and the border with El Salvador. Finally there's a single bus to Mariscos, leaving from outside the market in Puerto Barrios at 3pm.

A severely antiquated **train** service also runs between Guatemala City and Puerto Barrios. Scheduled to take eight hours, the trip has been known to take as long as twenty, and could well go out of service in the near future as the company is burdened by massive debts. The trains are used by only the poorest of Guatemalans and the staunchest of rail enthusiasts. For the moment the train sets out from both ends at 7am on Tuesday and Saturday.

From the dock at the bottom of 12 Avenida two daily **ferries** leave Puerto Barrios for Livingston; at 10.30am and 5pm, returning at 5am and 2pm. The trip takes around one and a half hours, although departure times are subject to sudden changes so it's worth checking as soon as you arrive in Puerto Barrios. For Punta Gorda in **Belize** a ferry leaves on Tuesday and Friday at 7.30am, from the dock at the end of 9 Calle, calling in at Livingston on the way. You have to clear immigration before you can buy a ticket. Both the ticket office and the immigration office are in 9 Calle close to the dock and open from 7am to noon and 2 to 5pm.

Livingston and the Río Dulce

North of Puerto Barrios the **Bay of Amatique** is ringed with a bank of lush green hills, rising straight out of the Caribbean and coated in tropical rainforest. Halfway between Puerto Barrios and the border with Belize, at the mouth of the Río Dulce, is **LIVINGSTON**. Reached only by boat, Livingston not only enjoys a superb setting, but it's also the only Carib town in Guatemala, and the only place that you can sample the laid-back atmosphere of their life, surrounded by a strange hybrid of Guatemalan and Caribbean culture, in which marimba mixes with Marley. Along with several Belizean centres, Livingston provides the focus for a displaced people who are now strung out across the Bay of Amatique and southern Belize. Their history begins on the island of St·Vincent, where their pure bred ancestors intermarried with shipwrecked sailors and runaway slaves. In 1795 they staged a rebellion against British rule, were defeated, and resettled on the island of Roatan off Honduras, from where they migrated to the mainland.

Today their culture incorporates elements of indigenous Indian belief with African and *Ladino* constituents, and in Belize in particular they have recently attempted to revive their independent cultural identity as "Garifuna" people. For the rest of Guatemalans, who've always had a problem accepting indigenous cultures, the Caribs are a mysterious and mistrusted phenomenon. They are subjected not only to the same prejudices that plague the Indian population, but also viewed with a strange awe that gives rise to a range of fanciful myths. Uninformed commentators have argued that their society is matriarchal, polygamous, and directed by a secret royal family. Accusations of voodoo and cannibalism are commonplace too, and it's often claimed that the women speak a language incomprehensible to the men, passing it on only to their daughters.

At the bottom of all this is a unique and unusual culture, although in Livingston itself it's fast being swamped by the more modern rhythms of twentieth-century Caribbean culture. Among the young, Bob Marley, dreadlocks and weed are becoming more important than the spirit house and the mythical journey from Roatan, which are central to traditional Garifuna culture. Nevertheless Livingston is still the centre for a number of small and traditional villages strung out along the coast, and it has a powerful, relaxed atmosphere of its own.

Eating, sleeping and other practicalities

Getting your bearings in Livingston is fairly straightforward as there's really only one street. **Hotels** are in plentiful supply, and one of the best is the *Casa Rosada*, about 300 metres along the shore to the left of the dock. Right on the water, this has lovely double rooms for $10, with a minimum stay of two days. On the way to the *Casa Rosada* you pass the *Hotel Caribe* (cheaper at $4), and further up the main street is the *Río Dulce*, an impressive wooden building with rooms for $2: the upstairs rooms are the better ones and the hotel has a bit of a record for theft, so take care. Further into town, taking the left turn along the main street, you eventually come to the *African Place*, a bizarre building that includes a restaurant and has several rooms for rent. The rooms are good and cost around $4, more for a private bathroom. Finally there's the *Flamingo*, on the beach down behind the *African Place*, a German-owned hotel in a walled compound. Once again the rooms are very well kept and cost around $4.

There are also plenty of places to **eat**, one of the best being the *African Place*, which has a good range of unusual dishes, including delicious fish with curry sauce. Other than this your best bet is to try one of the small *comedores* on the main street, all of which do a fantastic line in simple fried fish. The *Comedor Coni* and the *Livingston* are two personal favourites, both very simple, friendly and cheap. For a good fruit juice, or a tropical breakfast, try the *MC Tropical* opposite the *Río Dulce* hotel. For evening **entertainment** there are plenty of hard drinking bars, a pool hall, and several clubs, both in town and out along the coast, where local people go to drink and dance, particularly at weekends.

As for the other practicalities of life, there's a **laundry service** at the *Hotel Río Dulce* if you can't summon the energy to wash your clothes; the **immigration office**, for an exit stamp if you're heading for Belize or an entrance stamp if you've just arrived, is a block or so behind the *Río Dulce*; *Guatel*, for long-distance phone calls, is on the main street; and you can usually change travellers' cheques, at a fairly poor rate, in one of the shops (try the *Almacen Koo Wong*) – there is no bank.

Las Siete Altares

While there's not really that much to do in Livingston itself, other than relaxing in local style, there are a few things roundabout that are worth a visit. Sadly the local beaches are not of the Caribbean dream variety, and they tend to be strewn with seaweed, but there are plenty of pleasant places to take a swim. Everywhere you'll find that the sand slopes into the sea very gradually. The most popular trip out of town, however, is to **Las Siete Altares**, a waterfall about 5km along the beach. To get there you just walk down onto the beach below the *African Place*, past the *Flamingo*, and follow the sand. After a couple of kilometres you come to a small river, which you have to wade across, and beyond this the beach eventually peters out. Just before it does so there's a path in to the left, which you should follow inland. In a short while it brings you to the first of the falls, the lowest of three or four cascades. To reach the others you have to scramble up over it and follow the water: all of the falls are idyllic places to swim, but the highest one is the best of all.

The Río Dulce, from Livingston to El Relleno

Another very good reason for coming to Livingston is to travel up the Río Dulce, a truly spectacular trip that takes you into the hills behind the town and eventually brings you to the main road about 30km upriver. It's the scenery that's the main attraction, but along the way there are a couple of places where you can stop off for a while. Mail boats do the trip twice a week, and this is the cheapest way to travel, but if you can gather a group of five or six people it's worth hiring a boat and taking your time. If you really want to explore the river, searching out its wildlife or exploring the inlets, then you'll certainly need to hire a boat – you can find them fairly easily in both Livingston and El Relleno.

From Livingston the river heads into a daunting gorge, between sheer rock faces a hundred metres or so in height. Clinging to the sides is a wall of tropical vegetation and cascading vines, and here and there you might see some white herons or flocks of squawking parakeets. A few kilometres into the gorge there's a spot, known to most of the boatmen, where warm sulphurous waters emerge from the base of the cliff, a great place for a swim.

After another five or six kilometres the gorge opens out into a small lake, **El Golfete**, and on the northern shore is the **Biotopo de Chocón Machacas**, a government-sponsored nature reserve designed to protect the habitat of the manatee or sea cow, a threatened species that's seen around here from time to time. The manatee is a massive seal-shaped mammal that lives in both sea and freshwater and, according to some, gave rise to the myth of the mermaid. Female manatees breast-feed their young, clutching them in their flippers, but are not as dainty as traditional mermaids, weighing up to a ton. They are exceptionally timid too, so you're very unlikely to see one.

The reserve is also there to protect the forest that still covers much of the lake's shore, and there are some specially cut trails where you might catch sight of a bird or two, or if you've plenty of time and patience a tapir or jaguar. The reserve also has a jetty where boats dock, which is great to swim from. Visitors are welcome to camp here, but you'll need to bring all your own food.

El Relleno and the Castillo de Felipe

Heading on upstream, across the Golfete, the river closes in again and passes the marina at **EL RELLENO**. This part of the Río Dulce is a favourite playground for wealthy Guatemalans, with boats and hotels that would put parts of California to shame. Here also the road for the Petén crosses the river and the boat trip comes to an end, although you might try and include a stop at the Castillo, an old Spanish castle on the other side of the bridge.

The village of El Relleno, also known as Río Dulce, is little more than a truck stop, where traffic for the Petén pauses before the long stretch to Flores. The road is lined with cheap *comedores* and *tiendas*, and from here you can pick up buses in either direction. If you're heading towards Guatemala City or Puerto Barrios then the best bet is to take a minibus going to Morales (every half-hour) and get out at the Ruidosa junction, where you can flag down a bus. If you're heading for the Petén then the last direct bus passes at about 3pm; after that you might be able to hitch as far as Poptún, or you can spend the night here in El Relleno, and head on in the morning. The village has plenty of cheap hotels – the *Hotel Marilu*, in the centre, and the *Hospedaje Del Río* are both cheap and basic.

If you have an hour or so to spare then it's well worth heading out to the **Castillo San Felipe**, a kilometre upstream, which marks the entrance to Lake Izabal. The fort is a tribute to the audacity of English pirates, who used to sail up the Río Dulce and into the lake in order to steal supplies and harass mule trains. The Spanish were so infuriated by this that they built the fortress to seal off the entrance to the lake and a chain was strung across the river. In later years the castle was used as a prison, but these days it has been restored and landscaped, and looks exactly like a miniature medieval castle: the recent improvements haven't done any harm and it's still well worth a visit, with a maze of tiny rooms and staircases, and fantastically thick walls. Alongside the castle there's a café, a swimming pool and a tennis court. About 300 metres away the *Hotel Humberto*, one of the best places to stay around El Relleno, charges around $2, the only disadvantage being that it's a bit far from the road if you're just passing through.

THE EASTERN HIGHLANDS

The eastern end of the highlands, connecting Guatemala City with El Salvador, has to rank as the least visited part of the entire country. Here the population is almost entirely latinised, speaking Spanish and wearing western clothes, although by blood many are pure-bred Indians. Only in a couple of isolated areas do they still speak Pocoman, the area's original indigenous language: this is closely related to Kekchi, the language spoken around Cobán. The *Ladinos* of the east have a reputation for behaving like cowboys, and violent demonstrations of macho pride are common in these parts. This part of the country is also a stronghold of right-wing politics.

The landscape of this eastern area lacks the immediate appeal of the western highlands. Not only is it lower, but in general its features are less clearly defined. The volcanoes, unlike the neatly symmetrical cones of the west, are badly eroded, merging with the lower-lying hills. But the lower altitude does have a positive side: the hills are that much more fertile, and the broad valleys are lush with vegetation, similar in many ways to the highlands of El Salvador.

On the whole you're unlikely to head in this direction unless you're on your way to the border with El Salvador, in which case your best bet is to travel directly to **San Salvador** by pullman. It's a route that takes you through the southern side of the eastern highlands, and several companies can get you from one capital to the other in little over eight hours. If, however, you decide to explore this part of the country, then the best route takes you right through the central area, from **Jutiapa** to **Jalapa**, and then north to **Esquipulas**. The roads are poor but the scenery is superb, taking you across vast valleys and over great ranges of hills.

Alternatively you can head into the northern side of the eastern highlands, along a good road that branches off the Caribbean highway and connects the towns of **Zacapa**, **Chiquimula** and **Esquipulas**. From here you can head on into Honduras and El Salvador, or make a short trip to the ruins of **Copán** in Honduras, the very best of the southern Maya sites. Heading out this way the landscape is very different, with dry hills and dusty fields, but once again the population is very latinised and urbanised.

From Guatemala City to El Salvador

Although there are several possible routes between the capital and the El Salvadorean border, it's the highland route, passing through Cuilapa, that draws the most traffic. This is not only the fastest connection between the two countries but also offers the most spectacular scenery, weaving through a series of lush valleys. The highway leaves through the southern suburbs of Zona 10, and climbs steeply out of the city, passing the hillside villas of the wealthy. At the top it reaches a high plateau from which you get a good view of the eastern side of the Pacaya volcano. There are few towns out this way: the only place before CUILAPA, some 70km from the capital, is the small roadside settlement BARBERENA. Cuilapa's claim to fame is that it is supposedly the very "centre of the Americas" – which doesn't actually make it an interesting place to stop. There are a couple of hotels if you get stuck, and a branch road that heads south to the coastal town of **Chiquimulilla** (with buses every hour or so).

Eleven kilometres beyond Cuilapa the highway splits at the **El Molino junction**. The southern fork, highway CA8, is the most direct route to the border, heading straight for the crossing at **VALLE NUEVO**, less than 50km away. This road is straight, fast and scenic, but the border crossing is little more than a customs post and there's nowhere to stay either there or on the way.

The northern fork, CA1, is the continuation of the **Pan-American highway**. This road is much slower, as it passes through most of the main towns and is served only by second-class buses, but it's also considerably more interesting. If you're heading directly for El Salvador then the southern branch is the one to stick with, and if you wait at the junction a pullman for San Salvador will turn up sooner or later.

The Pan-American Highway: Jutiapa

Heading west from El Molino, the Pan-American highway turns towards the mountains, running through an isolated valley of sugar cane and then climbing onto a high plateau. Here the landscape is more characteristic of the eastern highlands, with its open valleys and low ridges overshadowed by a huge eroded volcano.

Bypassing the small town of QUESADA, the road arrives at **JUTIAPA**, the main town in this part of the country. The centre of trade and transport for the entire eastern region, this is a busy and not particularly attractive place, with a steady stream of buses to and from the border and the capital, and to all other parts of the east, from Jalapa to Esquipulas. If you decide to **stay** there are plenty of places to choose from. For those on a tight budget the cheapest places are around the bus terminal, and the *Pension Gloria*, near the main road, charges a couple of dollars for a basic room. The *Hotel España*, on the other hand, is impeccably kept and very popular with local businessmen: all rooms have private bathrooms and for $10 three meals are included in the price – $5 with only one meal. The *Posada Belen* ($3) is another spotless place, with rooms set off a leafy courtyard.

Hourly **buses** pass through Jutiapa heading for the border and for Guatemala City, pulling in at the bus terminal, right in the middle of town. Jutiapa is also the starting point for a trip across the eastern highlands to Chiquimula or Esquipulas (see below). The quickest route takes you directly to Esquipulas, through Ipala, and there are buses from Jutiapa that head this way. But if you'd rather take your time and see the best of this part of the country then take a bus to Jalapa, spend the night there, and then press on to Chiquimula.

Asunción Mita and the border at San Cristóbal

Heading on from Jutiapa towards the border with El Salvador the Pan-American highway runs through EL PROGRESO, where the roads to Jalapa and to Ipala (for the direct route to Chiquimula or Esquipulas) branch off to the north. Beyond here the road drops into yet another vast open valley, and arrives at the small town of **ASUNCIÓN MITA**, 45 minutes from Jutiapa, half an hour from the border. Despite its jaded appearance, Asunción has a considerable past: founded, according to Indian records, in 1449, and captured by the Spanish in 1550, it was an important staging post on the royal route to Panama in colonial times. More recently there was a railway that ran through here from Guatemala City. Nowadays, about its only significance is as the last town before the border – if you arrive here in the evening it's easiest to stay the night and cross into El Salvador the next day. The *Hotel Selecta* ($2), right beside the road, is a comfortable sort of place that also has a restaurant; the *Pension Central*, between the road and the centre of town, is cheaper at $1.

For real archaeological enthusiasts there are some ruins about 4km to the east of Asunción Mita along the main road – opposite the *INDECA* building. There's not much to see, but if you rummage around in the fields you should find them – a series of small mounds. According to legend an old man and a young girl rose out of a lake and built the mounds as a monument to Quetzalcoatl.

The **border**, 21km to the south, is connected to Asunción Mita by a stream of buses and minibuses. The actual crossing point is marked by the small town of **SAN CRISTÓBAL**, where there are a couple of basic *pensiones* – the best of these is the *Pension Hernandez*, a block or so to the south of the main road. The last bus for Guatemala City leaves the border at 3pm, and the last minibus for Asunción Mita leaves at around 5pm.

Jalapa to Ipala

Any trip through the eastern highlands should include the road **between Ipala and Jalapa**, which takes you through some truly breathtaking scenery. This is not actually on the way to anywhere, and it's a fairly long and exhausting trip, but if you've had enough of the tourist overkill of the western highlands and don't mind a bumpy ride, then it makes a refreshing change.

From Jutiapa direct buses run to Jalapa, passing through a huge bowl-shaped valley and the towns of MONJAS and MORAZÁN. **JALAPA** itself – where you'll almost certainly have to spend the night – is a prosperous but isolated town in the heart of the eastern highlands. Set away from all the major roads, its bus terminal links all the smaller towns and villages of the area, and is consequently very busy. A paved road runs from here to SANARATE, on the main road from Guatemala City to Puerto Barrios, much the fastest route back to the capital. Alternatively there's a very rough road to Guatemala City which goes via MATAQUESQUINTLA and SAN JOSÉ PINULA – a route I'd only recommend to the hardy and patient as it takes a couple of days. The chances are that you'll arrive in Jalapa fairly late and have to stay the night here; not a bad prospect as the *Hotel Casa del Viajero* has to rate as one of finest budget hotels in the entire country. It's a charming and relaxed sort of place, with a restaurant that has the atmosphere of an Austrian taverna.

Heading on from Jalapa towards Chiquimula and Esquipulas the road climbs into the hills for the most beautiful section of the entire trip, leading up onto a high ridge, with superb views, and then dropping down to the isolated villages of SAN PEDRO PINULA and **SAN LUIS JILOTEPÉQUE**, two outposts of Indian culture. The plaza of San Luis is particularly impressive, with two massive ceiba trees, a colonial church, and a couple of replica stelae from Copán. On Sunday the plaza is the scene of a vast Indian market. If you get stuck here, or find the place so intriguing that you want to stay for a while, there are two fairly basic *pensiones*.

Fourteen kilometres beyond San Luis, this back road joins the main road from Jutiapa at **IPALA**. This is an important crossroads: Jutiapa is to the south, Jalapa west, Chiquimula north and Esquipulas east, and there are buses to all of these places. The village itself is built on an open plain at the base of the Volcán de Ipala, which looks more like a rounded hill. The cone, inactive for hundreds of years, is now filled by a small lake, to which you can walk from the village. There are two grubby *pensiones* in Ipala, the *Catarina* and the *Ipalteca*, but if you can you're better off pushing on to one of the larger towns.

The north: Zacapa, Chiquimula and Esquipulas

What is true of the entire eastern highlands is particularly true of the string of towns which run along the northern side of the mountains. Here eastern machismo is at its most potent and hardly anyone lives outside the towns. The vast majority of the population are *Ladinos*, and furiously proud of it, with a reputation for quick tempers and violent responses. The three towns are, however, the most accessible in the eastern highlands, with a good road and fast bus service from the capital. They also offer access to two particularly interesting sites: the Maya ruins at **Copán** in Honduras, and the shrine of the **Black Christ** in Esquipulas.

The direct road branches off the Caribbean highway at the Río Hondo junction, running through dry, dusty hills to Zacapa, and on through Chiquimula and Esquipulas to the three-way border with Honduras and El Salvador. Before Zacapa the road passes the small town of **ESTANZUELA**, which, oddly enough, has its own museum of palaeontology – the study of earliest man. The museum, **El Museo de Paleontología Bryan Patterson**, is dedicated to an American scientist who worked in the area for many years: hence its presence in this tiny backwater. The exhibits, which include the fossil of a blue whale, manatee bones, a giant armadillo's shell, and the entire skeleton of a mastodon said to be some 50,000 years old, are equally unexpected. There are also some more recent exhibits such as a small Maya tomb, transported here from a site a kilometre or so away, and in the basement some copies of Copán stelae and one or two originals.

The museum is open daily from 8am to 5pm, admission free, and has a certain amateur charm to it. It's certainly well worth a look if you happen to be in the area with an hour to spare. To get here take any bus between El Rancho and Zacapa – including all the buses heading between Guatemala City and Esquipulas – ask the driver to drop you at the village, and simply walk straight through it, along the main street, until you come to the museum. Since it's the only museum for hundreds of kilometres, it shouldn't prove too hard to find.

Zacapa

Just 13km from the Río Hondo junction, **ZACAPA** is reached from the main road by twin bridges across the Río Grande. The town itself is elongated in shape, strung out between the plaza and the railway station. Its atmosphere is dominated by two things: *Ladino* culture and the surrounding desert, which is irrigated to produce tobacco. There's no particular reason to visit Zacapa, but it's pleasant enough if you do, and there are some hot springs a few kilometres to the south. The market is large, sprawling and busy through most of the week, and the plaza is relaxed and tree-lined, with some of the finest public loos in all of Guatemala. On the plaza you'll find a branch of the *Banco de Guatemala*, the **post office**, and a *Guatel* office for long-distance phone calls.

If you do decide to stay there are two **hotels** of note; the Chinese-run *Hotel Wong*, 6 Calle 12–53, is very good value at $2, and around the corner you'll find the *Hotel Central*, in 7 Calle beside the market, which is a bargain at $1. There's not much to do in the evenings in Zacapa, although there are a cinema and pool hall on the main street, 4 Calle, which is also where you'll find most of the places to eat.

The **bus** terminal in Zacapa is a kilometre or so from the centre of town and you need to take a local bus to get there: these leave from outside the *Banco G & T* on the plaza. From the terminal buses leave hourly for Guatemala City, Chiquimula and Esquipulas. There are also minibuses that run between the junction at El Rancho and all of the towns out this way. In Zacapa these can be found in 6 Calle, near the *Hotel Wong*; they don't run to any timetable but departures are regular. If you're coming from Guatemala City to Zacapa there are plenty of buses from the Zona 1 terminal at 19 Calle and 9 Avenida. **Trains** also pass through Zacapa, on a twice-weekly basis, although the timetable is very hard to predict as the service is unreliable at the best of times. To get to the train station follow 4 Calle downhill from the plaza.

The hot springs of Santa Marta

The one good reason for stopping off in Zacapa is to take a trip to the luxurious **Aguas Thermales Santa Marta**, four or five kilometres south of town. There are no buses out this way so you'll either have to walk (in which case you might be able to hitch some of the way) or go by taxi. To get to the hot springs on foot, walk up the street to the right of the church in Zacapa's plaza, past the *Banco de Guatemala*. After four blocks you come to a small park where you want to take the first left, then the next right and then another left. This brings you onto a track that heads out of town across a small river – stick with this track as it heads on through the fields and after about three kilometres it will start to drop into another small valley. Just as it does so take the left-hand fork, at the end of which you'll find the baths.

The bathing rooms are set off a small courtyard in a beautiful old building, built on a vaguely colonial model. Inside each room there's a huge tiled tub, filled with naturally heated water, and the experience is superbly relaxing, sending you to the brink of sleep – if not beyond. The baths are open daily from 8am to 4pm, and there's a small entrance fee.

Chiquimula

From Zacapa the main road continues in the direction of the border, heading up over a low pass and into a great open valley. Set to one side of this is the town of **CHIQUIMULA**, another bustling *Ladino* stronghold. Chiquimula is the largest of these three towns and its plaza functions as the main regional bus terminal, permanently congested by the coming and going of assorted traffic. Other than this it has few unusual features except for a massive ruined colonial church, on the edge of town beside the main road. The church was damaged in the 1765 earthquake, and its ruins have gradually been left behind as the town has moved since then.

There's no particular reason to pause in Chiquimula but it is the starting point for the routes to Copán in Honduras and back through Ipala to Jalapa, so you might end up here for the night. If so the *Hotel Chiquimula* on the plaza is alright but overpriced at $4 (all rooms have private showers); the *Pension Hernandez*, further down the hill, is better value at $3; and the *Pension España* is cheaper still at $2. Or if you're really counting the pennies try the *Casa del Viajero*, on 8 Avenida opposite the *Shell* petrol station.

Buses to Guatemala City and Esquipulas leave the central plaza every hour or so, and to Puerto Barrios until 3pm. There are buses to Ipala four or five times a day, and also to the border at El Florido, for Copán in Honduras, every hour from 9am to 3pm.

Esquipulas

We returned to breakfast, and afterwards set out to visit the only object of interest, the great church of the pilgrimage, the Holy Place of Central America. Every year, on the fifteenth of January, pilgrims visit it, even from Peru and Mexico; the latter being a journey not exceeded in hardship by the pilgrimage to Mecca. As in the east, "it is not forbidden to trade during the pilgrimage", and when there are no wars to make the roads unsafe eighty thousand people have assembled among the mountains to barter and pay homage to "our Lord of Esquipulas".

John Lloyd Stephens, 1841.

The final town on this eastern highway is **ESQUIPULAS**, which, now as in Stephens' day, has a single point of interest. Arriving from Chiquimula the bus winds through the hills, beneath craggy outcrops and forested peaks, emerging suddenly at the lip of a huge bowl-shaped valley. On one side of this, just below the road, is Esquipulas itself. The place is entirely dominated by the perfectly white twin domes of the church, brilliantly floodlit at night: beneath it the rest of the town is a messy sprawl of cheap hotels, souvenir stalls and overpriced restaurants.

The pilgrimage, which continues throughout the year, is what the town is all about, and it has generated numerous sidelines, creating a booming resort where people from all over Central America come to worship, eat, drink and relax.

The principal day of pilgrimage, when the religious significance of the shrine is at its most potent, is January 15. Even the smallest villages will save enough money to send a representative or two on this occasion, their send-off and return invariably marked by religious services. These plus the thousands who can afford to come in their own right ensure that the numbers attending are still as high as in Stephens' day, filling the town to bursting and beyond. Buses chartered from all over Guatemala choke the streets, while the most devoted pilgrims of all arrive on foot (and some even on their knees for the last bit). There's a smaller pilgrimage annually on March 9, and crowds of the faithful visiting at any time of year.

The history of the pilgrimage probably dates back to before the conquest, when the valley was controlled by Chief Esquipulas. Even then it was the site of an important religious shrine, perhaps connected with the nearby Maya site of Copán. When the Spanish arrived the chief was keen to avoid the normal bloodshed and chose to surrender without a fight; the grateful Spaniards named the city they founded at the site in his honour. The famed colonial sculptor Quirio Cataño was then commissioned to carve an image of Christ for the church constructed in the middle of the new town, and in order to make it more likely to appeal to the local Indians he chose to carve it from balsam, a dark wood. (Another version has it that Cataño was hired by Indians after one of their number had seen a vision of a dark Christ on this spot.) In any event the Image was installed in the church in 1595, and soon accredited with miraculous powers. But things really took off in 1737 when the bishop of Guatemala, Pardo de Figueroa, was cured of a chronic ailment on a trip to Esquipulas. The bishop ordered the construction of a new church, which was completed in 1758, and had his body buried beneath the altar.

While all this might seem fairly straightforward it doesn't explain why this figure has become the most revered in a country full of miracle-working saints. One possible explanation is that it offers the Indians, who until recently dominated the pilgrimage, a chance to combine pre-Columbian and Catholic worship. It's known that the Maya pantheon included several black deities such as Ek Ahua, the black lord, who was served by seven retainers, and Ek-chuach, the tall black one, who protected travellers. When Aldous Huxley visited the shrine in 1934 his thoughts were along these lines:

> *So what draws the worshippers is probably less the saintliness of the historic Jesus than the magical sootiness of his image . . . numinosity is in inverse ratio to luminosity.*

Inside the **church** today there's a constant scurry of hushed devotion amid clouds of smoke and incense. In the nave pilgrims approach the Image on their knees, while others light candles, mouth supplication or simply stand in silent crowds. The Image itself is most closely approached by a separate, side entrance where you can join the queue to shuffle past beneath it and pause briefly in front before being shoved on by the crowds behind. Back outside you'll find yourself among crowds of souvenir and relic salesmen, and pilgrims who, duty done, are ready to head off to eat and drink away the rest of their stay. Many pilgrims also visit a set of nearby **caves** said to have miraculous powers and there are some **hot baths** – ideal for ritual ablution.

Practical details

When it comes to staying in Esquipulas you'll find yourself amongst hundreds of visitors at any time of year. **Hotels** probably outnumber private homes and there are new ones springing up all the time. In 1988 plans for a massive luxury hotel were unveiled, to provide for the influx of wealthy pilgrims. Bargains, however, are in short supply and the bulk of the budget hotels are grubby and bare, with tiny monk-like cells – this isn't designed to enhance the mood of pilgrimage but simply to up the number of guests. Many of the cheapest places are opposite the church and the best plan is to look at a few before you decide, as they're all right next door to each other. The *Pension Lemus* is one of the better ones, or try the *San Antonio*, *La Favorita* or *Paris*. There are also dozens of **restaurants** and **bars**, most of them overpriced by Guatemalan standards, and a lone cinema.

Rutas Orientales run a superb **bus** service between Guatemala City and Esquipulas, with departures every half-hour. Their office in Guatemala City is at 19 Calle 8–18, Zona 1, and in Esquipulas it's on the main street. There are also direct buses to Puerto Barrios at 6.30am, 7.15am, 8.30am and 9.30am, and across the highlands to Ipala and Jutiapa. If you're heading from Esquipulas to the ruins of Copán you'll need to catch a bus to Chiquimula and change there.

On to the borders: El Salvador and Honduras

The **Honduran** border crossing at **Agua Caliente** is just 10km from Esquipulas and served by a regular shuttle of minibuses that leave from the main street; the El Florido crossing, which is more convenient if you're heading for the ruins of Copán, is reached by bus from Chiquimula. There's a **Honduran consulate** (weekdays 8.30am–4pm) in the *Hotel Payaqui* in Esquipulas, beside the church. **The border with El Salvador** is about 24km from Esquipulas, down a branch road that splits from the main road just before you arrive at the town. Minibuses and buses serve this border too, but there's no Salvadorean consulate in Esquipulas.

Copán

Across the border in Honduras, less than a day's journey from Guatemala City, are the ruins of **Copán**, one of the most impressive of all Maya sites. Its architecture may not be as impressive as the likes of Tikal or Chichén Itzá, but in other ways it is more than their equal. As at Quiriguá – and indeed all southern Maya sites – the buildings themselves are relatively low. Here the most impressive features are not the temples themselves, but the carvings that decorate them and the stelae that surround them. Maya artists at Copán and Quiriguá developed astounding skills and carved superbly rounded portraits and deep-set glyphs, many of which are still well preserved. Copán's most famous structure is the Hieroglyphic Stairway, the longest Maya text in existence, containing some 2000 glyphs carved onto a flight of sixty stone steps.

It's just possible to see the ruins as a day trip from Guatemala, but to make it worth your while and really take in the splendours of the site it would be a better idea to spend a night in Honduras. The best plan is to set out early from Guatemala so that you'll be in Copán by lunchtime, spend the afternoon at the ruins, and return the next morning – transport from the ruins to the border is virtually non-existent after 1pm. There's no need to get a visa as the border guards are particularly understanding and operate a special system of temporary entry, whereby they give you an entrance stamp on a piece of paper and then throw it away when you come back into Guatemala – that way it won't invalidate your Guatemalan visa.

Getting there and staying at the ruins

Wherever you're coming from you first need to get to **Chiquimula**, a three-hour trip from Guatemala City (buses leave every hour or so from the terminal in Zona 1, at 18 Calle and 9 Avenida; any bus going to Esquipulas will pass through Chiquimula). From the plaza in Chiquimula small second-class buses depart for the trip to **El Florido** and the border with Honduras every hour between 9am and 3pm, usually packed. Twenty minutes up the road, in the direction of Esquipulas, the road for the border branches off to the left at the **Vado Hondo junction**. The journey through the Sierra del Espíritu Santo to El Florido is rough and dusty: in the few small villages along the way the people are mostly Chorti-speaking Indians, the remnants of an isolated Indian group who've largely abandoned traditional ways, although you might see some local-style *huipiles*. The journey from Chiquimula to the border takes about two and a half hours.

At **EL FLORIDO** you'll find the most rudimentary of border posts, open from 7am to 6pm. Here you'll be charged around $1 for an exit fee and $3 for an entrance fee, depending on the mood of the day. Explain to the border guards that you intend to go no further than *Las Ruinas* (the ruins) and they'll give you a temporary entrance stamp, which saves a lot of hassle. If on the other hand you're heading on into Honduras then make sure you get the real thing. Money changers operate on both sides of the border, but you can also find them, or rather they'll find you, in the village: there's also a bank there.

On the Honduran side a series of trucks, minibuses and buses provide transport to the village of **LAS RUINAS DE COPÁN**, 12km from the border and only a short walk from the site. Once a small farming settlement, Las Ruinas is now at least as much dependent on the ruins for a livelihood, housing the site museum and providing accommodation for visitors.

If you set out early enough from Guatemala you should reach the village around midday, all being well. Before heading out to the ruins you need to find somewhere to **stay** and drop off your stuff. There are plenty of reasonable places that charge around $2, the best of them the *Hotel Las Brisas de Copán* and the *Hotel Marina Annexo*; the *Hotel Honduras*, *Hotel Pena* and *Hotel Patty* are also good. If you feel the need for a bit more luxury then try the *Hotel Marina* or the *Maya*, both of which charge around $5. For some reason hotels in Copán only give you a sheet, which may seem enough in the heat of the day but leaves you freezing at night – so ask for a blanket.

When it comes to **eating** there are several basic *comedores* and a more civilised restaurant in the *Hotel Patty*, but as always the cheapest place to eat is the market. Other than eating and sleeping there's not much to do in the evenings, although there are a couple of cinemas.

On the village's main plaza is the site **museum** (daily 8am–4pm; small fee) which displays some of the miscellaneous bits and pieces that were unearthed amongst the ruins, as well as some of the larger pieces from outlying areas. There's some fantastic carving, as well as jade, obsidian, ceramics and human skulls. The main marker from the ball court is also kept here, and there's a replica of stela B.

Moving on
Heading **back to El Florido** and the border there are trucks and buses through-out the morning, with the last departure at around 1pm. From El Florido to **Chiquimula** there are buses every hour or two from 8am to 4pm. If you want to go on **into Honduras** then you need to take a bus to **San Pedro Sula**, about four hours away, from where there are buses to **Tegucigalpa**.

Copán – a short history of the site

In recent years great strides have been made in understanding the history of Copán, although it's important to remember that the site lies at the southern limit of Maya civilisation and was largely cut off from the other sites, except for Quiriguá, with which it was heavily involved.

Archaeologists now believe that the valley was first inhabited around 1000 BC. Graves dating from 900 BC include a carved jade necklace from the Motagua valley in Guatemala, indicating the existence of trade in luxury goods. The next piece of evidence comes from the grave of a shaman who died in 450 AD and was buried along with a codex and some animals' teeth, perhaps the tools of his trade.

In the sixth century Copán emerged as a substantial city and we know that its emblem glyph was first used in 564 AD, and that the ruler depicted on Quiriguá's Monument 26 was either the fourth of fifth member of Copán's ruling dynasty. It's believed that in these early days Quiriguá, and possibly the entire southern region, was under the control of Copán. Few concrete details are known, however, until the rule of Smoke Imix (628–695 AD) when the area was develop-ing fast. Finds from this era include grinding stones, sophisticated pottery and obsidian blades.

From then on much of our information about Copán is gleaned from the stelae at Quiriguá. In 731 AD Quiriguá's independent emblem glyph emerges for the first time, which probably indicated that the city was starting to break away from Copán. Around this time Copán's ruler was 18 Rabbit (Smoke Imix's son), and his rival at Quiriguá was Cauac Sky. Competition between the two centres came to a head in 737, a date recorded on several of Quiriguá's stelae, when 18 Rabbit was captured by Cauac Sky, probably during a raid on Copán. This event was the start of a boom period in the fortunes of Quiriguá, but it marked a downturn for Copán. 18 Rabbit was succeeded by a short-lived ruler, Smoke Monkey (738–749), and there was little new building during these uncertain years. Political stability returned in 749, when Smoke Shell succeeded, and the city prospered until his death in 763. During his reign the famous hieroglyphic stairway, perhaps the most impressive piece of Maya architecture anywhere, was built. Smoke Shell's son, Yax Pac, took office on July 2, 736, but despite frantic attempts to continue the building boom the city went into decline. Skeletal remains from this period indicate malnutrition and disease, and with the population some-where around 20,000, food resources were by no means adequate. Yax Pac died in the winter of 820, ending the dynastic line of Copán.

Glyph references to 18 Rabbit, God K and Copán

The site came to light again soon after the conquest, in 1576, when it was described by Don Diego de Palacios, although at the time nobody showed much interest. It wasn't until the nineteenth century that the world began to take notice, when John Lloyd Stephens published an account of it, complete with superb illustrations by Frederick Catherwood. Stephens was at the time acting as the American ambassador to Central America, but as he could find no stable government he spent most of his time in search of ancient ruins. In true American style he managed to buy the ruins of Copán, planning to chop the site up and transport it to the States:

> *The reader is perhaps curious to know how old cities sell in Central America. Like other articles of trade, they are regulated by the quality and by the quantity in the market, and the demand; but, not being staple articles, like cotton and indigo, they were held at fancy prices and at that time were dull of sale. I paid fifty dollars for Copán. There was never any difficulty about the price. I offered the sum for which Don Jose María thought me only a fool; if I had offered more, he would probably have considered me something worse.*
>
> John Lloyd Stephens, 1834.

These days the site is in the Honduran government's hands, but American money is still very much involved. The first scientific exploration of the site was carried out between 1891 and 1894 by the Peabody Museum of Harvard, the second major investigation by the Carnegie Institute in Washington. This second project, which began in 1935, included the diversion of the Río Copán which was carving into the site. Finally the Hondurans themselves have got their hands in, and the ruins are now being studied by the *Instituto Hondureño de Antropología y Historia* .

The ruins

The ruins themselves, open daily from 8am to 4pm, are a few kilometres from the village and the walk between the two takes you past some interesting stelae. If you stick to the path – which is on the left-hand side of the road – you'll get a better view of these, just a brief taster to whet your appetite for things to come.

At the entrance to the site there's a **visitors' centre**, where you buy your ticket, a small cafeteria, and an exhibition that includes photos of the reconstruction work and a model of the city as it once was. From here you have to walk a couple of hundred metres further to the tall fence that surrounds the ruins, and a gate guarded by two superb macaws. Once inside you can either walk straight ahead, and into the Central Plaza, or bear off to the right and approach it via an indirect route. Personally I'd recommend this second approach, which takes you through the East and West courts, saving the splendours of the plaza till last.

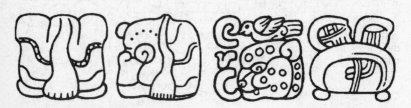

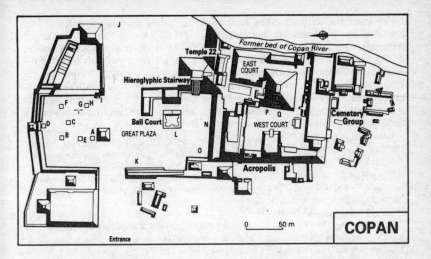

COPAN

The East and West Courts

When you head to the right you'll arrive first in the **West Court**, a small, confined area that forms part of the main acropolis. The most famous feature here is **Altar Q**, at the base of Pyramid 16. The Altar was carved in 776 AD, and was originally thought to have been connected with the lunar cycle. Recent studies, however, have suggested that it was dedicated to the young ruler Yax Pac (also known as New Sun-at-Horizon). The top of the altar is carved with six hieroglyphic blocks, while its sides are decorated with sixteen cross-legged figures, all seated on cushions. For a long time the significance of all this remained a mystery, but in recent years archaeologists have come up with a coherent theory. All of the figures, who represent previous rulers of Copán, are pointing towards a portrait of Yax Pac, who is receiving a ceremonial staff from Mah K'ina Yax K'uk Mo, the city's first ruler. The monument is therefore endorsing Yax Pac's right to rule, clear evidence of the importance of dynastic power structures. Behind this altar archaeologists found a small **crypt** containing the remains of a macaw and fifteen big cats, possibly sacrificed in honour of Yax Pac and his ancestors.

On the northern side of the court is a large terraced **viewing stand**, which is in fact one side of the Central Acropolis. Its panels are decorated with worn carvings and some odd-looking figures, including two monkey gods.

Climbing the stairs on the east side of the court, behind Altar Q, brings you into the **East Court**, larger than the West but still intimate compared to the main plaza. The sides of this court are more elaborate than those of the West Court, and standing in the central dip you're surrounded by austere carvings. The best of these are the great jaguar heads, each as large as a man. The small hollows in their eyes would once have held pieces of jade, or polished obsidian. In the middle of the staircase, flanked by the jaguars, is a rectangular Venus mask, also carved in superb deep relief.

At the southern end of the East Court is **Structure 18**, a small square building with carved panels – although the process of reconstruction has revealed one or

two gaps in the sequence. The floor of
this structure has been dug up to reveal
a magnificent tomb, probably that of one
of Copán's later rulers, Sun-at-Horizon.
Unfortunately by the time archaeologists unearthed it the tomb was virtually
empty, and had probably been looted on
a number of occasions. To the south of
Structure 18 is the so-called **Cemetery
Group**, which was once thought to have
been a burial site, although current
thinking has it marked out as a residential complex, possibly the home of
Copán's ruling elite. As yet it remains
hidden in the trees and little work has

Glyph, Stela 19

been done in this part of the site. Walking back from here towards the main part of
the ruins, along the eastern edge of the court, you get a superb view over the Río
Copán. Between here and the river there used to be another building, Temple 20,
but the force of the river swept it away long ago. The river is now diverted, to steer
it clear of the site and prevent any further damage.

At the northern end of the court, separating it from the main plaza, is **Temple
22**, one of Copán's most impressive buildings. Some of the stonework is astonishingly simple while other sections, particularly around the door frames, are superbly intricate, decorated with outlandish carving. Above the doorway is the body of
a double-headed snake, its heads resting on two figures which in turn are
supported by skulls. At the corners of the temple are portraits of the long-nosed
rain god Chaac, a favourite Maya deity. The quality of the carving on Temple 22
has led archaeologists to suggest that the East Court may have been Copán's
most important plaza. Such carving is unique in the southern Maya area, and
even at Quiriguá carving of this quality is confined to stelae. Only in the Yucatán,
at sites such as Kabáh and Chicanna, is there anything that can compare with
this, or buildings decorated with anything approaching similar skill.

The Great Plaza
The Great Plaza is the hallmark of Copán and sums up its finest features and peculiar architectural attributes. At the southern end of the plaza the **Hieroglyphic
Court** is pressed up against the Central Acropolis. On one side is the **Temple of
the Inscriptions**, a great towering stairway. At its base is **Stela N**, another classic
piece of Copán carving with portraits on the two main faces and glyphs down the
sides. The Great Plaza is strewn with these stelae, all of them magnificently carved
and most exceptionally well preserved. The depth of the relief has protected the
nooks and crannies, and in some of these you can still see flakes of paint: originally
the carvings and buildings would have been painted in a whole range of colours,
but it's only the red that seems to have survived. The style of carving is similar to
that of Quiriguá, and at both sites the portraits of assorted rulers dominate the
decoration, with surrounding glyphs that give details of events and dates from the
period of their rule. Here at Copán most of the carving has yet to be decoded:
Stela J is perhaps the most unusual, decorated in a kind of woven pattern which is
found at only one other place in the entire Maya world, Quiriguá.

On the left-hand side of the Hieroglyphic Court is the famed **Hieroglyphic Stairway**, the most astonishing work of all. The stairway is made up of some 63 stone steps, and every block is carved to form part of the glyphic sequence – a total of between 1500 and 2200 glyphs. It forms the longest known Maya hieroglyphic text, but sadly the sequence is so jumbled that a complete interpretation is still a long way off. The easiest part to understand is the dates, and these range from 544 AD to 744 AD. At the base of the stairway is **Stela M**, which records a solar eclipse in 756 AD.

To the north of the Hieroglyphic Court, Copán's **Ball Court** is one of the few Maya courts that still has a paved floor. Again the entire plaza would once have been paved like this, and probably painted too. The court dates from 775 AD, and beneath if there are two previous versions. The rooms that line the sides of the court, overlooking the playing area, would probably have been used by priests and members of the elite as they observed the ritual of the game.

As for the rest of the plaza, its main appeal lies in the various stelae, Copán's greatest feature. The vivid quality of the carving remains wonderfully clear and the portraits still have an eerie presence to them. It is these carvings, above all else, that separate Copán from all other sites. **Stela A**, which dates from 731 AD, has incredibly deep carving, although much is now eroded. Its sides include a total of 52 glyphs, better preserved than the main faces. **Stela B** is one of the more controversial stones, with a figure that some see as oriental, supporting theories of mass migration from the east. **Stela C** (782) is one the earliest stones to have faces on both sides, and like many of the central stelae it has an altar at its base, carved in the shape of a turtle. **Stela D**, at the northern end of the plaza, depicts 18 Rabbit (who is also on Stela 4). His hair is long and he has a beard, a fashion that he may well have taken with him when he was captured by Cauac Sky, the ruler of Quiriguá, in 737 AD. There are other stelae and altars dotted all around the main plaza, all of them following the same basic pattern, ranging from the fierce-looking **Stela F** to the faceless **Stela J**, entirely covered in glyphs.

fiestas

January
El Progreso (near Jutiapa) kicks off the fiesta year in the eastern highlands. The action lasts from the 12th to the 15th and the final day is the most important. **Cabañas** (near Zacapa) has a fiesta from the 19th to 21st, in honour of San Sebastian, in which the 19th is the main day. **Ipala** has its fiesta, which includes some traditional dances and bullfighting, from the 20th to 26th: the 23rd is the main day. Also, of course, the great pilgrimage to Esquipulas on the 15th.

February
San Pedro Pinula, one of the most traditional places in the east, has a fiesta from the 1st to 4th, in which the final day is the main one. **Monjas** has a fiesta from the 5th to 10th, with the 7th as the main day. **Río Hondo** (on the main road near Zacapa) has its fiesta from the 24th to 28th, with the 26th as the principal day. Both **Pasaco** (in the department of Jutiapa) and **Huite** (near Zacapa) have moveable fiestas around carnival time.

March
Jerez (in the department of Jutiapa) has a fiesta in honour of San Nicolas Tolentino from the 3rd to 5th, with the last day as the main one. There's a smaller day of pilgrimage to the Black Christ of Esquipulas on the 9th. **Moyuta** (near Jutiapa) and **Olapa** (near Chiquimula) both have fiestas from the 12th to 15th. **Morales**, which is a town with little to celebrate but its lust for life, has a fiesta from the 15th to 21st, with the main day on the 19th. **Jocotán** (halfway between Chiquimula and El Florido) has a moveable fiesta in March.

April

April is a quiet month in the east but **La Unión** (near Zacapa) has a fiesta from the 22nd to 25th.

May

Jalapa has its fiesta from the 2nd to 5th, in which the 3rd is the main day. **Gualán** (which is near Zacapa) has a fiesta from the 5th to 9th.

June

The only June fiesta out this way is in **Usumatlán**, from the 23rd to 26th.

July

Puerto Barrios has its fiesta from the 16th to 22nd, with the main day on the 19th: this has something of a reputation for its (enjoyably) wild celebrations. **Jocotán** (near Chiquimula) has its fiesta from the 22nd to 26th. **Esquipulas** has a fiesta in honour of Santiago Apostol from the 23rd to 27th.

August

Chiquimula has its fiesta from the 11th to 18th, with the main day on the 15th: sure to be a good

one, this also includes bullfighting. Over on the other side of the highlands, **Asunción Mita** has a fiesta from the 12th to 15th. **San Luis Jilotepéque** has its fiesta for a single day on the 25th.

September

Sansare (between Jalapa and Sanarate) has its fiesta from the 22nd to 25th, with the 24th as the main day.

November

Sanarate celebrates from the 7th to 14th and **Jutiapa** from the 10th to 16th, with the middle day as the main day. **Quesada** (near Jutiapa) has a fiesta from the 26th to 30th.

December

Zacapa has its fiesta from the 4th to 9th, with the main day on the 8th, and **San Luis Jilotepéque** from the 13th to 16th. **Cuilapa** goes wild from the 22nd to 27th, and **Livingston** from the 24th to 31st: the latter has to be one of the best places in the country to spend a Christmas of Caribbean carnival.

travel details

Once again bus is the best way to get around. For the northeastern area you simply take a bus to either Puerto Barrios or Esquipulas, as these pass through all the main towns in between. To travel into the central highland area you need to catch a bus heading for Jutiapa, and change buses there.

Buses
The Motagua Valley

Buses for **Puerto Barrios** leave Guatemala City hourly from the terminal at 9 Avenida and 18 Calle in Zona 1. The very best of these, luxury pullmans, are run by *Litegua* (whose actual office is at 15 Calle 10–40), with departures from 5.30am to 5pm. In Puerto Barrios their office is on 6 Avenida, between 9 and 10 Calles, from where there are buses to Guatemala City from 1am to 4pm. The trip takes about six hours and tickets can be bought in advance. All buses run past the entrance road for **Quiriguá**, which is about four hours from Guatemala City, and virtually everywhere else along the way except **Morales** and **Bananera**: for these you can change at the

Ruidosa junction where the road to the Petén turns off.

From Puerto Barrios there are buses to **Morales and Bananera** every hour or so, and to **Esquipulas** during the morning. There's also a daily bus to **Mariscos** at 3pm.

From Morales and Bananera there are regular buses and minibuses to **Río Dulce**, and you can also pick up buses to the **Petén** here.

To Mariscos there's a direct bus from 18 Calle and 9 Avenida in Guatemala City at 6am, and one from Puerto Barrios at 3pm – you can also hitch to Mariscos from the **La Trinchera** junction on the main Caribbean highway.

The Eastern Highlands

To Esquipulas there are regular pullman buses, run by *Rutas Orientales*, that leave from 19 Calle and 9 Avenida in Zona 1, Guatemala City, every half-hour. These call in at **Zacapa** and **Chiquimula**. If you're coming from Puerto Barrios or the Petén and want to head out this way then you can pick up one of these buses at the **Río Hondo junction** on the Caribbean highway.

From Esquipulas there are buses every half-hour to Guatemala City, and a regular flow of mini-buses and buses to the borders with El Salvador and Honduras. There are also buses to **Jutiapa** and **Jalapa**, and during the morning to **Puerto Barrios**.

From Chiquimula there are three or four buses a day, between 9am and 3pm, to the **El Florido** border crossing, from where there are trucks and buses to **Copán** in Honduras. There's also a fairly regular service to **Ipala**, from where there are buses to **Jalapa**.

To Jutiapa there are buses every hour or so from the Zona 4 bus terminal in Guatemala City, and most of these go on to **Asunción Mita** and **San Cristóbal Frontera** – the border with El Salvador. The last bus from the border to Guatemala City is at 2.30pm. All buses between Guatemala City and Jutiapa pass through **Cuilapa**, from where there are hourly buses to **Chiquimulilla**.

From Jutiapa there are buses to all parts of the eastern highlands, including **Esquipulas**, **Ipala** and **Jalapa**.

To San Salvador several companies run a direct service from Guatemala City via the **Valle Nuevo** border crossing – the entire trip takes around eight hours. The companies serving this route include *Mermex*, *Taca* and *Trascomer*, and between them they lay on a departure every hour. Their offices are all at the junction of 1 Calle and 5 Avenida in Zona 4, Guatemala City.

Boats

From Puerto Barrios to Livingston there's a daily ferry service at 10.30am and 5pm, returning at 5am and 2pm. On Tuesday and Friday a boat leaves at 7.30am for **Punta Gorda** in Belize, via Livingston.

From Livingston up the Río Dulce there's a twice-weekly mail boat, on Tuesdays and Fridays, but if you can get together five or six people then it's just as cheap to hire a boat.

From Mariscos to El Estor a ferry leaves daily at 1pm, returning at 5am.

CHAPTER FIVE

COBAN AND THE VERAPACES

W hile essentially a continuation of Guatemala's western highlands, the mountains of Alta and Baja Verapaz have always been set apart in a number of ways: in physical terms the flat-bottomed Salamá valley and the mist-soaked hills of Cobán are certainly unlike any of the other mountainous areas. **Baja Verapaz**, the more southerly of these two departments, is sparsely populated, a mixture of deep river valleys, dry hills and lush tropical forest. A single road runs through the department, connecting the towns of **Salamá**, **Rabinal** and **Cubulco**, while the rest of the land is dotted with tiny hamlets. **Alta Verapaz**, the wettest and greenest of Guatemala's highlands, occupies the higher land to the north. Local people say it rains for thirteen months a year here, alternating between straightforward downpour and the drizzle of the *Chipi-chipi*, a misty rain that hangs interminably on the hills. The capital of Alta Verapaz is **Cobán**, from where roads head north into the Petén, west to El Quiché, and east to the shores of Lake Izabal.

The history of the Verapaces is also quite distinct. Long before the conquest its people, the **Rabinal** nation, had earned themselves a unique reputation as the most bloodthirsty of all the tribes, said to sacrifice every prisoner that they took. Their greatest enemies were the Quichés, with whom it's said they were at war for a century. So ferocious were the Rabinal that not even the Spanish could contain them by force. Alvarado's army was unable to make any headway against them, and eventually he gave up trying to control the area, naming it *Tierra de Guerra*, the land of war.

The church, however, couldn't allow so many heathen souls to go to waste, and under the leadership of **Fray Bartolomé de Las Casas**, the so-called apostle of the Indians, they made a deal with the *conquistadores*. If Alvarado would agree to keep all armed men out of the area for five years, the priests would bring it under control. In 1537 Las Casas himself, accompanied by three other Dominican friars, set out into the highlands. Here they befriended the Rabinal chiefs, and learning the local dialects they translated devotional hymns and taught them to the bemused Indians. By 1538 they had made considerable progress, converting large numbers of Indians and persuading them to move from their scattered hillside homes to the new Spanish-style villages. At the end of the five years the famous and invincible Rabinales were transformed into Spanish subjects, and the king of Spain renamed the province *Verapaz*, "true peace".

Since the colonial era the Verapaces have remained isolated and in many ways independent: all their trade bypassed the capital by taking a direct route to the Caribbean, along the Río Polochic and out through Lake Izabal. The area really started to develop with the coffee boom at the turn of the century, when German

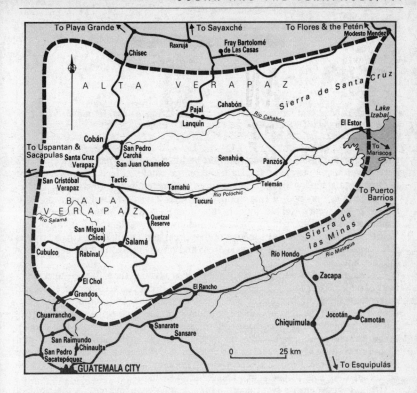

immigrants flooded into the country to buy and run *fincas*, particularly in Alta Verapaz. By 1914 about half of all Guatemalan coffee was grown on German-owned lands and Germany bought half of the exported produce. Around Cobán the new immigrants intermarried with local families and established an island of European sophistication. A railway was built along the Polochic valley and Alta Verapaz became almost totally independent. This situation was brought to an end by World War II, when the Americans insisted that Guatemala do something about the enemy presence, and the government was forced to expel the landowners, many of whom were unashamed in their support for Hitler.

Although the Verapaces are now well connected to the capital and their economy is integrated with the rest of the country, the area is still dependent on the production of coffee, and Cobán is still dominated by the huge coffee *fincas*. Here and there, too, hints of the Germanic influence survive.

Taken as a whole, however, the Verapaces remain very much Indian country: Baja Verapaz has a small Quiché outpost around Rabinal, and in Alta Verapaz the Indian population, largely **Pokomchí** and **Kekchí** speakers, the two languages of the **Pokoman group**, is predominant. The production of coffee has cut deep into their land and their way of life, and traditional costume is worn less here than in the western highlands. Not so long ago each village had a recognisable costume, and only in the last decade or so have many of the decorative local *huipiles* gone out of use. In their place many Indians have adopted a more universal Kekchí

MARKET DAYS	
Monday	**Saturday**
Tucurú. Senahú.	Senahú.
Tuesday	**Sunday**
Cubulco. Chisec. El Chol. Lanquín.	Cubulco. Chisec. Purulhá.
Purulhá. Rabinal. San Jerónimo. San	Rabinal. Salamá. San Jerónimo. Santa
Cristóbal Verapaz. Tres Cruces.	Cruz. Verapaz. Tactic.

costume, using the loose hanging *huipile* and locally made *cortes*. Coffee bushes have driven many people off the land, and on the whole Indians are now confined to the marginal land, with all prime territory dominated by the *fincas*.

The northern section of Alta Verapaz includes a slice of the Petén rainforest, and in recent years Kekchí Indians have fanned out into this empty expanse, reaching the Río Salinas in the west and making their way across the border into Belize. Here they carve out sections of the forest and attempt to farm, a process that threatens the future of the rainforest and offers little long-term security for the migrants.

For visitors the Verapaces are perhaps less inviting than the western highlands, and far fewer tourists make it out this way. But if you've time and energy to spare then these highlands include a few unique sites and some adventurous trips. The hub of the area is **Cobán**, nowadays subdued and somewhat miserable, but still the place from which to set out to explore. In Baja Verapaz, if you happen to be around at the right time of year, the towns of **Salamá**, **Rabinal** and **Cubulco** all have famous fiestas, and in August Cobán itself hosts the **National Folklore Festival**. From Cubulco you can continue on foot, over the Sierra de Chuacús, to Joyabaj, a spectacular and exhausting hike.

Heading between the two departments, beside the main road, is the **quetzal sanctuary**, where you can occasionally see one of Central America's rarest birds, prized since the earliest of times. Heading out to the north of Cobán you can reach the beautiful **Semuc Champey**, a natural set of bathing pools surrounded by lush tropical forest. Cobán is also the starting point for three seldom-travelled back routes: east down the Río Polochic to **Lake Izabal**, north through Pajal to **Fray Bartolomé de Las Casas** (for connections to Sayaxché), or west to **Uspantán** for connections to Santa Cruz del Quiché and Nebaj (or all the way across to Huehuetenango).

Baja Verapaz

A strange but dramatic mix of dry hills and fertile valleys, Baja Verapaz is crossed by a skeletal road network, with only the towns of Salamá, Rabinal and Cubulco served by buses. All of these have interesting markets and are famed for their fiestas, where you'll see some unique traditional dances. The other big attraction is the quetzal sanctuary, set to one side of the main road to Cobán.

The main approach to both departments is from the Caribbean highway, where the road to the highlands branches off at the **El Rancho** junction. As this road climbs steadily into the hills, the dusty browns and dry yellows of the Motagua valley soon give way to an explosion of greens, in dense pine forests that offer superb views. All too often, though, the mountains are shrouded in a blanket of cloud. Forty-eight kilometres from the junction is **La Cumbre de Santa Elena**, where the road for the main towns of Baja Verapaz turns off to the west, immediately starting to drop towards the floor of the Salamá valley. Surrounded by steep hillsides, with a level floodplain at its base, the valley appears entirely cut off from the outside world.

Here at its eastern end is the village of **SAN JERÓNIMO**, which is bypassed by the road for Salamá. In the early days of the conquest Dominican priests built a church and convent here and planted vineyards, eventually producing a wine that earned the village something of a reputation. In 1845, after the religious orders were abolished, an Englishman replaced the vines with sugar cane and began brewing an *aguardiente* that became equally famous. These days the area still produces cane, and a fair amount of alcohol, although the English connection is long gone. Minibuses connect Salamá and San Jerónimo, but there's no particular reason to visit the village unless you're exceptionally keen on *aguardiente*.

Salamá, Rabinal and Cubulco

At the western end of the valley is **SALAMÁ**, capital of the department of Baja Verapaz. The town has a relaxed and prosperous air to it, and like many of the places out this way its population is largely latinised. There's not much to do here, other than browsing in the Sunday market, though a couple of things are worth a look. On the edge of town is a crumbling colonial bridge, now used only by pedestrians, and the old church, currently under restoration, is also interesting, with huge altars running down either side, darkened by age. The fiesta in Salamá runs from September 17 to 21. If you decide to **stay** then the *Hotel Tezulutlán* ($4) is a gorgeous old building with rooms set around a spotless and leafy courtyard, and there's a bank and a post office on the plaza.

Nine **buses** a day head out in this direction from Guatemala City, leaving the Zona 1 terminal at 19 Calle and 9 Avenida between 5.45am and 4.45pm. Three of them terminate here in Salamá, three stop at Rabinal and three (all morning departures) continue all the way to Cubulco: heading back, the last bus leaves Cubulco at 2pm. At Salamá the tarmac ends and the road continues west, climbing out of the valley over a low pass, through a gap in the hills, to SAN MIGUEL CHICAJ, a small and traditional village clustered around a colonial church. Beyond here the road climbs again, this time to a greater height, reaching a pass with magnificent views across the surrounding hills, stepping away into the distance.

An hour or so from Salamá you arrive in **RABINAL**, another isolated farming town that's also dominated by a large colonial church. Here the proportion of Indian inhabitants is considerably higher, making both the Sunday market and the fiesta well worth a visit. Founded in 1537 by Bartolomé de Las Casas himself, Rabinal was the first of the settlements in his peaceful conquest of the Rabinal nation: about three kilometres to the northwest are the ruins of one of their fortified cities. Nowadays the place is best known for its oranges, claimed to be the best in the country – and they certainly taste like it.

Rabinal's **fiesta**, January 25–29, is famous above all for its dances. The most notorious of these, an extended dance drama known as the *Rabinal Achi*, was last performed in 1856, but many other unique routines are still performed. The *Patzca*, for example, is a ceremony calling for good harvests, using masks that portray a swelling below the jaw and wooden sticks engraved with serpents, birds

Details from Chixoy Valley vase

and human heads. If you can't make it for the fiesta the Sunday market is a good second best. There are two fairly simple hotels in Rabinal, the *Hospedaje Caballeros* and the *Pension Motagua*.

Leaving Rabinal the roads heads on to the west, climbing yet another high ridge with fantastic views to the left, into the uninhabited mountain ranges. To the north, in one of the deep river valleys, is the Chixoy hydroelectric plant, where over three-quarters of Guatemala's electricity is generated.

Another hour of rough road brings you down into the next valley, and **CUBULCO**. Another isolated, latinised town, surrounded on all sides by steep forested mountains, Cubulco is again most worth visiting for its fiesta. This is one of the few places where you can still see the *Palo Volador*, a pre-conquest ritual in which men throw themselves from a thirty-metre pole with a rope tied around their leg, spinning down towards the ground as the rope unravels, and hopefully landing on their feet. It's as dangerous as it looks, particularly when you bear in mind that most of the dancers are blind drunk: in 1988 a drunken dancer fell from the top of the pole, killing himself. The fiesta still goes on, though, as riotous as ever, with the main action taking place on January 23. The best place to stay is in the large *Farmacía* in the centre of town, and there are several good *comedores* in the market.

On from Cubulco: the back routes

If you'd rather not leave the valley the same way that you arrived, there are two other options. One bus a day, leaving Cubulco at 9am, heads back to Rabinal and then, instead of heading for La Cumbre and the main road, turns south, crossing the spine of the Sierra de Chuacús, and dropping directly down towards Guatemala City. The trip takes you over rough roads for around nine hours, through EL CHOL, GRANADOS and SAN JUAN SACATEPÉQUEZ, but the mountain views and the sense of leaving the beaten track help to take the pain out of it all.

Hiking from Cubulco to Joyabaj

If you'd rather leave the roads altogether, then an even less travelled route takes you out of the valley on foot, also over the Sierra de Chuacús, to Joyabaj. The hike takes between eight and ten hours, but if you have a tent it's probably best to break the trip halfway at the village of **TRES CRUCES**: if you don't have one you'll probably be able to find a floor to sleep on. The views, as you tramp over a huge ridge and through a mixture of pine forest and farmland, are of course spectacular.

The hills around Cubulco are covered in a complex network of paths so it's well worth getting someone to point you in the right direction, and asking plenty of people along the way – for the first half of the walk it's better to ask for Tres Cruces rather than Joyabaj. Broadly speaking the path bears up to the right as it climbs the hillside to the south of Cubulco, crossing the mountain range after about three hours. On the other side is an open, bowl-shaped valley, where to reach Tres Cruces you walk along the top of the ridge that marks the right-hand side of the valley – heading south from the pass. Don't drop down into the valley until you reach Tres Cruces. The village itself is the smallest of rural hamlets, perched high on the spine of the ridge, and far from the reach of the nearest road. On Thursday mornings the tiny plaza is crammed with traders who assemble for the market, but otherwise there's nothing but a couple of simple *tiendas*. Beyond Tres Cruces you drop down into the valley that cuts in to the right (west) of the ridge, and then follow the dirt road out of the valley, onto the larger Joyabaj to Pachalum road – turn right for Joyabaj (p.95).

Towards Alta Verapaz: the Quetzal Sanctuary

Heading for Cobán, and deeper into the highlands, the main road sweeps straight past the turning for Salamá and on around endless tight curves below forested hillsides. Just before the village of PURULHÁ is the **Biotopo del Quetzal**, a 1153-hectare nature reserve designed to protect the habitat of the quetzal. The national symbol – with the honour of lending its name to a unit of currency – this rare bird also has a distinguished past and an uncertain future. The feathers of the quetzal were sacred from the earliest of times, and in the strange cult of Quetzalcoatl, which spread its influence throughout Mesoamerica, the quetzal was incorporated into the plumed serpent, a supremely powerful deity. (The great Quiché leader Gucumatz, who built their capital at Utatlán, was also known as "plumed serpent".) To the Maya the quetzal was so sacred that killing the bird was a capital offence, and the bird is also thought to have been the *Nahual*, or spiritual protector, of the Indian chiefs. When Tecún Umán faced Alvarado in hand-to-hand combat his headdress sprouted the long green feathers of the quetzal. And when the *conquistadores* founded a city adjacent to the battleground they named it Quezaltenango, the place of the quetzals.

In modern Guatemala the quetzal has been adopted as the national symbol, and its image saturates the entire country, appearing in every imaginable context from *huipiles* to bank notes. Citizens honoured by the president are awarded the "Order of the Quetzal", and the bird is also considered a symbol of freedom, as caged quetzals die from the rigours of confinement. Despite all this the sweeping tide of deforestation threatens the very existence of the quetzal, and the sanctuary is about the only concrete step that has been taken to save it.

The more resplendent of the birds, and the source of the famed feathers, is the male. Their heads are crowned with a plume of brilliant green, the chest and lower belly is a rich crimson, and stretching out behind are the unmistakeable long, golden-green tail feathers. The females, on the other hand, are an unremarkable brownish colour. The birds nest in holes drilled into dead trees, laying one or two eggs at the start of the rainy season, usually in April or May, and just before and just after this is the best time of year to visit if you hope to see them.

The reserve is a steep and dense rainforest, through which the Río Colorado cascades towards the valley floor. Two paths have so far been cut into the undergrowth, each completing a circuit that takes you up into the woods and around above the reserve headquarters. There are fairly large numbers of quetzals hidden in the forest, but they're extremely elusive. Dawn is the best time to catch a glimpse of one, but you just might get lucky at any time of day. In general they tend to spend the nights up in the high forest and float across the road as dawn breaks, to spend the days in the forest below. New paths, probably completed by the time you read this, are being cut into the forest below the road, so during the day that's probably the best place to go in search of a sighting. Whether or not you see a quetzal, the forest itself, usually damp with mist, is well worth a visit: a profusion of lichens, ferns, mosses, bromeliads and orchids, spread out beneath the towering canopy.

The reserve is open daily from 6am to 5pm, and there are camping and hammock spaces, and a stream-fed pool for bathing. A kilometre or so past the entrance to the reserve is the *Pension Los Ranchitos* where a bed in one of two wooden huts costs around $2. There's no electricity and the *comedor's* menu is usually limited to eggs and beans. **Buses** running to or from Cobán pass the entrance hourly, but make sure they know you want to be dropped at the Biotopo as it's easy to miss.

Alta Verapaz

Beyond the quetzal sanctuary the main road crosses into the department of Alta Verapaz, and another 13km takes you beyond the forests and into a luxuriant alpine valley of cattle pastures hemmed in by steep hillsides. Here the hills are always gloriously green, a feature which firmly marks the landscape of Alta Verapaz.

The first place of any size is **TACTIC**, a small town adjacent to the main road which most buses run straight through. Tactic has earned its ounce of fame as the site of the *Pozo Vivo*, the living well. A sign points the way to this decidedly odd attraction opposite the northern entrance road. The well itself is a small pool that appears motionless at first, until your eye catches the odd swirl in the mud – local legend has it that the water only comes to life when approached. The colonial church in the village is also worth a look, as is the Chi-ixim chapel high above the town. If you fancy a cool swim then the *Balneario Cham-che*, a crystal-clear spring-fed pool, is on the other side of the main road, opposite the centre of town. If you decide to stay in Tactic the *Pension Central*, on the main street to the north of the plaza, is simple and cheap, or if it's full you can try the *Pension Sulmy*.

Further towards Cobán, the turning for **SAN CRISTÓBAL VERAPAZ** peels off to the left. A tranquil, pretty town surrounded by fields of sugar cane and coffee, it's set on the banks of **Lake Cristóbal**, a favourite spot for swimming and fishing. Legend has it that the lake was formed in 1590 as a result of a dispute between a priest and local Indians over the celebration of pagan rites. According to one version the earth split and swallowed the Indians, sealing their graves with the water, while another has it that the priest fled hurling maledictions, and these were so heavy that they created a depression which then filled with water. The Pokomchí-speaking Indians of San Cristóbal are among the last vestiges of one of the smallest and oldest highland tribes.

West from San Cristóbal the rough road continues to **Uspantán** (in the western highlands) from where buses run to Santa Cruz del Quiché, via Sacapulas, for connections to Nebaj and Huehuetenango. To head out this way you can either hitch from San Cristóbal or catch the bus that leaves San Pedro Carchá at noon, passing through the plaza in Cobán ten minutes later, and reaching San Cristóbal after about another half-hour.

Cobán

The heart of these rain-soaked hills and the capital of the department is **COBÁN**, where the paved highway comes to an end. The town has something of a dull atmosphere, weary and inactive, and the air is usually damp and often cold. Despite all this it's the largest town in the Verapaces so if you're heading up this way you're likely to be here for a night or two.

Cobán's imperial heyday, when it stood at the centre of its own isolated world, is now long gone, and the glory well faded. The plaza, however, remains an impressive triangle, dominated by the cathedral, from which the town drops away on all sides. A block behind the cathedral is the market, bustling with trade during the day, and surrounded by cheap food stalls at night. Life in Cobán revolves around coffee; the sedate restaurants and overflowing supermarket are a tribute to the town's affluence, and the crowds that sleep in the market and plaza, assembling in the bus terminal to search for work, are migrant labourers heading for the plantations. Since a fast road linked Cobán with the capital, the *finqueros*, wealthy owners of the coffee plantations, have mostly moved to Guatemala City, but a small residue still base themselves in Cobán. Hints of the days of German control can still be found here and there, whether in the architecture, incorporating the occasional suggestion of Bavarian grandeur, or the posters of the fatherland that are peeling from the walls of the cinema.

Sleeping and eating

Unless you happened to coincide with the August fiestas you'll probably only pause here for a day at the most before heading off into the hills, out to the villages, or on to some other part of the country. There are however plenty of **hotels** in town. The cheapest is the *Pension Familiar* ($1), a grubby sort of place at the plaza's pointed end that's a favourite with local traders. Two roads lead from this end of the plaza: on the higher of the two are the *Banco de Guatemala* and the **post office**; take the second right off this and you'll find the *Hotel Monterrey* and the better *La Paz*, both of which are good value at $2. In the other direction, down the side of the cathedral, is the *Hotel Central* ($2).

When it comes to **eating** in Cobán you have a simple choice between fancy European-style restaurants and very basic, cheap *comedores*. The smartest places are opposite the *Banco de Guatemala*, where you'll find the *Pizzeria El Molino* and the *Pastelería Mus Mus Hab*. *Ticos*, right down the other end of town in 1 Calle, is another fairly sophisticated place, serving everything from steaks to pancakes. Also on 1 Calle are the *Comedor El Rey* and the *Restaurant Belice*, both of which serve cheaper Guatemalan food. Halfway between the two is the *Cafe Central*, at the end of an arcade in 1 Calle, beside the cathedral. It's open until 11pm and does good snacks and sandwiches. As for really cheap food, your best bet as always is the market, but remember that it's closed by sunset.

Cobán is quiet at the best of times, but particularly so in the evenings. There are however two **cinemas**, one in the plaza and the other a little way down 1 Calle.

Buses

Transportes Monja Blanca, sometimes called *Escobar*, run one of Guatemala's best bus services, with regular departures between Guatemala City and Cobán. In Cobán their office is on the corner of 4 Avenida and 0 Calle, with departures hourly from 3am to 4pm. In Guatemala City the office is at 8 Avenida 15–16, Zona

1, and buses leave hourly from 6am to 5pm. The trip takes four or five hours. One bus a day, leaving the plaza in San Pedro Carchá at noon, goes to **Uspantán**, for connections to Sacapulas, Nebaj and Quiché.

The times of buses to local destinations – Senahú, El Estor, Lanquín and Cahabón – are listed in the relevant passages. These either leave from the terminal, down the hill behind the town hall, or from the plaza in San Pedro Carchá.

San Pedro Carchá

SAN PEDRO CARCHÁ is only a few kilometres away, and connected by a regular shuttle of buses. Carchá is a smaller and poorer version of Cobán, with none of the coffee money and a greater percentage of Indians. These days the two towns are merging into a single urban sprawl, and many of the buses that go on towards the Petén, or even over to Uspantán, leave from Carchá. If you're planning a speedy departure then you might prefer to stay here in the *Pension Central*, just off the plaza. Some buses from Guatemala City continue to Carchá, others stop at Cobán, in which case you'll have to catch a local bus between the two. These leave from outside the cinema on 1 Avenida in Cobán and from the plaza in Carchá.

If you're here at the weekend then the **regional museum** (weekends only 9am–noon & 2–5pm), in the street beside the church, is worth a visit. It houses a collection of Maya artefacts, dolls dressed in local costumes, and a mouldy collection of stuffed birds and animals, including the inevitable moulting quetzal. Another excursion takes you a couple of kilometres from the centre of town to the **Balneario Lisas**, a stretch of cool water that's a popular spot for swimming. To get there walk along the main street beside the church and take the third turning on the right. Follow this street for about a kilometre, and take the right-hand fork at the end.

East to Lanquín, Semuc Champey and beyond

To the northeast of Cobán a rough, badly maintained road heads off into the hills, connecting a string of coffee *fincas*. For the first few kilometres the hills are closed in around the road, but as it drops down into the richer land to the north the valleys open out. Their precipitous sides are patched with cornfields and the level central land is saved for the all-important coffee bushes. As the bus lurches along the road, clinging to the sides of the ridges, there are fantastic views of the valleys below.

The road divides at the **Pajal** junction (43km from Cobán), where one branch turns north to Sebol and Fray Bartolomé de Las Casas and the other cuts down into the valley to **LANQUÍN** (another 12km). Here you'll find a fairly nondescript village, surrounded by the usual acres of coffee, with two fairly simple places to stay: the *Tienda Mary* and the house next to the *Farmacía Divina Providencia*. The latter is the better, and also serves meals. There are two good reasons for stopping in Lanquín: the **Lanquín caves** and the natural pools at Semuc Champey. The first of these is close to town, only a couple of kilometres away. To find the caves simply walk to the river and follow it upstream until it disappears beneath a huge rock face. The caves themselves, a maze of dripping, bat-infested chambers, stretch for three kilometres underground at least – possibly a good deal more. A walkway, complete with ladders and chains, has been cut through the first few hundred metres and electric lights have been installed, which makes it all substantially easier, though it remains dauntingly slippery. Before you set out from the village ask in the Municipalidad if they can turn on the lights, but fix the fee before you set off. A small car park near the entrance to the caves has a covered shelter where you're welcome to camp or sling your hammock.

The extraordinary pools at **Semuc Champey** are considerably harder to reach, but also a great deal more spectacular. It takes four or five extremely gruelling hours to get there, but if the walk is hell the pools are close to paradise. To get there, set out from the village along the gravel road that heads to the south, away from the river. Once beyond the houses this starts to climb its way back and forth, out of the valley and down into another, and then wanders on through thick tropical vegetation where bananas and coffee grow beside scruffy thatched huts. Just as you start to lose hope the river appears below the road, but there's a little way to go yet. The road heads upstream for a kilometre or so before crossing on a suspension bridge. On the other side of this you want to turn to the right and head on upstream, first on the road and then along a muddy track that brings you, at long last, to the pools. Here you'll find a staircase of turquoise waters suspended on a natural limestone bridge, with a series of idyllic pools in which you can swim – though watch out for sharp edges. The bulk of the river runs underground beneath the bridge: if you walk a few hundred metres up the valley you can see where the water plunges furiously into a cavern that cuts under the pools to emerge below.

If you do decide to set out for Semuc Champey then take along plenty of water, as the walk is often sweltering and always exhausting. If you have a tent or a hammock it makes sense to stay the night – there's a thatched shelter, and the altitude is sufficiently low to keep the air warm in the evenings.

Beyond Lanquín the road continues to CAHABÓN (which has a basic *pension*), another 24km to the east, and from there an even rougher road heads south to PANZÓS (see below). In the rare event of the road being in a good enough state of repair there's an occasional bus between these two places, but normally transport is by the pick-ups that carry people and property between them.

Buses to Cahabón, passing through Lanquín, leave San Pedro Carchá three times a day, the first at 5.30am, and take about three hours. From Lanquín to San Pedro Carchá they leave at 5am, 8am and 2pm. Buses pass Pajal for **Fray Bartolomé de Las Casas** (see p.227) twice daily in the mornings.

Down the Polochic valley to Lake Izabal

If you're planning to head out towards the Caribbean from Cobán, or simply interested in taking a short trip along backroads, then the Polochic valley is an ideal place to spend the day being bounced around inside a bus. To reach the head of the valley you have to travel south from Cobán, along the main road to Guatemala City, and then shortly after Tactic you leave the luxury of tarmac and head off into the valley. The scenery is strongly characteristic of the highlands of Alta Verapaz: V-shaped valleys where coffee commands the best land and fields of maize cling to the upper slopes wherever they can. The villages are untidy-looking places where Pokoman Indians live, now largely latinised and seldom wearing the brilliant red *huipiles* that are traditional here.

The first village in the upper end of the valley is TAMAHÚ, and below that is TUCURÚ, beyond which the valley starts to open out and the river loses its frantic energy to wander gently across the floodplain. Here cattle pastures replace the coffee bushes, and both the villages and the people have a more tropical look about them. Next is TELEMÁN, the largest of the squalid trading centres in this lower section of the valley.

A side trip to Senahú

From Telemán a side road branches off to the north and climbs high into the lush hills, past row upon row of neatly ranked coffee bushes. As it winds upwards a superb view opens out across the level valley floor below, exposing the river's swirling meanders as it runs through a series of oxbows and cut-offs.

Set back behind the first ridge of hills, the small coffee centre of **SENAHÚ** sits in a steep-sided bowl. The village itself is a fairly unremarkable farming settlement, but the setting is spectacular to say the least. If you find yourself drawn by the hills of Alta Verapaz then Senahú is the ideal starting point for a short wander in their midst.

Away to the northwest a gravel road runs to the *Finca El Volcán*, occasionally served by buses, and beyond there you can continue towards **Semuc Champey** (see above), passing the *Finca Arenal* en route. The walk takes at least three days, and with the uncertainty of local weather conditions you can expect to be regularly soaked, but the dauntingly hilly countryside and the superb fertility of the vegetation make it all worthwhile. The best way to find the route is to hire a guide in Senahú, but you do pass several substantial *fincas* where you can ask the way.

Panzós and El Estor

Heading on down the Polochic valley you reach **PANZÓS**, the largest of the valley villages. Its name means "place of the green waters", a reference to the swamps which surround the river, infested with alligators and bird life. It was here in Panzós that the old Verapaz railway from the Caribbean coast ended, and goods were transferred to boats for the journey across Lake Izabal. These days you have to go all the way to the lake shore at El Estor to find the ferry. In 1970 Panzós made a brief appearance in international headlines when a group of *campesinos* attending a meeting to settle land disputes were gunned down by the army and local police. About 100 men, women and children were killed, and the event is generally regarded as a landmark in the history of political violence in Guatemala, after which the situation deteriorated rapidly.

Beyond Panzós the road pushes on towards Lake Izabal, and just before it reaches El Estor it passes a huge and deserted nickel plant, yet another monument to disastrous foreign investment. In the mid-Sixties, prompted by a chance discovery of high grade nickel deposits, the *International Nickel Company of Canada* formed *Exmibal (Exploraciones y Explotaciones Mineras de Izabal)*, who then built and developed the mine and processing plant. After thirteen years of study and delay the plant opened in 1977, functioned for a couple of years at reduced capacity, and was then shut down as a result of technical problems and the plummeting price of nickel. Today the great, ghost-like structure stands deserted, surrounded by the prefabricated huts that would have housed its workforce.

In **EL ESTOR** itself, a kilometre or so further on, life has settled back into the provincial stupor from which the nickel boom briefly aroused it. In fact the nickel wasn't the first foreign presence here: the town's name is said to have derived from a local mispronunciation of the name given to it by English pirates, who came up here to buy supplies ("The Store"). These days no-one comes here to buy anything, and the only boat that drops by is the **ferry for Mariscos**, which leaves daily at 5am, returning at 1pm. On the other side it's met by two buses, one to Guatemala City and the other for Puerto Barrios. The best hotel in El Estor is the *Vista del Lago* ($2), right beside the dock with great views across the water; the cheapest is the *Hospedaje Santa Clara* ($1). There's not a lot to do in town, but if you find yourself with an afternoon to spare there's a canyon in the hills behind which is an excellent place for a swim.

Buses for El Estor leave the terminal in Cobán at 5am, 8am and 11am, and from El Estor to Cobán at 5am, 7am and 8.30am: they take six or seven hours.

fiestas

The Verapaces are famous for their fiestas, and in Baja Verapaz especially you'll see an unusual range of traditional dances. In addition to this, Cobán hosts the **National Fiesta of Folklore**, at the start of August, which is attended by indigenous groups from throughout the country.

January
Rabinal's fiesta, famed for its traditional dances, runs from the 19th to 25th, with the most important events saved for the final day. **Tamahú** has a fiesta from the 22nd to 25th, where the 25th is also the main day.

May
Santa Cruz Verapaz has a fiesta from the 1st to 4th, including the dances of *Los Chuntos*, *Vendos* and *Mamah-Num*. **Tucurú** celebrates from the 4th to 9th, with the main day on the 8th.

June
Senahú has its fiesta from the 9th to 13th, with the main day on the 13th. In **Purulhá** the action is from the 10th to 13th, with the principal day on the 13th. **San Juan Chamelco** has a fiesta from the 21st to 24th, in honour of San Juan Bautista. In **San Pedro Carchá** the fiesta is from the 24th to 29th, with the main day on the 29th: here you may witness the dances of *Moros y Cristianos* and *Los Diablos*. **Chisec** has a fiesta from the 25th to 30th, with the main day on the 29th.

July
Cubulco has a very large fiesta from the 20th to 25th, in honour of Santiago Apostol. The dances include the *Palo Volador*, *Toritos*, *Los 5 Toros* and *El Chico Mudo*, amongst others. **San Cristóbal Verapaz** has a fiesta from the 21st to 26th, also in honour of Santiago.

August
The fiesta in **Cobán** lasts from the 31st July to 6th August, and is immediately followed by the **National Fiesta of Folklore**. **Tactic**'s fiesta is from the 11th to 16th, with the main day on the 15th. In **Lanquín** the fiesta runs from the 22nd to 28th, with the main day on the last day. In **Chajal** the fiesta takes place from the 23rd to 28th, and in **Panzós** it lasts from the 23rd to 30th.

September
Cahabón has a fiesta from the 4th to 8th, with the main day on the 6th. **Salamá** has its fiesta from the 17th to 21st, with the principal day on the 17th. In **San Miguel Chicaj** the fiesta runs from the 25th to 29th, and in **San Jerónimo** from the 27th through to October 10.

December
Santa Cruz El Chol has a fiesta from the 6th to 8th, with the main day on the 8th.

travel details

Buses
Baja Verapaz

Salamateca have offices in Guatemala City at 19 Calle 9 Avenida, Zona 1, with buses leaving at the following times.

From Guatemala City to Rabinal at 5.45am, 12.30pm and 2.30pm; to Cubulco at 7.45am, 9.45am and 11.30am; to Salamá at 1.30pm, 3.30pm and 4.45pm.

To Guatemala City from Cubulco at 2.30am, 4.30am and 2pm; from Rabinal at 4.30am, 8.30am and noon; from Salamá at 4am and 8.30am.

A daily bus from Guatemala City **to Cubulco via El Chol** leaves from the Zona 4 terminal at about 4am, and from Cubulco on the return journey at 9am.

Heading for Baja Verapaz from Cobán or from Guatemala City you can also take any bus between Cobán and the capital and get off at **La Cumbre de Santa Elena**, from where minibuses run to Salamá.

Alta Verapaz

Guatemala City to Cobán services, calling at all points in between including the Biotopo and Tactic, are run by *Monja Blanca*. In Guatemala City their office is at 8 Avenida 15–16, Zona 1, and in Cobán at 4 Avenida and 0 Calle. They leave Guatemala City hourly from 6am to 5pm, and they leave Cobán hourly from 3am to 4pm. (Most of the buses are pullmans and the trip takes 4–5 hours.)

Cobán to Tactic and San Cristóbal Verapaz every hour or so from the terminal down the hill behind the Municipalidad.

Cobán to Senahú one bus at 6am which can be caught outside the *Hotel Chipi Chipi*, a block or so behind the cathedral. The trip to Senahú takes around 7hr. From Senahú to Cobán the bus leaves at 4am, but you should check this the night before.

Cobán to El Estor from the terminal in Cobán at 5am, 8am and 11am, returning from Estor at 5am, 7am and 8.30am. The trip takes around 7hr and the third bus sometimes doesn't operate so it's safer to stick to the first two.

San Pedro Carchá to Uspantán (5hr) one bus a day at noon. From Uspantán there's a connecting bus to Santa Cruz del Quiché, which passes through Sacapulas for connections to Nebaj. The bus for San Pedro Carchá leaves Uspantán at 5am.

San Pedro Carchá to Fray Bartolomé de Las Casas daily at 6am, and sometimes a second bus mid-morning and a third at midday. One dawn departure also goes to Raxruja, further to the west of Las Casas, from where there are pick-ups to **Sayaxché**. If this doesn't materialise take the first bus to Las Casas and then a pick-up to Sayaxché. Coming the other way a bus leaves Las Casas for Carchá at 6am.

San Pedro Carchá to Cahabón three buses a day, passing through **Lanquín**, the first at 5.30am; returning buses pass through Lanquín at 6am, 8am and 2pm (3hr to Lanquín, 4hr to Cahabón).

CHAPTER SIX

THE PETEN

T he vast northern department of **El Petén** occupies about a third of Guatemala but contains less than two percent of the population. This huge and featureless expanse of swamps, dry savannahs and tropical rainforest forms part of an untamed wilderness that stretches into the Lacandon forest of southern Mexico and across the Maya mountains to Belize. Totally unlike any other part of the country, much of it is all but untouched, with ancient ceiba and mahogany trees that tower fifty metres above the forest floor. Undisturbed for so long, the area is also extraordinarily rich in **wildlife**. Some 285 species of bird have been sighted at Tikal alone, including a great range of hummingbirds, toucans, blue and white herons, hawks, buzzards, wild turkeys, motmot (a bird of paradise) and even the elusive quetzal, revered since Maya times. Many of these can be seen quite easily, moving through the forest in the early morning and evening, when their cries fill the air. Beneath the forest canopy are many other species that are far harder to locate. Among the mammals are the massive tapir or mountain cow, ocelots, deer, coatis, jaguars, monkeys and many others, and there are also crocodiles and thousands of species of plants, snakes, insects and butterflies.

Recently however, this position of privileged isolation has been threatened by moves to colonise the country's final frontier. Waves of **settlers**, lured by offers of free land, have cleared enormous tracts of jungle, while oil exploration has brought with it mountains of money and machinery, cutting new roads deep into the forest. The jungle also provides shelter for some of Guatemala's guerrilla armies, in particular the FAR (Rebel Armed Forces), who occasionally emerge to confront the army. In part this explains why the government is so keen to develop the region, but in practice the conflict has led to many of the settlers becoming refugees, driven across the border into Mexico. The oil industry, too, has withdrawn from some of the worst-hit areas. In the last few years, however, the situation has improved considerably, and fighting is now confined to a few of the most remote border areas.

The new interest in the region is in fact something of a reawakening, as the Petén was once the heartland of the **Maya civilisation**, which reached here from the highlands some 2500 years ago. A total of 102 Maya sites have been reported in the Petén area: many of them still lie completely buried in the jungle, while others are known only to local people. Here Maya culture reached its height of architectural, scientific and artistic achievement during the Classic Period, roughly 300 to 900 AD. Great cities rose out of the forest, surrounded by smaller satellite centres and acres of raised and irrigated fields. **Tikal** and **El Mirador** are among the largest and most spectacular of all Maya ruins – Tikal alone has some 3000 buildings – but they represent only a fraction of what was once here. At the close of the tenth century the cities were mysteriously abandoned, and many of the people moved north to the Yucatán where Maya civilisation continued to flourish until the twelfth century.

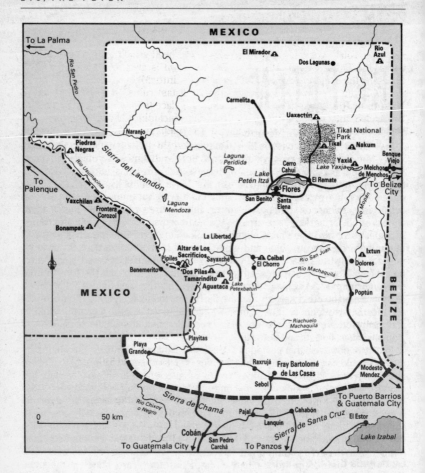

By the time the Spanish arrived the area had been partially recolonised by the Itzá, a group of Toltec-Maya (originally from the Yucatán) who inhabited the land around Lake Petén Itzá. The forest proved so impenetrable that it wasn't brought under Spanish control until 1697, more than 150 years after they had conquered the rest of the country. Although the Itzá resisted persistent attempts to Christianise them, their lakeside capital was eventually conquered and destroyed by Martín de Ursúa and his army, thus bringing about the defeat of the last independent Maya tribe.

The Spanish had little enthusiasm for the Petén, and under their rule it remained a backwater, with nothing to offer but a steady trickle of chicle – the basic ingredient of chewing gum, which is bled from sapodilla trees. Independence saw no great change, and it wasn't until 1970 that the Petén became genuinely accessible by car. Even today the network of roads is skeletal, and many of them are impassable in the wet season.

The hub of the department is **Lake Petén Itzá** where the three adjacent towns of **Flores**, **Santa Elena** and **San Benito** together form the only settlement of any size. You'll inevitably arrive here, if only to head straight out to the ruins of **Tikal**, the Petén's prime attraction. But the town is also the starting point for buses to the **Belize border**, and for a **route into Mexico** along the Río San Pedro. If you plan to reach any of the more distant ruins – **El Mirador**, Yaxjá, **Nakum** or **Río Azul** – then Flores is again the place to be based. To the south is **Sayaxché**, surrounded by yet more Maya sites including **Ceibal**, where you can see some of the best-preserved carving in the Petén. From Sayaxché you can also set off down the Río de la Pasión to **Mexico** and the ruins of **Yaxchilán**, or take an alternative route back to Guatemala City – via Cobán in Alta Verapaz.

Getting to the Petén

Most visitors arrive in the Petén by bus or plane directly from the capital; **by air** it's a short fifty-minute hop, **by bus** it can take anywhere between ten and twenty hours. If you travel overland be warned that the jungles of the Petén still play host to some of the country's guerrillas, who occasionally stop buses in order to re-educate the passengers. Although it's frightening you needn't worry as they're only interested in lecturing you, and possibly extracting a dollar or two as war tax.

Plane tickets can be bought from any travel agent in Guatemala City and from several hotels or the airport in Flores. There are usually four flights a day, and at the time of writing the schedule was as follows: *Aerovias* leave Guatemala City at 7am, returning from Flores at 4pm; *Aeroquetzal* fly Guatemala City to Flores at 7.15am, also returning at 4pm; and *Tapsa* leave Guatemala City at 7.30am and 3pm, returning at 8.30am and 4pm. In addition *Aviateca* have two flights a week, on Friday and Sunday afternoon. A return ticket costs around $100 and the planes sometimes get booked up in the peak season – July and August.

Buses from Guatemala City are run by *Fuente del Norte*, 17 Calle 8–46, Zona 1, who have an office beside the market in Santa Elena (on the lakeshore opposite Flores). From Guatemala City they leave at 11pm (*especial*), 2am and 7am, and from Santa Elena at 10pm (*especial*), 5am and 11am. It's always a good idea to book a seat in advance, particularly if you plan to travel on the *especial*.

Guatemala City to Flores

If you do decide to take the **bus** there are two ways to ease the pain; either catch the *servicio especial* – a fast bus with pullman-style seats that leaves Guatemala City at 11pm and takes around ten hours – or make the trip in stages. The total distance by road is 554km, and all buses (except the *especial*) make a stop in **Morales** on the Caribbean highway (p.175). Shortly afterwards, the road to the Petén turns north at the **Ruidosa junction**, soon crossing the Río Dulce, stopping-off place for the boat to or from Livingston. From here it continues through MODESTO MÉNDEZ – where the tarmac ends – and on through SAN LUÍS to POPTÚN, about 100km short of Flores, and the best place to break the trip. On the edge of the village is the *Finca Ixobel*, a working farm run by Americans Mike and Carole DeVine. In the cool foothills of the Maya mountains, surrounded by lush pine forests, it's a relaxing place to settle into; swimming in the pond, walking in the forest, and stuffing yourself with delicious home-grown food. Many an over-night stop here becomes a week-long stay. There's a guesthouse ($2), camping or hammock space, and tree houses; and for both food and accommodation you run up a tab and pay when you leave. To get to the *finca* ask the bus driver to drop you at the gate, from where its about a kilometre's walk. There are several cheap *pensiones* in the village as well, the best of them in the *Restaurante Ixobel*, which is under the same ownership as the *finca* and also serves delicious food. There's also a *Guatel* office, for long-distance phone calls, and a bank.

The limestone hills surrounding the *finca* are riddled with **caves**. Two of these can be reached as day trips (the larger of them contains an underground waterfall) but the most impressive is **Naj Tunich** ("stone house"), a full day's hike from the *finca*. Discovered in 1980, Naj Tunich is massive, reaching 850 metres underground. Its walls are decorated with Maya murals which, in addition to depictions of religious ceremonies and the ball game, include several graphic and well-preserved drawings of erotic scenes, a feature found nowhere else in Maya art. Alongside these are extensive hieroglyphic texts (a total of 400 glyphs), all etched in black charcoal. Amongst the deities that are drawn here are the twins Hanahpu and Xbalanque, who are the main characters in the Popol Vuh, a Quiché text found in the Guatemalan highlands. Caves were sacred to the ancient Maya, who believed them to be entrances to Xibalda, the dreaded underworld. The glyphs and pottery found here all date to a relatively short period from 733 to 762 AD.

Three-day trips to the cave (for a minimum of three people) can be made from the *finca* for $30, which includes the price of food, a guide and a mule. There's a possibility that the cave will be closed to tourists in the near future because of damage done to it by visitors, so if you're heading this way especially to see it, check first with the tourist office in Guatemala City.

Another twenty kilometres north of Poptún, the village of DOLORES is set back from the road and bypassed by most buses. It was founded in 1708 as an outpost for missionaries working out of Cobán. An hour's walk to the north are the Maya ruins of **Ixkún**, a medium-sized site made up of eight plazas. It remains unrestored with little to see, but if you do want to visit the site then it's possible as a day trip from Poptún.

Buses run from Poptún to Guatemala City (up to 10hr), via Río Dulce, at 2.30am, 5am*, 9am and 2.30pm; and to Flores (4hr) at 8am*, 10.30am*, 11am, 1pm, 2pm and 3.30pm (*local bus, starting in Poptún).

Other possible routes to the Petén

Coming from the Guatemalan highlands you can also reach the Petén along the back roads **from Cobán** in the highlands of Alta Verapaz, a long, exhausting and adventurous route covered in more detail on p.227. If you're coming **from Belize or Mexico** you can also enter the country through the Petén. The most obvious route is from Belize, through the border at Melchor de Mencos, but there are also two river routes that bring you through from Palenque or Tenosique in Mexico. All of these are described later in this chapter.

Flores, Santa Elena and San Benito

Officially **FLORES** is still the capital of the Petén, but in practice its position of importance belongs to quieter times that are now long past. The town fills the island of San Andrés in Lake Petén Itzá, a cluster of cobbled streets and ageing houses built around a twin-domed church. Connected to the mainland by a gravel causeway, its sedate, old-world atmosphere is rarely disturbed by the changes that are transforming the rest of the Petén. The modern emphasis lies across the water in the merging towns of **SANTA ELENA** and **SAN BENITO**, both of which belong to the era of expansion. Santa Elena, opposite Flores at the other end of the gravel causeway, is strung out between the airport and the sprawling market. It includes several hotels, the offices of the bus companies, and a well-established residential area. San Benito, further to the west, is in the forefront of the new frontier, complete with rough bars, sleazy hotels and mud-lined streets. The three once distinct towns are now often lumped together under the single name of Flores.

The site of **Tayasal**, capital of the Itzás until their conquest in 1697, lay on the island not far from modern Flores. Cortes passed through here in 1525, on his way south to Honduras, leaving behind a sick horse which he promised to send for. In 1618 two Franciscan friars arrived to find the people worshipping a large white idol in the shape of a horse called *Tzimin Chac*, the thunder horse. Unable to persuade the Indians to renounce their religion they smashed the idol and left. Subsequent visitors were less well received; in 1622 a military expedition of twenty men was invited into the city by Canek, chief of the Itzás, where they were set upon and sacrificed to the idols. The town was eventually destroyed by Martín de Ursúa and an army of 235 in 1697. The following year the island of San Andrés was fortified for use as a penal colony, and Flores itself was founded in 1700.

Eating and sleeping

If you're just passing through then **Santa Elena** is the most convenient place to stay. The *Hotel San Juan* – $5 with a private bathroom, $2 without – is a new building on the main street, which conveniently doubles as the office of the *Pinita* bus company. Beside the entrance to the causeway are the *Hotel Jade*, a tall scruffy building which is good value at $1, and the *Don Quijote*, which has small rooms for about $2.

If you decide that you'd rather stay in **Flores** itself, hotels tend to be more expensive. The cheapest is the *Pension Universal*, a grubby place about halfway around the island, down a little alley to the left just after the restaurant *Palacio Maya*. Basic rooms go for $2, and the nicest are on the top floor where they catch the wind. A little bit more expensive, but better, are the *Hotel Itzá*, which faces the lake, and the *Hotel Santana*, also known as the *Anexo Petén*, on the left-hand edge of the island just behind the big *Hotel Yum Kak*. More upmarket still is the friendly *Hotel Petén* – $10 with a private bathroom, $8 without – where some rooms have fans.

Good, cheap places to eat are in short supply. The cafés in the hotels *San Juan* and *Santana* are safe standbys, as is the *Cafeteria Arco Iris* in Calle Centro America, or there are three very good but fairly expensive places in Flores: the *Jungla* (slow service), the *Gran Jaguar* and the *Mesa de los Mayas* which sometimes serves the local delicacy of armadillo and other exotic local dishes. The only other available entertainment is at two **cinemas** on the main street in San Benito, the *Nelly* and the *Palacio*.

Other practicalities

If you need to **change money** there's a *Banco de Guatemala* in Flores, or you can try the *Hotel San Juan* in Santa Elena – worse rates but longer hours. There's a *Guatel* office in Santa Elena, and **post offices** in both Flores and Santa Elena. **Plane tickets** for Guatemala City can be bought at the airport or the hotels *San*

Juan and *Petén*, both of which also hire out minibuses. Several local **car hire** firms operate from the airport, and *Hertz* have an office in the *Hotel Tziquinaha*, on the airport road. For trips within the Petén, **information**, transport and **guides** can be arranged through Ricardo, the local *Inguat* representative, who you'll find at the airport every day except Monday. The people who run the *Hotel Petén* are also very helpful and will rent out minibuses to groups heading anywhere in the Petén or even as far as Belize.

Moving on, *Pinita* **buses**, for destinations within the Petén, leave from the *Hotel San Juan* in Santa Elena, and others from the market in San Benito. For Guatemala City, *Fuente del Norte* is on the San Benito side of the market.

Around Flores

For most people Flores is no more than a base for overnight stops, but if you have a few hours to spare the lake and hills offer a couple of interesting diversions. The most obvious excursion is a **trip on the lake**. Boatmen in Flores can arrange to take you around a circuit that takes in a *mirador* on the peninsula opposite and the **Petencito zoo**, which has a small collection of local wildlife, pausing for a swim along the way. The fee is negotiable but it's obviously cheaper if you can get together a group of four of five people. You'll find the boatmen and their boats in Flores behind the *Hotel Yum Kak*.

Alternatively you can visit one of the numerous **caves** in the hills behind Santa Elena. The most accessible of these is **Aktun Kan** – simply follow the Flores causeway through Santa Elena, turn left when it forks in front of a small hill, and then take the first right. The cave is also known as *La Cueva de la Serpiente*, and is the legendary home of an enormous snake: there's a small entrance fee, for which the guard will turn on the lights and explain to you some of the bizarre names given to the shapes inside.

Further afield, on the eastern edge of the lake, is the recently developed **Cerro Cahui Wildlife Reserve**. Set up primarily for the protection of the ocellated turkey, the reserve contains the full range of Petén wildlife in an area of well-preserved rainforest. The minibus that leaves the market in Santa Elena for Jobompiche at 11am goes to the reserve, or you can take a Tikal bus to **El Remate** and walk from there. You can camp in the reserve or at the nearby *Gringo Perdido*, which also has a small restaurant.

Tikal

Just sixty-five kilometres from Flores, towering above the rainforest, are the ruins of **Tikal**, possibly the most magnificent of all Maya sites. The ruins are dominated by five enormous temples: steep-sided granite pyramids that rise some forty metres from the forest floor. Around them are literally thousands of other structures, many still hidden beneath mounds of earth.

The site itself is surrounded by the **Tikal National Park**, a protected area of some 370 square kilometres. The trees around the ruins are home to hundreds of species including spider monkeys, toucans and parakeets. The sheer scale of the place is overwhelming, and its atmosphere spellbinding. Whether you can spare as little as an hour or as much as a week, it's always worth the trip.

Getting there

The best way to reach the ruins is in one of the tourist minibuses – VW combis known as *colectivos* – that meet flights from the capital and also leave from the *Hotel Petén* (in Flores) and the *Hotel San Juan* (in Santa Elena) between 6am and 7am, returning at around 3pm or 4pm. There's also an unreliable local bus service that leaves the *Hotel San Juan* at 6am and noon, returning at 7am and 1pm – the minibus costs twice as much but takes half as long. Entrance to the national park costs $2 a day and you're expected to pay again if you stay overnight, although this is rarely enforced. The ruins themselves are open from 6am to 5pm, and extensions to 8pm can be obtained from the *Inspectoría* (a small white hut on the left at the entrance to the ruins).

If you're travelling between Tikal and Belize there's usually no need to go all the way to Flores: instead get off at **El Cruce** – the three-way junction at the eastern end of Lake Petén Itzá – to change buses. It's only safe to do this in the morning; otherwise you could end up at the junction for longer than you expected.

Eating and sleeping at the site

Plane and bus schedules are designed to make it easy to visit the ruins as a day trip from Flores or Guatemala City, but if you can spare the time it's well worth staying overnight. This is partly because you'll need the extra time to do justice to the ruins themselves, but more importantly to spend dawn and dusk at the site, when the forest canopy bursts into a frenzy of sound and activity. The air fills with the screech of toucans and the roar of howler monkeys, while flocks of parakeets wheel around the temples, and bats launch themselves into the night. With a bit of luck you might even see a fox sneak across one of the plazas.

There are three **hotels** at the ruins, all of them overpriced. The cheapest is the *Jungle Lodge*, where they charge $3.50 for a bare room, and a lot more for a bungalow. At the *Jaguar Inn* you'll pay a little under $10, and at the *Tikal Inn* a little over, for which you get a private shower and the use of a pool.

Alternatively – for no charge – there's a cleared space where you can **camp** or sling a **hammock** under one of the thatched shelters. Hammocks and mosquito nets (essential in the wet season) can be hired, either at the camp site or from the *Comedor Imperio Maya* for $2 (with a $3 deposit). During the dry season you'll also need a blanket of some sort as the nights can be cold. At the entrance to the campsite there's a shower block, but there's hardly ever any water.

There are also three simple *comedores*, all of which offer a limited menu featuring the traditional Guatemalan specialities of eggs, beans and chicken. For a more extensive but expensive menu there's a restaurant in the *Jaguar Inn*.

The site museum and other facilities

In between the hotels is a one-room **museum** (9am–5pm; closes 4pm at weekends; entrance $1) which houses some of the artefacts found in the ruins, including tools, jewellery, pottery, a reconstructed tomb, obsidian, jade and the remains of stela 29, one of the oldest pieces of carving found at Tikal, dating from 292 AD. There are also some interesting photographs that show the process of clearing and reconsolidating the ruins, revealing the extent to which they've been restored.

At the entrance to the ruins there's a **post office**, a handful of shops, and a visitors' centre that serves no apparent purpose. Two **books** of note are usually available. The best guide to the site is *Tikal, A Handbook to the Ancient Maya Ruins,* written by Michael Coe, who was director of archaeology at the site between 1962 and 1969. The other is *The Birds of Tikal*, by no means comprehensive but still useful for identifying some of the hundreds of species.

The rise and fall of Tikal

According to archaeological evidence the first occupants of Tikal arrived around 700 BC, probably attracted by its position raised above surrounding seasonal swamps and by the availability of flint for making tools and weapons. There's nothing to suggest that it was a particularly large settlement at this time, only simple burials and a few pieces of ceramics found beneath the North Acropolis. The first definite evidence of buildings dates from 500 BC, and by about 200 BC the first ceremonial structures had emerged, including the first version of the **North Acropolis**.

Two hundred years later the **Great Plaza** had begun to take shape and Tikal was already established as a major site with a large permanent population. For the next two hundred years art and architecture became increasingly ornate and sophisticated. The styles that were to dominate throughout the Classic Period were all perfected in these early years, and by 250 AD all the major architectural traits were well established. Despite this Tikal remained very much a secondary centre, dominated, along with the rest of the area, by **El Mirador**, a massive city about 65km to the north.

The closing years of the **Preclassic** era were marked by the eruption of the Ilopango volcano in El Salvador, which covered a huge area of the highlands, including much of Guatemala and Honduras, in a thick layer of volcanic ash. Trade routes were disrupted and alliance patterns altered. The ensuing years saw the decline and abandonment of El Mirador, and the rise of Tikal as the centre of trade, science and religion. At this time Tikal was allied with the powerful highland centre of Kaminaljuyú – on the site of modern Guatemala City – which was itself allied with Teotihuacán, the city that dominated what is now central Mexico. Backed by this formidable combination, Tikal became the greatest of lowland centres, its influence reaching to Copán in Honduras and Yaxchilán on the Usumacinta, monopolising the crucial lowland trade routes. The **population** grew to somewhere between 50,000 and 100,000, expanding to cover an area of around thirty square kilometres. Debate still rages about the exact function of Tikal, but it's now widely accepted that it was a real city. The elite lived in the centre, possibly housed in the area around the Central Acropolis, and the ordinary people in small residential compounds dotted around the core of the site.

For 300 years the city enjoyed a sustained period of **growth and prosperity**, at the very heart of Maya civilisation. In the middle of the sixth century it suffered a setback, and building programmes were briefly suspended. This was probably caused by the upheavals in Mexico, where Teotihuacán was in decline. Tikal's importance was severely curtailed by the fall of its northern ally, and from now on the other lowland centres began to develop greater independence. Nevertheless Tikal was still the most important of them, revitalised by a powerful ruling dynasty, and magnificent temples were still under construction as late as 889 AD.

What brought about Tikal's final **downfall** remains a mystery, but what is certain is that around 900 AD the entire lowland Maya civilisation collapsed, with much of the population moving north to the Yucatán. Possible causes range from earthquake to popular uprising, but the evidence points in no particular direction.

Afterwards the site was used from time to time by other groups, who worshipped here and repositioned many of the stelae, but it was never occupied again.

After the mysterious decline little is known of the site until 1695 when Father Avendano, lost in the maze of swamps, stumbled upon a "variety of old buildings". The colonial powers were distinctly unimpressed by the Petén and for the next 150 years the ruins were left to the jungle. In 1848 they were rediscovered by a government expedition led by Modesto Méndez. Later in the nineteenth century a Swiss scientist visited the site and removed the beautifully carved wooden lintels from the tops of Temples 1 and 4 – they are currently in a museum in Basel – and in 1881 the English archaeologist Maudslay took the first photographs of the ruins, showing the main temples cloaked in tropical vegetation.

Until 1951 the site could only be reached – with considerable difficulty – on horseback, and although there was a steady trickle of visitors the ruins remained mostly uncleared. Then in the early Fifties an airstrip was constructed by the Guatemalan army, paving the way for an invasion of archaeologists and tourists. In 1956 the Tikal project was started in order to mount one of the most comprehensive investigations ever carried out at a Maya site. By the time it was completed in 1970 the report stretched to 28 volumes and included the work of 113 archaeologists – despite which astonishingly little is known for certain about the ruins or their history.

The ruins

The sheer scale of the ruins at Tikal can at first seem daunting. But even if you make it only to the main plaza, and spend a hour relaxing on top of a temple, you certainly won't be disappointed. The central area, with its five main temples, forms by far the most impressive section; if you start to explore beyond this you can wander seemingly forever into the maze of smaller structures and outlying complexes.

From the entrance to the Great Plaza

Walking into the ruins the first structures that you come to are the romantically named **Complex Q** and **Complex R**. These are two of seven sets of twin pyramids that were built to mark the passing of each *katun*, a period of twenty 360-day years. This is an architectural feature found only at Tikal and Nakum, a site to the east. Only one of this particular pair of pyramids is restored, with the stelae and altars re-erected in front of it. The stelae at the base of the pyramid are blank, as a result of erosion, but there's a superbly carved example in the small enclosure that's set to one side, recording the ascension to the throne of Chitam, Tikal's last known ruler, in the month of the parrot 768 AD. He is portrayed in full regalia, complete with an enormous sweeping headdress and the staff of authority.

Following the path as it bears around to the left you approach the back of Temple 1 through the **East Plaza**. On the left side, behind a small ball court, is a broad platform supporting a series of small buildings known as the **marketplace**, and in the southeast corner of the plaza is an imposing temple, beneath which were found the remains of several severed heads, the victims of human sacrifice. Behind the marketplace is the **Sweat House**, which may have been the site of a kind of sauna similar to those used by highland Indians today. It's thought that Maya priests would take a sweat bath in order to cleanse themselves before conducting religious rituals.

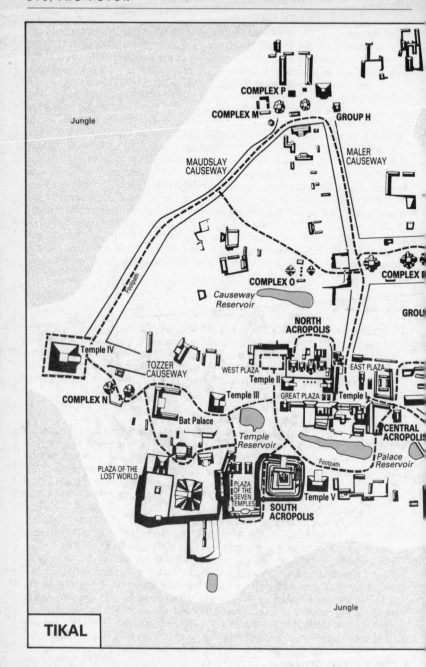

COMPLEX P

COMPLEX M

GROUP H

Jungle

MALER
CAUSEWAY

MAUDSLAY
CAUSEWAY

Footpath

COMPLEX O

COMPLEX P

*Causeway
Reservoir*

GROU

**NORTH
ACROPOLIS**

Temple IV

TOZZER
CAUSEWAY

WEST PLAZA

EAST PLAZA

Temple II

COMPLEX N

Temple III

GREAT PLAZA

Temple I

Bat Palace

*Temple
Reservoir*

**CENTRAL
ACROPOLIS**

Footpath

*Palace
Reservoir*

PLAZA OF THE
LOST WORLD

PLAZA
OF THE
SEVEN
TEMPLES

Temple V

**SOUTH
ACROPOLIS**

Jungle

TIKAL

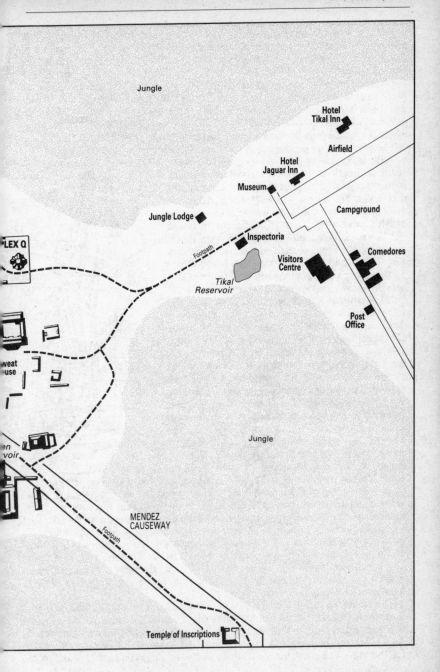

From here a few short steps bring you to the **Great Plaza**, the heart of the ancient city. Surrounded by four massive structures, this was the focus of ceremonial and religious activity at Tikal for around a thousand years, and was still in use long after the rest of the city had been abandoned. The earliest structure is the North Acropolis: the two great temples, which disrupted its original north–south axis, weren't built until the eighth century. The plaza covers an area of one and a half acres, and beneath today's grass there are four layers of paving, the oldest of which dates from about 150 BC and the latest from 700 AD. Both of the two main temples can be climbed, and although they're very steep and the ascent can be a hair-raising experience, it's well worth it once you get to the top.

Temple 1, towering 44 metres above the plaza, is the hallmark of Tikal – it's also known as the Jaguar Temple because of the jaguar carved in its door lintel. The temple was built as a burial monument, and its core contained the magnificent **tomb of Ah Cacau**, who ascended Tikal's throne in 682 AD. It was actually built in 721 AD, after his death, under the direction of his son and successor Yax Kin Caan Chac. The skeleton was found facing north, surrounded by an assortment of jade, pearls, seashells and stingray spines, which were a traditional symbol of human sacrifice. There was also some magnificent pottery, depicting a journey to the underworld made in a canoe rowed by mythical animal figures: a reconstruction of the tomb is on show at the site museum. Hundreds of tons of flint and rubble were poured on top of the completed tomb and the temple was then built around this, with a staircase of thick plastered blocks running up the front. The staircase currently in use was a construction staircase, over which the final surface would have been built. The whole thing is topped by a three-room structure and a hollow roof comb that was once painted in cream, red and possibly green. On the front of the

Maya prisoner incised on a bone
from Temple 1 tomb, Tikal

comb it's just possible to make out a seated figure and a stylised serpent. The view from the top of the temple is incredible; raised just above the height of the forest canopy, the great plaza is spread out below you, with the complex structures of the North Acropolis to the right and the Central Acropolis to the left.

Standing opposite, like a squat version of Temple 1, is **Temple 2** – known as the Temple of the Masks. On this second temple the central stairway is flanked by two grotesque masks, now heavily eroded. As yet no tomb has been found beneath the temple, which stands 38 metres high, although with its roof comb intact it would have equalled Temple 1. The echo from the top of either of these temples is fantastically clear and crisp.

The **North Acropolis**, which fills the whole north side of the plaza, is one of the most complex structures in the entire Maya world. In traditional Maya style it was built and rebuilt on top of itself, and beneath the twelve temples that can be seen today are the remains of about a hundred other structures. As early as 100 BC the Maya had constructed elaborate platforms supporting temples and tombs here: in about 250 AD the entire thing was torn down and rebuilt as a platform and four vaulted temples, each of which was rebuilt twice during early Classic times. Archaeologists have removed some of the surface to reveal these earlier structures, including two ten-foot-high masks. In 1959 a trench was dug deep beneath the platform, unearthing a bizarre burial chamber in which the body of a priest lay surrounded by nine retainers killed for the occasion, turtles, a crocodile, and a mass of pottery.

In front of the North Acropolis are two lines of **stelae** with circular altars at their bases, all of which were originally painted a brilliant red. These were once thought to show images of the gods, but archaeologists now believe the carvings are of members of Tikal's ruling elite. Many of them (throughout the site) bear the marks of ritual defacement, which was carried out when one ruler replaced another and thought to erase any latent powers that his image may have retained. Many of the ones here were set up in their current positions long after the decline of the city, by people who still worshipped here.

The Central Acropolis and Temple 5
On the other side of the plaza is the **Central Acropolis**, a maze of tiny interconnecting rooms and stairways built around six smallish courtyards. These buildings are usually referred to as palaces rather than temples, although their precise use remains a mystery. The possibilities include law courts, temporary retreats, administrative centres, and homes for Tikal's elite. What we do know is that they were constantly altered and adapted, with rooms, walls and doorways added and repositioned on a regular basis. The large two-storey building in Court 2 is known as **Maler's Palace**, named after the archaeologist Teobert Maler who made it his home during expeditions in 1895 and 1904.

Behind the acropolis is the palace reservoir, which is one of at least twelve clay-lined pools that were fed by a series of channels with rainwater from all over the city. Further behind the central acropolis is **Temple 5** – 58 metres in height – which supports a tiny single room. Climbing the temple isn't that easy as you have to scramble over all sorts of rocks and roots, but the view from the top is superb, with a great profile of Temple 1 and a side view of the central plaza.

From the West Plaza to Temple 4
Behind Temple 2 is the **West Plaza**, dominated by a large Late Classic temple on the north side, and scattered with various altars and stelae. Like those in the main plaza these stelae owe their present position to Post Classic people, who rearranged many of the smaller monuments. From here the **Tozzer Causeway** – one of the raised routes that connected the main parts of the city – goes west to **Temple 3**, which is 55 metres high and still covered in jungle vegetation. A fragment of stela 24, found at the base of the temple, gives it the date 810 AD.

Around the back of the temple is a huge palace complex of which only the so-called **Bat Palace** has been restored. Further down the causeway, on the left-hand side, is **Complex N**, another set of twin pyramids. In the northern enclosure of the complex is the superbly carved **stela 16**, showing the ruler Ah Cacau. The altar at its base has a sculptured scene and a text that possibly refers to the death of his wife.

At the end of the Tozzer Causeway is **Temple 4**, the tallest of all the Tikal structures at a massive 64 metres (210 feet) high. At the top are three rooms, separated from each other by walls twelve metres thick: to reach them you have to scramble over more roots and rocks, and finally up a metal ladder around the side of the pyramid. Slow and exhausting as this is, it's always worth it. All around you the green carpet of the canopy stretches out to the horizon, interrupted only by the great roof-combs of the other temples. At any time this view is enthralling – at sunset or sunrise it's unbeatable.

From Temple 4 the **Maudslay Causeway** leads to **Group H**, which includes two more twin-pyramid structures, and from here the Maler Causeway leads back down to the East Plaza, past yet another set.

The Mundo Perdido, the Plaza of the Seven Temples and the Temple of the Inscriptions

The other main buildings in the centre of Tikal are to the south of the Central Acropolis. Here you'll find the **Plaza of the Seven Temples**, reached by a trail from Temple 3, which forms part of a complex that dates back to before Christ. There's an unusual triple ball court on the north side of the plaza, and to the east is the unexcavated Southern Acropolis. To the west of this is the **Mundo Perdido**, or lost world. The main feature here is the the great pyramid, a 32-metre-high structure whose surface hides four earlier versions, the first dating from 700 BC. Little is known about the ruins in this part of the site but archaeologists hope that further research will help to explain the early history of Tikal.

Finally there's the **Temple of the Inscriptions**, reached along the Méndez Causeway from the East Plaza behind Temple 1. The temple (only discovered in 1951) is about a kilometre from the plaza. It's famous for the forty-foot roof comb, the back of which is a huge hieroglyphic text, only just visible these days.

Outside the main area are countless smaller **unrestored structures**. Compared to the scale and magnificence of what you've seen already they're not that impressive, but it can be exciting to explore nevertheless, and there's a real feeling of discovery when you do find something interesting. If you're hungry for more, arm yourself with a good map (the best is in Coe's guide to the ruins), and set out to explore some of the rarely visited outlying sections. Tikal is certain to exhaust you before you exhaust it.

Uaxactún

Twenty-four kilometres to the north of Tikal, strung out along the sides of an airstrip, are the village and ruins of **UAXACTÚN**. Substantially smaller than Tikal, and totally unrestored, the ruins are thought to date from the same period,

Detail from Uaxactún vase

although there's also evidence of much earlier occupation and the main group is known to have been rebuilt over a period of 500 years. The most interesting buildings are in group E, to the east of the airstrip, where three temples, built side by side, are arranged to function as an observatory. Viewed from the top of a third temple the sun rises behind the north temple on the longest day of the year, and behind the southern one on the shortest day. It's an architectural pattern that was first discovered here but has since been found at a number of other sites.

Beneath one of these temples the famous **E-VII** was unearthed, the oldest building ever found in the Petén. Its three phases of construction probably date back to 2000 BC, but still seem connected with much later Maya architecture. The original pyramid had a simple staircase up the front, flanked by two stucco masks, and post holes in the top suggest that it may have been covered by a thatched shelter.

The site is perhaps a little disappointing after the grandeur of Tikal, but if you're planning a stroll through the forest then this is a good spot to make for, and it's always interesting to see unrestored ruins.

A dirt track links Tikal with Uaxactún – a five- or six-hour walk – but it's easy to lose your way so make sure you get good directions before setting out. The trail starts from

Drawing from polychrome Uaxactún plate

a point between the museum and the *Jungle Inn* and the first section is fairly well marked. On the rare occasions that the road is in a good enough state of repair, the *Pinita* buses to Tikal continue to Uaxactún, returning the same day. It's easy enough to find camping or hammock space and a meal of tortillas and beans at the site.

El Mirador and Río Azul

Way to the north of Tikal are two other substantial ruins, both unrestored and for the most part uncleared. The bulk of the temples lie beneath mounds of earth, their sides coated in vegetation, and only the tallest roof-combs are still visible. These sites, still totally dominated by the jungle, have a unique atmosphere. Doubtless in a year or two they'll be reached by road – indeed a dirt track already gets as far as Río Azul – but for the moment they are well beyond the reach of the average visitor.

El Mirador

EL MIRADOR is the larger of the two, a massive complex the scale of which certainly matches Tikal and may even surpass it. Discovered in 1926, it dates from an earlier period than Tikal, when it was the dominant city in the Petén. Little work has been done here, and not much is known about its history, but it's clear that the site represents the peak of Preclassic Maya culture, which was perhaps far more sophisticated than was once believed. The most impressive features are a series of massive pyramid structures, each of which supports three smaller pyramids. The largest of these, the **Dante Complex**, rises in three stages to a height of seventy metres, making it the tallest known Maya structure, while in the western part of the site the **Tigre Pyramid** is 43 metres high. In all, El Mirador has five temples that rise above the forest canopy.

The site can only be reached by an exhausting two-day jungle hike from the village of **CARMELITA**, a small centre for the gathering of chicle, 64km from Flores. This trip offers an exceptional chance to see virtually untouched forest, though the walk is by no means a gentle stroll. Inside the forest the canopy shuts out the rays of the sun, cocooning you in the moist half-light of the forest floor; a world of orchids, vines, mosses, huge arching palms and ferns.

To get to Carmelita, take a boat from Flores across Lake Petén Itzá to the village of SAN ANDRÉS, on the northern shore. From here you can hitch a ride along the branch road to Carmelita, where you'll easily find a guide to take you out to the site. Expect to pay around $10 a day for a guide and a donkey, and to spend five or six days on the round trip. The journey is almost impossible in the rainy season, and is best attempted in January or February.

Río Azul

Although not on the same scale as Tikal or El Mirador, **RÍO AZUL** is another interesting and remote site. One hundred and seventy-seven kilometres from Flores, in the northeast corner of the Petén, it was only discovered in 1962. The city and its suburbs had a population of around 5000, scattered across 750 acres: several incredible tombs have been unearthed here, painted with vivid red glyphs and lined with white plaster. One of these contained the remains of one of the sons of Stormy Sky, Tikal's great expansionist ruler, suggesting that the city may have been founded by Tikal to consolidate the border of its empire. Sadly, the site was subjected to extensive looting after its discovery, with a gang of up to eighty men plundering the tombs in the rainy season, when archaeological teams retreated to Flores. Today there are two resident guards.

The rough road that connects the ruins with the outside world is barely passable, and the three-day round trip by jeep involves frequent stops to clear the road as you go. Trips can be arranged by Ricardo, the *Inguat* representative in Flores. He charges around $100 per person for the three days.

Sayaxché and around

Southwest of Flores, on a lazy bend in the Río de la Pasión, **SAYAXCHÉ** is an easy-going jungle town, from where you can arrange to visit the forest and its huge collection of archaeological remains. At the junction of road and river, it's an important point for the storage of grain and cattle, and the source of supplies for a vast surrounding area. It's also an ideal base from which to explore the forested wilderness and the complex network of rivers and swamps that cuts through it. This system has been an important trade route since Maya times, and there are several interesting ruins in the area. Upstream is **Ceibal**, a small but beautiful site in a wonderful jungle setting. To the south is **Lake Petexbatún**, on the shores of which are the ruins of **Dos Pilas**, **Aguateca** and **Tamarindito**. These sites are fairly small but visiting them – for which you'll need to hire a horse or a boat – always offers great opportunities to wander in the forest and watch the wildlife. Heading downriver, to the **Río Usumacinta**, you pass the ruins of **Altar de los Sacrificios**, and beyond that the river runs along the Mexican border and past the sites of **Yaxchilán** and **Piedras Negras**, among the hardest to reach of all Maya sites.

Getting to Sayaxché is fairly straightforward, with two *Pinita* buses a day from Flores (at 6am and 1pm, returning at the same times) along the 62km – two to three hours – of rough road. On the way you pass through the town of LA LIBERTAD, which was the capital of the Petén for a short spell in the nineteenth century, and the army post at EL SUBINE, where buses are often searched by teenage troops. The bus brings you as far as the north bank of the Río de la Pasión, directly opposite Sayaxché. Motorised canoes ferry bus passengers across, and there's also a large, flat-bottomed barge that can take trucks and buses.

The best **hotel** in Sayaxché is the *Guayacan*, an old wooden building right beside the river, whose basement is often flooded in the rainy season. Rooms go for between $3 and $5, depending on whether they have a bathroom or not. Julio Godoy, who owns the hotel, used to guide big-game hunters until hunting was outlawed and still knows the area extremely well, so if you need someone to point you in the right direction he's the man to ask. For a cheaper room try the *Hospedaje Mayapan* ($1), left down the street above the *Hotel Guayacan*. There are plenty of reasonable places to **eat**, and one of the best is *La Montana*, whose owner Julian's enthusiasm for helping travellers is matched only by his knowledge of the area. He arranges trips for groups of six or more to all of the places mentioned above for around $30 a day – or to anywhere else you might care to visit. If Julian can't help you he'll always know someone who can, whether you want to hire a fishing rod or a jeep.

The ruins of Ceibal

The most accessible and impressive of the nearby sites is **Ceibal**, which you can reach either by land or river. By boat it's easy enough to make it there and back in an afternoon; by road it should be a day trip, although you may end up stranded at the entrance road waiting for a truck. If you have a tent or hammock (with a mosquito net) you might as well stay – bring some food to share with the guards and you'll always be welcome. Not much commercial river traffic heads upstream, so you'll probably have to hire a boat – ask around at the waterfront and be prepared to haggle: boats take up to six people and generally charge around $30. Two hours on the boat is followed by a 45-minute walk through towering rainforest. By road Ceibal is just 17km from Sayaxché, but there's not much traffic and you'll almost certainly have to walk half the way. Trucks that leave Sayaxché in the mornings for EL PARAISO pass the entrance road to the ruins, from where it's an eight-kilometre walk to the site itself.

Surrounded by untouched forest and shaded by huge ceiba trees, **the ruins** of Ceibal are partially cleared and restored, and beautifully landscaped into a mixture of open plazas and untamed jungle. Many of the largest temples still lie buried under mounds of earth. Although it can't match the enormity of Tikal, Ceibal does have some quite outstanding carving, superbly preserved by the use of very hard stone. The two main plazas are dotted with lovely stelae, centred around two low platforms. Fragments of stucco found on these platforms suggest that they were originally decorated with ornate friezes, and painted in brilliant shades of red, blue, green, pink, black and beige. During the Classic Period Ceibal was a relatively minor site, but it grew rapidly between 830 and 930 AD, apparently after falling under the control of colonists from what is now Mexico. In this period it was the largest southern lowland site, with an estimated population of around 10,000, and the influence of the outsiders is clearly visible in the carving: speech scrolls, straight noses, waist-length hair and serpent motifs are all decidedly non-Maya. The architecture is also very different from that of the Classic Maya sites, including round platforms that are usually associated with the Quetzalcoatl cult, which we know spread from the north at the start of the Postclassic Period, around 1000 AD.

Lake Petexbatún

A similar distance to the south of Sayaxché is **Lake Petexbatún**, whose waters contain plentiful supplies of snook and bass, and whose shores abound with wildlife and Maya remains. The ruins themselves are small and unrestored, but they make interesting goals as part of a trip into the forest, and the sheer number of them suggests that the lake was an important trading centre for the Maya. **Dos Pilas** – the only site with guards and hence the best place to stay – is the obvious place to head for first. A 45-minute boat trip from Sayaxché takes you to RANCHO EL CARIBE, from where it's a further twelve kilometres on foot to the ruins. Some days, particularly Sundays, you may be able to get a lift as far as Rancho El Caribe (where it's also possible to camp), but if not you'll have to hire a boat: if you can get together a group of three or four it's well worth hiring a boat and guide to take you on a two- or three-day trip around the lake. The simplest way to do this is to talk to Julian in the *Montana* in Sayaxché, who'll be able to arrange things for you. There are plenty of options – touring the lake on foot, by boat or on horseback – but whichever you opt for you'll need to hire a guide.

As always you should bring a tent or hammock and mosquito net, and enough food to share with the guards. Using Dos Pilas as a base you can fish in the lake, ask the guards to guide you to the nearby sites of **Tamarindito** and **Arroyo de Piedras** (both of which can be reached on foot) or make the canoe trip to **Aguateca** – an hour by boat and another hour on foot. The ruins of Aguateca, discovered in 1957, are situated on a hill above one of the streams that feeds into Lake Petexbatún, divided in half by a great cleft in the rock; again there are some finely carved stelae. If you feel the need for a hot bath there are some naturally heated springs on the shores of the lake.

Towards the highlands: Raxruja and Fray Bartolomé de Las Casas

Sayaxché is also the starting point for an adventurous route back to Guatemala City, via Cobán in the highlands of Alta Verapaz. At 9am each morning a motley collection of trucks and pick-ups meet the bus from Flores, hustling up business for the four- to five-hour trip south to **RAXRUJA**.

Leaving Sayaxché the trucks continue to pick up passengers along the way, cramming every conceivable space. The road to the south is often in a poor state of repair, swamped by lakes of mud, but the truck drivers are particularly intrepid. Once you reach Raxruja the shape of the land starts to change, as the flat expanse of the Petén gives way to the rolling foothills of the highlands. The area is known as the Northern Transversal Strip, and is the source of much contentious political debate in Guatemala. In the Seventies it was earmarked for development as a possible solution to the need for new farmland and pressures for agrarian reform, but widespread corruption ensured that huge parcels of land, complete with their valuable mineral resources, were dispersed no further than the generals: the land was dubbed "Generals' Strip". Since then oil reserves have been developed around Playa Grande, in the west of the strip, and the area has seen heavy fighting between the army and guerrillas. If you decide to head in this direction bear in mind that the army will wonder why.

If at Raxruja you decide you can't go on, the *Hospedaje Agua Verde* does offer rooms, but it's really a last resort and you'd do better to press on. Trucks go west from here to PLAYA GRANDE on the banks of the Río Salinas, but it's hard to get beyond there. The road does continue west some distance and is planned eventually to get to **Barillas** (p.140) – even now it's possible to travel overland this way, an interesting but potentially hazardous route as the undeveloped land in the middle is one of the last hideouts of the guerrilla armies. Alternatively you could attempt to travel down the river – in which case you'll need plenty of time and patience. You're more likely to want to travel east from Raxruja to **FRAY BARTOLOMÉ DE LAS CASAS**, a couple of hours away. There are three **hotels** here, the best of which is the *Pension Ralios* ($1), and buses to San Pedro Carchá (8hr) and Guatemala City (11hr). For some reason Fray Bartolomé de Las Casas has been left off most maps of Guatemala, and the junction of **Sebol** is marked instead. Sebol is at the junction of the main Cobán–Raxruja and Fray Bartolomé de Las Casas–Raxruja roads, and is little more than a cluster of houses and a bridge, with no hotels.

Routes to Mexico

River trade between Guatemala and Mexico is increasing rapidly, as are the number of tourists making a couple of obscure border crossings, either with the cargo boats that make the trip **from Sayaxché** to Benemerito, on the Mexican bank of the Río Usumacinta, several times a week, or **from Flores** via Naranjo and along the Río San Pedro to La Palma in Mexico. Neither route is exactly crowded with gringos, but both are increasingly well-organised and used to seeing foreign faces. Border formalities are relatively straightforward on the San Pedro route, where there's a Guatemalan immigration office in Naranjo and a Mexican one in La Palma, less so on the Usumacinta. Heading into Mexico this way it's crucial to remember that there's no immigration post in Sayaxché. The nearest place that you can get your passport stamped is the airport in Santa Elena (Flores), though Mexican entrance stamps are available at a number of places on the west side of the Usumacinta. It's easy enough to cross the border without getting your passport stamped, but it could easily lead to trouble at a later date. If you enter Mexico without getting a Mexican entry stamp you'll almost certainly live to regret it and could well end up in a Mexican police station for hours, while they leaf through FBI photographs and try to identify you.

From Sayaxché to Benemerito

Downriver from Sayaxché the **Río de la Pasión** snakes its way through an area of forest and swamp that is gradually being occupied by a mixture of well-organised farming cooperatives and impoverished migrants. Along the way tiny river turtles bask on exposed rocks, white herons fish in the shallows and snakes occasionally slither across the surface of the river. There are two main land-marks: a slick American mission on the left-hand bank and the army post at PIPILES on the right, which marks the point where the Río Salinas and the Río de la Pasión merge to form the Río Usumacinta. At Pipiles all boats have to stop and their passengers are required to present their papers, while luggage is usually searched.

On the north bank of the river is the small Maya site of **Altar de Los Sacrificios**, discovered by Teobert Maler in 1895. The site, commanding an important river junction, is one of the oldest in the Petén, but these days there's not much to see beyond a solitary stela. The beach below, which is exposed in the dry season, is often scattered with tiny fragments of Maya pottery, uncovered as the river eats into the base of the site, carving into ancient burials.

From Pipiles it's possible to head **up the Río Salinas**, south along the Mexican border, through an isolated area visited only by traders buying maize and selling soft drinks and aspirin. Between trips these entrepreneurial geniuses can be found in Sayaxché, loading and unloading their boats, and for a small fee they might take a passenger or two. Most boats only go part of the way up the Salinas, but if you're really determined you can travel all the way to **Playa Grande**, and there join the road east to Raxruja and Fray Bartolomé de Las Casas. This is a rough trip for which you'll need a hammock, a mosquito net, a week or two, and a great deal of patience.

Following the **Usumacinta** downstream from Pipiles you arrive at BENEMERITO in Mexico, a sprawling frontier town that marks the end of a new dirt road from Palenque. Passengers from Sayaxché are charged a few dollars for what is usually an eight-hour trip, although boats with business along the way can take a couple of days to get this far. Benemerito is the destination of most of the cargo traffic, but if you're in a hurry, or want to go further down the Usumacinta (to Yaxchilán), you can hire a fast boat. Expect to pay around $70 from Sayaxché to Benemerito (4hr), or double that to Yaxchilán (8hr). From Benemerito you can head on to Yaxchilán by boat or road, though the latter (by bus to Frontera Corozal and then by boat from there) is a lot cheaper. In Benemerito a large *tienda* beside the dock has rooms to let and will usually change money (though don't expect a particularly good rate), and there are several *comedores* on the main road, which runs through the village parallel to the river, about a kilometre from it.

Buses leave Benemerito for Palenque (9hr) at 5.30am, 7am and 9am. (Coming from Palenque, buses for Benemerito leave from the *Mercado Nuevo* at 5am, 8am and 11am.) The first **immigration post** that you'll pass is a couple of kilometres outside Benemerito, where the road for Palenque crosses the Río Lacantún – ask the bus driver to stop for you while you go in and pick up a tourist card.

Inside Mexico: by road from Benemerito to Frontera Corozal

Between Benemerito and Palenque two branch roads leave the main route. The first runs to the riverside village of Frontera Corozal, the nearest settlement to the Maya site of Yaxchilán, and the second to Betel, where there's a small *pension* and from where you can walk to the ruins of Bonampak.

Heading for Yaxchilán this way you need to get off the bus at the junction for **FRONTERA COROZAL** and hitch from here to the village, a distance of about 20km. (The road has recently been upgraded and at the time of writing the bridge was being completely rebuilt, so it is likely that the village will now be served by a daily bus service from Palenque – even so it's likely to be quicker to hitch). In the village itself there's no hotel or *pension*, although again this may well have changed by now as the whole area is being opened up. However if you ask around you'll certainly be able to find somewhere to sling a hammock and you should be able to camp on the football pitch, once the evening game has drawn to a close. The village does have a couple of simple *comedores* and an immigration post – so if you arrive directly by boat from Sayaxché you can get a tourist card here. There are very few commercial boats that do the trip between Corozal and Sayaxché, but if you're in a group of five or more you could always hire a boat to take you there, which should take a day or so. Boats to **Yaxchilán** can be hired at the waterfront and charge around $25 for the round trip: they can usually take ten people.

By river to Yaxchilán and Piedras Negras

Heading on down the **Río Usumacinta**, which marks out the border between Guatemala and Mexico, you pass through dense tropical rainforest, occasionally cleared to make way for pioneer villages and cattle ranches, particularly along the Mexican bank. In the past the border area has been the scene of fighting between the Guatemalan army and guerrilla forces, but these days you're unlikely to meet either.

There's little commercial river traffic between Benemerito and Frontera Corozal, so if you plan to make the trip you'll almost certainly have to hire your own boat. Boats for Yaxchilán can be hired in both Benemerito and Frontera Corozal, though it's considerable easier in the latter, which is much closer to the ruins. If you're coming from Guatemala and plan to travel all the way to Yaxchilán then it's cheaper to hire a boat for the whole trip – speak to Julian in Sayaxché.

Below Benemerito the first place of any interest is the **Planchon de Figuras**, at the mouth of the Río Lacantún, which feeds into the Usumacinta from the Mexican side. One of the least known and most unusual of all Maya sites (though hardly a site in the conventional sense), this consists of a superb collection of graffiti carved into a great slab of limestone that slopes into the river. Its origin is completely unknown but the designs, including birds, animals, temples and eroded glyphs, are certainly Maya. A little further downriver is the Chorro waterfall, a series of beautiful cascades some 30km before **Frontera Corozal**, and beyond there it's another 15km to Yaxchilán.

The ruins of **Yaxchilán** are undeniably the most spectacular Maya site on the Usumacinta, in a magical site on the Mexican bank, spread out over several steep hills that are surrounded on three sides by a great loop in the river. This is an important position, and carvings at Yaxchilán, like those at the neighbouring sites of Bonampak and Piedras Negras, tell of repeated conflict with the surrounding Maya centres. By 514 AD, when its emblem glyph was used for the first time, Yaxchilán was already a place of some size, but its era of greatness was launched by the ruler Shield Jaguar, who came to power in 682, and extended the city's sphere of influence through a campaign of conquest. At this stage it was sufficiently powerful to form a military alliance that included not only the Usumacinta centres but also Tikal and Palenque. Shield Jaguar was succeeded by Bird Jaguar III, possibly his son, who seems to have continued the campaign of aggressive military expansion. Less is known about the later years in Yaxchilán, although building continued well into the Late Classic so the site was probably occupied until at least 900 AD.

What you see today is a series of plazas, temples and ball courts strung out along the raised banks of the river, while the low hills in the centre of the site are topped with impressive palaces. The structures are all fairly low, but each of the main temples supports a massive honeycombed roof, decorated with stucco carvings. The quality of this carving is yet again exceptional, though many of the best pieces have been removed to museums around the world: one set of particularly fine lintels is displayed in the British Museum. However more recent finds, including some incredibly well-preserved carving, remain on site. When the layers of vegetation are peeled back the original stonework appears unaffected by the last thousand years, with flecks of red paint still clinging to the surface. Yaxchilán's architecture focuses heavily on the river, and the remains of a built-up bank suggest that it might have been the site of a bridge or toll gate.

Until fairly recently the site was still used by Lacandon Indians, who came here to burn incense, worship, and leave offerings to their gods. The whole place still has a magical atmosphere, with the energy of the forest, overwhelming in its fertility, threatening to consume the ruins. The forest here is relatively undisturbed and buzzes with life; toucans and spider monkeys loiter in the trees while bats are now the main inhabitants of the palaces and temples.

Arriving at the site by boat you'll be met by one of the guards, who live here to ward off the ever-present threat of looting. The guards are happy to show you round the site, though they generally ask a small fee for their labours. You're welcome to camp here too, though mosquitoes can be a problem – whether you're staying or not – particularly in the rainy season.

Heading on downstream from Yaxchilán the current quickens and the river drops through two massive canyons. The first of these, the **Cañon de San Jose**, is a narrow corridor of rock sealed in by cliffs 300 metres in height; the second, the **Cañon de las Iguanas**, is less dramatic. Travel on this part of the river is a treacherous experience and really only possible on white-water rafts: any smaller craft have to be carried around the two canyons, and under no circumstances is it possible to travel upriver.

Below the rapids, the ruins of **PIEDRAS NEGRAS** stand on the Guatemalan side of the river. Despite the fact that the ruins here are possibly as extensive as those of Tikal, this is one of the least accessible and least visited of Maya sites.

Human sacrifice depicted on
Stela II, Piedras Negras

Many of the very best carvings are now on display in the National Museum of Archaeology in Guatemala City, where they're a great deal easier to see, but there's still plenty to experience if you make it to Piedras Negras. The site was closely allied with Yaxchilán, and probably under its rule at various times: its name is a reference to the stones that line the river bank at this point. Maps of this area often show an airstrip alongside Piedras Negras, but this has long been lost to the jungle, so don't count on landing here.

Beyond Piedras Negras the river cuts a sluggish path towards the Atlantic, joined by the Río San Juan just below Tenosique in Mexico. Periodically both Guatemalan

and Mexican governments have planned to develop the Usumacinta for hydroe-
lectricity, a scheme that would drown most of the Maya sites below the new
water level. Nothing has yet come of several decades of talk, however, and it now
seems unlikely that the project will ever go ahead.

Seven-day **trips down the Usumacinta**, from Sayaxché to Tenosique, covering all the sites mentioned above and shooting the rapids, are run by *Maya
Expeditions*, 3 Avenida 16–52, Zona 10, Guatemala City.

Naranjo and the San Pedro River route into Mexico

The most direct route **from Flores to Mexico** takes you along the Río San
Pedro, through an area of remote forest. The river trip starts in **NARANJO**, a
small settlement in the northwest of the Petén. *Pinita* buses from Flores run
there at 5am and 1pm, returning at the same times, and the trip takes between
five and six hours, over rough roads. Once you reach Naranjo, a bit of a dump
which consists of little more than an army base, an immigration post and a grimy
hotel, you need to hunt out the boat owner. He usually makes the trip to Mexico
in the early morning, returning in the afternoon, but this depends on the number
of passengers – a minimum of four – and his mood. If he does plan to leave in the
early morning there's nothing to do but go to bed, getting up early to handle the
Guatemalan immigration and customs procedures, for which you'll be charged a
small fee.

Heading downriver, the next port of call is the Mexican immigration post,
about an hour away. Beyond that another three hours brings you to **LA PALMA**
in Mexico, a small riverside village with bus connections to Tenosique. There's
nothing much in La Palma, but at a hut beside the river you can buy cold beer
and food, and sling your hammock if you miss the bus. This same hut, owned by
Nicolás Valencia, is the place to wait if you're heading into Guatemala by the
afternoon boat. Nicolás is something of an entrepreneur and seems to have a
share in the boat business. He also changes money at a bad rate, though if you're
in need of *pesos* or *quetzales* it's the best you'll get.

Coming from Guatemala you're unlikely to miss the last (5pm) bus, but if you
do you've little choice but to stay the night – the first out is at 8am. From
Tenosique there are train connections to Palenque and bus connections to all
parts of Mexico. Coming into Guatemala the boat from La Palma waits for the
1pm bus from Tenosique, leaving at 2 or 3pm and arriving in Naranjo at 7 or 8pm.

From Flores to Belize

The hundred kilometres from Flores to the border with Belize takes you through
another sparsely inhabited section of the Petén, a journey of around three hours
by bus. Buses leave from the *Hotel San Juan* in Santa Elena at 5am, 7am, 10am,
11am and 3pm, and it's a good idea to set out early in order to make the bus
connections inside Belize and reach San Ignacio or Belize City the same day: if
you catch the 5am bus you can go straight through to Chetumal, in Mexico, the
same day. Coming directly from Tikal in the early morning you can get out at El
Cruce, the road junction halfway between the site and Flores, and catch a passing
bus from there. Once again you should set off early to avoid getting stranded.

Lake Yaxjá and the ruins of Yaxjá and Nakum

About halfway to the border, **Lake Yaxjá** is a shallow limestone depression, similar to Lake Petén Itzá, ringed by dense rainforest. The lake is home to two Maya sites and offers access to a third, Nakum, to the north. These are remote, demanding a couple of days or more, and you'll need hammocks and food at the very least.

The main Flores to Belize road passes about eight kilometres to the south of the lake – ask the driver to drop you at the turning if you want to go there. It's a sweltering two-hour walk along the branch road to reach the lake, where the road heads around to the right towards a *finca*. To make it to **the ruins of Yaxjá** you want to bear off to the left instead, along a smaller track. At the ruins you'll find a couple of guards, who are permanently stationed here to ward off potential looters. Stuck out in the wilderness they're always pleased to see strangers and will be glad to show you around. If you haven't brought a tent they'll find you a spot to sling a hammock and let you share their fire to cook on: as always it's a good idea to bring enough food to share with them as they'll doubtless be surviving on a monotonous diet of fish and week-old tortillas.

The ruins of Yaxjá were rediscovered in 1904 and remain totally unrestored, spread out across nine plazas. Don't expect any of the manicured splendour of Tikal, but do count on real atmosphere as you attempt to discover the many features still half hidden by the forest. The most unusual aspect of Yaxjá is that the town appears to have been laid out on a grid pattern, more typical of Teotihuacán than of the less systematic growth of a Maya centre.

There are also some ruins on a small island in the lake, known as **Topoxte**. These aren't particularly impressive, but again there's one very unusual feature: everything is built on a miniature scale, including tiny temples and stelae. Inevitably an American archaeologist has suggested that the site is evidence of a race of pigmy Maya.

About 20km to the north of Lake Yaxjá are the ruins of **Nakum**, a somewhat larger site that is also unrestored. The site is made up of two main groups of buildings, and the most impressive structure is the residential-style palace, which has forty separate rooms and is similar to the North Acropolis at Tikal. It's thought that Nakum was a trading post in the Tikal empire, funnelling goods to and from the Caribbean coast, a role for which it is ideally situated at the headwaters of the Río Holmul. Once again there are a couple of guards permanently posted at the site and they'll be more than willing to show you around and find a spot for you to sling a hammock or pitch a tent.

If you'd rather not walk back to the road from Nakum then it's also possible to **walk to Tikal** in a day, a distance of around 25km. To do this you'll need to persuade one of the guards to act as a **guide** as there's nothing marking the route. Alternatively you could bring a guide with you for the entire trip, which is certainly the best course of action if you're in a group. To arrange a guide, speak to Ricardo, the *Inguat* representative in Flores, and expect to pay around $30 per day for a guided trip from Flores to Yaxjá, Nakum and Tikal. Trips can also be arranged through *Tivoli Travel* (4 Calle 0–43 in Santa Elena), who offer a horse-riding adventure along this route, which can include a day's fishing in the lake. If you'd rather make the trip the other way around, from Tikal to Yaxjá, you should be able to arrange a guide from Tikal if you ask around amongst the guards at the site, all of whom know the area well. Approached from this direction, however, the circuit is somewhat anti-climactic, as the sites get smaller and smaller.

Melchor de Menchos and the border

MELCHOR DE MENCHOS marks the Guatemalan side of the Belize–Guatemala border. There are several cheap hotels and *comedores* here, though little worth savouring: just before you leave Guatemala there's one last tourist shop, just in case you wish you'd bought more in the highlands or have a few *quetzales* to get rid of.

The Guatemalan and Belizean border posts are on opposite banks of the Belize River, and despite the countries' differences border formalities are fairly straightforward. Once in Belize you'll find buses for Belize City every hour or so, though to catch most of these you have to travel by shared taxi to the town of **Benque Viejo**, a couple of kilometres inside Belize, where you'll also find the first hotels. If you can muster a small group and are in a real hurry to travel to Belize City or through to the border with Mexico, then you might consider hiring a minibus for the trip, which will enable you to make it to Mexico in a day. To hire a minibus contact the *Hotel Petén* in Flores.

If you're heading in the other direction there are buses **from Melchor de Menchos to Flores** at 3am, 5am, 8am, 11am and 3pm, and again it's well worth setting out early, when the bus service is at its best.

fiestas

The Petén may not offer Guatemala's finest fiestas, but those that there are have the energy that is typical of *Ladino* culture, and feature fireworks and heavy drinking. In some of the smaller villages you'll also see traditional dances and hear the sounds of the marimba – transported here from the highlands as are many of the inhabitants of the Petén. The list below is short, mainly because there really aren't that many towns or people in the Petén.

January
Flores has its fiesta from the 12th to 15th: the final day is the most dramatic.

March
San José has a small fiesta from the 10th to 19th.

April
Poptún's fiesta from the 27th to 1st May, is held in honour of San Pedro Martír de Merona.

May
San Benito has a fiesta from the 1st to 9th, which is sure to be wild and very drunken. The border town of **Melchor de Menchos** has its fiesta from the 15th to 22nd, with the last day as the main day. **Dolores** has a fiesta from the 23rd to 31st, with the principal day on the 28th.

June
Sayaxché has a fiesta from the 6th to 13th, in honour of San Antonio de Padua, which would be well worth travelling to.

July
Santa Ana has its action from the 18th to 26th.

August
San Luís has a fiesta from the 16th to 25th, with the main day on the last day.

October
San Francisco's fiesta runs from the 1st to 4th.

November
San Andrés, across the lake from Flores, has a fiesta from the 21st to 30th, with the last day as the main day.

December
Finally **La Libertad** has it's fiesta from the 9th to 12th.

travel details

Buses

Guatemala City to Flores (12–18hr). *Fuente del Norte* (17 Calle 8–46, Zona 1, Guatemala City) at 11pm, 2am and 7pm. **Flores to Guatemala City** at 10pm, 5am and 11am. All of these pass through **Poptún**.

Flores to Tikal (45min). Minibuses from the *Hotel Petén* and *Hotel San Juan* at around 7am – returning at around 5pm – and from the airport connecting with planes from Guatemala City. There is also an unreliable local *Pinita* bus that leaves the *Hotel San Juan* at 6am and noon, returning at 7am and 1pm. If the road is passable these buses go on to **Uaxactún**.

Flores to Sayaxché (2hr). *Pinita* (at the *Hotel San Juan*) have buses at 6am and 1pm. Same times for return services from Sayaxché to Flores. Heading on **from Sayaxché** there are no scheduled services to Benemerito (by boat) or Raxruja

(by truck) but there's a fairly regular flow of traffic to both.

Flores to Melchor de Menchos (3hr). *Pinita* run buses at 5am, 7am, 10am, 11am and 3pm, returning 3am, 5am, 8am, 11am and 3pm. The early bus from Flores can take you right through Belize to Chetumal the same day.

Flores to El Naranjo (5–6hr). *Pinita* buses run at 5am and 1pm, returning at the same times. **From Naranjo** the boat to La Palma in Mexico has no regular schedule but usually leaves in the early morning.

Planes

Guatemala City to Flores (50min). *Aerovias*, *Aeroquetzal* and *Tapsa* fly daily. Outward flights are in the early morning, around 7am, returns at around 5pm. *Aviateca* fly on Friday and Sunday afternoons.

PART THREE

BELIZE

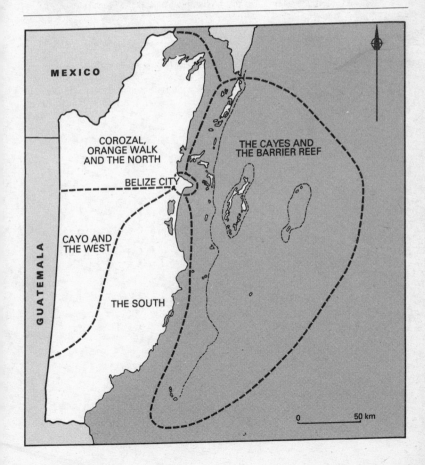

MEXICO

COROZAL,
ORANGE WALK
AND THE NORTH

THE CAYES AND
THE BARRIER REEF

BELIZE CITY

CAYO AND
THE WEST

GUATEMALA

THE SOUTH

0   50 km

Introduction

Belize is an anomaly. Peaceful, democratic, English-speaking, it seems in many ways not to belong in Central America at all. And indeed, to an extent, it is more a Caribbean nation than a Latin one, looking out from the coast rather than inland for its trade and alliances. On the other hand it has plenty of distinctively Central American features too, above all a blend of cultures and races that includes, in a tiny population, Maya, *mestizo*, African, European and others. Spanish runs a close second as a spoken language to the rich local *Creole*.

The peaceful atmosphere, together with the spectacular natural beauty of the coast and landscape, has started to draw increasing numbers of tourists every year. Well over half of them are from North America, but a large number come from Europe, with numbers of British visitors up by 400 percent over the last four years. Belize is by no means crowded, though: although it's barely bigger than Wales it has the lowest population density in Central America, and its land area is balanced by an almost equivalent amount of territorial waters, giving visitors plenty of scope to explore little-visited islands as well as the heartland of the ancient Maya culture.

There are now one or two package deals from the UK to Belize – and quite a few from the US – but it's still an ideal place to travel independently. There are numerous small hotels, starting from about the price of a youth hostel, inexpensive restaurants and plenty of public transport. Belizeans are extremely friendly and are genuinely pleased when visitors enjoy their country.

Physically the land increases in elevation as you head south and west and the population decreases correspondingly. The highest land in Belize is the rugged hilly area in the south-central region, where the granite peaks of the Maya Mountains rise to over 1000 metres. The main rivers rise in the west and flow north or east to the Caribbean. In the Cretaceous limestone of the western mountains, rivers have formed some of the largest cave systems in the world, few of which have been fully explored.

Offshore, the Barrier Reef, cayes and coral atolls shelter a vast number of marine species and protect the mainland from the ocean swell. The coastal waters are shallow and very productive: brilliant for divers and fishermen alike.

Beneath the sand the coastal shelf is a continuation of the limestone on the mainland, with more caves and sinkholes.

■ Where to go

Northern Belize is relatively flat and often swampy, with a large proportion of agricultural land. As everywhere in Belize there are Maya ruins and nature reserves here. **Cuello**, near Orange Walk, is the oldest known Maya site and there are nature reserves at **Shipstern** and **Crooked Tree**. Adjacent to the Guatemalan border is the potentially vast **Rio Bravo Conservation Area**.

The largest of the cayes, **Ambergris Caye**, is about the size of Barbados and is becoming extremely popular. More than half of all tourists to Belize have the resorts of **San Pedro**, the only town on the island, as their destination. **Caye Caulker**, to the south, is also being developed, though without the same North American urgency as Ambergris Caye; it's the most popular of the islands with independent travellers. Many of the other cayes are more difficult to reach, but trips can be arranged and dedicated divers and naturalists will find them very rewarding. Even on the cayes, however, there are relatively few **beaches** suitable for swimming, and the mainland coast is almost entirely low-lying, swampy and covered in mangroves. The lagoons inland offer superb wildlife habitats and a visit to **Lamanai**, on the shores of New River Lagoon, combines a nature safari with an ancient Maya centre.

Almost every visitor will have to spend at least some time in **Belize City**, even if only passing through. It's the hub of the country's transport system, for both inland and the cayes. First-time visitors may be shocked initially by the decaying buildings and the pollution of the river but there are ways to spend several pleasant hours in this former outpost of the British Empire, now the bustling commercial heart of the country.

For those interested in seeing the abundant tropical flora and fauna, anywhere in Belize is wonderful; an astonishing array of birds are readily visible, making **nature tourism** increasingly popular. In the west **San Ignacio** has everything for the eco-tourist: Maya ruins and rainforest, rivers and caves, and accommodation in every price range. The magnificent ruin of **Xunantunich** is at the road and riverside on the way to the Guatemalan border and **Caracol**, the largest Maya site in Belize, can be visited from here. The capital, **Belmopan**, is primarily an administrative centre though it does house the **archaeological vault** containing masses of Maya treasures.

The main town of the south-central region, **Dangriga**, is very small and acts mainly as a market for the citrus-growing area of the Stann Creek valley. Local people are now realising the potential of Dangriga as a base for tourism on the central cayes (little developed at present) and for visiting the **Maya Mountains** and the **Cockscomb Basin Jaguar Preserve**. Further south than this the road following the narrow coastal plain is unpaved. The few villages are located on the coast, with the delightful **Placencia** at the tip of a long, curving peninsula. **Punta Gorda**, the main town of Toledo District, is very small indeed and most tourists are here on their way to or from the ferry to **Livingston** in Guatemala. However, if you venture inland you'll find the villages of the **Mopan** and **Kekchi** Maya set in some of the most stunning countryside in Belize. **San Antonio** is the largest and has the only accommodation, but others are equally interesting with caves and rivers and the Maya ruins of **Lubaantun**, **Uxbenka** and **Pusilha** within reach.

Getting Around

With just four main roads, and only two that are tarmacked – the Northern and Western highways – Belize doesn't offer a great range of options when it comes to getting around. But, as always, it makes the most of what it's got, with boats, planes, buses and trucks making it possible to get just about anywhere – eventually. The main areas are well served by public transport, but it can take a while to get to some of the more distant corners of the country, where rough roads and heavy rainfall often conspire to disrupt the best laid plans.

■ Buses

Buses are by far the most popular mode of transport. The service on the Northern and Western highways, to the borders with Mexico and Guatemala, is particularly good, with departures every hour or so. In the north the buses actually cross the border and go into the Mexican town of Chetumal, but heading west they're allowed no further than the Belizean customs post. On these two routes the main companies are *Batty* (54 East Collet Canal, Belize City) and *Novelo* (19 West Collet Canal, Belize City). The Hummingbird and Southern highways, to Dangriga and Punta Gorda, are not so well provided for. However *Z-Line* (Magazine Road, Belize City) run four daily buses to Dangriga and one a day to Punta Gorda – which is a good 10–12 hours from Belize City. On all of these routes tickets can be bought in advance from the offices in Belize City, but if you get on the bus somewhere along its route then you can pay the driver, which is what most people do. The vast majority of buses are second-class, although a couple of luxury express buses do run to Chetumal.

If you're heading away from the main highways then you'll be relying on the **local bus services** operated by smaller local companies. In most cases these own just one bus, so a breakdown can bring the whole service to a halt. Local buses run to many of the smaller villages, and they operate alongside a fleet of **trucks** that also form part of the informal transport network, serving small and out of the way places. The service tends to be very slow indeed, catering to everyone's needs – providing they're not in a hurry.

The details for both types of bus service are given in the text, but be warned that services are greatly reduced on Sunday. If you stick to the buses you'll find that travel is cheap: the journey from Belize City to Chetumal, for example, will cost around US$10.

■ Driving

Driving in Belize is subject to the same limitations as bus travel. The Northern and Western highways offer easy motoring and smooth roads, but in the south the roads are rough and distances are long. Any car will be able to take you through the north with ease, but if you want to head off the beaten track or make your way down south then you'll need high clearance and four-wheel drive. The best guide to Belize's roads is Emory King's *Driver's Guide to Beautiful Belize*, which is sold at petrol stations throughout the country and offers a characteristically Belizean account of the network. If you're driving your own car then bear in mind that **lead-free petrol** is not available in Belize, and nor are many parts. Bring an assortment of spares, in case things should go wrong. **Insurance** is available from an agent just inside the border or in Belize City – it will cover you against damage to third parties, but fully comprehensive cover is not available. If you're heading into Guatemala, the only way to go is west, as the ferry to Guatemala from Punta Gorda doesn't take cars.

As in Guatemala, **car hire** is very expensive, but cars, Jeeps and Land Rovers are available from several companies in Belize City – their addresses are listed in the text.

■ Cycling

Seeing Belize from a **bike** is fairly straightforward, particularly in the north and west where there's not all that much traffic and the roads are well surfaced. Cycling is popular and you'll be well received wherever you go, although you'll only find spares and repairs in Belize City. Again you'll need to think twice before you head south, where a mountain bike is virtually a necessity: remember that bikes can always be carried on top of buses, so if you think your wheels won't survive the rigour of the Southern highway then you can always sit back and take it easy.

■ Hitching

In the more remote parts of Belize the bus service will probably only operate once a day, if at all, and unless you have your own car, **hitching** is the only other option. The main drawback is the shortage of traffic, but if cars do pass they'll usually offer you a lift. Bear in mind that many local trucks also operate as buses and you're expected to offer the driver some money.

■ Boats and Ferries

Although there's no scheduled **ferry** service to the islands, there are daily boats from Belize City to Caye Caulker and San Pedro. There's also a fairly regular shuttle of boats between these two islands. The only coastal boat service is a twice-weekly ferry from Punta Gorda to Livingston and Puerto Barrios in Guatemala.

Boats can also be **chartered** for travel along the rivers and out amongst the islands. If you're planning to explore the country's river network then San Ignacio is the ideal base, with canoes readily available to hire for an hour or a week. Canoes can also be rented in Placencia for trips on the Monkey River, which is ideal for bird-watching, and from Shipyard for trips to the ruins of Lamanai. Out on the islands you can charter a boat to spend a few hours on the reef, snorkelling and fishing. Some boatmen will also take tourists on a sailing tour of the cayes for a week or so,

camping along the way. If you've come to Belize to go diving then you might want to consider a live-aboard **dive boat**. Several of these operate out of Belize City, and their contact addresses are listed there.

■ Planes

Within Belize *Maya Airways* and *Tropic Air* offer a scheduled service to all of the main towns and out to San Pedro. There are two or three daily **flights** on each of the main routes – from Belize City to Punta Gorda, Independence, Dangriga, Corozal and San Pedro. A flight from Belize City to San Pedro costs around US$17 one way, and all flights leave from the Municipal Airstrip, about a kilometre north of the centre of Belize City. Again the service is very limited on Sunday.

If you can afford it, this is a good way to travel – especially to the south, where buses take a while, or out to San Pedro, when you get superb views of the hills and the clear blue sea, skimming along at low altitude in a small plane.

There are also **flights to Guatemala City** and to Flores if you're heading that way and can't face the rigours of the road.

Sleeping

Hotels in Belize fall into two categories; the first catering for big-spending American tourists, and the second for local people and budget travellers. All Belizean accommodation is expensive by Central American standards, and certainly in comparison with Guatemala, with a simple room usually costing at least BZ$10 (US$5) for facilities no better than a cheap Guatemalan hotel, and in some places you won't find anything for less than BZ$15. You'll probably end up in a basic sort of room with a shared bathroom at the end of the corridor, and if you want the luxury of a private bathroom then expect to pay at least BZ$15. Price fluctuations are fairly unpredictable and oddly enough Belize City offers some of the best budget accommodation in the whole country, while in Orange Walk there's very little available. Out on Caye Caulker prices are reasonable but in San Pedro everything is overpriced. Elsewhere you won't have any problem finding a decent and inexpensive room. The exception to every rule is Belmopan, where there are only three hotels, the cheapest charging BZ$50 for a single: if you have things to do in Belmopan it's better to stay in San Ignacio, which is far more pleasant anyway.

Finding a room is no problem as all the towns are so small that you can see what's on offer in no time, and walk between all the hotels. Even in Belize City most of the hotels are within a kilometre of the Swing Bridge. On the whole there's always accommodation available, but during the peak season, from July to September and around Christmas time, you may have to look a little longer. Checking-in is typically informal and only in very organised establishments will you be expected to sign a register or go so far as listing your passport number. In most cases you simply pay your money and take your room. It's a good idea, however, to take a look at the room before parting with your cash: check that the fan works and that it's reasonably insect-proof – although a good fan will keep most beasts at bay. Insects are only really a problem on the islands where, when the wind drops, the sandflies will get at you however well you're protected.

■ Camping

With Belizean prices outstripping those in the rest of Central America you might consider **camping** as a way of keeping within a tight budget. You'll easily be able to find somewhere to pitch a tent or sling a hammock in the coastal villages like Placencia and Hopkins, or out on Caye Caulker, although in San Pedro restrictions tend to be a little tougher. You can also camp out in the area around San Ignacio, where some of the local ranches offer campsites for passing travellers, surrounded by lush tropical forest. Sadly there are only two places where you can pitch tent in the Mountain Pine Ridge Forest Reserve – at the entrance and at Augustine – which would otherwise be ideal for camping. In the north you should also be able to camp out at or near the ruins of Lamanai and Altun Ha, and at the Crooked Tree Wildlife Reserve and the Burrell Boom Baboon Sanctuary. Down south a tent will enable you to spend some time wandering inland, around the Maya villages and ancient ruins, and there's a superb campsite beside the Blue Creek.

Communications

Thanks to its recent colonial entanglement with Britain, Belize is blessed with excellent telecommunications and postal networks, and particularly well connected to Europe. Belizean stamps are also fantastically beautiful.

■ Mail

Belizean postal services are perhaps the most efficient in Central America, although they're also probably the most expensive. **Incoming mail** is kept at the main post office in Belize City, which is on the northern side of the Swing Bridge – open 8am–noon and 1–5pm – for a couple of months, and if it's not collected then they return it to the sender. If you want to collect your mail from the post office have it sent to *Poste Restante, The Main Post Office, Belize City,* you'll need some kind of ID, preferably a passport, to pick it up. Although this is fairly reliable, *American Express* are safer still – their office is at *Belize Global Travel,* 41 Albert Street, Belize City, and you'll need to show an *American Express* credit card or travellers' cheque to pick up your mail.

Sending letters and cards home is easy enough, if a little slow, and the stamps, decorated with coral formations and tropical fish, are a considerable added bonus. A normal air-mail letter takes around ten days to reach Europe, a week to the States. If you're sending a **parcel** then you have to go to the special parcel office, in Church Street, Belize City. Parcels leaving the country have to be wrapped in a cardboard box, inspected by customs, and tied with string. A parcel sent to Europe by sea, which is a lot cheaper than air mail, might take as long as two months to arrive but it will usually get there eventually.

■ Phones

Belize has a surprisingly modern phone system. The first phone reached Belize in 1902 and today the country has some of the latest satellite communications hardware. It's easy enough to dial direct into and out of Belize: a call to Europe will cost you BZ$6 per minute, and to the States BZ$3.20 per minute. To dial direct, the code for Britain is 0044, then the local code less its initial zero. To reach the States phone 001, then the city and local codes; Guatemala is 00502.

The main office of *Belize Telecommunications Limited* (BTL) is at 1 Church Street, Belize City (daily 8am–9pm), but you can make a call from the BTL office in any town in the country – you can even dial direct from Caye Caulker. Many smaller villages have a shared "comunity telephone", which may have just one public phone in the exchange or a few extensions in homes and elsewhere.

PHONE CODES IN BELIZE

Belize City ☎02	Punta Gorda ☎07
Orange Walk ☎03	Belmopan ☎08
Corozal ☎04	San Ignacio ☎092
Dangriga ☎05	Benque Viejo ☎093
Independence/	Caye Caulker ☎022
Placencia ☎06	San Pedro ☎026

■ Media

Although Belize, with its English-language media, can make a welcome break in a world of Spanish, this doesn't necessarily mean that it's very easy to keep in touch with what's happening in the rest of the world. In Belize City you should be able to get hold of copies of *Time* and *Newsweek*, and perhaps even *The Economist*. **Foreign newspapers** are rarely available for sale, but copies of British newspapers – usually *The Times* and *The Telegraph* – are kept at the Bliss Institute in Belize City: they get there about a week after publication. The *Book Centre*, on Regent Street West in Belize City, has the largest selection of magazines and newspapers in the country.

There are five **local newspapers**: *The People's Pulse*, *The Reporter*, *The Belize Times* and *The Amandala*, all of which are published weekly and most of which stick religiously to a party line. Local news, normally reported in a very nationalistic manner, takes pride of place and international stories receive very little attention indeed. *Belize Currents*, a bi-monthly magazine published in the US, is also readily available in Belize: expensive and aimed mainly at would-be property buyers, it nevertheless has some excellent colour photography and occasional interesting articles on Maya sites or Belizean wildlife

There are two national **television** stations, channels 7 and 9, which show an almost uninterrupted stream of imported American shows, mixed in with a few news programmes – their best features are the locally produced homemade adverts and short fillers. Some towns and villages also have **cable TV**, giving them access to American soaps and a steady diet of films.

There are also two **radio** stations, *Radio One*, which broadcasts on 830, 910, 930 and 940 KHZ, and on 91.1 and 3.28 MHZ, and *Friends*, which broadcasts on 88.9MHZ. For the most part they're rather dull music stations, sponsored by the government, and from time to time they run plays from the BBC and short snippets from the World Service news. You can also pick up other Caribbean stations, which come wafting in across the sea and blast out pure reggae. If you have a short-wave receiver you will be able to pick up BBC Radio 2, broadcast on the Armed Forces' network BFBS, and the BBC World Service.

Eating and Drinking

Belizean food is a distinctive mix of Latin America and the Caribbean, with Creole cuisine dominating the scene but plenty of other influences playing an important part. Mexican empanadas are as common as chow mein and hamburgers. In a few places Belizean food is a real treat, and the seafood is particularly good, but in all too many it's a neglected art, conforming to a single simple recipe – beans and rice.

■ Where to eat

The quality of the food rarely bears much relation to the appearance of the restaurant, and a full range of rough *comedores*, **bars**, **cafés** and smooth-looking **restaurants** are on offer. Out on the islands and in the small seashore villages some restaurants are little more than thatched shelters, with open sides and sand floors, while in Belize City and San Ignacio you'll find polished floors, tablecloths and napkins. Only in Belize City, though, do you have much to choose from, with fast food and snack bars sprouting on street corners but one or two surprisingly elegant restaurants as well. Even here most places are somewhere between the two, serving up good food but not too concerned about presentation.

In very small villages, such as Burrell Boom or Hopkins, where there is no restaurant, you should be able to find someone who cooks for passing travellers. There's usually somebody who fill this role on a regular basis, and local people should be able to point you in the right direction. This is often a great opportunity to sample the delights of traditional Creole food.

Travelling, you'll find that food often comes to you as street traders offer up tacos, empanadas, fish burgers and fruit to waiting bus passengers. The practice isn't quite as common as elsewhere in Central America but it still makes a pleasant diversion on most journeys.

Most Belizeans eat their main meal in the evenings, but in a country noted for its informality anything goes, and if you want to eat steak for breakfast and scrambled eggs for dinner nobody will be at all bothered. For **vegetarians** the pickings are slim as Belizeans have never had much enthusiasm for the land. The fruit here is good and there are some locally produced vegetables, largely thanks to the Mennonites, but they're hard to come by. A walk through any Belizean market, with its tiny piles of withered fruit and veg (mostly onions, tomatoes and potatoes), is an accurate representation of the way in which such food is viewed here. Your best hope is within the **Chinese** community, who run restaurants in all of the main towns.

◼ What to eat

The basis of any **Creole** meal is **beans** and **rice**, and in small restaurants and cafés this type of food features heavily. In many cases it means exactly that, and nothing more, but usually it's served with **chicken**, **fish** or **beef**, and backed up by some kind of sauce, often cooked with the beans. Vegetables are scarce in Creole food but there's often a side dish of fried **bananas** or **plantains**. At its best Creole food is delicious, taking the best from the sea and mixing it with the smooth taste of coconut, another favourite ingredient, and a range of herbs and spices. But all too often what you get is a stodgy mass, with little in the way of flavour. Often, too, you'll find an Anglicised version of Creole cooking, still based on seafood, rice and beans, but including **steaks**, **chips** and deep-fried **chicken**.

Seafood is almost always excellent. **Red snapper** is invariably fantastic, and you might also try a **shark steak**, **conch fritters** or a plate of **fresh shrimps**; avoid **turtle** steaks however –

they're still on the menu in many places, but they're a protected species, threatened with extinction. Out on Caye Caulker the food is often exceptional, and the only worry is that you might get bored of **lobster**. Anticipating that possibility they serve it up in an amazing range of dishes: lobster curry, lobster chow mein, lobster and scrambled eggs, or even pasta with lobster sauce.

From time to time you might also come across local **game**. The **gibnut** (paca) is a local favourite, and was served up to the Queen when she was last in Belize (it was described by the British tabloids as a type of rat; in fact it's a herbivorous rodent, about the size of a badger, that looks like a giant guinea pig). **Brocket deer** and **armadillo** are also eaten by local people, but they rarely make their way into restaurants.

Chinese food will probably turn out to be an important part of your trip, and when there's little else on offer Belize's Chinese restaurants are always a safe bet. In Belize City some of them are very good indeed, but elsewhere they tend to look a little run-down and serve bland food. Other Belizean ethnic minorities are now starting to break into the restaurant trade; in Belize City you can now eat **Japanese** and **Middle Eastern** food, and there's an excellent **Sri Lankan** restaurant in San Ignacio, serving superb curries.

Travelling around you'll also be confronted by an array of snacks. On the whole these tend to be Mexican and Guatemalan delicacies such as **empanadas**, **tamales**, **tacos** and **chiles rellenos**, but you'll also come across local specialities like **fish burgers** and **coconut bread**.

◼ Drinks

The most basic **drinks** to accompany food are water, beer and Coke. All three are available at every restaurant and bar. Belizean **beer**, *Belikin*, is extremely popular, selling for a little over US$1 a bottle (more out on the cayes) or slightly less for the lighter *Crown Beer*. imported European and American beers cost roughly double. Tap **water** is not to be recommended, but mineral water is available in bottles, as is a predictable range of fairly cheap soft drinks including **Sprite**, **Fanta** and **Pepsi**.

Some locally produced **wines** are sold in shops and restaurants, mostly made from fruit and cashew nuts (and tasting like it), and you can also get hold of imported wine, which is far from cheap. Local **rum** is the best deal in Belizean alcohol, however. Both dark and clear varieties are made in Belize, brewed in true Caribbean style, and tasting delicious. Many Belizeans like to mix rum with condensed milk – known as *rum-popo*. Locally produced gin, brandy and vodka are also available – cheap, and fairly nasty.

One last drink that deserves a mention is **seaweed**, a strange blend of actual seaweed, milk, cinnamon, sugar and cream. If you see someone selling this on a street corner, give it a try.

Opening Hours and Holidays

It's very difficult to be specific about **opening hours** in Belize, as people tend to take each day as it comes and open up when the mood takes them, but in general most places are open 8am– noon and 3–8pm. Some shops and businesses work a half-day on Wednesday and Saturday, and everything is liable to close early on Friday, with the weekend coming up. Banks and government offices are only open Monday to Friday. Watch out for **Sundays**, when everybody takes it easy; shops, and sometimes restaurants, are closed, the bus service is severely limited, and few internal flights operate. Archaeological sites, however, are open every day.

The main **public holidays**, when virtually everything will be closed, are shown below.

PUBLIC HOLIDAYS
January 1 New Year's Day
March 9 Baron Bliss Day
Good Friday
Holy Saturday
Easter Monday
May 1 Labour Day
May 24 Commonwealth Day
September 10 National Day
September 21 Independence Day
October 12 Columbus Day
November 19 Garifuna Settlement Day
December 25–26 Christmas

Fiestas and Entertainment

In Belize it's only in the outlying areas, such as around San Ignacio and in the Maya villages of the south, that you'll find traditional village fiestas. Elsewhere national celebrations are the main excuse for a day-long party, and the rhythms of the Caribbean dominate the proceedings. But here you'll feel less of an outsider and always be welcome to dance and drink with the locals. The main celebrations are National Day (September 10), Independence Day (September 21), Columbus Day (October 12) and Garifuna Settlement Day (November 19), all of which are celebrated across the country.

You will, however, find plenty of entertainment at any time, as Belizeans are great partyers, and music is a crucial part of the country's culture.

◼ Dance

Traditional dance is still practised by two ethnic groups in Belize: the Maya and the Garifuna. The best time to see Garifuna dances is Garifuna Settlement Day (November 19), and the best place to see them is either Dangriga or Hopkins. Maya dances are still performed at fiestas in the south and west. The village of San José Succotz, to the west of San Ignacio, has fiestas on March 19 (St Joseph) and May 3 (Holy Cross), while down south you'll find traditional fiestas in San Antonio around January 17, and in San Pedro towards the end of June. In many ways these fiestas resemble their counterparts in Guatemala.

Elsewhere modern music and **modern dance** is the mood of the day. Dance is very much a part of Creole culture and all national celebrations are marked by open-air dances. Almost all villages, and particularly those along the coast, have their own discos, with dancing going on into the small hours. Dancers take their lead from the Caribbean, merging styles from Jamaica and Cuba.

◼ Music

Belizean **music** is a lively mixture of Caribbean and Latin American rhythms with haunting melodies played on Maya instruments. Creole music combines all the elements, but many individual styles are thriving too – see the section in *Contexts* on "Music in Belize". It has to be said, though, that ninety percent of what you'll actually hear will be **reggae**, and the sounds of Bob Marley dominate the airwaves.

Modern Latin American music is also popular; *merengue*, *salsa* and even Mexican *mariachi* are all heard throughout Belize, though perhaps more in the north and west, where the Spanish speaking population is that much larger.

But everywhere you go you'll hear music, either played or performed: look out especially for anything advertised as a *Jumpup*, an apt Belizean term for a dance. The term covers a multitude of sins: one great one had posters inviting people to a "Big massive jumpup", scheduled to end when "food gone, rum gone and people gone".

■ Sport

Sport in Belize is a reflection of the local environment, and most of what's on offer is connected to the water in some way. Sport **fishing** is popular, particularly out on the atolls, where wealthy tourists spend their time and money in pursuit of a whole range of fish. **Sailing**, **diving** and **snorkelling** are also extremely popular. Diving courses, for experts or beginners, are run in San Pedro, Caye Caulker and Placencia. If you want to book a course in advance then look at the listings for these places in the text, or write to *Personalised Services*, 91 North Front Street, Belize City, and they'll be able to send you details of all that's on offer: if you're planning a fishing trip they should also be able to give you information on fishing lodges. Away from the coast "**tubing**" – floating down rivers in a giant inner tube – is a popular pastime, particularly in the Cayo district. Many canoe-hire firms can arrange this for you. **Caving** is not really known in Belize and can be dangerous. There are few qualified cavers, but one exception is Logan McNatt, a peace corps veteran who now lives in Belmopan. Contact him there at PO Box 195 for details of tours.

The main spectator sport is **football**, although there aren't many level stretches of ground on which to play. Nevertheless this is probably the national game, closely followed by basketball. Athletics is also popular, as are most American sports, at least on TV: softball, baseball and American football. As in the rest of Central America, **cycling** is closely followed and there are sometimes races in Belize, though scope for these is limited given the state of the roads.

Finally there are a number of **horseracing** meets around New Year.

■ Film

A couple of well-known **films** have been shot in Belize – *The Mosquito Coast* and *The Dogs of War* – but there's no local film industry as such. Nevertheless, going to the movies is popular and there are two cinemas in Belize City, one in San Ignacio and one in Orange Walk. In other towns they show films from time to time, usually on a Saturday night, in the town hall. Most of what's on offer is imported directly from the States and new films get this far south with amazing speed. Some are even released in Belize before they reach Europe.

On **TV** you can watch American soaps and local news programmes. Most towns also have cable, serving up a steady diet of American films. A good series of locally produced **videos** is available, "The Best of Belize All Over", showing slices of local life to the accompaniment of great local music – unfortunately they're only suitable for playing on US equipment. For more info contact Great Belize Productions, 17 Regent Street, Belize City (☎77781).

Crafts, Markets and Shops

Compared to its neighbours, Belize has little to offer in terms of traditional **crafts** or local **markets**. The latter are particularly poor, and hardly worth visiting, but here and there you might come across some impressive local crafts. Many of these are dependent on the destruction of the reef, so think twice before you buy. They include black coral, often made into jewellery, and tortoise shells, which look far better on their rightful owners. If you're desperate to take home a souvenir then stick with wood carvings, which are often superb – the best are made from *zericote* or mahogany – clothing, or a good bottle of Belizean rum.

For **everyday shopping** you'll find some kind of shop in every village in Belize, however small, and if you have the time to hunt around, most things you'd find in Europe are also available in Belize. Luxury items, such as electrical goods and cameras, tend to be very expensive, as do other imported goods, including tinned food. Film is a little more expensive than at home, but easy to get hold of.

Trouble and Harassment

Belize has earned itself something of a reputation for criminal activities, and while it's true that the capital has a high crime rate, it certainly doesn't live up to some of the stories you may hear. The atmosphere on the streets can be intimidating, but on the whole petty crime is the only common pest and violence is very rare indeed. Nevertheless it pays to be aware of the dangers.

■ Crime

There are really two centres of crime in Belize: Belize City and Orange Walk, which is the centre of the Belizean drugs industry. The capital is perhaps the greatest worry as petty theft is now fairly common. The majority of cases involve **break-ins** at hotels. When you're out searching for a room bear this in mind and avoid places that seem over-exposed. Out and about there's also always a slight danger of **pickpockets** and **petty theft**, but this is certainly no greater here than in the surrounding countries, and with a bit of common sense you've nothing to fear. There's also a chance of something more serious happening, such as a **mugging**. During the daytime there's little to worry about, unless you go wandering off into particularly poor neighbourhoods. However at night you should stick to the main streets and it's not a good idea to go out alone, particularly for women. If you arrive in Belize City at night take a taxi to find a hotel, as the bus stations are in a particularly derelict part of town – although it's not bad enough to worry about daylight arrivals.

Having said all this, muggings are really not that common, and your greatest fear is the mood of intimidation on the streets, which makes Belize City feel far more dangerous than it is.

■ Harassment

Verbal abuse is certainly the most threatening aspect of life on the streets in Belize. Again the only real problem is Belize City, where there are always plenty of people hanging out on the streets, commenting on all that passes by. The inevitable "Hey, white boy/white chick – what's happening?" will soon become a familiar sound. At first it can all seem very threatening, as you struggle through the city, your mind full of terrifying tales. But if you take the time to stop and talk, you'll find the vast majority of these people simply want to know where you're from, and where you're heading . . . and perhaps to offer you a deal on boat trips, money exchange, or even bum a dollar or two. Once you realise that they mean no harm the whole experience of Belize City will be infinitely more enjoyable. Obviously the situation is a little more serious for women, and the abuse tends to be more offensive. But once again, annoying though it is, it's unlikely that anything will come of it and if you face a Belizean head-on they'll almost always ease up.

■ Drugs

Marijuana, **cocaine** and **crack** are all readily available in Belize, particularly in Belize City, Orange Walk and Caye Caulker. Whether you like it or not you'll receive regular offers; if you don't then just brush them off, if you do then prices are cheap and quality is high. However all such substances are illegal, and despite the fact that dope is smoked openly in the streets, the police do arrest people for possession of marijuana: they particularly enjoy catching tourists. So if you want to indulge in this local pastime then be discreet. If you're caught you'll probably end up spending a couple of days in jail and paying a fine of several hundred US dollars: expect no sympathy from your embassy.

Directory

AIRPORT TAX Leaving Belize by air you'll have to pay an airport tax of BZ$20: transit passengers who've been in the country for less than 24 hours don't have to pay.

BAGS If you're camping or travelling long-term you may need a rucksack, and if you've got a lot of stuff these are often easier to carry. But for shorter visits you can make do with something lighter and less cumbersome. A light nylon holdall should have enough space for a sleeping bag and clothes, and works out a lot easier if you're travelling by bus.

BEGGARS are rare in Belize and those that there are don't fit the Latin American mould. Most operate in Belize City and aim exclusively at tourists, bumming a bottle of beer or a dollar or two. They tend to be persistent but harmless.

CONTRACEPTION Condoms are available from chemists in Belize City, as are some brands of the pill. But in either case I'd always recommend bringing enough to last the trip. If you're using the pill – or any other orally administered drug – bear in mind that severe diarrhoea can reduce its efficacy.

ELECTRICITY The mains supply is 110 volts AC with American-style two flat pin sockets. Electrical equipment made for the States and Canada should be OK, but ask in your hotel before you do anything as the electricity supply is far from reliable. Some hotels and small villages have their electricity supplied by local generators, and the voltage is then much lower.

EMBASSIES AND CONSULATES The vast majority of embassies and consulates are still in Belize City, but the British High Commission, the Panamanian Consulate and the Venezuelan Embassy have all moved to Belmopan. Addresses are listed in the section on Belize City.

EMERGENCIES Emergency numbers in Belize City are: Police – ☎02/2210; Belize Hospital – ☎02/77251.

GAY LIFE There's no open gay community in Belize and the cities are too small to support any exclusively gay bars. Things here are easy-going so you needn't expect any great hassle, but it's probably still a good idea to be discreet in order to avoid verbal abuse.

LAUNDRY The addresses of laundry services are listed in the sections on Belize City and San Ignacio, which are the only towns that have any kind of laundry service. Elsewhere you can usually get away with doing your laundry in your hotel room.

ODD ESSENTIALS Insect repellent and sun tan lotion are a good idea, and both are available in Belize. I'd also recommend a flashlight and alarm clock for catching early-morning buses.

STUDENT CARDS won't do any harm – but in Belize they're not likely to do you much good either.

TAMPONS are generally available from chemists in Belize City, and you can always get hold of sanitary towels, which are sold in all towns and villages.

TIME ZONES Belize is on Central Standard Time, six hours behind Greenwich Mean Time and the same as Guatemala.

TIPS Tipping is by no means standard practice in Belize but then again it is often done, so it's really up to you.

TOILETS Public toilets are very rare indeed, though there is one on the main square in Belmopan which may mark the shape of things to come. In hotels and restaurants standards are extremely variable, but toilets are never considered a high priority. On the whole toilet paper is provided, but it's always a good idea to travel with your own roll, just in case.

TOURIST OFFICE The only real tourist office in Belize is at 53 Regent Street, Belize City (open weekdays 8am–noon and 1–5pm; ☎02/77213), but there's also an information booth open at the airport for incoming flights, and numerous offices of the *Belize Tourist Industry Association* (BTIA) around the country. Although this is really an industry organisation, they do try to help with information and especially complaints about hotel standards or service: head office is at 99 Albert Street, Belize City (☎02/75717).

WEIGHTS AND MEASURES The imperial system of pounds and ounces, miles, yards, feet and inches, is still used in Belize, although this book is metric throughout. See box on p.30.

THE WOMEN'S MOVEMENT Women in Belize are a good deal more liberated than many of their sisters in Latin America: male emigration has traditionally left women as the head of many Belizean households, and they play an important part in some industries, especially in the service sector. The Government of Belize has a Policy Statement on Women outlining the efforts taken to implement equal rights and advance the status of women. To this end the government enhanced the role of the Women's Bureau (established in 1980) and renamed it (perhaps inaptly) as the Department of Women's Affairs in 1986. The department acts as an umbrella organisation for all women's groups in the country and assists with income-generating projects. *Cottage Industries* at 26 Albert Street, Belize City, sells crafts made by women all over Belize and it is also where you'll find Sister Panton, an active organiser and supporter of the women's movement. The director of the *Women Against Violence Against Women* movement in Belize, Dorla Bowman, can be contacted on ☎02/72852.

WORK There's virtually no chance of finding temporary work in Belize as at least half of the population is underemployed. Work permits are only on offer to those who can prove their ability to support themselves without endangering the job of a Belizean.

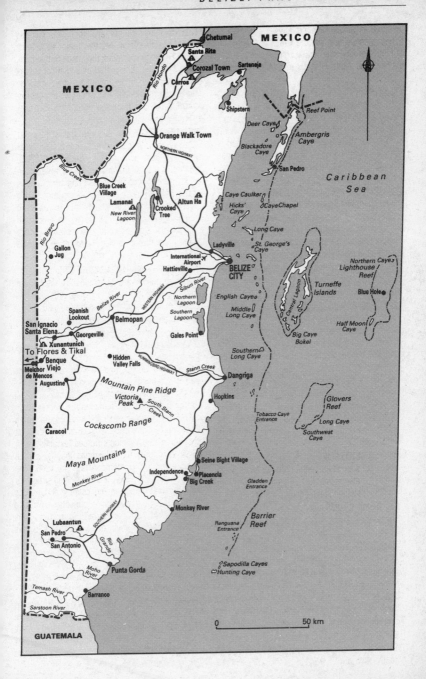

MEXICO

Chetumal
Santa Rita
Corozal Town
Cerros
Sarteneja

Shipstern

MEXICO

Rio Hondo

Orange Walk Town
NORTHERN HIGHWAY

Deer Cayes

Blackadore
Caye

Ambergris
Caye

Blue Creek

Blue Creek
Village
Lamanai
New River
Lagoon
Crooked
Tree
Altun Ha

San Pedro

Caribbean
Sea

Caye Caulker
Hicks'
Caye
Caye Chapel

Rio Bravo

Gallon
Jug

Long Caye

St. George's
Caye

Ladyville

International
Airport
Hattieville

BELIZE
CITY

Northern Cayes
Lighthouse
Reef

Blue Hole

Blue Creek

Belize River

Spanish
Lookout

Belmopan

Sibun River

Northern
Lagoon

Southern
Lagoon

English Caye

Middle
Long Caye

Turneffe
Islands

Central Lagoon

Half Moon
Caye

San Ignacio
Santa Elena
Georgeville
Xunantunich
To Flores & Tikal
Benque
Melchor Viejo
de Mencos
Augustine

WESTERN HIGHWAY

Hidden
Valley Falls

HUMMINGBIRD HIGHWAY

Gales Point

Mountain Pine Ridge

Victoria
Peak
South Stann
Creek

Cockscomb Range

Caracol

Stann Creek

Dangriga

Hopkins

Southern
Long Caye

Big Caye
Bokel

Glovers
Reef

Long Caye

Southwest
Caye

Tobacco Caye
Entrance

Maya Mountains

Monkey River

Independence

Seine Bight Village

Placencia
Big Creek

Gladden
Entrance

SOUTHERN HIGHWAY

Monkey River

Lubaantun
San Pedro
San Antonio

Rio Grande

Moho
River

Punta Gorda

Ranguana
Entrance

Barrier
Reef

Temash River

Barranco

Sarstoon River

Sapodilla Cayes
Hunting Caye

0   50 km

GUATEMALA

CHAPTER SEVEN

COROZAL, ORANGE WALK AND THE NORTH

Northern Belize is an expanse of relatively level land, where swamps, savannahs and lagoons are mixed with rainforest and farmland. For many years this part of the country was largely inaccessible and had closer ties with Mexico – where most of the original settlers came from – than Belize City. The Indian and *mestizo* farming communities were connected by a skeletal network of dirt tracks, while boats plied the route between Belize City and Corozal. In 1930, however, the Northern highway brought the region into contact with the rest of the country, opening up the area to further waves of settlers.

Today the largest town in the north is **Orange Walk**, the main centre for sugar production. Further to the north is **Corozal**, a small and peaceful Caribbean town with a strong Mexican element – scarcely surprising as the town is just twenty minutes from the Mexican border. Throughout the north Spanish is as common as Creole, and there's a mild Latin flavour to both of these towns.

The main attractions in northern Belize are **Maya ruins** and **wildlife reserves**. The largest of the ruins is **Altun Ha**, to the north of Belize City, while **Lamanai**, on the shores of the New River Lagoon, features some impressive pyramids. Both sites are difficult to reach, and Lamanai is accessible by road only in the dry season. The smaller sites include **Cuello**, to the west of Orange Walk, and **Santa Rita** and **Cerros**, both near Corozal.

The four wildlife reserves each offer a different approach to conservation, and an insight into different environments. The most northerly of them is the **Shipstern Reserve**, where a section of tropical forest is preserved with the income from a butterfly farm. At the **Crooked Tree Wildlife Sanctuary** a network of rivers and lagoons offers protection to a range of migratory birds, and at the **Bermudian Landing Community Baboon Sanctuary** a group of farmers have combined agriculture with conservation, much to the benefit of the black howler monkey. By far the largest and most ambitious conservation project, however, is the **Río Bravo Conservation Area**, comprising over 250,000 acres of tropical forest and river systems in the west of Orange Walk district. This vast, practically unspoilt area, containing several Maya sites, adjoins the border with Guatemala and stretches to Mexico in the north, opening the door to the exciting possibility of a three-nation natural reserve.

Travelling in the north is fairly straightforward if you stick to the main highway. *Venus* and *Batty* between them operate bus services every hour from 4am to 7pm between Belize City and Chetumal, calling at Orange Walk and Corozal. Smaller roads and centres are served by a fairly regular flow of trucks and buses,

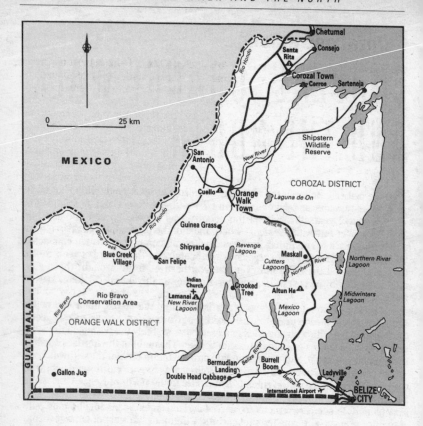

and several companies now operate **tours** to the Maya sites and nature reserves, though these can be expensive.

The border

Heading into Belize from Mexico you can pick up a bus for Belize City at the new terminal in **Chetumal**. This will take you to the **Santa Elena** border crossing, on the Río Hondo. The Mexican immigration and customs posts are on the northern bank; when you're finished there, simply walk across the bridge to their Belizean counterparts – the bus waits to pick you up again at Belizean immigration. Border formalities take just a matter of minutes, but to enter Belize you'll need to prove that you can afford to stay for a while. Don't try to bring in cheaper cigarettes or liquor from Mexico – imports are prohibited. Most travellers will be given a thirty-day visa, which can be extended in Belize City or Belmopan, although impecunious visitors are sometimes offered 24 hours or less. The **moneychangers** encountered on the Belize side will not rip you off, and if you're carrying US dollars in cash it's possible to negotiate a slightly better rate than the standard two Belize dollars for one American dollar. For details of the bus service to Belize City, see "Travel Details" at the end of the chapter.

Corozal and around

Continuing south, the road meets the sea at **COROZAL**, Belize's most northerly town, just twenty minutes from Chetumal. The original settlement was founded in 1849 by refugees from the massacre in Bacalar, Mexico, who were hounded south by the Caste Wars. Today's grid-pattern town is a neat mix of Mexican and Caribbean, its appearance largely due to reconstruction in the wake of Hurricane Janet in 1955. This is a fertile area – the town's name derives from the cohune tree, which the Maya recognised as an indicator of fecundity – and in the recent past much of the land was planted with sugar cane; tumbling sugar prices have now forced farmers to try a range of alternative crops, often with great success.

There's not much to do in Corozal, but it's an agreeable place to spend the day if you're heading to or from the Mexican border, with its shoreline shaded by palm trees and fanned by the sea breeze. The town hall is worth a look, painted with a graphic local history, and the remains of a small fort – built to ward off Indian attacks – can still be seen in one corner of the plaza. Also worth a visit is Brian Noquera's winery, producing excellent local fruit wines including cashew – the local favourite. Columbus Day celebrations in Corozal are particularly lively, Mexican fiesta merging with Caribbean carnival.

Two small Maya sites can be visited from Corozal. The closest is **Santa Rita**, on the northern side of the town. To get there follow the main road in the direction of the border, and when it divides take the left-hand fork, which soon brings you to the hospital, the power plant, and the raised Maya site; only a few minutes' walk. Founded around 1500 BC, Santa Rita was in all probability the powerful Maya city known as Chetumal, which dominated the trade of the area. It was still a thriving settlement in 1531 AD, when the *conquistador* Alonso Davila entered the town, which had been abandoned by the Maya; he was driven out almost immediately by Na Chan Kan, the Maya chief, and his Spanish adviser Gonzalo Guerro. Pottery found here has connected Santa Rita with other sites in the Yucatán, while some superb murals seem similar to those at Tulum. You won't be spellbound by its enormity, though, as only a fraction of the site has been unearthed, exposing a few simple chambers and some wall carvings. Some of the best finds, especially ceramics, are now on show in the Archaeological Vault in Belmopan (see p.296).

The second site, **Cerros**, is a late Preclassic centre on the southern shore of Corozal Bay, and includes tombs, ball courts and a 22-metre-high temple – though, once again, most of the site remains unexcavated. Cerros is best reached by boat; you can easily hire one at the dock in Corozal. In the dry season it's possible to drive to the site through the villages of Chunos, Progreso and Copper Bank.

Practicalities

In Corozal itself the cheapest **hotel** is the *Capri* (☎2042), on the seafront at the southern end, where small musty rooms cost BZ$8; there's a bar and dance floor downstairs, so it can get a bit noisy. On the main road opposite the *Capri* is the *Bumper Chinese Restaurant*, which serves a mix of Belizean and Chinese food. Another reasonable hotel, *Nestor's* on Fifth Avenue (☎2354), has doubles for BZ$15. The *Hotel Maya*, on the main road at the southern entrance to Corozal, costs BZ$28 single: well worth it, with excellent Spanish food. A little way out of town, to the south, is the *Caribbean Trailer Park* (☎2045), where you can camp for BZ$3, or rent a two-bed cabin for BZ$40. *Joe's Caribbean Restaurant*, in the middle of the park, serves good cheap food, but closes for a siesta at 1pm.

For a touch of luxury, *Tony's*, a kilometre to the south of Corozal (☎2055), has a pristine bar, a wonderful restaurant, and a moderately priced hotel, with rooms at BZ$36. North along the coast, CONSEJO has a resort hotel, the *Adventure Inn* (☎2187), on Consejo Shores – beautiful but expensive. A few kilometres from the border, a road leads to Four Miles Lagoon, where you can **camp** on the shore.

There are three **banks** in Corozal – *The Bank of Nova Scotia*, *Barclays* and the *Belize Bank* – open Monday to Friday 8am to 1pm, plus 3 to 6pm on Fridays only.

All **buses** between Belize City and Chetumal pass through Corozal, more or less hourly in each direction. For the border (20min) they pass through more or less on the hour from 7am to 9pm, for Belize City (3hr) on the half-hour from 5.30am to 7.30pm. The *Venus* bus depot is near the northern edge of town opposite the *Shell* station, *Batty* buses stop on the road outside, just round the corner. *Maya Airways* operate daily **flights** to San Pedro and Belize City at 8am and 3.30pm, while *Tropic Air* operate scheduled flights at 10am and 3.30pm. Tickets can be bought from *Jal's* travel agency, on Fourth Avenue (☎22163).

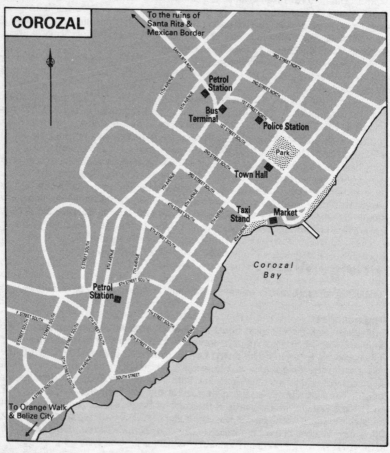

Sarteneja and the Shipstern Reserve

The **Sarteneja peninsula**, jutting out towards the Yucatán in the northeast of Belize, is an area that until recently could only be reached by boat. Its largest village is **SARTENEJA**, a lobster-fishing centre whose population of Spanish-speaking *mestizos* used to transport their supplies by boat from Chetumal before the road was built. Since the region's closest links have always been with Mexico, the idea of Belize nationality is still fairly novel here.

The rest of the peninsula is virtually uninhabited, covered with dense forests that support an amazing array of wildlife. In 1981 the **Shipstern Wildlife Reserve** was established to protect 31 square miles of this environment. The bulk of the reserve is made up of what's technically known as "tropical moist forest", although it contains only a few mature trees as the area was wiped clean by Hurricane Janet in 1955. It also includes some wide belts of savannah – covered in coarse grasses, palms and broad-leaved trees – and a section of the Shipstern Lagoon, a shallow stretch of water dotted with mangrove islands.

The reserve is a birdwatcher's paradise. The lagoon system supports blue-winged teal, American coot, thirteen species of egret and huge flocks of lesser scaup, while the forest is home to fly-catchers, warblers, keel-billed toucans, collared aracari and at least five species of parrot. In addition to this there are crocodiles, manatees, coatis, jaguars, peccaries, deer, racoons, pumas and an abundance of weird and wonderful insects and butterflies.

The butterfly farm adjacent to the site headquarters helps the reserve to pay its way, exporting pupae to butterfly farms in Britain, such as those at Syon Park, the Edinburgh Butterfly House and Stratford-upon-Avon. If you'd like to spend some time exploring the reserve via the specially cut trails that run through it, you can stay at the site headquarters for a small fee.

To get there you need to catch the **bus** which leaves Belize City at noon (from the *Shell* station on North Front Street) and passes through Orange Walk at around 2pm, stopping outside *The People's Store*. The trip from Belize City to Sarteneja takes around three hours, and the bus returns at 3am. The reserve itself is just beside the road about 10km to the south of the village – ask the bus driver to drop you.

Orange Walk

ORANGE WALK, with a population of just under 10,000, is the largest town in the north of Belize and the centre of a busy agricultural region. Like Corozal, it was founded by *mestizo* refugees fleeing from the Caste Wars in Yucatán in 1849, who chose as their site an area that had long been used for logger camps. These new outsiders faced bitter resistance from the local Indians, and the people of Orange Walk were often confronted by war parties. In 1872, spurred on by news of Indian uprisings in the Yucatán, the local Icaiche Maya under the leadership of Canul launched an attack on Orange Walk, having previously demanded protection money from the settlers. The West India Regiment, who had earlier come off worse in a skirmish with Canul's forces, were sent to sort things out, and Canul was slain in the subsequent engagement, after which the situation calmed down. Nowadays the few remaining Icaiche Maya live in the village of BOTES, on the Guatemalan border near the Río Hondo.

In recent times Orange Walk has expanded rapidly, with the growth of the sugar and citrus industries, although after sugar prices fell marijuana became a more profitable option. The land around Blue Creek and Shipyard has also been developed by **Mennonite** settlers, members of a Protestant religious group who choose to farm without the assistance of modern technology. The Mennonites arose from the radical Anabaptist movement of the sixteenth century and are named after the Dutch priest Menno Simons, leader of the community in its formative years. Recurring government restrictions on their lifestyle, especially regarding their pacifist objection to military service, forced them to move repeatedly. Having removed to Switzerland they travelled on to Prussia, and in 1663 a group of Mennonites emigrated to North America. After World War I they migrated from Canada to Mexico, arriving in Belize in 1958. Perseverance and hard work made them successful farmers, and in recent years prosperity has caused drastic changes in their lives. The Mennonite Church in Belize is increasingly split into a modernist section – who use electricity and power tools, and drive trucks, tractors and even cars – and the traditionalists, who prefer stricter interpretation of their beliefs. Members of the Mennonite community, easily recognisable in their denim dungarees, can be seen trading their produce and buying supplies in Belize City every day.

Practicalities

Orange Walk itself is not particularly attractive, so unless you plan to visit the ruins of Cuello or Lamanai (see below) there's little reason to stop here. What's more, cheap **accommodation** is limited, and if you're on a tight budget the only options are *Jane's Guest Houses* – one in Bakers Street and the other in Market Lane – both of which charge BZ$15 for a simple single room. The more upmarket *Baron's Hotel*, on Corozal Road (☎22518), charges BZ$31 for a double, for which you get to use the swimming pool and disco.

There are several good Chinese **restaurants** in town, a few bars, three banks, a theatre that shows films at the weekends, and some sleazy clubs. The last group includes the *Club America*, which doubles as a brothel and is ominously referred to as *Vietnam*.

All **buses** running between Belize City and Chetumal pass through Orange Walk, heading north on the hour and south on the half-hour.

Maya sites near Orange Walk

Although the Maya sites in northern Belize were the source of some of the most important archaeological finds anywhere in the Maya world, they are not (with the possible exception of Lamanai) as monumentally spectacular as some in the Yucatán. The area around Orange Walk contains some of the most productive arable farmland in Belize, and this was also the case in Maya times – aerial surveys in the late Seventies revealed evidence of raised fields and a network of irrigation canals, showing that the Maya practised skilful intensive agriculture. In the Postclassic era this region became part of the powerful Maya state of Chactemal, controlling the trade in cacao beans (which were used as currency) grown in the valleys of the Hondo and New rivers. For a while the Maya here were even able to resist the *conquistadores*, and long after nominal Spanish rule had been established in 1544 there were frequent Maya rebellions: in 1638 they drove the Spanish out and burned the church at Lamanai.

Cuello

Cuello, one of the earliest and most important known Maya sites, lies about 5km to the west of Orange Walk. Its discovery in 1973, by Norman Hammond, changed archaeologists' ideas about the sophistication of the early Maya. Previous theories had set the beginnings of Maya civilisation at around 1000 BC, but some of the finds at Cuello – including low house platforms, human burials, food remains, pottery and jade from the Motagua valley in Guatemala – indicate that it was founded by 1500 BC, and probably occupied for almost 3000 years. Unfortunately the site itself isn't very impressive, and there's not much to look at except a single small pyramid and several earth-covered mounds.

The ruins are behind a factory where *Cuello Rum* is made; the site is on their land so you should ask permission to visit the ruins by phoning ☎22141. To get to Cuello you can simply walk west from the plaza in Orange Walk (for a little under an hour); you can take the San Felipe bus, which passes the junction of Bakers Lane and Victoria Avenue in Orange Walk at around 10am and heads out past the factory; or you can take a taxi, for around BZ$10 return.

Nohmul

Situated on the Orange Walk/Corozal boundary just west of the village of San Pablo, **Nohmul** (Great Mound) is a major ceremonial centre with origins in the Late Formative Period. The ruins cover a large area, comprising two groups connected by a causeway, with several plazas around them. The main structure is an "acropolis" platform surmounted by a later pyramid which, owing to the site's position on a limestone ridge, is the highest point in the area. Nohmul was abandoned during the Classic Period, to be reoccupied by a Yucatecan elite during the Early Postclassic. As has occurred at so many of Belize's Maya sites, looters have plundered the ruins and at least one structure has been demolished for road fill – an incalculable tragedy.

Nohmul lies amid sugar-cane fields, 2km west of the village of SAN PABLO, which is 12km north of Orange Walk on the Northern highway. Any bus between Corozal and Orange Walk goes through the village. To visit, contact Estevan Itzab, in the house across from the village water tower.

Lamanai

Though they can't match the scale of the great sites in Mexico and Guatemala, the ruins of **Lamanai** are among the most impressive in Belize, and their setting on the New River Lagoon – in the 950-acre Archaeological Reserve (now the only jungle for miles around) – gives Lamanai a special quality that is long gone from sites served by a torrent of tourist buses.

Lamanai is one of only a few sites where the original Maya name is known – it means "Submerged Crocodile", hence the numerous representations of crocodiles here. The site was occupied until the sixteenth century, when Spanish missionaries built a church alongside to lure the Indians from their heathen ways. There are fifty or sixty structures, the majority of them still buried beneath mounds of earth.

The most impressive feature is the prosaically named N10-43, a massive **Late Preclassic temple**, the largest Preclassic structure in the entire Maya area, though later modified extensively. The view across the surrounding forest from the top is magnificent. Structure P9-56 is a sixth-century pyramid with a four-metre-high mask carved in the side; it overlies several smaller and older buildings, the earliest being a superbly preserved temple from around 100 BC. Traces of later settlers can be seen around the nearby village of INDIAN CHURCH: to the south of the village are the ruins of two churches built by Spanish missionaries, and to the west are the remains of a nineteenth-century sugar mill, built by Confederate refugees from the American Civil War.

Getting to Lamanai is neither easy nor cheap, and it's best to get together three or four people to keep the costs down. Setting out from Orange Walk you need to take a truck to either GUINEA GRASS or SHIPYARD, two small villages on the New River: trucks leave from *The People's Store*, on Main Street in Orange Walk, at around 10am. At either of these villages you'll be able to hire a boat to get you to the ruins themselves, for BZ$100–150. In Guinea Grass ask for Santiago Cima, who has a couple of boats and can usually spare the time to take you upriver, which takes around an hour. At the site there are guards who will charge you BZ$2 for a tour of the ruins.

Gilly's Inland Tours operate an overnight excursion from Belize City to Lamanai for US$125 per person (minimum of four); details from *Belize Air Travel Services*, 31 Regent Street, Belize City (☎77630). Better value is Mr Godoy, an expert local guide who offers tours to Cuello, Lamanai and Crooked Tree; contact him at 4 Trial Farm, Orange Walk (☎22969). If you're in a hurry to get to Lamanai, phone Mr Bader Hassan on ☎32/2115; he lives in Tower Hill, just off the highway near the turning for Guinea Grass, and has great local knowledge and several reliable (if expensive) vehicles, including a cabin cruiser that's ideal for group trips to the ruins. In the dry season, Lamanai can also be reached by dirt road from Orange Walk via SAN FELIPE.

Crooked Tree and south to Belize City

Heading south from Orange Walk you pass the branch road for the **Crooked Tree Wildlife Sanctuary**, a reserve that takes in a vast area of inland waterways, logwood swamps and lagoons. Founded in 1984 by the Belize Audubon Society and covering four separate lagoons and 3000 acres, it provides an ideal resting place for thousands of **migrating birds**, such as snail kites, tiger-herons, snowy egrets, ospreys and black-collared hawks. The reserve's most famous visitor is the **jabiru stork**, the largest flying bird in the New World, with a wingspan of eight feet. Belize has the biggest nesting population of jabiru storks: they arrive in November, the young hatch in April or May, and they leave just before the rainy season gets under way. If you set off to explore the lagoons you might also catch a glimpse of howler monkeys, crocodiles, coatis, turtles or iguanas.

In the middle of the reserve is the village of **CROOKED TREE**, 3km from the main road. One of the oldest inland villages in the country, its existence is based on fishing and farming – some of the mango and cashew trees are reckoned to be over a hundred years old. There's a visitors' centre in the village but no accommodation, so if you want to see the reserve it's a good idea to take an organised tour from Belize City. *Jal's Travel and Tours*, 148 North Front Street, run two standard trips, but a full day trip, including a boat ride into the lagoon, costs US$70. If you can't afford this, try hitching or walking to the village, from where you can wander through the reserve or hire your own boat – but set out early. There are two daily buses to Crooked Tree from Belize City but their schedule is hard to keep track of – ask in Orange Walk or at *Batty's* in Belize City.

The Río Bravo Conservation Area

In the far west of Orange Walk district is the **Río Bravo Conservation Area**, a 250,000-acre tract set aside for conservation, research and sustained-yield forests. Formed by private purchase and an agreement with the original owner of the land, Barry Bowen, to manage his remaining land under strict conservation restrictions, plus a gift of 42,000 acres from *Coca-Cola*, the reserve is now managed by the *Programme For Belize*, which was initiated in 1988 by the Massachusetts Audubon Society and launched in Britain in 1989 by Gerald and Lee Durrell. The entire area could soon become part of a tri-national **Maya Peace Park**, united with the Calakmul Biosphere Reserve in Mexico and the Maya Biosphere Reserve in Guatemala.

All five of Belize's native species of cat can be found here, as well as monkeys, crocodiles, tapirs and 250 bird species. Maya ruins are plentiful throughout the conservation area, and **accommodation** is available at *Chan Chich Lodge*, near **GALLON JUG** (a part of the reserve that is still owned by Barry Bowen). The modern thatched cabanas here are set in the middle of a Classic Period Maya plaza, and prices are US$50 single and US$65 double – extra for meals. This private enterprise promotes social exclusivity at a site where government ownership and control should ensure accessibility for all, but at least the year-round presence of the visitors and staff does prevent looting. At some times of the year it may also be possible to stay in the cabins used by the archaeologists. **Transport** to this remote site is difficult. There is a private airstrip at Gallon Jug, to which you could charter a plane for three people for around US$150 from Belize City or airport, or you can drive in from the village of Orange Walk near Belmopan (not to be confused with the major town in the north). For more information ask at the office of the *Programme For Belize* (see Chapter Eight, *Belize City*) or write to *Chan Chich Lodge*, PO Box 37, Belize City.

The Ruins of Altun Ha

Fifty-five kilometres north of Belize City and just nine kilometres from the sea is the impressive Maya site of **Altun Ha**, which was occupied from around 1000 BC until its abandonment in 900 AD. Its population probably peaked at 3000 inhabitants, and it must always have been sustained as much by trade as agriculture: its position close to the Caribbean coast suggests as much, and trade objects including obsidian, jade and shells were found here. Neither jade nor obsidian occur naturally in Belize, and both are very important in Maya ceremony. The jade here would have been traded from the Motagua Valley in Guatemala and much of it would probably have been shipped onwards to the north.

The core of Altun Ha (site entrance BZ$3) is clustered around two Classic Period plazas, both dotted with palm trees. Entering from the road, you come first to Plaza A. Large temples enclose it on all four sides, and a magnificent tomb has been discovered beneath Temple A-1 – **The Temple of the Green Tomb**. Dating from 550 AD, this yielded a total of 300 pieces, including jade, jewellery, stingray spines, skin, flints and the remains of a Maya book. Temple A-6, which has been particularly badly damaged, contains two parallel rooms, each about 48 metres long, and each with 13 doorways in an exterior wall.

The adjacent Plaza B is dominated by the site's largest temple, **The Temple of the Masonry Altars**, the last in a sequence of superimposed buildings raised on this spot. This was probably the main focus of religious ceremonies, with a single stairway running up the front to an altar at the top. Several priestly tombs have been uncovered within the main structure, but most of them had been desecrated, possibly in the political turmoil that preceded the abandonment of the site. Only two of the tombs were found intact, and in one of these archaeologists discovered a carved jade head of **Kinich Ahau**, the Maya sun god. Standing 14.9cm high, it was the largest carved jade to be found anywhere in the Maya world at the time of its discovery in 1968; today it's kept hidden away in the vaults of the Belize Bank as there is no national museum to display it.

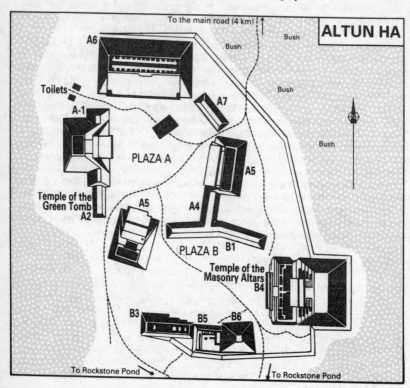

Outside these two main plazas there are several other areas of interest, though little else has been restored, despite recent archaeological work. A short trail leads south to **Rockstone Pond**, which was dammed in Maya times and at the eastern edge of which stands another medium-sized temple. Built in the second century AD, this contained offerings that came from the great city of Teotihuacán in the Valley of Mexico.

Polychrome plate from Sun God's Tomb

The site is fairly difficult to get to as there's no bus service along the delightful branch road (the former Northern highway) that leads here. However, trucks run from the market in Belize City to the village of **MASKALL**, about 2km from Altun Ha, or you should be able to hitch. There's no accommodation at the site, so it's a choice between camping nearby (ask the caretaker), hitching back to the capital, or going on to Maskall, where you should be able to find somewhere to stay in someone's house or a place to camp. The only nearby rooms are at the expensive **Maruba Resort** (☎03/22199), at the 40.5 mile post on the Northern highway.

The Bermudian Landing Community Baboon Sanctuary

The **Community Baboon Sanctuary** is one of the most interesting conservation projects in Belize, and almost certainly the most cost-effective. It was established in 1985 by Dr Rob Horwich and a group of local farmers (with help from the World Wide Fund for Nature), who adopted a voluntary code of practice which harmonised their own needs with those of the wildlife. A mixture of farmland and broad-leaved forest along the banks of the Belize river, the sanctuary coordinates eight villages and over 100 landowners in a project that combines conservation, education and tourism.

The main focus of attention is the **black howler monkey** (locally known as a baboon), an endangered sub-species of howler that exists only in Belize, Guatemala and Mexico. They generally live in groups of between four and eight, and spend the day wandering through the leaf canopy feasting on leaves, flowers and fruits. At dawn and dusk they let rip with the infamous howl, a deep and rasping roar that carries for miles. The sanctuary is also home to around 200 bird species, with iguanas, anteaters, deer, peccaries and coatis among other animals to be seen. Special trails have been cut through the forest so that visitors can see it at its best, and there's an excellent guidebook that tells you everything there is to know about the reserve and its inhabitants. There's an interpretative visitors' centre too, home to Belize's first natural history museum.

The village of **BERMUDIAN LANDING** is at the heart of the area, an old logging centre that dates back to the seventeenth century. Accommodation is available here at the visitors' centre, where you can also pitch a tent for a small fee, and meals can be arranged with local families. It's a small place, so you should let them know that you're coming, particularly if you plan to stay the night. The sanctuary manager is Mr Fallet Young, and you can get in touch with him on ☎02/44405. **Buses** run from Belize City to the sanctuary at 1.30pm: Mr Oswald McFadzean has a bus that leaves from the corner of Orange Street and Mussel Street, and Mr Sydney Russel has a bus that leaves from the corner of Orange Street and George Street. They run every day except Sunday, and return from Bermudian Landing at 5.30am. Once you get there you can either wander the trails on your own or hire a guide.

On the way out to Bermudian Landing you'll pass a turning to BURRELL BOOM, on the Belize River, reached by an old ferry. If you have your own vehicle and are heading directly west you can save time and considerable distance by cutting down through Burrell Boom to **Hattieville**, on the Western highway, thus avoiding Belize City altogether.

The approach to Belize City

Back on the Northern highway there's not much else to stop for. At LADYVILLE you pass the **International Airport** and there's a branch road to AIRPORT CAMP, the main base of the British Forces in Belize. Situated on the north side of the runways are the barracks for an infantry battalion, the headquarters units of the Army and Royal Air Force, and a detachment of Harrier jets. At the junction of the Northern highway and the road to the camp, the *International Hotel* (☎025/2150) is a modern building offering air-conditioned rooms for about BZ$50 single, and possibly the worst food and service in the country. The side road to the airport is the next one south of the hotel, a two-kilometre walk; there are no buses all the way to the airport.

Now it's only 15km to Belize City and, with the road very close to the river, heavy rain sometimes causes flooding on this stretch. If you notice a large concrete building on the left-hand side of the road called *Raoul's Rose Garden* you may care to know that it's not a nursery in the horticultural sense but a recently rebuilt brothel. The Haulover Bridge takes the road over the mouth of the Belize River, where the *Río Haul Motel* (☎44859) charges BZ$50 for a double room: next door, on the coast, is the attractive *Privateer* bar and restaurant, often with live music at weekends. Beyond this point you begin to enter the spreading suburbs of Belize City, where expensive houses are constructed on reclaimed mangrove swamps.

travel details

Buses
From Chetumal to Belize City (4hr 15min) via **Corozal** (1hr 30min) and **Orange Walk** (2hr 30min): *Batty* departures at 2.30am (express) and then every two hours from 4am to 6pm, with an express service at 2pm. From **Belize City to Chetumal** departures from *Batty's* terminal, 54 East Collet Canal, every two hours from 4am to 6pm, with the 6am and 6pm runs being express services. At the time of writing *Venus* schedules for the same route are undergoing major changes, but they previously operated every odd hour, from 5am to 7pm.

For **Sarteneja** the *Perez* bus leaves the *Shell* station on North Front Street in Belize City at noon, passing Orange Walk at about 2pm and arriving around an hour later.

For the **Bermudian Landing Baboon Sanctuary** there are two buses daily (except Sun), both leaving at 1.30pm. One departs from the corner of Orange Street and Mussel Street, the other from the corner of Orange Street and George Street.

Planes
Maya Airways and *Tropic Air* both operate two daily flights **from Corozal to San Pedro and Belize City**.

CHAPTER EIGHT

BELIZE CITY

The narrow and crowded streets of **Belize City** can initially be daunting to anyone who has been prepared by the usual tales of crime-ridden urban decay. Admittedly at first glance the city is unprepossessing. Its buildings – many of them dilapidated wooden structures – stand right at the edge of the road, and few pavements offer refuge to pedestrians from the ever increasing numbers of cars and trucks. Narrow bridges force the traffic to cross in single file over almost stagnant canals, which are still used for much of the city's drainage. Vultures circle overhead or sit with drooping wings on rotting riverside jetties. The overall impression is that the place has never recovered from some great calamity – an explanation that is at least partly true. Belize has suffered several devastating hurricanes, the latest in October 1961, when Hurricane Hattie tore the city apart with winds of 150mph, leaving a layer of thick black mud as the storm receded. The hazards of Belize City, however, are often reported by those who have never been here. If you approach the city with an open mind and take some precautions with your belongings, you may well be pleasantly surprised.

Most visitors hurry through on their way to catch their next bus or a boat out to the cayes, but the city has a distinguished history, a handful of interesting sights, and an astonishing energy. The 60,000 people of Belize City represent every ethnic group in the country, with the **Creole** descendants of former slaves and Baymen forming the dominant element and generating an easy-going Caribbean atmosphere. The streets are busy from early morning to late evening, alive with a street culture based on rum, reggae and hustle.

HASSLE

Walking in Belize City **in daylight** is perfectly safe if you observe common-sense rules. Be civil, don't provoke trouble by arguing too forcefully, and never show large sums of money on the street, especially American dollars – there are money changers who will give you better than the usual fixed rate of two dollars Belize for one US, but tourists are ripped off every day changing money on the street. Women wearing very short shorts or skirts will attract verbal abuse from the local studs. Be discreet if you smoke dope. Marijuana might be readily available, but it is illegal, and busting tourists can help a policeman get promoted.

Most people are friendly and chatty, but quite a few may want to sell you drugs or bum a dollar or two. The best advice is to stay cool – few of the hustlers are really persistent if you make it clear you're not interested.

At **night** it's a different matter. Anyone alone is in danger of being mugged, even in what appears to be a quiet area, and you shouldn't venture out with more than your immediate requirements in cash about your person. Walking in pairs is safer and you'll soon learn to spot dangerous situations. Especially menacing are the streets over the South Side Canal, towards the bus stations – take a taxi if you arrive by bus in the dark. Try to avoid the *Mesopotamia* and *King's Park* areas at night.

A brief history

Exactly how Belize came by its name is something of a mystery, but there are plenty of possibilities. It could be a corruption of "Willis", the name of a famous English pirate who may have landed here in 1638, and a similar claim is made for Peter Wallace, a Scotsman who founded a colony here in 1620. Those preferring a more ancient origin believe the name to be derived from *beliz*, a Maya word meaning "muddy", or from the Maya term *belekin*, meaning "towards the east". Another possibility is that it is a corruption of the French word *balise* – "beacon" – as there may have been a light marking the estuary of the Belize River.

What is known is that by the late seventeenth century buccaneers were cutting logwood in this region and that a settlement at the mouth of the river was used during the rainy season, the mangrove swamp being consolidated with wood chips, loose coral and rum bottles. By the eighteenth century Belize Town was well established as a centre for the logwood cutters, their families and their slaves; after the rains had floated the logs downriver the men returned here to drink and brawl, with huge Christmas celebrations going on for weeks. The sea front contained the houses of the **Baymen**, as the settlers called themselves; the slaves lived in cabins on the south side of Haulover Creek, with various tribal groups occupying separate areas.

The core of the settlement was on St George's Caye until a Spanish raid in 1779, when many of the inhabitants were captured and several of the Baymen fled. They returned in 1783, when Spain agreed to recognise the rights of the British settlers, and their new mainland capital soon grew into the main centre of the logwood and mahogany trade on the Bay of Honduras. Spanish raids continued, however, until the Battle of St George's Caye in 1798, when the settlers achieved victory with British naval help – a success that reinforced the bond with the British government.

The nineteenth century saw the increasing influence of **British expatriates**, colonial-style wooden housing dominating the shoreline as the "Scots clique" began to clean up the town's image and take control of its administration. Belize also became a base for Anglican missionaries: in 1812 the Anglican cathedral of St John was built to serve a diocese that stretched from Belize to Panama.

Fires in 1804, 1806 and 1856 necessitated extensive rebuilding, and there were epidemics of cholera, yellow fever and smallpox in this period too. Despite these reversals, the town grew with immigration from the West Indies and refugees from the Caste Wars in the Yucatán. In 1862 Belize became the colony of **British Honduras**, with Belize City as the administrative centre, and in 1871 Belize was officially declared a Crown Colony, with a resident governor appointed by Britain.

For the people of Belize the twentieth century has been dominated by uncertainty over their relationship with the "mother country". In 1914 thousands of Belizeans volunteered to assist the war effort, but when they arrived in the Middle East they were confronted by a wall of prejudice and racism, and consigned to labour battalions. In 1919 the returning soldiers rioted in Belize City, an event that marked the onset of black consciousness and the beginning of the **independence movement**.

On September 10, 1931, the city was celebrating the anniversary of the Battle of St George's Caye when it was hit by a massive **hurricane** that uprooted houses, flooded the entire city and killed about 1000 people – ten percent of the population. Disaster relief was slow to arrive and many parts of the city were left in a state of squalid poverty. This neglect, together with the effects of the Depression, gave added momentum to the campaign for independence, and the city saw numerous rallies and marches in an upsurge of defiance against the British colonial authorities. In 1961 the city was again ravaged by a hurricane: 262 people died, and the damage was so serious that plans were made to relocate the capital inland at Belmopan. (Hattieville, on the Western highway, began life as a refuge for those fleeing the hurricane.) The official attitude was that Belize City would soon become a redundant backwater as Belmopan grew, but in fact few people chose to leave for the sterile "new town" atmosphere of Belmopan, and Belize City remains by far the most populous place in the country.

Belize gained internal self-government in 1964, and the goal of **full independence** was reached in 1981, with Belize joining the Commonwealth as a sovereign state. Loyalty to the monarchy remains strong, though – as demonstrated by the tumultuous welcome given to the Queen in 1985. Since independence the rise of foreign investment and tourism has made an impact, and Belize City is now benefiting (and suffering) from a major construction boom. Work has now commenced on a Belize *Ramada Inn*, which gives some idea of the extent of foreign tourist investment.

Orientation, transport and accommodation

A quick glance at the map shows that the city is divided neatly into north and south halves by the **Haulover Creek**, a delta branch of the Belize River. The pivotal point of the city centre is the **Swing Bridge**, always busy with traffic and opened twice a day to allow larger vessels up and down the river.

North of the Swing Bridge things tend to be slightly more upmarket; here you'll find the most expensive hotels, most of the embassies and consulates, and – in the Kings Park area – some very luxurious houses. **South** of the Swing Bridge is the market and commercial zone, with banks, offices and supermarkets; the foreshore is the prestige area here, with an expensive hotel and the Governor's residence. West of the main thoroughfares of Regent and Albert streets is an area of impoverished and insanitary buildings – unsafe after dark.

The city is small enough to make **walking** the easiest way to get around, and if you make your way to the Swing Bridge you'll find all the hotels within easy reach on foot. There are also plenty of **taxis**, which run from the bus terminals and the taxi rank on Albert Street, by Central Park.

Buses, boats and planes

The four main **bus companies** in Belize have their terminals in the same western area of the city, around the Collet Canal and Magazine Road, a particularly derelict part of town known as Mesopotamia. It's less than a kilometre from the centre and you can easily walk to any of the hotels listed below, or take a taxi for BZ$3, plus BZ$1 for each extra person (see "Listings" for details).

If you're planning to go straight to the cayes you should be able to get a **boat** to Caye Caulker until about 4pm from *A&R's Shell Station* on North Front Street, by the Swing Bridge (fare BZ$12). For San Pedro on Ambergris Caye, a boat leaves the dock of the *Belle Vue Hotel*, 5 Southern Foreshore, at 4pm (fare BZ$20).

Boats returning from the cayes pull in at *A&R's* petrol station, from where it's a short walk to any of the hotels or bus depots. Taxis are usually waiting to take passengers to the International Airport (fare BZ$25).

Belize City has two **airports**, neither of them served by buses. International flights land at the **Phillip Goldson International Airport**, 17km northwest of the city at Ladyville, just off the Northern highway (see p.260). Arriving here can be chaotic, with a crush of people waiting anxiously for the trolleys to trundle in with their luggage. Not infrequently baggage has been left on board, to return from San Salvador or Tegucigalpa in a couple of days. The new terminal, to be opened soon, should end at least some of the overcrowding. If you land here the best way to get into town is to share a taxi (fare BZ$25), or walk to the highway (1.5km) and try to flag down a bus or truck. If you're leaving from here arrive early, and expect to pay BZ$20 departure tax.

Domestic flights come and go from the **Municipal Airport**, a few kilometres north of the town centre, on the shores of the Caribbean. Taxis are always available (BZ$5), or it's a twenty-minute walk.

Hotels

There are at least forty **hotels** in Belize City, around a third of which are in the budget category of BZ$9 to BZ$16 single, with at least another half-dozen in the medium price range of BZ$16 to BZ$45 single. The selection below covers most of the budget places. For a more comprehensive list, pick up a copy of *Where to stay in Belize* from the **tourist bureau**, 53 Regent Street (☎77213).

A couple of points to note at the start. The **youth hostel** marked on the free city map supplied by the tourist bureau is not a tourist facility but an institution for problem children. Another one to avoid is *Han's Guest House*, at 53 Queen Street; strongly recommended by many guides, it is in fact scruffy and overpriced.

One of the best-value hotels in the country is the *Sea Side Guest House*, 3 Prince Street (☎78339), half a block from the southern foreshore, where a shared room is BZ$9 per person and you really can see the sea. Clean and well-run by an extremely helpful American couple, the *Sea Side* is a meeting place for European travellers in a youth-hostel type atmosphere. Breakfast and evening meals are available if you book – delicious food and cheaper than a restaurant.

Another favourite with European and North American visitors is the *North Front Street Guest House*, 124 North Front Street (☎77596; BZ$15 single, BZ$21 double). This is a friendly guesthouse, good for information and handy for boats to Caye Caulker, which depart just a block away. Meals are available and breakfast is the best value in town; but the shower area is basic and can get crowded. There are several similarly priced hotels in this area, including the *Bon Aventure*, right next door (☎44248), and *Dim's Mira Rio* (☎44970) across the road, where all rooms have a washbasin and toilet. The bar at *Dim's Mira Rio* is worth a visit for local atmosphere and information – a verandah extends over the river and boat owners often call in for a beer – and simple but tasty Creole food is available. This is also the meeting place for trips to *Ricardo's Beach Huts* (see p.289), run by the same family. Another nearby hotel worth trying is the *Hotel Bell*, 140 North Front Street (☎31083; BZ$15 single); this is the nearest hotel to the boat dock, and the owner, a friendly guy called Juan Ricardo Clarke-Bell, can book passage on boats to Caye Caulker for BZ$10 instead of the usual BZ$12.

Marin's Travelodge, towards the hospital at 6 Craig Street (☎45166; BZ$12 single, BZ$16 double), is comfortable, clean and really quiet, in contrast to the bustle of the *Sea Side* or *Front Street Guest House*; the showers are excellent and the rooms well furnished.

The manager of the inexpensive and basic *Vinats*, 8 Gabourel Lane, near the junction with Handyside Street (BZ$15 single), also runs *Vinats Guest House* at 37 Regent Street West – a dodgy area if you're alone, but close to the bus stations.

Some of the Asian-run shops on Albert Street also have hotels above them and at 11 Dean Street – which crosses Albert Street – there's the Chinese-owned *America Hotel*.

Another cheap hotel worth trying is the *Dominique Hotel*, 9 Douglas Jones Street (BZ$12 single, BZ$18 double), but this is further away from the centre. Finally in the budget category there's the *Riverview Hotel*, 25 Regent Street West (BZ$13 single); rooms are basic – though some more expensive ones have air conditioning – and showers even more so, but security is good, which is important around the bus station, a part of town that can be rowdy late at night. Further down the street is *Marr's Hotel,* which is best avoided for this reason.

Recommendations in the medium price category begin with the *Belcove Hotel*, 9 Regent Street West (☎73054; BZ$25 single, BZ$30 double), where you're paying extra for a balcony over the river with a view of the Swing Bridge. There's also a certain thrill of being on the edge of the dangerous part of town, though the hotel itself is quite secure. The owner, Danny Weir, has many tales to tell of Belize, both city and country. Trips to the reef at Gallows Point are organised from here (US$20 for the day, including lunch) – the best chance to visit the reef for those with only a day in Belize City.

Mom's Triangle Inn, 11 Handyside Street (☎45073; BZ$30–50 single), is one of the best-known hotels in Belize among American visitors. It's now situated a few blocks north of the "Triangle" area (on the south side of the Swing Bridge), but many guides still advertise the old location and wax lyrical about the homely American-style atmosphere. Unfortunately Mom herself died a few years ago, and although the rooms are comfortable and air-conditioned, the place now lives largely on its reputation – in the restaurant prices are high and service is slack. Yet *Mom's* is still – for American visitors – an almost obligatory port of call.

Freddie's Guest House, 86 Eve Street (☎44396; BZ$25 single, BZ$35 double), has only three rooms, but is secure and peaceful; it's on the edge of the city near the waterfront, along the road from the Center for Environmental Studies.

The drab and uninspiring view from the street belies the charming interior of *Glenthorne Manor*, a large and very comfortable colonial-style house off Queen Street at 27 Barrack Road (☎44212; BZ$45 double, including breakfast).

Yet more expensive, the *Mopan Hotel*, next to the tourist bureau at 55 Regent Street (☎7544516), is a large, almost rambling wooden building with some newer additions, where prices are BZ$58 single, BZ$84 double, with triples available. Run by avid conservationists Jean and Tom Shaw, both of whom are a mine of information on Belize, it's much used by expedition members, naturalists, writers and scientists. The Shaws also have some accommodation at *Shawfields*, their own nature reserve on a lagoon just west of the city.

Even if *Four Fort Street* (at the obvious address; ☎45638) is beyond your reach at BZ$70 single, BZ$90 double (including breakfast), it's a delightful building to visit or have a meal, and the food is good value. A large colonial house, it has been expertly restored, with large, well-decorated rooms cooled by ceiling fans. A spacious balcony extends from the dining room, a great place to relax, despite the view of customs sheds and a filling station.

The flagship of Belize City's hotels is the *Fort George*, 2 Marine Parade, with a large private dock on the north side of the harbour mouth. It's far too expensive for the ordinary traveller (about US$150 double), but the hotel's public areas and grounds are an oasis of peace and tranquillity on the edge of the sea, away from the city centre. The hotel pool is the only one available to the public in Belize City: you're officially charged (about US$5) to use it, but if you look respectable and buy a drink at the bar you can generally get in free. The new seven-storey extension, looking (at least in the context of Belize) like something out of downtown Denver, offers panoramic views from its roof.

The *Bellevue Hotel*, 5 Southern Foreshore, is the premier hotel on the south side of the Swing Bridge. The upstairs bar is worth a visit – they even serve tea in the afternoon – and the disco is a focal point of the city's nightlife, with live music at weekends. Rooms are expensive – US$80–100 a night for a single.

The *Caribbean Trailer Court*, 5224 Barracks Road (☎45086), provides **camping** facilities and parking for RVs. It's quite a way from the city centre, though, and the high possibility of theft makes it a very dodgy prospect.

Around the City

Richard Davies, a British traveller in the mid-nineteenth century, wrote of the city: "There is much to be said for Belize, for in its way it was one of the prettiest ports at which we touched, and its cleanliness and order ... were in great contrast to the ports we visited later as to make them most remarkable." Most of the features that elicited this praise have now gone. In some other cities, **wooden colonial buildings** like those of Belize would be preserved as heritage showpieces, but here their only chance of escaping decrepitude is to be turned into a hotel or restaurant. Yet even in cases where the decay is too advanced to restore the paintwork, balconies and carved railings, the old wooden structures are more pleasing than the concrete blocks which have replaced so many of them.

Before the construction of the first wooden bridge in the early 1800s, cattle were winched over the waterway that divides the city – hence the name Haulover Creek. The present **Swing Bridge**, made in Liverpool and opened in 1923, is the only manually operated swing bridge left in the world. At 5.30am and 5.30pm the endless parade of vehicles and people is halted by policemen, and the process of turning begins. Using long poles inserted into a capstan, four men gradually lever the bridge around until it's pointing in the direction of the harbour mouth. During the few minutes that the bridge is open the river traffic is heavier than that on the roads, and traffic is snarled up across the whole city. A new swing bridge is planned a few blocks upriver of the present one.

The south side

The south side is generally the older section of the city: in the early days the elite lived in the seafront houses while the back streets were inhabited by slaves and labourers. These days it's the commercial centre, with the main shopping streets, banks and travel agencies.

The **covered market** by the Swing Bridge was built in 1820 on the site of an even earlier market. Some of its functions have been taken over by the fishing co-op on North Front Street and the farmers' market by the Belcan bridge, but it's still a busy spot. For those sensitive to the exploitation of sea life, the sight of giant sea turtles and many smaller freshwater ones lying upturned, helplessly awaiting their dismemberment, is enough to churn the stomach. If you think nothing could live in the stinkingly polluted river, take a look as the fish remains are dumped – the water is alive with writhing, evil-looking catfish, thriving on the spoils. Vastly more appealing are the stalls of tropical fruit and veg in the main market and in the street outside, with many delicious bargains. A note for film fans: the *Mona Lisa Hotel*, just past the market, was used as a set in the film of Paul Theroux's *The Mosquito Coast*, shot in Belize in 1985.

Albert Street, running south from the Swing Bridge past the rotating Coca-Cola clock – a reminder of the importance of that company in the economy of Belize – is the main commercial thoroughfare. On the parallel Regent Street are the former colonial administration and court buildings, known as the **Court House**. These well-preserved examples of colonial architecture, with their columns and fine wrought iron, were completed in 1926 after an earlier building on the same site was destroyed by fire. The Court House overlooks a patch of grass and trees ambitiously known as Central Park, with a dry ornamental fountain as a centrepiece.

A block or two behind the Court House, on the waterfront, is the **Bliss Institute**, which looks like a squat airport control tower, but is in fact the cultural centre of Belize City (Mon–Fri 8.30am–noon & 2–8pm, Sat morning only). The Institute was funded by the legacy of a moderately eccentric Englishman with a Portuguese title, Baron Bliss. A keen fisherman, he arrived off the coast of Belize in 1926 after hearing about the tremendous amount of game fish in local waters. Unfortunately he became ill and died without ever having been ashore, but he must have been impressed by whatever fish he did catch, as he left most of his estate to the colony. This became the Bliss Trust, which has been used on various projects, helping to build markets and improve roads and water supplies. Grateful for his generosity, the authorities declared March 9, the date of his death, Baron Bliss Day.

The Bliss building is the home of the **National Arts Council** and hosts exhibitions, concerts and plays. Just inside the entrance are stelae and altars from Caracol, priceless examples of Maya art that seem to have been dumped in a corner while somewhere is found to display them; a small plaque gives an account of the scenes depicted on the stones. Upstairs you'll find the national library and copies of English newspapers – a welcome luxury for homesick travellers.

At the far end of Albert Street stands **St John's Cathedral**, the oldest Anglican Cathedral in Central America, and one of the oldest buildings in Belize. Looking like a large English parish church transplanted to the Caribbean, it was begun in 1812, its red bricks being brought over as ballast in British ships; the main structure, roof and mahogany beams have survived over 150 years of tropical heat and hurricanes in good condition. Here, in great pomp and ceremony, the Kings of the Mosquito Coast were crowned between 1815 and 1845, taking the title to a British Protectorate that extended along the coast of Honduras and Nicaragua. The Mosquito Indians were keen to maintain their links with Britain to avoid Spanish colonial rule, and thus their kings were crowned and their children baptised in Belize's cathedral.

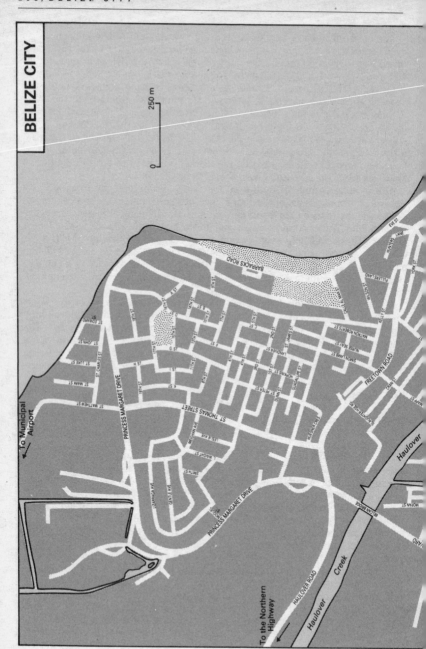

BELIZE CITY

To Municipal Airport

250 m
0

BARRACKS ROAD

PRINCESS MARGARET DRIVE

ST. THOMAS STREET

ST JOHN ST
ST CHARLES ST
ST LUKE ST
ST MARK ST
ST MATTHEW ST

PRINCESS MARGARET DRIVE

FREETOWN ROAD

Haulover

Haulover Creek

Haulover

HAULOVER ROAD

To the Northern Highway

West of the cathedral is the **Yarborough Cemetery**, which was used until the end of the nineteenth century, when it reached full capacity. The graves have fallen into a state of disrepair but a browse will reveal fascinating tales of piracy and murder inscribed on the fallen stones. Most of the occupants are from the elite: the cemetery is named after a magistrate who owned the land and allowed the burial of prominent people here from 1781 – commoners were admitted only after 1870.

Toward the sea front from the cathedral is the white-painted, green-lawned **Government House**, formerly the residence of the Governor when Belize was a British Colony. At the very end of this strip of land is **Bird's Isle**, connected to the mainland by a narrow wooden causeway. There's a roller-skating rink on the island (skates can be hired), and it's also a venue for reggae concerts and parties.

Naturalists will gain from a visit to the **Belize Audubon Society**, just beyond the *Bellevue Hotel* at 49 Southern Foreshore. They have books, maps and posters, and organise slide shows and talks on aspects of wildlife and conservation. The Society has established several wildlife reserves in Belize and participates in conservation education. Also in this area are the offices of the **Programme for Belize**, founded in Britain in May 1989 to save over 250,000 acres of the country's rainforest. Call in at the headquarters at 1 King Street (☎75616/7) for up-to-date news from the enthusiastic staff.

Admiral Burnaby's Coffee Shop and Art Gallery, 9 Regent Street, is a good place to call in for breakfast, coffee or a cold drink while exploring the city. Run by Emory King, a well-known figure in Belize City and the author of several books, including a walking tour of the city, *Burnaby's* has books, maps, guides and tapes of Belizean music for sale and the walls are adorned with the work of local artists.

The north side

On the north side of the Swing Bridge is the **Paslow Building**, a vast, run-down structure built entirely of wood, housing the post office on the ground floor and other government offices above. Opposite is the Fire Station, still containing a few relics from the past but now with several modern fire engines – reassuring in a city with so many wooden buildings.

Heading east along the shore, you pass the **Custom House** and adjacent wharves, beyond which is the lighthouse and the tomb of Baron Bliss, Belize's greatest benefactor. Walking around the shoreline you pass the *Fort George Hotel* and **Memorial Park**, which honours the Belizean dead of World War I. In this area are several well-preserved colonial mansions, many of the finest of which have been taken over by embassies and upmarket hotels. A superb example is the American embassy, further along the shore.

Beyond the US Embassy is the city gaol, as grim as you might expect, and then comes Eve Street and the Belize City Hospital, which, in spite of looking as though a good gust of wind would demolish it, has a high standard of medical care. Also on Eve Street is the **Belize Center for Environmental Studies**, a non-profit institution established to assess the quality of Belize's natural environment and co-ordinate efforts to protect it; worth a visit for anyone seriously interested in Belize's natural and cultural history. It's also the home of the Association for Belizean Archaeology, formed to preserve archaeological sites and artefacts, which has started a fund to establish a museum in Belize.

Eating, drinking, nightlife and shops

The multitude of **restaurants** in Belize City don't offer much in the way of variety. There's the tasty but monotonous **Creole** fare of rice and beans, plenty of **seafood** and **steaks**, and lots of **Chinese restaurants**. Vegetables other than cabbage, carrots, onions and peppers are in short supply, and a salad might consist of small quantities of these sliced. Greasy fried chicken is available from small restaurants all over the city as a takeaway item, a Belizean favourite known as "dollar chicken" – whatever the price. The big hotels have their own restaurants, naturally quite expensive.

For reasonably priced dishes try the *Caribbean Restaurant* on Regent Street at the junction with Prince Street; a Chinese restaurant, it also has T-bone steak and pork chop specials in large portions. The *Marlin*, next to the *Belcove Hotel* in Regent Street West, serves good local food; it has a covered verandah overlooking the river. Nearby, next to the *Bliss Hotel* on Water Lane, is the *Aberdeen Restaurant*, serving inexpensive Chinese food and owned by the same family who run the *Aberdeen* on Caye Caulker. *Macy's* on Bishop Street is a great Creole restaurant, a favourite with locals and extremely busy at lunchtime. *Archies* and *Chon San* on Collett Street are good-value Chinese restaurants.

Across the Swing Bridge, on Queen Street, the *Upstairs Café* serves good Taiwanese food and is a popular place for drinks in the evening; the balcony over the street is a favourite spot for people-watching. It's often noisy and crowded with British soldiers – they're boisterous rather than troublesome. All around here are more Chinese restaurants, all with similar menus and reasonable prices: next door is the *Ganchou*, opposite is the *China Town*, and further down the street is the *Hong Kong*. The *Shangri La*, with a huge sign saying *Hard Rock Café*, has a large bar and dining area; it also has a balcony that is less crowded than the *Upstairs Café*. For really large portions go to the *Chon Saan II*, opposite the *Texaco* station on North Front Street – that's if you can stomach the gory Chinese videos showing in the "dinning room", as the sign says.

Undisturbed views of quiet foreshore, blue sea and offshore islands are a major attraction of the vaguely Chinese *Chateau Caribbean*, 6 Marine Parade. A wide flight of steps leads to the cool first-floor restaurant where the prices are more reasonable than you might expect from the white linen and gleaming cutlery, although beyond anyone on a tight budget at upwards of BZ$13 for a main course; order something inexpensive and forget for a while the heat and noise of the city.

For a fairly priced splurge in relaxing surroundings, have dinner at the *Fort Street Restaurant*, 4 Fort Street. A superb four-course meal is only BZ$19, though the price is sure to rise soon; it does great fruit breakfasts too.

Still a favourite amongst travellers is *Mom's*, 11 Handyside Street (see "Hotels"), where they serve Creole dishes, American breakfasts, burgers and sandwiches. For Middle Eastern food try the *Nile*, 49 Eve Street, where you'll find kebabs and hummus, and for pizza try the *Pizza House* on King Street.

Bars

The more sophisticated and air-conditioned **bars** are to be found in the most expensive establishments, and there aren't many of those. At the lowest end of the scale there are dimly lit dives where you might be offered drugs or be robbed, but most likely will have a thoroughly enjoyable time meeting easy-going and hard-drinking Belizeans. There are also several equally interesting places between the two extremes, most of them in restaurants and hotels – for example, the *Marlin* restaurant and *Dim's Mira Rio* hotel (details for both above).

Nightlife, though not as wild as it used to be, is becoming more reliable and the quality of bands is improving all the time. The *Big Apple* **disco** on North Front Street isn't very interesting; better is *The Pub*, further along the street, with an air-conditioned dance floor. The *Fort George* and the *Bellevue* hold regular dances and the *Upstairs Café* has **live music** on Thursday evenings. The *Lumberyard Bar*, on the river bank just out of town on the Northern highway, also has live reggae bands but can get out of hand – good on Saturday lunchtimes. Belize City has two **cinemas**, the *Majestic* on Queen Street and the *Palace* on Albert Street. These usually have two showings a day, at 5pm and 8pm, the main features being imported American action, war and martial arts movies.

Shopping and souvenirs

If you're shopping for **food**, the main **supermarkets** – *Brodie's* and *Romac's* – are worth a look; they are on Albert Street, just past the park, and their selection of food is quite good if expensive, reflecting the fact that much is imported. Milk and other dairy products, produced by Mennonite farmers (see p.254), are delicious and good quality. *Kee's Bakery*, 53 Queen Street, sells excellent wholewheat and French bread. Naturally enough, local **fruit** is cheap and plentiful, though highly seasonal – Belizean citrus fruits are among the best in the world.

You may well be approached by street peddlers selling **wood carvings**, often exquisitely executed, of dolphins, jaguars, ships and other subjects. If you're interested in these as souvenirs, do a deal on the spot, as there's a terrific mark-up in the hotel gift shops. (Of course be careful about showing money on the street.) The zericote wood of which they are made is said to grow only in Belize, and they make quite unusual gifts. Another gift option is a set of wildly colourful Belize **stamps**, often expertly depicting the animals and plants of the country; relatively cheap and easy to post home, they are available from the Belize Philatelic Society, 91 North Front Street, above *The Pub* disco. **T-shirts**, some with Rasta or Creole slogans, make distinctive Belizean gifts: some of the best bargains are to be found at the Chinese and Indian stores along Albert Street and Queen Street. *Cottage Industries*, 26 Albert Street, has a good selection of local handicrafts, as does *Di Creole*, 7 Graboural Lane, which also sells some unique T-shirts at non-tourist prices.

Souvenirs you should **not buy** are **shells**, **coral**, **turtle products** – indeed **marine curios** of any kind. By resisting the temptation to buy reef souvenirs you will be helping to preserve them alive. Many animal and plant souvenirs you may be offered in Belize are listed in Appendix I to CITES (Convention on International Trade in Endangered Species) and their trade is prohibited, so you wouldn't be allowed to bring them into the US, Canada or Europe anyway. Protected species include the cats of Belize, monkeys, many birds of prey and parrots, all marine turtles, other reptiles and nearly all orchids.

Listings

Airlines *TACA* are represented by *Global Travel*, 41 Albert Street (☎77185), where you can confirm return flights. *Continental* are at 24 Queen Street (☎78463); *Eastern* are at 26 Queen Street (☎78646). *Tan Sahsa* have their office in the Valencia Building, New Road (☎77080 in town, ☎025/2062 at the airport). *Aerovias* operate flights between Belize City, Flores and Guatemala City; their agents are the *Mopan Hotel* (☎75445). *Western Caribbean Airlines* may again be operating to Honduras: check with *Belize Global Travel*, 41 Albert Street (☎77363).

Maya and *Tropic* are the domestic airlines, with daily flights to Sarteneja, Corozal, San Pedro, Dangriga, Big Creek and Punta Gorda. *Tropic* also operate a daily service to Cancún in Mexico. These and other charter companies also offer charters to any airstrip of your choice in Belize, and all domestic flights are extremely good value. *Maya* are at 6 Fort Street (☎77215 in the city, ☎44032 at the airport); *Tropic* have their office at the Municipal Airstrip (☎45671, or ☎026/2012 in San Pedro).

American Express Main Belize office at *Belize Global Travel*, 41 Albert Street, (☎77363); this is the safest place to receive mail, and has a fax service too.

Banks The *Atlantic*, *Bank of Nova Scotia*, *Belize Bank* and *Barclays* all have their main Belize branches on Albert Street, and are open Mon–Thurs 9am–1pm and Fri 9am–1pm & 3–6pm. Travellers' cheques and cash can be changed at many shops, hotels and restaurants, and cash can sometimes be changed on the streets at a slightly better rate, but take care. The banks can change travellers' cheques into American dollars (to a limit of US$100) if you can produce a plane or bus ticket to prove that you're soon to leave the country, though you may have to get a permit from the Central Bank on Bishop Street first.

Boats There are scheduled departures to San Pedro on Ambergris Caye from the *Belle Vue Hotel* dock on the Southern Foreshore and to Caye Caulker from *A&R's Shell Station*, North Front Street, near the Swing Bridge. For detailed information, see the section on the cayes.

Books The *Belize Book Shop*, on Regent Street opposite the *Mopan Hotel*, has the largest selection of books in the city, and the *Book Centre*, 114 North Front Street, near the Swing Bridge, has a fairly good selection of magazines and some books. Many of the larger hotels also sell books, magazines and newspapers and *Mom's Triangle* sells copies of *Time*, *Newsweek* and *The Miami Herald*. The *Budget Discount Store*, near the Fire Station on North Front Street has a huge selection of second-hand paperbacks. For more serious reading on Belize and around check out the SPEAR library on North Front Street.

Buses Schedules for each part of the country are listed at the end of the relevant chapters. All the bus companies are in the same area, along the Collet Canal and Magazine Road, a short walk from the centre of town. *Batty* (☎72025) cover the route to the north and Chetumal in Mexico, and west to San Ignacio; *Venus* (☎73354) also cover the north; *Novelo* (☎77372) cover the western route to Benque Viejo and the Guatemalan border; and *Z-Line* (☎73937) cover the southern route to Dangriga and Punta Gorda. All buses heading west and south call at Belmopan.

Car hire All the main companies offer cars, Jeeps and Land Rovers for between BZ$150 and BZ$200 a day. You'll have to leave either a credit card, travellers' cheques or a large cash deposit. A word of **warning**: comprehensive insurance is not available in Belize so the hirer is likely to be held liable for any damage, however caused, to the vehicle. Check carefully before signing anything. Hire companies include: *Avis*, Fort George Plaza (☎78637); *National*, 126 Freetown Road (☎31586) and at the airport (☎025/2117); *Smith and Sons*, also at the airport (☎73779), the only company likely to allow you to take a car into Guatemala or Mexico; and *Sutherland*, 127 Neal Pen Road (☎7358). *Fandango's*, 66 Freetown Road (☎31554), rent **scooters** for use in the city, for BZ$7 per hour or BZ$22 per day.

Embassies Despite the fact that the official capital has moved to Belmopan, the majority of embassies have stuck it out in Belize City; normally they are open weekday mornings. Panama and Venezuela have moved to Belmopan, and Guatemala is unrepresented in Belize, the nearest consul being in Chetumal. The British High Commission is based in Belmopan (☎08/22146), but operates a consular clinic in Belize City at 11 St Marks Street, Kings Park, near the Municipal Airstrip (Mon 9–11am). The US Embassy is at 29 Gabourel Lane, at the corner of Hutson Street (☎77161). Others include:

Mexico (for tourist cards) 20 Park Street on the seafront (☎45367).

Costa Rica 8 18th Street (☎44796).

El Salvador 120 New Road (☎44318).

Honduras 91 North Front Street (☎45889).

Immigration The Belize Immigration Office is at 115 Barrack Road, on the top floor above a hardware shop (Mon–Thurs 8.30–11.30am & 1–4pm, Fri closing at 3.30pm; ☎77273). An extension of stay will cost you BZ$5.

Laundry Many hotels offer a laundry service, but if yours doesn't you can go to *Carry's Laundry*, 41 Hyde Lane (Mon–Sat 8am–5.30pm) or *The Belize Laundromat*, 7 Craig Street (Mon–Sat 7am–8pm).

Maps Superb topographical maps of Belize are sold at the Survey Department, above the post office on Queen Street. A two-sheet map covering the whole country at a scale of 1:250,000 costs BZ$10 per sheet, and there is a series of 44 sheets at a scale of 1:50,000, again covering the whole country, costing BZ$3 per sheet. Other specialist offerings include geological maps and a land-use map. Maps can also be obtained from the Ministry of Natural Resources in Belmopan.

Post The main post office is in the Paslow Building, on the corner of Queen Street, immediately north of the Swing Bridge (Mon–Thurs 8am–noon & 1–3pm, Fri closing at 4.30pm). *Poste restante* is on the ground floor. The **parcel office** is on Church Street, across the Swing Bridge, just past *Barclays* bank. Sending a parcel is a fairly elaborate process, as you need to put the parcel in a box, wrap it in brown paper and – if you want to insure the contents – tie it with string. This can be done very quickly at the hardware store opposite for a small fee. The post office offers a reasonably efficient service but be careful of sending anything valuable – thefts have been known to happen.

Taxis Fares within the city are fixed by the government at BZ$3 for one person plus BZ$2 for each extra person, and BZ$5 to the Municipal Airstrip. For other journeys agree the fare in advance. If you arrive at night it's advisable to take a taxi: they can usually be found at the airports, the bus stations or by the park.

Telephones The main office of *BTL*, Belize's privately owned phone company, is on Church Street (daily 8am–9pm). International calls are quickly and easily made from the luxury of their air-conditioned office; the service is very efficient and much cheaper than calling from neighbouring countries. There are now several **payphones** in Belize City.

Tourist Office The Belize Tourist Bureau main office is at 53 Regent Street (☎77213; weekdays 8am–noon & 1–5pm). The staff are friendly and knowledgeable, giving free bus timetables, a hotel guide and a city map. The relatively new *Belize Tourism Industry Association*, at 99 Albert Street, co-ordinates the tourist industry and has branches in most towns. The local *BTIA* representative will usually be helpful when you're travelling around the country.

Travel Agents There are a number of travel agents in the city; most at least as good as the ones at home, while the smaller ones specialise in local flights, tours and packages. The largest agency is *Belize Global Travel*, 41 Albert Street (☎77363), and others include *Belize Air Travel*, 28 Regent Street (☎73174), *Caribbean Holidays*, 81 Albert Street (☎72593) and *Universal Travel*, on Handyside Street (☎30964). All of these can book domestic and international flights. For tours to inland Belize or the reef and islands try *Jals* at 148 North Front Street (☎45407), or *Personalised Services* at 91 North Front Street (☎77593). A new local tour agency is *Native Guide Tours*, on Water Lane opposite the *Bliss Hotel* (☎75819).

travel details

Buses
North

Belize City to **Chetumal** (4hr 15min) via **Orange Walk** (2hr) and **Corozal** (3hr) from *Batty's* terminal, 54 East Collet Canal (☎72025), every two hours from 4am to 6pm: express services at 6am and 6pm. At the time of writing *Venus* schedules for the same route were undergoing major changes, but they previously operated every odd hour, 5am to 7pm, from Magazine Road (☎73354).

Urbina runs a daily service to **Orange Walk**, departing from Cinderella Plaza at 1pm.

For **Sarteneja** the *Perez* bus leaves the *Shell* station on North Front Street at noon, for a journey of at least three hours.

For the **Bermudian Landing Baboon Sanctuary** there are two buses daily (except

Sun), both leaving at 1.30pm. One departs from the corner of Orange Street and Mussel Street, the other from the corner of Orange Street and George Street.

West

Batty run a service from **Belize City** to **San Ignacio** (2hr 30min) via Belmopan (1hr 30min): the 6.30am bus goes to the border, the rest terminate at San Ignacio. *Novelo*, 19 West Collet Canal (☎77372), cover the same route, terminating at **Benque Viejo**, with departures hourly from 11am until 6pm. The Sunday service is more limited.

South

The Southern highway doesn't have anything like the same number of buses running along it as the Northern and Western highways, and trips into the south will inevitably take a day or two, travelling via Dangriga. *Z-Line* buses from **Belize City to Dangriga** (3hr) depart from Magazine Road at 10am, 11am, 1pm, 3pm and 4pm: the first two will make the connection for Punta Gorda the same day. There are also daily through buses to Punta Gorda, though not entirely reliable.

Boats

There are frequent boats to Ambergris Caye (San Pedro) and Caye Caulker, but not to any strict timetable: see the Cayes chapter for details.

Planes

There are **international flights** from Belize airport to Miami, New York, New Orleans, Houston, LA and others, and four flights a week with *Aerovias* (Thurs, Fri, Sat & Sun at 3.10pm) from the international airport to **Flores** (35min) and **Guatemala City** (2hr). There may also be a service with *Western Caribbean Airlines* to **La Ceiba** (Honduras).

Maya Airways and *Tropic Air* both operate two daily flights from the municipal airfield **to Corozal** and **to San Pedro**. *Maya Airways* have flights from Belize City to **Dangriga**, **Independence** and **Punta Gorda** at 8am, 11am and 2pm. *Tropic Air* also operate flights on this route daily at 4.30pm.

CHAPTER NINE

THE CAYES AND THE BARRIER REEF

Belize's spectacular **Barrier Reef**, with its dazzling variety of underwater life and string of exquisitely beautiful islands – known as cayes – is the main attraction for most first-time visitors to Belize. The coral reef runs the entire length of the Belize coastline at a distance of 15km to 40km from the mainland, and is the longest barrier reef in the western hemisphere. One of the richest marine ecosystems on earth, it's a paradise for scuba divers

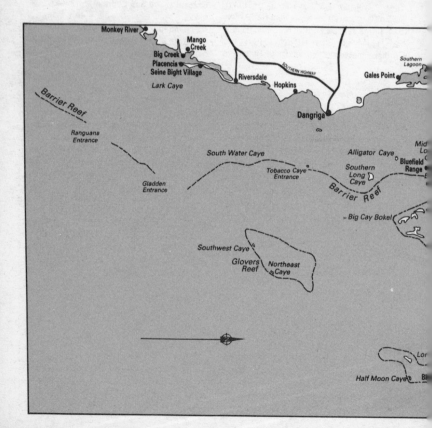

and snorkellers, the incredible coral formations teeming with hundreds of species of brilliantly coloured fish. The entire area of reef, islands and coastline has been proposed as a **World Heritage Site** – in other words, a place of such significance that its "deterioration or disappearance" would constitute "a harmful impoverishment of the heritage of all nations of the world", to quote the criterion of the World Heritage Convention. Official classification would enable funds from UNESCO to be used for protection of the reef, which is essential as Belize itself lacks the necessary resources. Unfortunately Belize is not a party to the World Heritage Convention. At present nature reserves include the **Hol Chan Marine Reserve** off San Pedro and **Half Moon Caye Natural Monument**, part of Lighthouse Reef.

Most of the **Cayes** (pronounced "keys") lie in shallow water behind the shelter of the reef, with a limestone ridge forming larger low-lying islands to the north, while smaller, less frequently visited outcrops are clustered toward the southern end of the chain – often merely a stand of palms and a strip of sand. Though the cayes form only a tiny proportion of Belize's total land area, their tourism and lobster fishing accounts for a substantial amount of the country's foreign currency earnings. In recent years the town of **San Pedro**, on **Ambergris Caye**, has under-

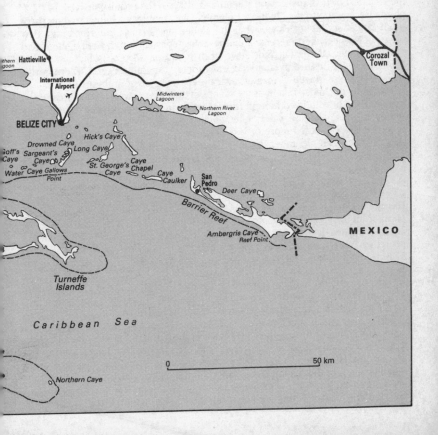

gone a transition from a predominantly fishing economy to one geared to commercial tourism; **Caye Caulker**, to the south, is less – but increasingly – developed, and remains popular with budget-minded travellers. But in all, only about twenty out of a total of over 450 cayes have any tourist development, and in some instances this amounts to just a single, exclusive tourist lodge. Many of the other cayes are populated only by communities of fishermen, whose settlements fluctuate with the season.

Beyond the chain of islands and the coral reef are Belize's three **atolls**: the **Turneffe Islands**, **Glovers Reef** and **Lighthouse Reef**. Here the coral reaches the surface, enclosing a shallow lagoon, with some cayes lying right on top of the encircling reef. These tropical idylls all now have small, expensive hotels offering sport fishing and diving to big-spending visitors.

The Cayes from the Maya to the present

The earliest inhabitants of the cayes were **Maya Indians** or their ancestors, and by the Classic Period (300–900 AD) the Maya had developed an extensive trade network stretching from the Yucatán to Honduras, with settlements on several of the islands. Some of these were still inhabited when the Spanish arrived: in 1502, on his last voyage to the "Indies", Columbus was met by an Indian trading party in an immense dugout canoe when he landed on Guanaja, off Honduras. Few traces of Maya civilisation remain on the cayes today, although shell mounds and other evidence of coastal trade have been found on several islands, including Moho Caye off Belize City and Wild Cane Caye near Punta Gorda. There is also the small ruin of **Marco Gonzalez**, near the southern tip of Ambergris Caye.

Probably the most infamous residents of the cayes were the **buccaneers**, usually British, who lived here in the sixteenth and seventeeth centuries, taking refuge in these shallow waters after plundering the Spanish treasure ships. In time the pirates settled more or less permanently on some of the northern and central cayes. But life under the Jolly Roger became too hot for them in the late 1600s, after Britain agreed to stamp out privateering under the terms of the Madrid Treaties.

After this, some turned to logwood cutting in the mainland's swamps, but the cutters (the Baymen) kept their dwellings on the cayes – and more specifically **St George's Caye** – because their cool breezes and fresh water offered a welcome break from the steaming swamps where the logwood grew. The population of the cayes remained low during the seventeenth and eighteenth centuries, but the settlement on St George's Caye was regarded by the Baymen as their capital until 1779, when a Spanish force destroyed the settlement and imprisoned 140 of the Baymen and 250 of their slaves. The Baymen returned in 1783, and took revenge on the Spanish fleet in the celebrated Battle of St George's Caye in 1798. However, although the elite of the Baymen still kept homes on St George's Caye, from then on the population of the islands began to decline as Belize Town (later City) grew.

Fishermen and turtlers continued to use the cayes as a base for their operations, and refugees fleeing the Caste Wars in the Yucatán towards the end of the last century also settled on the islands, but only in small numbers. During this century the island population has increased steadily, and a boom came with the establishment of the fishing co-operatives in the 1960s, which offered the fishermen improved traps, ice plants, and access to the export market. There's now a threat of the lobster-fishing industry destroying itself by overfishing.

At around the same time there was another boom, as the cayes of Belize, particularly Caye Caulker, became a hangout on the hippy trail, and then began to attract more lucrative custom. The islanders generally welcomed these new visitors: rooms were rented and hotels built, and a new prosperity began to transform island life. Luxuries not usually associated with small fishing communities – colour televisions, telephones, skiffs with outboard motors – are evidence of the effects of tourism.

Diving, fishing and taking it easy

The increasing popularity of Belize as a holiday destination has led to an escalation in land prices, and real estate offices proliferate San Pedro's main streets, tempting wealthy visitors to invest in a Caribbean island. Luckily most of the islands are too small and remote to entice the developers. Indeed, getting to many of the cayes and atolls can be a problem, especially if you're limited by time and finances. One way to visit the more isolated places is to see if a visiting yacht owner needs a crew (they're not all millionaires); alternatively, if you can get together a group of three or four, you might hire a boat for a week or so – easily done on Caye Caulker – and let a local boatman show you the lesser-known parts of the reef.

Life on the cayes is superbly relaxing, tempting you to take it easy in a hammock, feast on seafood, and sip rum as the sun sets. The most accessible and cheapest of the islands is **Caye Caulker**, and if you feel the urge to see what's beneath the waves it's easily done from here or Ambergris Caye. **Divers** can visit sites of almost unbelievable beauty and isolation, either joining a group day trip or staying at a lodge on the edge of the reef. This kind of fun can be expensive, though. **Snorkelling** is a far cheaper option, and often just as rewarding. Again trips are on offer on both of the main cayes, visiting three of four different reef sites in a day, each revealing a new coral landscape and array of tropical fish.

Birdwatching, as anywhere in Belize, is fascinating. Around 200 species live in or visit the coastal areas and cayes, from ospreys to sandpipers and flamingoes to finches. Many otherwise rare birds are relatively common here; for instance, the preservation of the red-footed booby on **Half Moon Caye** was the main reason for establishing a National Monument there in 1982.

The reef offers some of the best sport **fishing** in the world – for grouper, pompano, cubera snapper and rock fish – while the Turneffe flats are ideal for fly fishing, with huge numbers of tarpon, permit and red snapper. Deep-sea fishing yields large catches of marlin, sailfish, wahoo and tuna, and even if you can't afford to follow in the wake of Hemingway, you'll still be able to cast a hand-line over the side, and perhaps pull up a small barracuda for your tea. Most snorkelling trips can also include a chance to do a bit of fishing, and if you have a word with the boatman he'll make sure you don't go home empty-handed.

Ambergris Caye

The most northerly and by far the largest of the cayes is **Ambergris Caye**, separated from Mexico by a narrow but deep channel that was dug by the Maya. The island's main attraction is the former fishing village of **SAN PEDRO**, facing the reef just a few kilometres from the southern tip, 58km northeast of Belize City. If you fly into San Pedro, which is the way most visitors arrive, the views are breathtaking: the sea appears so clear and shallow as to barely cover the sandy bed, and the mainland and other islands stand out clearly. Probably the best view is of the reef's white crest, dramatically separating the vivid blue of the open sea from the turquoise water on its leeward side. The aircraft fly at so low an altitude, under 100 metres, that photographs taken from inside the cabin generally turn out well.

As you land at the tiny airstrip, with the sea on each side, a glimpse at San Pedro shows the town taking up the whole width of the island. It's not a large town, but its population of 2000 is the highest on any of the cayes. You're never more than a stone's throw from the Caribbean, but in the built-up area most of the palms have been cut down, and in recent years traffic has increased considerably, creating deep ruts in the sandy streets. If you want a guide to the history, biology and geology of the caye, *The Field Guide to Ambergris Caye*, by RL Woods and others, is available in San Pedro and in some hotels and bookshops in Belize City. Richie Woods himself, a Belizean marine biologist, can often be found around San Pedro – a mine of information.

Coming and going

Flying to San Pedro is the easiest approach. Both *Maya Airways* and *Tropic Air* operate several flights a day from the Municipal Airport in Belize City (7am–4.30pm) in 4- to 28-seater aircraft. *Maya* also fly from San Pedro to Corozal, stopping at Sarteneja, so you could use this route to reach the Mexican border without going back to Belize City. For information in Belize City telephone ☎7215 or ☎2312 for *Maya*, or ☎45671 for *Tropic*. On the island it's easy enough to walk to the airstrip to book a flight.

Boats from Belize City to San Pedro are not as frequent as to Caye Caulker, and the journey takes longer. The most reliable is the *Andrea*, leaving from the dock of the *Belle Vue Hotel* at 4pm from Monday to Friday and 1pm Saturday, returning to Belize City at 7am (BZ$20 each way). Skiffs sometimes leave from the Swing Bridge area: the *Triple J* is one that boasts a regular schedule, leaving at 9am and returning from San Pedro at 4pm. In theory the *Miss Belize* operates a daily passenger service, but "engine trouble" seems to be a perpetual problem. With the rate of development in San Pedro there's sure to be an increase in traffic, so just ask around at the bridge. For an even cheaper ride, ask any of the **cargo boats** at Custom Wharf (near the Fort George lighthouse) if they would take a passenger.

Travelling **from San Pedro** to other cayes isn't very easy, though you might meet a fishing boat or yachtsman heading somewhere. Any boat with C.C. on the side, followed by numbers, is from **Caye Caulker**; they generally arrive in San Pedro in the early afternoon, at the dock beside the *Tackle Box*, and you'll probably be able to get a ride back with one of these for around BZ$20.

San Pedro practicalities

All the hotels and restaurants can be reached on foot from the airstrip, with the exception of a few extremely expensive resorts north of the town, whose clients are met by the hotel's boat. The three main streets, running parallel to the beach, were formerly called Front, Middle and Back streets, but now have been given names in keeping with the new upmarket image – Barrier Reef Drive, Tarpon Avenue and so on – most locals stick to the old names. In any case it's impossible to get lost, and the few reasonably priced hotels are located just a short distance from each other on these three streets.

The tourist industry here caters mainly for North American package tours (be warned that many prices are quoted in US dollars), and the hotels, restaurants and bars in San Pedro include some of the most exclusive in the whole country; most of the cheaper places are in San Pedro itself, which is also where most of the action takes place, particularly in the evenings. Avoid San Pedro at Christmas, New Year and Easter unless you've booked a room. There's nowhere that you can **camp** legally, and sleeping rough is not recommended.

Hotels

The first of the lower-priced hotels is *Rubie's* (☎2063), a short walk from the airstrip along Barrier Reef Drive, the street nearest the beach, opposite the **post office**; rooms in this clean, comfortable, family-run hotel (BZ$20 single, BZ$45 double) are often booked out. There's only one place cheaper – *Milo's* (☎2033), at the end of the street, on the left just before the *Paradise Hotel*; the rooms here are basic, at BZ$15 for a single, BZ$20 for a double. Above a grocery shop on Middle Street, *Martha's* (☎2053) is the same price as *Rubie's*, as is the *Lourdes Hotel* (☎2066) nearby. *Lily's Caribeña*, on the front, is a little more expensive. These are the only places within reach of the budget traveller.

Slightly more expensive than the budget hotels are the *San Pedrano* (☎2054), good value for BZ$30, with private bath and a spacious verandah, the *Tomas Hotel*, and the *Sea Breeze*. Higher still are the *Barrier Reef* and the *Coral Beach Hotel*, and there are many on a scale that rises to *The Belizean Hotel*, which will set you back almost US$500 a night. They're all easily found along the front.

Eating and drinking

As you might expect, seafood is prominent on most **restaurant** menus, but the prices charged are generally higher than elsewhere in Belize. There are several Chinese restaurants, the cheaper ones representing the best value on the island. Near the airstrip *The Hut* is popular, with Belizean and American-style food at reasonable prices; unfortunately, varnished turtle shells decorate the walls – an all too frequent sight in Belizean bars. *Elvie's Kitchen*, across the road from *Martha's Hotel*, is the place for burger and fries, with delicious fruit drinks in the style of Mexican *licuados*; a huge tree, possibly the biggest on the island, dominates the centre of the room. Further down the street, the *Katanga Shack* appears promising from the outside, with a cheapish menu; inside, the decor of jaguar and ocelot skins and yet more turtle shells is tasteless and depressing. Expensive pizza is served at *Fidos*, on the beachfront behind *All Island Rentals*, a travel agency that could be useful for information. The *Spindrift Hotel*, next to the *Atlantic Bank*, advertises "gourmet Italian dining", which is a rarity in Belize.

Buying your own food isn't particularly cheap either: there's no market and the grocery stores are stocked with imported canned goods, including tuna from Japan. Cooking it might also be a problem, as it's not so easy in San Pedro to improvise your own beach barbecue as it is on other islands.

Sandals Pub (next to *Milo's*), with its name spelled out in redundant flip-flops nailed to the wall, is a friendly **bar** where the prices not quite as outrageous as most, and the cool sand floor is a treat for your feet. For real nightlife there's *Big Daddy's* **disco**, in and around a beach bar near the main dock, often with a lively reggae band. The entertainment in San Pedro becomes more sophisticated every year, and walking around you'll soon discover what's on and where. Some of the hotels have thoroughly fancy bars, but back from the main street are a couple of

small **cantinas**, where you can buy a beer or a bottle of rum and drink with the locals.

The Tackle Box bar, situated at the end of the pier belonging to the *Coral Beach Hotel*, is one of the principal attractions for day-trip visitors to the island, because in front of it, in the sea, is a small pen housing a considerable number of turtles, sharks, stingrays and barracudas. Many of the animals exhibit signs of extreme stress, often bunching up together at the farthest point of the pen, as far away as possible from the noise and lights of the bar. This depressing spectacle exists for one reason only, to make money. Expressions of disgust at this exploitation of marine life may, eventually, free these creatures, which are often held illegally. Letters of protest can be sent to either The Director of Tourism, Belize Tourist Bureau, PO Box 325, 53 Regent Street, Belize City, or The Reserve Manager, Hol Chan Marine Reserve, Town Hall, San Pedro, Ambergris Caye.

Travel agents and banks

There are a couple of **travel agencies** on Front Street, *Amigo Travel* and *All Island Rentals*, for local packages and trips throughout Belize. Bigger and possibly better is *Belize Travel Haus*, now home of *Universal Travel*, at the airstrip; they can provide all the usual services, including local and international flights. There are branches of the *Atlantic Bank* and the *Royal Bank*; but you needn't worry about **changing money** as travellers' cheques and US dollars are accepted – even preferred – everywhere.

Exploring the reef and the caye

The water is the focus of daytime entertainment, from sunbathing on the docks to windsurfing, sailing, fishing, diving and snorkelling. Many hotels will rent equipment and there are several specialist **dive-shops**, where you can be taught to scuba dive. An open water certification, which takes novices up to the standard of fully qualified sport diver, costs around US$285–350. For qualified divers a two-tank dive costs around US$35 including tanks, weights, air and boat.

For anyone who has never dived in the tropics before, the reefs near San Pedro are fine, but experienced divers looking for high-voltage diving will be sorely disappointed. This is a heavily used area, which has been subjected to intensive fishing for some time and much of the reef has been plundered by souvenir hunters. To experience the **best diving in Belize** you need to take a trip out to one of the atolls, and several **live-aboard dive boats** are based in San Pedro; most of them sleep five or six, and they have to be booked well in advance. The *Manta IV*, for instance, charges US$219 for a three-day trip to the Blue Hole and Half Moon Caye, both on Lighthouse Reef; the price includes six dives (with three wall dives) and all meals, but not equipment. The *Manta IV* also has the only shark cage in the western Caribbean; a two-day shark-feeding and photo expedition costs around US$300. For information telephone ☎2371 or contact the *Holiday Hotel* in San Pedro on ☎2014. For up-to-date information on all the available live-aboard packages contact *Personalized Services*, PO Box 1158, Belize City (☎02/77593/4). Less ambitiously, day trips to the **Turneffe Islands** are on offer from *Bottom Time Dive Shop* (☎2348), who charge US$80 for two dives, including equipment and lunch.

Snorkelling trips are available from most of the hotels; they cost around BZ$30 for a day, the best of them taking in the Hol Chan Marine Reserve (see below). If you've never put on mask and fins before, you'll be well rewarded by practising from the *Paradise Hotel* pier, where shoals of colourful fish are constantly in view. If you'd rather not get wet at all, there are also some glass-bottomed boats which offer trips of a couple of hours for BZ$15.

Before going snorkelling or diving, whet your appetite with a visit to the excellent **Hol Chan Marine Reserve office** on Front Street next to *Amigo Travel*. There are photographs, maps and other displays on the reserve, and the staff will be pleased to answer your questions. They can also tell you if the USAID **conch hatchery**, just to the north of the main part of town beyond the *Paradise Hotel*, is open to visitors. If it is, Linda Reyes, the young and enthusiastic project manager, will allow you to have a look at the tiny conches in various stages of growth prior to being released onto the sea bed, where they replenish the vast numbers taken by fishermen.

Sailboards and **Hobie Cats** are available for rent, but they tend to be expensive; *Ramon's Reef Resort* has the largest selection. You can also rent **bikes** and mopeds from *Amigo Travel*, to explore the rough track running north and south from the town. Heading south, you could ride at least part of the way to **Marco Gonzalez**, a Maya ruin near the southern tip of the island. The site is hard to find and there's not a lot to see, but studies have shown it was an important trade centre, with close links to Lamanai.

Travelling north, hotels stretch for miles along the coast, though they are often spaced well apart. Beyond the furthest hotels the track becomes more difficult, with thick bush and mangrove lagoons making progress slow and sweaty. There is a surprising amount of wildlife, including deer, peccary and even a few of the cats of Belize. Turtles nest on some northern beaches, and volunteers are needed to patrol the nest sites when the eggs are being laid: contact the Belize Audubon Society or the Hol Chan Reserve office.

The Hol Chan Marine Reserve

The Hol Chan reserve takes its name from the Maya for "little channel", and it is this eponymous break in the reef that forms the focus of the reserve. Established in 1987, it is divided into three zones – covering a total of five square miles – that preserve a comprehensive cross-section of the marine environment, from coral reef through seagrass beds to mangroves. All three habitats are closely linked: many reef fish feed on the seagrass beds, and the mangroves are a nursery area for juvenile fish.

Feeding of fish sometimes takes place here, with the consequence that tourists congregate here, both on the water and in it. You'll have a more peaceful time on another part of the reef, and might see more fish as well as less trampled corals. A great deal of damage has already been caused by snorkellers standing on the coral or holding onto outcrops for a better look – in fact, on all the easily accessible areas of the reef you will clearly see the white patches of dead corals, especially on the large brain coral heads. The motto should be "look but don't touch", as the the protective cells are easily stripped away from the polyps, thereby allowing algae to enter. Keeping your distance is in your own best interests too: most coral will sting and some can cause agonising burns, while even brushing against the razor-sharp ridges on the reef top can cause cuts that are slow to heal.

Caye Caulker

South of Ambergris Caye and 35km northeast of Belize City, **Caye Caulker** is the most accessible island for the independent traveller, and long a favourite spot for backpackers on the "gringo trail". Until recently, tourism existed almost as a sideline to the island's main source of income, **lobster fishing**, which has kept the place going for over twenty years.

Although the lobster catch increased for many years after the setting up of the fishing co-ops, the deployment of more traps over an ever wider area led to the rapid depletion of the **spiny lobster**, which were once so common they could be scooped onto the beaches with palm fronds. Today their numbers are dangerously low, and specimens smaller than the legal 4oz are frequently taken and sold to local restaurants. Last season some catches were so low that the fishermen were taking the traps in by mid-January, even though the legal season isn't over until mid-March. In parallel with this decline there has been an increase in the number of hotels and bars, as the islanders have cashed in on an alternative source of income. Fishermen have become barmen, and fishing boats now offer snorkelling trips; new hotels are being built, older ones improved, and prices – low for years – have begun to rise.

For the moment Caye Caulker is still relaxed and easy-going, maintaining a laid-back atmosphere and avoiding the commercialism of San Pedro. It has less concrete and many more palm trees, and there are only half a dozen vehicles on the island's sand paths. There's little air conditioning either, which is fine most of the time, when a cooling breeze blows in from the sea, but can mean some very sticky moments if the breeze dies. **Sandflies and mosquitoes** can cause almost unbearable annoyance on calm days. Sandflies are worse: they are inactive in breezy conditions, but at other times a good **insect repellent** is essential (though even that does not seem to last very long). Some swear by Avon's *Skin-So-Soft*.

Coming and going

Travel to Caye Caulker is entirely by **boat**; a site was partly cleared for an airstrip over a decade ago, but the project appears to be abandoned, much to the relief of islanders and visitors. Passenger boats for Caye Caulker, known locally as "skiffs" (as opposed to a canoe-shaped "dory"), tie up behind *A&R's Shell Service Station* on North Front Street in Belize City. Finding them is no problem, as you'll be persistently approached by boys in the street asking if you want to go to the islands. "Chocolate", the owner of *Soledad* (who gets a mention in most of the guidebooks), is usually the first to leave at around 11am, but there are several other reliable operators: few leave on time, whatever they might promise. Jerry, who runs *Blue Wave*, is perhaps the most punctual, and you can safely leave your luggage with any of the Caye Caulker boat owners if you want a look round the city before you leave – but don't pay anyone until you're safely landed on Caye Caulker.

The journey takes around fifty minutes and has cost BZ$12 for many years, though the increase in fuel prices makes a rise inevitable soon. You'll be dropped off at one of the piers at the front of the island, usually at the longest one, known as the "front bridge".

A swift way of getting to Caye Caulker from the international airport is to fly to Caye Chapel and phone Caye Caulker for a boat to pick you up; ask at the airport or when you land on Caye Chapel. This is actually cheaper than taking a taxi from the airport then catching a boat to the island.

Leaving for Belize City, most boats pass the "front bridge" looking for passengers between 6.30 and 7am. Few, if any, leave later than this, so if you've a plane to catch you have to be up early (you can reach the international airport by 8.30am if you take a taxi from the dock in Belize City). Recently some boats have been offering an afternoon service, leaving at around 3pm from the *Reef Hotel* dock – but don't rely on this if you really need to get home. If you want to get to one of the **other cayes**, ask around amongst the boatmen in the early morning. You'll probably find someone who'll take you to **San Pedro** for BZ$20, if not less, but if you're planning to go further afield, to one of the small or uninhabited islands, you'll probably have to hire someone specifically to take you there.

Hotels

Most of the year it's easy enough to find an inexpensive room in one of the small clapboard hotels, but to arrive at Christmas or New Year without somewhere to stay could mean a sleepless night guarding your belongings on the beach.

Even the furthest **hotels** are no more than ten minutes' walk from the main dock. Strolling **north** for a few hundred metres, past the park and police station, you come to *Riva's Guest House* (☎2127/2165), above the *Aberdeen* Chinese restaurant; it's basic and clean (and you get a fan), and is in the lowest price range, costing BZ$12.50 for a double room. The balcony gives a great view of the passing traffic (mostly pedestrian) and palm fronds dipping in the breeze – and the restaurant below is good value. Next door the recently extended and repainted *Mira Mar* is about the same price. Behind these is another small cheap place, the *Sandy Lane Hotel* (near the BTL office, for telephone services), while half a block further on is the recently revamped and renamed *Reef Hotel* (☎2196), which has hot water and a private bathroom for every room. Secure and well-run, the *Reef* is popular with groups, and the busy bar has live music at times; the summer rates are BZ$25 single, BZ$30 double and BZ$40 triple – in winter it's about BZ$10 more. The *Reef*'s original owner, Billy Martinez, has a restaurant next door (*Martinez Caribbean Inn*; ☎2113) and recently started renting rooms. Next comes the *Rainbow*, a two-storey concrete building that offers little in the way of ambience or privacy: the rooms open right onto the path past the hotel and the view is of recently cut-down mangroves. Right at the end, past the *Cabanas* bar (☎2200), is a new development of cabins for rent, called simply *The Split*.

South from the main dock are at least another dozen hotels. First is the *Vega's Far Inn* (☎2142), where prices are steep by Caye Caulker standards, but the owners pride themselves on the security and have the only place for **camping** on the island: Maria Vegas is the local BTIA representative and offers tourist information. Further on you'll find *Lena's* and *Deisey's*, both of which offer basic budget rooms, and on the block opposite there's *Marin's* and the *Hideaway Hotel*. *Edith's*, on the corner, now has hot water and is slightly higher priced, though if you book a boat ride back to Belize City here you get a BZ$2 discount. Overlooking the cemetery is the *Tropical Paradise Hotel* (☎2124), whose smart-looking huts are pricey but good quality, with air conditioning and private bathrooms with hot water. Right next door is the *Tropical Paradise* **ice cream parlour** and restaurant – a popular spot for breakfast, though again it isn't the cheapest on the island. Walk along the beach through the coconut grove and you come to the new *Seebeez*, which is expensive (BZ$60 double) and closes during the summer; there's a bar and restaurant below.

Next along is *Tom's Hotel* (☎2102), a large hotel for Caye Caulker (20 rooms), and fine value at BZ$12. There's **snorkelling equipment** for guests to hire, and the owner runs excellent trips to the reef. Further on, situated right on the beach, is *The Anchorage*, which is built in the style of Maya houses and consists of whitewashed oval huts with thatched roofs; it might be too expensive if you're on your own, but can be a bargain if you're sharing, and definitely has the best location on the island. *Ignacio's Beach Huts*, just past *The Anchorage*, are the ultimate in budget accommodation at just BZ$7 per person. A little way beyond *Ignacio's* is the last hotel on the south end of the island, *Shirley's Guest House* (☎2145), which is worth the walk if you want peace and quiet; the rooms are comfortable and clean, slightly more expensive than average at around BZ$35 for a double, but still good value.

If you're planning an extended stay, there are often a few **houses for rent** – ask around or see the sign by the football field.

Eating, drinking and entertainment

Good home cooking, large portions and very reasonable prices are features of all the island's **restaurants**, half of which you'll pass while looking for a hotel room. Lobster is served in every imaginable dish, from curry to chow mein; seafood generally is good value, accompanied as a rule by rice or potatoes. Fresh vegetables are often in short supply (as throughout Belize), the usual ones being cabbage, carrots and onions.

Along the **main street** (no street names here), one block back from the shore, are *Marin's Restaurant*, with a shady outdoor dining area, and the particularly good *Rodriguez Home Restaurant*, a favourite; a few yards down a side path is *Syd's Bar*, which serves great food, but unfortunately is not often open. Just past here is *Glenda's*, where you can buy fresh orange juice, rolls and cake. The **post office**, down at the south end of the street, is not only a mini-supermarket and gift shop, but has recently added a restaurant that stays open in the evenings.

There are several shops on the island where you can buy food, but be warned that bread and milk sell out quickly. As you walk around you might see young girls selling bread or pastries from bowls balanced on their heads, and it's always worth seeing what delicious snacks they have. Also, many houses advertise banana bread, coconut cakes and other home-baked goodies.

Pirates Disco, at the crossing of the main streets in the centre of the village, is the focal point of island **nightlife**, and there are often as many music fans hanging around outside as there are inside. On most evenings the social scene oscillates between here and the *Reef* bar, the island's other main watering hole. Most people are friendly enough, but as the evening wears on and drink takes its toll it can get rowdy. Caye Caulker is a favourite weekend R & R destination for British soldiers, who are often very young and get drunk quickly, when the macho tendency takes over. Be careful with your money – Caye Caulker has a criminal element and a drug problem, but only two policemen.

Otherwise, evening entertainment mostly consists of relaxing over dinner or a drink, or gazing at the tropical night sky. Television – beamed down by satellite and soon to reach the island by cable – is a feature of most bars, with baseball, game shows and soaps as the programming staples. Home-made commercials and brief fillers of Belizean scenes and wildlife provide a touch of local interest.

Exploring the reef from Caye Caulker

There's not that much to do on Caye Caulker, which is a good excuse for loafing about and relaxing. **Trips to the reef** are easily arranged, provided four or five people want to go, and the cost should be no more than BZ$8–10 each. Most of the boatmen hang out on the shore by the *Reef Hotel* in the early morning, and plenty of people will offer to take you. An extended sailing trip to the uninhabited reefs and islands is not cheap, but better value here than in Belize City – try *Seaing is Belizing* (☎2189), where James Beveridge offers, for example, five-day trips for around US$250 for two people.

The reef is definitely an experience not to be missed, swimming along coral canyons surrounded by an astonishing range of fish, with perhaps even the ominous shape of a shark or two (these will almost certainly be harmless nurse sharks). Snorkellers should be aware of the fragility of the reef and be careful not to touch any coral – even sand stirred up by fins can damage corals. Most reef trips last several hours and take in several sites, often including the protected Hol Chan Marine Reserve (see above); some also include fishing along the way. Dolphins will often accompany the boat on the way to the reef.

For a really well-informed tour of the reef contact Ellen MacRae at the *Galeria Hicaco* (☎2178): as a marine biologist, she can explain exactly what it is you're seeing in this amazing underwater world. She also does slide shows and conducts **Audubon bird walks**, which are introductions to the dozens of bird species of the caye – waders from herons to sandpipers, with pelicans, spoonbills and the ever-present frigate birds swooping with pinpoint accuracy on morsels of fish. (Opposite the *Galeria* is a small house where Rainy Burns makes lovely framed glass ornaments.)

Other good reef trips are offered by Bobby Heusner in his sailboat *Sea Hawk* (he also runs camping trips to the atolls), and Gamusa in the *Hot Duck*, with an easy-going Rasta crew. If you'd like to learn underwater photography then get in touch, again, with James Beveridge at *Seaing is Belizing*, his house is by the football field, and he and his wife Dorothy run an interesting gift shop that sells photos, slides and film (you can also get film developed here). They also do slide shows and operate a book exchange service.

Sub-aqua diving is available from *Belize Diving Services* (☎2143), by the football field, expertly run by an American couple, Frank and Jane Bounting, who offer some of the best-value diving in Belize; Frank offers night-diving and is a cave diving expert – one of the world's largest single-chamber underwater caves runs right beneath Caye Caulker. Two-tank dives for qualified divers cost US$35 including equipment, and a four-day course should cost around US$300, which is cheap by Caribbean standards. They also have good quality **snorkelling equipment for hire** (some of the stuff offered by hotels

tends to be old and leaky). A new dive shop – *Frenchie's* – opened last year just north of Frank's; Frenchie is a young man from Caye Caulker trained by Frank, and charges similar prices. The diving here is good, but not as good as Belize's reputation in diving circles suggests. To experience the best that Belize has to offer you should take a live-aboard dive trip to the outer atolls – see comments under "Ambergris Caye".

You'll see signs for **fishing trips** as you walk around. Some of the best are operated by Porfilio Guzman (☎2152), Roly Rosado and Rally; ask for them by name – any of the locals will direct you.

Swimming isn't really possible from the shore since the water's too shallow. You have to leap off the end of piers or go to "the cut", a deep channel at the north end of the village created in 1961 when Hurricane Hattie sliced Caye Caulker in two. Here you can see the damage done when mangroves are cut down – the cut was narrower before this area was developed, now there's a desperate attempt to build shore defences. The northern part of the island is long and narrow, mainly covered in mangroves and thick vegetation that comes right down to the shore. These mangrove shallows swarm with small fish called "sardines" by the fishermen, who use them as bait to catch snapper. **Salt-water crocodiles** are sometimes seen here, but you're more likely to find them on the Turneffe Islands or in the more remote coastal areas.

Walking round the island you might also meet Phillip Lewis, otherwise known as **Karate**, a renowned artist and writer in Belize who helped design the paper currency. His hand-drawn maps of Caye Caulker are featured in most bars and restaurants, and as his work increases in maturity it also becomes more expensive. Ray Axillou – "Cap'n Ray" as he likes to be known – is another resident Caye Caulker author. He's published two books of espionage, intrigue and skullduggery set in Belize, *The Belize Connection* and *The Belize Vortex*. The hero, suffering incredible hardships, just about saves the western world, and is based (very loosely) on Ray's own experiences in Belize. An entertaining read.

The rest of the reef

Although the only villages anywhere on the reef are Caye Caulker and San Pedro, there are several other islands that can be visited, some of them supporting fishing camps or upmarket resorts, others completely uninhabited. Caye Caulker is within day-trip distance of some of these, and there are also a couple of isolated islands where the budget-minded traveller can find reasonably priced accommodation. Bear in mind that tourism in Belize is developing each year, so there are likely to be more hotels and resorts on offer than are given here.

In addition to the places mentioned below, there are other superbly isolated hotels – called lodges in deference to their American guests – on a few reefs and cayes. **Prices**, which are not low, include transport from Belize City or the International Airport, accommodation, all meals, and usually diving or fishing. The attraction of these lodges is the "simple life" scenario. Buildings are low-key, wooden and sometimes thatched, and the group you're with will probably be the only people staying there. There are no telephones (most are in radio contact with Belize City), electricity is supplied by generator, and views of palm trees curving over turquoise water reinforce the sense of isolation.

Caye Chapel and Long Caye

As a diversion during a snorkelling trip you could visit **Caye Chapel**, immediately south of Caye Caulker. Quite different from Caye Caulker, Caye Chapel is privately owned and has an airstrip, a golf course, a marina and a hotel, the *Pyramid Island Resort*. The beaches are cleaned daily and the bar is open all day – perfect for a cold beer after a hard day's snorkelling. It was on Caye Chapel that the defeated Spanish fleet paused for a few days after the **Battle of St George's Caye** in 1798, and some of their dead are buried on the island. Flights from Belize City to San Pedro pick up passengers on Caye Chapel.

Long Caye, south of Caye Chapel, is a low-lying mangrove caye; practically uninhabited, but about to be developed – a small hotel is being built.

English Caye, Goff's Caye and St George's Caye

The tiny islands of **English Caye** and **Goff's Caye** are popular as organised day trips from Belize City, but no regular transport goes to them. The *Gallows Point Resort*, about 15km from Belize City, is right on the edge of the reef, on Gallows Point, the site of hangings in earlier days. It's not cheap at BZ$240 per day, but day trips from Belize City cost around US$25 per person – contact Danny Weir at the *Belcove Hotel* ☎02/3054.

St George's Caye, also around 15km from Belize City, served as capital for the Baymen of the eighteenth century, but doesn't offer any rewards for the casual visitor. However, for those interested in Belizean history there's a small graveyard on the southern tip of the island, with the graves of early settlers. The only **hotel**, *St George's Lodge*, charges around US$150 per night and is chiefly a diving resort. A very small island, St George's Caye has some luxury holiday villas and is home to a few fishermen, as well as an adventure training centre for the British Forces in Belize.

The Bluefield Range

In the **Bluefield Range** cayes, 35km southeast of Belize City, there's the opportunity to stay on a remote fishing camp at a more affordable price. *Ricardo's Beach Huts* offer simple, comfortable accommodation right on the water, in huts built on stilts. The freshly caught fish and lobsters are included in the price of the two-night stay, as are meals and transport from Belize City: if there are at least three in the group it costs US$60 per person from April to December, and US$80 in high season. Tent sites (US$2.50 per person) are also available, but you still have to pay for transport and meals. Ricardo Castillo is a reliable, expert fishing guide and practises conservation of the reef (he's one of the few fishermen who puts back undersized lobsters). For more information ask at *Dim's Mira Rio* bar, 59 North Front Street, Belize City (☎02/44970) – trips begin here, and they make the necessary arrangements – or contact *Personalised Services* in Belize City (☎02/77593) who can contact Ricardo by radio.

The Turneffe Islands

Though shown on many maps as a single large island, the **Turneffe Islands** are an oval archipelago 60km long, enclosed by a beautiful coral reef. Situated 40km from Belize City, they consist mainly of low-lying mangrove and sandbanks around a shallow lagoon, and are virtually uninhabited. There are two places offering accommodation here, on the two small areas of dry land large enough to support buildings. *Turneffe Flats* on the windward, eastern side costs US$1200 per person for a week's fishing, including the airfare from Miami, New Orleans or Houston (☎02/45634). *Turneffe Island Lodge*, at the southern tip of the islands on Caye Bokel, is US$1000 per person for a week of diving, even more for fishing (contact PO Box 480, Belize City; ☎02/2331). *Personalised Services* can again arrange for trips if you're already in Belize, still extremely expensive.

Tobacco Reef and the south

Further south is the **Tobacco Reef**, where there's some reasonably priced accommodation on **Tobacco Caye**, reached from Dangriga (see p.315). The cayes in the far south of Belize are at present little developed for tourism, and between Dangriga and Punta Gorda are dozens of isolated reefs and islands. From the village of Placencia you can take trips to **Laughing Bird Caye**, and the most southerly islands, the **Sapodilla Cayes**, can be explored from Punta Gorda.

Glover's Reef

Glover's Reef is the furthest away of all – a large, almost deserted atoll over 100km southeast of Belize City. Accommodation here is offered by *Glovers Reef Resort* (☎05/2006), where an eleven-day diving package will cost you around US$1500, including airfare from Miami. A new hotel is the *Manta Reef Resort* (PO Box 215, Belize City; ☎02/45606). This kind of isolated splendour is expensive, but you won't find better anywhere in the Caribbean.

Lighthouse Reef and Half Moon Caye

About 100km to the east of Belize City, at the outer reaches of the reef, is the **Lighthouse Reef Lagoon**, made famous by Jacques Cousteau, who visited Belize in the Seventies. There are two main attractions out here, the Blue Hole and the Half Moon Caye Natural Monument, and it was the first of these that attracted the attention of Cousteau. The **Blue Hole** is a shaft about 90m in diameter, which drops through the bottom of the lagoon and opens out into a complex network of caves and crevices. Its depth gives it a peculiar deep blue colour and according to local legend it's home to an enormous sea monster. Cousteau's investigations have shown that the caves underlie the entire reef, and that the sea has simply punctured their roof at the site of the Blue Hole.

The **Half Moon Caye Natural Monument**, the first marine conservation area in Belize, was declared a national park in 1982. Its lighthouse was first built in 1820 and was not always effective: several wrecks testify to the dangers of the reef. The 45-acre caye is divided into two distinct ecosystems: in the west, guano from thousands of seabirds fertilises the soil, allowing the growth of dense vegetation, while the eastern half has mostly coconut palms growing in the sand. A total of 98 bird species have been recorded here, including frigate birds, ospreys, mangrove warblers, white-crowned pigeons and – most important of all – a resident population of 4000 red-footed boobies, one of only two nesting colonies in the Caribbean. The boobies came by their name because they had no fear of man, enabling sailors to kill them in their thousands. They still exhibit no fear and move only reluctantly when visitors stroll through them. The nesting area of the birds is accessible from a viewing platform built by the Belize Audubon Society. Apart from the birds, the island supports iguanas and lizards, and both loggerhead and hawksbill turtles nest on the beaches, which also attract the biggest land crabs in Belize.

There's no accommodation for visitors, but **camping** is allowed with the permission of the Audubon Society. Remember to bring your own food and water and register with the park warden when you arrive.

Although it is possible to visit the Blue Hole and Half Moon Caye as a day trip from either of the main cayes or Belize City, hiring a boat will be quite expensive. If you'd like to spend some time birdwatching and snorkelling here, you could get someone reliable to drop you on the island and come back in a day or two. At the time of writing there is a plan to build two hotels on Northern Caye on Lighthouse Reef; for more information check with a travel agent in Belize City.

travel details

Boats

The chief way of getting to or between the islands is of course by boat, but only San Pedro (on Ambergris Caye) and Caye Caulker have anything resembling a regular service: other than these it's a question of hitching a lift with someone who's going, or hiring a boat – both possibilities covered in the text.

From **Belize City to San Pedro** (1hr 20min) the most reliable boat is the *Andrea*, leaving from the dock of the *Belle Vue Hotel* at 4pm Mon–Fri and 1pm Sat, returning to Belize City at 7am. Skiffs sometimes leave from the Swing Bridge area: the *Triple J* is one that boasts a regular schedule, leaving at 9am and returning from San Pedro at 4pm. In theory the *Miss Belize* operates a daily passenger service, but "engine trouble" seems to be a perpetual problem. Cargo boats leave from Custom Wharf (near the Fort George lighthouse).

Travelling from **San Pedro to other cayes** isn't very easy, though you might meet a fishing boat or yachtsman heading somewhere. Any boat with C.C. on the side, followed by numbers, is from **Caye Caulker** – they generally arrive in San Pedro in the early afternoon, at the dock beside the *Tackle Box*.

Passenger boats from **Belize City to Caye Caulker** (50min) tie up behind *A&R's Shell Service Station* on North Front Street. Finding them is no problem, as you'll be persistently approached by boys in the street asking if you want to go to the islands. "Chocolate", the owner of *Soledad*, is usually the first to leave at around 11am, but there are several other reliable operators: few leave on time, whatever they might promise. Jerry, who runs *Blue Wave*, is perhaps the most punctual. Returning, all the boats pass the "front bridge" looking for passengers, between 6.30 and 7am. Few, if any, leave later than this, though recently there have been boats leaving the *Reef Hotel* dock at around 3pm.

For transport from Caye Caulker to the **other cayes**, ask around amongst the boatmen in the early morning. You should find someone who's going to **San Pedro**, but if you're heading for one of the small or uninhabited islands you'll probably have to hire someone to take you there.

Planes

Both *Maya Airways* and *Tropic Air* operate several flights a day from the Municipal Airport in Belize City (7am–4.30pm) **to San Pedro** in five- or six-seater aircraft. *Maya* also fly from San Pedro to Corozal, stopping at Sarteneja, so you could use this route to reach the Mexican border without going back to Belize City.

For **Caye Caulker** you can fly from the International or Municipal Airport to Caye Chapel and call Caye Caulker for a boat to pick you up; ask at the airport or when you land on Caye Chapel. Any flight to or from San Pedro will land at Caye Chapel if requested.

CHAPTER TEN

CAYO AND THE WEST

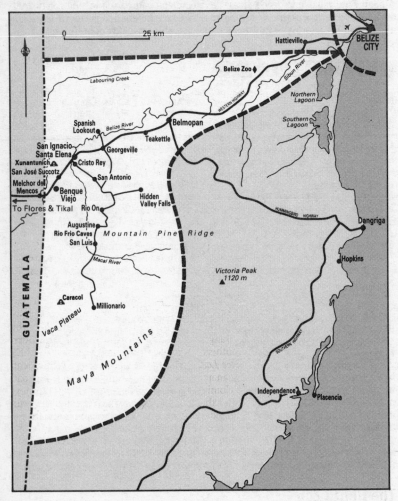

H eading west from Belize City to the Guatemalan border you travel through a wide range of landscapes – from open grassland to rolling hills and dense tropical forest. It's a journey that takes you from the heat and humidity of the coast to the lush foothills of the Maya mountains, and into an area increasingly influenced by Spanish-speaking *mestizos*, including large numbers of refugees from other Central American countries.

A single road connects Belize City with the Guatemalan border. This is the Western highway, a fast, paved route that leaves Belize City through mangrove swamps and heads inland across a stretch of open savannah scattered with pine trees. Before reaching Belmopan the road passes a couple of places of interest: the **Belize Zoo**, well worth a visit if you're interested in the country's natural history, and **Guanacaste Park**, a relatively small reserve designed to protect a section of the original forest. Beyond this is the Belizean capital, **Belmopan**, which was established in 1970 and looks something like an unfinished college campus.

Heading further west you start to climb into the foothills of the Maya mountains, a beautiful area where the air is clear and the land astonishingly fertile. South of the road, **Mountain Pine Ridge** is a pleasantly cool region of hills and pine woods traversed by a network of good dirt roads. The chief town hereabouts is **San Ignacio**, the ideal spot to use as a base for exploring the forests, rivers and ruins of central Belize. San Ignacio, the main town of Cayo district, is becoming known as a centre for Belize's growing "eco-tourism" industry. The ruins of **Caracol**, the largest Maya site in Belize and a focus for current archaeological research, lie deep in the jungle of the Vaca plateau, south of San Ignacio.

From San Ignacio the Guatemalan border, marked by the Mopan branch of the Belize River, is only another 15km further west. On the Belizean side is the town of **Benque Viejo del Carmen**. As you approach the town you pass **Xunantunich**, a Maya ruin from which you can view the Guatemalan province of **El Petén**.

Belize City to Belmopan

Leaving Belize City to the west, the main road skirts along the shoreline, running behind a tangle of mangrove swamps and past **Cucumber Beach Wharf**, a graveyard for the rusting hulks of beached ships. A few kilometres beyond the outskirts of the city you cross the **Sir John Burden Canal**, an inland waterway that connects the Belize River with the Sibun River. This is the route taken by small boats travelling down to Dangriga, via the **Northern and Southern Lagoons**. At the south end of Southern Lagoon is the small village of GALES POINT, with a hotel called *Manatee Lodge* (BZ$100 at least), where visitors can be virtually guaranteed a sight of manatee. The village is connected by a dirt road to Dangriga, 25km to the south. Continuing on the Western highway the next place is HATTIEVILLE, named after the 1961 hurricane which created the refugees who initially populated it. The village started life as a temporary shelter for the homeless, but since then it has become rather more permanent.

The curious steep hills on the left are limestone outcrops, quarried for road-building. The highest of them is **Gracie Rock**, near the Sibun River, the set of fictional "Geronimo" in the film of *The Mosquito Coast*. The set's ruin still stands.

The Belize Zoo

The first point of interest out this way is the **Belize Zoo**. Originally set up in 1983 by Sharon Matola, after an ambitious wildlife film (Path of the Raingods, Parts 1–4) left her with a collection of semi-tame animals, the zoo is organised around the theme of "a walk through Belize", with a trail that takes you into the pinelands, the forest edge, the rainforest and the river forest, introducing a selection of animals from each environment. The residents include a Baird's tapir (locally known as a mountain cow) called April who is well known to the schoolchildren of Belize. All the cats to be found in Belize are represented and some, including the jaguars, have bred successfully. There is a wide range of birds (including toucans, macaws, a spectacled owl and several vultures), and other residents include monkeys (both spider and howler), a crocodile and an assortment of snakes.

The zoo is actively involved in conservation and captive breeding, and runs a series of outreach programmes that tour Belize's schools, teaching children about their country's wildlife. All children in Belize are encouraged to visit the zoo, which has a policy of free admission for school groups. The zoo's efforts are an important part of the struggle to protect Belize's natural history, and it aims to encourage the support of local people. A new and better site for the zoo has been planned for some time, with a development scheme donated by zoo architects from Seattle, Washington. The new site is next to the old one, at mile 30, and may be open by the time you read this.

To get to the zoo take any bus heading between Belize City and Belmopan and ask the driver to drop you; you'll easily spot it, as there's a sign on the highway. There's a bit of a walk from here (over a kilometre), though if you know what time you're arriving they'll pick you up – phone ☎02/45523. The entrance fee is BZ$10 for non-Belizeans and includes a guided tour on which every animal is introduced personally by your guide: it's highly enjoyable, and the money goes to a worthwhile cause.

On towards Belmopan

Beyond the zoo is the branch road to the village of CHURCHYARD, on the Sibun River, and next comes *J.B.'s Bar*, an ideal place to stop and quench your thirst. This is an old favourite with the British Army, whose mementoes deck the walls alongside a word of thanks from Harrison Ford and the crew of *The Mosquito Coast. J.B.'s* marks the boundary between the Belize and Cayo districts, and here the open expanse of pine and savannah gives way to the dense bush and tropical rainforest of the interior. The road continues, well-surfaced and fast, to the junction with the Southern highway. A track on the right leads to "**The Valley of Peace**", a UN-sponsored resettlement camp for refugees from Guatemala and El Salvador, and landless Belizeans.

Shortly before the turning for Belmopan another track leads off to the right, this time to the **Banana Bank Ranch** (☎08/23180) on the north bank of the Belize River, crossed by an ancient ferry. The ranch is owned by an American couple, John and Carolyn Carr, who offer horse-riding, canoeing, swimming and trips into the surrounding area. The ranch also has a small collection of animals (including a tame jaguar) and a tiny Maya ruin. Accommodation costs around BZ$35, and a couple of hours on horseback will set you back BZ$25. If you're planning to stay for a while then phone ahead and they'll pick you up from Belmopan.

Guanacaste Park

At the junction for Belmopan is **Guanacaste Park**, a small (and mosquito-ridden) wildlife reserve where you can wander through a superb area of lush tropical forest. Founded in 1973 and officially dedicated as a National Reserve in 1988, the park covers a total area of 21 hectares, bordered by the highway,

Roaring Creek and the Belize River. The main attraction is a huge guanacaste or tubroos tree, a vast, spreading hardwood that supports some 35 other species and reaches a height of 40 metres. Hanging from its limbs are a huge range of bromeliads, orchids, ferns, cacti and strangler figs, which blossom spectacularly at the end of the rainy season. The wood of the tree is particularly hard and partially water-resistant, and it's traditionally favoured for use as feeding troughs, dugout canoes, and mortars for hulling rice. This specimen escaped being felled because the trunk split into three near the base. A good-sized guanacaste can produce two or three canoes. In season the tree produces ear-shaped fruit that are a favourite food for cattle.

Other botanical attractions include young mahogany trees, cohune palms, a cotton tree and quamwood, while the forest floor is a mass of ferns, mosses and vines. As the park is so close to the road your chances of seeing any four-footed **wildlife** are fairly slim, but armadillos, white-tailed deer, jaguarundi, opossums and agouti have nevertheless all been seen here, and recently a small number of howler monkeys have used the park as a feeding ground. Birds also abound, with around fifty species frequenting the park. These include blue-crowned motmots, black-faced ant-thrushes, black-headed trogons, red-lored parrots and squirrel cuckoos.

There's an information booth near the entrance and four or five short **trails** to take you on tours through the park and along the banks of the Belize River. Sadly there's only a single mature guanacaste tree, but the rest of the park is just as fascinating and offers a very accessible glimpse of the Belizean forest. To get to the park take any bus heading between Belmopan and either San Ignacio or Belize City, and get off at the junction between the main road and the start of the Hummingbird highway, just a couple of kilometres from Belmopan itself.

Belmopan

From the Guanacaste Park the main road splits; one branch (the Western highway) pushes on towards San Ignacio and the Guatemalan border, while the other turns south to **BELMOPAN**, where it becomes the pot-holed Hummingbird highway, heading all the way to Dangriga. Belmopan itself is an unlikely capital city – Belize's answer to Washington and Brasília. Arriving in the bus station the first thing that strikes you is a sense of space, as moving to Belmopan is an opportunity that few Belizeans have taken up. Government offices and their staff (given no option) have moved here, but Belize City remains very much the country's social and cultural centre.

Belmopan was designed to embody the country's cultural roots and its name combines the words Belize and Mopan, the language spoken by local Maya Indians. The layout of the main government buildings is modelled on a Maya city, grouped around a central plaza: some of the main buildings incorporate a version of the traditional roof comb. In classic new-town terms Belmopan was meant to symbolise the dawn of a new era, with tree-lined avenues, banks, a couple of embassies and telecommunications worthy of a world centre. In fact it has all the essential ingredients except one: there are hardly any people! The long, grey concrete administrative buildings are set away from the road, surrounded by grassy space.

The city was founded in 1970 after Hurricane Hattie had swept much of Belize City into the sea. The government decided to use the disaster as a chance to move to higher ground and, in a Brasília-style bid to focus development on the interior, the planners chose the site of Belmopan. The population of this new capital was planned at 5000 for the first few years, eventually rising to 30,000. Today, however, it stands rooted at around 4000, and Belizeans still prefer the congestion of Belize City to the boredom of Belmopan.

If you're in the area though, there's one thing well worth a visit: the **archaeological vault**. This is a locked strongroom which houses all of Belize's finest archaeological treasures. Sadly the government can't afford a real museum and in its absence this is the only place where priceless artefacts are safe from theft. A visit to the vault is extraordinary, and certainly like no other museum you've ever seen. A member of the Archaeology Department opens the huge lock and you crowd into the vault. On the wooden shelves are hundreds of pottery bowls, mostly broken but with some superb specimens intact. In foam-padded boxes are exquisite gold and jade ear plugs, beautiful jade and shell necklaces, delicate obsidian blades obtained from trade with Mexico, and a Maya whistle, in working order. There are beautiful painted vessels with a hole in them to symbolise death, a stone hatchet with its original wooden handle, stone effigies and carvings, and skulls showing how the Maya deformed the heads of infants by flattening the forehead with a board. The list goes on; what you see here, impressive though it is, is only a fraction of the cultural highlights of a powerful and advanced civilisation. Some of the most beautiful works of art are huge eccentric flints found in burial sites. If you've seen any of Belize's Maya sites and you're interested in the archaeology of the country, try to visit the vault. It's open from 1.30 to 4.30pm on Monday, Wednesday and Friday, but you have to book your visit two days in advance by phoning ☎08/22106.

Practicalities

Buses from Belize City to San Ignacio, Benque Viejo and Dangriga all pass through Belmopan, so there's at least one an hour from 6.30am to 6.30pm: it's a good idea to pick up some food or a cold drink here, especially if you're heading south. Unless you've come to see the archaeological vault, however, or need to visit a government department, there's no particular reason to stay any longer than it takes your bus to leave. While you wait, the best **restaurant** is the *Caladium*, right beside the bus terminal, though *Yoli's*, next to the petrol station, has more attractive surroundings. Nearby you'll also find the banks, the post office, and a small **market**. At the top of the market square is the Ministry of Natural Resources, where you can buy **maps**. The **British High Commission** is on Half Moon Avenue, behind the National Assembly building (☎08/22146; they also have a consular clinic in Belize City), and the **US Embassy** has an office here (☎08/22617). The office of the **phone** company is beside the large satellite dish, and the **immigration** office is in the main administrative building. If you missed a chance to buy souvenirs and you're leaving Belize it's worth calling in at *El Caracol*, 32 Macaw Avenue (☎08/22394), where you'll find a good selection of reasonably priced art and gifts.

Hotels in Belmopan cater for the needs and expense accounts of diplomats and aid officials, so if for any reason you think you need to be here for a day or two it's far cheaper and far more interesting to stay in San Ignacio. If you have to stay then the *Circle A Lodge*, 37 Half Moon Street, is the cheapest at BZ$50, while the *Bull Frog Inn*, nearby at 23 Half Moon Avenue, charges BZ$56: the *Belmopan Convention Hotel*, near the bus terminal, is twice as expensive.

Belmopan to San Ignacio

After leaving Belmopan the scenery becomes more rugged, with thickly forested ridges always in view to the south. The road stays close to the valley of the Belize River, passing through a series of villages: ROARING CREEK, TEAKETTLE, ONTARIO and UNITEDVILLE. At mile 62 is *Caesar's Place*, where Caesar Sherrard runs a café and bed and breakfast guesthouse (☎092/2341; around BZ$45). Caesar makes jewellery and carvings, and he knows a lot about Belize, so it's a good place to visit.

In GEORGEVILLE a track to the south leads to **Mountain Pine Ridge** (covered later). This is the Chiquibul Road, reaching deep into the forest, crossing the Macal River at the Guacamallo Bridge, and it's here that you should get off if you're hitching to AUGUSTINE, the Forest Reserve HQ. The road is used, infrequently, by villagers and foresters, but you're only allowed to camp at the entrance or in Augustine. You really need a four-wheel drive vehicle to properly explore this fascinating and exciting area of hills and jungle, though a mountain bike would also be great. Eleven kilometres along the road is *Mountain Equestrian Trails*, where you'll find expensive but very comfortable accommodation in a forest setting. They offer horse-riding and trips in the Pine Ridge.

South of the highway, between Barton and Roaring creeks, is **Society Hall Nature Reserve**, around 7000 acres of semi-deciduous rainforest with an array of Belizean wildlife. It's a privately-owned reserve but there are plans for a visitors' centre and camping facilities. If you fancy spending some time in the rainforest (in fairly basic accommodation) you can volunteer for work in the reserve; write to Svea Dietrich-Ward, PO Box 206, Belmopan, Belize.

At **Central Farm** research is carried out to find suitable crops and farm animals for Belize. Past here, on the right, is the road to SPANISH LOOKOUT, a successful Mennonite farming community. And right at the side of the highway is the British Army's **Holdfast Camp**, the base for an infantry company. Now there are farms and houses all the way to SANTA ELENA, San Ignacio's sister town on the eastern bank of the Macal River. The river is crossed by the Hawksworth Bridge, built in 1949 and still the only suspension bridge in Belize.

San Ignacio and around

About 35 kilometres west of Belmopan, **SAN IGNACIO** stands at the heart of the Cayo district on the banks of the Macal River, a town that draws together much of the best in inland Belize. The focus of west-central Belize, it's surrounded by fast-flowing rivers that tumble towards the coast, and the forested hills which begin here roll all the way across Guatemala and south to the Maya mountains. It's an ideal base from which to explore inland Belize, offering good food, inexpensive hotels and restaurants, and frequent bus connections. The population is a typically varied racial mix: *mestizos* dominate and Spanish is the main language, but you'll also hear plenty of English and see Creoles, Maya Indians, Mennonites, Lebanese, Chinese and even Sri Lankans. People here are relaxed and friendly (no hustlers) and you very soon pick up the atmosphere – peaceful yet invigorating. The evenings are cool and the days fresh, a welcome break from the sweltering heat of the coast.

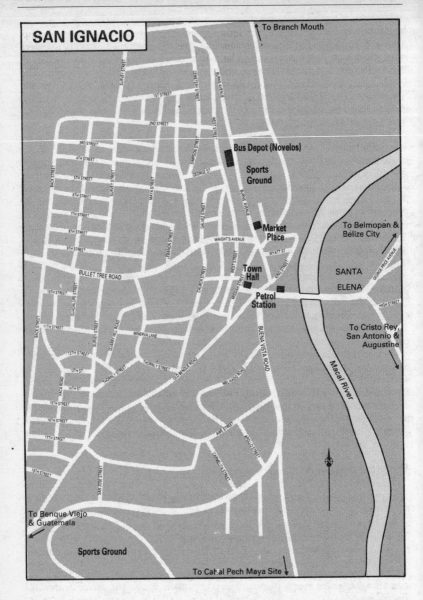

Until the Western highway was built in the 1930s (the western part of the road wasn't paved until the 1980s), local transport was by mule or water. It could take ten days of paddling to reach San Ignacio from Belize City, though later small steamers made the trip. Nowadays river traffic, which had almost died out, is enjoying something of a revival as increasing numbers of tourists take river trips.

Like many places in Belize, San Ignacio probably started life as a logging camp. A map drawn up in 1787 simply states that the Indians of this general area were "in friendship with the Baymen". In later years it was a centre for the shipment of chicle, the sap of the sapodilla tree, and the basic ingredient of chewing gum. The *chicleros*, as the collectors of chicle were called, were self-reliant and knew the forest intimately, including the location of most, if not all, Maya ruins – when the demand for Maya artefacts sent black-market prices rocketing later this century, many of them turned to looting.

The name originally given to this central area was **El Cayo**, the same word that the Spanish used to describe the offshore islands. It's an apt description of the area, in a peninsula between two parallel rivers, and also a measure of how isolated the early settlers felt, surrounded by the forest. It wasn't just mosquitoes and jungle they had to fear, for the forest was also home to a Maya group who valued their independence. **Tipu**, a Maya city that probably stood at Negroman on the Macal River, was the capital of the province of Dzuluinicob, where for years the Indians resisted attempts to Christianise them. The early wave of conquest, in 1544, made only a little impact here, and the area was a centre of rebellion in the following decades. Two Spanish friars arrived in 1618, but a year later one of the friars found that the entire population was still practising idolatry. The idols were smashed and the native priests flogged, but by the end of the year the Indians had again driven out the Spaniards. Four years later, Indians from Tipu worked as guides in an expedition against the Itzá and in 1641 the friars returned, determined to Christianise the inhabitants. To express their defiance the pagan priests conducted a mock mass, using tortillas, and then threw out the friars. From then on little is known about Tipu, although it must have remained an outpost of Maya civilisation, providing refuge to other Maya fleeing from Spanish rule. It retained at least a measure of independence until 1707 when the population was forcibly removed to Lake Petén Itzá. Nothing remains of the city, although there are plenty of other Maya ruins in the area, including Cahal Pech, in San Ignacio itself.

Nowadays the administrative capital of Cayo district, San Ignacio is a rich agricultural centre, and the surrounding valleys are used to farm citrus fruit and graze cattle. When Belizeans refer to Cayo they usually mean the town of San Ignacio and not Cayo district.

Practical details

Before you do anything in San Ignacio step into *Eva's* restaurant, 22 Burns Avenue, and have a word with the owner Bob Jones, who knows all there is to know about San Ignacio and the surrounding area. Whether you're in search of a hotel for a cheap overnight stop or a country cottage for a week of luxury, Bob will be able to point you in the right direction.

The very cheapest **hotels** are in Santa Elena on the other side of the suspension bridge, where you'll find the *Grand Hotel* and a small hotel above the health-food shop: other than price these have nothing to recommend them and if you can afford it you're much better off in San Ignacio itself. The *Hotel Central*, 24 Burns Avenue (BZ$15), and the *Imperial Hotel*, 22 Burns Avenue, above *Eva's* are both reasonable: certainly better than the *Jaguar Hotel* across the street (BZ$15 single, BZ$20 double). The *Jaguar* does have a good restaurant, though, decorated with gorgeous murals, and can serve delicious local food when it's being organised properly. The *Hi-Et Hotel* (BZ$12 single), at the corner of West and Waight Streets, is the cheapest in town and a personal favourite. You can order simple breakfasts here and they also do laundry. Slightly smarter is the *Hotel Belmoral*, 17 Burns Avenue, which has hot water and charges BZ$20 single – more for a room with a private bathroom. The most expensive hotel in town is *The San Ignacio Hotel*, on Buena Vista Street (☎2125), with a superb location on the hill overlooking the valley, just a ten-minute walk from the town centre. Prices are high at the height of the season (winter) but come down to around BZ$50 double in summer. The restaurant is good value, even for budget travellers, and eating here enables you to use the pool. Across the road and higher up the hill is the *Piache Hotel* (☎2032; BZ$30 single, BZ$40 double, less in the low season), a very friendly place with an outdoor bar and great views, run by Mrs Ethel Ellis, whose daughter Zoila wrote *On Heroes, Lizards and Passion* (see "Books" in *Contexts*). See the following section for possible **campsites** and places to stay in the country around San Ignacio.

San Ignacio also has some very good **restaurants**. *Eva's* is the best place for a filling meal at a reasonable price. They serve delicious chille con carne, locally caught fish, and some delicious Creole dishes. A little way up the street, at 27 Burns Avenue, is the *Serendib*, serving Sri Lankan curries and seafood; not all that cheap but well worth it. For cheap Chinese food and large portions try the *Tai San* or *Maxims*. The best **club** is the *Cahal Pech Tavern*, a huge thatch structure towering high above the town. Bands play regularly here, and the action lasts from lunchtime till late. Other possibilities are the *Blue Angel* and *Shangri-La*.

The *Belize Bank* (Mon–Thur 8am–1pm, Fri 8am–1pm & 3–6pm) is on Burns Avenue, as is the *BTL* office (for phone calls; Mon–Fri 8am–noon & 1–4pm, Sat 8am–noon), under *Cano's Gift Shop*. **Market day** is Saturday and well worth a visit if you're cooking for yourself; the market is one of the best in Belize, with farmers bringing in produce, much of which has been picked that morning. The **post office** is above the police station, on the San Ignacio side of the bridge. **Buses** to San Ignacio stop in the marketplace, behind the *Hotel Belmoral*. Both *Batty* and *Novelo* have regular services to Belize City (2hr 30min) and the border (30min), more or less hourly throughout the day (the first to the border at 9am). *Shaws* also run a good service to and from Belmopan, with five buses a day. San Ignacio has no **airport**, but planes can be chartered to land at Central Farm.

Cottages and campsites near San Ignacio

In the area around San Ignacio there are a number of ranches offering **cottage-style accommodation** and organised trips. On the whole their standards are very high and they cater to big-spending Americans who come here after a week on the reef; a phenomenon known as a "surf and turf holiday". Prices usually start at around BZ$100 a day, but if you can afford it then your every need will be looked after. They're often booked up in the peak season (between Christmas and Easter) but can offer reduced prices in the rainy season (if they're open). If you're booked in they'll send someone to pick you up; if not you may have to take a taxi as none (apart from *Nabitunich*) are near the main road. Most offer horse-riding, birdwatching, canoeing, delicious home-made food and various trips in the surrounding area.

The cheapest and closest of them is *Las Casitas* (☎2506; BZ$38 double; meals BZ$8) at Branch Mouth (see below), within walking distance of San Ignacio. *Maya Mountain Lodge* (☎2162; around BZ$150 double), along the Cristo Rey road from Santa Elena, bills itself as an "educational field station" and offers comfortable cabanas and a fine reference library. *Windy Hill Cottages* (☎2017/2055), west of San Ignacio at Graceland Ranch, is one of the newest. They have a pool and offer horse-riding, a nature trail and canoeing on the Mopan River. Down a long track on the right from the road and across the Mopan River is *El Indio Perdido* (contact through *Eva's* or on ☎2188). Run by a lovely European woman, Collette Gross, this is a wonderfully relaxing location, surrounded by rich farmland and jungle and offering a chance to kayak or raft down the clear, jade-green river. The cabins are beautifully furnished and the food is superb.

Further along is the turning for *Chaa Creek Cottages*, *Duploys* and *Ix Chel Farm*. *Chaa Creek* (☎2037) has a great reputation and is very luxurious but is also one of the most expensive of all: the cottages are delightful, high above the river, surrounded by jungle. Next door is *Ix Chel Farm* (contact on ☎2188), named after the Maya goddess of medicine. Here Drs. Greg Shropshire and Rosita Arvigo study the plants of the tropical forest for their medicinal uses. There is accommodation available and seminars are held in natural healing and healthy living. *Duploys*, further along, is again very expensive.

Opposite the *Chaa Creek* turning is *Nabitunich* (☎2061), beautifully situated below the ruins of Xunantunich, and run by Rudi and Margaret Juan, two of the friendliest people in Belize. *Nabitunich* is just a short walk from the highway and out of high season offers good accommodation within the reach of backpackers. Margaret, a nurse originally from Lancashire, plans to open a clinic for local people when funds permit.

If you want to **camp**, the *Jungleview Campground*, a few kilometres upriver from San Ignacio, used to be recommended but is now rather run-down and not really worth the BZ$15 they charge. Robert Huether, of the *Front Street Guest House* in Belize City, plans to build a campsite and some cabanas further upstream at Black Rock: check in Belize City or San Ignacio if anything has come of this. Meanwhile, to get to *Jungleview* by road, walk over the suspension bridge and along the road until you come to a sign for the *Maya Mountain Lodge*. Follow the sign and walk on past the lodge for another two kilometres.

Trips from San Ignacio

San Ignacio's best feature is its location. The river and the surrounding countryside, with its hills, farms, streams and forest, are equally inviting, and there are many ways to enjoy them – on foot, by boat or even on horseback. Perhaps the easiest introduction is the twenty-minute walk to **Branch Mouth**, where the Macal and Mopan rivers merge peacefully to form the Belize River. The track leads north from the football field, past rich farmland, with thick vegetation, tropical flowers and butterflies on either side. Some of the fields you pass belong to *Marathon Tropical Farms*, whose owner, Robert Gougler, allows interested visitors to have a look at the heliconias, flowering ginger and other tropical plants being grown for export: ask permission first. At the confluence of the rivers is a huge tree, with branches arching over the jade water. A rusting iron mooring ring in the trunk is a reminder of the past importance of river transport; now there are swallows skimming the surface, flocks of parrots flying overhead and scores of tiny fish in the water.

At the relatively inexpensive resort of *Las Casitas*, across the water, you can hire horses for BZ$5 per hour, take guided jungle hikes, or rent a canoe. The village of BULLET TREE FALLS is a walk or short ride away – from here you can visit the ruins of **Pilar**, one of Belize's largest Classic Maya centres. The site is little excavated but contains at least fifteen plazas with palaces, stepped platforms and a ball court. An unusual feature is a low wall running west, probably into Guatemala.

If the idea of a lengthy **canoe trip** appeals, *Float Belize* will rent canoes for a leisurely, week-long float down to Belize City, camping on the way. Trips of any duration can be arranged and naturally it's less expensive if you travel in a group. Prices start at around BZ$36 a day, or BZ$70 for an overnight trip, with the Belize City voyage costing around BZ$450 for two people. To contact Scott Cast, who runs *Float Belize,* ask at *Eva's* or phone on ☎2188. If you want a slightly cheaper canoe trip, ask for Tony at *Eva's* bar. Tony or Clifford will paddle you expertly upriver for a whole day for only BZ$25, and you'll see far more wildlife under their guidance than you ever would alone. Pack a lunch or stop for a sandwich at the *Chaa Creek* resort.

This trip is the best way to experience the river, see the other places to stay and visit the **Panti Medicinal Trail**, the botanical version of the Belize Zoo. The tour takes you through the forest to seek out and explain the medicinal properties of many of the plants. It was named after Don Eligio Panti, a Maya bush doctor who passed on his skills to Dr Arvigo at *Ix Chel Farm*: she now acts as a guide and also sells home-made remedies, including natural insect repellent. The trail runs along the banks of the Macal River, where you can see a whole range of traditional medicinal plants, some of which are also used in modern medicine. The medical knowledge of the Maya was extensive, and the trail is fascinating: there are vines which provide fresh water like a tap; poisonwood, with oozing black sap and with the antidote always growing nearby; and the bark of the negrito tree, once sold for its weight in gold in Europe as a cure for dysentery. In addition you'll see specimens of the tropical hardwoods of the jungle which have been exploited for economic reasons. If you're with a group you can book a tour of the trail in advance through *Ix Chel Farm* (contact through ☎2188), but Dr Arvigo's services are expensive and it's perfectly easy to follow the trail on your own. Get there by river or by the track to *Chaa Creek* – at the entrance you pay a small fee (there's a box if no-one's around) and self-guiding handbooks are available to take along.

If you prefer to travel on **horseback** there are several places which hire out horses. *Las Casitas* is very good value, *Windy Hill Cottages* is ideally situated for a trip to Xunantunich, but their horses are pricey at BZ$60 for a half-day. They also hire out canoes at BZ$50 for a day. The *Jungleview Campground,* which also rents out horses, tends to be cheaper.

The Mountain Pine Ridge

To the south of San Ignacio the **Mountain Pine Ridge Forest Reserve** is a spectacular range of rolling hills and jagged peaks that runs parallel to the border with Guatemala. The peaks themselves are some of the oldest rocks in Central America, granite intrusions that have thrust up from below and are part of the bedrock that underlies the entire isthmus. In amongst this there are also some sections of limestone, riddled with superb caves, the most accessible of which are the **Rio Frio Caves**, near Augustine. For the most part the landscape is beautifully open, a mixture of grassland and pine forest, although in the warmth of the river valleys the vegetation is thicker, verging on the tropical, and eventually giving way to rainforest. Fertility is ensured by plentiful rainfall – rainfall that also renders the smooth, sandy roads impassable in the rainy season. The rains feed a number of small streams, most of which run off into the Macal and Belize rivers. One of the most scenic is the **Rio On**, rushing over cataracts and forming a gorge; a sight of tremendous natural beauty within view of the picnic shelter. On the northern side of the ridge are the **1000-Foot Falls**: actually over 1600 feet (488m) and the highest in Central America. The long, slender plume of water becomes lost in the valley below, giving rise to their other, more poetic name – **Hidden Valley Falls**.

The ridge is virtually uninhabited except for one or two tourist lodges and one small settlement, **AUGUSTINE**, site of the reserve headquarters. The whole area is perfect for **hiking**, but **camping** is allowed only at Augustine and at the Pincherichito Gate, near San Antonio, and officially you need permission from the forestry department in Belmopan (though in practice you'll almost certainly be allowed to if you ask nicely when you arrive). So, although it's fairly hard to explore this part of the country on your own, as you have to rely on hitching from place to place, it can be very rewarding. If you set off early you should be able to make it to the 1000-Foot Falls and back in a day, hitching some of the way and then walking the last few kilometres.

There are two **entrance roads** to the reserve, one from the village of **Georgeville**, on the Western highway, and the other from Santa Elena, along the Cristo Rey road and through SAN ANTONIO. Three kilometres east of San Antonio are the ruins of **Pacbitun**, a major ceremonial centre dating from 1000 BC. This is one of the oldest known Preclassic sites in Belize, and continued to flourish throughout the Classic Period. The hills all around contain Maya farming terraces and farmhouse mounds. Pacbitun, meaning "stones set in the earth", has at least 24 temple pyramids, a ball court and several raised causeways. To visit the site contact the owner of the land, Mr Tzul, at his house about 1km after leaving San Antonio.

Not far beyond San Antonio the two roads meet, and begin a steady climb towards the entrance to the reserve proper, about 18km from Georgeville. Here you have to enter your name in the visitors' book (to ensure there's no illegal camping), and there's information on the reserve as well as toilets and drinking water. Entering the reserve, the dense, leafy forest is quickly replaced by pine trees. After three kilometres a branch road heads off to the left, running for 7km (about an hour and a half's walk) to a point which overlooks the **1000-Foot Falls**.

Back on the main road, another 18km ride brings you to the **Rio On**, a gorgeous spot for a swim, where the river forms pools between huge granite boulders before plunging into a gorge. Another eight kilometres and you reach the reserve headquarters at Augustine, a few kilometres beyond which are the **Rio Frio Caves**, at the end of the road. A trail leads down through the forest from the parking area to the main cave, carved beneath a small hill. The Rio Frio flows right through the cave and out the other side of the hill, and you can follow its course through the entire length of the cave, bringing you out into the open at its other entrance. On either side of the river here are sandy beaches, while inside the cave, whose mouth is massive, you'll find an impressive collection of stalactites.

The ruins of Caracol

Beyond Augustine the main ridges of the Maya Mountains rise up to the south, while to the west is the Vaca plateau, a fantastically isolated wilderness. Here the ruins of **Caracol**, the largest known Maya site in Belize, were lost in the rainforest for several centuries until their rediscovery by *chicleros* in 1936. They were first systematically explored by A H Anderson in 1938: he named the site "Caracol" – Spanish for snail – because of the large numbers of snail shells found there. Other archaeologists visited and made

Modelled stucco mask found at Caracol

excavations in the 1950s but early reports took a long time to reach the public domain as many documents were destroyed by Hurricane Hattie in 1961. In 1978–9 Paul Healy of Trent University examined the agricultural terraces surrounding Caracol and a detailed report was finally published in 1981. In 1985 the first detailed, full-scale excavation of the site, the "Caracol Project", began under the auspices of Drs Arlen and Diane Chase of the University of Central Florida – it's expected to take at least ten years.

Caracol covers over three square kilometres, with at least 32 large structures and twelve smaller ones around five main plazas. The largest pyramid, **Canaa**, is the tallest in Belize at 42 metres, and several others are over twenty metres high. The dates on stelae and tombs suggest an extremely long occupation, with the population peaking at the height of the Classic Period, around 700 AD. Carvings on altars tell of war between Caracol and Tikal, with power over a huge area alternating between the two great cities. One altar gives a date of 562 AD for Caracol's victory over Tikal, a victory that set the seal on the city's rise to power: soon afterwards it embarked on a major building programme. Archaeological research has revealed some superb tombs, with lintels of iron-hard sapodilla wood supporting the entrances and painted texts decorating the walls. Sadly the site is so isolated that archaeologists can only work in the spring and summer months and in the past it has been badly looted while they were away. At the start of the 1985 season, for example, an advance party of archaeologists found smouldering fires, left by a team of looters who had barely left in time. Today the site is guarded throughout the year by a permanent team of caretakers and the British Army and Belize Defense Force make frequent patrolling visits.

Fifteen kilometres beyond Caracol is the vast **Chiquibul Cave System**, the longest cave system in Central America containing what is reputed to be the largest cave chamber in the western hemisphere. To explore the caves requires a properly organised expedition. The entire area is dotted with caves and sinkholes, which must have been known to the ancient Maya and perhaps used for ceremonies.

Emblem glyph from Caracol

Getting there

The cheapest way to explore the Mountain Pine Ridge is by **hitching** in from Georgeville, in which case you'll need to set off early and can't expect to get any further

A TRIP TO CARACOL

Starting at San Ignacio around 8am the route taken by Chris in the Unimog (see over) crosses the Hawksworth Bridge to Santa Elena then turns right onto the dirt road to Cristo Rey and San Antonio. The scenery is immediately riveting as you travel along the Macal River valley, through forest and rich farmland. Around San Antonio, a Mopan Maya village, are numerous mounds and temple platforms. In fact so plentiful are the ancient Maya remains in the fields that the whole area must have been a major centre of population.

After this the road heads into the Forest Reserve and at the gate you're signed in. The first real break comes at the Rio On where you have a welcome chance to cool off in the river. The part of the journey through the Pine Ridge is fascinating, with bromeliads and orchids growing in profusion on the pines and the track crossing clear, rushing creeks; but the best is yet to come. The Macal River is crossed again, this time at the low Guacamallo Bridge, only inches above the river. Now begins the ascent to the Vaca plateau, with thick rainforest on either side. Sitting in the vehicle you're viewing the forest at a height of about eight feet, enabling you to see above the underbrush, possibly catching a glimpse of the inhabitants of the forest. On my visit a couple of trees had fallen across the trail; it obviously hadn't been used by a vehicle for months. The winch on the Unimog pulled them to one side.

The first signs of a ruined city are tree-covered mounds in the forest, then suddenly the shining, impressive bulk of Canaa, the largest pyramid, looms over a cleared plaza. There are huts for archaeologists and workers here, and solar panels to provide electricity. The only other people were two caretakers, one of whom, Benjamin Pantí, was my guide.

Benjamin spends a great deal of his time at the site and so is truly an expert on Caracol and the surrounding forest. It was an amazing experience, virtually alone in this great abandoned city, and Benjamin was eager to show me around. He was genuinely upset as he showed me altars and stelae, deliberately broken by logging tractors driving over them in the 1930s. Beneath Canaa a series of looted tombs still have traces of the original painted glyphs on the walls. At the top of this freshly restored structure is a small plaza and an altar here revealed signs of a female ruler. The horizon is bounded by jungle-covered peaks, through which it's only three hours on foot to the Guatemalan border. Benjamin showed me the intact altar he discovered in the plaza as he was planting corn. This clearly depicts two bound captives with a row of glyphs above and between them and has been dated at 810 AD. One of the most awe-inspiring sights in this fantastic city is an immense ceiba tree, with enormous buttress roots twice as high as a man. The ceiba was sacred to the Maya and this magnificent specimen is at least 700 years old. Looking at it you cannot help but wonder at the nature of the relationship between the Maya and their forest. The reservoir, built by the Maya, is still in use when the archaeologists are in residence and the camp was being prepared for their return in February.

The site is a **Natural Monument Reserve**, a haven for wildlife as well as archaeologists. There were beautiful ocellated turkeys feeding in the plazas and at night tapirs dine on the succulent shoots growing on cleared areas.

The trip back is largely in the dark, offering a chance to see the night creatures, most of which seem unconcerned by the bright headlights. Of course it is difficult to identify these creatures and this promotes discussion of what it was someone saw. By the time you reach San Ignacio you're aware of having experienced a fascinating slice of Belizean natural history, as well as being extremely tired.

Peter Eltringham

than 1000-Foot Falls before time runs out and you have to head for home. Trucks also travel to Augustine, from where you can walk to the Rio Frio caves, and where it's possible to camp. Unless you have your own vehicle the next best option is a tour by **taxi**. If you can muster three or four people it'll cost around BZ$175 to hire a taxi for the day, which will give you time to see 1000-Foot Falls, the Rio On and the Rio Frio caves. It's also possible to **hike** in, of course: in her book, *Backpacking in Mexico and Central America*, Hilary Bradt describes in detail a hike visiting 1000-Foot Falls. Plans are now advanced for a tourist lodge with six cabins near the waterfall, to be called *Hidden Valley Inn*.

If your heart's set on seeing **Caracol** you'll need to embark on a substantial expedition. A sturdy, high-clearance four-wheel drive vehicle will manage the forest tracks in the dry season and if archaeologists are working on the site the road will normally be clear. Alternatively you can go to Caracol on horseback; several lodges in the area offer a four-day trip into the mountains, taking in Caracol. In late 1989, however, a surprisingly comfortable vehicle began a new service to Caracol, making this amazing site much more accessible. This vehicle is a Daimler-Benz Unimog driven by its friendly, knowledgeable owner Chris Heckert. Chris, originally from Germany, shipped the Unimog to Florida and drove it down to Belize. The trip to Caracol costs BZ$100 per person, takes at least ten hours and offers a chance to see Maya villages, the Pine Ridge, Rio On, tropical rainforest and of course Caracol itself. Contact Chris at *Eva's* bar in San Ignacio, and see the account on p.305 for more detail.

Succotz and the ruins of Xunantunich

Back on the Western highway, the village of **SAN JOSE SUCCOTZ** lies about 10km west of San Ignacio, right beside the Mopan River just before Benque Viejo. It's a very traditional village in many ways, inhabited largely by Maya Indians, who celebrate fiestas here on March 19 and May 3. Under colonial administration the Indians of Succotz sided with the British, a stance which angered other Indian groups, such as the Icaiche, who burnt it to the ground in 1867. Today it's pretty quiet, and the main reason to visit outside fiesta times is to get to the ruins of **Xunantunich** (pronounced Shun-an-tun-ich), "the Stone Maiden", a Classic Period ceremonial centre.

The site was explored in the 1890s by Dr Thomas Gann, a British medical officer, and in 1904 Teobalt Maler of the Peabody Museum took photographs and made a plan of the largest structure, A–6, commonly known as **El Castillo**. Gann returned in 1924 and excavated large numbers of burial goods and removed the

carved glyphs of Altar 1, the whereabouts of which are now unknown. The British archaeologist J Eric S Thompson excavated a residential group in 1938, unearthing pottery, obsidian, jade, a spindle, seashells, stingray spines and hammers. Later excavations have revealed signs of an earthquake in about 900 AD, which apparently caused the city to be abandoned. Based on this evidence some archaeologists have suggested earthquakes as the main cause of the downfall of the lowland Maya civilisation (which happened around that time), although there's little

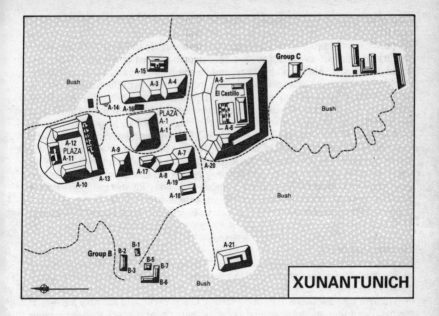

corroboration from other sites. However it does seem likely that the destruction put an end to building at Xunantunich, as the last temple dates from 849 AD.

To get to the site from Succotz you have to cross the river on the old chain ferry, which operates from 8am to 5pm with a break for lunch around midday. From the bank a track leads through the forest for a couple of kilometres to the ruins, where you pay the entrance fee of BZ$3. **The site** itself is built on top of an artificially flattened hill and includes five plazas in all, although the remaining structures are grouped around just three of them. The track brings you out into plaza A–2, with large structures on three sides. Plaza A–3, to the right, is almost completely enclosed by a low, acropolis-like building, and plaza A–1, to the left, is dominated by El Castillo, the city's largest building. This massive pyramid rises to a height of over forty metres and until recently was celebrated as Belize's tallest building, though Canaa at Caracol is now known to be taller. As so often the building is layered, with later versions built on top of earlier ones. It was once ringed by a decorative stucco frieze carved with abstract designs, human faces and jaguar heads: this has been extensively restored. On your way to El Castillo take a look at the stelae, now beneath thatched covers, that once stood at the base of the temple. The climb up El Castillo can be terrifying, but the views from the top are superb, with the forest stretching out all around and the rest of the ancient city mapped out beneath you.

If you want to carry on exploring Maya sites, the ruins of **Actuncan** are a couple of kilometres to the north. **Accommodation** in Succotz is provided by the *Rancho Los Amigos* (☎093/2261), a couple of kilometres from the road, down a signed track. Here an American couple, Edward and Virginia Jenkins, have cabins for BZ$25, with vegetarian meals if required.

Benque Viejo and the border

The final town before the Guatemalan border is **BENQUE VIEJO DEL CARMEN**, just half an hour from San Ignacio, where Guatemala and Belize are mixed in almost equal proportions and Spanish is certainly the dominant language. It's a quiet little place with little to offer the passing traveller, but if you're heading through then you may end up here for the night. The *Hospedaje Roxy*, 70 St Joseph Street, is easily the cheapest **hotel** in town, at only BZ$6, but is decidedly sleazy: if you're on a tight budget I'd recommend going over the border to **MELCHOR DE MENCOS**, where you'll find the same standard for much less. The *Okis Hotel*, on George Street (BZ$10), is a better bet, or the *Maya Hotel*, 11 George Street, is also reasonable at BZ$15 for a regular room, BZ$25 for the luxury of a private bathroom. There are only two **restaurants** in Benque: the *Riverside*, on George Street, and the canteen-style *Okis Restaurant*. For evening entertainment at weekends, films are shown at the *Teatro Impala*.

The **bus terminal** is on George Street, with departures for Belize City hourly from 4am to 11am.

Crossing the border

The border itself is a little under 2km beyond Benque Viejo. Some **buses** continue all the way to the Belizean immigration post, but if yours doesn't there are plenty of taxis that provide a shuttle service for a few dollars. The border is open from 6am to midnight but there might be a charge late at night, and possibly a siesta in the middle of the day, from around noon to 2pm. There is no charge for leaving Belize, but Guatemala charges a Q3 entry (and exit) tax. Guatemalan **tourist cards** (which should be free but rarely are) and even visas (US$10) can be issued here. If you do need a visa, however, you'd be very unwise to leave it this late: although the immigration staff will generally give you a permit to travel to Tikal or to visit the market in Melchor de Mencos, just over the bridge, there's no guarantee. If you get refused the nearest Guatemalan consulate is in Chetumal, Mexico. There are a couple of restaurants and cantinas at the border; they're not up to much but then nor are the ones in Melchor itself. Just over the bridge is a gift shop, *Nina Kaufman*, where visitors can buy Guatemalan textiles and other souvenirs – the best item, though, is the tourist map of Guatemala, which is virtually unobtainable in Belize. Buses to **Flores** (see p.212) leave from Melchor.

travel details

Buses

Batty, 54 East Collet Canal, Belize City (☎72025), run a service from **Belize City to San Ignacio** (2hr 30min) via Belmopan, the 6.30am bus goes to the border; those at 8am, 9am and 10am terminate at San Ignacio.

Novelo, 19 West Collet Canal, Belize City (☎77372), have buses from **Belize City to Benque Viejo** hourly from 11am to 6pm.

From the border to Belize City, *Novelo* buses run from Benque Viejo hourly from 4am to 11am. *Batty* have a 1pm service from the border and then departures from San Ignacio at 1pm, 2pm, 3pm and 4pm.

All of the above buses pass through **Belmopan** (1hr 30min from Belize City, 1hr from San Ignacio), as do those heading to or from **Dangriga** in the south (five a day; 1hr 30min). There are also five buses a day (*Shaws*) directly **between Belmopan and San Ignacio**.

CHAPTER ELEVEN

THE SOUTH

To the south of Belmopan Belize is at its wildest. Here the central area is dominated by the Maya Mountains, which slope down towards the coast through a series of forested ridges amongst which tracts of the dense, towering **rainforest** survive virtually untouched by the logging industry. It includes superb mature forest, rich in wildlife, although many of the exposed hillsides were swept clean by Hurricane Hattie in 1961. The **coastal strip** is a

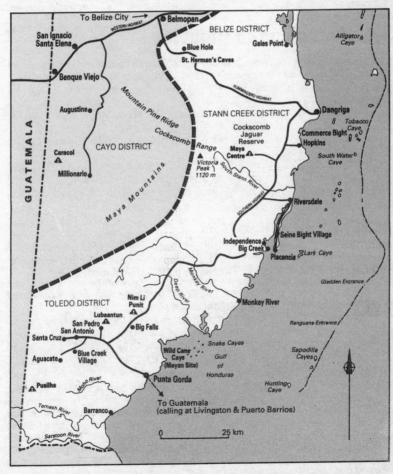

narrow band of savannah and swamp, hemmed in by the sea and the mountains, while the shoreline is a mixture of mangrove swamps and sandy bays.

The largest town in the south is **Dangriga**, which has much in common with Belize City and is the focus for the **Garifuna** people, descendants of the Caribs. Heading south from Dangriga you pass the small seashore settlements of **Hopkins** and **Placencia**, two idyllic Caribbean fishing villages. Placencia is starting to develop a tourist trade and can offer more in the way of facilities, including reef trips, while Hopkins remains pretty remote. In the mountains behind is the **Cockscomb Wildlife Sanctuary**, a reserve designed to protect the area's sizeable jaguar population and a good place to explore the forest – but don't count on seeing a jaguar. The Southern highway comes to an end in **Punta Gorda**, a final outpost, from where you can head south to Guatemala, or visit Maya villages and ruins in the southern foothills of the Maya Mountains.

The Hummingbird Highway

The **Hummingbird Highway**, heading south from Belmopan to Dangriga, is an accurate introduction to the rigours of travel in southern Belize. Despite its fancy name it's a poorly surfaced, severely pot-holed road. The scenery, though, is considerable compensation for any hardship, as the road heads steadily uphill through lush forest, with the eastern slopes of the **Maya Mountains**, coated in greenery, rising to the right. Most of this is untouched, but here and there Salvadorean or Guatemalan refugees have hacked down a swathe of jungle to plant *milpas* of maize and beans.

The hills you pass form part of a ridge of limestone mountains that's riddled with underground rivers and caves. About 19km out of Belmopan the road crosses the **Caves Branch River**: the upper reaches of this valley hold some of Belize's finest caves.

The Blue Hole and St Herman's Cave

A few kilometres further on is the **Blue Hole**, an excellent spot for a swim and the start of a path to St Herman's Cave. The hole is in fact a short stretch of river that emerges from its underground course to flow on the surface for about fifty metres before disappearing beneath another rock face. Its turquoise waters, cool and fresh, are surrounded by dense forest, and overhung with vines, mosses and ferns: there's no better place for a refreshing dip.

St Herman's Cave is about half an hour away, on the other side of the hill above the pool. The walk between the two (the trail starts from the highway, just beside the entrance to the Blue Hole) takes you along a series of steep and sweaty trails, and over wooden staircases that climb the ridge before dropping down on the other side. Once you're over the ridge you'll find the cave to your left, at the base of a hill, its entrance squashed beneath a vast, dripping rock face. To get back to the road you can either return along the same route, and cool off at the Blue Hole, or simply follow the track out of the valley, which brings you to the highway in about ten minutes.

To get to the Blue Hole take any bus travelling between Dangriga and Belmopan, and ask the driver to drop you; but make sure there'll be another one along in a while as there's nowhere to stay in the area. If you're driving then be warned that cars left unattended at the Blue Hole are sometimes tampered with.

On towards Dangriga

Beyond the Blue Hole the Hummingbird highway runs past the *Hummingbird Hershey* factory, where locally grown cacao is transformed into sweets for the American market – the legendary *Hershey Bars*. Bouncing on between the pot-holes, the road eventually crosses a low pass, beyond which is the *Over The Top Cool Spot*, a favourite watering hole that marks the start of the descent. Two miles further on you'll come to *Palacio's Place*, a new roadside bar with excellent swimming facilities.

This point also marks the start of the **Stann Creek valley**, which is the centre of the Belizean citrus fruit industry. Bananas were the first crop to be grown here, and by 1891 half a million stems were being exported through Stann Creek (now Dangriga) every year. However the banana boom came to an abrupt end in 1906, when disease destroyed the crop, and afterwards the government set out to foster the growth of citrus fruits instead. Between 1908 and 1937 the valley was even served by a small railway, and by 1945 the citrus industry was well established.

Today it accounts for about ten percent of the country's exports, and is heralded as one of the nation's great success stories, although for the largely Guatemalan labour force, housed in rows of scruffy huts, conditions are little better than on the oppressive coffee *fincas* at home. The presence of tropical parasites, such as the leaf-eating ant, has forced the planters to resort to powerful insecticides, including DDT. Two giant pulping plants beside the road produce concentrate for export.

Dangriga

The Hummingbird highway comes to an end at MIDDLESEX and continues as the Stann Creek Valley Road. About seven miles before Dangriga the Southern highway to Punta Gorda turns off. The spot is marked by a dilapidated bus stop, and from here the tarmac returns for the last few kilometres into **DANGRIGA** (formerly known as Stann Creek), whose population of around 10,000 makes it the largest town in southern Belize. The town's businesses are gradually waking up to the increasing role played by tourism and there's recently been a minor hotel-building boom along the dusty main street. This is partly due to the local people wanting their share of the cake and partly to Dangriga's fortunate position as a base for visiting the offshore islands and the mountains inland.

A bustling but decaying strip of wooden houses that runs along behind the beach, the town is cut in two by the waters of the North Stann Creek, which empties into the sea right through the middle. In many ways it resembles a much smaller version of Belize City, with less of the sleaze, though at the far end of town *The Harlem Club* establishes a connection which is hard to deny. Culturally Dangriga serves as the centre of the **Garifuna**, one of the country's largest ethnic minorities, who are of mixed Caribbean and African descent.

The Garifuna

The Garifuna trace their history back to the island of **St Vincent**, one of the Windward Islands in the eastern Caribbean. At the time of Columbus's discovery of the Americas the islands of the Lesser Antilles had recently been inhabited by Indians from the South American mainland, who had subdued their previous inhabitants, the Arawaks. They called themselves *Kalipuna*, but the Spanish called them *Caribs*, their word for cannibal. The natives the Europeans encountered were descendants of Carib men and Arawak women.

In the early seventeenth century Britain and France vied for control of the islands, fighting each other and the Caribs. The admixture of African blood came in 1635 when two Spanish ships, carrying slaves from Nigeria to their colonies in America, were wrecked off St Vincent and the survivors took refuge on the island. At first there was conflict between the Indians and the Blacks, but the Caribs had been weakened by wars and disease and eventually the predominant race was black, with some Indian blood. They were known as the **Black Caribs**.

For most of the seventeenth and eighteenth centuries St Vincent was nominally under British control but in practice in possession of the Caribs. Britain attempted to gain full control of St Vincent in 1763 but was driven off by the Caribs, with French assistance. Another attempt twenty years later was more successful, and in 1783 the British imposed a treaty on the Caribs, allowing them over half the island: this was never accepted by the Caribs, however, who continued to defy British rule. This defiance led to frequent battles, in which the French consistently lent their support to the Caribs. The last serious attempt by the Caribs to establish their independence took place in 1795, when both sides suffered horrendous casualties. The Caribs lost their leader, Chief Joseph Chatoyer, and on June 10, 1796, after a year of bitter fighting, the French and Caribs surrendered to the British.

The colonial authorities could not allow a free black society to survive amongst slave-owning European settlers so it was decided to deport the Carib population. They were hunted down, their homes (and in the process their culture) destroyed, and hundreds died of starvation and disease. The survivors, 4300 Black Caribs and 100 Yellow Caribs, were transported to the nearby island of Balliceaux. In six months over half of them had died, many of yellow fever. On March 3, 1797, the remaining survivors were loaded aboard ships and sent to **Roatan**, one of the Bay Islands, off the coast of Honduras. One of the ships was captured by the Spanish and taken to Trujillo, on the mainland, and barely 2000 Caribs lived to make the landing on Roatan, where the British abandoned them.

Perhaps in response to pleas for help from the Caribs, who continued to die on Roatan, the Spanish Commandante of Trujillo arrived and took possession of the island, shipping the 1700 survivors to Trujillo where they were in demand as labourers. The Spanish had never made a success of agriculture here and the arrival of the Caribs, who were proficient at growing crops, benefited the colony considerably. The boys were conscripted and the Carib men became known as good soldiers and mercenaries. Soon they began to move to other areas along the coast, and in 1802 150 of them were brought as wood-cutting labourers to work in Stann Creek and Punta Gorda. Their intimate knowledge of the rivers and coast also made them expert smugglers, evading Spanish laws forbidding trade with the British in Belize. Their military skills were even more useful and by 1819 a Carib colonel was commander of the garrison at San Felipe in Guatemala, while in 1820 two Carib soldiers received (posthumous) awards from the king of Spain for their bravery in the defence of Trujillo.

Throughout the early years of the **nineteenth century** small numbers of Caribs moved up the coast to Belize, and although in 1811 Superintendent Barrow of Belize ordered the expulsion of all Caribs it had little effect: when European settlers arrived in Stann Creek in 1823 Caribs were already there and were hired to clear land. The largest single migration to Belize took place in 1832 when vast numbers fled from Honduras, by then part of the Central American Republic, after they had supported the wrong side in a failed revolution to overthrow the Republican government. It is this arrival which is today celebrated as Garifuna Settlement Day, though it seems likely many arrived both before and after.

In 1825 the first Methodist missionaries arrived in Belize, and by 1828 they had begun to visit Stann Creek, or "Carib Town" as the settlers knew it. They were outraged to discover a bizarre mix of Catholicism, ancestor worship and polygamy, in which the main form of worship was "devil dancing", but they had little success in their struggle to Christianise the Caribs beyond the adoption of various new rituals: when John Lloyd Stephens visited Punta Gorda in 1839 the women were eager to have their children baptised and he even became a godfather.

By the start of this century the Caribs or Garifuna were well established in the Stann Creek area, with the women employed in bagging and stacking cohune nuts and the men working in agriculture. Throughout the nineteenth and twentieth centuries the Garifuna travelled widely in search of work. To start with they confined themselves to Central America (where they can still be found all along the Caribbean coast from Honduras to Mexico), but in World War II Caribs manned both British and US merchant ships. Since then trips to the States have become an important part of the local economy and there are small Garifuna communities in New York, New Orleans, Los Angeles and even in London.

Since the early 1980s Garifuna culture has undergone something of a revival, and as a part of this movement the town was renamed Dangriga, a Garifuna word meaning "standing waters". The most important day in the Garifuna calendar is November 19, **Garifuna Settlement Day**, which in Dangriga is a day of wild celebration, when the town erupts with music, dance, drink and dope. A group of local people re-enact the arrival from Roatan, landing on the beach in dugout canoes. Christmas and New Year are also celebrated in true Garifuna style and the town is home to some of the country's most popular artists, including painters, drum makers, the Waribagabaga Dancers and the Turtle Shell Band.

The Town

Dangriga is not the most exciting of places, and although the atmosphere is enjoyably laid-back there's really not a lot to do during the day: people come here mainly because it's the best centre for visiting south-central Belize, the cayes offshore and the jaguar reserve inland. There isn't much to see as you walk around the town but if you're staying overnight it's worth calling in at *P J's Gift Shop*, 3 Lemon Street (you'll see the sign on Commerce Street), where there's a BTIA **tourist information** centre, and you can get up to date information about hotels while you're looking at the books, T-shirts and crafts on display. Another interesting shop is the *Dangriga Art Centre*, south of the bridge on St Vincent Street, with locally made baskets and drums and good tapes of Garifuna music.

If you arrive by **bus** from Belize City you'll be dropped on the main street just by the bridge. The *Z-Line* office, where they sell tickets and answer questions about overdue buses, is in *The Tropic Zone Club*. Continuing south, there are buses from Dangriga to Punta Gorda at 3pm and 4.30pm, and from Dangriga to Independence at 3.30pm. The bus to Placencia leaves from outside the *Hub* restaurant at 2.30pm on Monday, Wednesday, Friday and Saturday, calling at the turn-offs for Hopkins, Sittee River and Maya Centre. Departures to Belize City are at 5am, 6am, 9am and 10am.

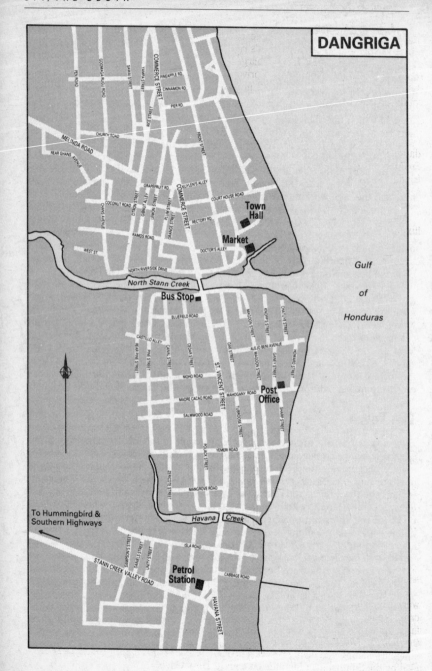

DANGRIGA

PEN ROAD

GODMALA RUGU ROAD

SIWA STREET

TAMPA STREET

COMMERCE STREET

PINEAPPLE RD.

CINNAMON RD.

PIER RD.

MELINDA ROAD

CHURCH ROAD

FRONT STREET

BEAR GHANS AVENUE

GRAPEFRUIT RD.

CRUYLEN'S ALLEY

COURT HOUSE ROAD

Town Hall

CHANG AVENUE

COCONUT ROAD

CITRON STREET

DONUT ALLEY

HONEY

PLUM STREET

LIME STREET

JELLY STREET

COMMERCE STREET

RECTORY RD.

Market

RAMOS ROAD

WEST ST.

DOCTOR'S ALLEY

NORTH RIVERSIDE DRIVE

North Stann Creek

Bus Stop

BLUEFIELD ROAD

CASTILLO ALLEY

REAR PINE STREET

PINE STREET

CANAL STREET

CEDAR STREET

ST. VINCENT STREET

OAK STREET

MAGOON STREET

KNOPPS STREET

CHATUYE STREET

ALEJO BENI AVENUE

MAGOON STREET

LANET STREET

HOWARD STREET

MOHO ROAD

MADRE CACAO ROAD

MAHOGANY ROAD

Post Office

SALMWOOD ROAD

TUBROOSE STREET

SHARP STREET

POLLACK STREET

YEMERI ROAD

ZERICOTE STREET

MANGROVE ROAD

Gulf

of

Honduras

To Hummingbird & Southern Highways

Havana *Creek*

SAMPSON'S STREET

DANE'S STREET

UNITY STREET

ISLA ROAD

STANN CREEK VALLEY ROAD

Petrol Station

CABBAGE ROAD

HAVANA STREET

The *Riverside Hotel*, with simple rooms for BZ$15, is the most convenient place to stay for new arrivals, as it's right beside the bridge. On the other side of the river, the *Hub Guest House* charges the same for a slightly better standard room, or BZ$25 for a room with a private bathroom. Other inexpensive hotels on the main street (Commerce Street north of the bridge, St Vincent Street to the south) are the *Tropical Hotel* and the *Chameleon* at around BZ$12. Cheaper still is the *Caialina*, 37 Cedar Street, at only BZ$7.50 single. The *Rio Mar Hotel*, 1 Waight Street (☎22201; BZ$20 single, BZ$30 double), is a personal favourite, right by the sea at the river mouth. It's also the place to find out about accommodation on Tobacco Caye; ask the owner Maurice Stanley. Just before this is *Sophie's*, on Chatuye Street, a new hotel run by Sophie herself, an exuberantly friendly Belizean recently returned from the United States. The balcony has fine sea and river views and downstairs is a good local restaurant, serving Creole and Garifuna food.

Another new hotel is the *Bonefish*, 15 Mahogany Road (☎22165). This is in the luxury category with cable TV, hot water, carpeting and air conditioning. Also in the luxury range is the *Pelican Beach Hotel* (☎22044), on the northern side of town, which charges BZ$75 for a single. The hotel also has accommodation on South Water Caye, about ten kilometres offshore, where they charge the same rates. Both these hotels can arrange fishing **tours** and inland trips.

If you're in search of a reasonably priced **meal** try *Burger King*, which is not what you might think and does good rice, chicken, fruit juices, fish and conch soup, a Garifuna delicacy. There's also a restaurant in the *Hub Guest House*, plus several good Chinese restaurants on the main street. Also worth trying are *Le Elegante*, 8 Ramos Road, and the *Sea Flame* on Commerce Street. The *Sea Flame* also has reasonable rooms and the owners plan an offshore resort hotel.

There are two **banks**, *Barclays* and *The Bank of Nova Scotia*, both on the main street. The **post office** is on Caney Street, in the southern half of town, a block back from the sea. The **market** is by the river, but it's very small – for other groceries try the *Southern Pride* supermarket, by *Barclays Bank*. Also here is a payphone and the BTL office.

There's no shortage of **bars**, though some, particularly those calling themselves clubs, like *The Kennedy Club*, *The Culture Club* and the *Harlem Club*, are particularly dubious-looking, both inside and out.

Maya Airways have flights from Belize City to Dangriga at 8am, 11am and 2pm, which go on to Independence and Punta Gorda. Flights from Dangriga to Belize City leave at 10am, 1pm and 5pm, and you can buy tickets from the *Pelican Beach Hotel* or from the shop on the main street where you see a *Maya Airways* sign. *Tropic Air* also operate scheduled flights to Dangriga.

Offshore

About twenty kilometres off Dangriga is the **Tobacco Reef**, a superb section of the barrier reef with some small cayes scattered along its length. These cayes were originally farmed by the first Puritan settlers and are named after their main crop. Some of them now have tourist accommodation. **South Water Caye** is fairly upmarket and has accommodation owned by *The Pelican Beach Hotel* and the *Bonefish Hotel*. Also on South Water Caye is *Blue Marlin Lodge* (☎22296), an expensive fishing and diving resort. The *Pelican Beach* also has a research station used by the Smithsonian Institute on **Carrie Bow Caye**.

Tobacco Caye, ideally situated right in the middle of the reef, has several options. There's a house that sleeps six owned by Roland Jackson (about BZ$50) and some small cabins owned by Elwood Fairweather (BZ$25), and by the time you read this *Island Camps* should have opened too (BZ$20 to camp, BZ$25 for transport); for more information check with Mark Bradley or Maurice Stanley at the *Rio Mar Hotel* in Dangriga. Whichever you choose you'll find yourself on a remote Caribbean island with lobster fishermen as your neighbours, and surrounded by a perfect stretch of reef, ideal for fishing, snorkelling and diving.

To get to Tobacco Caye you can ask around on the river in Dangriga, where someone will know someone who's heading that way, but for more reliable information check at the *Rio Mar*. A ride out there (40min) costs around BZ$25.

The Southern Highway

To the south of Dangriga the country becomes more mountainous, with such development as there is restricted to the coastal lowlands. The road deteriorates and the towns and villages are increasingly isolated. Setting off in this direction is the Southern highway, 160km of pot-holed and deeply rutted road. Unlike the Hummingbird highway this stretch has never had the honour of tarmac, though the road surface is frequently graded and in the last few years a number of bridges have been built by a British company, high above the water level. It should be passable except during the very worst rainstorms. For the entire distance the road is set back from the coast, running beneath the peaks of the Maya Mountains, often passing through pine forest and vast banana estates. There are several branch roads leading off to idyllic coastal villages, the best of which are **Hopkins** and **Placencia**. From the village of **Maya Centre** another road leads west, into the Cockscomb basin and to the **Jaguar Preserve**.

Just before the highway comes to an end in **Punta Gorda** another road leads west into the southern foothills of the Maya Mountains. Here are some delightful Maya villages with many ruins in the surrounding hills. Punta Gorda is the southernmost town in Belize, from where the only onward transport is a twice-weekly ferry service to **Livingston** in Guatemala.

Hopkins

HOPKINS, a twenty-minute boat ride south of Dangriga, has to be one of the most relaxing destinations in Belize. The village, stretching for over a kilometre along a shallow, gently curving bay, is home to around 1000 Garifuna people. They make a living from small-scale farming and fishing, often paddling dugout canoes to pull up fish traps, or using baited handlines. Their houses, built closely together, are small wooden structures, thickly shaded by palm trees and usually raised on stilts to allow air to circulate, though there are still many built on the simple Maya design of poles and a thatched roof. The views from the sea, looking back towards the village, with the high ridges of the Maya Mountains in the background, are breathtakingly beautiful. All of the villagers, and the children in particular, are exuberantly friendly and you'll be made to feel welcome. They're also proud of their traditions, and celebrate Garifuna Settlement Day, November 19, enthusiastically: singing, dancing and above all beating the drums, which are an integral part of their culture, in a orgy of rhythm.

Not on the usual tourist circuit, Hopkins sees few visitors and if you visit you have to be prepared to live in almost a different age. At the moment the village offers little in the way of **accommodation**. *Hopkins Paradise*, at the junction of the road leading to the Southern highway, is a collection of cabanas with ambitious names such as *Manhattan* and *Brooklyn*, built over a drained swamp. It doesn't really live up to its name, although the owner, Rosita Estrada, has some choice land at the northern end of Hopkins, and plans to develop tourist bungalows there. At the south end, on the beach, is *Sandy Beach Lodge* (☎2033), which has half a dozen basic rooms for BZ$25 double. Run by Alberta Casimiro and other women of Hopkins, this is the only women's co-operative in Belize and looks set for a promising future. An alternative is to ask if anyone has a house or a spare room to rent, or to **camp**. The latter will attract hordes of smiling, giggling children, fascinated by this novel entertainment.

There are no proper **restaurants** in Hopkins, though the hotels will make arrangements for meals; if you ask around you'll be shown houses where you can eat delicious Garifuna food if you book in advance. It's a good idea to buy some supplies in Dangriga and ask if anyone will let you cook them; you'll be invited to join in the life of a family and may find a cheap house to rent. A few small shops offer basic supplies and there's a post office.

The village is still without electricity, although there are telephones, so a **flashlight** is essential. The few **bars** are lit by generators on special occasions, but usually illumination is provided by candles or kerosene lamps. There's no piped water either, so you should be careful about its use (both from a conservation and a health point of view): drinking water is saved in rain barrels; water for washing is dredged up from wells, as you can tell by its appearance. The main drawbacks to the peace of Hopkins are the crowing of the roosters and the howling of the dogs, both of which conspire to keep the nights short. There must be at least one dog for every person and none appear to be owned or cared for, they just exist as best they can – and continually reproduce.

Getting there

There's a **truck** from Dangriga to Hopkins most days at 3pm (check on the main street or by the bridge in Dangriga) and Mr Nunez has a truck leaving Hopkins for Dangriga at 6.30am on Mondays, Wednesdays and Fridays, returning from Dangriga at 11am. The best and quickest way to arrive in Hopkins, however, is by boat. Ask around where the boats tie up by the bridge if anyone from Hopkins is in town – they'll probably be willing to give you a lift back with them and possibly even arrange accommodation as well.

The Cockscomb Basin Jaguar Preserve

The jagged peaks of the **Maya Mountains** rise to the west of the Southern highway, their lower slopes covered in dense rainforest. The tallest of them are the summits of the Cockscomb range, which rises to 1120 metres at Victoria Peak, the highest mountain in Belize*. Beneath the ridges is a sweeping bowl which was declared a wildlife sanctuary in 1986 and is today the **Cockscomb Basin**

*The very latest maps show a new mountain, Elizabeth Peak, as being 51m higher, though this is not yet officially recognised. It's in an inaccessible part of the far south of the Maya Mountains, beyond Caracol.

Jaguar Preserve. A rough track connects the reserve with the main highway, branching off at the village of MAYA CENTRE. Heading towards the reserve it runs through towering forest, fording a couple of fresh, clear streams before it crosses the Cabbage Hall Gap and drops into the Cockscomb basin. Any **bus** heading between Dangriga and Punta Gorda, Placencia or Independence will pass Maya Centre.

The reserve itself covers 390 square kilometres and was chosen because of concern about its large jaguar population. The area was inhabited in Maya times, and the ruins of **Chucil Balam**, a small Classic Period ceremonial centre, still lie hidden in the forest. It was also exploited by the mahogany loggers, and the names of their abandoned camps, such as "Sale si se puede" (leave if you can) and "Go to Hell Camp", illustrate how they felt about life in the forest. More recently many of the larger trees were brought down by Hurricane Hattie in 1961, and the basin now includes a mixture of mature trees and dense secondary forest, with a canopy height of between fifteen and fifty metres. Technically it's a tropical moist forest, with an annual rainfall of 180 inches which feeds a complex network of streams and rivers, all of which eventually run into the Swasey River and the South Stann Creek.

The forest is home to a sizeable percentage of Belize's **plant and animal species**. Among the mammals are tapir, otter, coati, deer, anteater, armadillo and of course jaguar. Over 290 species of bird have also been recorded so far, including the endangered scarlet macaw, the great curassow, the keel-billed toucan and the king vulture. And there's an abundance of reptiles and amphibians, including the red-eyed tree frog, the boa constrictor and the deadly fer-de-lance (known as tommy-goff in Belize). The forest itself is made up of a fantastic range of plant species, including orchids, giant tree ferns, airplants and trees such as banak, cohune, mahogany and ceiba. It's an ideal environment for serious birdwatching, exploring the forest, or seeking out the ever-evasive wildlife. Special trails have been cut to give visitors a taste of the forest's diversity, although your chances of actually seeing a **jaguar** are very slim.

To get to the reserve you'll have to walk or drive the ten kilometres from Maya Centre on the main Southern highway. At the reserve headquarters you'll find an excellent visitors' centre, a **campground** and some fairly simple but comfortable **accommodation**. It costs BZ$15 to stay in a bunk or BZ$3 to camp. No food is available, so you'll have to carry your own, but you don't need to carry fuel if you're staying in the huts as there's a gas stove. According to the rules you should have a **permit** to stay overnight in the reserve: they're obtainable from the Belize Audubon Society in Belize City, the *Pelican Beach Resort* in Dangriga, or from the site headquarters. Sign in at the craft centre in Maya Centre, run by the women of the village, before entering the reserve.

The walk from Maya Centre to the reserve headquarters takes a couple of hours and is gently uphill. At the visitors' centre, a cleared grassy area surrounded by beautiful tropical foliage, you'll find the cabins, with the campsite a little further on. The **trails** that start here take you along the river banks, through the forest or even, if you're suitably prepared, on a two-day hike to Victoria Peak. The **Ben's Bluff Trail**, for example, is a strenuous but worthwhile hike from the riverside to the top of a forested ridge – where there's a great view of the entire Cockscomb basin – with a chance to cool off in a delightful rocky pool on the way back.

About 10km before Maya Centre you pass the turn-off for **Possum Point**, an ecological field station run by Paul and Mary Shave who operate the *Sittee River Scenic Park*. Here you can stay in cottages or camp on tent platforms on the river front, and there are courses in tropical field ecology. The station also has a marine laboratory on Wee Wee Caye, 12km offshore, to teach the biology of the coral reef.

Placencia and around

However you reach **PLACENCIA** (and it will be especially welcome after the bus ride from Belize City or Belmopan) you can be confident that you'll get a chance to relax. It's a small, laid-back fishing village, catering to an increasing number of tourists. Shaded by palm trees, cooled by the sea breeze, and perched on the tip of a long, narrow, sandy peninsula, 75km south of Dangriga, Placencia is light years from the hassle of Belize City. A good dirt road connects the village with the Southern highway, turning east to RIVERSDALE, then south through MAYA BEACH and SEINE BIGHT, a Garifuna village where you may be able to find accommodation. Seine Bight is reputed to have been founded by privateers in 1629 and was possibly given its present name by French fishermen deported from Newfoundland after Britain gained control of Canada. The road down the peninsula is always in sight of water; the Caribbean Sea on one side and mangrove lagoons on the other, a suitable introduction to the tranquillity of life on the beach. Once you've settled in it's all too easy to become entranced by Placencia's unhurried ways, and moving on soon becomes a proposition you'd rather not contemplate.

Rum Point Inn, the first outpost of tourism as you approach Placencia, is very expensive (US$100 a night in the high season). Next is *Kitty's* (☎2027), the only **dive-shop** in Placencia, where a double room costs US$35 a day or you can rent an apartment for US$150 a week: you can also **camp** here. Then comes the *Turtle Inn*, in a delightful setting, but again not for budget travellers at US$50 a night. Further along is *The Cove* (☎2024), expensive at US$65 a day in winter, though the price includes all meals and accommodation is in spacious, comfortable bungalows on the beach.

Once you reach Placencia village proper there's a wide choice of pleasant, inexpensive **accommodation**, and you should have no problem finding a room provided you don't arrive at Christmas or New Year without a booking. Possibilities begin at the sidewalk, a mile-long walkway that winds through the palm trees like an elongated garden path, and was for years Placencia's main road. *Clive's*, at the northern end of the sidewalk, is the cheapest place to stay, with cabins for rent and camping at only BZ$1.50. A favourite with visitors is the *Sea Spray Hotel* (BZ$31.50 double), run by Doris Leslie, a friendly woman who's a mine of information and has a library of paperbacks for exchange. For about BZ$10 you can stay at *Ran's Travel Lodge*, a personal favourite, which is behind the *Galley Restaurant*, or nearby at *Miss Cuncu's* shop, where you might be able to get room and board. The *Stone Crab*, just in front of the market, has inexpensive rooms and an excellent restaurant.

Follow a path to the right of the dock and you'll come to *E-Lee's Hotel*, with reasonable rooms at BZ$12.50 single, BZ$24 double. Adjacent to the hotel is the recently built *Tentacles Bar*, with sea views and cold beer. Right at the southern point is the post office, where Janice Leslie has four recently built cabins right on the beach with great views of the bay for between US$40 and US$60 per day. Her husband, Gino, runs snorkelling trips and has a canoe for rent. This is also the location of the public telephone.

There are plenty of **restaurants** in Placencia, most of which you'll have seen while looking for a room; *Jene's*, *J&L's* and *The Galley* all serve Creole food (rice and beans) with chicken, seafood, burgers and the like. Sometimes fresh baked pastries and coconut bread are also on offer and there is a bakery. The **market** is the main place for produce or any other shopping: get there early as goods are soon sold out.

The evenings in Placencia are as relaxed as the days and there are plenty of **bars**, ideal for drinking rum and watching the sun set. A pleasant walk north takes you along the beach to *Kitty's*, an excellent example, with prices no higher than elsewhere (BZ$2.50 a beer) and great bar snacks. There's also satellite TV, which attracts American football fans at weekends, and a large library with a wide selection of books, especially on Belize and Latin America. Non-residents can also use the bars at *The Cove* or the *Turtle Inn*. If you feel the urge to dance then try the *Cozy Corner Disco*, which keeps unpredictable hours but sometimes opens up later in the evening.

Getting to Placencia

The easiest way to reach Placencia is by regular *Maya Airways* or *Tropic Air* flights to **BIG CREEK** (on the "mainland" – the airstrip at Placencia is not in use at present) then by boat across the lagoon to Placencia. It helps to know if other passengers are going to be met, as boats only connect with the plane by prior arrangement. The fare can be either free or BZ$10, depending on where you're staying. If you get stuck, phone the post office in Placencia (☎06/2946) and they'll send a boat over. There's a hotel at the airstrip, the *Toucan Inn* (BZ$92 per night), where you can get a good breakfast or have a drink in the *Tipsy Toucan Bar*. Next door is the *Belize Bank*, open only on Friday mornings.

Although it's marked as separate on most maps, MANGO CREEK is in fact the same place as **INDEPENDENCE**. Some people use one name and some the other, but in fact Mango Creek is the name of the creek, so that end of town is referred to by that name, and Independence (named for Belize's independence) begins at the road junction. The residents of Placencia come here to do their shopping, so you can usually find a boat willing to take you across the lagoon if you go to the dock. **Buses** to Independence leave from Dangriga at about 3.30pm, although a more straightforward option is the direct bus from Dangriga to Placencia, which leaves Dangriga at 2.30pm four times a week, returning at 5am. Big Creek is the banana port of Belize and seems to be growing every week: *Fyffes* are currently organising the clearance of the harbour with a dredge brought from Holland.

If you do get stuck here, the *Hello Hotel* (☎06/2011) in Independence will charge you at least BZ$15 for an unsavoury, roach-infested room. Ask at the store for the key. There is another hotel, but it's even worse and could have fallen down by now. The restaurant opposite the *Hello* is very basic and they had run out of food when I ordered a meal. The best advice is to try not to get stranded in Independence for the night!

Around Placencia, offshore and inland

If you take to the water from Placencia you'll find that the main **reef** here is quite a way out (30km). Here are the **Silk Cayes**, where the Barrier Reef begins to break into several smaller reefs and cayes. There are also many smaller islands and coral heads closer to shore, including the **Bugle Cayes** and **Lark Caye**. Some of the main hotels run trips to **Laughing Bird Caye** but this can be expensive. For cheaper fishing or snorkelling trips shop around; ask at the dock, at *Ran's Travel Lodge*, the *Seaspray*, *E-Lee's*, or try Gino at the post office. You'll need to get together a group to bring the cost down. Trips can be tailor-made to your preference and your pocket, and you can do anything from an afternoon on the water to a week of camping, fishing, snorkelling and sailing. For **scuba-diving**, sailing and jungle trips check at *Kitty's*.

Other trips venture **inland**, up the thickly forested banks of the **Monkey River**, teeming with fish, bird life and, naturally enough, monkeys. Manatee can occasionally be seen in the lagoons, though all you're likely to spot is a startled expression or a series of ripples as the shy giant swims powerfully for cover. Again these trips are primarily for the more affluent visitors, but you should be able to negotiate a good deal with Gino. He'll rent you a canoe and a tent, plan your trip, and turn you loose. Again you can opt for three days on the Bladen or Monkey rivers, or an afternoon messing around in the mangrove swamps, any of which are rich in wildlife and ideal for cruising without a motor. But be warned that it's easy to get lost and darkness falls quickly in the tropics, so it's best to have a guide.

The Far South

Beyond the Placencia and Independence junctions, the Southern highway leaves the banana plants and the small, grim settlements squashed beside the plantation roads, twisting at first through pine forests, then jungle, crossing numerous creeks and rivers. There are few villages along the way and no more gas stations until the Punta Gorda turn-off – a place which was not lightly named "The Dump".

About 35km north of Punta Gorda is **NIM LI PUNIT**, a Late Classic Maya site that was possibly allied to nearby Lubaantun. The site was discovered in 1976 and a total of 25 stelae were found, of which eight were carved, including one that measured nine metres in height, the tallest yet found in Belize. Unfortunately the site was badly looted soon after its discovery: archaeological work did not begin until 1983 and in 1986 another stela and a royal tomb were unearthed. The site is about a kilometre west of the Southern highway (a sign points the way), surrounded by the fields of the nearby Maya village of INDIAN CREEK. Just below the turn-off for the ruins is *Whitney's* store, which is better stocked than many shops in Punta Gorda and has fresh bread every day.

A little further south, the **road to Silver Creek** branches off to the right. If you have your own vehicle you can use this route to visit the Maya villages and the ruins of Lubaantun. Near the village of **BIG FALLS** is the only **hot spring** in Belize, a luxurious spot for a warm bath. The spring is on a farm belonging to Peter Alaman, who also runs a small shop. Ask permission if you want to camp and it'll cost a few dollars. Don't expect to have it all to yourself at weekends, however, as the pools are a popular picnic spot.

To get to either of the above you'll have to try your luck hitching along the Southern highway or catch a lift on a bus heading between Punta Gorda and Dangriga.

Punta Gorda

The Southern highway eventually comes to an end in **PUNTA GORDA**, the last town in Belize and the heart of the isolated **Toledo district**, an area that has always been hard to reach and remains largely overlooked by planners and developers. The town consists basically of five streets – Front Street, Main Street, Back Street, West Street and Far West Street – all of which run parallel to the shoreline. It probably started life as a logging settlement, and we know that Caribs from the island of Roatan were brought here in the early part of the nineteenth century to work as labourers.

To the north of Punta Gorda are the remains of the Toledo settlement, which was founded in 1867 by emigrants from the US. Many of the original settlers soon drifted home, discouraged by the torrential downpours and the rigours of frontier life, but their numbers were boosted by Methodists from Mississippi. The Methodists were deeply committed to the settlement and, despite a cholera epidemic in 1868, they managed to clear 160 acres. By 1870 sugar was the main product, with twelve separate estates running their own mills. The settlement reached its peak in 1890, after which it was threatened by falling sugar prices. Most farmers moved into the production of alcohol, but for the Methodists this was out of the question, and they preferred to feed molasses to their cattle or simply throw it in the rivers. By 1910 their community was destitute, although it was largely as a result of their struggle that Toledo was permanently settled.

Today's town is populated by a mixture of *mestizos*, Garifunas, Maya Indians, Lebanese, Chinese and Creoles, and is the focal point for a large number of villages and farming settlements in the district. It's also the nearest town to Rideau Camp, the main British Army base in the south, and several of the bars are forever England, decked out with regimental mascots and football scarves and frequented by local prostitutes.

Hotels and restaurants

There aren't many hotels in Punta Gorda, but for the moment there are more than enough to meet demand. For budget travellers, *Foster's Hotel*, 19 Main Street, is probably the best value in town, or there's *Mahung's*, on the corner of Main Street and North Street, both of which charge BZ$10. On Front Street the *Wahima*, just past the bakery, is the cheapest in town at BZ$15 for a double: basic but friendly with a small adjacent bar. In the town centre there's the *Lux Drive Inn*, 37 Front Street, scruffy and overpriced at BZ$25, and the *Miramar*, 95 Front Street, which is also overpriced at BZ$75. If you do want something more upmarket try the *Saint Charles Inn*, 21 King Street, which is spotlessly clean and charges BZ$30 for a room with a private bathroom.

Previous visitors to Punta Gorda may remember *Nature's Way Guest House*, at 65 Front Street, run by "Chet" (William Schmitt), as being the best hotel in town. This is now the headquarters of a USAID agricultural project in Toledo but Chet, who knows southern Belize as well as anybody, is still around and may have rooms for rent or be able to provide information. **Restaurants** are not at their best in Punta Gorda, but there's a decent Chinese one on Front Street, or you can

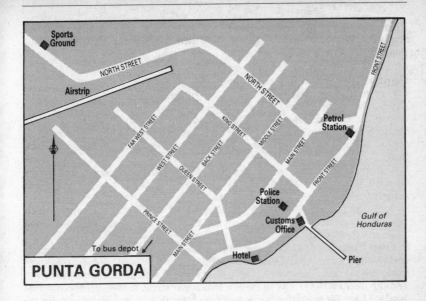

eat at the *Lux Drive Inn* or the *Airport Café* at the landing strip. *Bobby's Restaurant* on Main Street serves good Belizean food. Punta Gorda is full of people with new ideas and may well have changed by the time you read this. The *Hotel Isabel*, on Front Street, should reopen soon, and *Toledo Travel* hope to open a travel agency at 52 Front Street. There are certain to be more hotels and packages on offer as tourism in Toledo takes off in the near future.

Buses, boats and planes

The best **buses** to Punta Gorda are run by *Z-Line*, who have an onward connection from Dangriga to Punta Gorda at 3pm, returning at 5am. *Williams Bus Service*, Pound Yard, Belize City, also have a bus from Belize City to Punta Gorda but this is less reliable. The *James* bus meets the ferry on its arrival in Punta Gorda (see below) and continues to Belize City. The new **bus terminal** is at the south end of town, opposite the BDF barracks. *Maya Airways* have **flights** from Belize City to Punta Gorda, calling in at Dangriga, at 8am, 11am and 2pm, returning at 9.25am, 12.25pm and 3.25pm. Only the last of these runs on Sunday. In Punta Gorda tickets can be bought at Bob Pennell's hardware store on Main Street, and cost about BZ$80. *Tropic Air* have a flight leaving the municipal airstrip in Belize City at 4.30pm, returning from Punta Gorda at 7am

If you want to continue south, a **ferry** runs to Guatemala twice a week, leaving at 2.30pm on Tuesday and Friday. Tickets are sold on the day only, from 8.30am (you need to show your passport to get one) at the office of *Agencia de Lineas Maritimas Puerto Santo Tomás de Castillo Izabal Guatemala*, which is at 24 Middle Street. Before you leave, get an exit stamp from the police station beside the dock. The ferry takes you to Livingston (p.177) first of all, and goes on to Puerto Barrios (p.176). From Puerto Barrios it runs on Tuesday and Friday at 7.30am, dropping in at Livingston at 9am.

Out to sea: the cayes and the coast

The cayes and reefs off Punta Gorda mark the southern end of Belize's Barrier Reef. The main reef has already started to break up here, leaving several clusters of islands, each surrounded by a small independent reef. The closest to Punta Gorda are the **Snake Cayes**, hundreds of tiny islands in the mouth of a large bay, where the shoreline is a complex maze of mangrove swamps. On Wild Cane Caye archaeologists have found evidence of a Maya coastal trade centre. Further out, in the Gulf of Honduras, are the **Sapodilla Cayes**, the largest of which, Hunting Caye, has a small army post on it and is frequented by Guatemalan as well as Belizean day-trippers. There is a proposal to designate Hunting Caye as a park.

The whole area receives little attention from international tourism and is very interesting to explore. If you'd like to spend a day or two out on the reef talk to someone with a boat in Punta Gorda, such as Bobby of *Bobby's Bar*, who organises trips for the army. Livingston, at the mouth of the Río Dulce in Guatemala, is becoming a centre for sailing charters and there are often boats sailing between there and Punta Gorda.

From Punta Gorda you can see range upon range of mountains in Guatemala and Honduras, but the Belizean **coastline** south of here is flat and sparsely populated. Rivers meander across a coastal plain covered with thick tropical rainforest, and the Temash River has the tallest mangrove forest in the country along its banks. In the far south the Sarstoon River, navigable by small boats, forms the border with Guatemala. The only village is **BARRANCO**, a small Garifuna settlement of 200 people. There's no tourist accommodation at the moment, although *Barefoot Adventures* used to run a campsite here.

Towards the mountains: Maya villages and Maya ruins

Heading inland from Punta Gorda towards the foothills of the Maya Mountains, you meet yet another uniquely Belizean culture. Here Mopan Maya are mixed with Kekchi-speaking Indians from the Verapaz highlands of Guatemala. For the most part each group keeps to its own villages, language and traditions, although both are partially integrated into modern Belizean life and many speak English. Guatemalan families have been arriving here for the last hundred years or so, escaping repression and a shortage of land at home, and founding new villages deep in the forest. It's estimated that about twelve families a year still cross the border to settle in land-rich Belize, along routes that have been used for generations. Several of the villages are connected by road and there's a basic bus service, although moving around isn't that easy and in many places you'll have to rely on hitching, despite the fact that there isn't much traffic.

The Mopan Maya village of **SAN ANTONIO**, perched on a small hilltop, is the easiest to reach, as it's served by a regular bus service from Punta Gorda (*Chun's*, from the Civic Centre) with daily departures at 4pm, returning at 5am. It also has the benefit of *Bol's Hill Top Hotel* (BZ$10 single) which has simple rooms and superb views, and is a good place for information on local natural history and archaeology. The area is rich in wildlife, surrounded by jungle-clad hills and swift-flowing rivers. Further south and west are the villages of the Kekchi Maya, fairly recent immigrants who still retain strong cultural links with their way of life in Guatemala.

The founders of San Antonio were from the Guatemalan village of San Luís, just across the border, and they maintain many age-old traditions. Amongst other things the Indians of San Luís brought with them their patron saint, and opposite *Bol's Hotel* is the church of San Luís Rey, currently looked after by American nuns. The church is the third to stand on the site (two previous versions were destroyed by fire) and its most remarkable feature is a set of superb stained-glass windows, donated by the people of Saint Louis, Missouri. The Indians also adhere to their own pre-Columbian traditions and their fiestas – the main one takes place on June 13, and features masked dances and much heavy drinking.

If you walk (or hitch) west from San Antonio for about 7km towards the village of SANTA CRUZ, you'll come to the ruins of **Ux Ben Ka**, a fairly small Maya site. The site's caretaker lives in Santa Cruz, to protect it from further looting. Ux Ben Ka's existence only became known to archaeologists in 1984 after reports of looting in the area. As you climb the hill before the village you'll be able to recognise the shape of two tree-covered mounds to your left. Some salvage work has been carried out and a map produced with help from the British Army, but the site has not been fully excavated. You can still make out a couple of pyramids and a plaza, and there are several badly eroded stelae, protected by thatched shelters. The site is superbly positioned on an exposed hilltop, with great views towards the coast.

Blue Creek and Pusilha

About four kilometres before the village of San Antonio a branch road heads off south and west to the village of **BLUE CREEK**, where the main attraction is the village's namesake – a beautiful stretch of water that runs through magnificent rainforest. Whether you're walking or driving you won't miss the river, as the road crosses it just before it enters the village.

To get to the best spot for swimming, walk upriver along the right-hand bank (facing upstream), and in about ten minutes you'll come to a lovely turquoise pool, where the army has recently built a picnic site with a shelter. Heading on upriver the source, where the water gushes from beneath a mossy rock face, is about another fifteen minutes' walk. Alongside this is the entrance to the **Hokeb Ha** cave, which is fairly easy to explore. The entire area is made up of limestone bedrock honeycombed with caves, many of which were sacred to the Maya, and doubtless there are still plenty of others waiting to be rediscovered. An entrance fee will soon be charged to visit the cave.

Further to the west of Blue Creek is the Kekchi village of AGUACATE and beyond that the road climbs a ridge leading to the valley of the Moho River, near the border with Guatemala. Further up the valley are the ruins of **Pusilha**, a large ceremonial centre. The city is built alongside the river on a small hilltop and although many of the buildings are quite extensive, none is very tall, reaching a maximum height of just five or six metres. The site has yielded an astonishing number of carved monuments and stelae, including zoomorphs in a style similar to those at Quiriguá in Guatemala. This has led archaeologists to suggest that at some stage Pusilha may have been under the control of Quiriguá. The site's most unusual feature is the remains of a stone bridge, which is unique in Maya architecture.

The ruins are only accessible by boat, on foot or on horseback, which makes the whole business rather expensive. If you'd like to see Pusilha, hire a horse and guide in Blue Creek or San Antonio, but try and make sure you're dealing with someone who knows what they're doing.

San Pedro and the ruins of Lubaantun

To visit the ruins of Lubaantun from San Antonio, get a lift along the road to the Southern Highway and turn left at the track leading to **SAN PEDRO COLUMBIA**, a Kekchi village. There's no bus to San Pedro but the bus to San Antonio will drop you at the entrance road, about 3km from the village, and there's sometimes a truck waiting there to ferry passengers over the final section of their journey. Head through the village and cross the Columbia River, just beyond which you'll see the track to the ruins, a few hundred metres on the left. If you ask in the village one of the older boys will gladly show you the way; the ruins are a twenty-minute walk from the village. There's nowhere to stay in San Pedro, although you'll have no problem finding somewhere to camp.

Lubaantun, which means "Place of the Fallen Stones" in modern Maya but isn't the original name, is a major Late Classic ceremonial centre that originally covered quite a large area. The site is on a high ridge and from the top of the tallest building you can (just) see the Caribbean, over 30km away. The Maya architects shaped and filled the hillside, with retaining walls as much as ten metres high. Some restoration has begun and the pyramids are quite impressive, as is the surrounding forest.

It now seems that the site was only occupied briefly, from 700 to 890 AD, very near the end of the Classic Period. There are five main plazas with eleven major structures and three ball courts. The architecture is unusual in a number of ways: for instance there are no stelae or sculpted monuments other than ball-court markers, and the whole site is essentially a single acropolis, constructed on a series of low ridges. Another unusual feature is the absence of mortar, which was usually used by Maya builders. In this case the stone blocks are carved with particular precision and fitted together, Inca style, without anything to bind them. The plainness and monumentality of Lubaantun's architecture is again similar to the later buildings at Quiriguá, in Guatemala, and there may have been some connection between the two sites.

Lubaantun was brought to the attention of the colonial authorities in 1903 and the governor sent Thomas Gann to investigate. A survey in 1915 revealed many structures, and three ball-court markers were removed and taken to the Peabody Museum. The British Museum expedition of 1926 was joined in 1927 by J Eric S Thompson, who was to become the most renowned Maya expert of his time. No further excavations took place for over forty years until Norman Hammond mapped the site in 1970. From his work he produced a reconstruction of life in Lubaantun, showing the inhabitants' connection with communities on the coast and inland. The wealth of Lubaantun was created by the production of cacao beans, used as money by the civilisations of Mesoamerica.

Perhaps the most enigmatic find came in 1926, when the famous **Crystal Skull** was unearthed here. This skull, which is made from pure rock crystal, was apparently found beneath an altar by Anna Mitchell-Hedges, the adopted daughter of the expedition's leader, F A Mitchell-Hedges. By a stroke of luck the find happened to coincide with her seventeenth birthday, and the skull was then given to the local Indians, who in turn presented it to Anna's father as a token of their gratitude for the help he had given them. Today it is still in the possession of Anna Mitchell-Hedges, who lives in Kitchener, Ontario. In the Museum of Mankind in London there's another crystal skull which – according to Dr G M Morant, an anthropologist who examined both skulls in 1936 – is a copy of the one found at Lubaantun. He also concluded that both of the life-size crystal skulls

Late Classic figurine found at Lubaantun

are modelled on the same original human head, but could give no answer as to their true age and origin.

Mystery and controversy still surrounds the skulls (there's a similar, smaller crystal skull in the Musée de l'Homme in Paris). It's possible that the "discovery" was a birthday gift for Anna, placed there by her father who had acquired it on his previous travels, although she strenuously denies the allegation. She has said she will disclose the full story of how the crystal skull came to be in her (and her father's) possession when she is ready. The label on the Museum of Mankind's skull is suitably vague: "Possibly from Mexico, age uncertain . . . resembles in style the Mixtec carving of Fifteenth Century Mexico, though some lines on the teeth appear to be cut with a jeweller's wheel. If so it may have been made after the Spanish Conquest."

travel details

The Southern highway doesn't have anything like the same number of buses running along it as the Northern and Western highways, and trips into the south will inevitably take a day or two. The main routes are listed below; other buses to the smaller villages are covered in the text.

Buses
Belize City to Dangriga (3hr) is best covered by *Z-Line*, from Magazine Road, Belize City. They leave Belize City at 10am, 11am, 1pm, 3pm and 4pm (only the first two will make the connection for Punta Gorda) and Dangriga at 5am, 6am, 9am, 10am and 3pm.

Dangriga to Placencia four a week at 2.30pm (Mon, Wed, Fri, Sat), returning from **Placencia to Dangriga** at 5am.

Dangriga to Independence daily at 3.30pm, and from **Independence to Dangriga** at 6am.

Dangriga to Punta Gorda *Z-Line* daily at 3pm, returning at 5am; also an unreliable daily *Williams* bus from **Belize City to Punta Gorda** (12hr) and a *James* bus that meets the ferry from Guatemala and runs to Belize City.

Flights
Maya Airways have flights from **Belize City to Dangriga** at 8am, 11am and 2pm, which go on to **Independence** and **Punta Gorda**. Flights from Punta Gorda to Belize City leave at 9.25am, 12.25pm and 3.25pm. *Tropic Air* also operate scheduled flights, leaving Belize City at 4.30pm and returning from Punta Gorda at 7am.

Ferries
The twice-weekly **ferry** from **Punta Gorda to Livingston and Puerto Barrios** in Guatemala leaves at 2.30pm on Tuesday and Friday. It runs from Puerto Barrios, also on Tuesday and Friday, at 7.30am, dropping in at Livingston at 9am.

PART FOUR

THE
CONTEXTS

HISTORY

Not until the early nineteenth century is it really possible to talk of Guatemala and Belize (or British Honduras) as we know them now. Their histories began to diverge, however, as early as the tenth century, with the collapse of the Classic Maya civilisation. It's that break which has been regarded as crucial here. The later histories are dealt with separately: before that the area has to be considered as part of Mesoamerica, which includes Mexico and the rest of Central America. This definition is designed to exclude the North American Indians (whose culture remained largely nomadic), and to bunch together the pre-Columbian civilisations of their southern neighbours.

By far the most important of these as far as Guatemala and Belize are concerned are the Maya, whose culture began to emerge here as early as 2000 BC and whose cities were at the height of their power and glory between 300 and 900 AD.

BEGINNINGS

Delving into the early history of Central America archaeologists are on uncertain ground, piecing together a rough idea on the basis of scattered archaeological remains and a handful of written texts. Prior to the advent of Maya civilisation very little is known about the area, and even the Maya remain fairly mysteri-

ous. Set out below is a brief overview of many separate theories, none of which can claim to dominate the academic debate. Over the last few years the situation has if anything become even more confused, as excavations of important new sites (especially in Belize) throw up information that casts doubt on many accepted notions. At any moment our whole understanding could be overturned by new discoveries, and there is certainly still a great deal to learn.

PREHISTORY

The earliest inhabitants of the Americas are thought to have crossed the Bering land bridge from Siberia to Alaska during the Fourth Ice Age, around 60,000 years ago, when sea levels were considerably lower than they are today. Successive waves of Stone Age hunters, travelling south along an ice-free corridor, had reached Central and South America by 15,000 BC. The first recognisable culture, known as **Clovis**, had emerged by 10,000 BC. Worked stone tools, including spearpoints, blades and scrapers, dating from 9000 BC, have been found in the Guatemalan highlands. In northern Belize the discovery of thousands of chert flakes, which may be man-made artefacts, at the Richmond Hill site could be evidence of human occupation 20,000 years ago.

In Mesoamerica, an area defined as stretching from north-central Mexico through Central America to Panama, the first settled pattern of development took place around 8000 BC, as a warming climate forced the hunter-gatherers to adapt to a different way of life. The glaciers were in retreat and the big game, which the hunters depended upon, became scarce due to the warmer, drier climate and possibly over-hunting. This period, in which the hunters turned to more intensive use of plant foods, is known as the **Archaic** and lasted until about 2000 BC. During this time the food plants vital to the subsequent development of agriculture, such as corn, beans, peppers, squash and probably maize, were domesticated.

In Belize, the subject of extensive investigation in the 1980s, there is evidence of Archaic sequences dating from 7500 BC until later than 2000 BC. An early language, known as Proto-Maya, was in use in the western highlands of Guatemala, and probably other places too. Recent research on ancient pollen samples indicates that 4000 years ago the Petén was an area of savannahs and broad-leaved woodlands. The current theory is that tropical forest did not appear until the Classic Period, by which time the Maya could more easily control its profuse growth.

THE EARLY MAYA

Somewhere between 2000 and 1500 BC we move into the **Preclassic**, a name used by archaeologists to describe the earliest developments in the history of the **Maya**, marking the first phase on a long road of evolution and increasing sophistication which culminates with the Classic (300–900 AD).

The names given to archaeological periods are often confusing. Current excavations seem to be pushing back the dates when the earliest breakthroughs were made, and the dates of each period vary according to what you read; but in general terms the tail end of the Archaic (5000–1500 BC) becomes the **Formative** or **Preclassic** (1500 BC–300 AD), in which the early Maya settled in villages, practised agriculture and began making pottery. Some of the earliest ceramics, found at Cuello in northern Belize, date from around 2000 BC (other artefacts from Cuello are dated as early as 2500 BC, making it the oldest Maya site yet found). Many of the temple mounds at Kaminaljuyú, on the outskirts of Guatemala City, are also Preclassic, although thorough excavation is impossible as the mounds are now largely covered by sprawling suburbs. Further evidence, from a site near Ocós on the Pacific coast of Guatemala, shows groups of between three and twenty family huts, some of which include small temples.

By the **Middle Preclassic** (1000 BC to 300 BC) similar pottery and artefacts, including red and orange jars, dishes of the *Mamon* style and stone *metates*, for grinding corn, are found throughout the Maya lands, from southern Guatemala to northern Yucatán. Temple mounds are still at their most basic and the entire culture remains village-based. However it's thought that some kind of Maya language was spoken throughout the area and that there was a substantial increase in the population. Religion, practised from a very early date, may have provided the stimulus and social cohesion to build bigger towns and, as in all early agricultural communities, food surpluses freed some to eventually become seers, priests and astronomers. However the Middle Preclassic is primarily marked by the spread of stable village life, with little in the way of sophisticated cultural advances.

Elsewhere in Mesoamerica, however, big changes were taking place that were to have a far-reaching impact throughout the region. The first great culture to emerge was the **Olmec** civilisation, originating in the coastal plain of Veracruz, in Mexico. The Olmecs, often regarded as the true ancestors of Maya culture, developed a complex polytheistic religion, an early writing system and a calendar known as the "Long Count", which was later adopted by the Maya.

Among the Maya, real advances in architecture came in the **Late Preclassic** (300 BC–300 AD), when the **Chicanel culture** dominated the northern and central areas. Large pyramids and temple platforms were built at Tikal, El Mirador, Río Azul, Kaminaljuyú and many other sites in Guatemala and Belize, in what amounted to an explosion of Maya culture. Traditionally these early Maya were painted as peaceful peasant farmers led by astronomer priests, but in fact these new cities were bloodthirsty, warring rivals. Trade was of vital importance in the Late Preclassic. Cerros, at the mouth of the New River in Belize, and Lamanai, on New River Lagoon, were great trading centres, probably continuing in this role right through the Classic and into the Postclassic period. The famous Maya corbelled arch (which was not a true arch, with a keystone, but consisted of two sides, each with stones overlapping until they eventually met, and thus could only span a relatively narrow gap) was developed in this period and the whole range of buildings became more ambitious. The question of what sparked this phase of rapid development is a subject of much debate. Some archaeologists argue that the area was injected with ideas from across the Pacific, while others see the catalyst as the Olmec culture from the Gulf of Mexico. Both groups agree, however, that writing and calendar systems spread south along the Pacific coast, which developed before the Petén area: in the archaeological sites around the modern town of Santa Lucía Cotzumalguapa there is much evidence of Olmec-style carving.

Rivalling the developments on the Pacific coast was the city of **Kaminaljuyú**, on the site of the modern capital of Guatemala, which dominated the central highlands in the early Preclassic. The principal centre in the Petén during this period was **El Mirador**, which reached a scale comparable to the later achievement at Tikal. El Mirador remains one of the least understood of the great Maya cities and its ruins will doubtless yield some important information on Preclassic Maya civilisation.

THE CLASSIC MAYA

The development that separates the Late Preclassic from the early **Classic Period** (300–900 AD) is the introduction of the Long Count calendar and a recognisable form of writing. This appears to have taken place by the fourth century AD and marks the beginning of the greatest phase of Maya achievement.

During the Classic Period all the cities we now know as ruined or restored sites were built, almost always over earlier structures. Elaborately carved **stelae**, bearing dates and emblem-glyphs, were erected at regular intervals. These tell of actual rulers and of historical events in their lives – battles, marriages, dynastic succession and so on. As these dates have come to be deciphered they have provided confirmation (or otherwise) of archaeological evidence, and offered a major insight into the nature of Maya dynastic rule.

Developments in the Maya area were still powerfully influenced by events to the north. The overbearing presence of the Olmecs was replaced by that of **Teotihuacán**, which dominated Central Mexico during the early Classic Period. Armed merchants, called *pochteca*, were operating in the early Classic, spreading the influence of Teotihuacán as far as the Petén and the Yucatán. They brought new styles of ceramics, alternative religious beliefs and perhaps preceded a complete military invasion. Whatever happened around 400 AD, the overwhelming power of Teotihuacán radically altered life in Maya lands. Influence spread south, via the Pacific coast, first to Kaminaljuyú on the site of modern Guatemala City and thence to the Petén, where Tikal's rise to power must have been helped by close links with Teotihuacán. Both cities prospered greatly: Kaminaljuyú was rebuilt in the style of Teotihuacán, and Tikal has a stela depicting a lord of Tikal on one side and a warrior from Teotihuacán on the other.

Exactly how the various centres related to one another is unclear, but it appears that large cities dominated specific regions but no city held sway throughout the Maya area. Broadly speaking the culture was made up of a federation of city states, bound together by a coherent religion and culture, and supporting a sophisticated trade network. The cities jostled for power and influence, a struggle that occasionally erupted into open warfare.

Intense wars were fought as rival cities sought to dominate one another, with no ruler appearing to gain ascendency for very long. There were clearly three or four main centres that dominated the region through an uncertain process of alliances. Tikal was certainly a powerful city, but at one time Caracol in Belize defeated Tikal, as a Caracol ball-court marker shows. Detailed carvings on wooden lintels and stone monuments depict elaborately costumed lords trampling on captives and spilling their own blood at propitious festivals, staged according to the dictates of the intricate and precise Maya calendar. Copán and Quiriguá were certainly important centres in the southern area, while the cities of the highlands were still in their infancy.

At the height of Maya power, advances were temporarily halted by what is known as the **Middle Classic Hiatus**, a period during which there was little new building at Tikal and

after which many smaller centres, once under the control of Tikal, became independent city states. The victory of Caracol over Tikal, some time around 550 AD, may have been a symptom or a cause of this, and certainly the collapse of Teotihuacán in the seventh century caused shock waves throughout the civilisations of Mesoamerica. In the Maya cities no stelae commemorating events were erected, and monuments and statues were defaced and damaged. In all likelihood the Maya centres suffered revolts, and warfare raged as rival lords strove to win political power.

However as the new kings established dynasties, now free of Teotihuacán's military or political control, the Maya cities flourished as never before. Architecture, astronomy and art reached degrees of sophistication unequalled by any other pre-Columbian society. Trade prospered and populations grew: Tikal had an estimated 40,000 people. Many Maya centres were larger than contemporary Western European cities, then in their "Dark Ages".

The prosperity and grandeur of the **Late Classic** (600–800 AD) reached all across the Maya lands; from Bonampak and Palenque in the west, to Labná, Sayil and Uxmal in the north, Altun Ha and Cerros in the east, and Copán and Quiriguá in the south, as well as hundreds of smaller centres. Masterpieces of painted pottery and carved jade (their most precious material) were created, often to be used as funerary offerings. Shell, bone and, rarely, marble were also exquisitely carved; temples were painted in brilliant colours, inside and out. Most of the pigments have faded long ago, but vestiges remain, enabling experts to reconstruct vivid images of the appearance of the ancient cities.

THE MAYA IN DECLINE

The days of glory were not to last very long however. By 750 AD political and social changes began to be felt; alliances and trade links broke down, wars increased and stelae recording periods of time were carved less frequently. Cities gradually became depopulated and new construction ceased in the central area after about 830 AD. Bonampak was abandoned before its famous murals could be completed, while many of the great sites along the Río Usumacinta (now part of the border between Guatemala and Mexico) were occupied by militaristic outsiders.

The reason for the decline is not (and may never be) known. Probably several factors contributed to the downfall of the Maya. The growth and demands of the unproductive elite may have led to a peasant revolt, while the increase in population put great strains on food production, possibly exhausting the fertility of the soil, and epidemics may have combined to cause the abandonment of city life. At the end of the Classic Period there appears to have been strife and disorder throughout Mesoamerica. The power vacuum left by the departing elite could have been partially filled by Putun or Chontal Maya moving into the Petén from Tabasco and Campeche in Mexico.

By the tenth century, the Maya had abandoned their central cities and those few Maya that remained were reduced to a fairly primitive state. But not all Maya cities were entirely deserted: those in northern Belize, in particular, survived to some degree, with Lamanai and other cities in the area remaining occupied throughout the **Postclassic** period (900 AD to Spanish Conquest); the Yucatán

peninsula, which appears to have escaped the worst of the depopulation, was conquered by the militaristic Toltecs who came from central Mexico in 987 AD. The invaders imposed their culture on the Maya, possibly introducing human sacrifice and creating a hybrid of Classic Maya culture.

GUATEMALA SINCE MAYA TIMES

The decline of Maya civilisation in the Petén lowlands meant a rapid depopulation of the heartland of the Maya, an event which prompted an influx of population into the surrounding areas, and in particular into the Yucatán peninsula in the north and the Guatemalan highlands to the south. These areas, formerly peripheral regions of relatively little development, now contained the last vestiges of Maya culture and it's at this time that the Guatemala area began to take on some of the local characteristics which are still in evidence today. By the end of the Classic Period there were small settlements throughout the highlands, usually built on open valley floors and supporting large populations with the use of terraced farming and irrigation. Little was to change in this basic village structure for several hundred years.

PRE-CONQUEST: THE HIGHLAND TRIBES

Towards the end of the thirteenth century, however, the great cities of the Yucatán, such as Chichén Itzá and Uxmal, which were now inhabited by groups of Toltec-Maya from the gulf coast of Mexico, were also abandoned. At around the same time there was an invasion of the central Guatemalan highlands, also by a group of **Toltec-Maya**, although whether they came from the Yucatán or from the Gulf of Mexico remains uncertain. Some argue that they travelled due south into the highlands along the Río Usumacinta and Río Chixoy valleys, while others claim that they came from further west and entered the area via the Pacific coast, which has always been a popular route for invading armies. Their numbers were probably small but their impact was profound, and following their arrival life in the highlands was radically altered.

What once had been a relatively settled, peaceful and religious society, became under the influence of the Toltecs fundamentally secular, aggressive and militaristic. The Toltec invaders were ruthlessly well organised and in no time at all they established themselves as a ruling elite, founding a series of competing empires. The greatest of these were the **Quiché**, who dominated the central area and had their capital, **Utatlán**, to the west of the modern town of Santa Cruz del Quiché. Next in line were the **Cakchiquel**, who were originally based to the south of the Quichés, around the modern town of Chichicastenango, but later moved their capital to **Iximché**. On the southern shores of Lake Atitlán the **Tzutujil** had their capital on the lower slopes of the San Pedro volcano. To the west the **Mam** occupied the area around the modern town of Huehuetenango, with their capital at **Zaculeu**, while the northern slopes of the Cuchumatanes were home to a collection of smaller groups such as the **Chuj**, the **Kanjabal**, and further to the east the **Aguatecas** and the **Ixil**. The eastern highlands, around the modern city of Cobán, were home to the notoriously fierce **Rabinal** nation, with the **Kekchi** to their north, while around the modern site of Guatemala City the land was controlled by the **Pokoman**, with their capital at **Mixco Viejo**. Finally along the Pacific coast the **Pipil**, a tribe that had also migrated from the north, occupied the lowlands.

The sheer numbers of these tribes give an impression of the extent to which the area was fragmented, and it's these same divisions, now surviving on the basis of language alone, that still shape the highlands today (see map p.377).

The Toltec rulers probably controlled only the dominant tribes – the Quiché, the Tzutujil, the Mam and the Cakchiquel – while their lesser neighbours were still made up entirely of Indians indigenous to the area. Arriving in the later part of the thirteenth century the Toltecs must have terrorised the local Quiché-Cakchiquel highlanders and gradually established themselves in a new, rigidly hierarchical society. They brought with them many northern traditions – elements of a Nahua-based language, new gods and an array of military skills – and fused these with local ideas. Many of the rulers' names are similar to those that were used in the Toltec heartland to the north, and they claimed to trace their ancestry to

Quetzalcoatl, a mythical ruling dynasty from the Toltec city of Tula. Shortly after the Spanish conquest the Quichés wrote an account of their history, the *Popol Vuh*, in which they lay claim to a Toltec pedigree, as do the Cakchiqueles in their account, *The Annals of the Cakchiqueles*.

The Toltec invaders were not content with overpowering just a tribe or two, so under the direction of their new rulers the Quichés began to expand their empire by conquering neighbouring tribes. Between 1400 and 1475 they embarked on a campaign of conquest that brought the Cakchiquel, the Mam and several other tribes under their control. At the height of their power around a million highlanders bowed to the word of the Quiché king. But in 1475 the man who had masterminded their expansion, the great Quiché ruler **Quicab**, died, and the empire lost much of its authority. The Cakchiqueles were the first to break from the fold, anticipating the death of Quicab and moving south to a new and fortified capital, Iximché, in around 1470. Shortly afterwards the other tribes managed to escape the grip of Quiché control and assert their independence. For the next fifty years or so the tribes were in a state of almost perpetual conflict, fighting for access to the inadequate supplies of farmland. All the archaeological remains from this era give evidence of this instability; gone are the valley-floor centres of pre-Toltec times, and in their place are fortified hilltop sites, surrounded by ravines and man-made ditches.

When the Spanish arrived, the highlands were in a state of crisis. The population had grown so fast that it had outstripped the food supply, forcing the tribes to fight for any available land in order to increase their agricultural capacity. With a growing sense of urgency both the Quichés and the Cakchiqueles had begun to encroach on the lowlands of the Pacific coast. The situation could hardly have been more favourable to the Spanish, who were able to foster this inter-tribal friction, playing one group off against another.

THE SPANISH CONQUEST

While the tribes of highland Guatemala were fighting it out amongst themselves their northern neighbours, in what is now Mexico, were confronting a new and ruthless enemy. In 1521 the Spanish *conquistadores* had captured the

Aztec capital at Tenochtitlan, and were starting to cast their net further afield. Amidst the horrors of the conquest there was one man whose evilness stood out above the rest, **Pedro de Alvarado**. He could hardly have been better suited to the job – dashingly handsome, ambitious, cunning, intelligent, ingenious, and ruthlessly cruel.

In 1523 Cortés despatched Alvarado to Guatemala, entreating him to use the minimum of force, "and to preach matters concerning our Holy Faith". His army included 120 horsemen, 173 horses, 300 soldiers and 200 Mexican Indian warriors, largely Tlaxcalans who had allied themselves with Cortés in the conquest of Mexico. Marching south they entered Guatemala along the Pacific coast, where they met with the first wave of resistance, a small army of Quiché warriors. These were no match for the Spaniards, who cut through their ranks with ease. From here Alvarado turned north, taking his troops up into the highlands and through a narrow mountain pass to the Quezaltenango valley, where they came upon the deserted city of **Xelaju**, a Quiché outpost.

Warned of the impending arrival of the Spanish the Quichés had struggled to build an alliance with the other tribes, but old rivalries proved too strong and the **Quiché** army stood alone. Three days later, on a nearby plain, they met the Spaniards in open warfare. It's said that the invading army was confronted by some 30,000 Quiché warriors, led by **Tecún Umán** in a headdress of quetzal feathers. Despite the huge disparity in numbers, sling-shot and foot soldiers were no match for cavalry and gunpowder, and the Spaniards were once again able to wade through the Indian ranks. Legend has it that the battle was brought to a close when Alvarado met Tecún Umán in hand-to-hand conflict – and cut him down.

Accepting this temporary setback, the Quichés decided to opt for a more diplomatic solution and invited the Spaniards to their capital **Utatlán**, where they planned to trap and destroy them. But when Alvarado saw their city he grew suspicious, and took several Quiché lords as prisoners. When hostilities erupted once again he killed the captives and had the city burnt to the ground.

Having dealt with the Quichés, Alvarado turned his attention to the other tribal groups.

The **Cakchiqueles**, recognising the military superiority of the Spanish, decided to form some kind of alliance with them and as a result of this the Spaniards established their first headquarters, in 1523, alongside the Cakchiquel capital of **Iximché**. From here they ranged far and wide, overpowering the countless smaller tribes. Travelling east, Alvarado's army met the **Tzutujiles** on the shores of Lake Atitlán. Here the first battle took place at a site near the modern village of Panajachel, and the second beneath the Tzutujil capital, at the base of the San Pedro volcano, where the Spaniards were helped by a force of Cakchiquel warriors who arrived on the scene in some 300 canoes. Moving on, the Spanish travelled southto the Pacific coast, where they overcame the **Pipiles** before making their way back to Iximché.

In 1524 Alvarado sent his brother Gonzalo on an expedition against the **Mames**, who were conquered after a month-long siege during which they holed up in their fortified capital **Zaculeu**. In 1525 Alvarado himself set out to take on the **Pokomans**, at their capital **Mixco Viejo**, where he came up against another army of some 3000 warriors. Once again they proved no match for the well disciplined Spanish ranks.

Despite this string of relatively easy gains it wasn't until well into the 1530s that Alvarado managed to assert control over the more remote parts of the highlands. Moving into the Cuchumatanes his forces were beaten back by the **Uspantecs**, and met fierce resistance from the Indians of the **Ixil**. And while Alvarado's soldiers were struggling to contain resistance in these isolated mountainous areas, problems also arose at the very heart of the campaign. In 1526 the Cakchiquel rose up against their Spanish allies, in response to demands for tribute; abandoning their capital the Indians moved into the mountains, from where they waged a guerrilla war against their former partners. As a result of this the Spanish were forced to abandon their base at Iximché, and moved instead to a site near the modern town of Antigua.

Here they established their first permanent capital, the city of **Santiago de los Caballeros**, on St Cecilia's Day, November 22, 1527. For ten years Indians toiled in the construction of the new city, neatly sited at the base of the Agua volcano, putting together a cathedral, a town hall, and a palace for Alvarado. The land within the city was given out to those who had fought alongside him, and plots on the edge of town were allocated to his remaining Indian allies.

Meanwhile, one particularly thorny problem for the Spanish was presented by the **Rabinal** and **Kekchi** Indians, who occupied what are now the Verapaz highlands. Despite all his efforts Alvarado was unable to conquer either of these tribes, who fought fiercely against the invading armies. In the end he gave up on the area, naming it *Tierra de Guerra* and abandoning all hopes of controlling it. This problem was eventually overcome by the church. In 1537 **Fray Bartolomé de Las Casas**, the "protector of the Indians", travelled into the area in a bid to persuade the locals to accept both Christianity and Spanish authority. Within three years the priests had succeeded where Alvarado's armies had failed, and the last of the highland tribes was brought under colonial control in 1540. Thus did the area earn its name of *Verapaz*, true peace.

Alvarado himself grew tired of the conquest, disappointed by the lack of plunder, and his reputation for brutality was spreading. He was forced to return to Spain to face charges of treason, but returned a free man with a young wife at his side. Life in the New World soon sent his bride to an early grave and Alvarado set out once again, in search of the great mineral wealth that had eluded him in Guatemala. First he travelled south to Peru, where it's said that Pizarro paid him to leave South America. He then returned to Spain once again, where he married **Beatriz de la Cueva**, his first wife's sister, and the two of them made their way back to Guatemala, where he dropped off his new bride before setting sail for the Spice Islands. Along the way he stopped in Mexico, to put down an Indian uprising, and was crushed to death beneath a rolling horse.

From 1524 to his death in 1541 Alvarado had ruled Guatemala as a personal fiefdom, desperately seeking adventure and wealth, and enslaving and abusing the local Indian population in order to finance his urge to explore. By the time of his death all the Indian tribes had been overcome, although local uprisings, which have persisted to this day, had already started to take place.

COLONIAL RULE

The early years of colonial rule were marked by a turmoil of uprisings and political wrangling, and while the death of Alvarado might have been expected to bring a degree of calm, it was in fact followed by fresh disaster. When his wife, Beatriz de la Cueva, heard of Alvarado's death she plunged the capital into a period of prolonged mourning. She had the entire palace painted black, both inside and out, and ordered the city authorities to appoint her as the new governor. Meanwhile the entire area was swept by a series of storms, and on the night of September 10, 1541, it was shaken by a massive earthquake. The sides of the Agua volcano shuddered, undermining the walls of the cone and releasing its contents. A great wall of mud and water swept down the side of the cone, and the city of Santiago was buried beneath it.

The surviving colonial authorities moved up the valley to a new site, where a second **Santiago de los Caballeros** was founded in the following year. This new city served as the administrative headquarters of the **Audiencia de Guatemala**, which was made up of six provinces; Costa Rica, Nicaragua, San Salvador, Honduras, Guatemala and Chiapas (now part of Mexico). With Alvarado out of the way the authorities began to build a new society, recreating the splendours of the motherland. Santiago was never endowed with the same wealth or freedom as Mexico City and Lima, but it was nevertheless the centre of political and religious power for two hundred years, accumulating a superb array of arts and architecture. By the mid-eighteenth century its population had reached some 80,000. Here colonial society was at its most developed, rigidly structured along racial lines with pure-bred Spaniards at the top, Indian slaves at the bottom, and a host of carefully defined racial strata in between. The city was regularly shaken by scandal, intrigue and earthquakes, and it was eventually destroyed in 1773 by the last of these, after which the capital was moved to its modern site.

Perhaps the greatest power in colonial Central America was the **church**. The first religious order to reach Guatemala was the **Franciscans**, who arrived with Alvarado himself, and by 1532 the **Mercedarians** and **Dominicans** had followed suit, with the **Jesuits** arriving shortly after. **Francisco Marroquín**, the country's first bishop, rewarded these early arrivals with huge concessions, taking in both land and Indians, which later enabled them to earn fortunes from sugar, wheat and indigo, income boosted by the fact that they were exempt from tax. In later years a whole range of other orders arrived in Santiago, and religious rivalry became an important shaping force in the colony. The wealth and power of the church fostered the splendour of the colonial capital, while ruthlessly exploiting the Indians and their land. In Santiago alone there were some eighty churches, and alongside these were schools, convents, hospitals, hermitages, craft centres and colleges. The religious orders became the main benefactors of the arts, amassing a wealth of tapestry, jewels, sculpture and painting, and staging concerts, fiestas and endless religious processions. Religious persecution was at its worst between 1572 and 1580, when the office of the **Inquisition** set up in Santiago, seeking out those who had failed to receive the faith and dealing with them harshly. Not much is known about the precise nature of the Guatemalan inquisition, however, as no written records have survived.

By the eighteenth century the power of the church had started to get out of control and the Spanish kings began to impose taxes on the religious orders, and to limit their power and freedom. The conflict between church and state came to a head in 1767, when Carlos III banished the Jesuits from the Spanish colonies.

The Spanish must have been disappointed with their conquest of Central America as it offered none of the instant plunder that had been found in Mexico and Peru. They found small amounts of silver around the modern town of Huehuetenango and a few grains of gold in the rivers of Honduras, but nothing that could compare with the vast resources of Potosí (a huge silver mine in Bolivia) or highland Mexico. In Central America the **colonial economy** was based on agriculture. The coastal area produced cacao, tobacco, cotton and, most valuable of all, indigo; the highlands were grazed with sheep and goats; and cattle, specially imported from Spain, were raised on coastal ranches. In the lowlands of the Petén and the jungles of the lower Motagua valley, the mosquitoes and forests remained unchallenged, although here and there certain aspects of the forest were developed; *chicle,* the raw material of chewing gum, was bled from the sapodilla trees, as was *sarsparilla*, used to treat syphilis.

At the heart of the colonial economy was the system of *repartamientos*, whereby the ruling classes were granted the rights to extract labour from the Indian population. It was this that established the process of Indians being transported to the Pacific coast to work the plantations, a pattern that is still a tremendous burden for the Indians of today.

Meanwhile in the capital it was graft and corruption that controlled the movement of money, with titles and appointments sold to the highest bidder. All of the colony's wealth was funnelled through the city, and it was only here that the monetary economy really developed.

The impact of the conquest was perhaps at its most serious in the highlands, where the **Indian population** had their lives totally restructured. The first stage in this process was the *reduccion*, whereby scattered Indian communities were combined into new Spanish-style towns and villages. Between 1543 and 1600 some 700 new settlements were created, each based around a Catholic church. Ostensibly the purpose was to enable the church to work on its new-found converts, but it also had the effect of pooling the available labour and making its exploitation that much easier. The highland villages were still bound up in an ancient system of subsistence farming, although its pattern was now disturbed by demands for tribute.

Indian **social structures** were also profoundly altered by post-conquest changes. The great central authorities that had dominated in pre-conquest times were now eradicated, replaced by local structures based in the new villages. *Caciques* (local chiefs) and *Alcaldes* (mayors) now held the bulk of local power, which was bestowed on them by the Church. In the distant corners of the highlands, however, priests were few and far between, only visiting the villages from time to time. Those that they left in charge developed not only their own power structures but also their own religion, mixing the new with the old. By the start of the nineteenth century the Indian population had largely recovered from the initial impact of the conquest and in many places these local structures became increasingly important. In each village *Cofradía* (broth-

erhood) groups were entrusted with the care of saints, while *Principales*, village elders, held the bulk of traditional authority, a situation that still persists today. Throughout the highlands village uprisings became increasingly common-place as the new indigenous culture became stronger and stronger.

Perhaps even more serious for the indigenous population than any social changes were the **diseases** that arrived with the *conquistadores*. Waves of plague, typhoid and fever swept through a population without any natural resistance to them. In the worst hit areas the Indian population was cut by some ninety percent, and in many parts of the country their numbers were halved.

Two centuries of colonial rule totally reshaped the structure of Guatemalan society, giving it new cities, a new religion, a transformed economy and a racist hierarchy. Nevertheless the impact of colonial rule was perhaps less marked than in many other parts of Latin America. Only two sizeable cities had emerged and the outlying areas had received little attention from the colonial authorities. While the indigenous population had been ruthlessly exploited and suffered enormous losses at the hands of foreign weapons and imported diseases, its culture was never eradicated. It simply absorbed the symbols and ideas of the new Spanish ideology, creating a dynamic synthesis that is neither Maya nor Catholic.

INDEPENDENCE

The racist nature of colonial rule had given birth to deep dissatisfaction amongst many groups in Central America. Spain's policy was to keep wealth and power in the hands of those born in Spain (*chapetones*), a policy that left growing numbers of *creoles* (including those of Spanish blood born in Guatemala) and *mestizos* (of mixed blood) resentful and hungry for power and change. (For the majority of the indigenous Indians, both power and wealth were way beyond their reach.) But those who desired change (and indeed Guatemala's entire history since independence) were locked in a struggle between **conservatives**, who sided with the church and the crown, and **liberals**, who advocated a secular and more egalitarian state. One result of the split was that Independence was not a clean break, but was declared several times.

The spark, as throughout Spanish America, was Napoleon's invasion of Spain and the abdication of King Fernando VII. In the chaos that followed a liberal constitution was imposed on Spain in 1812 and a mood of reform swept through the colonies. At the time Central America was under the control of **Brigadier Don Gabino Gainza**, the last of the Captains General. His one concern was to maintain the status quo, in which he was strongly backed by the wealthy landowners and the church hierarchy. Bowing to demands for independence, but still hoping to preserve the power structure, Gainza signed a formal **Act of Independence** on September 15, 1821, enshrining the authority of the church and seeking to preserve the old order under new leadership. Agustin de Iturbide, the short-lived emperor of newly independent Mexico, promptly sent troops to annexe Guatemala to the Mexican empire, a union which was to last less than a year.

A second Declaration of Independence, in 1823, joined the Central American states in a loose **federation**, adopting a constitution modelled on that of the United States, abolishing slavery and advocating liberal reforms. The federation however was doomed by the struggle between the countries and within each of them. The first president of the federation was **General Manuel José Acre**, a Salvadorean, who fought bitterly with his party and then founded a government of his own. This prompted others to do the same and the liberals of Salvador, Honduras and Guatemala united under the leadership of **Francisco Morazon**, a Honduran general. Under his rule **Mariano Galvez** became the chief of state in Guatemala: religious orders were abolished, the death penalty done away with, and trial by jury, a general school system, civil marriage and the Livingston law code were all instituted.

The liberal era, however, lasted little longer than the Mexican empire, and the reforming government was overthrown by a revolt from the mountains. Throughout the turmoil of independence, life in the highlands remained harsh, with the Indian population still bearing the burdens imposed on them by two centuries of colonial rule. In 1823 a cholera epidemic swept through the entire country, killing thousands, and only adding to the misery of life in the mountains. Seething with discontent, the Indians were united behind an illiterate but charismatic leader, the 23-year-old **Rafael Carrera**, under whose command they marched on Guatemala City.

Carrera respected no authority other than that of the church, and his immediate reforms swept aside the changes instituted by the liberal government. The religious orders were restored to their former position and traditional Spanish titles were reinstated. The conservatives had little in common with Carrera but they could see that he offered to uphold their position with a tremendous weight of popular support, and hence they sided with him. Under Carrera Guatemala fought a bitter war against Morazon and the federation, eventually establishing Guatemala as an independent republic in 1847. Carrera's other great challenge came from the state of **Los Altos**, which included much of the western highlands, and had established itself as an independent republic in defiance of him: it was a short-lived threat, however, and the state was soon brought back into the republic.

In 1865 Carrera died, at the age of 50, leaving the country ravaged by the chaos of his tyranny and inefficiency. He was succeeded by **Vicente Cerna**, another conservative, who was to rule for the next six years.

Meanwhile the liberal opposition was gathering momentum yet again and 1867 saw the first **liberal uprising**, led by **Serpio Cruz**. His bid for power was unsuccessful but it inspired two young liberals, Justo Rufino Barrios and Francisco Cruz, to follow suit. In the next few years they mounted several other unsuccessful revolts, and in 1870 Serpio Cruz was captured and hanged.

RUFINO BARRIOS AND THE COFFEE BOOM

1871 marked a major turning point in Guatemalan politics. In that year Rufino Barrios and Marcia García Ganados set out from Mexico with an army of just 45 men, entering Guatemala via the small border town of Cuilco. The **liberal revolution** thus set in motion was an astounding success, the army growing by the day as it approached the capital, which was finally taken on June 30, 1871. Ganados took the helm of the new liberal administration but held the presidency for just a few years, surrounding himself with ageing comrades and offering only very limited reforms.

Meanwhile, out in the district of Los Altos, **Rufino Barrios**, now a local military commander, was infuriated by the lack of action. In 1872 he marched his troops to the capital and installed them in the San José barracks, demanding immediate elections. These were granted and he won with ease. Barrios was a charismatic leader with tyrannical tendencies (the monuments to Barrios throughout the country testify to his sense of his own importance) who regarded himself as the great reformer and was intent on making sweeping changes. Above all he was a man of action. His most immediate acts were classic liberal gestures; the restructuring of the education system and an attack on the church. The University of San Carlos was secularised and modernised, while clerics were forbidden to wear the cloth and public religious processions were banned. The church was outraged and excommunicated Barrios, which prompted him to expel the archbishop in retaliation.

The new liberal perspective, though, was instilled with a deep arrogance and Barrios would tolerate no opposition, regarding his own racial and economic outlook as absolute. In order to ensure the success of his reforms he developed an effective network of secret police and struggled to make the army increasingly professional. In later years he founded the *politecnica*, an academy for young officers, and the army became an essential part of his political power base.

Alongside all this Barrios set about reforming agriculture, in which he presided over a boom period, largely as a result of the cultivation of **coffee**. It was this more than anything else that extinguished the era, and was to fundamentally reshape the country. When the liberals came to power coffee already accounted for half the value of the country's exports, and by 1884 the volume of output had increased five times. To foster this expansion Barrios founded a Ministry of Development, which extended the railway network (begun in 1880), established a national bank, and developed the ports of Champerico, San José and Iztapa to handle the growth in exports. Between 1870 and 1900 the volume of foreign trade increased twenty times.

All this had an enormous impact on Guatemalan **society**. Many of the new plantations were owned and run by German immigrants, and indeed the majority of the coffee eventually found its way to Germany. The newcomers soon formed a powerful elite, and although most of the Germans were later forced out of Guatemala (during World War II), their impact can still be felt: directly in the Verapaz highlands, and more subtly in the continuing presence of an extremely powerful clique, their wealth based on the income from plantation farming, who are still central to political life in Guatemala. The new liberal perspective maintained that foreign ideas were superior to indigenous ones, and while immigrants were welcomed with open arms the Indian population was still regarded as hopelessly inferior.

Indian society was also deeply affected by the needs of the coffee boom, and it was here that the new crop had the most damaging and lasting effect. Under the previous regime landowners had complained that the Indian population were reluctant to work on the plantations and that this endangered the coffee crop. Barrios was quick to respond to their needs and instituted a system of **forced labour**. In 1876 he ordered local political chiefs to make the necessary workers available: up to one-quarter of the male population could be dispatched to work on the *fincas*, and in addition to this the landowners continued to employ their old methods and debt peonage spread throughout the highlands. Conditions on the *fincas* were appalling and the Indian workforce was treated with utter contempt.

As a result of the coffee boom the Indians lost not only their freedom but also their land. From 1873 onwards the government began confiscating land that was either unused or communally owned, and selling it to the highest bidder. In some instances Indian villages were given small tracts of land taken from unproductive *fincas*, but in the vast majority of cases it was the Indians who lost their land to large coffee plantations. Huge amounts of land were seized, and land that had been communally owned for centuries was gobbled up by the new wave of agribusiness. In many areas the villagers rose up in defiance and there were significant **revolts** throughout the western highlands. In Momostenango some 500 armed men faced the authorities, only to find their village overrun by troops and their homes burnt to the ground. In Cantel troops shot all of the village officials, who were campaigning against plans to build a textile factory on their land. Throughout the latter years of the nineteenth and the early ones of the twentieth century, villages continued to rise up in defiance of demands on their land and labour. At the same time the loss of their most productive land forced the Indians to become dependent on seasonal labour, while attacks on their communities drove them into increasing introspection.

JORGE UBICO AND THE BANANA EMPIRE

Rufino Barrios was eventually killed in 1885 while fighting to recreate a unified Central America, and was succeeded by a string of short-lived, like-minded presidents. The next to hold power for any time was **Manuel Estrada Cabrera**, a stern authoritarian who restricted union organisation and supported the interests of big business. He ruled from 1898 until he was overthrown in 1920, by which time he was on the verge of insanity.

Meanwhile a new and exceptionally powerful player was becoming involved: the *United Fruit Company*, whose influence asserted itself over much of Central America in the early decades of the twentieth century, and was to exercise tremendous power over the next fifty years. The story of the *United Fruit Company* starts in Costa Rica, where a man named Minor Keith was contracted to build a railway from San José to the Pacific coast. Running short of money he was forced to plant bananas on land granted as part of the railway contract. The business proved so profitable that Keith merged his own *Tropical Trading and Transport Company* with his main rival *The Boston Fruit company*, to form the *United Fruit Company*.

The Company first moved into Guatemala in 1901, when it bought a small tract of land on which to grow bananas, and in 1904 it was awarded a contract to complete the railway from Guatemala City to Puerto Barríos. The company was also granted 100 feet on either side of the track, exempted from paying any tax for the next 99 years, and assured that the government wouldn't interfere with its activities. In 1912 the company was also granted ownership of the Pacific railway network and, as it already controlled the main Caribbean port, this gave it a virtual monopoly over transport. It was around this time that large-scale banana cultivation really took off ,and by 1934 the company controlled a massive amount of land, exporting around 3.5 million bunches of bananas annually, and reaping vast profits. In 1941 some 25,000 Guatemalans were employed in the banana industry.

The power of the *United Fruit Company* was by no means restricted to agriculture, and its influence was so pervasive that the company earned itself the nickname *El Pulpo*, "the octopus". Control of the transport network also gave it control over the coffee trade; by 1930 28 percent of the country's coffee output was handled by the company's Caribbean port, Puerto Barrios, and during the 1930s it cost as much to ship coffee from Guatemala to New Orleans as it did from Río de Janeiro to New Orleans.

Against this background the power of the Guatemalan government was severely limited, with the influence of the United States increasing alongside that of the *United Fruit Company*. In 1919 Guatemala faced a financial crisis and President Cabrera was ousted by a coup in the following year. He was replaced by **Carlos Herrera**, who represented the Union Party, a rare compromise between liberal and conservative politicians. Herrera refused to use the traditional weapons of tyranny and his reforms threatened to terminate *United Fruit Company* contracts. As a result of this Herrera was to last barely more than a year, replaced by **General José Maria Orellano** in December 1921. Orellano had no qualms about repressive measures and his minister of war, Jorge Ubico, killed some 290 opponents in 1926, the year in which Orellano died of a heart attack. His death prompted a bitter power struggle between Jorge Ubico, a fierce radical, and

Lazaro Chacon, who won the day and was elected as the new liberal President. In the next few years indigenous farmers began to express their anger at *United Fruit Company* monopoly, while the company demanded the renewal of long-standing contracts, squeezing Chacon from both sides. His rule came to an end in 1930, when he suffered a stroke.

The way was now clear for **Jorge Ubico**, a charismatic leader who was well connected with the ruling and land-owning elite. Ubico had risen fast through the ranks of local government as *jefe politico* in Alta Verapaz and Retalhuleu (greatly assisted by the patronage of his godfather Rufino Barrios), earning a reputation for efficiency and honesty. As president, however, he inherited financial disaster. Guatemala had been badly hit by the depression, accumulating debts of some $5 million: in response Ubico fought hard to expand the export market for Guatemalan produce, managing to sign trade agreements that exempted local coffee and bananas from import duties in the United States. But increased trade with the great American power was only possible at the expense of traditional links with Europe.

Within Guatemala Ubico steadfastly supported the *United Fruit Company* and the interests of US business. This relationship was of such importance that by 1940 ninety percent of all Guatemalan exports were being sold in the United States. Trade and diplomacy drew Guatemala ever closer to the United States, a relationship exemplified when Ubico, against his will, was forced to bow to US pressure for the expulsion of German landowners in the run up to World War II.

Internally, Ubico embarked on a radical programme of reform, including a sweeping drive against corruption and a massive road-building effort, which bought him great popularity in the provinces. Despite his liberal pretensions, however, Ubico sided firmly with big business when the chips were down, always offering his assistance to the *United Fruit Company* and other sections of the land-owning elite. The system of debt peonage was replaced by the **Vagrancy Law**, under which all landless peasants were forced to work 150 days a year. If they weren't needed by the *fincas* then their labour was used in the road-building programme or some other public works scheme. The power of landowners was further reinforced by a 1943 law that gave them the power to shoot poachers and vandals, and in effect landowners were given total authority over their workforce. Throughout his period of office Ubico ignored the rights and needs of the peasant population, who were still regarded as ignorant and backward, and as a result of this there were continued uprisings in the late 1930s and early 1940s.

Internal security was another obsession that was to dominate Ubico's years in office, as he became increasingly paranoid. He maintained that he was a reincarnation of Napoleon and was fascinated by all aspects of the military: he operated a network of spies and informers whom he regularly used to unleash waves of repression, particularly in the run-up to elections. In 1934, when he discovered an assassination plan, 300 people were killed in just two days. To prevent any further opposition he registered all printing presses in the country, and made discipline the cornerstone of state education.

But while Ubico tightened his grip on every aspect of government, the rumblings of opposition grew louder. In 1944 discontent erupted in a wave of student violence, and Ubico was finally forced to resign after 14 years of tyrannical rule. Power was transferred to **Juan Frederico Ponce Viades**, who attempted to continue in the same style, but by the end of the year he was also faced with open revolt, and finally the pair of them were driven into exile.

TEN YEARS OF "SPIRITUAL SOCIALISM"

The overthrow of Jorge Ubico released a wave of opposition that had been bottled up throughout his rule. Students, professionals, and young military officers demanded democracy and freedom. It was a mood that was to transform Guatemalan politics and so extreme a contrast to previous governments that the handover was dubbed **the 1944 revolution**.

Power was initially passed to a joint military and civilian junta, elections were planned, and in March 1945 a new constitution was instituted, extending suffrage to include all adults, and prohibiting the president from standing for a second term of office.

In the elections **Juan José Arevalo**, a teacher, was elected president with 85 percent of the vote. His political doctrine was dubbed "spiritual socialism", and he immediately set about effecting much-needed structural reforms. Under a new budget, a third of the government's income was allocated for social welfare, to be spent on the construction of schools and hospitals, a programme of immunisation, and a far-reaching literacy campaign. The vagrancy laws were abolished, a national development agency was founded, and in 1947 a labour code was adopted, ensuring workers the right to strike and to union representation.

The expulsion of German plantation owners during World War II had placed several large *fincas* in the hands of the state, and under Arevalo some of these were turned into cooperatives, while new laws protected tenant farmers from eviction. Other policies were intended to promote industrial and agricultural development: technical assistance and credit were made available to peasant farmers and there was some attempt to colonise the Petén.

In Arevalo's final years the pace of reform slackened somewhat as he concentrated on consolidating the gains made in early years and avoiding various attempts to overthrow him. Despite his popularity Arevalo was still wary of the traditional elite: church leaders, old-school army officers and wealthy landowners all resented the new wave of legislation and there were repeated coup attempts.

Elections were scheduled for 1950 and in the run-up the two main candidates were **Colonel Francisco Arana** and **Colonel Jacobo Arbenz**, both military members of the junta that had taken over at the end of the Ubico era. But in 1949 Arana, who was favoured by the right, was assassinated. Suspicion fell on Arbenz, who was backed by peasant organisations and unions, but there was no hard proof. For the actual vote Arana was replaced by **Brigadier Ydigoras Fuentes**, an army officer from the Ubico years.

Arbenz won the election with ease, taking 65 percent of the vote, and declared that he would transform the country into an independent capitalist nation and raise the standard of living. But the process of "overthrowing feudal society and ending economic dependency" was to lead to a direct confrontation between the new government and the American corporations which still dominated the economy.

Aware of the size of the task that confronted him, Arbenz enlisted the support of the masses, encouraging the participation of peasants in the programme of agrarian reform, and inciting the militancy of students and unions. He also attempted to break the great monopolies, building a state-run hydroelectric plant to rival the American-owned generating company, a highway to compete with the railway to the Caribbean, and planning a new port alongside Puerto Barrios, which was still owned by the *United Fruit Company*. At the same time Arbenz began a series of suits against foreign corporations, seeking unpaid taxes. Internally these measures aroused a mood of national pride, but they were strongly resented by the American companies whose empires were under attack.

The situation became even more serious with the **Law of Agrarian Reform**, which was passed in July 1952 and stated that idle and state-owned land would be distributed to the landless. Some of this land was to be rented out for a lifetime lease, but the bulk of it was handed over outright to the new owners, who were to pay a small percentage of its market value. The former owners of the land were to be compensated with government bonds, but the value of the land was calculated on the basis of the tax that they had been paying, usually a fraction of the true value.

The new laws outraged landowners, despite the fact that they were given the right to appeal. Between 1953 and 1954 around 884,000 hectares were redistributed to the benefit of some 100,000 peasant families. It was the first time since the arrival of the Spanish that the government had responded to the needs of the indigenous population, although some studies suggest that the whole thing confused the Indians, who were unsure how to respond. The landowner most seriously affected by the reforms was the *United Fruit Company*, which only farmed around 15 percent of its land holdings, and lost about half of its property.

As the pace of reform gathered, Arbenz began to take an increasingly radical stance. In 1951 the communist party was granted legal status, and in the next election four party members were elected to the legislature. But the Arbenz government was by no means a communist government, although it remained staunchly anti-American.

In the United States the press repeatedly accused the new Guatemalan government of being a communist beach-head in Central America, and the US government attempted to intervene on behalf of the *United Fruit Company*. Allen Dulles, the new director of the CIA, happened also to be a member of the company's board.

In 1953 President Eisenhower finally approved plans to overthrow the government. The CIA set up a small military invasion of Guatemala to depose Arbenz and install an alternative administration more suited to their tastes. A rag-tag army of exiles and mercenaries was put together in Honduras, and on June 18, 1954, Guatemala City was bombed with leaflets demanding the resignation of Arbenz. Aware that the army would never support him, Arbenz had bought a boat-load of Czechoslovakian arms, hoping to arm the people; but the guns were intercepted by the CIA before they reached Puerto Barrios. On the night of June 18, Guatemala was strafed with machine-gun fire while the invading army, described by Arbenz as "a heterogeneous Fruit Company expeditionary force", was getting closer to the city by the hour.

On June 27 Arbenz declared that he was relinquishing the presidency to **Colonel Carlos Enrique Diaz**, the army Chief of Staff. And on July 3 John Peurifoy, the American Ambassador to Guatemala, flew the new government to Guatemala aboard a US Air Force plane. Guatemala's attempt to escape the clutches of outside intervention and bring about social change had been brought to an abrupt end.

COUNTER-REVOLUTION AND MILITARY RULE

Following the overthrow of Arbenz it was the army that rose to fill the power vacuum, and they were to dominate politics for the next thirty years, sending the country into a spiral of violence and economic decline.

In 1954 the American Ambassador had persuaded a provisional government to accept **Castillo Armas** as the new president, and the gains of the previous ten years were immediately swept away. Hardest hit were the indigenous Indians – who had enjoyed the greatest benefits under the Arbenz administration – as *Ladino* rule was firmly reinstated. The constitution of 1945 was revoked and replaced by a more restrictive version; all illiterates were disenfranchised, left-wing parties were outlawed, and large numbers of unionists and agrarian reformers were simply executed. Restrictions placed on foreign investment were lifted and all the land that had been confiscated was returned to its previous owners. Meanwhile Armas surrounded himself with old-style Ubico supporters, attempting to reinstate the traditional elite and drawing heavily on US assistance in order to develop the economy.

To lend a degree of legitimacy to the administration Armas held a referendum in which voters were given the chance to support his rule (though what else was on offer was never made clear). With or without popular support, however, the new government had only limited backing from the armed forces, and coup rumblings continued throughout his period of office, which was brought to a close in 1957, when he was shot by his own bodyguard.

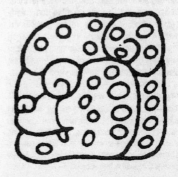

The assassination was followed by several months of political turmoil, out of which **Ydigoras** (who had stood against Arbenz in 1954, but declined an offer to lead the CIA invasion) emerged as the next president, representing the National Democratic Renovation Party. Ydigoras was to rule for five years, a period that was marked by corruption, incompetence, outrageous patronage and economic decline caused by a fall in coffee prices, although as some compensation the formation of the Central American Common Market helped to boost light industry. The government was so disastrous that it prompted opposition even from within the ranks of the elite. In 1960 a group of young military officers, led by **Marcos Yon Sosa** and **Turcios Lima**, attempted, without success, to take control, while in 1962 a large section of the Congress withdrew its support from the government.

Ydigoras was eventually overthrown when Arevalo threatened to return to Guatemala and contest the 1963 elections, which he might well have won. The possibility of another socialist government sent shock waves through the establishment in both Guatemala and the United States, and John F. Kennedy gave the go ahead for another coup. In 1963 the army* once more took control, under the leadership of **Perlata Azurdia**.

Perlata was president for just three years, during which he fiddled with the constitution and took his time in restoring the electoral process. Meanwhile the authoritarian nature of his government came up against the first wave of armed resistance. Two failed coupsters from 1960, Turcios Lima and Marco Yon Sosa, both army officers, took to the eastern highlands and waged a guerrilla war against the army. Both had been trained in counter-insurgency by the US army in Panama and, in their early twenties, they began to attack local army posts. A second organisation, FAR, emerged later that year, and the Guatemalan Labour Party (PGT) formed a shaky alliance with the guerrillas, attempting to represent their grie-

vances in the political arena and advocating a return to Arevalo's rule.

Perlata finally lost control in the the 1966 elections, which were won by **Julio Cesar Montenegro** of the centre-left *Partido Revolucionario*. Before taking office, however, Montenegro was forced to sign a pact with the military, obliging him to obey their instructions and giving the army a totally free hand in all affairs of national security. Montenegro was elected on July 1, and his first act was to offer an amnesty to the guerrillas: when this was rejected a ruthless counter-insurgency campaign swung into action (a pattern of events that was repeated in the early Eighties under Ríos Montt).

Under the command of **Colonel Carlos Arana Osorio**, "the Jackal of Zacapa", specially trained units, backed by US advisers, undermined peasant support for the guerrillas by terrorising the local population. The guerrillas were soon forced to spend much of their time on the move, and further damage was done to the movement by the death of Turcios Lima, in a car crash. By the end of the decade the guerrilla movement had been virtually eradicated in the eastern highlands, and its activities, greatly reduced, shifted to Guatemala City.

Meanwhile Montenegro declared his government to be "the third government of the revolution", aligning it with the socialist administrations of Arevalo and Arbenz. But despite the support of reformers, students, professionals and a large section of the middle classes, his hands were tied by the influence of the army. Above all else the administration was marked by the rise of political violence and the increasing power of an alliance between the army and the MLN, a right-wing political party. Political assassination became commonplace as "**death squads**" such as the *Mano Blanco* and *Ojo por Ojo* operated with impunity, killing peasant leaders, students, unionists and academics.

ECONOMIC DECLINE AND POLITICAL VIOLENCE

The history of Guatemala since 1970 has been dominated by electoral fraud and political violence. At the heart of the crisis is the injustice and inequality of Guatemalan society: for while the country remains fairly prosperous the benefits of its success never reach the poor, who are denied access to land, education or

---

*Since the time of Jorge Ubico the army had become increasingly professional and political, and following the overthrow of Arbenz it had received increasing amounts of US aid, expanding its influence to include a wide range of public works and infrastructure projects.

health care; forced instead to work in the coastal plantations that fuel the capital's affluence. The victims of this system have little to lose, while the ruling elite refuse to concede any ground.

In the 1970 elections the power of the military and the far right (represented by the MLN and PID) was confirmed, and **Colonel Arana Osorio**, who had directed the counterinsurgency campaign in the east, was elected as president. The turnout was under 50 percent, of which Arana polled just under half, giving him the votes of around 4 percent of the population (bearing in mind that only a small percentage of the population was enfranchised).

Once in power he set about eradicating armed opposition, declaring that "if it is necessary to turn the country into a cemetery in order to pacify it, I will not hesitate to do so". The reign of terror, conducted by both the armed forces and the "death squads", reached unprecedented levels. Once again the violence was to claim the lives of students, academics, opposition politicians, union leaders and agrarian reformers. According to one estimate there were 15,000 political killings during the first three years of Arana's rule.

The next round of presidential elections was held in 1974, and was contended by a broad coalition of centre-left parties under the banner of the National Opposition Front (FNO), headed by General Efraín Ríos Montt. The campaign was marked by manipulation and fraud on the part of the right, who pronounced their candidate, **Kjell Laugerud**, as the winner. The result caused uproar, and for several days the situation was extremely tense. Ríos Montt was eventually persuaded to accept defeat and packed off to a diplomatic post in Spain, although many had hoped that reforming elements within the armed forces would secure his right to the presidency.

Meanwhile, the feared severity of the Laugerud regime never materialised and instead he began to offer limited reforms, incorporating Christian Democrats into his government. Greater tolerance was shown towards union organisations and the cooperative movement, and the government launched a plan for the colonisation of the Petén and the Northern Transversal Strip in an attempt to provide more land. The army, though, continued

as ever to consolidate its authority, spreading its influence across a wider range of business and commercial interests, and challenging Laugerud's moderation.

All of this was interrupted by a massive **earthquake** on February 4, 1976. The quake left around 23,000 dead, 77,000 injured and a million homeless. For the most part it was the homes of the poor, built from makeshift materials and on unstable ground, that suffered the most, while subsistence farmers were caught out just as they were about to plant their corn. On the Caribbean coast Puerto Barrios was almost totally destroyed, and remained cut off from the capital for several months.

In the wake of the earthquake, during the process of reconstruction, fresh centres of regional control emerged on both sides of the political spectrum. The electoral process seemed to offer no respite from the injustice that was at the heart of Guatemalan society, and many of the victims felt the time had come to take action. A revived trade union organisation championed the cause of the majority, while a new guerrilla organisation, The Guerrilla Army of the Poor (EGP), emerged in the Ixil area, and army operations became increasingly ferocious. In 1977 President Carter suspended all military aid to Guatemala because of the country's appalling human rights record.

In the following year, 1978, Guatemala's elections were once again dominated by the army, who engineered a victory for **Brigadier General Fernando Lucas García**, who'd served as Defence Minister in the Laugerud administration. The run-up to the elections was marred by serious disturbances in Guatemala City, after bus fares were doubled. Lucas García promised to bring the situation under control and things took a significant turn for the worse as the new administration unleashed a fresh wave of violence. All opposition groups met with severe repression, as did journalists, trade unionists and academics. Conditions throughout the country were deteriorating rapidly, and the economy was severely struck by a fall in commodity prices, while several guerrilla armies were developing strongholds in the highlands.

As chaos threatened, the army resorted to extreme measures, and within a month there was a major massacre. In the village of

Panzos, Alta Verapaz, a group of local people were cut down by soldiers when they arrived for a meeting – 100 were left dead. In Guatemala City the situation became so dangerous that political parties were driven underground. Two leading members of the Social Democrat party, who were expected to win the next election, lost their lives in 1979. Once they were out of the way the government turned on the Christian Democrats, killing over 100 of their members, and forcing **Vinicio Cerezo**, the party's leader, into hiding.

Throughout the Lucas administration the **army** became increasingly powerful and the death toll rose steadily. In rural areas the war against the guerrillas was reaching new heights as army casualties rose to 250 a month, and the demand for conscripts grew rapidly. The four main guerrilla groups had an estimated 6000 combatants and some 250,000 unarmed collaborators. Under the Lucas administration the horrors of **repression** were at their most intense, both in the highlands and in the cities. The victims again included students, journalists, academics, politicians, priests, lawyers, teachers, unionists, and above all peasant farmers, massacred in their hundreds. Accurate figures are impossible to calculate but it's estimated that around 25,000 Guatemalans were killed during the four years of the Lucas regime.

But while high ranking officers became more and more involved in big business and political wrangling, the officers in the field began to feel deserted. Here there was growing discontent as a result of repeated military failures, inefficiency and a shortage of supplies, despite increased military aid from Israel.

RÍOS MONTT

The 1982 elections were again manipulated by the far right, who ensured a victory for **Aníbal Guevara**. However on March 23 a group of young military officers led a successful coup, which installed **General Efraín Ríos Montt** (who had been denied the post in 1974) as the head of a three-member junta. The coup leaders argued that they had been left with no option as the ruling elite had overridden the electoral process three times in the last eight years, and the takeover was supported by the majority of the opposition parties.

Ríos Montt was a committed Christian, a member of the *Iglesia del Verbo*, and throughout his rule Sunday-night television was dominated by presidential sermons. Above all he was determined to restore law and order, eradicate corruption, and defeat the guerrillas, with the ultimate aim of restoring "authentic democracy". Government officials were issued with identity cards inscribed with the words "I do not steal. I do not lie".

In the immediate aftermath of the coup things improved dramatically. In the cities repression dropped overnight, a welcome relief after the turmoil of the Lucas regime. Corrupt police and army officers were forced to resign, and trade and tourism began to return.

However, in the highlands the war intensified, as Ríos Montt declared that he would defeat the guerrillas by Christmas. Throughout June they were offered **amnesty** if they turned themselves in to the authorities, but once the month was passed (and only a handful had accepted) the army descended on the highlands with renewed vigour. Montt had instituted a new "code of conduct" for the army, binding soldiers not to "take a pin from the villagers" and not to "make romantic overtures to the women of the region". The army set about destroying the guerrillas' infrastructure, by undermining their support within the community. In those villages that had been "pacified" the local men were organised into Civil Defence Patrols (PACs), armed with ancient rifles, and told to patrol the countryside. Those who refused were denounced as "subversives". Thus the people of the villages were forced to take sides, caught between the attraction of guerrilla propaganda and the sheer brutality of the armed forces.

Ríos Montt's bizarre blend of stern morality and ruthlessness was as successful as it was murderous, and the army was soon making significant gains against the guerrillas. In late 1982 President Reagan decided that Ríos Montt had been given a "bum rap", and restored American military aid. Meanwhile the "state of siege" became a "state of alarm", under which special tribunals were given the power to try and execute suspects. By the middle of 1983 Ríos Montt was facing growing pressure from all sides. Leaders of the Catholic church were outraged by the influx of evangelical preachers, while politicians, businessmen, farmers and professionals were angered by the lack of progress towards democratic rule, and landowners were frightened by rumours of land reform.

In August 1983 Ríos Montt was overthrown by yet another military coup, this one backed by a US government keen to see Guatemala set on the road to democracy. The new president was **General Mejía Víctores**, and although the death squads and disappearances continued, elections were held for an 88-member Constituent Assembly, which was given the task of drawing up a new constitution, in preparation for presidential elections.

Under Víctores there was an upturn in the level of rural repression, though the process of reconstruction initiated by Ríos Montt continued. Internal refugees were rehoused in "model villages", where they were under the control of the army. Scarcely any money was available for rebuilding the devastated communities, and it was often widows and orphans who were left to construct their own homes. In the Ixil Triangle alone the war had displaced 60,000 people (72 percent of the population), and nine model villages were built to replace 49 that had been destroyed. Nationwide a total of 440 villages had been destroyed and around 100,000 had lost their lives.

In 1985 presidential elections were held, the first free vote in Guatemala for thirty years.

VINICIO CEREZO AND DEMOCRATIC RULE

The elections were won by **Vinicio Cerezo**, a Christian Democrat whose father had served in the Arbenz administration. Cerezo was by no means associated with the traditional ruling elite and had himself been the intended victim of several assassination attempts. His election victory was the result of a sweeping wave of popular support, and in the run-up to the election he offered a programme of reform that would rid the country of repression.

Once in office, however, Cerezo was aware that his room for manoeuvre was subject to severe limitations, and declared that the army still held 75 percent of the power. From the outset he could promise little: "I'm a politician not a magician. Why promise what I cannot deliver? All I commit myself to doing is opening up the political space, giving democracy a chance."

Throughout his five-year rule Cerezo has offered a **non-confrontational approach**, seeking above all else to avoid upsetting the powerful alliance of business interests, landowners and generals. To protect himself Cerezo courted the support of a group of sympathetic officers, and with their aid he survived several coup attempts. But the administration remained trapped in the middle; the right accused Cerezo of communist leanings, while the left claimed that he was evading his commitment to reform.

Political killings dropped off a great deal under civilian rule, although they by no means stopped. Murder was still a daily event in Guatemala in the late Eighties and the war between the army and the guerrillas still raged in remote corners of the highlands. In Guatemala City the death squads still operated freely, and while no one accused Cerezo of involvement in the killings, they were often carried out by policemen or soldiers.

It's certainly true that the early years of civilian rule created a breathing space in Guatemala, but as the decade drew to a close it was clear that the army was still actively controlling political opposition. Having forsaken the role of government, the generals allowed Cerezo to take office, presenting an acceptable face to the world, but the army continued to control the countryside. In 1988 violence was again on the increase, and in the village of El Aguacate, in the department of Chimaltenango, 22 corpses were found in a shallow grave. Army and guerrillas have blamed each other for the massacre, by far the most serious under Cerezo's rule, but as yet no proof has emerged (which may in itself be an indication of official involvement). Urban killings and "disappearances" were also on the increase in the final years of Cerezo's rule. In February 1989 there were 220 killings, of which 82 were politically motivated. It now appears that the Cerezo administration has failed to stem the tide of violence.

The country's leading human rights organisation, The Mutual Support Group (GAM), have repeatedly called for an investigation into the fate of the "**disappeared**". But while Cerezo has chosen to forget the past, and ongoing abuses go unpunished, GAM's leaders have also become victims of the death squads. The present political climate has fostered the growth of numerous pressure groups and protests are now a regular feature of Guatemalan life.

A general thaw in the political climate brought fresh demands for reform. Sixty-five percent of the population still live below the official poverty line, and little was done to meet their needs in terms of education, health care or employment. The thirst for land reform reared its head once again, and under the leadership of Padre Andrés Girón, some 35,000 peasants demanded action. Girón's approach was direct. He accused business interests of "exploiting and killing our people. We want the south coast, that's where the wealth of Guatemala lies". Cerezo has avoided the issue and in a bid to appease the business community he has also steered clear of any significant tax reform or privatisation policy. (Padre Girón has also been the intended victim of an assassination attempt.) Meanwhile the teachers, postal workers and farm labourers have all been on strike, demanding action on human rights and economic reform.

The Guatemalan economy has been hit badly by falling commodity prices (most notably the price of coffee), and here also the president has little room to manoeuvre. Despite the fact that Guatemalan income tax is among the lowest in the world, any move to increase tax receipts is met with bitter resistance from the land-owning classes. However Cerezo did successfully negotiate a loan from the IMF and has instituted a series of austerity measures designed to revitalise the economy after decades of decline.

PRESIDENTIAL ELECTIONS: NOVEMBER 1990

As this book went to press, presidential elections were scheduled for November 1990, though the list of candidates was still unclear. The constitution prevents Cerezo from standing for re-election, and he has endorsed the candidacy of Alfonso Cabrera, although Cerezo's wife has also threatened to stand (much to the embarrassment of the Christian Democratic party). General Ríos Montt, who retains much popularity in the countryside, is said to stand a good chance of winning, and Padre Andrés Girón has also suggested that he may stand for election.

BELIZEAN HISTORY SINCE THE DECLINE OF CLASSIC MAYAN CIVILISATION

From around 900 AD, and the break-up of Classic Maya civilisation, the Belize area was largely independent, but it remains impossible to separate the early history of Belize from that of the surrounding areas of El Petén in Guatemala or the Yucatán of Mexico, where small tribal groups fought bitterly to maintain their independence.

After the collapse of lowland Maya civilisation in the ninth century and the invasion of the Toltecs in 987 AD, the Yucatán Peninsula became the main centre of Maya political and social life. To the south, however, the Belize area was never entirely deserted and many of the cities here not only survived but prospered long after those in the Yucatán.

Relatively little is known of this period of decline. Chichén Itzá, the great centre in the Yucatán, was abandoned early in the thirteenth century, and thereafter power moved to Mayapan. This in turn declined in the fifteenth century and many of the inhabitants moved south into the jungles of the Petén. In the years leading up to the Spanish conquest the Yucatán and northern Belize consisted of over a dozen rival provinces, bound up in a cycle of competition and conflict.

THE FIRST EUROPEANS

The general assumption that Belize was practically deserted by the time Europeans arrived is now widely discredited. In fact the Maya towns and provinces, though no longer powerful city-states with far-reaching trade links, were still vigorously independent, as the Spanish found to their cost on several occasions.

The northern part of Belize, possibly reaching as far south as the Northern River, was part of the Maya province of **Chactemal**, later known as Chetumal. Its capital was not at the Mexican city of the same name, but probably a site now known as **Santa Rita**, in present day Corozal. Chetumal was a wealthy province, producing cacao and honey, and covering an area from Maskall in Belize to northern Lake Bacalar in Mexico. Trade, alliances and wars kept Chetumal in contact with surrounding Maya states up to and beyond the Spanish conquest of Aztec Mexico.

Further south the forests were thicker and the ridge of the Maya Mountains intruded across the land. To the Maya of Chetumal this area was known as *Dzuluinicob* – "land of foreigners". The capital of this province was **Tipu**, possibly located at Baking Pot on the Belize River or, more likely, Negroman, located on the Macal River, south of San Ignacio. The Maya here controlled the upper Belize River valley and put up strenuous resistance to attempts by the Spanish to subdue and convert them. The struggle was to continue with simmering resentment until 1707 when the population of Tipu was forcibly removed to Lake Petén Itzá.

The first **Europeans** to set eyes on the mainland of Belize were the Spanish sailors Pinzon and de Solis in 1506 or 1508, on a voyage round the Bay of Honduras, but they didn't attempt a landing. In 1511 a small group of Spanish sailors, shipwrecked off Jamaica, managed to reach land on the southern coast of Yucatán. This first, accidental, contact between European and Maya was fatal for some of the shipwrecked Spaniards. Five were immediately sacrificed, some escaped and some became slaves.

It is possible that at least one of the escapees regained contact with his fellow countrymen because **Cortés** knew of the existence of two survivors of the shipwreck when he reached Yucatán in 1519. He sent for them after he had established his force on Cozumel. Geronimo de Aguilar immediately joined Cortés, but the other survivor, Gonzalo Guerrero (the archaeologist Eric Thompson calls him the first European to make Belize his home), refused. Guerrero eventually married the daughter of Nachankan, the chief of Chetumal, and was to become a crucial military adviser to the Maya in their subsequent resistance to Spanish domination. Cortés, meanwhile, sailed north around Yucatán and into the Bay of Campeche to land at Veracruz: the destruction of the Aztec Empire promised greater glory and pillage.

In the early years of the conquest few reports were made of contact with the Maya in the east, possibly because the Spanish themselves had heard no stories of gold or treasure – their overriding obsession. In 1525 Cortés himself almost certainly passed through the extreme south of Belize on his epic march from Veracruz in Mexico to punish a rebellious subordinate in a recently established town on the Gulf of Honduras. The course of his march took Cortés and his retinue of 140 Spanish soldiers and 3000 Indians across the heartland of the Maya, which still contained many thriving towns and cities. They traversed largely unknown territory – jungles, swamps, tropical rivers and mountains, heading through Tabasco, Chiapas and the Petén. Cortés was welcomed at Tayasal on Lake Petén Itzá by Can Ek, chief of the Itzá, who had heard of Cortés' cruelty in conquering the Aztecs and decided not to oppose him. The expedition continued southwards, to the valley of the Sarstoon River, the present boundary with Guatemala, either following that river to the coast or crossing it and following the Río Dulce. The destination was San Gil de Buena Vista at the mouth of the Río Dulce, the recently renamed and relocated Maya town of Nito, a Late Postclassic trading centre on the Río Dulce.

After pacifying the rebels Cortés sailed north to Mexico, without apparently realising Yucatán was a peninsula. Despite previous expeditions, including landings on the island of Cozumel and the settlement of Salamanca on the mainland near Xelha, it was not until 1528, when Francisco de Montejo sailed south along the coast of Yucatán to Honduras, that the Spanish realised that the Yucatán was not an island.

ATTEMPTED CONQUEST

At the time of the conquest, the Maya of Yucatán and Belize were not united into a single empire. Postclassic society in the northern lowlands consisted of numerous city-states, fighting rivals or forming alliances to gain temporary advantage. The leaders of these provinces were accustomed to dealing with enemies and fighting to retain their independence, which is one reason why the Spanish found the Yucatán and Belize such a difficult area to subdue.

In Mexico and Peru it had proved relatively simple to capture and eventually kill the "living god", leader of a militaristic, unified and highly organised society, and replace him with an equally despotic Spanish ruler. However here the situation was very different, and similar in many ways to that in the highlands of Guatemala.

The first stage in the attempted conquest of Yucatán was the granting of permission by the Spanish crown to **Francisco de Montejo** to colonise "the islands of Cozumel and Yucatán". He established a small settlement at Salamanca, but this was not safe from attack, so in 1528 he sailed south to find a more secure location for a permanent Spanish colony. At the same time his lieutenant, **Alonso Davila**, was to lead an overland expedition to the south. Neither was particularly successful; Davila encountered hostile Maya a short distance south and Montejo was forced to turn away from Chetumal by Maya under the leadership of Gonzalo Guerrero.

A second attempt by Davila to found a town at Chetumal, in 1531, was also short-lived. On this occasion the Maya had abandoned the town, on the advice of Guerrero who realised they could not defeat the Spanish outright, and it was occupied by Davila and renamed **Villa Real**. This was the first attempt by Spain to conquer and settle the area later to become Belize. Once established, however, Davila and his troops were continually harassed by the Maya when searching for food and were driven out eighteen months later, fleeing south along the coast of Belize and eventually reaching Omoa in Honduras.

Montejo's vision of a vast province of the Spanish empire comprising the whole of Yucatán, Chiapas and Honduras was not to be fulfilled. His son, Montejo the Younger, completed the conquest of Yucatán, establishing the capital at **Mérida** in 1542. Montejo himself was occupied further south, in the sparsely settled, ill-defined area of Honduras. From 1535 to 1544 he was *Adelantado* of Yucatán and Governor of Honduras-Higueras, which would have included Belize. With the establishment of the *Audiencia de los Confines* in 1544 Montejo lost control of Honduras, but he still considered the area north of the Río Dulce to be part of Yucatán and within his domain. Expeditions he sent in 1546–7 to the Río Dulce were opposed by the Dominicans working there to peacefully convert the Maya, and by 1549 he was forced to abandon the idea of a settlement, his authority restricted to Yucatán alone.

For some years after Montejo and Davila's unsuccessful attempts to conquer Chetumal, northern Belize remained independent. Chetumal regained its important trading links and was obviously also a powerful military force, in 1542 sending fifty war canoes 200 miles to Omoa in Honduras to assist local Indians in their fight against the Spanish.

Late in 1543, however, **Gaspar Pacheco**, his son Melchor and his nephew Alonso began another chapter in the sickeningly familiar tale of Spanish atrocities, advancing on Chetumal, destroying food and ruthlessly slaughtering the Indians. In a letter to Spain, Fray Lorenzo de Bienvenida wrote: "Nero was not more cruel (than Alonso Pacheco). He passed through and reached a province called Chetumal, which was at peace. . . . This captain with his own hands committed outrages: he killed many with the garrote, saying 'This is a good rod with which to punish these people'."

In 1544 the Pachecos had subdued Maya resistance sufficiently to found a town on Lake Bacalar and claim *encomienda* (tribute) from villages in Chetumal. It is likely that the Pachecos also conquered parts of the province of Dzuluinicob to the south, though there was strong opposition to Spanish control with uprisings in Yucatán and Chetumal. Tipu, for a time at least, was the centre of an alliance between Chetumal and Dzuluinicob, showing that there was still organised resistance to Spanish domination.

During the second half of the sixteenth century missions were established, including one at Lamanai, and the Spanish, with difficulty, strengthened their hold over northern Belize. The resentment that was always present under the surface, however, boiled over into total rebellion in 1638, forcing Spain to abandon the area of Chetumal and Tipu completely.

In the mid-seventeenth century the nearest permanent Spanish settlements to Belize were at Salamanca de Bacalar in Yucatán and Lake Izabal in Guatemala. Records are scarce but it is possible that the Maya of Belize were under some form of Spanish influence even if they were not under Spanish rule. Perhaps the determination of Maya resistance deterred Spain from attempting to colonise the area; perhaps the experience of cruelty and oppression which followed conquest caused the Maya to flee to inaccessible forests in an attempt to retain their independence. Repeated **expeditions** were mounted by friars and colonial leaders during the seventeenth century: one unsuccessful *entrada* led by Fray Fuensalida in 1641 attempted to convert the people of Tipu, but there was little, if any, Spanish contact until 1695, when a Spanish mission met Itzá leaders to discuss the **surrender of the Itzá**. The negotiations were fruitless and in 1697 Spanish forces attacked Tayasal (on Lake Petén Itzá), bringing Maya independence to an end, at least in theory.

Events didn't all go in favour of the Spanish even now. In the late seventeenth century Bacalar was abandoned after years of **Indian and pirate attacks**. Spain's forces were simply too stretched to cope with securing and administering the vast (and relatively gold-free) territory from Campeche to Honduras. English, and later British, trade and territorial ambitions in the sixteenth century focused on America, bringing her into almost continuous conflict with Spain. The capture of Jamaica in 1655, after 150 years of Spanish rule, gave Britain a base in the Caribbean from which she could harass Spanish shipping and support the growth of her colonies.

THE ARRIVAL OF THE BRITISH

The failure of the Spanish authorities to clearly delineate the southern boundary of Yucatán subsequently allowed **buccaneers** (primarily British) to find refuge along the coast of Belize and ultimately led to Guatemala's claim to the territory of British Honduras and refusal to recognise Belize's independence. Had Spain effectively occupied the area between Yucatán and Honduras it is unlikely that British influence would have been allowed to become established. When Spain did take action on various occasions to expel the British settlers (Baymen), there was confusion over whether the Captain-General of Yucatán or Guatemala maintained jurisdiction in the area. Consequently the Baymen were able to return in the absence of any permanent Spanish outposts on the coast.

British incursions along the Bay of Honduras were first made by buccaneers, resting and seeking refuge after raids on Spanish ships and settlements. Some of the great Elizabethan sailors such as Raleigh, Hawkins and Drake may have landed on the coast of Belize, although there are no records to prove this. (Indeed records referring to settlements, even temporary camps, are scarce: while the dates of the establishment of other British colonies in the Caribbean are known, there was no attempt on the part of the British government to colonise Belize.)

Britain was not the only power interested in establishing colonies in this lucrative area of the Caribbean, with both **France** and the **Netherlands** keen to establish a foothold. Companies were set up to equip privateers, really government-sanctioned pirate ships, to raid the Spanish treasure fleets. Treasure wasn't always easy to come by and sometimes they would plunder the piles of logwood, cut and awaiting shipment to Spain.

In due course the cutting of **logwood** was to become an important industry in Belize. The wood itself, hard and extremely heavy, was worth £90 to £110 per ton and the trade was controlled by Spain. Back in Europe logwood was used in the expanding textile industry to dye woollens black, red and grey. Naturally such an abundance of convertible wealth attracted the buccaneers, once they learned of its importance. By the mid-seventeenth century, and possibly as early as 1640, British buccaneers had settled on the coasts of Campeche and the Spanish Caribbean.

The signing of the **Godolphin Treaty** of 1670 between Britain and Spain recognised the right of Britain to own and occupy the territories in the Americas she held at the time of signing. This acknowledgement by Spain was partly to control the activities of the buccaneers (already outlawed in a treaty of 1667) and partly to ease tension between the two powers in the face of increasing French might in Europe and the Caribbean. However it was never intended that this treaty would legitimise the existing British settlements or the cutting of logwood on the coast from Mexico · to Panama, which Spain clearly regarded as her own domain.

Of course the logwood cutters did not simply go away and Spain's attitude to the trade was ambivalent, with local officials tending to ignore it. For the next 130 years **British settlements** on the western shore of the Caribbean periodically came under attack whenever Spain sought to defend her interests, but the settlements on the coasts of Campeche, Yucatán, Belize and the Mosquito Coast were on the periphery of much wider and, to the Great Powers of the period, more important issues. France and Holland as well as Britain and Spain were building empires and competing for trade across the globe. The attention of the governments of these countries rarely rested upon the humid and insect-ridden swamps where the logwood cutters, who were becoming known as **Baymen**, worked and lived. Treaties were signed, edicts passed and the British government, while wishing to profit from the trade in logwood, did not wish to get involved in the question of whether or not the Baymen were British subjects. For the most part they were left to their own devices.

Life in the logwood camps was uncomfortable to say the least. Though the wood was mainly cut in the dry season, the men often had to wait until the rains to float it down the rivers to be stored for shipment. The Baymen lived in rough huts thatched with palmetto leaves, surviving on provisions brought by ships from Jamaica. These ships also brought rum, which the Baymen drank with relish whenever it was available; an English merchant (writing in 1726) reports: "Rum Punch is their Drink, which they'll sometimes sit several Days at . . . for while the Liquor is moving they don't care to leave it."

Though many of the cutters had "voluntarily" given up buccaneering, raiding of Spanish ships still occurred in the later years of the seventeenth century, only to be punished by Spain whenever she had the will and opportu-

nity. An attack by Spain on settlers in the Bay of Campeche left the survivors imprisoned in Mexico and led to Belize becoming the main centre for logwood cutting. (Some cutters did return to Campeche but in further attacks in 1716 and 1735 Spain again destroyed the settlements.)

Attacks by Spanish forces, from both Yucatán and Petén, on the settlements in the Belize River valley occurred throughout the eighteenth century, with the Baymen being driven out on several occasions. Increasingly though, Britain – at war with Spain from 1739 to 1748 (The War of Jenkins' Ear) and France from 1743 to 1748 (The War of Austrian Succession) began to admit a measure of responsibility for the protection of the settlers – for the British there was little to lose.

In 1746, in response to requests from the Baymen, the Governor of Jamaica sent troops to Belize, but this assistance didn't stop the Spanish laying waste to the settlement in 1747 and again in 1754. The **Paris Peace Treaty** of 1763 was the first (of many) to allow the British to cut logwood, but since it did not define boundaries the Governor of Yucatán sent troops from Bacalar to ensure that the cutters confined themselves to the Belize River. The Baymen complained at this interference and in 1765 the Commander-in-Chief at Jamaica, Admiral Burnaby, visited Belize to ensure that the provisions of the treaty, vague though they were, were upheld. As so often in reports of naval officers concerning the condition of the settlers he found them in "a state of Anarchy and Confusion". The admiral decided the Baymen needed laws and regulations. His rules, known as **Burnaby's Code**, were a simple set of laws concerning the maintenance of justice in a remote and uncouth area where the British government did not care to become too closely involved. They gave authority to a bench of magistrates to hold quarterly courts with the power to impose fines, supported by a jury. The Baymen attached an importance to the Code (though they apparently rarely obeyed it) beyond that which Burnaby intended, and even voted to increase its scope a year later.

Decades of Spanish attacks had fostered in the settlers a spirit of defiance and self-reliance, with a realisation that British rule was preferable to Spanish, as long as they could choose which of its institutions to accept.

THE BATTLE OF SAINT GEORGE'S CAYE

The **Battle of St George's Caye** was the culmination of over a century of antagonism, boundary disputes and mutual suspicion between the Spanish colonial authorities and the woodcutting (ex-buccaneering) Baymen. Relations were never secure: the Spanish feared raids on their treasure ships, the Baymen feared being driven out of what was ostensibly Spanish territory.

In 1779 Spain (then allied with France on the side of the American colonies) had sent a fleet under the Commandant of Bacalar to Belize and captured all the inhabitants of St George's Caye, then the chief settlement of the Baymen, imprisoning them in Mérida and later Havana.

The Versailles Peace Treaty (1783) did little to resolve the question of the Bay settlement but a Convention signed three years later in London granted concessions to the Baymen. Logwood (and other timber) could be cut as far as the Sibun River; St George's Caye could be inhabited but no plantations were to be established. The clause which rankled the independent-minded settlers most was that no fortifications were allowed and no system of government could be established without approval from Madrid. True to their "turbulent and unsettled disposition", the Baymen ignored the strictures of the Convention, cutting wood where they pleased and being generally unruly. After 1791 the settlement was without even the little-regarded authority of a Superintendent appointed by the Governor of Jamaica.

With the outbreak of war between Britain and Spain in 1796 the settlers appealed for help in their defence to Lord Balcarres, the Governor of Jamaica. In spite of his own difficulties in Jamaica, Balcarres sent a small amount of gunpowder and arms to the settlement and in December a **Lieutenant-Colonel Barrow** was despatched to Belize as Superintendent, to command the settlers in the event of hostilities. Under the supervision of Colonel Barrow the settlers prepared for war, albeit grudgingly.

A vital **Public Meeting**, held on June 1, 1797, decided by 65 votes to 51 to defend the settlement rather than evacuate. A few companies of troops were sent from Jamaica and slaves were released from woodcutting to be armed and trained. The sloop **HMS Merlin** was stationed in the Bay, local vessels were armed, gun rafts built and an attack was expected at any time. Throughout the next year the mood of the defenders vacillated between aggression and despair. Martial law was imposed, all men of military age were ordered to Belize Town and buildings on St George's Caye were pulled down to prevent their use by the enemy. As late as August 1798, 53 of the Baymen wrote to Barrow asking him for help in their request to Lord Balcarres that they be removed to safety in the Bahamas or Jamaica; the plea was ignored. The Baymen (and their slaves) would have to defend themselves with the scant resources at their disposal.

The available local support for HMS Merlin consisted of the sloops *Towser*, *Tickler* and *Mermaid*, with one gun each, and the schooners *Swinger* and *Teazer*, each armed with six four-pounders, and seven gun-flats (rafts) armed with one nine-pound gun each.

The **Spanish fleet** assembled by the Governor of Yucatán, one Don Arturo O'Neill Tirone, sailed from Bacalar early in September. There were reported to be 32 vessels, including 16 heavily armed men-of-war and 2000 troops – on 3 September, 1798, look-out boats north of Belize Town sighted them. The main body of the Spanish fleet remained in deep water beyond the reef while five ships attempted to force their way over Montego Caye Shoals, just north of St George's Caye. They were repulsed by the three sloops and the next day the Spanish tried again to force a passage, but again they were beaten back, this time withdrawing to the safety of the main fleet. That evening, September 4, stakes placed by the Spanish to mark the reefs and channels were removed by the defenders, who knew these waters well. Yet another attempt was mounted on September 5 to break through Montego Caye Shoals, and was again unsuccessful.

Colonel Barrow and Captain Moss of the *Merlin* correctly guessed the Spanish would now try to seize St George's Caye. The *Merlin*, and part of the Baymen's tiny fleet, sailed there on the evening of the September 5, securing it just as twelve of the heaviest Spanish warships were attempting to do the same. The Spanish, frustrated by these setbacks, withdrew to their anchorage between Long Caye and Caye Chapel.

The next few days must have passed anxiously for both sides: the Spanish, with their massive firepower severely restricted by the shallow water; and the Baymen with their small but highly manoeuvrable fleet, awaiting the impending attack. On the morning of **September 10, 1798,** fourteen of the largest Spanish ships sailed to within a mile and a half of St George's Caye. Five vessels, packed with troops, anchored to the east of the caye. The other nine, armed with eighteen- and twenty-four-pounder cannon and towing launches loaded with soldiers, formed a line abreast and began firing.

In the centre of the channel Captain Moss of HMS *Merlin* held his fire; the Spanish broadsides were falling short. At 1.30pm he gave the order to open fire. Guns blazing, the small fleet swept forward, wreaking havoc among the heavy and crowded Spanish warships. The battle was fast and furious; the Baymen's slaves at least as eager to fight the Spanish as their masters were. Although a dory was sent to Belize to summon Colonel Barrow to join in the fight and the troops immediately set off in any craft available, they arrived too late to take part in the action.

The Spanish fleet, already weakened by desertions and yellow fever, suffered heavy losses and fled in disorder to Caye Chapel. They remained there for five days, burying some of their dead on the island. On the morning of September 16 the Spanish sailed for Bacalar, defeated and still harassed by the Baymen, who captured a packet-boat that evening and took five prisoners.

Though a victory was won against almost overwhelming odds, the Battle of St George's Caye was not by itself decisive. No one in the Bay settlement was sure that the Spanish would not once again attempt to remove the Baymen by force. The legal status was as before: a settlement where the inhabitants could cut timber but did not constitute a territory of the British empire. Sovereign rights remained, nominally at least, with the Spanish crown, though it was never clear which of the neighbouring *Audiencias*, Mexico or Guatemala, had responsibility for implementing the numerous treaties and agreements between Britain and Spain.

In purely practical terms the power of the Spanish empire was waning while the British empire was consolidating and expanding. But in Belize the slaves were still slaves though they had fought valiantly alongside the Baymen: their owners expected them to go back to cutting mahogany. Emancipation came no earlier than elsewhere in the British empire.

In 1898 the centenary of the battle, September 10, was established as a national holiday, St George's Caye Day, still jubilantly observed today.

SETTLERS AND SLAVES

The population of the Honduras settlements during the century following the arrival of the first buccaneers had never been more than a few hundred, their livelihoods dependent on the attitude of the adjacent Spanish colonies. In order to gain concessions from Spain favourable to the Belize settlement, Britain had agreed to relinquish claims to the Mosquito Shore (along the coasts of Honduras and Nicaragua, including the Bay Islands) in the **Convention of 1786**. Many of the aggrieved inhabitants displaced by the Convention settled in Belize and by 1790 the population had reached over 2900 – of whom over 2100 were slaves.

A report by a Spanish missionary in 1724 mentions the ownership of **slaves** by Englishmen, and it is unlikely that slaves were brought in (from Jamaica and Bermuda) much before that time. Over the years the view that slavery in Belize was somehow less harsh than elsewhere has emerged. It's a misconception that may have arisen because of the differences between plantation slavery, as practised in the West Indies, and the mainly forest labour that Belize slaves were employed upon. A number of slave revolts from 1745 to 1820 show that relations between master and slave were not as amicable as some would like to believe. The whites in the settlement, always vastly outnumbered by their slaves, feared rebellion at least as much as they feared attack by the Spanish, requesting help from Jamaica on several occasions. The biggest (and arguably most successful) revolt occurred in 1773 when six white men were murdered and at least eleven slaves escaped across the Río Hondo, where they were promised asylum by the Spanish authorities. Spain was not displaying altruism with this policy, as encouraging slaves to flee the Belize settlement was calculated to weaken its economy.

In spite of revolts, the nature of slavery in Belize was very different from that on the sugar plantations in the West Indies. The work of cutting mahogany, which had overtaken logwood as the principal export by the 1760s, involved small gangs working in the forest on their own or on a fairly harmonious level with an overseer. The slaves were armed, with firearms in some cases, to hunt for food and for protection against Indians. Skills developed in searching for the trees, cutting them down and transporting them to the coast, gave the slaves involved a status and a position of trust which their masters depended upon for the continuation of their own way of life. Manumission, whereby a slave might purchase his freedom or be freed as a gift or as a bequest in a will, was much more frequent in Belize than in the Caribbean islands, perhaps an indication of the greater informality in Belizean society. However treatment could still be harsh and little protection was offered by the law. The owner could inflict up to thirty-nine lashes or imprison his slaves, and if a slave was hanged for rebellion or assault the owner could be compensated for the loss of his property.

Ironically it was the Abolition Act of 1807, which made it illegal for British subjects to carry on the African slave trade, but not to transport slaves from one British colony to another, which gave the settlers in Belize recognition as **British subjects**. If Belize was not a colony (which it clearly was not) then slaves could not be transported between Jamaica and the settlement. Superintendent Arthur, the British government's representative and upholder of the law in Belize, decided that the settlers in Belize were British subjects and as such forbidden to engage in the slave trade. The **Abolition Act of 1833** ended slavery throughout the British empire, and a special clause was written to include Belize.

As the gangs of woodcutters advanced further into the forests, searching for mahogany which was of increasing value in furniture-making, they came into contact with scattered bands of Maya. For centuries the Indians had been driven from their homelands, taking refuge from European settlers and missionaries. The Baymen, however, had no wish to colonise or convert the Maya, so there was little conflict in the early and mid-eighteenth century.

THE SETTLEMENT BECOMES A COLONY

The consolidation of British logging interests in the late eighteenth century led to grudging, tentative steps toward recognition from Spain. A form of British colonial government gradually became established, though the settlement did not achieve **colony status** until 1862. Since the 1730s the settlers had been electing magistrates at the Public Meeting which, in the democratic spirit of the time, gave only property-owning white males a vote. Free coloured men were allowed to vote at the Public Meeting after 1808, though they had to prove five years' residence and own property worth £200 (against a white's one year and £100). The **Public Meeting** had its origins in the early years of the settlement, as the need arose for a rudimentary form of government to bring order to the lawless and independent logwood cutters. The Meeting, at first informal, slowly assumed importance, and members voted to grant powers to the magistrates to hold courts and impose fines. Burnaby's Code in 1765 had reinforced and enlarged the jurisdiction of the magistrates and also allowed the laws passed to be enforced by the captain of a British naval ship. Frequently, visiting naval officers reported on the settlers inability to keep the laws, generally finding Belize in disorder, even anarchy.

These early examples of Britain's acceptance of some form of responsibility for the settlers led to the appointment in 1784 of the first **Superintendent**, Captain Despard, who took up his position in 1786. The office of Superintendent, always held by an army officer, appears to have been a difficult one. They often faced an awkward, unsupportive Public Meeting which wanted to run affairs in the settlement without "interference" from London. Gradually, though, during the first half of the nineteenth century, the powers of the Superintendent grew, while those of the magistrates lessened. Magistrates, elected but unpaid, had traditionally shouldered the burden of public office, including the finance of the settlement – collecting taxes, deciding on expenditure and administering justice. The election of magistrates ceased in 1832, after which they were appointed by the Superintendent, with the approval of the Colonial Office. Progress towards an elected **Legislative Assembly**, along the lines of those in British colonies, was made, and the office of Superintendent took on the role (though not the title) of a Lieutenant-Governor of a colony.

In 1854 a Legislative Assembly was finally formed, consisting of eighteen elected men and three appointees of the Superintendent. A Speaker was elected from among the Assembly and the beginnings of colonial-rule parliamentary democracy were established. The Assembly began petitioning for recognition as a colony, arguing that British Honduras, in fact if not in law, was already a British colony. Earl Grey, at the Colonial Office, supported the Assembly and Palmerston, British Prime Minister from 1855, agreed. On May 12, 1862 the settlements in Belize, with the boundaries that still exist today, became the **Colony of British Honduras**.

MEXICAN AND GUATEMALAN CLAIMS

After the Battle of St George's Caye in 1798 Spain continued to maintain her claim to the territory between the Hondo and Sarstoon rivers, and the **Treaty of Amiens** in 1802 required Britain to hand back to Spain the territory captured during the war. In spite of the long-standing occupation by the Baymen, who showed no sign of leaving, Spain took this to include Belize. But in the face of gathering difficulties in her empire, and Britain's decision to assist the settlers in their defence of the settlement, Spain's claim became increasingly unsupportable.

Independence, achieved by Mexico in 1821, signalled the end of the Spanish empire in the Americas. Guatemala, briefly ruled by Mexico following independence, became, in 1823, a part of the United Provinces of Central America, a loosely-knit and inherently unstable federation consisting of the republics of El Salvador, Honduras, Nicaragua, Costa Rica and Guatemala. The federation was never recognised by Britain and it fell apart in 1839.

The years between the collapse of the Spanish empire in America and the close of the nineteenth century were filled with claim and counter-claim, treaties made and broken – a situation not entirely resolved today.

Mexico, in spite of years of internal strife, war with the United States in 1846, the Caste Wars of 1847 and a period of British, French and Spanish occupation in the 1860s, continued to claim British Honduras as an extension of Yucatán. This was unacceptable to the British government and eventually, after numerous diplomatic exchanges, an **Anglo-Mexican Treaty** was ratified in 1897. However Mexico stated that should Guatemala revive any of her claims to British Honduras then she (Mexico) would press her claim to the land north of the Sibun River.

Guatemala's claim has been the source of more belligerent disagreement with Britain, and there's no doubt that the British government shares much of the blame for the confusion. In treaty after treaty Britain regarded Belize as a territory, under Spanish sovereignty, where British subjects had a right to cut timber. Long after Spain's expulsion from the area, Britain maintained the fiction that Spain held sovereignty, and her refusal to recognise Central America was to complicate relations with Guatemala after it had emerged from the dissolution of the federation.

Guatemala's claim to the territory of Belize rested upon the acceptance in international law of *uti possidetis* – the right of a colony which successfully gains independence from a colonial authority to inherit the rights and territory of that authority at the time of independence. This presumed that the entire territory of British Honduras (Belize) had been under Spanish control in 1821 and that the premise of *uti possidetis* was valid. The British position was that Spain hadn't effectively occupied Belize at the time of Guatemala's independence, therefore Guatemala's claim was invalid.

In a vain attempt to reach a settlement Britain and Guatemala signed a treaty in 1859 which has been the subject of controversy ever since. This treaty, in the British view, settled the boundaries of Belize and Guatemala in their existing positions. Guatemala interpreted it differently – as a disguised treaty of cession of the territory outlined, not confirmation of the boundaries. With such a gulf of interpretation it's no wonder the dispute ground on for so many years, keeping international lawyers busy and several times threatening to erupt in war.

The most controversial clause of the Treaty was the addition of Article 7 – the agreement to build a road between Belize City and Guatemala City. For various reasons the road was never built, but a route was surveyed in 1859 and a costing given of £100,000. The disputes were no nearer resolution when the settlement became the colony of British Honduras in 1862. An additional Convention in 1863 failed because Guatemala was at war with El Salvador and by 1864 the British Foreign Office was of the opinion that the Convention was invalid because Guatemala had failed to ratify.

Throughout the 1860s Article 7 was the source of numerous exchanges between Britain and Guatemala, but the British government failed to vote any funds for construction of the road, claiming Guatemala had no intention of complying with the convention.

CASTE WARS AND INDIAN UPRISING

The terrible, bloody **Caste War** of Yucatán began with a Maya uprising at Valladolid in January 1847. The Indians, supplied with arms and ammunition from Belize, sacked the town and over the next year terror spread throughout the peninsula. From 1848, as Mexico sent troops to put down the rebellion, thousands of

Maya and *mestizo* refugees fled to Belize. Some returned but many stayed, increasing the population of Corozal and Orange Walk and clearing the land for agriculture.

The Santa Cruz Maya, occupying a virtually independent territory north of the Belizean border, were not subdued by Mexico until 1901, and the border between Belize and Mexico was fluid, with many refugees settling in Belize. Mexico's claim, in 1864, to the territory extending to the Sarstoon River enraged the Santa Cruz Maya, who resisted Mexico's attempts to defeat them and took it to mean that Mexico intended to occupy the territory. British settlers were justifiably afraid of **Indian attack** which, when it came, was from the Icaiche, not the Santa Cruz.

The Icaiche, supported by Mexico and led by Marcus Canul, attacked a mahogany camp on the Río Bravo in 1866, capturing dozens of prisoners, who were later ransomed. The Indian raids caused panic in Belize, appeals for help were sent to Jamaica and troops were sent for the defence of the colony. Even Canul's death in 1872 after a raid on Orange Walk did not put an end to the raids. Corozal became a military base and although the attacks lessened the danger wasn't over until the 1890s. The ruling class in Belize City were unwilling to vote funds for the defence of the northern areas under threat, while the British government objected to the cost of extra troops.

Partly as a result of arguments about raising finance, the Legislative Assembly dissolved itself in 1870 and was replaced by a **Legislative Council**. This enabled the British government to establish a Crown Colony form of government in 1871, in line with colonial policy throughout the West Indies. **Agriculture**, hitherto unimportant, began to play an increasing role in the economy. The arrival of Yucatecans, many of them small farmers, during the Caste Wars, and the introduction of new crops and forestry techniques, gradually changed the economic base.

TROUBLED TIMES: THE EARLY TWENTIETH CENTURY

By 1900, free for the moment from worries about external threats, Belize was an integral, though minor, colony of the British empire. The population in the census of 1901 was 37,500, of whom 28,500 were born in the colony.

Comfortable complacency set in; the economy stagnated and the predominantly white property owners could foresee no change to their rule. The workers in the forests and on the estates were mainly black, the descendants of former slaves, known locally as "creoles". Wages were low and employers maintained strict controls over their workers – up to three months' imprisonment for missing a day's work.

The start of **World War I** in 1914 caused a rush of volunteers to defend the empire and a limited period of prosperity began in Belize as demand for forest products increased. The troops from Belize, however, were not thought capable of fighting and instead were employed on river transport in British-held Mesopotamia. On their return in 1919, humiliated and disillusioned by their role, bitterness exploded into violence and the troops were joined by thousands of Belize City's population (including the police) in looting and rioting.

The status of workers had improved little over the last century and the Depression years of the Thirties brought extreme hardship. The mechanisation of forestry in the 1920s caused even more unemployment, and a disastrous hurricane in 1931 compounded the misery. The disaster prompted workers to organise in 1934 after a relief programme initiated by the governor was a dismal failure. Their leader, Antonio Soberanis, was imprisoned after attempting to post mail for pickets at a sawmill who had been arrested.

The colonial government responded by passing restrictive laws, banning marches, and increasing the powers of the governor to deal with disturbances.

TOWARDS INDEPENDENCE

World War II again gave a boost to forestry and the opportunity for many Belizeans to work in Britain or on merchant ships. Conditions for the returning soldiers and workers at the end of the war were, however, no better than they had been at the end of World War I. Property and income qualifications limited the franchise to only 2.8 percent of the population by 1948, and political power lay with a wealthy elite who controlled the Executive Council, and with the governor, a Foreign Office appointee. The devaluation of the British Honduras dollar at the end of 1949 caused more hardship and reinforced the belief that Belize was manipulated for the benefit of the ruling class.

A cautious report on constitutional reform in 1951 only increased calls for "one man, one vote" and violent political incidents occurred during the 1952 **National Strike**. A **new constitution**, based on recommendations of the 1951 report, was approved and in 1954 elections were held in which all literate adults over 21 could vote These elections were won with an overwhelming majority by the **Peoples' United Party** (PUP), led by **George Price**. A semblance of ministerial government was introduced in 1955 but the governor retained control of financial measures and the elected members of the Executive Council did not have a clear majority. Ministerial power was extended in 1960 and at the general election in 1961 all parties stated their intention to pursue full independence for Belize.

The delay in achieving independence was caused largely by Guatemala's still unresolved claim to Belize. In 1933 Guatemala had begun to renew her claim as she saw it under the 1859 Treaty. Guatemala had various motives in pursuing the claim among them national pride and an attempt to focus attention away from problems at home. The claim took a more formal, potentially dangerous, turn in 1945 with Guatemala declaring "Belice" as an integral province of her national territory.

In spite of the territorial dispute Belize was granted full **internal self government** in 1964, intended after a relatively short time to lead to complete independence, as was the policy throughout the Commonwealth. The British government, through the governor, remained responsible for defence, foreign affairs and internal security. The Assembly became a bicameral system with a Senate, whose eight members were appointed by the governor after consultation, and a House of Representatives consisting entirely of elected members.

Meanwhile the **dispute with Guatemala** regained prominence: numerous meetings between Britain and Guatemala to solve the problem by diplomatic means got nowhere. Joint control was proposed, but this was unacceptable to Belize, as was any settlement involving concessions of Belizean territory. At least twice, in 1972 and 1977, Guatemala moved troops to the border and threatened to invade, but prompt British reinforcements, especially the deployment of Harrier jets, dissuaded her. The situation remained tense but international opinion was gradually in favour of Belizean independence.

In 1975 the Non-Aligned Movement gave its full support for an independent Belize and in 1976 President Omar Torrijos of Panama campaigned on Belize's behalf throughout Latin America. With the overthrow of Somoza in 1979 the Sandinista government of Nicaragua gave full support to Belize. The most important demonstration of worldwide endorsement of Belize's right to self-determination was the **UN resolution** passed in 1980, demanding secure independence, with all territory intact, before the next session. This time 139 countries voted in favour, with none against.

Further negotiations with Guatemala began and some progress was made, but complete agreement could not be reached. Guatemala still insisted on some territorial concessions. On March 11, 1981, Britain, Guatemala and Belize released the "Heads of Agreement", a document listing subjects for future discussion, which would, they hoped, result in a peaceful solution of the long-standing dispute. Guatemala agreed to recognise the independence of Belize, on condition agreement was reached on points Guatemala considered vital to her interests. These included "use and enjoyment" of certain cayes, free port facilities, cooperation in security and a non-aggression pact, but were not clearly specified.

Belize's response was that **independence** could not be delayed any longer and further negotiations could take place after independence. Accordingly, on September 21, 1981, Belize became an independent country within the British Commonwealth, with Queen Elizabeth II as Head of State. In a unique decision British troops were to remain in Belize, to ensure the territorial integrity of the new nation. In 1988 Guatemala and Belize established a Joint Commission to work towards a "just and honourable" solution to the border dispute: not much progress has been made, but at least it occupies plenty of diplomats and civil servants.

The government of Belize formed by the PUP with George Price as Premier – he had held power through various constitutions and Assemblies since 1954 – continued in power until the general election of 1984. Then thirty years of one-party domination came to an end as the United Democratic Party (UDP), led by **Manuel Esquivel**, began their first term in office.

The new government encouraged private enterprise and foreign investment, policies which have had some success in reducing foreign debt, but despite the introduction of high tariffs they have not managed to stem the flow of imported luxury goods. Sugar is still the main export, but citrus products, bananas and timber exports are increasingly important. Tourism too brings more foreign exchange, mainly US dollars, each year. Belize has a highly literate population (93 percent of adults) and prospects for improvements in living conditions are good. The 1980s were "the decade of agricultural self sufficiency" and major steps have been taken to realise that goal. For the moment, though, Belize remains heavily dependent on foreign aid and money sent back from the States by migrant workers.

In September 1989 George Price and the PUP were elected once again by the narrowest of margins, gaining 50.02 percent of the votes cast.

CHRONOLOGY: THE MAYA

25,000 BC	**Palaeo-Indian**	First waves of nomadic hunters from the north.
20,000 BC		Worked stone chips in northern Belize.
9000 BC		Stone tools in Guatemalan highlands.
7500 BC	**Archaic Period**	Evidence of settled agricultural communities throughout Mesoamerica, maize cultivated and animals domesticated.
4500 BC	First Maya-speaking groups settle in western Guatemala, around Huehuetenango	
2000 BC	First evidence of Maya settlement in Belize.	House platforms, pottery and middens at **Cuello**.
1500 BC	**Preclassic or Formative Period** Divided into: Early: 1500–1000 BC Middle: 1000–300 BC Late: 300BC–300AD	During this period the Maya began building the centres which developed into the great cities of the Classic Period. Trade, of vital importance, increased, and contact with the **Olmec** people of Mexico brought many cultural developments including a calendar and new gods. **Kaminaljuyú** dominates highland Guatemala, while **El Mirador** is the most important city in the east.
300 AD	**Classic Period** Maya culture reaches its high point – introduction of the Long Count **calendar**, used to mark events on carved stelae and monuments	The Central Lowlands are thickly populated, with almost all the sites now known flourishing. In the Early Classic the influence of **Teotihuacán** was strong: client cities like **Kaminaljuyú** and **Tikal** were particularly successful. Later, and especially after the fall of Teotihuacán, more and more cities flourish: Tikal remains important but is defeated in battle at least once by **Caracol**. The great buildings today associated with the Maya almost all date from the Classic Period.
900 AD	**Postclassic Period** Decline of Classic civilisations in Mexico as well as Guatemala and Belize, for reasons which remain unclear.	Population decline and total abandonment of many important Maya centres. Others, however, like **Lamanai** in Belize, do survive and indeed remain relatively prosperous throughout the Postclassic period.
987 AD	**Toltec** invasion of Yucatán.	Toltec culture grafted onto Maya: possible Mexican influence on Maya in Guatemala and Belize.
c.1200	Cities of the Yucatán abandoned – major movement south of Toltec-Maya population. Toltecs come to dominate many of the Guatemalan highland tribes.	In Belize many of the Maya cities continue to thrive, while in Guatemala the village-based highland society familiar today is developing.
1400–1475	**Quiché** overrun much of highland Guatemala, conquering their rivals. After 1475 their power declines and tribes splinter again.	Quiché capital at **Utatlán**; Cakchiquel version at **Iximché**.
1519	**Cortés** lands in Mexico.	
1521	Aztec capital of Tenochtitlán falls to Spanish.	
1523	**Alvarado** arrives in Guatemala.	

GUATEMALA AND BELIZE

1523–40   **Spanish conquest** of Guatemala proceeds: first Spanish capital founded 1527.

Only sporadic advances in Belize area.

1541   Alvarado dies; new capital founded at **Antigua**.

1543   **Alonso Pacheco** brutally conquers Corozal area.

17th c.   **Colonial rule** is gradually established throughout Guatemala. Antigua is the capital of the whole of Central America. Power of the church grows.

Spain claims sovereignty over Belize, but never effectively colonises the area. British and other **pirates** use the coast as a refuge.

1697   Conquest of the Itzá at Tayasal on Lake Petén Itzá: the last of the independent Maya.

18th c.   Colonial Guatemala remains a backwater, with no great riches for the Spanish.

Conflict between Spanish authorities and increasingly established settlers (Baymen): they are driven out several times but always return. First slaves arrive from Africa. Britain increasingly prepared to defend settlers' rights.

1779   Spanish troops capture Baymen and imprison them on Cuba.

1798   **Battle of St George's Caye**; settlers defeat Spanish fleet with British aid.

1821   Mexico and Central America gain **independence** from Spain; Guatemala annexed by Mexico, then joins Central American Federation.

All sides claim Belize.

1832   **Garifuna** arrive from Roatan.

1847   Guatemala becomes republic independent of Central America under **Rafael Carrera**.

Caste Wars in Yucatán.

1850   Clayton Bulwer Treaty and other agreements aim to end dispute between Guatemala and Britain over Belize, but no real conclusion is reached.

1862   Belize officially becomes part of British Empire as Colony of **British Honduras**.

1867   First **liberal uprising** under Serpio Cruz.

1871   Liberal revolution, **Rufino Barrios** becomes president. Start of coffee boom.

Status raised to **Crown Colony**.

1919   Belizean troops riot on return from World War I: the start of nationalist sentiment which grows through the century.

1930   **Jorge Ubico** president – banana boom and height of **United Fruit Company** power.

1944-54   "Spiritual Socialism" presidencies of Arevalo and Arbenz: ended by CIA-backed military **coup**.

1949   British Honduras dollar devalued: resultant hardships strengthen anti-colonial feeling. **PUP** formed in 1950. Universal adult suffrage introduced.

1954   Castillo Armas president: the start of **military rule** and a series of military-backed dictators.

1960s   First **guerrilla** actions, rapidly followed by repressive clampdowns and rise of **death squads** under Colonel Carlos Arana.

Guatemalan claims to Belize renewed, delaying independence. Full **internal self-government** granted in 1964.

1970   **Colonel Arana Osorio** president.

1974   Electoral fraud wins presidency for Kjell Laugerud.

1976   **Earthquake** leaves 23,000 dead, million homeless.

1978   **Lucas García** president, wholesale repression, thousands die.

1981   Belize becomes **independent**.

1982   **Ríos Montt** president: situation improves.

1984   Manuel Esquivel and UDP elected.

1986   **Vinicio Cerezo** elected: return to civilian rule though power of the military remains great.

THE MAYA ACHIEVEMENT

For some three thousand years before the arrival of the Spanish, Maya civilisation dominated Central America, leaving behind some of the most impressive and mysterious architecture in the entire continent. At their peak, around 300 AD, Maya cities were far larger and more elaborate than anything that existed in Europe at the time. Their culture was complex and sophisticated, fostering the highest standards of engineering, astronomy, stone-carving and mathematics, as well as an intricate writing system.

To appreciate all this you have to see for yourself the remains of the great centres. Despite centuries of neglect and abuse they are still astounding, their main temples towering above the forest roof. Stone monuments, however, leave much of the story untold and there is still a great deal that we have to learn about Maya civilisation. What follows is the briefest of introductions to the subject, hopefully just enough to whet your appetite for the immense volumes that have been written on it.

MAYA SOCIETY

While the remains of the great Maya sites are a testament to the scale and sophistication of Maya civilisation, they offer little insight into

daily life in Maya times. To reconstruct the lives of ordinary people archaeologists have turned to the smaller **residential groups** that surround the main sites and are littered with the remains of household utensils, including pottery, bones and farming tools. These groups are made up of simple stone or adobe structures, each of which was home to a single family. The groups as a whole probably housed an extended family, who would have farmed and hunted together and may well have specialised in some trade or craft. Those who lived in these groups were the commoners, their lives largely dependent on agriculture. Maize, beans, cacao, squash, chillies and fruit trees were cultivated in raised and irrigated fields, while wild fruits were harvested from the surrounding forest. Much of the land was communally owned and groups of around twenty men worked in the fields together.

Maya **agriculture** was continuously adapting to the needs of a developing society and the early practice of slash and burn was soon replaced by more intensive and sophisticated methods to meet the needs of a growing population. Much of the land was terraced, drained or irrigated in order to improve its fertility and ensure that fields didn't have to lie fallow for long periods, as was the case with slash and burn. The large cities, today hemmed in by the forest, were once surrounded by open fields, canals and residential compounds; while slash and burn agriculture probably continued in marginal and outlying areas. Agriculture became a specialised profession and a large section of the population would have bought at least some of their food in markets, although all households still had a kitchen garden where they grew herbs and fruit.

Maize has always been the basis of the Maya **diet**, in ancient times as much as it is today. Once harvested it was made into *saka*, a corn-meal gruel, which was eaten with chilli as the first meal of the day. During the day labourers ate a mixture of corn dough and water, and we also know that *tamales* were a popular speciality. The main meal, eaten in the evenings, would have been similarly maize-based, although it may well have included meat and vegetables. As a supplement to this simple diet, deer, peccary, wild turkeys, duck, pigeons and quail were all hunted with bows and arrows or shot with blowguns. The Maya also

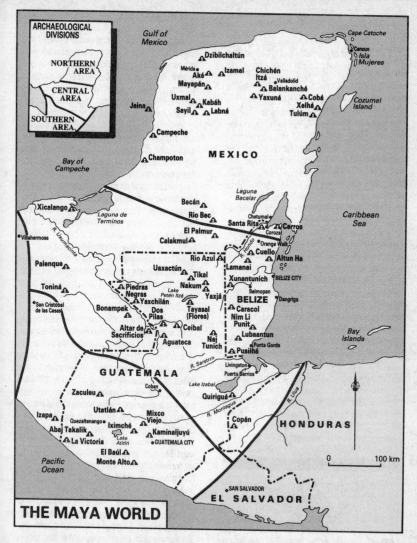

ARCHAEOLOGICAL DIVISIONS

NORTHERN AREA

CENTRAL AREA

SOUTHERN AREA

Gulf of Mexico

Cape Catoche

Cancun
Isla Mujeres

Dzibilchaltún

Mérida
Aké
Izamal
Chichén Itzá
Valladolid

Mayapán
Balankanché

Uxmal
Kabáh
Yaxuná
Cobá

Sayil
Labná
Xelhá

Jaina
Tulúm

Cozumel Island

Campeche

MEXICO

Champoton

Bay of Campeche

Laguna Bacalar

Becán

Xicalango

Laguna de Terminos

Rio Bec

Chetumal

Santa Rita
Cerros

Caribbean Sea

El Palmar
Corozal

Villahermosa

Calakmul

Orange Walk
Cuello

Palenque

Rio Azul

Lamanai
Altun Ha

Toniná

Uaxactún
Tikal
Nakum

Xunantunich
BELIZE CITY

Piedras Negras
Lake Petén Itzá

San Cristóbal de las Casas

Yaxchilán
Yaxjá

Belmopan

Bonampak
Dos Pilas

Tayasal (Flores)

BELIZE
Caracol
Dangriga

Altar de Sacrificios
Ceibal

Nim Li Punit

Aguateca
Naj Tunich

Lubaantun

Pusilhá
Punta Gorda

Bay Islands

R. Sarstrrn

Livingston
Puerto Barrios

GUATEMALA

Coban
Lake Izabal

Zaculeu

Quiriguá

R. Montagua

R. Ulua

Utatlán
Mixco Viejo

Izapa
Quezaltenango
Iximché

Copán

HONDURAS

Abaj Takalik
Lake Atitlán
Kaminaljuyú

La Victoria
GUATEMALA CITY

El Baúl
Monte Alto

Pacific Ocean

0   100 km

SAN SALVADOR

EL SALVADOR

THE MAYA WORLD

made use of dogs, both for hunting and eating. Fish were also eaten, and the remains of fish hooks and nets have been found in some sites, while those living on the coast traded dried fish far inland. The forest provided firewood, and cotton was cultivated to be dyed with natural colours and then spun into cloth.

The main sites represent larger versions of the basic residential groups, housing the most powerful families and their assorted retainers. Beyond this these centres transcended the limits of family ties, taking on larger political, religious and administrative roles, and as Maya society developed they became small cities. The principal occupants were a small number of priestly rulers, but others included bureaucrats, merchants, warriors, architects and assorted craftsmen – an emerging middle class. At the highest level this **hierarchy** was controlled by a series of hereditary positions, with a single chief at its head.

The relationship between the cities and the land, drawn up along feudal lines, was at the heart of Maya life. The peasant farmers supported the ruling class by providing labour – building and maintaining the temples and palaces – food and other basic goods. In return the **elite** provided the peasantry with leadership, direction, protection and above all else the security of their knowledge of calendrics and supernatural prophecy. This knowledge was thought to be the basis of successful agriculture, and the priests were relied upon to divine the appropriate time to plant and harvest.

In turn, the sites themselves were structured into a hierarchy of control. At times a single city, such as Tikal or El Mirador, dominated vast areas, controlling all of the smaller sites, while at other times smaller centres operated independently. A complex structure of **alliances** bound the various sites together and there were periodic outbursts of open **warfare**. The distance between the larger sites averaged around 30km, and between these were a myriad of smaller settlements, religious centres and residential groups. The structure of these alliances can be traced in the use of emblem glyphs. Only those of the main centres are used in isolation, while the names of smaller sites are used in conjunction with those of their larger patrons. Trade and warfare between the large centres was commonplace as the cities were bound up in an endless round of competition and conflict.

THE MAYA CALENDAR

The cornerstone of all Maya thinking was an obsession with **time**. For both practical and mythical reasons the Maya developed a highly sophisticated understanding of arithmetics, calendrics and astronomy, all of which they believed gave them the power to understand and predict events. All great occasions were interpreted on the basis of the Maya calendar, and it was this precise understanding of time which gave the ruling elite its authority. The majority of carving, on temples and stelae, records the exact date at which rulers were born, ascended to power, and died.

The basis of all Maya **calculation** was a vigesimal counting system, which used multi-

ples of twenty. All figures were written with a combination of three symbols – a shell to denote zero, a dot for one and a bar for five – which you can still see on many stelae. When calculating calendrical systems the Maya used a slightly different notation known as the head-variant system, in which each number from one to twenty was represented by a deity, the head of which was used to represent the number.

When it comes to the Maya **calendar** things start to get a little more complicated as they used a number of different counting systems depending on why it was that they were calculating the date.

The basic unit of the Maya calendar was the day, or *kin*, and second was the *uinal*, a group of twenty days roughly equivalent to our month; but it's at the next level that things start to get complex as there are three different types of year. The **260-day almanac** (16 *uinals*) was used to calculate the timing of ceremonial events. Each day was associated with a particular deity that had strong influence over those born on that particular day. This calendar wasn't divided into months but had 260 distinct day names. (This system is still in use among the Cakchiquel Indians who name their children according to its structure, and celebrate fiestas according to its dictates.) A second calendar, the so-called "**vague year**" or *haab*, was made up of 18 *uinals* and five *kins*, a total of 365 days, making it a close approximation of the solar year. These two calendars weren't used in isolation but operated in parallel so that once every 52 years the new day of the solar year coincided with the same day in the 260-day almanac, a meeting that was regarded as very powerful and marked the start of a new era.

Finally the Maya had another system for marking the passing of history, which is used on dedicatory monuments. The system, known as the **long count**, is based on the great cycle of 13 *baktuns* (a period of 5128 years). The current period dates from 3114 BC and is destined to come to an end on December 10, 2012. The dates in this system simply record the number of days that have elapsed since the start of the current great cycle, a task that calls for ten different numbers – recording the equivalent of years, decades, centuries etc. In later years the Maya sculptors obviously tired of this exhaustive process and opted instead for the shortcut, an abbreviated version.

MAYA TIME – THE UNITS

1 *kin* = 24 hours.
20 *kins* = 1 *uinal*, or 20 days.
18 *uinals* = 1 *tun*, or 360 days.
20 *tuns* = 1 *katun*, or 7200 days.
20 *katuns* = 1 *baktuns*, or 144,000 days.
20 *baktuns* = 1 *pictun*, or 2,880,000 days.
20 *pictuns* = 1 *calabtun*, or 57,600,000 days.
20 *calabtuns* = 1 *kinchiltun*, or 1,152,000,000 days.
20 *kinchiltuns* = 1 *alautun*, or 23,040,000,000 days.

ASTRONOMY

Alongside their fascination with time the Maya were interested in the sky above them and devoted much time and energy to unravelling its patterns. Several large sites such as Copán, Uaxactún and Chichén Itzá have **observatories** carefully aligned with solar and lunar sequences.

The Maya showed a great understanding of **astronomy** and with their 365-day "vague year" were just half a day out in their calculations of the solar year, while at Copán, towards the end of the seventh century AD, Maya astronomers had calculated the lunar cycle at 29.53020 days, not too far off our current estimate of 29.53059. In the Dresden Codex their calculations extend to the 405 lunations over a period of 11,960 days, as part of a pattern that set out to predict eclipses. At the same time they had calculated with astonishing accuracy the movements of Venus, Mars and perhaps Mercury. Venus was of particular importance to the Maya as they linked its presence with success in war, and there are several stelae which recorded the presence of Venus as prompting the decision to attack.

RELIGION

Maya **cosmology** is by no means straightforward as at every stage an idea is balanced by its opposite and each part of the universe is made up of many layers. To the Maya this is the third version of the earth, the previous two having been destroyed by deluges. The current version is a flat surface, with four corners, each associated with a certain colour; white for north, red for east, yellow for south, and black for west, with green at the centre. Above this the sky is supported by four trees, each a different colour and species, which are also sometimes depicted as gods, known as *Bacabs*. At its centre the sky is supported by a ceiba tree. Above the sky is a heaven of thirteen layers, each of which had its own god, while the very top layer is overseen by an owl. However it was the underworld, *Xibalda*, "The Place of Fright", which was of greater importance to most Maya, as it was in this direction that they passed after death, on their way to the place of rest. The nine layers of hell were guarded by the "Lords of the Night", and deep caves were thought to connect with the underworld.

Woven into this universe the Maya recognised an incredible array of **gods**. Every divinity had four manifestations based upon colour and direction and many also had counterparts in the underworld and consorts of the opposite sex. In addition to this there was an extensive array of patron deities, each associated with a particular trade or particular class. Every activity from suicide to sex had its representative in the Maya pantheon. However to simplify matters some sources speak of a single dominant god, *Itzama* (Lizard House), the omnipotent inventor of writing and the patron of learning. His closest consort was *Ix Chel*, the goddess of weaving, childbirth and medicine. All the other gods were apparently descended from this pair.

RELIGIOUS RITUAL

The combined complexity of the Maya pantheon and calendar gave every day a particular significance and the ancient Maya were bound up in a demanding **cycle of religious ritual**. The main purpose of ritual was the procurement of success by appealing to the right god at the right time and in the right way. As every event, from planting to childbirth, was associated with a particular divinity, all of the main events in daily life demanded some kind of religious ritual and for the most important of these the Maya staged elaborate ceremonies.

While each ceremony had its own format there's a certain pattern that binds them all. For several days beforehand the participants fasted and remained abstinent, and the correct day was carefully chosen by priestly divination.

The main ceremony was dominated by the expulsion of all evil spirits, the burning of incense before the idols, a sacrifice (either animal or human), and blood-letting.

In divination rituals, used to foretell the pattern of future events or account for the cause of past events, the elite used various **drugs** to achieve altered states of consciousness. Perhaps the most obvious of these was alcohol, either made from fermented maize or a combination of honey and the bark of the balnche tree. Wild tobacco, which is considerably stronger than the modern domesticated version, was also smoked. The Maya also used a range of hallucinogenic mushrooms, all of which were appropriately named, but none more so than the *xibalbaj obox*, "underworld mushroom", and the *k'aizalah obox*, "lost judgement mushroom".

ARCHAEOLOGY IN BELIZE

Like almost everything in Belize, archaeology has made leaps and bounds in the last decade or so as researchers have unveiled a wealth of new material. What follows is written by Winnel Branche of the Belize Archaeology Department and illustrates the problems facing Belizean archaeology as it emerges into the limelight, under siege from foreign expeditions and looters.

The ancient Maya sites of Belize have seen activity since the late nineteenth century. During these early times British amateur archaeologists and both British and American museums kept up a lively interest in the artefacts that came out of these sites. Preservation of monuments was not yet "in" and techniques were far from subtle. In some cases dynamite was used to plunder the sites and Belizean artefacts often found their way, unmonitored, out of the country and into museums and private collections worldwide.

Since 1894 the ancient monuments and antiquities of Belize have had loosely structured legislation to protect them, but it was not until 1952 that a civil servant was made responsible for archaeology, and not until 1957 that a Department was formed to excavate, protect and preserve these remains. Since then scientific excavation of hundreds of sites in Belize has been carried out, with prior agreement from the Department of Archaeology, by universities, museums and scientific institutions from the USA, Canada and, to a lesser extent, Britain.

The Belize Department of Archaeology has grown from one member in 1957 to eight members of office staff in 1990. It monitors fieldwork and excavations carried out by foreign researchers in the country. It also performs small-scale salvage excavations in emergencies and is dedicated to the training of Belizeans to carry out all archaeological work in the country in full. A vital task is to prevent looting activities, which have become rampant in recent years, but all these efforts are hampered by the lack of resources. The Department also carries out educational activities including lectures, slide shows and travelling exhibitions in an attempt to sensitise the public on this part of their heritage. The responsibility of maintaining archaeological sites, especially those open to the public, falls to the Department, as does the safekeeping of the vast national collections, in the absence of a museum in Belize.

Since any immoveable man-made structure over 100 years old and any moveable man-made item over 150 years old are considered ancient monuments and artefacts respectively, the Department is also in charge of all the non-Maya historical and colonial remains.

There are now sixteen archaeological research teams visiting Belize annually, illustrating the fact that the Maya of Belize were not on the fringe of the Maya civilisation, as had previously been thought, but were in fact a core area of the Maya culture. Evidence has been found of extensive raised-field agriculture and irrigation canals in northern Belize and the oldest known site so far found in the Maya world is at Cuello, near Orange Walk. Even Tikal in Guatemala, once thought to be the centre of power of the lowland Maya, is now known to have been toppled at least once by Caracol, perhaps the largest site in Belize.

There has been increased interest lately in ancient Maya maritime trade, with coastal sites and those on the cayes receiving more attention. In addition the extensive cave systems which form a network under inland Belize have shown much evidence of use by the Maya. In 1984 the longest cave system in Central America, containing the largest cave room in the Western Hemisphere, was discovered in Belize. Known as the Chiquibul Cave System, exploration has revealed areas of concentration of Maya artefacts.

With the wealth of Maya remains in the country, it is hardly surprising but most unfortunate that looting of sites and the sale of antiquities on the black market is increasing. In Belize all ancient monuments and antiquities are owned by the State, whether on private or government land or under water. Residents are allowed to keep registered collections under licence, but the sale, purchase, import or export of antiquities is illegal and punishable under the law. Excavation and other scientific research can only be done with Department permission after conditions are agreed to. While this law is structured to prevent looting and destruction, it is also meant to keep the remains intact and within the country so that Belizeans and visitors can see the evidence of this splendid heritage.

INDIAN
GUATEMALA

A vital Indian culture is perhaps Guatemala's most unique feature. It's a strange blend of contradictions, and while the Indians themselves may appear quiet and humble, their costumes, fiestas and markets are a riot of colour, creativity and celebration. In many ways the Indians live in a world of their own, responding to local traditions and values and regarding themselves as Indians first and Guatemalans second.

It's generally accepted that indigenous Indians, the vast majority of whom live in the western highlands, make up about half of Guatemala's population, although it's extremely hard to define exactly who is an Indian. For the sake of the national census, people who think that they're Indians are classed as such, regardless of their parentage. And when it comes to defining Indians as a group, culture is more important than pedigree, as Indians define themselves through their relationships with their land, gods, villages and families. Holding aloof from the melting pot of modern Guatemalan society, Indians adhere instead to their traditional *costumbres*, codes of practice that govern every aspect of life.

As a result of this the only way to define Indian culture is by describing its main characteristics, acknowledging that all Indians will be a part of some of them, and accepting that many are neither Indian nor *Ladino*, but combine elements of both.

INDIAN CULTURE

When the Spanish set about destroying the Maya tribes of Guatemala they altered every aspect of life for the indigenous people, uprooting their social structures and reshaping their communities. Before the conquest the bulk of the population had lived scattered in the hills, paying tribute to a tribal elite, and surviving through subsistence farming and hunting. Under Spanish rule they were moved into new **villages**, known as *reducciones*, where their homes were clustered around a church and a marketplace. Horizons shrank rapidly as allegiances became very localised and tribal struc-

tures were replaced by the village hierarchies that still dominate the highlands today.

For the last 450 years the Indian population has suffered repeated **abuse**, as the predominantly white elite have exploited Indian land and labour, regarding the Indians themselves as an expendable commodity. But within their own communities the Indians were left pretty much to themselves and developed an astoundingly introspective culture that is permanently adapting to new threats, reshaping itself for the future. **Village life** has been insulated from the outside world and in many areas only a handful of the population speak fluent Spanish, the remainder speaking one of the 28 indigenous languages and dialects. Today's Indian culture includes elements of Maya, Spanish and modern American culture, blended together in a complex synthesis.

The vast majority of the Indian population still live by **subsistence farming**, their homes either spread across the hills or gathered in small villages. The land is farmed using the *milpa* system to produce beans, chillies, maize and squash – which have been the staple diet for thousands of years. To the Indians land is sacred and the need to own and farm it is central to their culture, despite the fact that few of them can survive by farming alone. Most are now forced to migrate to the coast for several months a year, where they work in appalling conditions on the **plantations**, in order to supplement their income. In some villages the economy is boosted by a local **craft**: in Momostenango they produce wool and blankets, around Lake Atitlán the villagers make reed mats, in Cotzal and San Pablo la Laguna they make rope, while other villages specialise in market gardening, pottery, flowers or textiles.

Family life is also rigidly traditional with large families very much a part of Indian culture. Marriage customs vary from place to place but in general the groom is expected to pay the bride's parents, and the couple may well live with their in-laws. If things don't work out separation isn't a great problem and men often take more that one wife (nor is it totally unheard of for a woman to live with two men). A man's place is in the fields and a woman's in the home, where she cooks, tends to the children, and weaves. Authority within the village is usually given to men, although in the Ixil area women are involved in all decision making.

INDIAN RELIGION

Every aspect of Indian life – from the birth of a child to the planting of corn – is loaded with religious significance, based on a complicated **fusion of the Maya pantheon and the Catholic religion**. Christ and the saints have taken their place alongside *Dios Mundo*, the God of the World, and *Hurakan*, the Heart of Heaven. The two religions have merged to form a hybrid, in which the outward forms of Catholicism are used to worship the ancient pantheon, a compromise that was probably fostered by Spanish priests. The symbol of the cross, for example, was well known to the Maya, used to signify the four winds of heaven, the four directions, and everlasting life. Today many of the deities have both Maya and Hispanic names, and are usually associated with a particular saint. All of the deities remain subordinate to a mighty and remote supreme being, and Christ takes a place in the upper echelons of the hierarchy.

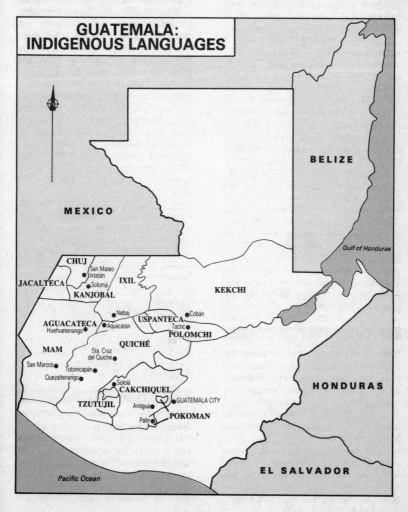

GUATEMALA: INDIGENOUS LANGUAGES

BELIZE

MEXICO

Gulf of Honduras

CHUJ
San Mateo Ixtatán
JACALTECA
Solomá
IXIL
KANJOBÁL
KEKCHI

Nebaj
AGUACATECA
Huehuetenango
Aquacatán
USPANTECA
Cobán
Tactic
POLOMCHI
QUICHÉ

MAM
Sta. Cruz del Quiché
San Marcos
Totonicapán
Quezaltenango
Sololá
CAKCHIQUEL
HONDURAS

TZUTUJIL
Antigua
GUATEMALA CITY

Palin
POKOMAN

EL SALVADOR

Pacific Ocean

For the Indians **God** is everywhere, bound up in the seasons, the mountains, the crops, the soil, the air and the sky. Every important event is marked by prayer and offerings, with disasters often attributed to divine intervention. Even more numerous than the gods are the **spirits** that are to be found in every imaginable object, binding together the universe. Each individual is born with a *nagual*, or spiritual counterpart, in the animal world, and his or her destiny is bound up with that particular animal. The spirits of dead ancestors are also ever-present, and have to be looked after by each successive generation.

Traditionally, **worship** is organised by the community's religious hierarchy. All office-holders are male and throughout their lives they progress through the system, moving from post to post. The various posts are grouped into *cofradías*, ritual brotherhoods, each of which is responsible for a particular saint. Throughout the year the saint is kept in the home of an elder member, and on the appointed date, in the midst of a fiesta, it's paraded through the streets, to spend the next year somewhere else. The elder responsible for the saint will have to pay for much of the fiesta, including costumes, alcohol and assorted offerings, but it's a responsibility, or *cargo*, that's considered a great honour. In the traditional village hierarchy it's these duties that give the elders a prominent role in village life, and through which they exercise their authority. Spending money on **fiestas** is really the only way that wealthy villagers can use their money in an acceptable way. (In some villages, such as Chichicastenango and Sololá, a *municipalidad indigena*, or Indian government, operates alongside the *cofradías*, and is similarly hierarchical. As men work their way up through the system they may well alternate between the civil and religious hierarchies.) However the *cofradías* don't necessarily confine themselves to the traditional list of saints, and have been known to foster "evil" saints, such as San Simón or **Maximón**, a drinking, smoking *Ladino* figure, sometimes referred to as Judas or Pedro de Alvarado.

On a more superstitious level, personal religious needs are catered for by **brujos**, native priests who communicate with the gods and spirits. This is usually done on behalf of an individual client who's in search of a blessing, and often takes places at shrines and caves in the mountains, with offerings of *copal*, a type of incense, and alcohol. They also make extensive use of old Maya sites, and small burnt patches of grass litter many of the ruins in the highlands. *Brujos* are also credited with the ability to cast spells, predict the future, and communicate with the dead. For specific medical problems Indians appeal to *zahorins*, who practise traditional medicine with a combination of invocation and herbs, and are closely associated with the *brujo* tradition.

Until the 1950s, when Catholic **missionaries** became active in the highlands, many Indians had no idea that there was a gulf between their own religion and orthodox Catholicism. To start with the missionaries drew most of their support from the younger generation, many of whom were frustrated by the rigidity of the village hierarchy. Gradually this has eroded the authority of the traditional religious system, undermining the *cofradías*, disapproving of traditional fiestas, and scorning the work of the *brujos*. As a part of this the reforming movement *Catholic Action*, in which the drive for orthodoxy was combined with an involvement in social issues, has also had a profound impact.

In the 1920s and 1930s the first Protestant missionaries, known as **evangelicos**, arrived in Guatemala, and their presence has also accelerated the decline of traditional religion. In the 1980s their numbers were greatly boosted by the influence of Ríos Montt, at a time when the Catholic church was suffering severe repression. These days there are at least 100 different sects in operation, backed by a huge injection of money from the States, and offering all sorts of incentives to fresh converts. But Indian religion is no stranger to oppression and despite the efforts of outsiders the *brujos* and *cofradías* are still in business, and fiestas remain drunken and vaguely pagan.

MARKETS AND FIESTAS

At the heart of the Indian economy is the **weekly market**, which is still central to life in the highlands and provides one of the best opportunities to see Indian life at close quarters. The majority of the Indian population still live by subsistence farming but spare a single day to gather together in the nearest village and trade their surplus produce. The market is as much a social occasion as an economic one and people come to talk, eat, drink, gossip and have a good time. In some places the action starts the night before with marimba music and heavy drinking.

On market day itself the village is filled by a steady flow of people, arriving by bus, on foot, or by donkey. In no time at all trading gets under way, and the plaza is soon buzzing with activity and humming with conversation, although raised voices are a rarity and the atmosphere is always subdued, with bargains struck after long and tortuous negotiations. Markets certainly don't operate in the way that westerners might expect and rival traders will happily set up alongside one another, more concerned about the day's conversation than the volume of trade.

The scale and atmosphere of markets varies from place to place. The country's largest is in San Francisco El Alto, on Friday, and draws traders from throughout the country. Other famous ones are the Friday market in Sololá, and the Thursday and Sunday markets in Chichicastenango, but almost every village has its day. Some of the very best are in tiny, isolated hamlets, high in the mountains.

Once a year every village, however small, indulges in an orgy of celebration in honour of its patron saint – you'll find a list of them at the end of each chapter. These **fiestas** are a great swirl of dance, music, religion, fireworks, eating and outrageous drinking, and express the vitality of indigenous culture. They usually centre on religious processions, in which the image of the local patron saint is paraded through the streets, accompanied by the elders of the *cofradía*, who dress in full regalia. (The members of the *cofradía* usually have special ceremonial costumes, superbly woven and beautifully decorated.) The larger fiestas also include funfairs and week-long markets. Traditional music is played with marimbas, drums and flutes; or professional bands are hired, blasting out popular tunes through crackling PA systems.

Dance is also very much a part of fiestas and incorporates routines and ideas that date from Maya times. Dance costumes are incredibly elaborate, covered in mirrors and sequins, and have to be hired for the occasion. Despite the cost, which is high by highland standards, the dancers see their role both as an obligation

– to tradition and the community – and an honour. Most of the dances form an extension of some vague dramatic tradition in which local history was retold in dance dramas, and are loosely based on historical events. The *Dance of the Conquistadores* is one of the most popular, modelled on the *Dance of the Moors* and introduced by the Spanish as a re-enactment of the conquest, although in some cases it's been instilled with a significance that can never have been intended by the Spanish. The dancers often see no connection with the conquest, but dance instead to release the spirits of the dead, a function perhaps closer to Maya religion than Catholicism. The *Palo Volador*, a dramatic dance in which men swing perilously to the ground from a twenty-metre pole, certainly dates from the pre-Columbian era (these days you'll only see it in Cubulco, Chichicastenango and Joyabaj), as does the *Dance of the Deer*, while the *Dance of the Bullfight* and the *Dance of the Volcano* relate incidents from the conquest itself. Most of the dances do have steps to them, but the dancers are usually blind drunk and sway around as best they can in time to the music, sometimes tumbling over each other or even passing out – so don't expect to see anything too dainty.

INDIAN COSTUME

To outsiders the most obvious and impressive feature of Indian culture is the **hand-woven cloth** that's worn by the majority of the women and some of the men. This, like so much else in the Indian world, is not simply a relic of the past but a living skill, responding to new ideas and impulses, and recreated by each generation.

Nevertheless **weaving** is one of the oldest of Maya skills, and was practised for centuries before the arrival of the Spanish. We know that the skill was highly valued and the Maya goddess Ix Che*l*, "she of the rainbow", who presided over childbirth, divination and healing, is often depicted at her loom. In pre-Columbian times the majority of the Indian population probably wore long white tunics, made from cotton, similar to those worn by the *Lacandones* today. In the highlands it's a style that has been largely superseded, although in some villages, such as Soloma and San Mateo Ixtatán, the basic format is still the same, now embellished with magnificent embroidery. We also know, from Maya tombs and sculptures, that the nobility wore elaborate headdresses and heavily decorated cloth, using blues and reds created with vegetable dyes. Here it seems that tunics and robes were also the fashion of the day.

After the conquest, the Indian nobility was virtually eradicated and the focus was shifted from large regional centres to small village communities. Meanwhile silk and wool were introduced by the Spanish, as were a whole range of new dyes. Not much is known about the development of Indian costume in colonial times, and it's impossible to say when or why each village developed a distinctive style of dress. Some argue that the styles were introduced by the Spanish as a means of control, rather like the branding of sheep, while others claim that they developed naturally from the introspective nature of village culture. The truth is probably to be found somewhere between the two, as we know that the Spanish influenced the development of traditional costume, introducing their own symbols, but that at times they had little influence over life in the villages.

WOMEN'S CLOTHING

Today there are around 150 villages where the women still wear **traditional costume**, each of which has its own patterns, designs and colours. What little we know of their development shows that the designs are constantly changing, taking on board new patterns and ideas. The advent of literacy, a recent development in most areas, means that modern *huipiles* might include the word *escuela* (school), the name of the village, or even the words *Coca Cola*. Synthetic thread, including garish silvers and golds, has also been absorbed into many of the patterns, and as village society starts to open up, some designs, once specific to a single village, are coming to be used throughout the country.

Nevertheless the basic style of the clothing worn by women has changed little since Maya times. The most significant development is simply that the **huipile**, which once hung loose, is now tucked into the skirt. Only in one or two places have the women added sleeves, or gathered their skirts, although in recent times young women have responded to outside influences and the latest generation of Indian

costumes tend to emphasise the shape of the body. But in defiance of modern fashion Indian women still wear their hair in an assortment of bizarre styles, ranging from the halos of Santiago Atitlán to the pom-poms of Aguacatán. Ceremonial *huipiles*, which are always the most spectacular, are still worn loose, in the style of the Maya.

The basic element of an Indian woman's costume remains the *huipile*, a loose fitting blouse, normally woven by the women themselves on a back-strap loom. All *huipiles* are intricately decorated, either as a part of the woven pattern or with complex embroidery, and it's these designs that are specific to each village. (To protect the embroidery some women wear their *huipiles* inside out, saving their full splendour for market days.) Ceremonial *huipiles*, reserved for fiestas, are usually more extravagant, often hanging low in the most traditional style. Under the *huipile* a skirt, or **corte**, is worn, and these are becoming increasingly standardised. The fabric is usually woven on a foot loom and is a simple piece of cloth, up to five metres long, that's joined to form a tube, into which the women step. Most common are the *jaspeado cortes* woven on looms in Salcajá, San Francisco Totonicapán and Cobán by commercial weavers, and tie-dyed in universally worn patterns. In some cases there are regional styles, but these tend to be used in a general area rather than specific villages: the brilliant reds of Nebaj and Cajul; the yellows of San Pedro and San Marcos; and the blues of the Huehuetenango area, for example. To add a touch of individuality to their skirts the women decorate them with thin strips of coloured embroidery, known as *randa*. And to hold them up they use elaborate **sashes**, woven in superb colours and intricate patterns, and often including decorative tassels. Perhaps the most outlandish part of women's costume is the headdress, which varies widely and seems to have no connection with modern styles. The most famous of these are the halos of Santiago Atitlán – forty-foot strips of cloth – while the turbans of Nebaj and Aguacatán are some of the finest. In addition to the cloth that they wear the women also weave **tzutes**, used to carry babies or food, and shawls that ward off the highland chill.

MEN'S CLOTHING

In the life of the Indian village men have had greater contact with the outside world, and as a result of this they have been more susceptible to change. From the outset their costume was influenced to a greater extent by the arrival of the Spanish, and today **men's traditional costume** is worn in only a few villages. The more traditional styles are generally reflected in ceremonial costume, while everyday clothes are heavily influenced by western styles. If you're around for a fiesta you'll probably see some fantastic costumes worn by men who wear jeans every other day of the year.

On the whole even "traditional costumes" now have more in common with shirt and trousers than the ancient loose-hanging tunic. Nevertheless men's costumes do include superb weaving and spectacular designs. Their jackets are particularly unusual, ranging from

REPRESSION OF THE INDIAN POPULATION

Throughout their history Guatemala's Indians have been severely victimised and exploited, but in the last two decades the situation has become increasingly serious, threatening the future of the entire indigenous population. Indians have always been the victims of racism, malnutrition and poor health care, suffering through the neglect of central government. However Guatemala's undeclared civil war has increased their burden immeasurably. In 1983 *Survival International* published an account of repression against the Indian population, which examined the way Indians were being selected for particularly brutal treatment. What follows is an extract from that report, which describes the situation at its very worst. Since then things have improved significantly:

Indians are reportedly bearing the brunt of the Guatemalan army's efforts to root out subversion. In May, *El Gráfico*, Guatemala's second largest newspaper, condemned the "genocide being carried out in the Indian regions of the country". A western European diplomat quoted on June 3 by the *New York Times* said, "Indians are systematically being destroyed as a group. . . .There is no break with the past". A priest in Huehuetenango told John Dinges in July that "the army is trying to kill every Indian alive". Guatemalan security forces do not always distinguish between innocent civilians and guerrillas, acknowledges General Ríos Montt. "Look, the problem of war is not just a question of who is shooting. For each one who is shooting there are ten behind him." His press secretary, Francisco Bianchi, adds: "The guerrillas won over many Indian collaborators. Therefore, the Indians were subversives, right? And how do you fight subversion? Clearly you had to kill Indians because they were collaborating with subversion. And then they say, 'You're massacring innocent people'. But they weren't innocent. They had sold out to subversion."

According to some reports, the government is also seeking to destroy once and for all the traditional Indian way of life. Measures are being aimed at the elimination of the several Indian languages still spoken in rural Guatemala. Young men conscripted into the army are stationed in regions where different languages are spoken and are forbidden to speak to each other in their own language. The army is said to aggressively discourage the use of Indian language by everyone else, whether in their own community or relocated in strategic hamlets (model villages). The Indians' distinctive traditional costume, which is such an important expression and symbol of their ethnic identity and pride, is taken from them and burned. The religious fiestas which used to be a feature of Indian life in rural Guatemala are forbidden with the claim that food prepared for these occasions will be given to the guerrillas. The musical instruments used in these fiestas are destroyed. The linkages between generations which permit and channel the transmission and continuation of cultural traditions are broken as the people are made orphans, losing their children, their parents, and their grandparents. Community solidarity is undermined by forcing men conscripted into the "civil patrols" to attack and kill their neighbours or fellow-villagers.

Not only are Indian customs, beliefs and traditions under attack but the economic and ecological basis for Indian existence is being destroyed. It is reported that when the army attacks an Indian community, the people's houses, belongings and crops are burned and their domestic animals are killed or illegally confiscated. Rivers and streams, sources of drinking water, are said to be poisoned. In certain areas extensive pine-forests are being burned down, in some cases set on fire by incendiary bombs thrown from helicopters.

ETHNIC BELIZE

Belize has a very mixed cultural background and the two largest ethnic groups, Creoles and *mestizos*, forming 75 percent of the population, are themselves descendants of very different ancestors. **Creoles**, descended from Africans brought to the West Indies as slaves and early white settlers, comprise about half the overall population. They form a large proportion of the population of Belize City, with scattered settlements in other towns and around the country. *Creole* is also the common language in Belize, a form of English similar to that spoken in those parts of the West Indies that were once part of the British empire.

The next largest group are *mestizos*, descended from Amerindians and early Spanish settlers and speaking Spanish as their first language. They are mainly located in the north and on Ambergris Caye and Caye Caulker, with a sizeable population in Cayo. Many of the ancestors of the present population fled to Belize during the Caste Wars of the Yucatán. In recent years many thousands of refugees from conflicts and repression in El Salvador, Guatemala and Honduras have settled in Belize, probably permanently, adding to the numbers of Spanish-speaking *mestizos*.

The **Maya Indians** in Belize are from three groups: the Yucatec, the Mopan and the Kekchi, and form about ten percent of the population. The Yucatecan Maya also entered Belize to escape the fighting in the Caste Wars and were soon acculturated into the *Ladino* way of life as small farmers. The Mopan Maya came to Belize in the 1880s and settled in the hills of Toledo and the area of Benque Viejo in the west. The last group of Maya, the Kekchi, came from the area around Cobán in Guatemala to work in cacao plantations in southern Belize. Small numbers still arrive in Belize each year, founding new villages in the southern district of Toledo.

The **Caribs** or **Garifuna** (see p.311) live mainly in Dangriga and in villages on the south coast, such as Hopkins and Seine Bight. They form about eight percent of the population. They are descended from shipwrecked and escaped slaves mingling with the last of the Carib Indians on the island of St Vincent, eventually settling in Belize in the nineteenth century.

Another group is the **East Indians**; relatively recent immigrants as apparently none of the earlier East Indians, brought as servants for the British administrators, left any descendants.

The **Mennonites** (see p.254), a German-speaking Protestant sect originating in the Swiss Alps, came to Belize from Mexico and Canada between 1958 and 1962, and now number about 6000, living in agricultural communities mainly in Orange Walk and Cayo, with a small settlement at Blue Creek in Toledo.

---

the superb reds of Nebaj, modelled on those worn by Spanish officers, to the ornate tuxedo-style of Sololá. (Those worn is Sololá seem to undergo regular changes, and the greys of late are now superseded by a very ornate white version.) In the Cuchumatanes the men wear **capixays**, small ponchos made from wool, and in San Juan Atitlán these seem remarkably similar to monks' habits. Other particularly unusual features are the **ponchitos**, short woollen skirts, worn in Nahuala and San Antonio Palopo; the superbly embroidered shorts of Santiago Atitlán and Santa Catarina Palopo; and the cowboy-style shirts of Todos Santos. And although fewer men wear traditional costume the styes that remain are astonishingly diverse, with their scarcity making them appear all the more outlandish. The **tzute**, a piece of cloth either worn on the head of folded on the shoulder, is of particular significance, often marking out an important member of the *cofradía*. In some villages the mayor, dressed in jeans and a T-shirt, will still wear a woven *tzute* on his shoulder as a symbol of office.

DESIGNS

The **designs** used in the traditional costume of both men and women are as diverse as the costumes themselves, an amazing collection of sophisticated patterns, using superb combinations of colour and shape. They include a range of animals, plants and people, as well as abstract designs, words and names. Many of them probably date from long before the conquest, and we know that the snake, the double-headed eagle, the sun and the moon were commonly used in Maya design, while the peacock, horse and chicken can only have been introduced after the arrival of the Spanish. The **quetzal** is perhaps the most universal feature and is certain to date from pre-conquest times, when the bird was seen as the spiritual protector of Quiché kings. The precise significance of the designs is as vague as their origins, although according to Lily de Jongh Osborne, an expert on Indian culture, designs once indicated the weaver's position within the social hierarchy, and could indicate their marital status. One particularly interesting design is the bat on the back of the jackets of Sololá, which dates back to the bat dynasty, among the last Cakchiquel rulers. In days gone by each level of the village hierarchy wore a different style of jacket, although today fashion is the prime consideration, and each generation is simply more outrageous than the last.

HUMAN RIGHTS IN GUATEMALA

Since the arrival of the Spanish, Guatemalan history has been characterised by political repression and economic exploitation, involving the denial of the most basic human rights. A horrifying catalogue of events stretches across the last 450 years, but reached levels as barbaric as any previously seen in the late 1970s and the early 1980s. The chief victims have always been the indigenous Indians, generally regarded as "backward", "ignorant" and dispensable. Today the story of Guatemalan repression is very much an unfinished history, despite the fact that the level of violence has declined significantly in the last few years.

THE EARLY YEARS

When **Pedro de Alvarado** arrived in Guatemala in 1523 he brought with him the notions of violent conquest and racist exploitation that have dominated the country to the present day. In the early years of the conquest towns were burnt to the ground and huge numbers of Indians were massacred and enslaved. At the same time they had to contend with repeated epidemics that were to halve their numbers. Once the initial conquest was over the survivors were systematically herded into villages, deprived of their land, and forced to work in the new plantations: a pattern that seems all too familiar in modern Guatemala.

Equally familiar is the response of the indigenous population, who rose in defiance. It took almost two centuries for their numbers to recover from the devastation of the conquest, but by the start of the eighteenth century uprisings were common. There were **Indian revolts** in 1708, 1743, 1760, 1764, 1770, 1803, 1817, 1818, 1820, 1838, 1839, 1898 and 1905, all of which met with severe repression.

Independence brought little change. Under **Rufino Barrios** (1873–1885) the demands of coffee put fresh strains on the Indian population, as their land and labour were once again exploited for the benefit of foreign investors and the ruling elite. Under **Jorge Ubico** (1931–1944) laws were introduced which obliged Indians to work on the plantations, and for the first time the government developed a network of spies and informers, giving it the capacity to deal directly with dissenting voices: a capacity it demonstrated in 1934, when Ubico discovered a plot to assassinate him and had some 300 people killed in just two days.

The most significant developments, at least in terms of human rights, came during the socialist governments of **Arevalo** and **Arbenz** (1945–1955) which, for the first time, sought to meet the needs of the indigenous population. Local organisations such as unions and cooperatives were free to operate, suffrage was extended to include all adults, health and schooling were expanded, and land was redistributed to the dispossessed. For the first time in the country's history the issues of inequality and injustice were taken by the horns.

However in 1954 the government was overthrown by a CIA--backed coup, which cleared the stage for military rule and ushered in the modern era of repression.

MILITARY RULE

Since the 1954 coup the army has dominated the government, operating in alliance with the land-owning elite and foreign business interests to consolidate the power of the right. Large-scale repression wasn't to begin until the mid-1960s, but directly after the takeover the army began gathering the names of those who had been active under the socialist administration. In association with the CIA they put together a list of some 70,000 people – a much-used reference source once the killing began.

The **guerrilla** movement, which developed out of an army revolt in 1960, was first active in the eastern highlands. Throughout the 1960s political violence was on the increase, aimed not just at the guerrillas, but at all political opponents and left-wing sympathisers. In the war against the guerrillas the army was unable to strike directly at their enemy, and opted instead to eradicate their support in the community. Between 1966 and 1977 some 10,000 non-combatants were killed in a bid to destroy a guerrilla force that numbered no more than 500; and by the early Seventies the guerrillas were on the run, unable to mount attacks or add to their numbers.

In other parts of the country there was a brutal clampdown on a range of "suspect" organisations. In Guatemala City this campaign gave birth to the "**death squads**", put together by the right-wing MLN (National Liberation Movement) and the army. The first to emerge was *Mano Blanco*, who swore "to eradicate national renegades and traitors to the fatherland". Today the death squads have become a permanent feature of Guatemalan politics, and they were active throughout the 1960s, 1970s and 1980s, assassinating unionists, left-wing politicians and students. Victims were usually abducted by men in unmarked cars, and later their bodies were found, dumped by the roadside, mutilated and tortured. Between 1970 and 1974, 15,325 people "disappeared".

By 1975 the guerrilla movement was once again on the rise, as were peasant organisations, cooperatives and unions, all inspired by the move towards **liberation theology**, under which the Catholic church began to campaign on social issues. The experience of 1954 proved to the Guatemalan people that their political options were severely restricted, and in the 1970s and 1980s they directed their energies towards grass-roots organisation and eventually armed uprising. But in response to this the repression continued, and in 1976 *Amnesty International* stated that a total of 20,000 Guatemalans had been killed in the previous decade.

The closing years of the 1970s saw a rapid polarisation of the situation that gave birth to a fresh wave of violence. The **guerrilla movements** were by now well established in many different parts of the country, as repression in the highlands drove increasing numbers to seek refuge in their ranks. At this stage there were four main organisations: the PGT (Guatemalan Workers Party), who operated in Guatemala City and on the Pacific coast, FAR (the Rebel Armed Forces), who fought throughout the Petén, EGP (the Guerrilla Army of the Poor), who had several fronts in northern Quiché, and ORPA (Organisation of People in Arms), who functioned in San Marcos and Quezaltenango.

The election of **Lucas García** in 1978 marked the onset of unprecedented mass repression. Once again the list of victims included left-wing politicians, labour leaders, lawyers, priests, nuns, teachers, unionists, academics and students, all of whom were regarded as subversive. In the highlands the war against the guerrillas also reached a new intensity, as selective killings were replaced by outright massacres. Once again the army found itself pitched against an elusive enemy and resorted to indiscriminate killings in a bid to undermine peasant support for the guerrillas.

Repression was so widespread that human rights organisations found it almost impossible to keep track of the situation, although certain incidents still came to light. In 1980 36 bodies were found in a mass grave outside Comalapa; in early 1981 17 people were killed in Santiago Atitlán; and in April 1981 *Oxfam* estimated that 1500 Indians had been killed in Chimaltenango in the previous two months. Precise numbers are impossible to calculate, but according to some estimates 25,000 died during the first four years of the Lucas administration, the vast majority killed either by the security forces or by the death squads, which were often operated by off-duty soldiers or policemen, and directed from an annexe of the National Palace.

RÍOS MONTT

In March 1982 Lucas was replaced by **General Efrían Ríos Montt**, and the situation improved significantly. The guerrillas were offered amnesty, death squad activity dropped off, and an office was set up to investigate the fate of the disappeared. But Ríos Montt had vowed to defeat the guerrillas by Christmas and in rural areas the level of violence did increase as the army began to make big gains in the fight against the guerrillas. In the early months of Ríos Montt's rule massacres were still commonplace as it took him some time to reshape the armed forces and provide an alternative to the brutal approach they had adopted under Lucas García. The campaign still claimed a heavy death toll, despite the downturn in indiscriminate slaughter. According to *Amnesty International* there were 2186 killings in the first four months of the new administration, and by now some 200,000 refugees had fled the country. *Amnesty's* report on the Ríos Montt administration (see box) is a catalogue of horror, though in many ways the events described were more typical of the Lucas García regime. However it does contain eyewitness accounts of army campaigns, which capture the full extent of repression in the highlands.

EYEWITNESS TESTIMONY

The following account, taken from an *Amnesty International* report, of a massacre in San Francisco Nentón, that took place on July 17, 1982, is one of the best documented of many such incidents. The events were related to a priest in a Mexican refugee camp by survivors of the massacre:

At 11am on Saturday 17 July the army arrived in San Francisco having passed through the nearby villages of Bulej and Yalambojoch. The army had previously visited the village on 24 June and had told the inhabitants that they could be killed if they were found not to be peacefully working in their homes and their fields. Soldiers had also said, however, that the villagers should not run away from the army, as it was there to defend them. On 17 July some 600 soldiers arrived on foot. A helicopter circled nearby and eventually landed. The military were accompanied by an ex-guerrilla, now in military uniform, who was apparently acting as the army's informer.

The people were told to assemble for a discussion with the colonel. It was the first day on which the village's new civil defense patrol was to have begun its duties. Some of the survivors said that the patrol, of 21, was taken away shortly after the arrival of the army and had not been seen since. They are presumed dead.

According to testimonies collected by priests, the villagers first sensed they were in danger when a man who survivors said had been "tied up like a pig" was brought before them by the soldiers. They knew he had not been involved in anything, and yet saw that he was being "punished". They also saw how "angry" the commander appeared to be and began to fear for themselves. They were first asked to unload the soldiers' supplies from the helicopter, which they did. The men were then shut up in the courthouse to begin praying "to make peace with God", as they were about to suffer. A survivor described how: "We pray, 11 o'clock, 12 o'clock passes. By now, everyone has come into town and been shut up. At 1 o'clock, it began: a blast of gunfire at the women, there in the church. It makes so much noise. All the little children are crying."

This witness went on to tell how the women who survived the initial gunfire were taken off in small groups to different houses by soldiers where they were killed, many apparently with machetes. After they had been killed, the houses were set on fire. This witness and the others interviewed, described a particularly atrocious killing they had seen, the murder of a child of about three. The child was disembowelled, as were several others, but kept screaming, until a soldier smashed his head

with a pole, then swung him by his feet and threw him into a burning house. "Yes", said the witness, "yes, I saw it. Yes, I saw how they threw him away, threw him into the house."

The witness continued: "At 2 o'clock, they began with all the men. They ordered them out of the courthouse in small groups, and then blasted them with gunfire. It went on and on. They tied up the men's hands and then 'bang, bang'. We couldn't see, we could only hear the noise of the guns. The killing took place in the courtyard outside the courthouse, then they'd throw the bodies into the church. They killed the three old people with a blunt machete, the way you would kill sheep."

Another witness described how the old were killed: "The old people said, 'What have we done, no, we are tired and old. We're not thinking of doing anything. We're not strong. We can't do anything any more.' But they said, 'You're not worth anything any more, even if you're tired, get out of there.' They dragged them out, and knifed them. They stabbed and cut them as if they were animals and they were laughing when they killed them. They killed them with a machete that had no teeth. They put one man on the table and cut open his chest, the poor man, and he was still alive, and so they started to cut his throat. They cut his throat slowly. He was suffering a lot. They were cutting people under the ribs, and blood came rushing out and they were laughing." Another survivor continued: "When they got to the end, they killed six people in the courthouse. One was a military commissioner. They didn't care. They killed him there at his table with his three policemen."

"By now it was 6.30pm. It was getting dark outside. They threw a bomb into the corner of the courthouse. It was bloody, two were killed. How the blood ran! It ran all over me. Then they fired at the remaining bodies in the courthouse. Then they threw all the bodies in a heap. They dragged people by the feet, as if they were animals. They threw me on top of the dead bodies."

One witness ended his testimony: "Father my heart is so heavy with pain for the dead, because of what I have seen. I saw how my brothers died. All of them: friends, godparents, everyone, as we are all brothers. My heart will cry for them the rest of my life. But they had committed no crime. Nobody said: 'This is your crime. Here is the proof.' They just killed them, that's all. That's how death came."

A list of the dead was compiled in Mexico on September 5. It included 302 people, 92 of whom were under twelve, and the youngest less than two months old.

Under Ríos Montt the army campaign was much more successful and the guerrillas were driven into the remote corners of the highlands. Soldiers swept through the mountains, rounding up those who had fled from previous campaigns and herding them into refugee camps, while villagers were forced to defend their own communities in Civil Defence Patrols. Those who returned from the mountains were put to work by the army, who fed and "re-educated" them.

Accounts of the army campaign under Ríos Montt are deeply divided. Some commentators see him as a significant reformer, who saved the rural population by transforming the approach of the army. On the other hand there are those who regard him as the most brutal of all Guatemala's rulers. Most Guatemalans, particularly those in the highlands, do seem to speak very highly of him and say that when he came to power he managed to put a stop to the indiscriminate violence which had plagued the country.

Ríos Montt was replaced by **Mejía Victores** in August 1983, and under the new administration there was a significant drop in the level of rural repression, although selective killings were still an everyday event. In 1984, however, the number of urban disappearances rose once again, with around fifty people abducted each month. In the highlands the process of reconstruction began. Guerrilla forces had dropped to around 1500, and although military campaigns continued, "model villages" were now being built to replace those that had been destroyed. Even so the conditions for refugees and survivors were still highly restricted and many large and impoverished communities are now made up entirely of widows and orphans.

Towards the end of 1985 the country faced its first free elections in thirty years, after a period that had seen 18 different administrations and cost the lives of 100,000 people. Another 38,000 had "disappeared", 440 villages had been destroyed, and 100,000 Guatemalans had fled to Mexico.

CIVILIAN RULE

In 1986 **Vinicio Cerezo** was elected as Guatemala's first civilian president for almost thirty years. Cerezo himself had on several occasions come close to assassination and members of his party, the Christian Democrats,

have been a favourite target for the death squads.

The new government ushered in a period of relative stability, although political killings are by no means a thing of the past. There are still countless abductions, assassinations and disappearances, with the victims drawn from the same groups as before. Between February 1986 and January 1987 there were at least 1000 killings, the vast majority attributable to the "death squads". And while no one accuses Cerezo himself of involvement in the killings, it does seem clear that they are carried out by members of the security forces, which is a measure of his inability to control them.

In rural areas the level of violence has dropped off significantly. At present there are probably around 2000 guerrillas, who only occasionally confront the army. Nevertheless abuses of the Indian population are still common, and they remain exploited and undernourished, while in some areas they are still caught up in the conflict and forced to patrol the countryside (despite guarantees that they would have the option not to). Little has been done to meet their needs in terms of land, health care or education. Internally there are thousands of refugees held in military camps, while around 100,000 remain in Mexico.

In 1988, violence began to increase once again and proof that the situation remains unresolved was provided in November of that year, when 22 bodies were found in a shallow grave near El Aguacate, a small village in the department of Chimaltenango. As yet there is no clear evidence to indicate who carried out the massacre, though recent testimonies suggest that the army was guilty: they blame the guerrillas.

While the killings continue there has been no serious attempt to find the bodies of the disappeared or to bring the guilty to trial: indeed shortly before taking office Cerezo was forced to pardon all crimes committed by the security forces. Many officers who were directly involved in the terror of the early 1980s still hold senior posts, and the army now receives enormous military aid from the US.

Cerezo himself remains preoccupied with holding on to power, fending off several coup attempts and attempting to build some kind of power base. As president he has adopted a non-confrontational approach which has not only ensured a reprieve for the guilty, but also allowed the continued abuse of human rights (on the other hand, it has at least maintained a civilian government). The judiciary remains powerless and the army unchallenged, while members of GAM, the country's most important human rights group, have themselves become targets of the death squads, their leaders joining the growing ranks of the disappeared.

For more information on human rights in Guatemala contact *Amnesty International*, 1 Easton Street, London WC1X 8DJ (☎071/833 1771), or *The Guatemalan Committee for Human Rights*, 83 Margaret Street, London W1N 7HB (☎071/631 4200); and see the "Books" section.

WILDLIFE AND THE ENVIRONMENT

Between them Guatemala and Belize embrace an astonishingly diverse collection of environments, ranging from the coral reefs of the Caribbean coast to the exposed central highlands of Guatemala, where the ground is often hard with frost. The wildlife of Central America is correspondingly varied; undisturbed forests provide a home to both temperate species from the north and tropical ones from the south, as well as a number of indigenous species found nowhere else in the world.

For the sake of organisation this piece traces the landscape from south to north, Pacific to Caribbean, exploring each of the environments along the way.

THE PACIFIC COAST

Guatemala's **Pacific coastline** is marked by a thin strip of black volcanic sand, pounded by the surf. There are no natural harbours and boats have to take their chances in the breakers or launch from one of the piers (though the purpose-built Puerto Quetzal now takes large, ocean-going ships). The sea itself provides a rich natural harvest of shrimp, tuna, snapper and mackerel, most of which go for export. The coastal waters are also ideal for sport fishing. A couple of kilometres offshore, dorado, which

grow to around forty pounds, are plentiful, while further out there are marlin, sailfish, wahoo and skipjack.

The **beach** itself rises from the water to form a large sandbank, dotted with palm trees, behind which the land drops off into low-lying mangrove swamps and canals. In the east, from San José to the border, the **Chiquimulilla Canal** runs behind the beach for around 100 kilometres. For most of the way it's no more than a narrow strip of water, but here and there it fans out into swamps, creating a maze of waterways that are an ideal breeding ground for young fish, waterfowl and a range of small mammals. The sandy shoreline is an ideal nesting site for **sea turtles**, which occasionally emerge from the water, drag themselves up the beach, and deposit a clutch of eggs before hauling their weight back into the water. At Monterrico, to the east of San José, a nature reserve protects a small section of the coastline for the benefit of the turtles, and with luck you might see one here. **The Monterrico Reserve** (p.166) is in fact the best place to see wildlife on the Pacific coast as it includes a superb mangrove swamp, typical of the area directly behind the beach, which you can easily explore by boat.

The **mangroves** are mixed in with water lilies, bulrushes and tropical hardwoods, amongst which you'll see **herons**, **kingfishers** and an array of **ducks** including **muscovies** and **white whistling ducks**. In the area around Monterrico flocks of **wood stork** are common, and you might also see the **white ibis** or the occasional **great jabiru**, a massive stork that nests in the area (and can also be

Jabiru

seen in Belize). With real perseverance and a bit of luck you might also catch a glimpse of a **racoon**, **anteater** or **opossum**. Other birds that you might see almost anywhere along the coast include **plovers**, **coots** and **terns**, and a number of winter migrants including **white** and **brown pelicans**.

Between the shore and the foothills of the highlands, the **coastal plain** is an intensely fertile and heavily farmed area, where volcanic and alluvial soils are ideal for sugar cane, cotton, palm oil, rubber plantations and cattle ranches. In recent years soya and sorgum, which require less labour, have been added to this list. Guatemala's coastal **agribusiness** is high cost and high yield: the soils are treated chemically and the crops regularly sprayed with a cocktail of pesticides, herbicides and fertilisers. There's little land that remains untouched by the hand of commercial agriculture so it's hard to imagine what all this once looked like, but it was almost certainly very similar to the Petén, a mixture of savannah and rainforest supporting a rich array of wildlife. These days it's only the swamps, steep hillsides and towering hedges that give any hint of its former glory, although beautiful flocks of white **snowy** and **cattle egrets** feed alongside the beef cattle.

Finally one particularly interesting lowland species is the **opendula**, a large oriole which builds a long woven nest hanging from trees and telephone wires. They tend to nest in colonies and a single tree might support fifty nests. You'll probably notice the nests more than the birds, but they thrive throughout Belize and Guatemala.

THE BOCA COSTA

Approaching the highlands, the coastal plain starts to slope up towards a string of volcanic cones, and this section of well drained hillside is known as the **Boca Costa**. The volcanic soils, high rainfall and good drainage conspire to make it ideal for growing **coffee**, and it's here that Guatemala's best crop is produced, with rows of olive-green bushes ranked beneath shady trees.

Where the land is unsuitable for coffee, lush tropical forest still grows, clinging to the hills. As you head up into the highlands, through deeply cleft valleys, you pass through some of this superb forest, dripping with moss-covered vines, bromeliads and orchids. The full value of this environment had remained unexplored for many years and the foundation of the **Faro Field Station**, on the southern slopes of the **Santiaguito** volcano, revealed an amazing undisturbed ecosystem, protected by the threat of volcanic eruption. Over 120 species of bird have been sighted here, including some real rarities such as **solitary eagles**, **quetzals** and **highland guans**. The **azure-rumped tanager**, seen here in June 1988, hadn't previously been sighted in Guatemala since the mid-nineteenth century.

THE HIGHLANDS

The highlands proper begin with a chain of **volcanoes**. There are 33 in all, running in a direct line from the southwest to the northeast. Most can be climbed in five or six hours and the view from the top is always superb. The highest is **Tajanulco** (4210 metres) which marks the Mexican border, and there are also three active cones: **Fuego**, **Pacaya** and **Santiaguito**, all of which belch sulphurous fumes, volcanic ash, and the occasional fountain of molten rock. Beneath the surface their subterranean fires heat the bedrock and there are several places where spring water emerges at near boiling point, offering the luxury of a hot bath (for the best of these see Almolonga, p.123).

On this southern side of the central highlands there are two large lakes, set in superb countryside and hemmed in by volcanic peaks. Both tell a sad tale of environmental mismanagement. **Lake Amatitlán**, to the south of Guatemala City, is further down the road to contamination, its waters already blackened by pollution and its shores ringed with holiday homes. It remains a popular picnic spot for the capital's not so rich. Further to the west is **Lake Atitlán**, still spectacularly beautiful, with crystal blue waters. There are moves afoot to develop this lake along the lines of Amatitlán and increasing tourist development threatens to damage the delicate ecological balance. The greatest damage so far was done by the introduction of the **black bass** in 1958, in a bid to create a sport fishery. The bass is a greedy, thuggish beast and in no time at all its presence had reshaped the food chain. Smaller fish were increasingly rare, as were crabs, frogs, insects and small mammals. Worst hit was the

Atitlán grebe, a small, flightless water bird that's found nowhere else in the world. Young grebes were gobbled up by the hungry bass and from 200 in 1960 their numbers fell to just 80 in 1964. Today the grebes have found refuge in a small reserve near the village of Santiago Atitlán, where an underwater net protects them from hungry predators. Meanwhile the beauty of Lake Atitlán remains under threat from overdevelopment, population growth and soil erosion.

On the northern side of the volcanic ridge are the **central valleys** of the highlands, a complex mixture of sweeping bowls, steep-sided valleys, open plateaux and jagged peaks. This central area is home to the vast majority of Guatemala's population and all the available land is intensely farmed, with hillsides carved into workable terraces and portioned up into a patchwork of small fields. Here the land is farmed by Indians using techniques that predate the arrival of the Spanish. The *milpa* is the mainstay of Indian farming practices; a field is planted with maize as the main crop, and beans, chillies and squash are grown beneath it at ground level. Traditionally the land is rotated between *milpa* and pasture, and also left fallow for a while, but in some areas it's now under constant pressure, the fertility of the soil is virtually exhausted and only with the assistance of fertiliser can it still produce a worthwhile crop. The pressure on land is immense and each generation is forced to farm more marginal territory, planting on steep hill-sides where exposed soil is soon washed into the valley below.

Some areas remain off-imits to farmers, however, and there are still vast tracts of the highlands that are **forested**. In the cool valleys of the central highlands pine trees dominate, intermixed with oak, cedar and fir, all of which occur naturally. To the south, on the volcanic slopes and in the warmth of deep-cut valleys, lush tropical forest thrives in a world kept permanently moist – similar in many ways to the forest of Verapaz, where constant rain fosters the growth of "high rainforest".

Heading on to the north the land rises to form several **mountain ranges**. The largest of these are the Cuchumatanes, a massive chain of granite peaks that reach a height of 3790 metres above the town of Huehuetenango. Further to the east there are several smaller ranges such as the Sierra de Chuacús, the Sierra de las Minas and the Sierra de Chama. The high peaks support stunted trees and open grassland, used for grazing sheep and cattle, but are too cold for maize or most other crops.

Birdlife is plentiful throughout the highlands; you'll see a variety of **hummingbirds**, flocks of screeching **parakeets**, **swifts**, **egrets** and the ever-present **vultures**. Slightly less commonplace are the **quails** and **wood partridges**, **white-tailed pigeons**, and several species of doves including the **little Inca** and the **white-winged dove**. Last but by no means least is the **quetzal**, revered since Maya times. The male quetzal has fantastic green tail-feathers which snake through the air as it flies: these have always been prized by hunters and even today the bird is very rare indeed. The only nature reserve in the highlands is the **Biotopo del Quetzal**, a protected area of high rainforest in the department of Baja Verapaz, where quetzals breed.

The highlands also support a number of small **mammals**, including foxes and small cats, although your chances of seeing these are very slim indeed.

THE RAINFORESTS OF THE PETÉN

To the north of the highlands the land drops away into the **rainforests** of the Petén, a massive area that's miraculously undisturbed, although recent oil finds, guerrilla war and migrant settlers are all putting fresh strain on this ecological wonderland. A 1981 United Nations report predicted that Guatemala will lose a third of its forest by the end of the century, and a report by the Guatemalan Commission for the Environment, published in 1990, claimed the country had lost forty percent of its forest cover in the last thirty years, prompting a significant drop in the amount of rainfall. The forest of the Petén extends across the Mexican border, where it merges with the Lacandon rainforest, and into Belize, where it skirts around the lower slopes of the Maya Mountains, reaching to the Caribbean coast.

Ninety percent of the Petén is still covered by **primary forest**, with a canopy that towers fifty metres above the forest floor, made up of hundreds of species of trees, including ceiba, mahogany, aguacate, ebony and sapodilla. The combination of a year-round growing season, plenty of moisture and millions of years of evolution have produced an environment that supports literally thousands of species of plants and trees. While temperate forests tend to be dominated by a single species – fir, oak or beech, say – it's diversity that characterises the tropical forest. Each species is specifically adapted to fit into a particular ecological niche, where it receives a precise amount of light and moisture.

It's a biological storehouse that has yet to be fully explored although it has already yielded some astonishing **discoveries**. Steroid hormones, such as cortizone, and diosgenin, the active ingredient in birth control pills, were developed from wild yams found in these forests; and tetrodoxin, which is derived from a species of Central American frog, is an anaesthetic 160,000 times stronger than cocaine.

Despite its size and diversity the forest is surprisingly **fragile**. It forms a closed system in which nutrients are continuously recycled, and decaying plant matter fuels new growth. The forest floor is a spongy mass of roots, fungi, mosses, bacteria and micro-organisms, in which nutrients are stored, broken down with the assistance of insects and chemical decay, and gradually released to the waiting roots and fresh seedlings. The thick canopy prevents much light reaching the forest floor, ensuring that the soil remains damp but warm, a hotbed of chemical activity. The death of a large tree prompts a flurry of growth as new light reaches the forest floor, and in no time at all a young tree rises to fill the gap. But once the trees are removed the soil is highly vulnerable, deprived of its main source of fertility. Exposed to the harsh tropical sun and direct rainfall, an area of cleared forest soon becomes prone to flooding and drought. Recently cleared land will contain enough nutrients for four or five years of good growth, but soon afterwards its usefulness declines rapidly and within twenty years it will be almost completely barren. If the trees are stripped from a large area soil erosion will silt the rivers and parched soils disrupt local rainfall patterns.

However **settlement** needn't mean the end of the rainforest, and in the past this area supported a huge population of Maya Indians, who probably numbered several million. (Although some archaeologists argue that

during Maya occupation the Petén was a mixture of savannah and grassland, and that relatively recent climatic changes have enabled it to evolve into rainforest.) Only one small group of Indians, the Lacandones, still farm the forest using traditional methods. They allow the existing trees to point them in the right direction, avoiding areas that support mahogany, as they tend to be too wet, and searching out ceiba and ramon trees, which thrive in rich, well drained soils. In April a patch of forest is burnt and then, to prevent soil erosion, planted with fast-growing trees such as bananas and papaya, and with root crops to fix the soil. A few weeks later they plant their main crops: maize and a selection of others, from garlic to sweet potatoes. Every inch of the soil is covered in growth, a method that mimics the forest and thereby protects the soil. The same land is cultivated for three or four years and then allowed to return to its wild state, although they continue to harvest from the fruit-bearing plants and in due course return to the same area. The whole process is in perfect harmony with the forest, extracting only what it can afford to lose and ensuring that it remains fertile. Sadly the Lacandones are a dying breed and traditional farming practices are now used by very few. In their place are waves of new settlers, burning the forest and planting grass for cattle. Neither the cattle, the farmers or the forest will survive long under such a system.

In its undisturbed state the rainforest is still superbly beautiful and is home to an incredible range of wildlife. Amongst the birds the **ocellated turkey**, found only in the Petén, is perhaps the most famous. But the forest is also home to **toucans**, **mot mots**, several species of **parrots** including **Aztec** and **green parakeets**, and the endangered **scarlet macaw**, which is said to live to at least fifty. As in the highlands, **hummingbirds**, **buzzards** and

Ocellated turkey

hawks are all common. A surprising number of these can be seen fairly easily in the **Tikal National Park**, particularly if you hang around until sunset.

Amongst the mammals you'll find **jaguars** (referred to as *tigre* in Guatemala and *tiger* in Belize), **peccary** (a type of wild boar), **brocket deer**, **opossums**, **weasels**, **porcupines**, **pumas**, **ocelots**, **armadillos** and several different species of **monkey**, including **spiders** and **howlers**, which emit a chilling deep-throated roar. The massive **tapir** (mountain cow) plunder through the forests, and the river banks are occupied by tiny **ridge-backed turtles** and **crocodiles**, while **egrets** and **kingfishers** fish from overhanging branches. The rivers and lakes of the Petén are correspondingly rich, packed with **snook**, **tarpon** and **mullet**.

THE MAYA MOUNTAINS

Heading to the west, the Maya Mountains rise up out of the forest, straddling the border with **Belize**. The mountains themselves are formed from a granite intrusion where the bedrock thrusts up through the surface limestone: the higher peaks are solid granite, but many of the lower ridges are formed from the original limestone and riddled with caves and underground rivers.

The lower slopes of the mountains support **moist tropical forest**, which is basically the same thing as full-blown rainforest, modified slightly by the cooler air. But higher up the dense growth gives way to scattered pine trees and rolling grassland. All of this high ground is across the border in Belize, protected in the **Mountain Pine Ridge Forest Reserve** (see p.302).

LOWLAND BELIZE

The rainforests of the Petén extend into **northern Belize**, where much of the low-lying land is swampy, mixed with shallow lagoons and sandy soils that are covered with pine forests and open savannah. There are three nature reserves in the north: the **Project for Belize**, which takes in a stretch of rainforest near the village of Gallon Jug; the **Crooked Tree Wildlife Reserve**, which protects several lagoons; and the **Shipstern Reserve**, which is on the Sarteneja peninsula. At the first of these

you'll see many of the same birds and mammals that are found across the border in Guatemala. At the Crooked Tree and Shipstern reserves you'll find **storks**, **toucans**, **lesser scaup** and perhaps even the odd **jaguar**.

In the south there's only a narrow stretch of land between the Maya Mountains and the coast, but heavy rainfall ensures the growth of lush tropical rainforest. Along the coast, large tracts of forest have been destroyed by hurricanes, and much of the existing forest cover is now dense secondary growth. The **Cockscomb Jaguar Reserve**, to the southwest of Dangriga, offers the best opportunity to explore the forest, and contains an unusually high population of jaguars. Otherwise the rainforests of Belize are very similar to those of Guatemala, supporting a wide range of mammals and birds. In many cases Belizean forest is even better preserved than that in Guatemala, as there's less pressure on the land.

THE CARIBBEAN COASTLINE AND THE BARRIER REEF

Belize's most unique environment is its Caribbean coastline and offshore barrier reef, dotted with small islands and atolls. The shoreline is largely made up of mangrove swamps, which, like those on the Pacific coast of Guatemala, are an ideal marine nursery. Young **stingrays** cruise through the tangle of roots, accompanied by baby **black-tipped sharks**, **bonefish** and small **barracudas**. The basis of the food chain is the nutrient-rich mud, held in place by the mangroves, while the roots themselves are home to **oysters** and **sponges**. The dominant plant species is the red mangrove, which thrives at the water's edge, although in due course it undermines its own environment by consolidating the sea bed until it becomes dry land, where the mangroves soon die off and other shrubs take over. The cutting down of mangroves, particularly on the cayes, exposes the land to the full force of the sea and can mean the end of a small and unstable island.

The mangrove swamps are also home to the **manatee**, an endangered species that looks rather like an overgrown seal. Manatees grow to four metres in length and can weigh as much as a ton, but are placid and shy, moving between the freshwater lagoons and the open sea. They were once common on the eastern seaboard of the United States but were hunted

CONSERVATION IN BELIZE

In **Guatemala** conservation organisations are thin on the ground, with most reserves administered by the government: for more information on wildlife reserves contact the tourist board at 7 Avenida 1–17, Centro Civico, Guatemala City. In **Belize**, however, conservation is being developed rapidly. In the last decade the country has placed itself in the forefront of "ecotourism" – hoping to capitalise on its rich natural environment for the benefit of the entire population, animal and human – but the country was in the conservation business long before it was on the tourist circuit, and today a whole range of organisations work here.

Conservation originally focused on forest reserves established by the colonial government to provide areas for timber exploitation, not primarily for nature preservation. In 1928, however, Half Moon Caye was established as a Crown Reserve to offer protection to the red-footed booby. Other bird and wildlife sanctuaries were established in the 1960s and 1970s, and since independence the government has taken measures to increase the land available for wildlife protection. The passing of the National Parks Act in 1981 provided the legal basis for establishing national parks, natural monuments and reserves. International voluntary organisations have been involved in conservation in Belize for many years and Belize is now earning a worldwide reputation for effective conservation of its tropical forest.

Nature reserves are covered in detail in the relevant chapters. Their success is due as much to the efforts of local communities to become involved in conservation as to the very necessary international organisations working in Belize. The variety of tropical land and marine ecosystems makes Belize, in spite of its small size, increasingly a focus of scientific research. Over seventy percent of land is still forested, with large areas of undisturbed wilderness and a vitally important coral reef. There are 4000 species of flowering plants, 533 bird species (including the rare harpy eagle), all five species of cats found in the Americas, the largest population of manatees outside the US, sea and river turtles, crocodiles and snakes, and countless insect species.

Among the **conservation organisations** at work in Belize are the following:

The Belize Audubon Society, founded in 1969, is the oldest conservation organisation in Belize and manages many of the country's reserves including Half Moon Caye and Guanacaste Park. Members receive a monthly newsletter about the progress of wildlife conservation in Belize. Foreign associate membership costs US$25 a year, from BAS, PO Box 1001, 49 Southern Foreshore, Belize City.

The Belize Zoo is becoming increasingly well known throughout the conservation world, especially in Britain after Gerald Durrell's visit in 1989. In Belize the zoo encourages schoolchildren to understand the natural environment by visits and the Outreach Programme. The zoo is easy to reach from Belize City (see p.293) and if you wish to support its aims individual membership is US$15. Write to Sharon Matola (the zoo's director), PO Box 474, Belize City.

The Belize Center for Environmental Studies is a non-profit organisation established in 1988 to promote sustainable use of Belize's natural resources. It also acts as a co-ordinating agency for conservation groups in Belize and for anyone overseas interested in Belize's environment. Studies made by the Center evaluate threats to the environment, and use may be made of its facilities by scientists, students, researchers and other interested parties. The Center publishes a bi-monthly newsletter and the *Center Environmental Quarterly*. For more information call at 55 Eve Street, Belize City (☎02/45545), or write to PO Box 666, Belize City.

The Programme for Belize is a recent addition to the armoury of conservation in Belize. Initiated in 1988 by the Massachusetts Audubon Society and launched in Britain in 1989, the PFB now manages over 250,000 acres in the Río Bravo Conservation Area. The Programme is raising money to buy land so that it can be held in trust for the people of Belize, with sufficient funds to enable the land to be managed for the benefit of wildlife. For more information visit the PFB office at 1 King Street, Belize City, or write to the UK representative, John Burton, PO Box 99, Saxmundham, Suffolk IP17 2LB.

The World Wide Fund for Nature supports a number of projects in Belize, ranging from the Community Baboon Sanctuary at Bermudian Landing to the Cockscomb Basin Jaguar Preserve (sponsored by Jaguar Cars). The *WWF Conservation Yearbook* contains an A–Z of Belizean wildlife. WWF's UK address is Panda House, Weyside Park, Godalming, Surrey GU7 1XR (☎0483/26444).

Manatee

for their meat and their numbers are now dangerously low.

Heading out to sea you reach the barrier reef, the longest in the western hemisphere, an almost continuous chain of coral that stretches from Mexico to Guatemala, between fifteen and forty kilometres offshore. Beneath the water is a world of astounding beauty, where fish and coral come in every imaginable colour. The corals grow like an underwater forest, with fields of grass carpeting the sea bed, overshadowed by the larger coral formations that feed off plankton wafting past in the current. Among these you'll find the **chalice sponge**, which is a garish pink, the **fire coral**, with hundreds of tiny tentacles, the delicate **feather-star crinoid**, and the **apartment sponge**, a tall thin tube with lots of small holes in it. The fish, including **angel** and **parrot fish**, several species of **stingrays** and **sharks**, **conger** and **moray eels**, **spotted goatfish**, and even a small striped fish call the **sergeant-major**, are just as unusual. The reef and its islands are also home to **marlin**, **barracuda**, three species of **turtle** – the hawksbill, the leatherhead and the green – **dolphins** and **salt -water crocodiles**.

For centuries the reef has been harvested by fishermen. In the past they caught manatees and turtles, but these days the **spiny lobster** and **conch** are the main catch, exported to the US. In the last two decades the fishing industry has been booming and the numbers of both of these have now gone into decline.

Many species, and in particular the turtles and manatees, both of which are considered great delicacies, are endangered, and on the southern tip of Ambergris Caye there's an underwater wildlife reserve, the **Hol Chan Marine Reserve**, which is a superb spot for snorkelling and diving. Wherever you enter the water, though, you stand a good chance of seeing a wide range of fish and corals.

Above the water the cayes are an ideal nesting ground for birds, providing protection from predators and surrounded by an inexhaustible food supply. At **Half Moon Caye**, right out on the eastern edge of the reef, there's a wildlife reserve designed to protect a breeding colony of 4000 **red-footed boobies**. Here you'll also see **frigate birds, ospreys, mangrove warblers** and **white-rowned pigeons**, amongst a total of 98 different species.

MUSIC IN BELIZE

For such a tiny country, Belize enjoys an exceptional range of musical styles and traditions. Whether your tastes run to the ethereal harp melodies of the Maya or the up-tempo *punta* of the Garifuna, or to calypso, marimba, *brukdown*, soca or steelpan, Belize is sure to have something to suit. Some visitors still complain about the noisiness of Belizean society and the volume at which the music is played, but if you can get into it, it's one of the quickest ways to the heart of Belizeans and their culture.

ROOTS

Until the demise of the Maya civilisation and the arrival of the Spanish, the indigenous **Maya** of Belize played a limited range of instruments drawn almost entirely from the flute and drum families. Drums were usually made from hollowed logs covered in goat skin. Rattles, gourd drums and the turtleshell provided further rhythmic accompaniment. Trumpets, flutes, bells, shells and whistles completed the instrumentation. Most music was ritual in character and could involve up to 800 dancers, although smaller ceremonial ensembles were more common. Sadly, the sounds of this now silent culture are no longer with us.

However, as befits a nation of immigrants, each new group arriving – the Europeans, the Creoles, the Mestizos and the Garifuna – brought with them new styles, vigour and variety which today inform and influence popular culture. The **Europeans** introduced much of the hardware and software for playing music: western musical instruments and sheet music, record players and discs, and most recently cassettes, compact discs and massive sound systems. The Schottische, quadrille, polka and waltz can be counted amongst their strictly musical innovations. From **Africa** via Jamaica, came an exciting melange of West African rhythms and melodies which also brought drums and stringed instruments into the mix.

A new syncretic style, nurtured in the logging camps and combining western instrumentation with specifically African inflections emerged in the late nineteenth century with the name "**Brukdown**". With a twentieth-century line-up of guitar, banjo, accordion, drums and the jawbone of an ass, *brukdown* remains a potent reminder of past Creole culture. Although the style is slowly fading, there are still several bands playing in and around Belize City of which **Mr Peter's Boom and Chime** is the best. **Brad Patico**, an accomplished guitarist and singer, similarly does his best to keep alive the Creole folk song tradition, and from his base in Burrel Boom collects old material, composes new songs and performs regularly to highly appreciative audiences. More recently, the "African" elements in Creole music have been expressed through wider pan-Caribbean styles like calypso, reggae, soca and rap.

Calypso enjoyed a brief period of pre-eminence and is still usually associated with **Lord Rhaburn's Combo**. The band can still be found performing regularly at the *Big Apple* but live appearances by Rhaburn himself are increasing rarities. Most other bands copy current hits with one or two original compositions thrown in: Youth Connection, Gilharry 7, Santino's Messengers and Brother David (particularly the last mentioned) can all provide an excellent evening's entertainment.

Mestizo communities (including the Mopan Maya) in the north and west of the country continue to favour **marimba** ensembles comprising half a dozen men playing two large wooden xylophones, perhaps supported by a double bass and a drum kit. Up to half a dozen bands play regularly in the Cayo district: Elfigo Panti, who doubles up as the knowledgeable tourist guide at Xunantunich, presides over the nation's pre-eminent marimba group – **Alma Belicena**. Orange Walk district boasts the country's sole brass band, playing a roots Mexican style, and just as leading marimba bands occasionally pop over from Flores in Guatemala, so too do Mexican **mariachi** bands occasionally appear. Nonetheless, traditional Mestizo music remains under threat as the youth turn to rock, rap and punta.

PUNTA ROCK

If Maya, Mestizo and Creole styles retain only a fragile hold on popular musical consciousness, it is the **Garifuna** who have catapulted to centre-stage over the last decade with the invention and development of **Punta Rock**. Descended from Carib Indians and African slaves, the Garifuna arrived in Belize in the early nineteenth century having been forcefully exiled from St Vincent by the British. With a distinct language and a vibrant, living culture, the Garifuna suffered a century of discrimination in Belize before re-establishing their individuality in the cultural renaissance of the early 1980s.

The key developments were the amplification of several traditional drum rhythms, the addition of new instruments such as the turtleshell, and the almost universal aversion to singing in anything but Garifuna. The new mood was pioneered by singer, guitarist and artist **Pen Cayetano** in Dangriga. His drum, guitar and brass arrangements provided the springboard for a number of Dangriga-based electric bands such as Sound City, Black Choral, Sounds Incorporated, and above all **Andy Palacio**, whose satirical 1988 hit "Bikini Panti" remains a national favourite. The **Waribagabaga drum and dance troupe**, formed in 1964, remain the chief guardians of more orthodox arrangements and should on no account be missed when they perform in Dangriga.

PLACES AND PEOPLE

Thursday evening is widely considered to mark the start of the weekend, and weekends are the best time to catch bands and other entertainment in **Belize City**. The *Big Apple*, *The Pub*, *Moby Dicks*, *Shangri-La*, *Lumba Yaad* and the *Privateer* usually offer live music, while bigger venues like *Bird's Isle* and the *Civic Auditorium* often host longer variety bills. Most

of the bigger hotels hire smaller outfits for residencies and special events and it would be a pity to leave Belize without hearing one of the several **one-man bands** which, with an array of electronic equipment and virtuoso keyboard skills, provide enjoyable dance music in less crowded settings. The most popular performers remain **Davonix**, **Steve Babb** and the talented **Magana**.

Caye Chapel offers live entertainment and beach barbecues on the last Saturday of every month, while neighbouring **San Pedro**, as the major tourist destination in Belize, guarantees some kind of entertainment throughout the tourist season. **Belmopan** is less well served. The *Bayman Inn*'s disco changes hands with a disruptive regularity while *Ed's Bar* in nearby Roaring Creek, despite its enjoyable dance-hall ambiance, can seldom guarantee a show. **San Ignacio**, capital of the Cayo district, presents far livelier options and residents of Belmopan clearly prefer the west to Belize City when it comes to weekend fun. Bands regularly perform at the *San Ignacio Hotel*, *Cahal Pech Tavern* and the *Blue Angel*, while the delightful Obandos entertain guests at their family-owned resort at *Las Casitas*.

In **Dangriga**, the *Riverside Disco* provides regular live music while **Pen Cayetano and the Turtleshell Band** can sometimes be found playing in the street in front of the art studio on a Friday night. **Punta Gorda**, **Benque Viejo** and **Corozal** seldom offer live music, but on the other hand the more rural areas do occasionally come up trumps with unexpected and informal performances. Placencia, Hopkins, Succotz, Bullet Tree, Ladyville, Burrell Boom, Consejo and Maskall all still entertain in the traditional way and luck alone will determine whether anything is happening on the night you happen to be there.

The large tourist **hotels** usually have something on offer as well, and it is always worth checking the *Pelican* in Dangriga, *Barons* in Orange Walk and the *Bellevue* and *Fort George* in Belize City.

OCCASIONS

Perhaps the best times to hear and see the full panoply of Belizean musical culture are the various **national events** which regularly punctuate the social calendar. Biggest and best are National Day (September 10) and Independence

Day (September 21) – dates which mark almost two weeks of festivities as Belize City comes close to the spirit and atmosphere of Caribbean carnival. Street parades, floats, block parties, "jump-ups" and late-night revelry characterise what are known locally as "The Celebrations".

Garifuna Settlement Day falls on November 19 and brings huge crowds to Dangriga for a long weekend of late nights, rum and rhythm. Mestizo communities celebrate with a number of very Latin type **fiestas** – bands, funfairs, sports and competitions. These are usually held around Easter and are soon followed by the **National Agricultural Show** held just outside Belmopan, when up to 50,000 people gather over three days for things both agricultural and recreational. All the country's top bands will appear at some stage during the weekend.

Occasionally the scene is further enlivened by visits from **Belizean musicians based in the States**. Los Angeles is the favourite destination for many Belizeans and prodigal sons like Chatuye, Jah Warriors, Poopa Curly and Sounds Incorporated usually try to come at least once a year. Calypso Rose is a regular visitor and late in 1989 the Mighty Sparrow from Trinidad put on several highly successful shows.

RECORDINGS

On an official level, the government takes a lively interest in local arts with a revitalised Arts Council based at the Bliss Institute. *Radio Belize* does its best to promote local talent but cable TV and pirate satellite stations steadily erode interest in local products. One recent initiative seeking to revitalise and preserve local music is the **SUNRISE project** – a community-based recording studio producing the best Belizean music available on cassette. They're sold at many big hotels and at record shops in most towns. Others groups, like Brother David, Messengers and Sounds Incorporated, have also produced good local cassettes and there are some signs that local record shops are beginning to respect the rights of musicians to also earn a living.

Of course there are those who do not fit into any of the tidy categories outlined above. Both the **Police Band** and the **Belize Defence Force Band** perform regularly and creditably. The **All-Stars Steel Band** plough a lonely furrow but are well-received wherever they play. There are also a number of small **jazz** outfits and some very gifted up and coming **female vocalists**. But on a national level, Punta still holds sway and there is no question, given the richness of the Garifuna traditional musical repertoire, that they will continue to develop new styles for decades to come. For their part, several young musicians are now experimenting with more traditional Mestizo melodies and rhythms. Mestizo Rock anyone?

Ronnie Graham

BOOKS

In the past Guatemala and Belize never inspired a great deal of literature; but in recent years the political turmoil has spawned a boom in books about Guatemala, while Belizean independence prompted a handful of new Belizean histories. Politics overshadows almost all books about Guatemala and most travel accounts deal with Central America as a whole, offering only a small slice of Belize or Guatemala. Be warned that many of the books listed below are very difficult to find.

TRAVEL

Anthony Daniels *Sweet Waist of America* (Hutchinson £14.95). The most recent and reasonable of Guatemalan travel books, and a delight to read. Daniels takes a refreshingly even-handed approach to the country and comes up with a fascinating cocktail of people and politics, discarding the stereotypes that litter most books on Central America. The book also includes some interesting interviews with prominent characters from Guatemala's recent history.

Patrick Marnham *So far from God . . .* (Penguin £3.95). A saddened and vaguely right-wing account of Marnham's travels through Central America, from the States to Panama (missing out Belize). Dotted with amusing anecdotes and interesting observations, the book was researched in 1984, and its description of Guatemala is dominated by the reign of terror. The Paraxtut massacre, mentioned by Marnham, has since been unmasked as a fabrication.

Aldous Huxley *Beyond the Mexique Bay* (Grafton £1.95). Huxley's travels, in 1934, took him from Belize through Guatemala to Mexico, swept on by his fascination for history and religion, and sprouting bizarre theories on the basis of everything he sees. There are some great descriptions of Maya sites and Indian culture, with superb one-liners summing up people and places.

Paul Theroux *The Old Patagonian Express* (Penguin £4.50). An epic train journey from Boston to Patagonia that takes in a couple of miserable trips in Guatemala, one on each of the country's railways. It's not too far off when it comes to life on Guatemala's railway network, although Theroux doesn't have much time for Guatemalans, dismissing them as unhelpful and taciturn.

Jeremy Paxman *Through the Volcanoes* (Michael Joseph £4.50). Similar in many ways to Patrick Marnham's book, this is another political travel account investigating the turmoil of Central America and finding solace in the calm of Costa Rica. Paxman's travels take him through all seven of the republics, including Belize, and he offers a good overview of the politics and history of the region.

Jonathan Evans Maslow *Bird of Life, Bird of Death* (Penguin £3.95). Again travel and political comment are merged as Maslow sets out in search of the quetzal, using the bird's uncertain future as a metaphor for contemporary Guatemala, and contrasting this with the success of the vulture. It's a sweeping account, very entertaining, but more concerned with impressing the reader than representing the truth. A great yarn, set in a country that's larger than life in every possible way, but in the end a naive and stereotypical image of Central American horror.

Ronald Wright *Time Among the Maya* (Bodley Head £14.95). A vivid and sympathetic account of his travels from Belize through Guatemala, Chiapas and Yucatán, meeting the Maya of today and exploring their obsession with time. The books twin points of interest are the ancient Maya and the recent violence. An encyclopaedic bibliography offers ideas for exploration in depth and the author's knowledge is evident in the superb historical insight he imparts through the book. Certainly one of the best recent travel books on the area: read it before you set off if you're planning a lengthy trip through remote Maya lands.

Nigel Pride *A Butterfly Sings to Pacaya* (Constable 1978). The author, accompanied by his wife and four-year-old son, travels south from the US border in a Jeep, heading through Mexico, Guatemala and Belize. A large section of the book is set in Maya areas, illustrated by the author's drawings of landscapes, people and animals. Though the travels took place over fifteen years ago the pleasures and privations they experience rarely appear dated: the description of the climb of Pacaya (a Guatemalan volcano) is one of the highlights of the book.

John Lloyd Stephens *Incidents of Travel in Central America, Chiapas, and Yucatán* (Century £3.95). Stephens was a classic nineteenth-century traveller. Acting as American ambassador to Central America he indulged his own enthusiasm for archaeology; while the republics fought it out amongst themselves he was wading through the jungle stumbling across ancient cities. His journals, told with superb Victorian pomposity punctuated with sudden waves of enthusiasm, make great reading. Some editions of the work include fantastic illustrations by Catherwood, which show the ruins overgrown with tropical rainforest.

FICTION AND AUTOBIOGRAPHY

Zee Edgell *Beka Lamb* (Heinemann £3.50). A young girl's account of growing up in Belize in the 1950s, in which the problems of adolescence are described alongside those of the Belizean independence movement. The book also explores everyday life in the colony, describing the powerful structure of matriarchal society and the influence of the Catholic church.

Norman Lewis *The Volcano Above Us* (Arena £3.99). A vaguely historical novel first published in 1957 that pulls together all the main elements of recent history in Guatemala: the banana company, trigger-happy troops and political upset. The image that it summons is one of depressing drudgery and eternal conflict, set against a background of repression and racism. In the light of what's happened since it has a certain prophetic quality, and remains gripping despite its miserable conclusions.

Paul Bowles *Up Above the World* (Arena £3.99). Paul Bowles is at his chilling, understated best in this novel based on his (and Jane Bowles's) experiences of Guatemala in the late 1930s. Jane Bowles also used the visit for fiction in *A Guatemalan Idyll* and other tales, recently republished in *Everything is Nice: Collected Stories of Jane Bowles* (Virago £5.95).

Victor Perera *Rites: A Guatemalan Boyhood* (Flamingo £3.50). An autobiographical account of a childhood in Guatemala City's Jewish community. It may not cast all that much light on the country, but nevertheless it's an interesting read, pulling together an unusual combination of cultures.

Zoila Ellis *On Heroes, Lizards and Passion* (Cubola Productions, Belize). A collection of seven short stories written by a Belizean woman with a deep understanding of her country's people and their culture.

Felicia Hernandez *Those Ridiculous Years* (Cubola Productions, Belize). A short autobiographical book about growing up in Dangriga thirty years ago.

Sharon Matola *Hoodwink the Owl* (Macmillan £3). A charming collection of children's stories relating the travels of Hoodwink as he searches for a safe home. The book is written by the founder of the Belize Zoo and carries a strong environmental message. The book also includes some illustrations by Allen Sutherland and Lee Turner.

Miguel Angel Asturias. Guatemala's most famous author, Asturias' work is deeply indebted to Guatemalan history and culture. *Hombres de Maiz* (Men of Maize; Verso £12.95) is generally regarded as his masterpiece, classically Latin American in its magic realist style, and bound up in the complexity of Indian culture. His other works include *El Señor Presidente*, a grotesque portrayal of social chaos and dictatorial rule, based on Asturias' own experience; *El Papa Verde*, which explores the murky world of the United Fruit Company; and *Weekend en Guatemala*, describing the downfall of the Arbenz government. Asturias died in 1974, having won the Nobel prize for literature.

Rodrigo Rey Rosa *Dust on her Tongue* (Peter Owen £8.95), *The Beggar's Knife* (Peter Owen £4.50). Two collections of stories by a young

Guatemalan writer, translated by Paul Bowles. The tales are brutal and lyrical, concerned, as Bowles commented, with "a present-day Central America troubled by atavistic memories of its sanguinary past". Highly recommended.

GUATEMALAN HISTORY, POLITICS, HUMAN RIGHTS

Jim Handy *Gift of the Devil* (Between the Lines, 1984). The best modern history of Guatemala, concise and readable with a sharp focus on the Indian population and the brief period of socialist government. Don't expect too much detail on the distant past as the book only explores it in order to set the modern reality in some kind of context, but if you're interested in the history of Guatemalan brutality then this is the book to read. Certainly not an objective perspective, it sets out to expose the development of oppression and point the finger at those who oppress.

Jean-Marie Simon *Eternal Spring – Eternal Tyranny* (Norton £20). Of all the books on human rights in Guatemala, this is the one that speaks with blinding authority and the utmost clarity. Combining the highest standards in photography with crisp text, there's no attempt to persuade you and the facts are allowed to speak for themselves, which they do with amazing strength. If you want to know what happened in Guatemala over the last twenty years or so there is no better book than this one. Again Simon clearly takes sides, aligning herself with the revolutionary left: there's no mention of any abuses committed by the guerrillas.

George Black *Garrison Guatemala* (Zed £5.95). An account of the militarisation of Guatemalan politics up to 1982. Black's condemnation is total: the conflict in Guatemala is seen as a battle to the death, with armed uprising the only possible solution and the probable outcome.

Stephen Schlesinger and Stephen Kinzer *Bitter Fruit: The Untold Story of the American Coup In Guatemala* (Anchor Books). As the title says, this book traces the American connection in the 1954 coup, delving into the murky water of United Fruit Company politics and proving that the invading army received its orders from the White House.

James Painter *Guatemala: False Hope, False Freedom* (Latin American Bureau £4.95). Another deeply depressing analysis of the situation in Guatemala today. First published in 1988, and revised in 1989, it's the most up-to-date account of the political situation, dealing with the failure of Cerezo's administration. It also includes an investigation into the roots of inequality and a summary of the main forces that help to perpetuate it. Alongside Jean-Marie Simon's book this will give you a real understanding of the situation.

Guatemala in Rebellion (Grove Press £10.75). A fascinating collection of historical snippets and eye-witness accounts tracing Guatemalan history from the arrival of the Spanish to 1983, in which the people involved are allowed to speak for themselves. They range from *conquistadores* to priests and Indians.

Guatemala: A Country Study. Published by the American army, this is a comprehensive overview of Guatemala, taking in everything from soil types to Indian languages. The style is dry, but the information superb.

George Lovell *Conquest and Survival in Colonial Guatemala* (McGill Queen's University Press). Very localised in its area of study, this book sets out to examine in intimate detail the rise and fall of the Indian population in the Cuchumatanes from 1500 to 1821.

Mario Payeras *Days of the Jungle* (Monthly Review Press £3.95). A slim volume originally written under the auspices of the EGP, one of Guatemala's main guerrilla armies. In this sense it's unique, as the voice of the guerrillas is rarely heard. Here one of their number tells of the early days of the organisation, as they enter Guatemala through the jungles of the northwest and attempt to establish contacts amongst the local population. There are, however, serious doubts about the accuracy of the story in the book.

Victor Montejo *Testimony: Death of a Guatemalan Village* (Kerbstone Press £6.50). Yet another horrifying account of murder and destruction. In this case it's the personal testimony of a school teacher, describing the arrival of the army in a small highland village and the killing that follows.

Amnesty International. If you're really interested in finding out about the human rights situation in Guatemala then get hold of an

Amnesty report. These are invariably clearly set out, homing straight in on the main issue and relying on very high standards of research.

Philip Berryman *Christians in Guatemala's Struggle* (Catholic Institute for International Relations £1.95). A very well informed and well written slim volume, covering the period from 1944 to 1984. Even if you're not particularly interested in the Christian angle, it offers a concise account of the political situation, seen through the eyes of the oppressed. It includes a great deal of information about the development of opposition to the oligarchy, particularly union organisation.

BELIZEAN HISTORY AND POLITICS

Narda Dobson *A History of Belize* (Longman Caribbean 1973). Excellent, authoritative account of Belize's history from Maya times through to the years prior to independence, detailing the early settlers, Spanish attempts to dislodge the British Baymen, and the numerous treaties between Britain and Spain (often ignored) to resolve territorial disputes. Doesn't cover modern history, though.

Nigel Bolland *Colonialism and Resistance in Belize* (Cubola Productions £10). Perhaps the most academic text on Belizean history, this adopts a staunchly Marxist stance, sweeping away many of the myths and much of the romance that surrounds the history of Belize.

Assad Shoman *Party Politics in Belize* (Cubola Productions, Belize). Less than a hundred pages in length, Shoman's book is nevertheless a highly detailed account of the development of party politics in Belize.

Among other **histories of Belize** the best are **William David Setzekon**'s *A Profile of the New Nation of Belize, formerly British Honduras* (Ohio University Press £8.95), which is easy going and approachable. For something more academic try *The Making of Modern Belize* by **C.H. Grant** (Cambridge). Inside Belize you'll also be able to buy copies of *The Baymen's Legacy – A Portrait of Belize City* and *A History of Belize – A Nation in the Making*, which are both straightforward and simple historical accounts, possibly written for use in schools.

CENTRAL AMERICAN POLITICS

James Dunkerley *Power in the Isthmus* (Verso £12.95). A detailed account of Central American politics which sadly excludes Belize and Panama. Nevertheless it offers a good summary of the situation in contemporary Central America, albeit in turgidly academic style.

Ralph Lee Woodward Jr *Central America; A Nation Divided* (Oxford University Press £8.95). More readable than the above, this is probably the best book for a general summary of the Central American situation, despite its daft title.

INDIGENOUS CULTURE

James D. Sexton. As an editor Sexton has published two excellent autobiographical accounts originally written by an anonymous Indian from somewhere on the south side of Lake Atitlán. The books give a real impression of life inside a modern Indian village, bound up in poverty, local politics and a mixture of Catholicism and superstition, and avoiding the stereotyping which usually characterises description of the Indian population. The earlier of the two is *Son of Tecún Umán* which takes us through from 1972 to 1977, while the second account, *Campesino*, leads up to 1982 and includes the worst years of political violence. Both books make fascinating reading and have a superb pace to them, in perfect harmony with life in the highlands. They're both published by Arizona University Press in hardback, and are hard to find (almost impossible in Britain): *Casa Andinista*, in Antigua, Guatemala, sometimes has copies.

Rigoberta Menchu *I . . . Rigoberta Menchu. An Indian Woman in Guatemala* (Verso £8.95). An unusual and fascinating account of life in the highlands, tracing the abuse of the Indian population and the rising tide of violence. It includes a chilling description of the military campaign and of the power and complexity of Indian culture, homing in on the enormous gulf between *Ladinos* and Indians.

Krystyna Deuss *Indian Costumes from Guatemala*. A rather sketchy survey of the traditional costumes worn in Guatemala, but still perhaps the best introduction to the subject, and certainly the most widely available.

Guisela Mayen de Castellanos *Tzute and hierarchy in Sololá.* Published by the Ixchel Museum and only available within Guatemala, this is a detailed and academic account of Indian costume and the complex hierarchy that it embodies. The book is somewhat dry in its approach but the research is superb and some of the information is fascinating.

Linda Asturias de Barrios *Comalapa: Native Dress and its Significance.* Also published by the Ixchel Museum and only available in Guatemala, this is another work of skilled academic research, investigating weaving skills and their place within modern Indian communities.

The Popol Vuh. The great poem of the Quichés, written shortly after the conquest and intended to preserve the tribe's knowledge of its history. It's an amazing swirl of ancient mythological characters and their wandering through the Quiché highlands, tracing Quiché ancestry back to the first man. There are several versions on offer and many of them are very half-hearted, including only a few lines from the original. The best version is translated by Dennis Tedlock and published by Touchstone in the USA at $9.95.

Hans Namuth *Los Todos Santeros* (Nishen). A splendid book of black and white photographs taken in the village of Todos Santos, to the north of Huehuetenango. The book was inspired by the work of anthropologist Maud Oakes – see below.

Byron Foster *Spirit Possession in the Garifuna Community of Belize* (Cubola Productions). The only offering on indigenous culture in Belize is by no means comprehensive. There's little background on Garifuna culture, and the main focus of the book is the actual experience of spirit possession, which is described by several Garifunas from southern Belize.

Maud Oakes. An anthropologist who spent many years in the Mam-speaking village of Todos Santos, north of Huehuetenango, Oakes' studies of life in the village were published in the 1940s and 1950s and still make fascinating reading. They include *Beyond the Windy Place* and *The Two Crosses of Todos Santos.*

Philip Werne *The Maya of Guatemala* (Minority Rights Group £2.50). A short study of repression and the Indians of Guatemala. Published in October 1989 and certainly the most up-to-date work on the subject.

ARCHAEOLOGY

Michael Coe *The Maya* (Thames and Hudson £5.95). As a clear and comprehensive introduction to Maya archaeology this is certainly the best on offer. Coe worked on the Tikal project for a number of years and is deeply experienced in this whole area of study. He has also written several more weighty, academic volumes, and *Tikal: A Handbook to the Ancient Maya Ruins* which is a superbly detailed account of the site. It's usually available at the ruins and includes a detailed map of the main area – essential for in-depth exploration.

Charles Gallenkamp *Maya* (Penguin £4.95). Perhaps a touch over-the-top on the sensational aspects of Maya archaeology, this is nonetheless another reasonable introduction to the subject. This book offers an overview of the history of Maya archaeology, taking you through the process of unravelling the complexity of the Maya world.

Robert Sharer *The Ancient Maya* (Stanford). If you really want to dig deep then this is a weighty account of Maya civilisation, more concerned with being scientifically accurate than readable. It's a long, dry account, but if you can spare the time you'll certainly end up well informed.

Eric S. Thompson. A major authority on the ancient Maya, Thompson's works include many academic studies: *The Rise and Fall of the Maya Civilisation* (University of Oklahoma Press) is one of the more aproachable. He is also the author of a very interesting study of Belizean history in the first two hundred years of Spanish colonial rule entitled *The Maya of Belize – Historical Chapters Since Columbus* (Cubola Productions). It's an interesting investigation into a little-studied area of Belizean history and casts some light on the tribes that weren't immediately conquered by the Spanish.

Carmack *Quichean Civilisation* (California). A thorough study of the Quichés and their history, drawing on archaeological evidence and accounts of the conquest. A useful insight into the structure of highland society at the time of the conquest.

Orellana *The Tzutujil Mayas* (University of Oklahoma Press). Another study of highland tribes. This one goes into greater depth when it comes to events since the conquest.

Warlords and Maize Men (Cubola, 1989). Subtitled "A Guide to the Maya Sites of Belize" and written by various experts, this is an excellent handbook to fifteen of the most accessible sites in Belize compiled by the *Association for Belizean Archaeology* and the Belizean government Department for Archaeology.

National Geographic also sponsor a good deal of archaeological research in the Maya area and it's always worth checking back issues for articles on Belize and Guatemala. The best recent issue was October 1989, which featured plans for the *Ruta Maya*, a route intended to connect all the great Maya sites, reaching from Honduras to Mexico.

WILDLIFE AND THE ENVIRONMENT

Smith, Trimm and Wayne *The Birds of Tikal* (The Natural History Press). This is sadly all that's on offer for budding ornithologists in Guatemala, but we should be thankful for small mercies. The book isn't available in Britain, but can usually be bought at Tikal.

Alan Rabinowitz *Jaguar* (Arbor House, New York, 1986). Written by a US zoologist studying jaguars for the New York Zoological Society in the early 1980s and living with a Maya family in the Cockscomb Basin, Belize. Rabinowitz was instrumental in the establishment of the Jaguar Reserve in 1984.

John C. Kricher *A Neotropical Companion* (Princeton University Press, 1989). Subtitled "An Introduction to the Animals, Plants and Ecosystems of the New World Tropics", this contains an amazing amount of valuable information for nature lovers. Researched mainly in Central America, so there's plenty that's directly relevant.

The Jungles of Central America (Time Life Books). A glossy trip through the wildernesses of Central America. By no means a comprehensive account of the area's wildlife but a good read nonetheless, with several good sections on Guatemala and Belize.

GUIDES, OLD AND NEW

Bruce Hunter *A Guide to Ancient Maya Ruins* (University of Oklahoma Press £9.10). The only guide that focuses exclusively on Maya ruins, this offers an account of all the most important Maya sites in Mexico, Guatemala and Belize. Many of the more obscure ruins are ignored, but it's well worth reading if you're into Maya sites.

Lily de Jongh Osborne *Four Keys to Guatemala* (1939, o/p). One of the best guides to Guatemala ever written, including a short piece on every aspect of the country's history and culture. Osborne also wrote a good book on arts and crafts produced in Indian Guatemala. Sadly both of these books are now out of print.

Hilary Bradt and Rob Rachowecki *Backpacking in Mexico and Central America* (Bradt Enterprises, £5.95). Written with real affection by dedicated walkers who enthuse about life in Central America. Having said that, the walks they describe are few and far between, although the background information is useful.

Trevor Long and Elizabeth Bell *Antigua Guatemala*. Published in Guatemala, this is the best guide to Antigua, replacing an older version by Mike Shawcross which is now out of print. The book is available from several shops in Antigua.

Emory King *Emory King's Driving Guide to Belize*. Worth a look if you're travelling around. The maps are perhaps a little too sketchy for complete accuracy but the book is typically Belizean: laid-back and easy-going. Emory King is something of a celebrity in Belize and has also written a humorous description of family life in Belize: *Hey Dad This is Belize*. These and other books written by him are only available in Belize.

Chiki Mallan *Guide to the Yucatán Peninsula, including Belize* (Moon Publications £11.95). Aimed primarily at the American market for tourists travelling around with their own cars. It covers an area from Tabasco and Chiapas to Belize. The Yucatán section is good but details are scarce when it comes to Belize.

A SINGLE COOK BOOK

Copeland Marks *False Tongues and Sunday Bread; A Guatemalan and Maya Cookbook* (Evans £12.95). Having travelled in Guatemala, and suffered the endless onslaught of beans and tortillas, you may be surprised to find that the country has an established culinary tradition. Copeland Marks, an American food writer, has spent years unearthing the finest Guatemalan recipes, from hen in chocolate sauce to the standard black beans. The book is a beautifully bound celebration of Guatemalan food as it should be. In Britain you can get it at *Books For Cooks*, 4 Blenheim Crescent, London W11 1NN (☎071/221 1992).

ONWARDS FROM BELIZE AND GUATEMALA

Leaving Guatemala or Belize the most obvious onward move is north to **MEXICO**, which is easily reached from either. Mexico is superbly beautiful and offers a wide range of attractions, certainly too many to go into here. Suffice to say that it is in many ways very different from Guatemala, but just as interesting. The landscape, the atmosphere and the culture will all come as a surprise to anyone who's immersed themselves in Central America. The sheer scale of Mexico can be a bit daunting after the miniature world of Guatemala and Belize, but the best way to get to grips with it is the *Rough Guide* to Mexico, by John Fisher, which will guide you around the pitfalls and steer you towards all that is best.

In Belize there's just one border point, taking you from Corozal in the north to the Mexican town of Chetumal, and buses out of Belize City run all the way, pausing for customs and immigration. In Guatemala there are a number of different possibilities. In the highlands you can cross the border at La Mesilla, reached from the Guatemalan town of Huehuetenango, and once across the border you can catch a bus to the Mexican towns of Comitán and San Cristóbal de Las Casas. Further south there are two bustling border crossings on the Pacific coast, Talisman and Tecún Umán, from both of which there are minibuses to Tapachula in Mexico. Most commercial traffic goes this way. Finally, and more adventurously, you can travel into Mexico by boat from the jungles of the Petén. The most popular of these trips takes you along the Río San Pedro from the Guatemalan settlement of Naranjo. This route is fairly well used, with established customs and immigration posts, and there's a boat that provides a daily shuttle between the two countries. You arrive in Mexico at the small village of La Palma, a bus ride from Tenosique. The second river route starts from the town of Sayaxché, and takes you along the Río de la Pasión to the Mexican border town of Benemerito. Here you'll have to hire your own boat, or hitch a ride with someone going downriver, and immigration procedures are a little tricky.

To get into Mexico Britons, EC nationals (except the French), Canadians and Americans need only a tourist card. These can usually be obtained at the border, although officially you should get hold of one beforehand, from a Mexican consulate. There are Mexican embassies in Belize City and Guatemala City, and consulates in Huehuetenango, Quezaltenango and Retalhuleu, so if you happen to be near one of these it's a good idea to get hold of a tourist card in advance. Australians, French and New Zealanders all need visas, which must be obtained from a Mexican embassy. (In London this is at 8 Halkin Street, London SW1X 7DW; for the addresses in Guatemala and Belize see the relevant sections.)

If you plan to head further north to the **USA** then get a visa at home, as the queues at American embassies in Guatemala, Belize and Mexico can literally stretch for weeks.

Heading south, the easiest country to reach is **EL SALVADOR**: direct buses run from Guatemala City to San Salvador. It's a beautiful place, with lush highland valleys, a string of volcanoes and some of the best surfing in Central America. El Salvador is also the most densely populated, Americanised and industrialised of the republics, and is ravaged by a bitter civil war, now in its eleventh year, which still claims the lives of around three people every day. Alfredo Christiani was elected as president in 1989, and the army remains firmly entrenched in a struggle against the FMLN, a left-wing guerrilla group who control some remote areas and have recently made startling gains. The abuse of basic human rights is commonplace, and abductions, torture and death squads are central to the army's campaign of terror. Bearing all this in mind you probably won't want to linger here, but this is still the quickest route from Guatemala to Nicaragua, and passing through is fairly straightforward. You should be able to get between the two countries in three days; the first night in San Salvador and the second in Choluteca, Honduras.

There are four border crossings connecting Guatemala with El Salvador. The most northerly, reached from the Guatemalan town of Esquipulas, and served only by a local bus service, is the least used. Further south are San

Cristóbal, reached from Asunción Mita, and Valle Nuevo, the most direct route, served by a regular flow of fast pullman buses that run between Guatemala City and San Salvador. And finally there's Ciudad Pedro de Alvarado, on the Pacific coast. The easiest way to travel between the two countries is on one of the direct buses which leave every hour or so from both capitals, taking around eight hours.

Visas for El Salvador are needed by Australians and New Zealanders and take a week or two to process, as applicants have to be checked out by the authorities in San Salvador. If you're just passing through it might be easier to travel through Honduras, which takes a day or so extra but is less hassle. Americans, Europeans and Canadians just need tourist cards, issued at the border.

Ignored by most travellers, **HONDURAS** is often seen as an unfortunate obstacle between Guatemala and Nicaragua. However it does have several interesting attractions: the Bay Islands, the ruins of Copán, Caribbean beaches and some superb scenery around Tegucigalpa. There are no direct connections between Belize and Honduras, but two border crossings connect Honduras with Guatemala. Most commercial traffic passes through Agua Caliente, which is reached from the Guatemalan town of Esquipulas. But if you're heading for the ruins of Copán then the crossing at El Florido, reached from Chiquimula, is far more suitable. Both routes bring you first to the industrial capital of San Pedro Sula, five hours from Tegucigalpa.

To get into Honduras you'll need a visa if you're from the USA, Canada, Australia, New Zealand, France, Portugal or Austria, and there are Honduran embassies in both Guatemala and Belize. Otherwise you don't even need a tourist card (it's normally possible to travel as far as the ruins of Copán – p.188 – without any formalities at all, regardless of where you're from).

Heading on south you reach **NICARAGUA**, which is badly scarred by years of conflict and natural disaster. While the war against the *contras* seems to be drawing to a close it will be many years before the country starts to recover from the combined impact of civil war, earthquake, hurricane and economic blockade. Nevertheless this is a lush tropical country and the people are relaxed, open and easy-going. You could even join the army of *internacionalistas* who are helping put the country back

together. Again Australians, New Zealanders and French, amongst others, need Nicaragua visas, but Britons, Americans and most other EC nationals do not. There are Nicaraguan embassies in Guatemala and Belize.

Continuing, **COSTA RICA** is the exception to the rule, a Central American country that is largely intact, where democracy is more or less operating, and where the army was abolished in 1948. The main attraction here is the wildlife, as there's a well developed system of national parks, protecting an array of habitats and an amazing number of different species. For American visitors Costa Rica is a favourite spot for winter holidays, offering superb beaches and tropical sunshine. Hardly anyone needs a visa to enter Costa Rica for a short stay, but be warned that the cost of living is high by Central American standards.

Last and probably least of the Central American republics is **PANAMA**, dominated by the Canal Zone. At the time of writing the country was still under American occupation following the overthrow of General Noriega, so the situation will doubtless have changed by the time you read this – hopefully for the better. Few travellers make it this far and if you're planning to travel on south bear in mind that the road comes to an end in Panama, starting up again across the border in Colombia. This trackless region of southern Panama is known as the Darien Gap and it can only be crossed on foot, a trek of two or three weeks, for which you'll need to be well prepared. In the north Panama is connected to Costa Rica by road.

If you plan to continue to **SOUTH AMERICA** then flights aren't necessarily any cheaper from Panama, and you might as well fly from somewhere further north. There are daily flights to northern Colombia from Belize and Guatemala, many of them including a stop over on the island of San Andrés: they're as cheap from here as anywhere else. There are also flights to most other capital cities on the continent.

One final possibility worthy of a mention is **CUBA**, which is fairly close to the tip of the Yucatán in Mexico. Flights from the USA are banned, so there are regular departures from Mexico City, Mérida and sometimes Guatemala City, to Havana. Particularly good value are two-week package deals, including accommodation, that are sometimes on offer from travel agents in Guatemala City.

LANGUAGE

Guatemala and Belize take in a bewildering collection of languages, probably numbering thirty in all, but fortunately for the traveller there are two that dominate – Spanish and English.

CREOLE

Creole may sound like English from a distance and as you listen to a few words you'll think that their meaning is clear, but as things move on you'll soon realise that complete comprehension is just out of reach. It's a beautifully warm and relaxed language, typically Caribbean, and loosely based on English but including elements of French, Spanish and Indian languages. Written Creole is a little easier to get to grips with, but it's hardly ever used. There is one compensation – almost anyone who can speak Creole can also speak English.

Just to give you a taste of Belizean Creole here are a couple of simple phrases:

Bad ting neda gat owner – Bad things never have owners.
Better belly bus dan good bikkle waste – It's better that the belly bursts than good victuals go to waste.
Cow no business eena haas gylop – Cows have no business in a horse race.

If you're after more of these then get yourself a copy of *Creole Proverbs of Belize*, which is usually available in Belize City.

SPANISH

The Spanish spoken in both Guatemala and Belize has a strong Latin American flavour to it and if you're used to the dainty intonation of Madrid or Granada then this may come as something of a surprise. Gone is the soft s, replaced by a crisp and clear version. If you're new to Spanish it's a lot easier to pick up than the native version. Everywhere you'll find people willing to make an effort to understand you, eager to speak to passing gringos.

The rules of **pronunciation** are pretty straightforward and, once you get to know them, strictly observed. Unless there's an accent, words ending in d, l, r and z are **stressed** on the last syllable, all others on the second last. All **vowels** are pure and short.

A somewhere between the "A" sound of back and that of father.
E as in get.
I as in police.
O as in hot.
U as in rule.
C is soft before E and I, hard otherwise: *cerca* is pronounced serka.
G works the same way, a guttural "H" sound (like the *ch* in loch) before E or I, a hard G elsewhere – *gigante* becomes "higante".
H is always silent.
J the same sound as a guttural G: *jamon* is pronounced hamon.
LL sounds like an English Y: *tortilla* is pronounced torteeya.
N is as in English unless it has a tilde (accent) over it, when it becomes NY: *mañana* sounds like manyana.
QU is pronounced like an English K.
R is rolled, RR doubly so.
V sounds more like B, *vino* becoming beano.
X is slightly softer than in English – sometimes almost SH – *Xela* is pronounced shela.
Z is the same as a soft C, so *cerveza* becomes servesa.

On the opposite page is a list of a few essential words and phrases (and see *Basics* for food lists), though if you're travelling for any length of time a dictionary or phrase book is obviously a worthwhile investment – some specifically Latin-American ones are available. If you're using a **dictionary**, remember that in Spanish CH, LL, and Ñ count as separate letters and are listed after the Cs, Ls, and Ns respectively.

BASICS

Yes, No	*Si, No*	Open, Closed	*Abierto/a, Cerrado/a*
Please, Thank you	*Por favor, Gracias*	With, Without	*Con, Sin*
Where, When	*Donde, Cuando*	Good, Bad	*Buen(o)/a, Mal(o)/a*
What, How much	*Qué, Cuanto*	Big, Small	*Gran(de), Pequeño/a*
Here, There	*Aqui, Alli*	More, Less	*Mas, Menos*
This, That	*Este, Eso*	Today, Tomorrow	*Hoy, Mañana*
Now, Later	*Ahora, Mas tarde*	Yesterday	*Ayer*

GREETINGS AND RESPONSES

Hello, Goodbye	*Ola, Adios*	Not at all/You're welcome	*De nada*
Good morning	*Buenos días*	Do you speak English?	*¿Habla (usted) Ingles?*
Good afternoon/night	*Buenas tardes/noches*	I don't speak Spanish	*(No) Hablo Castellano*
See you later	*Hasta luego*	My name is . . .	*Me llamo . . .*
Sorry	*Lo siento/disculpeme*	What's your name?	*¿Como se llama usted?*
Excuse me	*Con permiso/perdón*	I am English/	*Soy Ingles(a)/*
How are you?	*¿Como está (usted)?*	Australian	*Australiano(a).*
I (don't) understand	*(No) Entiendo*		

NEEDS – HOTELS AND TRANSPORT

I want	*Quiero*	Left, right, straight on	*Izquierda, derecha, derecho*
I'd like	*Quisiera*	Where is . . . ?	*¿Donde esta . . . ?*
Do you know . . . ?	*¿Sabe . . . ?*	. . . the bus station	*. . . el terminal de camionetas*
I don't know	*No se*	. . . the railway station	*. . . la estación de ferrocarriles*
There is (is there)?	*(¿)Hay(?)*	. . . the nearest bank	*. . . el banco mas cercano*
Give me . . . (one like that)	*Deme . . . (uno asi)*	. . . the post office	*. . . el correo/la oficina de correos*
Do you have . . . ?	*¿Tiene . . . ?*	. . . the toilet	*. . . el baño/sanitario*
. . . the time	*. . . la hora*	Where does the bus to . . . leave from?	*¿De donde sale la camioneta para . . . ?*
. . . a room	*. . . un cuarto*	Is this the train for Puerto Barrios?	*¿Es este el tren para Puerto Barrios?*
. . . with two beds/double bed	*. . . con dos camas/cama matrimonial*	I'd like a (return) ticket to . . .	*Quisiera un boleto (de ida y vuelta) para . . .*
It's for one person (two people)	*Es para una persona (dos personas)*	What time does it leave (arrive in . . .)?	*¿A qué hora sale (llega en . . .)?*
. . . for one night (one week)	*. . . para una noche (una semana)*	What is there to eat?	*¿Qué hay para comer?*
It's fine, how much is it?	*¿Está bien, cuanto es?*	What's that?	*¿Qué es eso?*
It's too expensive	*Es demasiado caro*	What's this called in Spanish?	*¿Como se llama este en Español?*
Don't you have anything cheaper?	*¿No tiene algo más barato?*		
Can one . . . ?	*¿Se puede . . . ?*		
. . . camp (near) here?	*¿ . . . acampar aqui (cerca)?*		
Is there a hotel nearby?	*¿Hay un hotel aquí cerca?*		
How do I get to . . . ?	*¿Por donde se va a . . . ?*		

NUMBERS AND DAYS

1	un/uno/una	20	veinte	1990	mil novocientos noventa
2	dos	21	veintiuno	1991	. . . y uno
3	tres	30	treinta	first	primero/a
4	cuatro	40	cuarenta	second	segundo/a
5	cinco	50	cincuenta	third	tercero/a
6	seis	60	sesenta		
7	siete	70	setenta		
8	ocho	80	ochenta	Monday	lunes
9	nueve	90	noventa	Tuesday	martes
10	diez	100	cien(to)	Wednesday	miercoles
11	once	101	ciento uno	Thursday	jueves
12	doce	200	doscientos	Friday	viernes
13	trece	201	doscientos uno	Saturday	sabado
14	catorce	500	quinientos	Sunday	domingo
15	quince	1000	mil		
16	diez y seis	2000	dos mil		

PHRASEBOOKS AND DICTIONARIES

Any good Spanish phrasebook or dictionary should see you through in Guatemala (Harrap ones are good); but specifically Latin-American ones are a help – like the *Berlitz Latin-American Phrasebook* (£2.95) – or you could try the *University of Chicago Dictionary of Latin-American Spanish* ($5.95).

GLOSSARY

AGUARDIENTE raw alcohol made from sugar cane.

AGUAS bottled fizzy drinks.

ALDEA a small settlement.

ALTIPLANO highland area of central Guatemala.

ATOL a drink usually made from maize dough, cooked with water, salt, sugar and milk. Can also be made from rice.

BARRANCA a steep-sided ravine.

BARRIO slum or shanty town.

BAYMAN early white settler in Belize.

BOCA COSTA western slopes of the Guatemalan highlands, prime coffee-growing country.

CAKCHIQUEL indigenous highland tribe occupying an area between Guatemala City and Lake Atitlán.

CAMIONETA a second-class bus. In other parts of Latin America the same word means a small truck or van.

CANTINA a local hard-drinking bar.

CAYE or **CAY** Belizean term for a small island.

CHICLE tree sap from which chewing gum is made.

CLASSIC period during which ancient Maya civilisation was at its height, usually given as 300–900 AD.

COFRADÍA religious brotherhood dedicated to the protection of a particular saint. These groups form the basis of religious and civil hierarchy in traditional highland society and combine Catholic and pagan practices.

COMEDOR basic Guatemalan restaurant, usually with just one or two things on the menu, always the cheapest places to eat.

CORRIENTE another name for a second-class bus.

CORTE traditional Guatemalan skirt.

COSTUMBRE a Guatemalan word for traditional customs of the highland Maya, usually of religious and cultural significance. The word often refers to traditions which owe more to paganism than to Catholicism.

CREOLE Belizean term used to describe those of Afro-Caribbean descent and the version of English that they speak.

DCG *Democracia Cristiana Guatemalteca* (Guatemalan Christian Democratic Party).

EGP *Ejercito Guerrillero de los Pobres* (Guerrilla Army of the Poor). A Guatemalan guerrilla group operating in the Ixil triangle and Ixcan areas.

EVANGELICO Christian evangelist or fundamentalist, often missionaries. Name given to numerous Protestant sects seeking converts in Central America.

FAR *Fuerzas Armadas Rebeldes* (Revolutionary Armed Forces). Another Guatemalan guerrilla group, operating mainly in the Petén.

FINCA plantation-style farm.

GLYPH element in Maya writing and carving, roughly the equivalent of a letter or numeral.

GRINGO any white person, not necessarily a term of abuse.

HOSPEDAJE another name for a small basic hotel.

HUIPILE woman's traditional blouse, usually woven or embroided.

INDIGENA indigenous person/Indian.

INGUAT Guatemalan tourist board.

I.V.A. seven percent sales tax.

IXIL highland tribe grouped around the three towns of the Ixil triangle – Nebaj, Chajul and Cotzal.

KEKCHI tribal group based in the Cobán area and Verapaz highlands.

LADINO a vague term. At its most specific it defines someone of mixed Spanish and Indian blood, but is more commonly used to describe a person of western culture, or who dresses in western style, be they of Indian or mix ed blood.

MAM Maya tribe occupying the west of the western highlands, the area around Huehuetenango.

MARIACHI Mexican musical style popular in Guatemala.

MARIMBA xylophone-like instrument used in traditional Guatemalan music, also used by the Belizean Maya.

MAYA a general term for the tribe who inhabited Guatemala, Honduras, southern Mexico and Belize since the earliest times, and still do.

MESTIZO a person of mixed Indian and Spanish blood, though like the term *Ladino* it has more cultural than racial significance.

METATE flat stone for grinding maize into flour.

MILPA maize field.

MLN *Movimiento de Liberacion Nacional* (National Liberation Movement). Right-wing political party in Guatemala.

NATURAL another term for an indigenous person.

PENSION simple hotel.

PGT *Partido Guatemalteco de Trabajadores* (Guatemalan Labour Party, also known as the Guatemalan Communist Party).

PIPIL indigenous tribal group which occupied much of the Pacific coast at the time of the conquest, but no longer survives.

PLANTATION farm (Belize).

POSTCLASSIC the period between the decline of Maya civilisation and the arrival of the Spanish, 900–1530 AD.

PRECLASSIC archaeological era preceding the blooming of Maya civilisation, usually given as 1500 BC–300 AD.

PULLMAN fast and comfortable bus, usually an old Greyhound.

PUP People's United Party (Belize).

QUICHÉ largest of the highland Maya tribes, centred on the town of Santa Cruz del Quiché.

SIERRA mountain range.

STELA free-standing carved monument. Most are of Maya origin.

TECÚN UMÁN last king of the Quiché tribe.

TIENDA shop.

TRAJE traditional costume.

TZUTE a headcloth or scarf worn as a part of traditional Indian costume.

TZUTUJIL indigenous tribal group occupying the land to the south of Lake Atitlán.

UDP United Democratic Party (Belize).

URNG *Unidad Revolucionaria Nacional Guatemalteca* (Guatemalan National Revolutionary Unity).

USAC *Universidad de San Carlos*/National University of San Carlos (Guatemala).

INDEX